Prehistoric Culture Change on the Colorado Plateau

The University of Arizona Press   Tucson

Publication of this book is made possible in part by a grant from the Peabody Coal Company.

Prehistoric Culture Change on the Colorado Plateau

Ten Thousand Years on Black Mesa

Edited by Shirley Powell and Francis E. Smiley

The University of Arizona Press
© 2002 The Arizona Board of Regents
♾ This book is printed on acid-free, archival-quality paper.
Manufactured in the United States of America
First Printing

07   06   05   04   03   02   6   5   4   3   2   1

Library of Congress Cataloging-in-Publication Data
Prehistoric culture change on the Colorado plateau : ten thousand years on Black Mesa /
Edited by Shirley Powell and Francis E. Smiley.
p.   cm.
Includes bibliographical references and index.
ISBN 0-8165-1439-9 (Cloth : alk. paper)
1. Indians of North America—Arizona—Black Mesa (Navajo County and Apache County)—
Antiquities.   2. Excavations (Archaeology)—Arizona—Black Mesa (Navajo County and Apache
County).   3. Black Mesa (Navajo County and Apache County, Ariz.)—Antiquities.   I. Powell,
Shirley.   II. Smiley, F. E.
E78.A7 P744   2002
979.1′35—dc21
2001006425

British Library Cataloguing-in-Publication Data
A catalogue record for this book is available from the British Library.

For the people of Black Mesa: past, present, and future

Contents

Foreword   Robert C. Euler   ix

Acknowledgments   Shirley Powell and Francis E. Smiley   xi

1   A History and Retrospective of the Black Mesa Archaeological
    Project   Shirley Powell, George J. Gumerman, and Francis E. Smiley   1

PART I   Hunters and Gatherers   13

2   Black Mesa before Agriculture: Paleoindian and Archaic Evidence
    Francis E. Smiley   15

PART II   Kayenta Farmers and Villagers   35

3   The First Black Mesa Farmers: The White Dog and Lolomai Phases
    Francis E. Smiley   37

4   Basketmaker III: Early Ceramic-Period Villages in the Kayenta Region
    Deborah L. Nichols   66

PART III   The Puebloan Dispersion   77

5   The Puebloan Florescence and Dispersion: Dinnebito and Beyond,
    A.D. 800–1150   Shirley Powell   79

**PART IV   Late Pueblo II and Pueblo III
in Kayenta-Branch Prehistory**   119

6   Late Pueblo II–Pueblo III in Kayenta-Branch Prehistory
    Jeffrey S. Dean   121

PART V   A View from the Present   159

7   *Hopit Navotiat*, Hopi Knowledge of History: Hopi Presence on Black
    Mesa   Leigh Kuwanwisiwma   161

8   The Navajos and Black Mesa   Miranda Warburton and
    Richard M. Begay   164

9   Black Mesa Present and Past   Shirley Powell and Francis E. Smiley
    182

References Cited   193

List of Contributors   217

Index   219

Foreword

I was sitting in my office at the Center for Anthropological Studies at Prescott College, Arizona, one spring morning in 1967 when the Vice President for Engineering of Peabody Coal Company called from St. Louis. I had no idea how he knew about me or my institution, and I was surprised. He wanted to know if I could conduct an archaeological survey of approximately 200 acres on Black Mesa, an area that Peabody had leased from the Bureau of Indian Affairs. He was negotiating at that time for the Hopi and Navajo Indians whose reservations encompassed the area. He also requested a survey of about seven miles of haul roads and one hundred miles of a coal slurry line from the proposed open-pit mine on Black Mesa westward.

Already I had been thinking about a project that would help train our students in field research, something almost unheard of in undergraduate institutions in those days. Such an approach to scholarly endeavor, even for freshmen, was a hallmark of the anthropological curriculum of the fledgling Prescott College, which had opened its doors only a year before.

I tried to mask my excitement about the possibilities of long-range future training for our students when I told the Peabody vice president that if he would send me topographic maps of the area and bounds of the initial work, I would send him a proposal and a cost estimate. Research designs would come later.

"That's the first decent thing I've heard from you archaeologists," the vice president said. He went on to indicate that he had earlier contacted an archaeological institution about the work, the director of which had said, "Don't worry about the cost, it's all for science."

The Peabody official's reply was, "Frankly, I can't run this coal company on that basis."

The budget for that initial survey was modest, and, armed with a simple letter of approval from Peabody and the necessary archaeological permits, the investigation was accomplished with $20 to spare. That cemented my relations with the company and paved the way for future contracts. Little did I realize then that with the unparalleled assistance of George Gumerman, who joined the Prescott College faculty and became field director of the Black Mesa Archaeological Project in 1968, our archaeological research on Black Mesa would continue virtually to the present.

The history of the Black Mesa Archaeological Project has been well documented in a multiauthored (Powell et al. 1983) *American Antiquity* article, "Fifteen Years on the Rock: Archaeological Research, Administration, and Compliance on Black Mesa, Arizona." That article discussed the project's move from Prescott College when that school unfortunately had to declare bankruptcy, to a one-year stint at Fort Lewis College in Durango, Colorado (where I had taken a faculty position), and then finally and productively to Southern Illinois University at Carbondale. There, the project blossomed under Gumerman's leadership and involved graduate students from many institutions as well as professional specialists from a number of disciplines related to archaeology. The support from Peabody Coal Company throughout has been to their great credit.

Another important synthesis and, it must be added, a cogent philosophical work that appeared about the same time was Gumerman's (1984) *A View from Black Mesa: The Changing Face of Archaeology*. Important portions of Gumerman's book related to how archaeological concepts and methods had changed since we had begun our work. It also dealt with those initial excavations and "nuisances" exacerbated by biting black gnats and the unfortunate fact that I had inadvertently situated our first camp on a rattlesnake den. Surely, that work was difficult, but lacking the bureaucratic complexities that hindered scholarly work in later years, it was both productive and enjoyable for students and staff.

A View from Black Mesa and the later synthesis, *People of the Mesa*, (Powell and Gumerman 1987) offered reconstructions of prehistoric Anasazi life on Black Mesa, noting the important correlates between the changing aspects of that life and the paleoenvironment. It seems to me that beyond the data produced from extensive surveys and literally hundreds of excavations, one of the most germane contributions has been the multidisciplinary investigations of the role that the past environment had in effecting culture change. These studies have been amply documented in at least two journal articles and one book (Euler et al. 1979; Dean et al. 1985; Gumerman 1988a).

Over the years that the Black Mesa Archaeological Project has functioned, not only have scholarly monographs detailing the work been published with regularity, but numerous papers have been presented at professional archaeological meetings, and many theses and dissertations have been authored by former participants in the project. In all, the Black Mesa Archaeological Project has resulted in innumerable publications, a creditable record for such a long-lived project, comparable to that of the Dolores Archaeological Project in southwestern Colorado (D. Breternitz 1993).

Now we have the final report of the Black Mesa project, one that integrates all the many studies that have been done over the past twenty years. It also reconstructs American Indian life there for some ten millennia. It has been a monumental task and one that has at last come to fruition. I am honored to have been asked to write this foreword and pleased that I had a role in the initial years of that endeavor.

Robert C. Euler
Prescott, Arizona
June 20, 1994

Acknowledgments

The vast number of people and the potential for overlooking some of those who made contributions to the Black Mesa Archaeological Project over the past thirty-four years are far too great for us to attempt to list even the principal contributors by name here. Moreover, we do not view any contributions as minor. Accordingly, we must rely on simply enumerating contributions by groups.

First and foremost, we thank the people of Black Mesa who made us welcome and made the discoveries described herein.

Second, we are grateful to the Peabody Coal Company for generous support over a period of decades, which continues with the subvention of the publication of this volume. We also thank the Peabody employees at the mine sites, at the headquarters facilities, and in the corporate structure for their help in the field, the laboratory, and numerous other venues.

We acknowledge the contributions of the scores of federal and state agency employees who provided regulatory guidance for the project.

Finally, we thank the hundreds of archaeologists from more than thirty universities who worked in the field, in the labs, and on the publication process. These individuals devoted substantial portions of their undergraduate, graduate, and professional careers to the survey, excavation, analysis, and publication of many hundreds of scholarly and public-oriented works on the archaeology and ethnology of Black Mesa.

These constitute few words for so much effort by so many people. The Black Mesa Archaeological Project stands as one of the longest-running and largest-scale projects in the history of American archaeology. No enterprise of this scale can succeed without such cooperation and dedication.

We thank you all.

Shirley Powell
Francis E. Smiley

Prehistoric Culture Change on the Colorado Plateau

CHAPTER 1

A History and Retrospective of the Black Mesa Archaeological Project

Shirley Powell, George J. Gumerman, and Francis E. Smiley

Most archaeologists would leap at the chance to begin a major research effort in an archaeologically unexplored region. Archaeologist Robert C. Euler took advantage of such an opportunity in 1967, establishing the Black Mesa Archaeological Project (BMAP). This volume, one consequence of that twenty-year, multimillion-dollar archaeological effort, examines and summarizes large-scale, intensive research focused on the previously unknown prehistoric and historic-period peoples of northern Black Mesa in northeastern Arizona.

For most researchers, and in today's terms, project funding that continued for two decades would constitute a luxurious situation. In contrast to today's large projects, Black Mesa field work extended over seventeen summers. BMAP archaeologists recognized and recovered the remains of ephemeral camps, early agricultural sites, Puebloan villages, and historic and modern-day settlements. The analytical and writing aspects of the project lasted another four years. The various kinds of sites resulted from about nine thousand years of periodic occupation by populations varying from as few as twenty people to, at most, several hundred. Seldom, if ever, have so many archaeologists labored so long to understand what so few people were doing.

Archaeological survey and excavation took place within the Peabody Coal Company Black Mesa leasehold on northern Black Mesa (figures 1.1 and 1.2). Black Mesa consists of a massive highland rising to eight thousand feet on the northern edge, gradually falling to the southwest, and terminating at the Hopi Mesas. Figure 1.3 offers a view across the north rim of Black Mesa, showing the dissected canyons and upland forests of northern Black Mesa.

Field work commenced in 1967 with the archaeological survey of Peabody access roads and potential mine sites and ended in 1983 with the completion of excavations. Analysis and production of final reports in 1987 concluded a twenty-year program continuously funded by Peabody Coal Company. BMAP crews intensively surveyed 256 km^2, identifying a total of 2,710 archaeological sites. Prehistoric occupations dating to both preceramic and Puebloan periods account for 1,671 sites. The other 1,039 sites date to the historic Navajo occupation. During the Black Mesa Archaeological Project, crews excavated 188 prehistoric and 27 historic-period Navajo sites, tested or mapped and made surface collections on 887 additional sites, and discovered 172 prehistoric burials.

The Black Mesa Archaeological Project obviously belongs to the category of southwestern archaeology called "Big Archaeology" (Rogge 1983). Big Archaeology began in the 1960s and appears to be rapidly waning with the realignment of federal priorities both in the allocation of research funds and in the nature of archaeological "treatments" in vogue in recent years. In any case, Big Archaeology produced benefits for Black Mesa research and research problems.

Because of the vast sums expended, professional archaeologists and members of the public tend to scrutinize Big Archaeology carefully, as indeed they should. Big Archaeology frequently occurs in the context of large-scale development projects that destroy archaeological remains. In such situations, researchers must always sample the archaeological remains in a study area. Generally in science, the term "sampling" appropriately connotes efficiency and high scientific standards. In most scientific endeavors, sampling saves money and means that researchers will afflict the rigors of some research regimen on only a small portion of a research population.

Unfortunately, in the harsh reality of research in salvage archaeological situations, sampling means that a (usually) small number of sites in the population can be saved through archaeological recovery but that a (usually) major portion of the site population will be destroyed. The sites will, in fact, be destroyed by the same development project that occasions the archaeological salvage in the first place. Because Big Archaeology

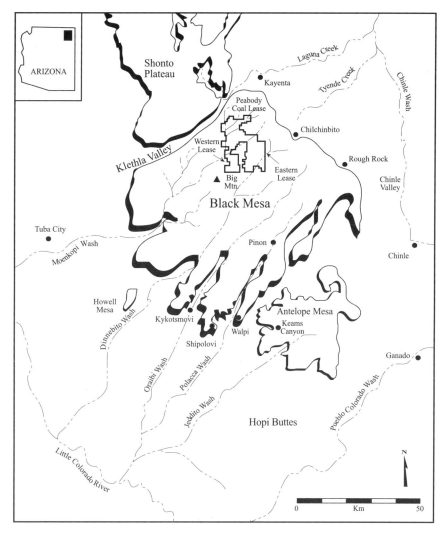

Figure 1.1 The northern Southwest, showing Black Mesa and the Peabody Coal Company leasehold.

usually proceeds only in a local area narrowly defined by the limits of development, additional problems stem from the discrepancy between project areas and the nature or distribution of archaeological remains. In other words, the nature of development and the intentions of the developers impose significant constraints on the degree to which even Big Archaeology may succeed in achieving scientifically valid samples and, therefore, valid results. Archaeologists face sampling inadequacies in nearly every field and laboratory undertaking, and so such situations tend to be usual. Nonetheless, archaeologists must clearly delineate the sampling limits of any

project and must, in drawing conclusions, take the sampling limits into account. The limits of development for BMAP consisted of an area roughly 18 km on a side, an area of over 300 km², far larger than most project areas. While we had a large project area, we remained constrained in terms of regional extrapolation. Accordingly, we have tried to hew to the criteria of inference that the sampling limits impose.

The relatively unspectacular objects of our BMAP investigations consisted of the material remains, and the relationships among these remains, left by small groups of people. For at least nine thousand years these

people hunted, gathered, farmed, and tended their herds on the vast and rugged upland pinyon-and-juniper-covered mesa. The lifeways of Black Mesa peoples appear similar to those of the inhabitants of comparable environments throughout the southern Colorado Plateau.

Reconstructing lifeways, however, proved difficult. Because the project spanned a period usually allocated to a whole human generation, BMAP researchers inevitably developed interesting and profound interpretive differences. Many differences accrued from the longevity of research, during which perceptions of the archaeology of different occupational time periods changed as new data from excavations and analysis accumulated. Other differences resulted from changing theoretical orientations within the discipline, which affected how we interpreted the remains. Still others arose because we enjoyed considerable monetary support that enabled us to underwrite research along many different analytical paths, allowing the exploration of avenues not always available to researchers in more limited excavation situations.

The Black Mesa project pursued an aggressive reporting program, resulting in the production of twelve reports that describe the findings of seventeen field seasons. Each report summarized the field work and synthesized our understanding of the archaeology at particular points in time. Not surprisingly, in view of the duration of the project and the number of researchers involved, the summaries sometimes appear contradictory. Most of the materials in the volumes focused on description and synthesis rather than on attempting extensive interpretation. The relatively few interpretations (e.g., Gumerman 1984; Parry and Smiley 1990; S. Plog 1986e; Powell 1983; Powell and Gumerman 1987) proceed from different databases and theoretical orientations. As a result, the differing interpretations have raised questions and caused controversy approximately equal to the answers provided. We attempt here to clarify such problems and to deal straightforwardly with the many still-unresolved interpretive disagreements.

This introduction has the multifaceted goal of providing context for the material that follows. The Black Mesa Archaeological Project operated within three quite distinct frames of reference, each with its own aims and limitations. The first of the frames of reference, that of the Peabody Coal Company, stemmed from the mining operation that provided the impetus for the archaeological investigations. Peabody's primary objective was to mine coal in compliance with federal and tribal legislation. The company generously supported the archaeological investigations. The generous levels of funding enabled BMAP to meet all compliance regulations so that the archaeological program never interfered with the coal mining.

A second frame of reference consisted of the regulations and regulatory machinery of a complex of federal agencies and the Hopi and Navajo tribes who monitored the archaeological program. The primary aim of the regulatory bureaucracy was also legal compliance, although at times particular agencies' interests produced differing interpretations of what constituted compliance.

The final frame of reference consisted of the research objectives of the many archaeologists whose collective goal involved recovering and interpreting data from the Peabody leasehold. Although some might view the interesting and profound interpretive differences of Black Mesa archaeologists as a project impediment, we see the difficulties in developing a single, integrated description and interpretation of Black Mesa cultural history both as inevitable and as an extremely interesting, scientifically fruitful phenomenon.

In fact, early recognition of the problems resulting from multiple interpretations became the source of one of the project's major strengths, fostering a great deal of introspection

Figure 1.2 Digitally shaded satellite photograph of the Black Mesa region showing approximately the same area as figure 1.1.

and reanalysis. The scientific method actually *requires* introspection and reanalysis. Introspection helps detect bias, a critical aspect of scientific research. Reanalysis helps check the replicability and reliability of research results and interpretations. During the long research process, we think we have learned something of the relationships between theory, method, and interpretation—especially the limits that theoretical orientations and methods place on the interpretive potential of the database. Accordingly,

our volume considers the frames of reference of big business, big government, and big research archaeology with, of course, an emphasis on the third—the archaeology of northern Black Mesa.

A Thumbnail History of Black Mesa Archaeology

In 1967, the Peabody Coal Company vice president for engineering contacted Robert C. Euler of Prescott College about archaeological work on

Figure 1.3 View to the northwest across the northern extent of Black Mesa. Navajo Mountain appears in the upper left distance (photograph by F. Smiley).

the Peabody Black Mesa leases. Euler undertook the ambitious project and conducted the first field research in the summer of 1968 as a field school (Gumerman 1970). Three supervisory archaeologists, ten undergraduate students, two cooks, and three local residents comprised that season's crew. Five Prescott College students performed laboratory analyses during the following fall semester. Prescott crews excavated eight of the fifty-six sites identified during survey.

The Prescott-based project, directed by George J. Gumerman, conducted the next five Black Mesa field seasons on approximately the same scale as the first season. In 1974, Prescott College declared bankruptcy and closed its doors but not before BMAP employees removed many survey and excavation records and artifact collections. The materials recovered first from the soils of Black Mesa, then from the chaos of Prescott College bankruptcy proceedings, currently reside at Southern Illinois Univer-

sity at Carbondale (SIUC). The Black Mesa materials that remained at Prescott, including most of the records from the 1971 through 1974 field seasons, disappeared in the legal chaos of the college's financial failure (Powell 1984b:1).

Euler coordinated the 1974 field season from Fort Lewis College in Durango, Colorado, at which he had accepted a faculty position. The following year, Euler took a position at Grand Canyon National Park. Euler handed the project to Gumerman, a former Euler student and its first field director. Gumerman moved BMAP to Southern Illinois University at Carbondale. Engaged in full-time teaching and administration, Gumerman hired Stephen Plog to direct the Black Mesa Archaeological Project.

BMAP continued to function as a field school from 1975 through 1977. During this period, the number of non-field-school personnel rose in response to Peabody's requirements for more work. In 1976 alone, more than

sixty-five students and staff occupied a project field camp designed to accommodate no more than thirty people. BMAP decided to discontinue the field school in 1977.

Plog set out the first explicitly stated research design (S. Plog 1978; Klesert 1979). Focusing on northern Black Mesa, Plog's design emphasized the roles of population increase and environmental variability in organizational and subsistence change. Much of the work performed during this stage of the project also reconsidered earlier descriptive generalizations, reevaluated data, and refined methods.

Plog accepted a position with the University of Virginia in 1978, and Shirley Powell was appointed BMAP director, continuing in that capacity until the project closed operations in 1987. During Powell's long tenure as BMAP director, a number of major changes occurred in the project structure and environment. The Peabody Coal Company, for example, underwent major internal reorganization, placing new personnel in the liaison positions that helped archaeology articulate with mining. At the same time, the intensity and scope of governmental monitoring of compliance with historic-preservation legislation increased dramatically. In part as a response to massively increased compliance paperwork requirements, the number of full-time, year-round BMAP personnel rose from one to fourteen.

The compliance process that had begun and had functioned for over a decade as a fairly straightforward structure became extremely complex. The Southwest Regional Office of the National Park Service (NPS) monitored all archaeological work conducted between 1967 and 1980. In 1977, the Memorandum of Agreement signed by Peabody Coal Company, the National Park Service, the Bureau of Indian Affairs, and the U.S. Geological Survey formalized the unofficial compliance and monitoring agreement. The agreement gave the National Park Service authority to provide technical assistance in the management of cultural resources on Indian lands. As lead agency, the NPS examined and distributed materials for additional evaluation and concurrence to other agencies, such as the Bureau of Indian Affairs (BIA) offices, the two tribes, and the Arizona State Historic Preservation Office (Powell et al. 1983).

In 1979, the Office of Surface Mining (OSM) notified the Peabody Coal Company that OSM had assumed lead-agency responsibility for cultural resources in the leasehold, by authority of the Surface Mining Control and Reclamation Act of 1977. The OSM attached stipulations to Peabody's 1981 to 1985 mine permit, giving OSM, BIA, the tribes, and the Arizona State Historic Preservation Office review authority but excluding the National Park Service. Paradoxically, the 1977 Memorandum of Agreement remained in effect, giving NPS lead-agency status. Additional bureaucratic confusion arose from a decision to shift responsibility for cultural resource management on Indian lands from the NPS to the BIA and by ambiguity

over the legality of OSM's regulatory authority on Indian lands in view of BIA jurisdiction. One set of regulations gave OSM responsibility for the cultural resources affected by surface mining; another set of regulations gave BIA responsibility for the cultural resources on Indian lands. The BIA and the tribes maintained control over archaeological mitigation through the archaeological-permit process, but at the same time, OSM maintained control through its powers of stipulation to Peabody's mine permit.

Despite these and other obstacles, BMAP personnel completed the archaeological program. Although BMAP closed operations in 1987, new legislation, such as the Native American Graves and Repatriation Act of 1990, continues to place requirements concerning cultural resources on Peabody (Spurr 1993). During the period of transition from relative regulatory simplicity to regulatory complexity, many agencies and individuals weighed in with advice and demands. Some federal agencies claimed we did far too much work, while others claimed we did too little. Nonetheless, the data-recovery program is complete, and the land is being mined. Projects of the size and scope of BMAP can easily fail. One can measure such failure along any one of the three reference dimensions set out above: those relating to archaeology, compliance issues, or business.

BMAP's successes in the two latter areas, compliance and business, appear clear. The project complied with all regulations, and the Peabody Coal Company received clearance to proceed with mining. From the business perspective, a complex compliance process came to a successful conclusion without the interruption of coal-mining operations.

The archaeological endeavor, as with any scientific enterprise, remains unfinished. In an important sense, the success of a large data-gathering operation like BMAP is a process. The materials, the field maps, and observations comprise a database that may never run out of surprises for archae-

ologists. The scholarly debates that turn on interpretation similarly continue without foreseeable conclusion. Sometimes in science, such processes take a long time.

From the perspective of publication, BMAP accomplished a great deal. BMAP researchers have produced hundreds of research publications. The publications take many forms, ranging from refereed journal articles, to technical field-work reports, to edited volumes, to topical research volumes, to chapters in general archaeological volumes. The research production also takes the form of doctoral dissertations, masters' theses, papers presented at professional meetings, and, finally, popular books that brought the vast project to the public.

From the perspective of data acquisition, huge quantities of information appear in the published reports, dissertations, and theses. From the perspective of collections curation, millions of recovered artifacts currently abide at the Center for Archaeological Investigations (CAI) at Southern Illinois University at Carbondale. The collections contain pottery, lithic artifacts, animal bones, ethnobotanical recovery, and other materials. In addition, BMAP recovered and reconstructed nearly a thousand ceramic vessels, so that one of the many highlights of the collection consists of the large, whole-pot collection housed in the University Museum at SIUC. Researchers have used the collections intensively for nearly two decades for a wide variety of researches. So, while we think that we have succeeded beyond our own and many others' expectations along a number of dimensions, the ultimate value of BMAP in the structure of scientific archaeology will be determined by the uses made of our work by past, current, and future scholars.

Although shortened by an Office of Surface Mining (OSM) directive (see below), the already extremely long BMAP run of field seasons supplied a great mass of data in terms of the sheer numbers of excavated sites (188 prehistoric and 27 Navajo), of intensity of survey (2,710 sites discovered, mapped, and collected), and of material recovery (millions of artifacts and samples). The project employed, trained, and was trained by hundreds of local region Navajo residents. In 1982, the project began recruiting and employing Hopi crews as well. In the later project years, the field camp housed over two hundred archaeologists, Navajo and Hopi excavation and lab personnel, cooks, and visitors. What began as a small-scale, but ambitious, field-school effort concluded as one of the largest archaeological projects ever conducted on a yearly basis.

Every summer, BMAP hired field archaeologists from universities all over the United States. Although the return rate remained high, the sheer size of the field effort insured large numbers of new personnel every summer. The incoming archaeologists encountered new cultures in the Navajo and Hopi people who staffed the excavation and the lab and who usually lived close to, even within, the project area. The new archaeologists encountered the culture of big-time surface mining, too, as haulage trucks with three-meter-high tires incapable of distinguishing a BMAP pickup truck from a small rock in the road rumbled by their excavations. They learned to pay attention to the periodic blast warnings and to enjoy the sight of a big "coal shot" in nearby pits, especially at night.

They learned that what they were doing was for keeps, because the mega-scale mining operations in the leasehold changed the landscape in fundamental ways every year. Arroyos were filled and transformed into high-speed haulage roads, whole ridges simply disappeared between field seasons, and long-wall pits moved at astonishing rates. The field crews' archaeological labors saved sites that would otherwise have disappeared in a 96-yard dragline bucket in the twinkling of an eye. Most archaeologists also learned that it was very difficult to have an uninteresting day on Black

Mesa. We know we never had any such days.

The new archaeologists brought in fresh ideas, training in a wide variety of specialties, and a great deal of energy. The returning BMAP veteran archaeologists brought experience, expertise, and a passion for the Black Mesa research. The research potential was open-ended. Both the BMAP research design and the BMAP funding level could absorb nearly any serious student with good ideas and energy. Accordingly, BMAP data and, often, funding underwrote large numbers of doctoral dissertations and masters' theses. Just as the archaeologists poured into the BMAP field camp each summer from everywhere, bringing fresh ideas and approaches, they returned to their universities each fall with a common Black Mesa experience. In this way, hundreds of serious students and senior researchers became affiliated with, or moved through, the process that was BMAP.

A decade after the cessation of Black Mesa field work, one of the authors asked an audience at a southwestern archaeological conference, how many of them had worked on Black Mesa. More than two-thirds of the audience raised hands, amidst a gasp of surprise from the BMAP veterans and nonveterans alike. We sometimes wonder whether a similar question put to all southwesternists active since 1968 might elicit a similar proportion of "yes" responses.

Lest this thumbnail history appear to project too smooth an image of field operations, we should point out that things did not always go perfectly. But they always went. Some of us got pickup trucks stuck between trees. Some of us staked, mapped, and collected a site *next* to the site we should have staked, mapped, and collected. Some of us took our crews to water bomb other crews working nearby. Some of us failed to note the stealthy approach of water bombers, and our crews paid the price. Some of us nearly rolled trucks trying to cross flooded and raging washes.

Some of us ripped out transmissions climbing rough slopes in two-wheel-drive trucks. Some of us forgot water when taking visitors on long hikes to Black Mesa rim cliff dwellings. These events and countless others kept life interesting in the field.

Data Recovery

Over the years, approaches to archaeological data recovery within the Peabody leasehold changed markedly. The twenty-year span of the project coincided with major changes in archaeological methods and theory. The changes in archaeological theory, standards, and techniques fostered changes in BMAP site selection, excavation techniques, and interpretive perspectives. Moreover, as regulations associated with federal legislation on cultural resources became formalized, regulatory requirements for archaeological data recovery changed as well. Finally, Peabody's scale of operations escalated over the years, accelerating the pace of activities. Accordingly, archaeological, regulatory, and business approaches changed significantly, and each impacted BMAP data-recovery techniques.

A major shift in BMAP's archaeological procedures occurred in 1975, coincident with the implementation of the new research design and with the project's move to SIUC. Lesser, but still important, changes happened in 1978, when the National Park Service took charge of overseeing compliance with federal legislation, and in 1980, when this responsibility shifted to the Office of Surface Mining. Also in 1980, Peabody decided to complete all archaeological work, independent of the Peabody mining schedules. To some extent, Peabody's decision came in response to changing regulations and shifting interpretations of the same regulations by the complex of federal agencies.

In a cryptic illustration of the regulatory climate during the last third of the project, a federal regulator told us, "You are a moving target." We remain, to this day, unsure of the regulator's precise meaning, but we took the statement as a general indicator of the extent to which regulators can create the context within which archaeological contractors must operate. The shifts just outlined had encumbered the compliance process to a point at which Peabody wanted closure. As of 1981, BMAP personnel planned field research extending through 1986. That same year, the OSM stipulated that field research be concluded in 1983 and that the project complete all research and writing by 1987. We were, indeed, a target—and we seemed to be moving.

Through a series of modifications in the research plans for the remaining two field seasons, BMAP personnel attempted to adjust the sampling strategies to compensate for the loss of three field seasons. By 1981, BMAP researchers understood the import of the large number of early agricultural sites and the early Puebloan sites in the leasehold. By this time, the apparent hiatus during the Basketmaker III period (from A.D. 400 through 800) appeared to be real, not a sampling problem. Small camp sites began to date to Archaic times, and evidence of human antiquity on Black Mesa increased geometrically.

During the final field seasons, Powell increased the emphasis she began in 1980 on Archaic, Basketmaker II, and early Puebloan sites in an effort to achieve useful samples of sites from all occupation time periods. The shift in sampling emphasis resulted in the recovery of the Southwest's largest sample of open-air Basketmaker II sites, a large sample of early Puebloan sites, and the definition of Archaic presence on Black Mesa that extended back to at least 9000 B.P. Although archaeologists usually consider most sites dated before about 8500 B.P. to be Paleoindian, the calibration of radiocarbon dates (Stuiver and Reimer 1993) from Black Mesa Archaic context pushes the Archaic dates further back (Parry and Smiley 1990).

What We Think We Know about the Archaeology of Northern Black Mesa

The Black Mesa project collected an immense quantity of information about a huge number of sites during its seventeen field seasons. Most of these sites have been described, analyzed, and used to identify and interpret patterns of cultural change on northern Black Mesa. BMAP published the information annually. In this volume, we attempt to tie together the various "yearly," preliminary interpretations and to present a coherent view of the prehistory of Black Mesa, along with our explanations of how and why the culture change occurred.

The history of the Black Mesa project parallels developments within the field of archaeology since the mid-1960s. Appropriate theoretical orientations, and questions derived from such orientations, arose from this "archaeological" context. Moreover, the research successes and failures were part of an interplay that contributed to ongoing changes in the discipline. There is no single, "correct" interpretation of what happened during Black Mesa's past, nor of why it happened. Instead, the years of research produced a mosaic of empirically verified patterns and plausible models. To understand how Black Mesa research fits into the greater picture of southwestern prehistory, we must distinguish between what we know, what we think we know (and why it is we are uncertain), and what we wish we knew (the new questions that have arisen as a result of our continued inquiries).

The First Interpretations

Black Mesa was a virtual archaeological unknown when excavations commenced in 1968. Members of the Rainbow Bridge–Monument Valley Expedition had excavated one Pueblo II–III site within the leasehold in 1936–1937, and they had recorded a large Pueblo III site on a promontory overlooking Oraibi Wash (Beals et al.

1945). Given the meager database, one objective of the Peabody/Black Mesa project involved filling an informational void between the comparatively well known Kayenta–Marsh Pass–Long House Valley area on the north and the Hopi Mesas–Hopi Buttes on the south.

Derived from his (Gumerman 1969, 1988b) Hopi Buttes research, George J. Gumerman, who directed BMAP between 1968 and 1974, initiated a comprehensive program of paleoenvironmental research. Gumerman integrated tree-ring, pollen, and geomorphological research with chronometric data to reconstruct the paleoenvironment. Gumerman's research received a bonus during this period: the discovery of Dead Juniper Wash in the central portion of Black Mesa. The buried forests of Dead Juniper Wash and nearby areas permitted extremely accurate temporal placement of major periods of alluvial deposition. Together, these data provided the context for environmentally based explanations of cultural change on northern Black Mesa.

The dendroclimatological record, extending back to the mid-seventh century A.D., the pollen, and the geomorphological data produced a mutually reinforcing scenario of rapid climatic oscillations overlain by a much longer period cycle of arroyo cutting and aggradation. Black Mesa researchers dated the environmental record, especially the dendroclimatological, at extremely high resolution, much higher than the patterns of cultural variation that the archaeologists sought to explain.

The correlation of the ceramic-period Black Mesa occupation with an apparent mesic interval (indicated by stream deposition), and the correlation of the abandonment of the mesa with a period of drought (indicated by stream channel erosion), suggested environmentally induced cultural change (Euler et al. 1979; Gumerman 1988a; T. Karlstrom et al. 1976). Particularly in the early versions, the cultural reconstructions tended to be simple, the correlations clear, and the interpretation both parsimonious and easily digestible. The initial interpretive structure provided just the sort of sacred cow that an energetic young researcher trained in an alternative paradigm could sink his teeth into—and he did.

Later Interpretations

Stephen Plog, who directed the Black Mesa project between 1975 and 1978, received his graduate training at the University of Michigan. Among their other shortcomings, he recognized that the interpretations of the Black Mesa cultural sequence failed to consider social organization. Plog knew the importance of integrating human social organization into culture-change models both as part of the environment to which the Black Mesa Anasazi adapted and as an Anasazi response to variation in the environment (S. Plog 1980b). Instead of a simple causal relationship between the physical environment and culture, Plog argued for complex systemic relationships linking the physical environment and culture.

Plog looked for and found great variation in cultural patterns. His refined chronometry suggested that the apparently close correlations between environmental cycles and cultural change failed, in fact, to be such a close fit. Alternatively, Plog suggested that the entire cultural system throughout the ceramic-period occupation could be characterized as unstable. Social variables played critical roles in both creating and ameliorating the instability. Plog saw the abandonment of northern Black Mesa not so much a catastrophic event precipitated by major physical environmental perturbations as it was the inevitable result of a series of deviation-amplifying processes.

Continued Methodological Refinements

Shirley Powell's tenure as BMAP director (1978 through 1987) coincided with a period of methodological inquiries and attempted research reconciliation (Stephen Plog was on her dissertation committee, and George Gumerman was her supervisor). Research performed during this third period of investigation provided substantial qualitative evidence for remarkable variation in subsistence and settlement strategies. Researchers used the floral, faunal, and settlement patterns to substantiate descriptive scenarios that emphasized highly variable responses to local conditions. A major problem, however, lay in the inability to link unequivocally human activities with material-culture patterning. The ubiquitous archaeological difficulties in linking activity to archaeological remains led, as it so often does, to interpretive ambiguities and competing reconstructions.

BMAP's Contributions

The Native American Graves Protection and Repatriation Act of 1990 (NAGPRA) and the 1992 amendments to the National Historic Preservation Act have changed the context in which archaeologists do archaeology. Today, laws and regulations compel archaeologists to consult with people having cultural affinity to archaeological remains. Archaeologists must, in many cases, change their ways of doing things. The Black Mesa Archaeological Project concluded all field work and most analyses before the development of the current perspective. Thus, BMAP operated as an archaeological project conducted, for the most part, by and for archaeologists. Given current legal requirements, BMAP's operations would doubtless be far different if it were happening today. We would be researching some topics never thought of fifteen years ago, and we would probably now avoid other topics that archaeologists used to consider "essential," particularly those requiring long-term access to human remains.

Through twenty years of great disciplinary and bureaucratic regulatory change, BMAP persisted and flourished. The scale of field research generally continued to increase until the end of field work. The project never suffered a hiatus, never failed to maintain compliance, and the BMAP personnel worked hard to uphold standards of field, laboratory, and analytical research.

Paleoenvironment and Culture Change

The paleoenvironment and its relationship to culture change provided an early and continuing research focus of the Black Mesa Archaeological Project. Multidisciplinary researchers used pollen, geomorphology, tree rings, and a wide range of archaeological remains to document a record of low- and high-frequency environmental shifts that corresponded with major cultural discontinuities. The research culminated with publication of *The Anasazi in a Changing Environment* (Gumerman 1988a), which proposed a dynamic for the interaction of culture and physical environment. Much contemporary research on the prehistoric Southwest follows explicitly the pioneering paleoenvironmental models generated by BMAP researchers.

Pre-Puebloan Archaeology on Black Mesa

Today, archaeologists recognize that northern Black Mesa hosted a vigorous early agricultural occupation. The early agricultural occupation that predates ceramics consists of small pit-structure settlements and camps that housed small Basketmaker II groups. Unlike the nearby Marsh Pass rockshelters explored by Kidder and Guernsey (1919), the Black Mesa Basketmaker II sites occur in the open and tend to have extremely low archaeological visibility.

During the project's initial field seasons, archaeologists identified few preceramic sites. In 1972, however, five years after BMAP began, Prescott College crews identified AZ D:7:102 (Prescott College), a large, early Puebloan site with surface architecture. The site lay on the proposed location of the coal-storage silos at the foot of Black Mesa in Klethla Valley. When the excavators started work on the site, they noted a spatially discrete lithic scatter on the northeast edge of the site. The scatter received a separate site number, D:7:103, and subsequent excavation and analyses verified the site as preceramic, probably dating to the late Archaic (Parry 1984; Ware 1984).

Thus alerted to the existence of preceramic sites in the vicinity of Black Mesa, BMAP personnel identified and excavated four preceramic sites on the mesa proper during the 1973 field season (Euler 1984). The intensive, systematic lease-area surveys of 1975 and 1980 identified more than a hundred lithic sites. Subsequent excavations and analyses documented Early Archaic, Middle Archaic, and Basketmaker II (Lolomai phase) occupations in the leasehold that dated to approximately 9000 B.P., 5000 B.P., and 1950–1650 B.P. respectively (Parry and Smiley 1990).

Origins of Agriculture in the Northern Southwest

A much better understanding of the agricultural transition, or Basketmaker II tradition, in the northern Southwest constitutes one of the major contributions of the project. The recovery of data from early agricultural sites and time to examine the data stem from the luxury of BMAP longevity. Partly because project priorities focused on Puebloan sites and partly because the early farming sites on Black Mesa, as elsewhere, manifest extremely low archaeological visibility, the Basketmaker II open-air sites came to light only in the fifth year (1972) of field work. In the frame of reference of most Big Archaeological enterprises of recent decades, such sites might never have been discovered, or, if discovered, only minimally excavated. Most large projects must hew to a five-year timeline, devoting three years to field work and two to analysis and writing. Under such constraints,

much might have been missed in the Peabody leasehold on Black Mesa.

During the 1950s and 1960s we archaeologists thought that prehistoric southwesterners had adopted corn agriculture and its accoutrements from Mesoamerican neighbors as a process of gradual change that required thousands of years. In this scenario, the adoption of agriculture fostered correspondingly gradual population growth, sedentism, and cultural complexity. We thought that farming had come to northeastern Arizona late, at about the time of Christ. In any case, the concentration on Basketmaker II site excavations from 1978 to 1983 revealed that small farming communities did, in fact, spring up on Black Mesa beginning soon after 2000 B.P. We also know that these groups descended from the rockshelter dwellers who began farming the Colorado Plateau at least a thousand years earlier. As a result of chronometric studies on the Black Mesa Basketmaker II sites and BMAP-sponsored radiocarbon dating of materials from museum collections from nearby regional sites (Smiley 1985, 1998b), we know that the introduction of farming occurred sometime before 3000 B.P.

Thus, advances in radiocarbon dating techniques and advances in techniques of interpretation for radiocarbon data, combined with new dates (many from northern Black Mesa), have substantially revised our interpretations (e.g., M. Berry 1982; Berry and Berry 1986; Smiley 1985, 1994; Wills 1988a, 1988b). The accumulated data currently suggest that agriculture had a much earlier introduction to the Southwest than originally thought, that agriculture spread rapidly, and that a considerable period of slow or no population growth may have followed the agricultural transition. Colorado Plateau peoples appear to have been quite mobile, ranging seasonally from rockshelters, until approximately 2000 B.P., at which time they began settling in the kinds of small, open-air settlements that Black Mesa archaeologists encountered and

excavated in substantial numbers (Smiley 1985, 1994:186, 1998b).

Ceramic Chronometry

The use of multivariate statistical techniques to determine associations between ceramic attributes and tree-ring dates derives from Stephen Plog's work in the Chevelon (Plog 1980b) and Black Mesa (Plog and Hantman 1979, 1986) regions of the Southwest. Plog's Black Mesa research both pioneered and refined these techniques, and subsequent Black Mesa researchers applied the techniques to grayware attributes (P. Reed 1981) and to traditional Tusayan White Ware types (Christenson and Bender 1994). Researchers working in other areas have borrowed these approaches to ceramic chronometry, often with mixed success (e.g., Ambler 1983), leading to controversy about the general applicability of the statistical models, although neither Plog nor his co-workers ever claimed that the techniques could be generally and indiscriminately applied. The controversies surrounding applications of such techniques have sparked much constructive debate (for example, drawing attention to some of the interpretive implications of chronometric techniques, especially the population-inflating tendencies of phase- vs. site-based dating [S. Plog 1986d]).

Adaptive Diversity

When the Black Mesa project began in the late 1960s, archaeologists tended to characterize prehistoric Puebloans as farmers who relied heavily on corn and beans for sustenance. The ideas that the prehistoric Puebloans occupied single villages for long spans of time and that the villages enjoyed social and economic autonomy derived from that characterization. The Black Mesa project spanned the development of techniques for recovering and analyzing materials previously ignored by field workers. Analyses, for example, of pollen and other plant microfossils, small faunal remains, and chemical residues of a vast array of organic and inorganic materials painted a picture of subsistence diversity. The prehistoric Puebloans relied on many more plant (Ford 1984) and animal (Leonard 1989; Semé 1984) resources than originally postulated. Such evidence led to the conclusions that site populations moved more frequently (Gilman 1983, 1987; Powell 1983), occupied sites for shorter spans of time (Hantman 1983), and achieved far higher levels of regional social and economic integration than originally thought (e.g., Green 1985; Hegmon 1986; S. Plog 1986a). These analyses have heightened our awareness of the immense variation represented in the material remains, a variation that raises many interpretive possibilities (Powell 1988).

Historic Archaeology

Most archaeological projects in the Southwest focused on prehistoric remains. The systematic investigation of historic remains began fairly recently, largely at the instigation of tribal historic preservation programs. The Black Mesa project stands as one of the first to record and analyze historic remains. The interest in historic remains stemmed, first, from the contribution that historic sites could make to understanding prehistoric remains (e.g., Powell 1983, 1984a; Russell and Dean 1985; Smiley 1985) and, second, from the potential for answering questions of general import (e.g., Blomberg 1983; Oswald 1993; Warburton 1985). Chapter 8 delineates the context for BMAP's changing policy toward historic remains, providing a fascinating commentary on the contemporary sociopolitics of archaeology.

The Sociopolitics of Archaeology

Finally, BMAP spanned several important trends in contemporary American culture, including the women's rights and Indian self-determination movements. BMAP acted as an important agent of the kinds of changes many now tend to take for granted in archaeology.

BMAP provided a strong model of leadership in the hiring of female archaeologists in both supervisory and nonsupervisory positions. In 1967, for example, when BMAP began, the project supervisory staff consisted entirely of men, and the field-worker cohort consisted mostly of men. Between 1967 and 1987 many changes took place: a woman, Shirley Powell, was the project's final director, serving for nine years; one of three assistant directors was a woman as well. Many women served in positions of supervisory crew chief and laboratory director while the project worked in the field and during the academic year when the project entered the analytical and writing modes. Many of the BMAP supervisory personnel (both men and women) have completed graduate training and now work as educators, researchers, administrators, and private contractors.

In tandem with leadership in providing opportunities for female archaeologists, BMAP broke with local archaeological tradition when George Gumerman instituted a policy of hiring Native American local residents for field and laboratory work. For the three final field seasons, the majority of the project's enormous summer payroll went to local residents, both Navajo and Hopi.

Later, Hopi and Navajo tribal officials asked why BMAP, with its academic connections, did not encourage local Navajo and Hopi students in their educational endeavors. Hindsight made the link obvious and the potential opportunity clear—an opportunity currently being pursued by the Navajo Nation Archaeology Department (Two Bears 1995) and the Hopi Tribe's Cultural Preservation Office through cooperative agreements with Northern Arizona University and Fort Lewis College.

Organization of This Volume

The organization of this volume reflects two major goals: (1) to present what we learned about Black Mesa prehistory and (2) to place the work of the Black Mesa Archaeological Project in a regional context. We are challenged to do justice to Black Mesa's prehistory, to air interpretive disputes about the exact nature of that prehistory, and to understand how Black Mesa fits into a larger, regional context. We have organized the chapters along the broadest possible temporal and spatial dimensions. Collectively the authors consider the entire span of human occupation of the Kayenta region, from Paleoindian times to the present. Although our perspective, for the most part, springs from archaeology, the volume also contains a chapter entitled "Hopit Navotiat, Hopi Knowledge of History" written by Leigh Kuwanwisiwma, director of the Hopi Tribe's Cultural Preservation Office (Chapter 7), and a chapter entitled "The Navajo and Black Mesa" by Miranda Warburton, manager of the Navajo Nation Archaeology Department—Northern Arizona University office, and Richard Begay formerly with the Navajo Nation Historic Preservation Department (Chapter 8).

Typically, a volume on the work of the Black Mesa Archaeological Project should focus on the project area (the Peabody leasehold) and on what was there—that is, the periods of occupation. However, the Black Mesa leasehold was not continuously occupied; periods of occupation (Archaic, Basketmaker II, early Puebloan, and historic [Navajo and Hopi]) were punctuated by periods represented by no archaeological remains (Paleoindian, Basketmaker III, and late Puebloan until approximately A.D. 1825). To integrate Black Mesa into Kayenta-area prehistory, it is important to understand both. Thus, despite the episodic occupation of northern Black Mesa, the volume considers the entire Kayenta region, covering the span from Paleoindian times to the present, including chapters on both the periods of occupation and periods of abandonment. Accordingly, the volume contains seven culture history chapters: Paleoindian and Archaic, Basketmaker II, Basketmaker III, early Puebloan (A.D. 825–1150), late Puebloan (A.D. 1150–1300), Navajo, and Hopi. Prehistoric populations lived on northern Black Mesa during only four of these periods (Archaic, Basketmaker II, early Puebloan, and Navajo).

The patterns of occupation and abandonment suggest regional, rather than local, adaptive mechanisms for coping with the environmental and sociopolitical variability of the Colorado Plateau, and we should not limit our efforts to the development of a Black Mesa prehistory solely confined to the Peabody leasehold. A number of researchers have raised questions about the spatial scale over which social systems would operate, and we find that different cultural mechanisms can operate within different spatial and temporal frameworks (S. Plog and Powell 1984; Wobst 1974). We consider the relationships among population density, subsistence strategies, and social organization and use these data to identify the regional context within which the Black Mesa people might have been operating during different time periods. These considerations combine to identify the appropriate spatial scale for each topic and each time period.

The volume concludes with an evaluation of the state of our knowledge about Black Mesa and the implications of our findings for other areas in the Southwest and for archaeology in general. The process of reevaluation of research results has generated a fascinating picture of multiple interpretations of a complex data set. However, even though the Black Mesa project is unusual in having been allowed the time and analytical scope for such problems to emerge, the potential for similar problems exists in every archaeological investigation. In fact, interpretive unity in smaller and shorter research efforts is usually illusory, often the product of a single, intellectually dominant principal investigator, of nonrepresentative samples, or of the short span of time devoted to field work and analyses. In short projects or in apparently interpretively clear project situations, the controversy inevitably emerges later.

BMAP can be understood and evaluated only in the intellectual context of American archaeology. The project began toward the end of the cultural-history phase in the Southwest, when chronology building, assignment of cultural affiliation, and "filling in the gaps" comprised major goals. BMAP's middle age spanned the wildly and unrealistically optimistic 1970s, when investigators often claimed that virtually any aspect of human behavior could be understood using archaeological techniques. In the early and mid-1980s, BMAP and American archaeology confronted reality. Many archaeologists during the period realized that our data and our understanding of data have never been as accurate or as plentiful as our questions required, at least to answer the questions with full confidence.

BMAP, then, consists of an enormous, long-term field and laboratory effort by hundreds of archaeologists and field and laboratory workers. The project had three different principal investigators, four different directors, and encompassed major paradigmatic and methodological changes in American archaeology. We hope that the chapters to follow provide a useful synthesis and interpretation of research that began three decades ago and both changed and reflected changes in American archaeology.

PART I

Hunters and Gatherers

Here we begin the chronological synthesis of Black Mesa Archaeological Project research, integrating it into the larger context of archaeological interpretations from the surrounding Kayenta region and beyond. Before the BMAP explorations, the region seemed largely devoid of evidence of preagricultural hunter-gatherer archaeological remains. Chapter 2, by Francis E. Smiley, traces the history of hunter-gatherer research in the northern Southwest, providing new evidence for the Paleoindian occupation of the surrounding region from sometime before 10,000 B.P. and for the Archaic occupation of Black Mesa itself.

Discussions of the paleoclimate during the late Pleistocene and Middle Holocene, the evidence for Paleoindian occupation of the Southwest, and general observations on the Paleoindian period provide context for understanding the Paleoindian/Archaic transitional evidence from Black Mesa. Archaic adaptive systems, time-honored frameworks for the southwestern Archaic, a reevaluation of Archaic period chronometry, and a review of archaeological evidence for the Archaic on Black Mesa and beyond prepare the reader for the transitions to agriculture and the development of villages.

CHAPTER 2

Black Mesa before Agriculture

Paleoindian and Archaic Evidence

Francis E. Smiley

Did Paleoindian groups hunt and gather on the Colorado Plateau and across Black Mesa around the close of the Pleistocene? Until relatively recently, the answer might have been, for lack of any but ephemeral evidence, just vaguely positive. Similarly, post-Pleistocene Archaic groups left, at best, only evanescent records across the greater region. While archaeologists assumed the reality of Paleoindian and Archaic occupations, the archaeological record remained, if not mute, then quiet, with few exceptions.

During several field seasons, Black Mesa Project researchers focused on ephemeral sites that might be "old," that is, preagricultural. To paraphrase Chapter 1, rarely have so many searched so intensively in an area of such limited size for so few old sites. Despite the best survey and testing efforts, Black Mesa evidence of the first seven or eight thousand years of human occupation remains limited, just as it does for the Southwest in general.

While the foregoing characterization of the preagricultural archaeological record may appear pessimistic, I do not so view it. In fact, survey crews *did* find and investigate *extremely* ephemeral sites, revealing a previously unsuspected Archaic presence that remains enigmatic.

Although this volume deals specifically with Black Mesa and the surrounding region, I examine the *earliest* human occupations in a larger context for two reasons. First, evidence of Paleoindian presence in the BMAP study area on Black Mesa and the pursuit, in particular, of Paleoindian studies in the larger region have begun to appear much more promising. Second, the Paleoindian and Archaic evidence in the Black Mesa region has previously been only generally outlined (Parry and Smiley 1990; Smiley and Andrews 1983) and requires fuller treatment to flesh out Black Mesa region prehistory.

In the sections below, I present summaries of the excavations at Tsosie Shelter on Black Mesa (Burgett et al. 1985) and the collections analysis for the Badger Springs site (Hesse et al. 1996, 2000) in the Inscription House area, as well as the Starling site near Kayenta that provide new information on the early human presence in the Black Mesa region. I think the evidence from these particular sites corroborates the kinds of inferred cultural and subsistence shifts documented elsewhere.

The Paleoindian Record in the Greater Black Mesa Region

To date, no Paleoindian evidence has come to light in the Black Mesa study area proper. Over the past few decades, however, a small but growing body of information increasingly attests to a regional Paleoindian occu-

pation at some level beginning before 11,000 B.P.

Before such data had begun to accumulate, the debate over human antiquity on the Colorado Plateau had interesting parallels to the early twentieth-century debates about human antiquity in the New World. Until the late 1920s, for example, New World humans were thought to be relatively recent arrivals, the occupation being on the order of only a few thousand years old (Meltzer 1989). Similarly, the Colorado Plateau archaeological record for a long while lacked in-situ Paleoindian evidence in the form of the clear association of human activity either with extinct fauna or with absolute-dated contexts.

The debate about human antiquity in the New World was resolved by the finds at Folsom and Clovis in New Mexico (Cook 1928; Brown 1928; Hrdlicka 1928). The finds provided solid, rapidly accepted evidence of the association between humans and extinct Pleistocene fauna (Meltzer 1989).

Like the general New World record, the Colorado Plateau literature, until a few years ago, provided no clearly documented evidence of, for example, in-situ Paleoindian camps, hunting activities, or kill sites. In addition, we still have a dearth of carefully excavated and dated evidence of such activities in the Black Mesa area. Such evidence does, however, exist as I describe below. Moreover, this evidence along with isolated projectile-point finds and in-situ lithic scatters suggests that Paleoindians exploited the Colorado Plateau in much the same manner, if not with the same apparent intensity, as described for Paleoindian groups on the High Plains (Frison 1978) or in southeastern Arizona (Haury 1953).

In the absence of a strong archaeological record of large data sets and dramatic sites, archaeologists often turn to paleoenvironmental studies as a means for determining the environmental constraints and possibilities for human occupation. Innumerable ethnographic studies document the sensitivity of hunter-gatherer societies to environment and to environmental change (Kelly 1995).

Black Mesa Paleoclimate in the Late Pleistocene and Early and Middle Holocene

Detailed Late Pleistocene and early-to mid-Holocene paleoclimatic data remain as scarce for the Black Mesa area as for the American Southwest in general. Detailed reconstructions from other regions in the northern Southwest, such as Petersen's work in the La Plata Mountains of southwestern Colorado (1981), can be only indirectly applied to Black Mesa. Such works do, however, provide a basis for broader comparisons. Researchers have developed a number of models of varying specificity over the past several decades. Figure 2.1 illustrates the paleoclimatic and cultural history constructs discussed in this chapter. Figures 2.2 and 2.3 show locations mentioned in the text in terms of the Greater Southwest, the Black Mesa region, and the BMAP study area on northern Black Mesa.

General Southwestern Models

Perhaps the best-known and most generally debated model of southwestern Holocene environments and environmental change is Antevs' (1955) tripartite schema (figure 2.1B). An-

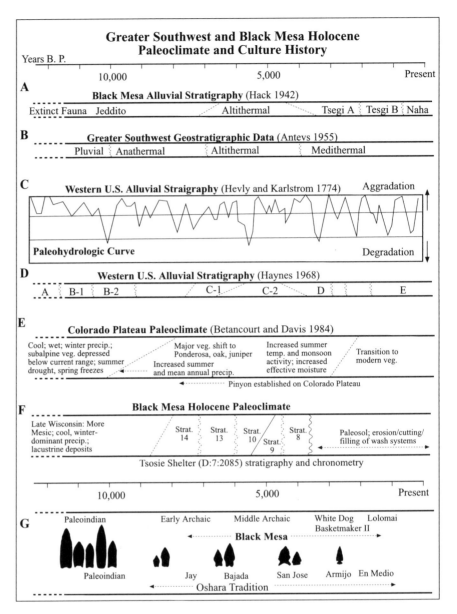

Figure 2.1 Paleoclimatic and cultural history constructs for the close of the Pleistocene.

tevs characterizes the early Holocene period, termed the "Anathermal" (10,000 to 7500 B.P.), as one of increasing average temperature during the withdrawal of the continental ice sheets. The following period, the Altithermal (7500 to 4000 B.P.) consisted of a period during which average temperatures continued to increase and conditions became more xeric. The subsequent Medithermal period (4000 B.P. to present) brought increased moisture and reduced temperatures from the postglacial maximum that had occurred during the Altithermal. Antevs' broadly drawn model thus

describes environmental variability observed in many parts of the world and that doubtless had significant impact on the demographics, social organization, and subsistence systems of foraging-adapted human groups.

Research in the northern Southwest and in the Black Mesa subregion generally affirms Antevs' reconstruction but also reveals a great deal more complexity than Antevs' schema contains. Such complexity tends largely to be a function of the localized interaction of topography with continental weather pattern changes, more accurate chronometric assessments of

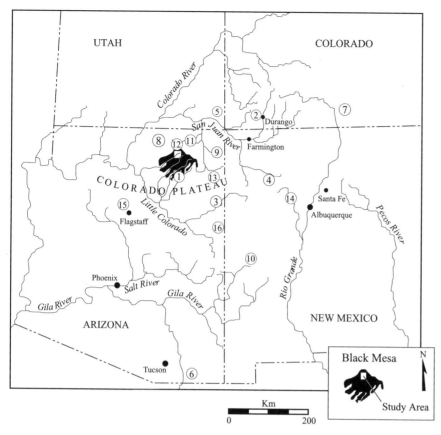

UTAH · COLORADO · Colorado River · San Juan River · Durango · Farmington · COLORADO PLATEAU · Little Colorado · Flagstaff · Santa Fe · Albuquerque · Pecos River · Rio Grande · Phoenix · Salt River · Gila River · Gila River · ARIZONA · NEW MEXICO · Tucson

Km 0 200

Black Mesa · N · Study Area

Figure 2.2 Map of the Greater Southwest, showing locations mentioned in the text. 1–Jeddito Wash; 2–La Plata Mountains; 3–Canyon de Chelly; 4–Chaco Wash; 5–Southeastern Utah; 6–Southeastern Arizona Paleoindian sites; 7–San Luis Valley; 8–Badger Springs site; 9–Prayer Rock District; 10–Quemado; 11–Starling site; 12–Marsh Pass, Tachini Point; 13–Hastqin site; 14–Arroyo Cuervo region; 15–San Francisco Volcanic Field; 16–Sanders.

depositional sequences, increasingly detailed palynological profiles, and more complete macrobotanical and faunal studies. While the chronology of climatic changes proposed by Antevs has held up well (Haynes 1968; Hevly and Karlstrom 1974), investigators disagree as to the directionality of these shifts (Betancourt and Davis 1984; Betancourt 1984; Betancourt et al. 1983; Petersen 1981; P. Martin 1963 [cf. Sayles 1965]).

In contrast to Antevs' simpler and more geographically general model, Hack, for example, focused on the Jeddito Valley in the Black Mesa local region (figure 2.1A). Hack, a member of the Peabody Museum Awatovi Expedition working in the Jeddito Valley between 1935 and 1939, developed the earliest comprehensive model specifically germane to Black Mesa (Hack

1942a). He divided the Holocene geomorphological sequence in the region into five basic intervals. He identified the Jeddito Formation as having been deposited under the more mesic late glacial climatic regime before 7000 B.P. on the basis of the Jeddito Valley data. The Jeddito formation contained elephant bones in one and possibly two localities (Hack 1942:50, figure 29). He identified an unconformity he termed the Jeddito/Tsegi "epicycle of erosion" that followed the Jeddito depositional interval. He suggested that the erosional interval lasted for a considerable period, given the extensive erosion of the previously deposited Jeddito formation materials during this period (1942:51). Concomitant with the Jeddito/Tsegi erosional period, he recognized widespread dune activity and concluded

that xeric conditions accompanied the erosional epicycle.

Hack further estimated that the subsequent deposition of Tsegi formation alluvium indicated a return to more mesic conditions and lasted from approximately 5000 to 800 B.P. His sequence finishes with a brief erosional epicycle (the Tsegi/Naha epicycle), followed by deposition of the Naha formation alluvium in relatively recent times. Although the basic sequence was originally worked out in the Jeddito Valley south of Black Mesa, Hack found correlative depositional stratigraphy on and around the Black Mesa landmass. Hack's reconstruction dovetails nicely with Antevs' pan-southwestern model (1955).

Much more recent work on the Black Mesa geomorphological and paleoclimatic history by Cooley (1962a), Cooley et al. (1969), and Hevly and Karlstrom (1974) finds little evidence to suggest problems with Hack's basic construct. However, refinements and more detailed models have added complexity, precision, and much higher resolution to the initial models.

The refinements for the preagricultural period of the Black Mesa subregion consist primarily of the "time-stratigraphic" modeling by T. Karlstrom et al. (1974), T. Karlstrom (1975), and Hevly and Karlstrom (1974) (figure 2.1C). Briefly, T. Karlstrom et al. (1976) developed a model for cyclical hydrological fluctuations sensitive to climatic conditions (see also Haynes 1968). T. Karlstrom (see also Hevly and Karlstrom 1974; T. Karlstrom et al. 1974; E. Karlstrom 1983; and Dean et al. 1985) views regional climatic change as consisting of cyclical mesic/xeric episodes that cause water tables to fluctuate, resulting in alluviation during moist periods and the downcutting of stream channels during more xeric intervals, when water tables drop (cf. Schumm 1977).

In particular, the research just cited documents a 550-year aggradational/degradational alluvial cycle over the past two millennia for Black Mesa. An excellent tree-ring record

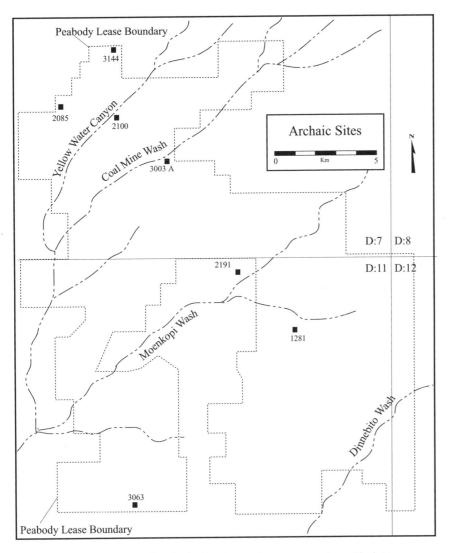

Figure 2.3 Black Mesa Archaeological Project study area on northern Black Mesa, showing the locations of Archaic sites.

and Karlstrom (1974) and that of Petersen (1981). Rather, the main points are, first, that the investigators detect complexity in the Holocene climatic record, and, second, they identify alternating mesic/xeric intervals. More specifically, Karlstrom describes the period 8000 to 5000 B.P. on Black Mesa as one "characterized by relatively dry but fluctuating climate" (1988). Although some researchers infer a long period of dry, hot conditions (e.g., the Altithermal; Hack 1942a; Antevs 1955), others find a great deal of intra-period variability in more detailed empirical data (e.g., Petersen 1981). The variability introduced by local topographic situations and the associated interaction with general atmospheric air-mass patterns compound the interpretive difficulties.

Thus, given the general agreement among students of southwestern paleoclimate on the general temporal boundaries of major climatic and accompanying floral and faunal shifts, these boundaries are viewed here as reasonably accurate and reflective of the conditions on Black Mesa during the preagricultural Holocene. The general Holocene sequence, accordingly, is reconstructed below, augmented where possible by data from recent archaeological and geomorphological investigations.

Black Mesa and Tsosie Shelter

The depositional sequence observed in the BMAP study area at Tsosie Shelter (D:7:2085; figures 2.3 and 2.4), a small, deeply stratified rockshelter in the northern portion of the study area provides a valuable example. Tsosie Shelter produced radiocarbon evidence of human occupation spanning the early and late-middle Holocene as well as during Puebloan times (Feathers and Stein 1985; E. Karlstrom 1985; Burgett et al. 1985; Trigg 1985).

Radiocarbon-dated cienega and lacustrine deposits in Coal Mine Wash, Red Peak Valley, and Yellow Water Canyon on Black Mesa indicate the existence of relatively mesic condi-

supports the validity of the cycle (Euler et al. 1979; Dean et al. 1985). Unfortunately, detailed empirical verification of the extrapolation of this curve into earlier portions of the Holocene (Hevly and Karlstrom 1974) on Black Mesa awaits additional work.

As figure 2.1C also indicates, the general sequence contains a series of oscillations throughout the Holocene. Oscillations of lesser amplitude between 7000 and 4000 B.P. suggest more stable conditions. This interval coincides closely with Hack's Jeddito/Tsegi erosional epicycle (1942a) and with Antevs' Altithermal (1955).

The critical feature of the curve consists of the short-term climatic

variability, that is, mesic/xeric cycles, within the more broadly defined Holocene periods in the reconstructions of Hack (1942a), Antevs (1955), Haynes (1968), Mehringer (1967) and Judge (1982). Figure 2.1, graphs D and E, illustrate selected sequences. In this respect, the complex and relatively detailed reconstruction of Holocene climate developed by Petersen (1981) using pollen data from the La Plata Mountains of southwestern Colorado suggests complex oscillations between relatively more mesic and xeric intervals.

I, however, make no claim here for a close correspondence between the detailed reconstruction of Hevly

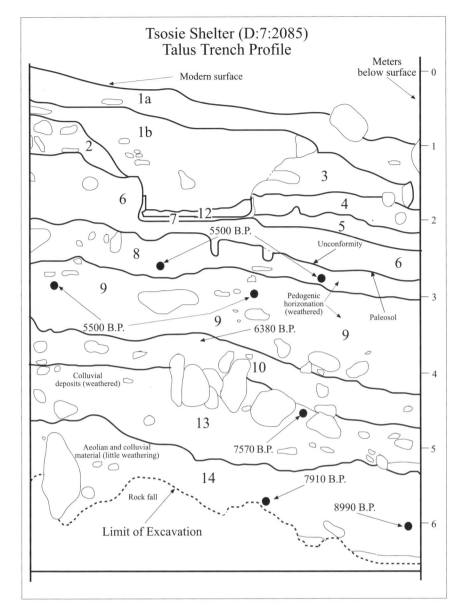

Figure 2.4 The depositional sequence at Tsosie Shelter, AZ D:7:2085 (after Burgett et al. 1985:figure 3.2).

tions at the beginning of the Holocene (ca. 10,000 to 8000 B.P.) (Eric Karlstrom, personal communication 1985; E. Karlstrom 1983:335). Figure 2.1F shows Karlstrom's early Holocene dates from wet deposits.

The wet deposits detected by Karlstrom (figure 2.1E and F) appear to have resulted from deposition in small lakes and from cienega conditions created by a rising water table. The temporal placement of the deposits fits well with the postulated post-glacial situations at Canyon de Chelly

(Betancourt and Davis 1984), Chaco Canyon (Betancourt et al. 1983), and in southeastern Utah (Betancourt 1984).

Studies based on macrofloral remains in fossil packrat (Neotoma) middens in these localities indicate the presence of conifers and the absence of both pinyon (*P. edulis*) and one-seed juniper (*J. monosperma*), from which investigators infer a cooler, more mesic climatic regime subject to spring freezes and summer drought in the context of a winter-dominant

precipitation regime. The studies further characterize the period as one of substantial biotic change during which pinyon, ponderosa, and one-seed juniper became established in the area by 8300 B.P.

E. Karlstrom characterizes Black Mesa geomorphic regime at the beginning of the Holocene as one of high water tables and alluvial filling of arroyo systems (Eric T. Karlstrom, personal communication 1985). Sometime before the close of the Pleistocene, the fluvial erosion of an outcrop of Wepo sandstone formed Tsosie Shelter and subsequently deposited gravels on the stream-course bottom of nearby Yazzie Wash. According to Karlstrom, at approximately 8000 B.P. the wash channel was at least four meters below the present level of the terrace. Moreover, springs are likely to have been active in the site vicinity and possibly at the site itself by this time.

By about 9000 B.P., the deeply stratified deposits at Tsosie Shelter (figures 2.1F and 2.4) begin to be informative of paleoclimatic events. All levels of the Tsosie Shelter sequence contained evidence of Early and Middle Holocene human occupation primarily in the form of lithic debitage and charcoal. The relevant deposits consisted of a number of mostly colluvial levels, five of which yielded radiocarbon dates on wood charcoal (Christenson and Parry 1985:451–454). All radiocarbon dates mentioned in this section have been calibrated using the Stuiver and Reimer (1993) radiocarbon calibration program, CALIB. The calibration process, pushing many of the determinations considerably further into the past, significantly increases the time depth of the Black Mesa occupation.

The earliest dated level at Tsosie Shelter, Stratum 14, produced a calibrated date at 8990 B.P. (Beta-9837). The dated material consisted of small pieces of scattered charcoal from the mid–lower portion of the approximately 60-cm-thick level at a depth of about six meters below the present surface. Another sample of scattered charcoal dating to 7910 B.P. (Beta-7201) derived from slightly higher in the same level (approximately 5.6 m below the present surface [see E. Karlstrom 1985:table B.1]). In this level, as in the undated Stratum 16 just below, the presence of both pinyon and juniper (*J. osteosperma*) as charred macrobotanicals (Ford et al. 1985; Trigg 1985) indicates that on Black Mesa, like the Canyon de Chelly and Chaco Canyon areas to the east, the Late Wisconsin (figure 2.1) climatic regime had given way to warmer conditions in which spring freezes tended to be less frequent and the advent of a summer monsoonal precipitation cycle lessened the possibility of mid- to late-summer drought.

Such conditions enabled the spread of pygmy conifer forest into the region. The presence of pinyon in the area accords well with the sequence developed by Betancourt and Davis (1984) and Betancourt and Van Devender (1983). Unfortunately, the stratigraphic record at Tsosie Shelter has not yet provided information on the actual timing of the Late Wisconsin/early Holocene vegetative succession.

Another interesting feature of Stratum 14 is that grain-sized analysis provided evidence of eolian deposition intermixed with the primarily colluvial deposit (Feathers and Stein 1985). Feathers and Stein also note that the deposit evidenced little chemical weathering, suggesting that it probably was sheltered by a roof overhang and was thus protected from moisture.

The next two strata above Stratum 14, Strata 13 and 10, consisted of generally similar composition, differing from one another only in color and separated by a diffuse boundary. Radiocarbon determinations on scattered charcoal placed Stratum 13 at 7570 B.P. (Beta-7200) and Stratum 10 at 6380 B.P. (Beta-10083). Feathers and Stein characterize the deposits as colluvial, noting both the apparently rapid rate of deposition and the large number of roof-fall blocks present in both levels. Feathers and Stein tenta-

tively suggest the strata were deposited during a wet interval. Direct corroborative evidence for deposition during a wet interval, however, remains scant.

The inference of the existence of a wet interval derives from the evidence of chemical weathering of these strata and rapid colluvial deposition from the surrounding steep slopes and mass wasting of material from the shelter itself. The depositional interval demarcated by the two radiocarbon determinations falls early in the xeric period (Antevs's Altithermal; Hack's Jeddito/Tsegi epicycle of erosion). If the evidence for a complex, alternating mesic/xeric cycle for Holocene climate is accurate, the occurrence of a relatively mesic interval during the period would hardly be surprising.

The tentatively identified mesic mid-Holocene interval also appears coeval with a warm, wet period in the La Plata Mountains (Petersen 1981). In addition, Betancourt and Davis (1984) and Betancourt and Van Devender (1983) assert that the mid-Holocene was a period of more mesic rather than more xeric conditions, although they agree with other assessments (Antevs 1955; Hevly and Karlstrom 1974) that infer higher average temperatures for this period (cf. P. Martin 1963). A definitive determination remains beyond the scope of available data.

In Strata 10 and 13, carbonized pinyon and juniper wood occur in relatively greater quantities than in the earlier levels below (Ford et al. 1985). The apparent quantitative increase in frequency of these species may, however, be a function of more intensive human occupation, a possibility bolstered by the higher frequency of artifactual material in Strata 10 and 13 (Burgett et al. 1985; Parry et al. 1985).

The next younger units, Strata 9 and 8, represent the final depositional intervals during preagricultural times at Tsosie Shelter. Radiocarbon determinations on multiple samples, each consisting of small, scattered chunks of charcoal, appear indistinguishable and provide an average age for the charcoal throughout these levels at approximately 5500 B.P. The two levels

can be distinguished from those below in that the differences between deposition events appear to result from soil-formation processes associated with intense weathering (Feathers and Stein 1985; Karlstrom 1985). In addition, the contact between Stratum 8 and the next younger level, Stratum 6, forms an unconformity representing a hiatus between Archaic-period deposition and deposition that occurred in the late Holocene.

The approximate temporal placement of the interval appears coeval with a period of widespread soil formation identified by Haynes (1968). The interval further coincides with a period of relative geomorphologic stability in the schema identified by Hevly and Karlstrom (1974). Feathers and Stein suggest that the pedogenic interval tended to be more xeric than preceding periods. E. Karlstrom (1985:391) further notes:

> The period between 4750 B.P. [now calibrated at about 5500 B.P.] and early Puebloan time is represented by . . . [a] . . . Haplargid soil. . . . This was a period of hiatus, nondeposition, soil formation, and perhaps erosion at the site. Based on alluvial stratigraphic records preserved elsewhere in the region, numerous and periodic cutting and filling cycles occurred in alluvial valleys during this period.

During the period in which Strata 8 and 9 formed, charred macrobotanical remains indicate the continued presence of pygmy conifer forest (Ford et al. 1985; Trigg 1985). Whether major vegetative shifts occurred on Black Mesa remains unknown, owing to the present low-resolution state of chronometric control for Holocene climatic, geomorphological, and paleobotanical events. The depositional hiatus and/or erosional events that might have accompanied such a hiatus preclude the presence of any record of a regional vegetative change in the test trench at Tsosie Shelter.

Thus, information on the Holocene climate of Black Mesa derives from general and local area reconstructions, from reconstructions of climate in neighboring regions, and from geomorphological and botanical studies on Black Mesa. Analysis of the suite of climatic reconstructions reveals interesting correlations between inferred Holocene events on Black Mesa and reconstructions from the Greater Southwest and other specific regions. The analysis also suggests notable disparities.

A Black Mesa Paleoclimatic Summary

The Holocene record on Black Mesa begins approximately 10,000 B.P. with radiocarbon-dated lacustrine sediments indicative of more mesic conditions than those of today. The temporal placement of the lacustrine sediments dovetails closely with general regional indications for a continuing Late Wisconsin climatic regime. Conditions at that time can be characterized as both cooler and more mesic, with mild winters, cool summers, spring freezes, mid-to-late summer droughts, and a winter-dominant precipitation cycle. Evidence from macrobotanical packrat midden studies in Chaco Canyon (Betancourt and Van Devender 1983), Canyon de Chelly (Betancourt and Davis 1984), and southeastern Utah (Betancourt 1984) indicates a major vegetation shift from conifer woodland to pygmy conifer (pinyon/juniper) forest over a wide area between 10,000 and 8000 B.P.

The macrobotanical record covering the period 8000 to 5500 B.P. at Tsosie Shelter on Black Mesa confirms the presence of pygmy-conifer forest sometime before 8000 B.P. but does not provide data to document the period of transition. The earliest known human occupation begins by about 9000 B.P. on Black Mesa. The presence of pinyon by 9000 B.P. further indicates a climatic shift to a monsoonal, mid-to-late summer precipitation cycle, with drier winters and fewer late-spring freezes (see Betancourt and Van Devender 1983).

Recent interpretations suggest that cyclical hydrologic and vegetation flux from 7500 to 4000 B.P., widely regarded as a warm, dry interval (Antevs 1955; Hack 1942a), stem from climatic oscillations from relatively mesic to xeric conditions. Moreover, the climatic oscillations indicate average temperature variation as well (Petersen 1981; Hevly and Karlstrom 1974). The Tsosie Shelter record indicates a period of rapid colluvial deposition, chemical weathering, and lack of soil formation for a portion of the period that can tentatively be interpreted as a wet cycle. The wet cycle corresponds to a warm, wet interval in the La Plata Mountains of southwestern Colorado and accords well with the suggestion by Betancourt and Van Devender (1983) that the Altithermal was a relatively mesic rather than xeric interval. Following the period, more xeric conditions appear to have been prevalent, although colluvial deposition continued but at a lesser rate at Tsosie Shelter (Feathers and Stein 1985). By approximately 4500 B.P., a nondepositional soil-forming interval ensued, lasting until approximately A.D. 800 (E. Karlstrom 1985).

A Sketch of Regional Paleoindian Occupation

Whether Late Pleistocene hunter-gatherers ever occupied the Colorado Plateau with any intensity remains an open question. That they moved widely about the vast regions of the western United States, including the Colorado Plateau, lies beyond doubt. Numerous well-documented finds from the High Plains, the Rockies, the Rio Grande Valley, and the southern Southwest attest to the Paleoindian presence. In view of the vast Paleoindian geographic distribution, we can imagine only with great difficulty that all of the ephemeral Paleoindian finds from the Colorado Plateau result from the curational behavior of later inhabitants. Agenbroad, in tracking Paleoindian archaeological finds and paleontological finds of Pleistocene megafauna notes, "Not surprisingly, there is a similarity in the distribution pattern of Clovis projectile points

and the distribution of known mammoth [paleontological] sites. Apparently, both mammoths and mammoth hunters frequented the well-watered portions of the Colorado Plateau, such as the Little Colorado, Colorado, San Juan, and Green Rivers as well as their major tributaries" (Agenbroad 1990:21).

The Black Mesa subregion has never been noted for the number or richness of Paleoindian finds. However, evidence for the pre-Archaic presence of hunter-gatherer groups has been slowly accumulating. The rate of accumulation and the nature of Black Mesa–Kayenta finds remain entirely in consonance with those of the Colorado Plateau and the Greater Southwest. Such finds tend to be limited to isolated projectile points or to artifact scatters in deflated localities. The accumulating evidence is tantalizing but provides very little absolute chronometric or site-pattern information. The occasional exceptions remain problematical, having received only nominal attention or having yet to be fully investigated.

Investigators have largely defined cultural complexes on the basis of distinctive, widely distributed Paleoindian projectile-point styles (figure 2.1G). Most, if not all, of the western North American complexes occur in the American Southwest, although in some instances only as isolated finds. In a few cases, however, unequivocal contexts and relatively rich assemblages shed light on the earliest Southwesterners.

The Clovis complex, well dated to 11,500–11,000 B.P. (Frison 1978:29) over much of North America, is thus far best expressed in the several mammoth kill sites in southeastern Arizona. Clovis sites like Lehner (Haury et al. 1959), Naco (Haury 1953), Murray Springs (Haynes 1973), and Escapule (Hemmings and Haynes 1969), among others (see Agenbroad 1990; B. Huckell 1982), have not been located in any other parts of the Colorado Plateau or the Southwest. Although a regional cluster of isolated finds and small sites occurs in central and south-central Arizona (Agenbroad 1967; B. Huckell 1982), the Colorado Plateau finds tend to be widely scattered and to show little tendency to cluster (see Schroedl 1977; Judge 1973). The only additional discoveries have been made in the Blackwater Draw locality of southeastern New Mexico (Hester 1975).

Succeeding the Clovis (Llano complex) peoples in the Southwest (as over most of North America), investigators date the Folsom peoples to the period between 11,000 and 10,000 B.P. (Frison 1978; Judge 1982). Folsom finds in the forms of isolated points and sites appear to occur with much greater frequency in the eastern Southwest than Clovis finds. The greater frequency of Folsom sites in that region suggests that the Folsom occupation may have been denser than that of the Clovis peoples who occupied the eastern region during the preceding millennium.

Folsom localities appear, in many instances, to be situated so as to allow inhabitants to monitor the movements of bison herds or to be close to kill and processing sites (Judge 1973; Frison 1978). Judge (1973) delineates a series of site types based on functional aspects of tool and debitage assemblages in the Rio Grande Valley of central New Mexico. Thus, in contrast to the archaeological record for Clovis times, in Folsom times we can identify functional site variation, and we can be assured we are observing more than a single aspect of settlement or subsistence behavior.

As has been a problem over much of the High Plains, the relatively high visibility of kill sites and the extremely ephemeral nature of base camp, monitoring, and processing sites (see Judge 1973) virtually insures that the early Paleoindian groups are best known from only a single aspect of their subsistence behavior: the communal hunting of large herbivores. Unfortunately, we cannot assume that communal kills reflect more than a single aspect of the hunting repertoire alone, since kill events are unlikely to have provided the yearly per capita

protein for such groups. Subsistence activities associated with gathering are even more poorly represented in the archaeological record.

In contrast to the eastern Southwest, Folsom materials occur across the Colorado Plateau and around the western Southwest but appear far less frequent (Agenbroad 1967, 1990; B. Huckell 1982; Schroedl 1977). Like Clovis materials, most evidence consists of isolated projectile points, although kill sites occur as well. For example, a handful of Folsom sites cluster in the San Luis Valley of southwestern Colorado, including the Zapata (Patterson and Agogino 1976), Linger (Hurst 1941; Dawson and Stanford 1975), and Cattle Guard (Emery and Stanford 1982) sites. Zapata and Linger are kills, each reported to have yielded the remains of five bison, while the Emery and Stanford reports interpret the Cattle Guard site as a Folsom camp. The apparent differentiation of site types in the San Luis Valley parallels, or at least complements, the findings of Judge (1973) in the Rio Grande Valley to the south.

Folsom finds on the Colorado Plateau, however, remain quite rare (B. Huckell 1982; Agenbroad 1967; Schroedl 1977). Davis (1985:11) described what he characterized as "one of the first Folsom sites on the Colorado Plateau documented with chronologically distinctive artifacts." The Montgomery site lies on a bench above the Green River in southeastern Utah, a few miles south of the town of Green River. Two fragmentary Folsom points, nearly two hundred tools, and more than seven hundred pieces of debitage make up the assemblage, all of which came from a deflated context. Because of the presence of artifact clusters on the site, Davis suggests the site is a base camp evidencing reoccupation (1985:11–12).

Plano points begin appearing by about 10,000 B.P., soon after Folsom materials. The Plano complex consists of a number of lanceolate point styles differing from the fluted Clovis and Folsom styles in plan shape and in the absence of the pronounced

basal fluting. The Plano cultures seem temporally distinct, though the best-dated sequences and those responsible for chronometric divisions come largely from the High Plains (Frison 1978). Plano finds remain scarce in the Southwest, although like Clovis and Folsom materials, we have likely seen only the tip of the iceberg in many subregions.

Judge's chronometric assessment of the preceramic sequence for the San Juan Basin (1982:22) agrees with most other such schemata (e.g., Frison 1978) as to the temporal placement of the Plano cultures. The earliest cultures produced what have been termed "unfluted Folsom points" that lie morphologically within the range of Folsom variability but lack basally struck thinning flutes. Many examples show the points to be finished products, not simply preforms. Unfluted types occur widely but sparsely in the Southern Plains and Southwest, but they are not limited to these areas. Subtypes include Plainview, Midland, Milnesand, Meserve, and Belen points; the meaning of the typological distinctions, however, is open to debate (Judge 1973).

The later Plano and terminal Paleoindian manifestation in the Southwest seems to be the Cody complex. Cody complex diagnostic points can easily be distinguished by long, narrow blades with very slightly but distinctly indented, parallel-sided bases, collateral pressure flaking, and pronounced median ridges. Cody sites have been found in central, western, and northwestern New Mexico (Judge 1973, 1982), and isolated finds have been reported from Utah (Schroedl 1977).

Two additional Plano manifestations deserve mention before turning to the local area Paleoindian data for Black Mesa. First is the Angostura complex, characterized by obliquely flaked lanceolate projectile points and not well known in Arizona (Frison 1978:37; Thomas 1994; Wormington 1957:138). Angostura materials may be present at the Badger Springs site just northwest of Black Mesa and described below. Dated between about 9300 and 6700 B.P. and distributed in the North American midcontinent from Alaska to Mexico (Thomas 1994:24), the Angostura point style remains poorly defined and has also been conflated with Jimmy Allen, Lusk, and Frederick complex points (Frison 1978:37).

A final Paleoindian complex known from the High Plains and other regions of the West derives its type name from the Hell Gap site in eastern Wyoming (Irwin-Williams et al. 1973). The distinctive and finely percussion-flaked Hell Gap points are relatively large and thick, with rounded shoulders and constricting bases. The Hell Gap style is strikingly similar to a number of Early Archaic point styles including Jay, Bajada, Lake Mojave, and Rio Grande. Although similarities exist between Hell Gap and later points, positively identified Hell Gap manifestations remain rare in the Southwest. In the Prayer Rock area approximately 80 km east of Black Mesa, Elizabeth Morris (1958) reports an isolated point, which she declines to classify (the Hell Gap type had not yet been defined when Morris reported the find [Judge 1982]). The excellent published photograph of the point shows a Hell Gap type morphologically similar to points from the Casper site assemblage of central Wyoming (Frison 1974, 1978). I have seen similar points in amateurs' collections, one reportedly found near Quemado, New Mexico, and another reportedly found near Flagstaff, Arizona. The type Hell Gap point is well dated to between 10,000 and 9500 B.P. on the High Plains (Frison 1978:23), and the general similarity of the Hell Gap type to Early Archaic Jay, Bajada, and others generates questions as to whether other Hell Gap materials may be incorrectly classified with post-Paleoindian assemblages. Without absolute dates on in-situ Colorado Plateau Hell Gap materials, however, the possibility remains moot.

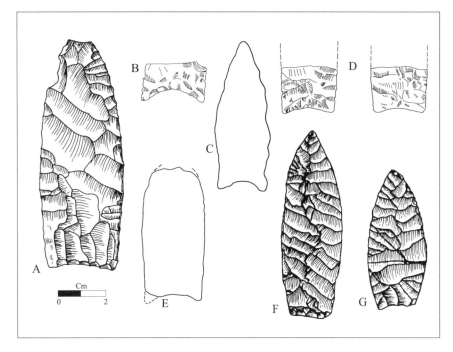

Figure 2.5 Paleoindian finds from the Kayenta area.

The Paleoindian Period and the Black Mesa Region

In previous assessments of the evidence for early humans in the Black Mesa subregion (Smiley and Andrews 1983; Nichols and Smiley 1984b), I have noted the absence of such finds both within the intensively surveyed Black Mesa study area and on Black Mesa in general. The single find from Black Mesa proper consists of a reworked Folsomlike point from the Hopi Mesas at the extreme southern reach of Black Mesa (figure 2.5c) reported by Gumerman (1966).

Several Paleoindian finds have been made in the Kayenta–Black Mesa area. The points I have directly observed or those for which photographs are available appear in figure 2.5, along with the Folsomlike point noted above (Gumerman 1966; figure 2.5c). The first of the points (figure 2.5a) is an isolated Clovis point found by an amateur in the area east of Kayenta (Ayers 1966).

A search of the Museum of Northern Arizona site files reveals a second Clovis find (not illustrated) from the general vicinity of the one reported by Ayers. Harrill (n.d., Museum of

Northern Arizona Site Files) recorded the locality of the additional find. Harrill reports that lithic manufacturing debris was also present as well as "other tool fragments."

A final Paleoindian point reported by Neely and Olson (1977:53) appears to be a Midland- or Plainview-like basal fragment (figure 2.5b). The fragment comes from a small lithic site (NA 8278) just north of Laguna Creek. In 1985, the Starling site, another discovery made by local residents in the area east of Kayenta, came to the attention of the author and William Parry. The Starling site consists of a large, dense, and varied lithic and groundstone scatter. The site seems to be oriented on a small source of unusually good Navajo chert near a seep, which in prehistoric times might have been a substantial spring.

The Starling site chert source is the only known actual quarry site for many kilometers, although Green identified numerous potential lithic sources in the area (1985). Preliminary inspection of the site revealed a number of nonlocal cherts, chalcedonies, and obsidian. In addition to a variety of Archaic projectile point styles (discussed in the sections to follow), the author noted a Plano point base of the Plainview type (figure 2.5d), generally placed contemporaneous with, or just after, Folsom-period materials. The fragment exhibited well-controlled, broad, transverse flaking, basal grinding, and a concave base. The probable in-haft fracture consisted of a transverse snap-break just distal to the extent of the lateral edge grinding. The raw material was a fine-grained, gray-green chert with no discernible inclusions.

The Kayenta area finds significantly enhance the documentation of Paleoindian presence. At least three finds, the Clovis point reported by Ayers (1966), the Plainview base found by the author, and the basal fragment from NA 8278, give some indication that early groups roamed the area and that the presence of the point specimens did not necessarily result from the curational behavior of later inhabitants.

The point reported by Ayers is of "mottled and speckled light grey to buff chert" and appeared to have been manufactured from a nodule of material available in the immediate vicinity (1966:76). The Plainview point from the Starling site, a fragmentary, non-reworked base, seems unlikely to have been curated and transported by later inhabitants. The Clovis reported by Harrill (n.d.) remains poorly documented, and at present, I can conclude only that its location in the context of chipping debris and in the general vicinity of the other finds lends some additional credence to the Paleoindian occupation in the Black Mesa subregion.

Another Paleoindian find in the Kayenta area comes from Tachini Point in the Marsh Pass area west of Kayenta. A Midland point, recovered during the excavation of a Tsegi-phase site (ca. A.D. 1250) by Cummings, has never been reported in print (William Parry, personal communication 1985; figure 2.5e). The point comes from Puebloan context, which makes its value in assessing the Paleoindian occupation dubious.

In areas surrounding, but more distant from, Black Mesa, more Paleoindian sites have been found. To the north near Green River, Utah, the Montgomery site (Davis 1985) attests to the probable presence of Folsom-age groups in the broader region. To the south, the Vernon site in the St. Johns area also appears to be a Folsom manifestation (Longacre and Graves 1976; Wilmsen 1970), and F. Plog mentions another "Folsom" site in the Winslow area, access to which was refused by the landowner (1981:51).

In the Sanders area southeast of Black Mesa, Danson (1961) illustrates three fluted specimens found by local residents and classed as Clovis-Folsom types. Danson also illustrates an additional parallel-oblique flaked lanceolate point without basal fluting and places it in the Angostura category.

The Badger Springs Angostura Site

Finally, the Badger Springs site, a small but comparatively rich site (NA 10924; AZ D:5:13) with Plano affiliation, was reported by Bernard Reimer of Inscription House Trading Post to Bruce Harrill (Harrill n.d.) of the Museum of Northern Arizona in 1970. The site was preliminarily interpreted as a camp and lay in a sand blowout approximately 15 km south of Inscription House Trading Post on the Kaibito Plateau.

The site yielded a rich assemblage of whole and fragmentary projectile points, chippage, tools, and groundstone, a human cranial fragment, teeth, and many pieces of cremated bone, possibly human (Hesse et al. 1996, 2000). The material appeared to be in situ, having been uncovered by the recent blowout (Harrill n.d.; Alexander Lindsay, personal communication 1981, 1985; Jeffrey S. Dean, personal communication 1985).

The projectile points tend to be narrow, well-flaked lanceolate types with some similarities to Agate Basin complex materials but which much more closely resemble Angostura points known from South Dakota to Mexico. The affiliation of the site

with the Angostura complex seems more probable on typological grounds and because Agate Basin materials remain virtually unknown on the Colorado Plateau and in the Southwest in general. Judge (1982:23), for example, notes the absence of Agate Basin materials in the San Juan Basin. The only other occurrence of Agate Basin materials is from the Blackwater Draw locality (Cordell 1984; Hester 1975) hundreds of kilometers to the southeast.

D. Lawler (Harrill n.d.) tentatively identified the bison skull from NA 10924, but this has not been viewed by the author. However, the author and William Parry inspected the lithic materials and the site locality in the fall of 1985. The site itself now consists of a deflated depression lying between two cornfields. We observed no remaining cultural materials during the 1985 visit, and the site appears to have been completely collected by local residents and during periodic visits by Harrill (n.d.) and by Alexander Lindsay (personal communication 1985) over the past thirty years.

The Badger Springs site assemblage consists of more than eighty-two items representing at least twenty individual points (Hesse et al. 1996). Figures 2.5f and 2.5g illustrate two complete examples from the Badger Springs site. The assemblage also contains debitage and other biface fragments.

Many of the projectile point fragments exhibit thermal alteration. Human bone also occurs at the site in highly fragmentary and either badly leached or burned condition. The burned projectile-point fragments and the small quantities of probably burned human bone suggest the possibility of the presence of a human cremation burial at the Badger Springs site (Hesse et al. 1996).

The Badger Springs site provides the best evidence of which I am aware for Paleoindian occupation of the immediate Black Mesa region. Although no absolute dates exist, the site appears to be a single-component phenomenon without the problematic presence of later Archaic or Puebloan materials. In concert with the Kayenta area in which materials of the Clovis and Plano (Folsom) age occur, NA 10924 helps to bolster the case for pre-Archaic occupation of the Black Mesa subregion.

Summary

In summary, the evidence for Paleo-indian occupation in the Black Mesa subregion (with notable exceptions) mirrors the situation elsewhere on the Colorado Plateau and in the Southwest in general. The majority of finds consist of a range of types of isolated projectile points, including Clovis, Plainview, Midland, Folsom, and Angostura materials. At least two finds come from later (Puebloan) context, and two sites near Black Mesa appear to retain some degree of contextual integrity (NA 10924 and the Starling site). The others consist of surface finds from ambiguous contexts.

Paleoindian/Archaic Transitional Evidence from Black Mesa

The newly calibrated radiocarbon determinations mentioned above for Tsosie Shelter suggest human occupation of the Mesa, itself, as early as 9000 B.P. These dates fall well before the frequently accepted terminal Paleoindian boundary between 8500 and 8000 B.P. Of course, the dates on which the Paleoindian boundary has been based could not then be calibrated either (Frison 1978), and so the "definitional" Paleoindian determinations can be assumed to represent significantly earlier calendar dates as well. Tsosie Shelter dates that fall before 8900 B.P. receive support from two other early sites, one (D:11:3063) on Black Mesa and the other, the Hastqin site, in the Ganado area (B. Huckell 1977). Both open-air camps, the two sites produced calibrated dates essentially coeval with the early strata at Tsosie Shelter.

While the sites just cited could be construed to be Paleoindian by conventional dating criteria, none

produced any diagnostic Paleoindian projectile points. In fact, the sites yielded a small assemblage of points that fit Early Archaic typologies (Smiley 1995a). The early dates for the sites probably do not alter the typological inclusion in particular cultural historical periods; rather, the new evidence changes the time frames of those culture historical periods. Accordingly, I discuss the sites in detail in the following Archaic sections.

General Observations on the Paleoindian Period

The paleoenvironmental reconstructions illustrated in figure 2.1 indicate the early Holocene occupational period to be one of fairly gradual but significant change in climate, fauna, and flora in the northern Southwest. Although no detailed data exist for the Black Mesa subregion, the available information fits virtually all proposed scenarios for the period.

Specifically, the retreat of the continental ice sheets in concert with general warming and air-mass flow-pattern changes, enabled the establishment of much of the modern-day vegetational regime by between 9000 and 8000 B.P. The early Holocene spruce/limber pine/pygmy conifer forest, probably interspersed with sage/grass parklands had been depressed up to 850 m below the present 2600 m ASL (Betancourt 1984). In concert with F. Plog (1981:52), I view it as likely that virtually the entire Black Mesa subregion was conifer parkland. The study area and surrounding region lie essentially between 1800 and 2450 m, well within the altitudinal reaches for such flora indicated by the various packrat midden studies (Betancourt and Van Devender 1983; Betancourt and Davis 1984; Betancourt 1984) in neighboring regions to the west and north.

Such a floral regime would not be ideal for either bison or mammoth, although paleontological discoveries suggest the presence of both (Hack 1942a:29; Agenbroad 1990). If the Paleoindian occupation of the area

was ephemeral and sporadic, the occupation seems likely to have been a function of both the inability of the area to support large numbers of herbivores, which were actually a "focal" resource (see discussion in Judge [1973, 1982]), and the general propensity of the human groups to maintain high mobility and low population density. Such faunal resources seem to have had a significant effect on the structuring of settlement and mobility decisions for early Holocene groups. The mobility of the bison herds alone, independent of herd size or regional packing, insures high residential mobility for hunter-gatherers dependent on the bison for a variety of subsistence needs (Frison 1978; Smiley 1979, 1995b).

Kelly and Todd examined Paleoindian groups in terms of subsistence concentration on large fauna. Such a hunting concentration, say Kelly and Todd, reduces the need to rely on detailed local knowledge of plant resources (1988). Given the Paleoindian archaeological record so far evident, one can easily imagine the Paleoindian occupations in terms of highly mobile, nontethered populations.

However, as the pinyon and juniper woodland and sage grassland became dominant over the subregion sometime before 8000 B.P., conditions might have significantly improved for grazing and, hence, hunting. Additionally, the sporadic but rich pinyon-nut mast would also have increased the viability of human groups using such areas. Thus, one might expect an increased Paleoindian presence in the period after about 10,000 B.P. The apparent late Plano materials and extinct bison remains recovered at NA 10924 indicate that successful hunting took place during the period. We simply do not know how intensively or how often such occupation occurred. In fact, and in general ways, the hypothetical high mobility, nontethered settlement pattern appears to persist on the northern Colorado Plateau for the next eight thousand years (Smiley 1997a).

A primary problem, perhaps *the*

problem, remains that despite the accumulating Paleoindian evidence, we still do not yet know the regional locational parameters for early human sites on the Colorado Plateau. The sites reviewed above suggest a variety of types, including camp, quarry, and hunting activities. The sites lie in a variety of topographic situations, but we have too little information to apply demographic or environmentally oriented models, as Judge (1973) has been able to do, for example, in the Rio Grande Valley.

The Black Mesa Archaic

The Southwest Archaic constitutes the longest of the broad cultural periods considered in this volume. Following the close of the Pleistocene, the associated faunal extinctions, and significant changes in the climatic and vegetative regimes, human populations in the Black Mesa region appear to have followed the classic southwestern pattern of greater reliance on vegetative and small animal resources. Though poorly represented on and around Black Mesa, the Archaic period remains particularly significant as precursor to the agricultural transition. The significance of the Archaic is heightened by the sheer volume of early agricultural period evidence in the Black Mesa region and the importance of the early agricultural material to southwestern prehistory.

In the following discussions of the Archaic, I wish to be clear that I view the Archaic both as an adaptation and as a temporal period. Accordingly, I apply the term "Archaic" only to hunter-gatherers and not to early agricultural populations. This must be said because some investigators writing about the early agricultural period and peoples of the southern Southwest tend to apply the terms "Archaic" or "Late Archaic" to early agriculturalists (Matson 1991:202; B. Huckell 1987). In fact, the several-millennium-long Archaic hunting-and-gathering adaptation comes to a close with the beginnings of food production. With the

agricultural transition, systems in the Southwest undergo changes not only in subsistence but in religious structure, settlement, social organization, technology, and population density (B. Huckell 1987, 1990; Smiley 1985, 1993, 1997e, 2000a, b, c; Wills 1988a; Matson 1991). Although some investigators see some continuity in the southern Southwest across the agricultural transition (Fish and Fish 1992; Wills 1988a), in the north, the changes appear dramatic and unequivocal.

Archaic Adaptation

The change in adaptation in the Southwest with the advent of agriculture suggests that a useful way to examine the long prelude to the agricultural fluorescence may be to contrast Archaic adaptations with the early agricultural period's process of changing human/land relationships. Embodied in this view is the fundamental idea that the advent of agricultural subsistence resulted in basic qualitative and quantitative alterations in human subsistence and social systems. These alterations seem to have behaved as positive feedback loops. The prelude to, and advent of, food production is of general interest to anthropologists for precisely the following reason: the transition to food production may have begun as a small systemic "kick" (e.g., Flannery 1968), but the shift had broad systemic consequences for the complexity, size, and density of human populations.

A number of general, timely reviews of the southwestern Archaic evidence have been published in recent years (Berry and Berry 1986; Matson 1991; Parry et al. 1985; Wills 1988a), and so I will not attempt a similarly detailed syntheses here. Instead, I examine certain models of early Holocene adaptation in terms of the Archaic data from the Black Mesa region.

The change in human/land relationships during the agricultural transition involved controlling the productivity of the natural environment; determining when, where,

and how much of specific kinds of resources would be produced; and making provision for resource availability during periods of low productivity. Archaeologists typically do not associate food production and storage with the organizational modes of the highly mobile hunter-gatherers who apparently inhabited virtually all regions of the Southwest for most of the Holocene. Consequently, one expects the adoption and assimilation of the technology and materials of food production by such groups, especially if the process occurs relatively quickly, to engender fundamental technological, subsistence, and social organizational changes. Such changes occurred, however, not as requirements but as consequences of adoption.

In a recent study, Wills views the transition as conscious decisions on the part of recipient groups and as predictable consequences of the availability of agricultural technology. Most important, the transition was economical in terms of group organizational investment (Wills 1988a, b). Wills sees Archaic development in the Southwest as a long trend in organizational change that results in preadaptation to modes of subsistence and settlement necessary to food production. In terms of Binford's conceptual continuum of subsistence, settlement, and mobility strategies for hunter-gatherer groups, the southwestern organizational change consists of a move from adaptations focused on *foraging* toward adaptations at the *collecting* end of the spectrum. That is, in many areas, populations appear to change from subsistence/mobility strategies that require hunter-gatherer groups to map onto resources over large areas through residential mobility toward modes of organization that require logistical structure.

The change involves a gradual movement toward logistical (e.g., Binford 1980) subsistence/mobility strategies that allow temporal and spatial resource distribution problems to be solved by task groups operating from base camps. The logistical settlement pattern thus assumes people will place the primary residential unit so that a variety of resources can be harvested by relatively short, task-specific excursions. Wills views the existence of more logistically oriented systems as a necessary precondition to farming. Under such circumstances, groups making the decision to adopt cultivation would require minimal organizational change (1988b).

Other researchers such as Berry and Berry (1986; see also M. Berry 1982) view the demographics of the Archaic period as a mosaic of populations and population movements that leave some regions of the Southwest nearly or completely depopulated for periods of time. This position does not necessarily contradict Wills' basic premise that population over the Southwest increased during the Archaic period and that group territories shrank in response. Wills does, however, see continuous occupation in all areas of the Southwest (1988a). Whether the Berry and Berry hypothesis of abandonment during some periods in some regions stems from sampling problems or from a real hiatus in human use of portions of the Southwest, notably the Colorado Plateau, remains to be seen.

The evidence from the Black Mesa regional and project area does, however, shed some light on the controversy, as should become apparent. In the sections to follow, I detail the Black Mesa Archaic occupation evidence as prelude to the agricultural transition. New chronometric data for the transition make possible improvements in the interpretation of sites and evidence previously thought to belong to what had been termed the "Late Archaic hunter-gatherer Hisatsinom phase" on Black Mesa (Smiley and Andrews 1983).

Time-Honored Frameworks for the Southwestern Archaic

Three primary conceptual frameworks provide structure for the interpretation of much of the Holocene prehistory of the Southwest. The two earliest

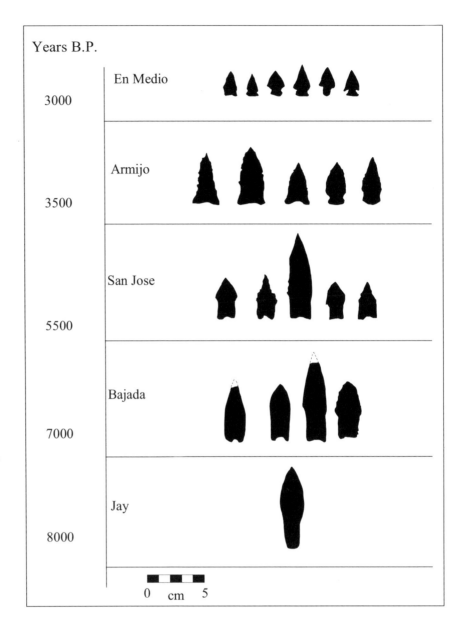

Figure 2.6   Projectile-point typology of the Oshara tradition (Irwin-Williams 1973).

schemes, the Desert Culture Tradition (Jennings 1978) and the Cochise Tradition (Sayles and Antevs 1941; Sayles 1984) primarily deal with the southern and western portions of the Southwest respectively. Although these chronologies have been criticized on chronometric and cultural grounds (Berry and Berry 1986), the systems remain in use. Having mentioned them, I refer the interested reader to the original sources.

The third general scheme of Archaic cultural history consists of Irwin-Williams' Oshara Tradition (1973), outlined in figure 2.1G, derived

from survey and excavation in the Arroyo Cuervo region of northwestern New Mexico, approximately 300 km southeast of Black Mesa. The Oshara construct (figure 2.6) attempts to explain preceramic variability in terms of cultural evolution (Irwin-Williams 1973:2) and recognizes settlement, subsistence, and technological variability among the phases. The Early Archaic (6000 to 3200 B.C.) under the Oshara schema consists of the Jay and Bajada phases identified by shouldered, almost lanceolate projectile points with ground convex, straight, or indented bases. The middle portion of the Archaic (3200 to 1800 B.C.), the San Jose phase, produces slightly shouldered or wide, side-notched, serrated projectile points that tend to be poorly dated and to occur widely over the northern Southwest. The final Archaic period phases in the Oshara construct consist of the Armijo (1800 to 800 B.C.) and En Medio (800 B.C. to A.D. 400) phases.

The Oshara Tradition, though based on the local sequence in the Arroyo Cuervo area, has been used over most of the northern Southwest. Most Oshara applications are a function of the absence of local chronological information. Until the basic chronometric and type artifact data appear in more detailed form, it is difficult to judge the extent to which the sequence can or should be adopted in other areas.

The adaptive models and the frameworks of cultural history devised over past decades to synthesize preceramic developments over major portions of the Southwest remain under scrutiny. This is a healthy process in which one expects changes in chronology and in the interpretive frames. In fact, as will be explained, the Black Mesa Archaic fails to conform in several respects to the models just described. The departures are particularly interesting and may result in the rethinking of some aspects of our current ideas about Archaic adaptations and chronologies.

The Archaic in the Greater Black Mesa Region

The new data on preagricultural human use of Black Mesa, gained primarily during the latter years of BMAP field work, have greatly increased the time depth of Black Mesa prehistory. Before 1972, for example, even the Basketmaker II occupation remained unknown in the study area, although the well-known Basketmaker burial/storage caves of the Marsh Pass area (Kidder and Guernsey 1919; Guernsey and Kidder 1921) lie only a few air kilometers from the northern

scarp of Black Mesa. Only in 1982, more than a decade after the beginning of field work, did radiocarbon-dated hearths and assemblages reveal that Early, Middle, and Late Archaic peoples had occupied Black Mesa.

Unlike the San Juan Basin, in which a large number of Archaic sites have come to light (Judge 1982; Reher 1977), the area immediately surrounding Black Mesa remains conspicuously depauperate in reported Archaic remains. However, much like the Paleoindian evidence discussed above, we have a slowly increasing corpus of data indicating that Archaic groups used the region on at least a sporadic and nonintensive basis.

The Black Mesa region Archaic presents other problems as well. A salient characteristic of the Archaic in the Southwest is the perpetual state of disarray in lithic typology (Smiley 1995). A second and equally vexing problem is the minuscule amount of chronometric information available for the thousands of sites that may be expected to fall into this long temporal interval (Cordell 1984:154; Judge 1982:21). Nowhere are these problems worse than in northeastern Arizona. Although such difficulties plague researchers, we have made some progress.

The Black Mesa project research has helped in several respects. Before 1980, BMAP had excavated only nine preceramic sites and had tested only three others. The relative lack of emphasis on pre-Puebloan archaeology resulted from the ephemeral nature of preceramic sites and the continuing interest in refining numerous aspects of the more visible and much richer Puebloan archaeological record.

Beginning with the 1980 field season, BMAP began to emphasize excavation of small, ephemeral lithic sites. BMAP excavated thirty such sites during the final four seasons. Most preceramic sites belonged to the early agricultural Basketmaker II period, but researchers originally assigned five to the Archaic, based on radiocarbon and artifactual data. Two other sites

located by BMAP survey personnel have also been identified as Archaic.

Traditional divisions of the Archaic into subperiods in the Southwest typically consist of a tripartite system (Irwin-Williams 1979; Wills 1988b). Although the particular temporal boundaries vary, the general schema consists of Early (8500 to 5000 B.P.), Middle (5000 to 3000 B.P.), and Late (3000 to 2000 B.P.) Archaic periods. The periods are defined on loosely dated projectile-point types and other aspects of assemblage variability (Irwin-Williams 1973, 1979; Sayles and Antevs 1941).

The diagnostic materials associated with dated preagricultural sites on Black Mesa, however, did not fit the divisions in a neat, unequivocal fashion. For example, excavators recovered Bajada and San Jose points in situ at a site that dates to approximately 9000 B.P. Both point styles date substantially later, however, in the Oshara Tradition schema of Irwin-Williams (1973). The possibility also exists that a Bajada-style point from the Hastqin site near Ganado (B. Huckell 1977) may be associated with hearths dating around 9000 B.P. On the other end of the temporal span, corner- and side-notched point varieties (typically considered late forms) from sites on Black Mesa have been recovered from sites the ages of which range from about 3800 to 2800 B.P.

One small site, NA 10824, consists of lithic debris and hearths exposed around the edges of a partially stabilized dune on a ridge just north of Long House ruin in Long House Valley north of Black Mesa (Museum of Northern Arizona site files; Jeffrey S. Dean, personal communication 1981). Although undated, projectile points from NA 10824 evidence serrations, side-notching, and straight bases and fit general late types such as Armijo and En Medio forms illustrated by Irwin-Williams (1973).

Another significant assemblage has been observed by the author and William Parry on the Starling site. While the Starling site, located near

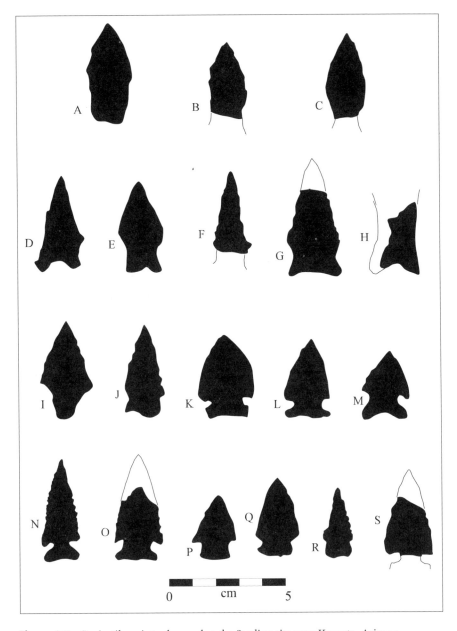

Figure 2.7 Projectile points observed at the Starling site near Kayenta, Arizona.

Kayenta, also produced some evidence of Paleoindian occupation (described above), Archaic materials occur on the site in abundance. Figure 2.7 illustrates points located and photographed on the site but not collected. During my several inspections of the site over the years, I identified at least one and possibly three Jay points assignable to the Early Archaic (figure 2.7a–c), several Pinto/San Jose types normally placed in the Middle Archaic (figure 2.7d–h), and numerous side-notched and corner-notched points typically

thought to date to Late Archaic times (figure 2.7i–s). The raw materials range from obsidian to chalcedony, including a wide variety of cherts.

In addition, surface collections made in various parts of the Navajo-Hopi Joint Use Area produced typical Pinto/San Jose forms as well as a shouldered, contracting stemmed specimen typical of Gypsum point forms (Bender 1979). Finally, the Hastqin site (AZ K:6:19; B. Huckell 1977) located near Ganado, Arizona, southeast of Black Mesa has yielded evi-

dence of a substantial Archaic occupation during the San Jose period. The Hastqin site produced radiocarbon dates on wood charcoal from hearths (Features 2 and 7) calibrated at 9240 B.P. (A-1694) and 8770 B.P. (A-1756) respectively. Excavations produced the Bajada-style point mentioned above (B. Huckell 1977) as well. The Bajada phase, though not securely dated, features a projectile-point style usually characterized as Early Archaic (Wills 1988a; Irwin-Williams 1973). The Hastqin site specimen could not be directly associated with the dated hearths, although B. Huckell characterizes the point as "heavily reworked" and apparently discarded at the site (1977:15).

The radiocarbon determinations clustering around 9000 B.P. fall earlier than, but not inconsistent with, an Early Archaic temporal assignment for at least some site components. The dates are also entirely consistent with those from two Black Mesa study-area sites, indicating that Early Archaic groups moved over the area during the early Holocene. The variety of point styles at the Hastqin site and the Starling site and the range of radiocarbon dates from at least one Black Mesa site (D:7:2085) indicate some level of Archaic presence over a period of several millennia. B. Huckell suggests the primary occupation at the Hastqin site occurred during the San Jose phase or Middle Archaic, based on morphological attributes of other projectile points from the Hastqin site(1977).

The short list of Archaic sites in the Black Mesa region just discussed illustrates the rudimentary state of current knowledge of preagricultural hunter-gatherer occupation. However, like the Paleoindian evidence cited above, the lack of systematic survey and general inattention to Archaic-period remains may explain the small sample size. On northeastern Black Mesa, the intensive survey and excavation work focused on small, ephemeral aceramic sites not only revealed the presence of Archaic groups in the project area but provide at least some evidence for use of the area over the entire span of the Archaic. One might reasonably expect the pattern to hold not only for Black Mesa but for the entire region.

Chronometry of the Black Mesa Archaic

Like the surrounding regions, the Black Mesa Archaic period can be divided at least into Early and Middle periods. The sites in the small sample of unequivocal Black Mesa Archaic sites range in age from approximately 9000 B.P. to approximately 5500 B.P. Depending on one's level of optimism, the nine radiocarbon dates from the two sites either leave no appreciable gaps across the span of the Archaic period or cover the period so sparsely that one could characterize the period as consisting entirely of gaps. One additional site (D:11:2191) yielded no datable material and has been placed in the Archaic period on the basis of its lithic assemblage.

Perhaps most informative for chronometric purposes is D:7:2085, Tsosie Shelter, described in detail in the foregoing paleoclimatic discussion. Figures 2.1F and 2.4 illustrate the placement of sampling units that yielded radiocarbon materials for assay. Figure 2.4 also shows the orderly stratigraphic progression of the dates from older to younger as one moves up the profile.

The earliest dated Tsosie Shelter stratum (14) at 8990 B.P. (B-5635) is contemporaneous with the two Early Archaic determinations from a site (D:11:3063) in the extreme southwest portion of the area. The two determinations from D:11:3063 fall at 8980 B.P. (Beta-5635) and 8550 B.P. (Beta-5634). Both dates derive from scattered charcoal recovered from small hearths.

Chronometric data from the Middle Archaic period (6000 to 4000 B.P.) continue to be more elusive. The best evidence for Middle Archaic occupation consists of radiocarbon-dated cultural strata (Stratum 8, 5570 B.P.; [Beta-9835] and Stratum 9, 5570

B.P., [Beta-9836]) at Tsosie Shelter. The determinations fall equivocally on the Early Archaic/Middle Archaic boundary. Although the two strata in question are unquestionably cultural levels, excavations yielded no diagnostic artifacts.

Other evidence for Middle Archaic occupation of the study area remains problematic. The evidence consists of a number of Pinto/San Jose-style points with bifurcate bases and serrated blades, occurring largely as isolated finds or in either equivocal Archaic or definitely non-Archaic contexts (Parry et al. 1985). To illustrate the context difficulties with much of the Archaic point sample, more than twenty Pinto/San Jose or Armijo/Concho points come from securely dated Basketmaker II or Puebloan contexts. As Parry et al. indicate, the possibility exists that some of the Basketmaker II or Puebloan sites that produced clearly Middle Archaic–style points have previously unrecognized Archaic components. However, most investigators would probably agree that later inhabitants of the area collected the points from original Archaic contexts (Parry et al. 1985:23).

To sum up the current interpretation of the chronology of the Black mesa hunter-gatherer occupation, the Black Mesa suite of radiocarbon dates provides relatively even coverage of the timeline from about 9000 to about 4000 B.P. Little should be made of the chronological coverage, however, since the sample remains too small to provide much statistical support. Any attempt to posit millennia of continuous habitation by Archaic groups in the general region or on Black Mesa would be irresponsible.

The best that can be responsibly said about the small suite of dates from two sites is that the coverage is remarkably even for so few dates. Further, the available data document the presence of Archaic hunter-gatherers in the study area and the surrounding region over most of the Holocene, sporadic and ephemeral though

the presence may have been. Unfortunately, the current suite of dates remains insufficient to resolve the controversy over the continuous or episodic occupation of the Colorado Plateau. The sample remains too small and the number of dated sites too few.

Whether Late Archaic sites exist remains open to question. Sites in the period initially assigned to the Hisatsinom phase (Smiley and Andrews 1983) now appear to fall within the White Dog phase, which begins with the onset of agriculture. Accordingly, these sites are likely to be campsites within the phase of the White Dog settlement system.

At one point, S. Plog (1986b) advocated elimination of the Hisatsinom phase, because it appeared to be undifferentiated from the Lolomai phase, which was then thought to be the only Basketmaker II manifestation and thought to begin around 2600 B.P. Subsequent work has established that the Lolomai-phase peoples were temporally discrete and adaptively different from the peoples of the Hisatstinom phase. The Lolomai phase, characterized by small, open-air agricultural settlements and camps, appears to begin after 2000 B.P. The small, short-term occupations or campsites D:7:2100, D:7:3003A, D:7:3144, D:11:1281, and D:11:2191 formerly assigned to the Hisatsinom phase fall significantly earlier than the Lolomai phase.

The problem of the Hisatsinom phase lies in explaining the existence of the several supposed Late Archaic sites just listed that appear to overlap temporally with the early Basketmaker II occupation of the region. Following Colton (1939) and Lipe (1970), I have called this earlier Basketmaker II manifestation the White Dog phase. The variant of the White Dog phase in the Black Mesa area can be defined by dates on cultigens from the "classic" Basketmaker II rockshelters of the region (Smiley 1994, 1997a, 2000c; Smiley et al. 1986). The White Dog phase may begin as early as 4000 B.P. and appears to involve agricultural subsistence focused on rockshelter use in the northern Southwest until about 2000 B.P. (Smiley 1994). The sites formerly classified as "Late Archaic," or Hisatsinom, on Black Mesa appear to date coevally with the White Dog phase and, as note above, likely comprise a component of the White Dog Phase settlement system.

Artifact Assemblages

The assemblages from the three Archaic-period manifestations at two sites in the Black Mesa study area consist overwhelmingly of chipped stone with a few groundstone items. As I have already indicated, the Archaic assemblages differ significantly from those of later Lolomai-phase and Puebloan-period assemblages. The differences include the average assemblage sizes, the diversity of chipped stone raw materials represented, the kinds and percentages of formal tools present, the stylistic attributes exhibited by projectile points, and the kinds of lithic reduction activities performed at the sites.

Archaic sites on Black Mesa typically produce much smaller chipped stone inventories, most sites yielding fewer than 200 items (Parry et al. 1985; Parry 1987a). In contrast, Basketmaker II Lolomai-phase occupations frequently yielded well over 1,000, and even small temporary camp localities sometimes produced thousands of pieces (Leonard et al. 1984c; Smiley et al. 1983). The Archaic sites have produced remarkably similar-sized inventories ranging from 151 to 178 pieces. The lithic sample from one of these sites, Tsosie Shelter (D:7:2085), derives solely from a 1 × 5 m test trench in buried Archaic levels. The small areal and volumetric sample of Archaic-age deposits from Tsosie Shelter yielded enough artifacts to suggest the total inventory could be expected to be substantially larger.

The patterns of lithic raw-material types found on Black Mesa Archaic sites also vary significantly from those

of later Basketmaker II and Puebloan assemblages. Various studies have examined the frequency patterns of raw material types in relation to models of raw materials procurement and the distribution of lithic raw material source locations in the greater Black Mesa region (Leonard et al. 1984c; Parry 1987b; Green 1985).

Accordingly, we can locate a large number of the sources of prehistoric raw materials. A general schema for classifying sources used in the studies just cited serves to categorize materials simultaneously by source distance from the Black Mesa study area and by quality of raw material. The finest-grained and highest-quality materials tend to come from greater distances, while the coarser, lower-quality materials come from local sources. Thus, obsidian and high-quality cherts and chalcedonies derive primarily from sources varying in distance from approximately 40 to over 200 km away. Locally available raw materials, including baked siltstones, poor-quality petrified woods, and quartzites, occur within and relatively near the study area.

The Archaic assemblages, particularly those attributed to the Early Archaic period (D:7:2085 and D:11:3063), contain higher percentages of nonlocal materials. The two Early Archaic site assemblages, moreover, contained unusual amounts of material from distant sources, those lying approximately 50 to 200 km away. The D:11:3063 assemblage featured 40 percent obsidian artifacts, and the small test at D:7:2085 yielded five obsidian flakes from Archaic levels. In addition, both sites produced vitreous petrified wood flakes also thought to come from distant sources (Parry et al. 1985). In contrast, obsidian artifacts tend to be extremely rare in Basketmaker II assemblages, even site assemblages numbering more than ten thousand pieces. In fact, in almost two decades of fieldwork on Black Mesa, less than two hundred pieces of obsidian have been recovered from all excavated and surface-collected sites

younger than the Early and Middle Archaic. The proportion of obsidian artifacts from non-Archaic contexts remains so small, compared to the total lithic assemblages from the Archaic contexts, as to barely register.

Parry (1987b) has made a detailed study of the structure of the lithic assemblages from Black Mesa sites of all periods. Parry's findings clearly distinguish Archaic sites from all other sites. At the same time, some variability is also evident within the small Archaic site sample. Basketmaker II sites typically produce assemblages containing over 90 percent baked siltstone (Parry 1987b:209; Leonard et al. 1984c). The average percentage for locally available baked siltstone on Archaic sites was 44 percent, compared to 91 percent for Basketmaker II sites. At the same time, Archaic assemblages averaged 39 percent nonlocal materials, while Basketmaker II sites yielded only 4 percent. The weights of waste flakes average far less than for flakes from the later sites of the Puebloan period for both locally available and nonlocal materials (Parry 1987b:213).

The variability among Archaic assemblages likely relates, as Parry et al. suggest, to "logistical factors, such as whether or not a need for additional tools arose while the people were camped on [Black Mesa]" (1985:18). Thus, the patterns of Archaic assemblage raw material indicate that groups tended to be transient, bringing with them much of the material for what little lithic manufacturing and maintenance they required (Parry 1987b:225).

The recent results of X-ray fluorescence characterization of obsidian artifacts from the two Black Mesa Early Archaic sites, Tsosie Shelter and D:11:3063, indicate that the obsidian came from the Government Mountain source in the San Francisco Volcanic Field. The Government Mountain source lies near Flagstaff, Arizona, approximately 200 km southwest of Black Mesa. The source characterization uses ratios of rubidium, strontium, and zirconium and the semiquantitative rapid-scan method (Christopher Stevenson, personal communication 1986).

With respect to lithic-reduction strategies, Parry (1987b) notes that compared to Basketmaker II assemblages, Archaic assemblages tend to contain more biface thinning debris on nonlocal materials. On the other hand, Basketmaker II groups tended to do more biface thinning on locally available siltstones than their Archaic counterparts.

Archaic assemblages on Black Mesa also evidenced other patterns of lithic reduction that differ from those of Basketmaker II sites, particularly in that Archaic groups apparently tended to bring both the locally available siltstones and nonlocal cherts and obsidians to sites in at least partially worked form (Parry 1987b). The tendency to perform some reduction away from sites may explain the higher frequencies of biface thinning debris and the relatively low frequencies of expedient flake tools.

The other major area of assemblage difference between sites assigned to the Archaic and later periods resides in artifact style. The only style-sensitive artifact category for Black Mesa and, in fact, for most southwestern Archaic assemblages consists of projectile points (see Wills 1988a). The sites assigned to the Early Archaic from the study area produced markedly different styles of points compared to, for example, the Basketmaker II assemblages. The two points recovered from D:11:3063 may be classed respectively as a Bajada/Jay type and a Pinto/San Jose type. Parry et al. (1985) note that investigators often associate Bajada points with the period between 6800 and 5200 B.P. and place San Jose–style points between about 5200 and 3800 B.P. (Irwin-Williams 1973). The presence of points of these styles on a site dated between 9000 and 8500 B.P. indicates that the early end of the temporal range of both point styles may substantially predate the ranges currently assigned to them within the Oshara Tradition.

As previously noted, points of styles typically associated with the Middle Archaic (5000 to 3000 B.P. Pinto/San Jose) have been recovered either as isolated finds or from Basketmaker II and Puebloan contexts. Thus, little can be said about Black Mesa temporal associations, with the exception of the point from an Early Archaic context already discussed. It is not likely that such points were moved great distances by later peoples. Moreover, I have observed Pinto/San Jose points with indented bases as well as shouldered points at the Starling site (figure 2.7a–c), and I think other such sites exist and will eventually be found on or around Black Mesa.

Like the chipped stone inventories, the groundstone assemblages tend to be proportionately small, consisting of one or two artifacts per site. Groundstone artifacts consist primarily of one-hand manos and small basin metates ostensibly used for processing wild seeds. Only the Archaic levels of Tsosie Shelter produced appreciable quantities of groundstone tools (five manos, four metate fragments; Christenson 1987a; Parry et al. 1985). Again, however, I emphasize that the Tsosie Shelter assemblage probably represents only a fraction of the total Archaic groundstone inventory at the site.

Archaic Subsistence

In the previous section, I outlined major resource exploitive strategies for Archaic-period groups on Black Mesa. However, information from two sites indicates the use of a variety of resources. Unfortunately, most sites, as small, ephemeral encampments subjected to erosional forces over several millennia, provide little in the way of organic preservation. Accordingly, the sites typically produce small samples of subsistence remains. Materials from the Archaic sites show marked similarities, even though the kinds of sites from which they derive differ significantly.

The best information comes from the levels at Tsosie Shelter. Flotation samples from Strata 14, 13, 10, and 9 (in order of absolute age from older to younger) indicated that Archaic groups used several seed-bearing annual and perennial plants. The most numerous specimens came from goosefoot (*Chenopodium*) and pigweed (*Amaranthus*) seeds, although purslane (*Portulaca*) and saltbush (*Atriplex*) occurred as well (Parry et al. 1985; Trigg 1985). The samples also contained trace amounts of prickly pear cactus (*Opuntia*), rice grass (*Oryzopsis*), beeweed (*Cleome*), and juniper (*Juniperus*). Faunal remains consisted primarily of cottontail (*Sylvilagus*; at least thirty-nine identifiable specimens) and jackrabbit (*Lepus*; at least five specimens). Analysis also recovered remains of smaller mammals, such as rock squirrels (*Spermophylus*) and pocket gophers (*Thomomys*; Parry et al. 1985).

The preponderance of goosefoot seeds in Early Archaic contexts parallels the findings of Reinhard et al. (1985)—at Dust Devil Cave, a sheltered site in southeastern Utah directly north of Black Mesa. Analysis of coprolites from Dust Devil Cave indicated that goosefoot seeds provided a significant component of the diet during Desha (Early Archaic ca. 8800 to 6800 B.P.) times.

Settlement and Demography

Over the several millennia of the Black Mesa Archaic, small hunter-gatherer groups must have made numerous visits, however brief. The small size of the sample of such sites recovered by the intensive survey and excavation program within the Black Mesa study area precludes any sort of definitive study of site locational criteria or population demography. However, as I have indicated elsewhere (Parry et al. 1985), the Archaic-period sites of which we have knowledge lie in a variety of geomorphic and topographic settings. The nature of the settings bears on our ability to generate even rudimentary estimates of relative site temporal occupation frequencies and site densities. Unfortunately, even the locational and geomorphic circumstances of the sites give confusing and contradictory evidence as to the actual intensity of the Archaic exploitation of Black Mesa. Geomorphic forces will have destroyed or buried a huge percentage of the sites. At the same time, I suspect that survey crews located most surviving sites, giving at least a nominally representative sample of the remaining Archaic evidence. Although we can never know what crews may have missed, I support the likelihood of reasonably accurate survey, first, because crews surveyed a number of areas more than once, reducing the chance of missing ephemeral sites. Second, crews focused specifically on the problem of identifying ephemeral camps and lithic scatters in the last two years of survey.

Given the range of site types, the problem lies in the difficulty of estimating the actual Archaic occupational density. On the one hand, the presence of at least one deeply buried site suggests that more such sites could be present. On the other hand, the presence of a site, D:11:3063, on a surface that has apparently remained geomorphically stable for millennia, indicates the capability of the survey effort to detect even the most ephemeral Archaic sites. Accordingly, the small number of located Archaic sites in the study area may well reflect a particularly low or sporadic level of Archaic exploitation of Black Mesa. The fact that large (siteless) expanses of Pleistocene and early and middle Holocene surfaces old enough to contain the remains of Archaic occupations lie exposed in the study area bolsters the argument for low-level or extremely sporadic occupation. In any case, the varied and geomorphically active environment of Black Mesa leads to conflicting interpretations of the intensity of Archaic occupations.

Whatever the nature of the universe of Archaic remains in the study area, site density appears to be far lower than that of adjacent regions, particularly the San Juan drainages to the east. Because the Black Mesa

Archaic site inventory contains only two sites within an area of 252 km^2, calculating a site-density figure would be specious. On the other hand, the Coal Gassification Project (CGP) survey in the Chaco region (Reher 1977) covered an area of approximately 151 km^2, identifying seventy-three Archaic sites and indicating an approximate site density vastly higher than that of Black Mesa. The ADAPT I Project survey in western New Mexico (Simmons 1982b) returned similar site-density figures. The ADAPT I survey of 67.3 km^2 located fifty-three Archaic sites, giving an approximate site density in the area of 0.64 sites/km^2.

The enormous differences in site density may stem from the environmental differences between the ADAPT I and CGP survey regions and that of Black Mesa. The environmental settings of the two New Mexico surveys consist of desert shrub/grassland communities in semiarid areas of dissected topography, with a major component of stabilized sand dunes (Donaldson 1982:93; Witter 1977). Contrasted with the dune and grassland settings, the canyons and wash systems of Black Mesa primarily feature pygmy conifer forest and sage communities on deeper alluvial soils. Reher and Witter (1977) and Simmons (1982a:925) have linked the location of Archaic sites to the comparative vegetative diversity offered by proximity to stabilized dune fields in the San Juan Basin. The extremely low site-density figures for Black Mesa may simply reflect a relatively light, sporadic occupation throughout the Archaic in a relatively depauperate environment.

Whether the vegetative productivity of northern Black Mesa fell below that of other areas in the San Juan Basin to the east remains an open question. However, if gathered plant foods made up a major share of the Archaic diet, as they almost certainly did, then the much greater Archaic site density in the San Juan Basin study areas may indicate the areas offered far more favorable conditions for hunter-gatherer subsistence. Obviously, the problems of geomorphic

forces acting to destroy or mask the presence of sites may be substantially different for northern Black Mesa than for the San Juan Basin areas, a possibility that must be kept in mind in analyzing site locational patterns.

Using, for the sake of argument, Steward's (1938) ethnographically derived Great Basin population estimates of approximately 1 person/40 km^2 (see Minnis 1985b:56), the 252 km^2 Black Mesa study area would have been occupied by only a family-sized group of five or six persons. The northern portion of Black Mesa, comprising an area of approximately 1600 km^2, could theoretically have supported a band-sized group of about forty persons.

The next step involves examining more specific diachronic models to determine whether the Black Mesa Archaic evidence exhibits any degree of fit. Wills' (1985, 1988a) construct may be of greatest interest to this study. Wills posits change in Archaic settlement and subsistence over the course of the Holocene. The change is toward more logistically organized systems in which residential mobility decreases in favor of the organizations of small task groups operating from base locations. Wills finds support for apparent decreases in territory size as a function of population increase. Changes in the stylistic content of projectile points indicate for Wills that by Late Archaic times (ca. 3000 to 2000 B.P.), information previously conveyed by projectile-point styles was embodied in more formalized intergroup exchange and communications policies. Vierra (1985:54) notes the association of subsistence/settlement systems operating in smaller territories with a tendency toward a greater logistical component in such systems as well. While Vierra speaks in terms of groups that have already adopted agriculture, Wills' (1985) model suggests that more logistically organized systems are, in essence, preadapted to the adoption of agriculture.

The problem of estimating territory sizes of prehistoric groups, however, remains predictably difficult.

One method involves the identification of the sources of lithic raw materials used by prehistoric groups (e.g., Reher and Frison 1980; Wilmsen 1974). Using the distance-to-source for materials in archaeological context provides a measure of the area exploited. A major problem inherent in such estimates consists of the difficulty in determining whether prehistoric groups obtained the materials directly (e.g., Binford 1979) or acquired the materials through exchange.

Materials from distant sources thus may indicate either access to extremely large territories or a developed exchange network between bands moving in relatively small territories. The former situation indicates a high degree of residential mobility; the latter, a system in which groups have developed social means for attaining indirect access to resources outside the area they directly exploit. In terms of the Archaic groups in question, either scenario typifies extensively organized societies at low population levels dependent on direct or indirect access to large territories to meet subsistence needs.

To return to a critical piece of evidence from the Archaic occupations of Black Mesa, the frequency of the occurrence on Archaic sites of obsidian from the San Francisco Volcanic Field over 200 km to the southeast of Black Mesa provides a clear temporal pattern. The Early Archaic components exhibit obsidian artifact frequencies far greater in absolute and relative terms than all other assemblages combined. Almost half the obsidian artifacts known from the almost two hundred excavated sites of all periods on Black Mesa come from the Early Archaic assemblages of Tsosie Shelter and D:11:3063. The Tsosie Shelter assemblage, we must remember, comprises a sample of only a 5 m² area, and the remaining deposits in the Archaic levels at Tsosie Shelter probably contain more than the five obsidian specimens recovered to date. In contrast, four sites formerly classified as Hisatsinom or Late

Archaic, and which I have now tentatively placed in the White Dog phase, produced only a single obsidian artifact, a finished projectile point found at D:11:1281. In addition, the obsidian assemblages from the two Early Archaic sites yielded obsidian-chipping debris, indicating that Archaic groups carried sufficient raw material to allow on-site manufacturing.

On balance, however, we may not be wise in making too much of the temporal patterns of the lithic raw material for so small a sample of sites. We can suggest that the apparent temporal pattern in obsidian frequencies among Archaic sites indicates that the late-period groups had less access to obsidian than the earlier groups. In terms of the subsistence territory/population model, one might tentatively infer relatively smaller territories and higher population density that reduced the need for mating and exchange networks over such vast areas. Compared to Archaic populations on Black Mesa, access through direct procurement or by exchange to the San Francisco Volcanic Field obsidian sources appears to have been much reduced for the populations of the White Dog phase. If greater site density during the White Dog phase is not merely a result of differential site preservation, then regional population increase appears unequivocal with the agricultural transition.

Obviously, we must consider the foregoing discussion in the context of small samples and the vagaries of preservation. The inferences for Black Mesa drawn from the concepts and models of Wills (1985, 1988a) and others remain tentative, and as all too often happens, we need larger area samples to make more definitive statements concerning the more than five millennia of the Black Mesa Archaic occupation.

Summary

In many respects the Black Mesa data from preagricultural use of the study area mirror those from many other

regions of the Southwest. In important ways, however, the data suggest a certain amount of temporal and regional variation. Black Mesa research has provided, through a small sample of radiocarbon dated sites, evidence for occupation during the preagricultural portion of the Holocene. That evidence indicates a sporadic, generally nonintensive occupation constrained by the relatively low resource supply of the mesa top. However, some evidence for a predictably broad diet and for reduction in territory size in the later portion of the period can tentatively be interpreted to result from population increase across the agricultural transition.

We also observe stylistic variability across the long Archaic interval, although the projectile-point styles associated with dated contexts on Black Mesa do not entirely reflect temporal assignments for similar styles in other portions of the northern Southwest. For example, both Bajada and Pinto/San Jose styles recovered from a site dating to over 8500 B.P. appear, on Black Mesa, to predate the temporal range accorded these types in Irwin-Williams' Oshara Tradition schema (1973). Our inferences on Archaic style remain extremely limited, and we have no nonlithic evidence to compare across the greater region, as Geib and Spurr (2000) have done with sandal styles from sheltered contexts. Even the limited investigation of Black Mesa rockshelters has not produced any Archaic perishables. Although the investigation of Black Mesa rockshelters remains limited to test excavations at D:7:618 and 619 (Smiley el al. 1986; Smiley 1994), deep soundings at both sites failed to reveal preagricultural occupations.

Finally, we must remember that the area surrounding Black Mesa has been subject to only patchy survey and excavation. A slowly accumulating but promising body of evidence suggests that both Archaic and Paleoindian occupations may be more plentiful than the present hard evidence would indicate.

PART II

Kayenta Farmers and Villagers

The early farmers of the northern Southwest left the most complete and detailed record of their lives and behavior of any such society in the world. The Black Mesa Archaeological Project amassed evidence for the northern Southwest's first agricultural populations, the chronology of the adaptation, and some of the best examples of early farming villages.

Departing from traditional treatments, Francis E. Smiley, author of Chapter 3, divides the early agricultural, or Basketmaker II, period into early and late phases. During the White Dog phase, agriculture spread across the Southwest, perhaps quite rapidly, followed by a considerable period of slow or no population growth. The prehistoric southwesterners first built villages during the subsequent Lolomai phase. Evidence for this period, largely from northern Black Mesa, includes dramatic shifts in site structure, content, and intersite relationships.

During the subsequent Basketmaker III period, people avoided the mesa-top habitat of northern Black Mesa, choosing instead to aggregate nearby in relatively large villages at lower elevations. In Chapter 4, "Basketmaker III: Early Ceramic–Period Villages in the Black Mesa Region," Deborah L. Nichols traces the history of research on these little-known people. These ancestral Puebloans were the first pottery makers in the region, leaving plentiful material remains to puzzle future generations.

CHAPTER 3

The First Black Mesa Farmers

The White Dog and Lolomai Phases

Francis E. Smiley

In the beginning, and for several years into BMAP, no one thought that preceramic farmers had occupied Black Mesa. Certainly, no one imagined that preceramic-period archaeology would become a significant focus of BMAP research. In the end, however, nearly 20 percent of excavated BMAP sites consisted of the remains of settlements and camps of the "Basketmaker II" peoples (Kidder 1927), preceramic early farming societies of the Colorado Plateau.

For the first half of the twentieth century, we knew Basketmaker II societies almost exclusively from the remarkable perishable assemblages recovered in rockshelters across the northern Southwest. One of the type localities for Basketmaker II cultures lies just a few air kilometers north of Black Mesa at Marsh Pass (Kidder and Guernsey 1919).

At the midpoint of the twentieth century, open-air sites came to light in the Four Corners region (Morris and Burgh 1954; Eddy and Dickey 1961; Matson and Lipe 1978). We wondered about the relationship between the rockshelter Basketmaker II peoples and the occupants of the small, open-air preceramic settlements, the nonperishable artifacts from which appear so similar to styles evident in the rockshelters.

Prior to mid-century, we did know that the "Basket Makers" or "elder brothers" of the cliff-dwellers, as the northern Southwest's early

rockshelter excavators termed them (Prudden 1897), farmed corn, stored the corn in caves, and buried the dead in the storage pits in the same caves. The "elder brothers" also made elegant baskets and other textiles but had no pottery.

The cultures of the rockshelters were clearly preceramic and clearly agricultural. The discovery of large numbers of open-air preceramic farming settlements on Black Mesa surprised us, and, because Basketmaker II groups appeared to constitute the foundations of later Puebloan societies, BMAP put a great deal of time and effort into the sites.

In the sections to follow, I examine Basketmaker II archaeology in a panregional framework that considers over a century of research and chronology building and details the nature of the long period of early agricultural adaptation. To do so, I begin at the beginnings of southwestern archaeology in the decades around the turn of the twentieth century.

Between about 1890 and 1920, the Wetherills, their associates, and the likes of Alfred Vincent Kidder and Samuel Guernsey unearthed remarkable assemblages of perishable remains from sheltered sites in the deeply incised canyons of the northern Southwest. The remains enabled these pioneer archaeologists to develop an interpretive framework for early agriculture in the northern Southwest.

The "Basket Makers," as excava-

tors initially termed the cave-dwelling farmers, appeared to predate the cliff-dwelling Puebloan peoples, but to what extent no one knew. In effect, no one could say beyond speculation exactly how or whether the Basket Makers might be connected to the Puebloan peoples who followed.

Now, as we move into the twenty-first century, my reading of the evidence suggests that the Basketmaker II peoples, as they have come to be known, occupy an evolutionarily significant intermediate position in the agricultural transition process. On the one hand, the Basketmaker peoples of the northern Southwest farmed, stored surpluses, and ceremoniously buried their dead in domestic context, all traits we usually associate with small-scale, tribal, agricultural societies. On the other hand, the early Basketmakers appear to occupy a position defined in social-organizational, settlement, and demographic terms that lies closer to structures usually ascribed to band-level hunting and gathering societies (Smiley 2000a, b, c; Robins and Hays-Gilpin 2000). The Basketmakers clearly fall somewhere between the band-level, nonfood-producing adaptation of the Archaic peoples and that of the agricultural, tribal, Puebloan societies.

Over a period as long as 2,500 years in the northern Southwest, the Basketmakers define and illustrate the transition from small-scale band to small-scale tribal societies; from *extensive* hunting and gathering adaptations to more *intensive* agriculture-dependent lifeways; from infrequent, nearly undetectable transitory regional occupation to location-specific, comparatively labor-intensive, and high-visibility occupation. For students of cultural evolution, the preceramic farming groups of the Colorado Plateau may provide the sort of transitional phase evidence that sheds significant light on agricultural transition processes.

Discovery and Chronology

The interpretive framework to which I alluded in the opening paragraphs took root in the 1890s, during a period of discovery and frenzied initial excavations in Grand Gulch and other areas of southeastern Utah (Prudden 1897; Pepper 1902). The framework matured in the context of scientific investigations before 1920 in the Marsh Pass area of northeastern Arizona (Kidder and Guernsey 1919; Guernsey and Kidder 1921). The general archaeological perception of "Basket Makers" endured for over a half-century. During the first three decades of the period, Basket Maker archaeology in the northern Southwest languished in a chronological backwater. The temporal relation between the Basket Makers and the Puebloans remained vague. Even the galvanizing chronometric breakthrough provided by tree-ring dating failed to help fix the chronological place of the Basket Makers in absolute time. Still, one of the most important aspects of the discovery of the Basket Makers was the revelation that the stratigraphic position of the preceramic cultures lay beneath the position of the ceramic-period cultures. The preceramic peoples were clearly older.

Early investigators used the term *Basket Makers* to emphasize the lack of ceramic technology in archaeological contexts. The term currently used, *Basketmaker II*, has come to connote peoples of the northern Southwest, organized in small groups, cultivating Mexican-derived domesticated

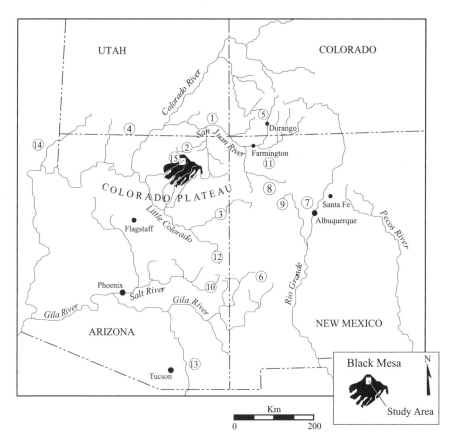

Figure 3.1 The Greater Southwest, showing locations mentioned in Chapter 3: 1–Grand Gulch, Cedar Mesa, Red Rocks Plateau; 2–Marsh Pass, White Dog Cave, Cave 1, Cave 2; 3–Canyon de Chelly, Canyon del Muerto; 4–Cave du Pont; 5–La Plata Mountains; 6–Bat Cave; 7–Albuquerque region; 8–Chaco region; 9–Arroyo Cuervo Region; 10–Cienega Valley; 11–Navajo Reservoir District; 12–Hay Hollow Valley; 13–Matty Canyon, San Pedro area; 14–Moapa region; 15–Three Fir Shelter.

plants, using dry caves and rockshelters as storage facilities, and marking stewardship of such facilities by placing the dead within the social context of the sites in comparatively rich funerary circumstances. A. V. Kidder (1927) affixed the Roman numeral "II" in his pan-southwestern cultural chronology, the Pecos Classification. Kidder assigned a "II" because he assumed an earlier, less developed culture would be discovered and could then take on the *Basketmaker I* designation.

Sites of the typical Basketmaker II rockshelter type occur in the Black Mesa region but not in the BMAP study area proper. To examine only the study area evidence would be to ignore 80 percent of the time depth of the early agricultural period and to miss a significant aspect of the

settlement variability. Thus, confining discussion to evidence from a limited area like the Peabody lease on Black Mesa leaves out a great deal of evolutionarily significant regional prehistory. Accordingly, I examine Basketmaker II archaeology across the region, as I did the Paleoindian and Archaic evidence in the preceding chapter.

Preceramic early agricultural remains are widely distributed in the Greater Southwest. The Black Mesa study area, alone, contains over one hundred open-air Basketmaker II sites. Figure 3.1 shows the regional locations of areas and sites mentioned in the text.

The extent of known Basketmaker II manifestations across the northern Southwest revealed by survey and excavation includes such famous research venues as the Grand Gulch region including the Red Rocks Plateau (Lipe 1970), Cedar Mesa (Lipe and Matson 1971; Matson and Dohm 1994), the Butler Wash area of southeastern Utah (Smiley and Robins 1997a; Smiley 2000b), and Navajo Mountain and Rainbow Plateau along the lower San Juan (Lindsay et al. 1968; Geib 1994; Geib and Spurr 2000). Other evidence for early agricultural occupations consists of numerous small pit-structure settlements and rockshelter sites scattered across the Greater Southwest. In the 1950s Eddy investigated Matty Canyon, a preceramic and intensively used locality in southeastern Arizona (Eddy 1958). In the decades to follow, numerous other sites and intensive investigations, for example, Cienega Creek, revealed early farming settlements established before 3000 B.P. (Huckell 1995).

In the Navajo Reservoir District of northwestern New Mexico, several small village sites have been reported by Eddy and Dickey (1961) and Eddy (1966). Numerous open-air sites have been located across the San Juan Basin as well (Reher 1977; Judge 1982). The Hay Hollow Valley and vicinity (Fritz 1974; Martin 1967) yielded important village and other open-site finds, and in the San Pedro area of southern Arizona several large and small open sites have also been investigated (Sayles and Antevs 1941; Huckell 1995; Roth 1992). Far to the west, preceramic agricultural sites assigned to the Moapa phase occur in the Virgin River area of southern Nevada.

Finally, Basketmaker II-like materials have been found in cave contexts in the western Sierra Madre in Chihuahua, Mexico (Mangelsdorf and Lister 1956). For obvious reasons, I do not attempt to list all investigations of Basketmaker II finds here, nor do I think that Basketmaker II settlement areas occur only in the specific localities and regions thus far investigated. The geographic range of Basketmaker II occupations continues to unfold as test excavations that have located the remains of early agricul-

tural camps in the Moab area of Utah demonstrate (Grant Fahrni, personnal communication 2000).

As the summary above indicates, the distribution of the archaeological remains of early farming societies in the northern Southwest covers a vast area and continues to develop. Still, the initial finds came from the Grand Gulch area of southeastern Utah (Prudden 1897; Pepper 1902; Smiley and Robins 1997a). In the early years of this century, the excavation of rich, well-preserved sites in southeastern Utah was followed by intensive excavations of similar sites in the Marsh Pass area west of Kayenta, Arizona, by Kidder and Guernsey (1919; Guernsey and Kidder 1921) and later work (Lockett and Hargrave 1953). Morris in Canyon del Muerto of northeastern Arizona (1925) and Nusbaum in Kane County, Utah (1922), made similar finds early in the last century.

In the late 1940s, important excavations by Morris and Burgh in the Durango, Colorado, area yielded tree-ring dates on open-air habitations that constituted the first absolute dates on preceramic agriculturalists. The tree-ring dates from Talus Village placed the Durango Basketmaker II sites between approximately A.D. 1 and A.D. 500 (1954). In the nearly complete absence of other reliable chronometric data, the Durango materials provided a chronometric anchor for early southwestern agriculture.

In addition to intensive excavations on Basketmaker II sites in the north, work at Bat Cave in western New Mexico produced the first radiocarbon evidence on early southwestern agricultural societies (Dick 1965; Wills 1988a). The Bat Cave work sparked the chronometric search for the entry of cultigens into the Southwest. The use of the original and problematic solid carbon method for dating samples and the mixing of discrete stratigraphic levels, however, resulted in problematic results (Wills 1988a).

The original Bat Cave estimates of about 6000 B.P. for early southwestern agriculture (Libby 1955) have not

withstood the refinement of the radiocarbon method and reanalysis of the stratigraphy (Wills 1988a:11). The early dates did, however, generate a great deal of research on agricultural origins and transition in the Southwest.

In the sections to follow, I divide the early agricultural, or Basketmaker II, period into early and late phases called the White Dog phase and Lolomai phase respectively. The White Dog phase of the Basketmaker II manifestation consists mainly of rockshelter sites used for storage, burial, and habitation. The Lolomai phase consists of open-air habitation and campsites.

I am not the first to propose a two-phase division for the Basketmaker phenomenon in the northern Southwest. Michael Berry (1982), for example, proposed doing so based on the chronometric evidence available in the early 1980s. Berry suggested that the open-air habitation sites, like those found on Black Mesa, in Hay Hollow Valley, and other places be placed in an early Basketmaker II phase beginning sometime around 2200 B.P. Berry placed the late Basketmaker II phase, consisting of the occupations in the Marsh Pass and other "classic" Basketmaker II caves, sometime after 1800 B.P. Given the chronometric information available at the time, Berry's construct was a reasonable estimate. However, research based on a great deal of new radiocarbon data established a different sequence. As should be apparent below, the acquisition of new radiocarbon data from sites across the northern Southwest has frequently and regularly required the revision of our timelines for early farming societies.

New information indicates that the occupations of classic Basketmaker II sites such as the Marsh Pass caves actually began well before 3000 B.P. In contrast, the open-air habitations on Black Mesa appear after 2000 B.P. The sequence appears to occur in reverse order from that proposed by Berry: first come the rockshelter-based "classic" Basketmaker II occupations, then open-air pit-structure settlements, although in some areas, open-air habitations appear earlier than on Black Mesa (Gilpin 1994; Geib and Spurr 2000).

Nonetheless, Berry's suggestion (1982) that the rockshelter and open-air Basketmaker occupations were temporally different phenomena remains accurate, in my view, although Berry's early agricultural period phase sequence has required revision. The radiocarbon data from Black Mesa and the surrounding region (Smiley 1985, 1994, 1997a, 2000a) point to the early use of rockshelters and caves in the region and the much later appearance of small, open-air habitation sites and villages.

The development of the currently recognized sequence has been a complex task and has taken many turns over the past two decades. In fact, the chronometry of the Basketmakers continues to develop as this volume goes to press. The real chronometric story of the early Colorado Plateau farmers begins with the original radiocarbon dates from Bat Cave mentioned above. Several exhaustive treatments of the radiocarbon evidence for early southwestern agriculture have appeared over the past fifteen years, and so I will not repeat the exercise here (see Berry and Berry 1986; Wills 1988; Matson 1991; Smiley 1994, 1997a). Given recent developments, however, a short review will help clarify a complex and apparently still fluid chronometric situation.

Although the earliest Bat Cave dates proved erroneously early at about 6000 B.P., by the late 1990s, a convincing body of evidence confirmed corn farming before 3000 B.P. from north of the San Juan and Colorado rivers in the north to the Mexico border in the south. Nevertheless, a pair of irksome, *even earlier* radiocarbon dates on corn continued to pose interpretive problems.

One of these troubling dates was from Three Fir Shelter (Smiley and Parry 1990; Smiley 1994) on northern Black Mesa, and another came from Bat Cave (Wills 1988a) in western New

Mexico. The two dates problematically suggested that southwestern food production might have begun as early as 4000 B.P.

While for years I have viewed with skeptical interest the calibrated radiocarbon date of approximately 3900 B.P. for corn from Three Fir Shelter on northern Black Mesa, new evidence from southern Arizona increases the probability that the Three Fir Shelter date and the similarly early date from Bat Cave may be accurate, if not precise. The Three Fir Shelter date has a two-sigma calibration range from 4412 to 3470 B.P., with an intercept at 3893 B.P. The Bat Cave date gives a two-sigma range from 4343 to 3884 B.P., with an intercept at 4086 B.P. (Smiley 1994; Wills 1988a; Stuiver and Reimer 1993). Recently, Lascaux and Hesse (in prep.) have reported new chronometric data relevant to the interpretations of the Bat Cave and Three Fir Shelter dates.

Lascaux and Hesse report that a corn kernel from a deeply buried thermal feature at Las Capas, a village of the early San Pedro phase in southern Arizona (AZ AA:12:111[ASM]), has produced a calibrated date at about 4000 B.P. The two-sigma calibration age estimate ranges from 4120 B.P. to 3860 B.P., with closely grouped multiple intercepts centered at about 3950 B.P. Another date on a mesquite bean from the same feature produced a calibrated age range from 4228 to 3897 B.P., with multiple intercepts centered at approximately 4000 B.P. A third date on *Chenopodium* from a nearby feature also closely supports the dates.

These new dates on cultigen and annual plant materials change the way we must view the early dates on corn from Three Fir Shelter and Bat Cave further north. The primary problem with the early dates from Black Mesa and Bat Cave has been the lack of supporting evidence from the southern Southwest from whence the cultigens must certainly have come. Clearly, the new dates just cited make four-thousand-year-old corn *possible* in the northern Southwest. We now have

five determinations with calibrated intercepts that cluster tightly around 4000 B.P.

I have argued elsewhere, based on the radiocarbon evidence and on cautious interpretation of the results of computer simulation of the diffusion of farming (Smiley 1994, 1995b, 1997d, 1997e), that agriculture spread rapidly across the Southwest. I based my earlier arguments on the apparent contemporaneity (in radiocarbon terms) of the earliest dates on corn in both the southern and northern Southwest at around 3000 B.P. (Huckell 1995; Smiley 1997e). In that context, the apparently anomalously early Black Mesa and Bat Cave dates (ca. 4,000 B.P.) appeared questionable on the grounds that corn farming was unlikely to have begun earlier in the north than in the south.

Now that the advent of corn agriculture by 4000 B.P. appears likely in the south, the same arguments for rapid dispersal of agriculture across the Southwest may remain viable. The early dates in the northern Southwest and in the southern Southwest appear remarkably coeval, at least in radiocarbon terms. The difference is that the onset of farming in both areas appears to fall much earlier than previously thought. So, as in many other cases (e.g., Berry 1982; Huckell 1995; Matson 1991; Smiley and Andrews 1983; Smiley 1985, 1994, 1998a; Wills 1988a), the received wisdom on the timing of the beginnings of southwestern agriculture appears to require significant revision.

Interesting as the new dates may be, however, I must interject a note of caution, at least with respect to inferences on the beginning dates for the White Dog phase in the northern Southwest. My cautionary note consists of the fact that any new interpretations raise the old problems of chronometric resolution and sample size. Achieving a degree of chronometric resolution in an archaeological situation requires a chronometric database sufficient to make supportable claims for contemporaneity or age differences among sites or objects or processes in the archaeological record. A high-resolution database requires sufficient numbers of dates on high-quality materials from reliable contexts (see Smiley 1997e, 1998a). We clearly do not yet have a high-resolution database on the earliest farmers. Nonetheless, the salient point here is that the calibrated intercepts of all five dates fall within a range of approximately one hundred and fifty years.

The interpretive framework I cautiously suggest hangs precariously from only five radiocarbon dates scattered across a vast space: three dates from the southern Southwest, one from Bat Cave in western New Mexico, and another from Three Fir Shelter in the northern Southwest. While all the dates are on reliable materials (cultigens or annuals [Smiley 1998a]) and from solid primary context, we must continue to entertain the probability of sample-size problems.

With such caveats foremost in mind, I tentatively advance the interpretation that farming appears to have begun in the southern areas around 4000 B.P. and to have rapidly diffused, or moved by a combination of diffusion and migration, into the northern regions soon after. Although for years I have hesitated to make too much of the early northern dates, we now have reason to reconsider the timing of the beginnings of the development of the cultures of the northern Southwest that are the subject of this volume.

Although attempts to date the earliest farmers occupied many investigators over the past couple of decades, other work enriched our knowledge of the variability of early farming settlement. Open-air sites consisting of one or two to ten or more pit structures, formal storage pits, and scatters of chipped-stone debris have been identified and excavated at widely scattered locations in the northern and southern Southwest. Early speculation about the existence of such open-air habitations was prompted by the apparent lack of both occupational debris and the remains of dwellings within the known caves (Guernsey and Kidder 1921:110).

Open habitation sites, such as those on Black Mesa, require vastly more labor to be put into dwellings and storage features than Archaic-period sites. Archaic sites, in fact, provide little evidence of any labor input. While the degree of Basketmaker dependence on domesticates continues to be debated (Matson and Chisholm 1986), the presence of corn in most open sites of all types attests to its significant, and probably primary, role in subsistence.

Early agricultural research in the Black Mesa project opened in the early 1970s with the discovery of preceramic, open-air sites in the study area that yielded corn macrofossils. While important open-air sites had been discovered in southwestern Colorado and other locales (Morris and Burgh 1954; Eddy 1966; Fritz 1974; Gumerman 1966), early southwestern farmers were best known from the late nineteenth- and early twentieth-century excavations of rockshelters in the northern Southwest. Thus, the interpretive framework for early farmers had little to say about small, open-air settlements with pit houses and storage pits.

The primary interpretive changes follow from increased field work and attention to absolute chronometry since the late 1970s. Field work and chronometric research on Black Mesa have contributed significantly to this effort. Thirty-five (nearly 20 percent) of the excavated Black Mesa sites of all types date to the early agricultural period, and the data from these and related excavations have helped move southwestern early agricultural researches forward in several areas.

First, and as detailed above, southwesternists in the Black Mesa region and others have extended the temporal range of preceramic agricultural societies further into the past. Second, the early agricultural period appears to be divisible into two phases on demographic and settlement evidence not only in the Black Mesa area (Smiley 1994, 2000a) but in the Tucson Basin as well (Huckell 1995). Third, the early agricultural phases appear even more distinct in socioeconomic, demographic, degree of residential mobility, and technological terms from the peoples and adaptations of the following ceramic period. Fourth, we have recognized whole new kinds of settlement systems in the behavioral repertoire of early southwestern farmers. Finally, we have begun to accrue enough evidence to investigate agricultural beginnings in the Southwest in terms of the rate of transition and the nature of process (Smiley 1997b). The information generated by BMAP has significantly increased the southwestern database on agricultural beginnings north of Mexico. I have noted elsewhere (Smiley 1994, 1997a) and reiterate here that we can now work from a far stronger analytical position than we could have only a few years ago.

The Environment

The period in question, from about 4000 B.P. to 1500 B.P., predates the temporal spans of high-resolution dendrochronological reconstructions of paleoenvironment (Dean et al. 1994; Dean 1988a), and we can examine the period only in terms of the general models discussed in previous chapters. The Altithermal had ameliorated, and effective moisture appears to have generally been increasing during the period 5000 to 4000 B.P. (Mehringer 1967; Petersen 1981). Petersen also provides evidence for more favorable conditions for the pinyon-juniper forest during this period in the La Plata Mountains of southwestern Colorado.

Dean et al. (1985) characterize the precipitation and groundwater regimes around and after about 2000 B.P. as cyclical and relatively regular. A period of high groundwater, aggrading floodplain conditions, and increased effective moisture appears to fall at about 2000 B.P., with other highs every 550 to 600 years.

Extrapolating this apparently regular hydrological cycle from 2000 B.P. into the past probably entails considerable risk. If we do the extrapolation, however, the curve suggests the possibility of more favorable hydrologic conditions at about 2500 B.P., 3100 B.P., 3700 B.P., and about 4300 B.P. Given the vagaries of climatic cycles and the lack of intra-phase chronological resolution, speculation as to a cause-and-effect relationship between early agriculture and climate remains on the thin ice. If the post-Altithermal pinyon increase in the La Plata Mountains documented by Petersen occurred across the northern Southwest, the expansion of the pinyon provided a significant subsistence element to augment hunter-gatherer or early farmer economies.

The Earliest Black Mesa Farmers: The White Dog Phase

In 1916 and in some of the earliest scientific excavations in Basketmaker II context in the Black Mesa area, an expedition from the Peabody Museum unearthed the desiccated but extremely well preserved body of a white dog (Guernsey and Kidder 1921:plate 15). The extraordinary find provided the name for the now-famous Basketmaker II rockshelter, White Dog Cave (figure 3.1), located in the southern extent of Comb Ridge, a linear sandstone feature that runs from northeastern Arizona north into southeastern Utah. Because White Dog Cave produced the most spectacular assemblages in the Marsh Pass region (Guernsey and Kidder 1921:10), other investigators (Colton 1939; Lipe 1966; Smiley 1994) have applied the term to the archaeological manifestation characterized by intensive use of rockshelters in the northern Southwest.

The period of earliest farming in the Black Mesa region, the White Dog phase, has only in the past decade been temporally defined as occurring before 2000 B.P. (Smiley 1994). The temporal definition remains vague on the early end but appears to begin sometime in the fourth millennium

B.P. (4000–3000 B.P.). The White Dog phase lasts until about 2000 B.P. As I argue above, the new evidence for corn farming by about 4000 B.P. may point to the similarly early agriculature in the White Dog phase.

The antiquity of the White Dog phase was unsuspected until 1985, when cultigens were assayed from Kidder's and Guernsey's Marsh Pass cave excavations that had taken place about seventy years before (Smiley 1985). Most investigators assumed that the *classic* Basketmaker II sites, as Berry has aptly termed the rockshelters, dated between 2000 and 1500 B.P. (M. Berry 1982; Smiley 1985). Also in 1985, excavations at Three Fir Shelter on northern Black Mesa produced radiocarbon dates in the same third millennium B.P. range and even earlier (Smiley et al. 1986; Smiley and Parry 1990; Smiley 1993, 1994). The body of dates on cultigens, all from the Marsh Pass region, confirmed that notions of the "late" arrival of agriculture in the northern Southwest should be reconsidered. More dates from materials from Three Fir Shelter produced a range of calibrated cultigen dates from about 4000 B.P. to about 1900 B.P.

The work at Three Fir Shelter had been designed to provide a conceptual and empirical bridge between the pioneering excavations of Kidder and Guernsey from 1914 to 1920 and the large body of early agricultural sites recovered during the Black Mesa project between 1973 and 1983. On the one hand, the Marsh Pass caves were thought to be storage and funerary facilities with rich perishable assemblages. These sites did not appear to Kidder and Guernsey to be habitations of the early farmers. On the other, the Black Mesa open-air sites were clearly habitations but with typically limited open-site, nonperishable assemblages comprised of stone and some bone materials.

The Black Mesa project study area contained no classic Basketmaker II, that is, rockshelter sites. Instead, a suite of open-air site types came to light, dating for the most part to a very limited period between about

1900 B.P. and 1600 B.P. (Smiley 1984, 1985, 1998a). The open-air sites in the study area revealed a great deal about site configuration and the range of variability in nonperishable artifacts. At the same time, the Basketmaker II "caves" in the greater region contained fabulous assemblages of highly perishable materials. The problem was that no absolute dates were available from the Basketmaker II caves. Thus, until the middle 1980s, the relationship between the people using the caves and the groups responsible for constructing the open-air habitation sites on Black Mesa remained murky. The primary ties between the various bodies of research in the two areas had consisted of a general suite of traits, namely, the styles of projectile points, lack of ceramics, and ample evidence of corn agriculture.

Given recent chronometric discoveries, however, the use of caves and rockshelters in the Marsh Pass region appears to begin long before the regular construction of open-air habitations. The advent of open-air habitations does not, however, signal the end of the use of rockshelters. Rockshelter dates place these excellent natural preservational facilities in use contemporaneously with the small open-air settlements. The designation "White Dog phase" sets the earlier period of primary use of natural shelters in the Marsh Pass region apart from the subsequent appearance of open-air settlements. I think the shift signifies a significant change in settlement and population evident in the development of habitation and earthen storage facilities in sandy loams and in bedrock settings, rather than in the rockshelters.

White Dog Phase Settlement on Black Mesa: Basketmaker II "Caves"

Although descriptions of Basketmaker II caves and the cornucopia of perishable materials they tended to contain trickled out of the intensive, almost frenzied excavations in the canyons of Grand Gulch in the 1890s (Pepper 1897), no one undertook the

Figure 3.2 Aerial view to the northwest of Three Fir Shelter on northern Black Mesa (photograph by F. Smiley).

task of systematically publishing the nature of Basketmaker II recovery until nearly twenty-five years later. Kidder and Guernsey set important standards when, in 1919, they described and illustrated finds from their Marsh Pass region excavations of 1914–1915. They continued the high standards in subsequent monographs (Guernsey and Kidder 1921; Guernsey 1931).

The sheltered sites unearthed by scientists and laymen alike between 1893 and 1935, from southern Utah to the Four Corners region and from Marsh Pass to Canyon de Chelly, contained strikingly similar assemblages. The two most prominent aspects of recovery, human burials in storage facilities and the storage facilities with associated corn, represent significant changes in human subsistence, social organization, and ideology over

the ways of Archaic peoples. Panregional artifact similarities showed clear parallels and connections among populations across the great region and eventually to other southwestern regions such as the Tucson Basin (Berry and Berry 1986; B. Huckell 1995; Matson 1991).

Three Fir Shelter in the north rim area of Black Mesa, shown in figure 3.2, is the nearest Basketmaker II rockshelter to the Black Mesa study area in which significant excavations have been conducted. Three Fir Shelter exhibits all but a few of the traits found in the sites near Marsh Pass, lacking, thus far, only evidence of burials. Because only about 8 percent of the shelter floor has been excavated, the probability of the presence of burials remains.

Three Fir Shelter provides an excellent example of Basketmaker II

regional material culture assemblage. Projectile points, for example, recovered from both rockshelters and open sites, suggest wide regional contact among Basketmaker II groups. The basic corner- and side-notched point types apparently enjoyed wide distribution. For example, the basic point styles identified by Morris and Burgh (1954:figure 29) in Durango can be seen in collections from Kidder and Guernsey's excavations in the Marsh Pass area. The widely recognized San Pedro side-notched, triangular-bladed atlatl dart point has been identified from the San Pedro drainage in southeastern Arizona to the Four Corners area in the northern Southwest.

The side- and corner-notched styles for dart points also appear in open-air habitation site assemblages from Black Mesa (Christenson 1987a; Matson 1991) and from southwest-

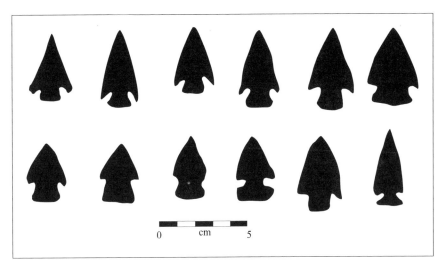

Figure 3.3 Basketmaker II projectile-point forms identified by Morris and Burgh (1954).

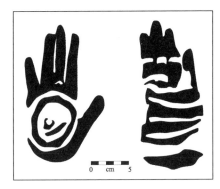

Figure 3.4 Embellished hand prints from the walls of Three Fir Shelter.

ern Colorado (Morris and Burgh 1954). Figure 3.3 illustrates the point typology developed by Morris and Burgh (1954) and which characterizes the variability in Basketmaker II point forms. While the age ranges of occupations in the sheltered sites appear to cover more than a thousand years and the open-air habitations appear to fall in the centuries around 2000 B.P., the point styles seem to persist across time and space for more than a millennium.

Perhaps the most spectacular artifacts recovered from the classic Basketmaker caves are the baskets and other textiles. Among the traits of items in textile assemblages, the list of similarities includes infants' cradles, string bags, scissor snares, many types of baskets, aspects of basket construction, and cordage of all weights and states of manufacture.

Morris and Burgh (1954) compared assemblages and other site traits, finding that about 70 percent of the characteristics observed appeared to be shared regionally. Matson, examining the materials from Basketmaker II sites over a wide area, notes both similarities and significant differences (Matson 1991:46–49). Morris and Burgh concluded that the San Pedro culture might have been ancestral to that of the Durango and other Basketmaker groups.

In addition to assemblage ma-

terials, the Basketmaker caves of the White Dog phase nearly universally contained sizeable storage facilities, mostly excavated into shelter floors and lined with slabs or with bark or grass. Both types appear in most sites. The primary common characteristic here is the construction of simple storage facilities within the habitation area.

Evidence for habitation in the shelters of the White Dog phase consists of considerable midden deposits containing well-preserved organic debris from textile industries, food processing, and other domestic activities. Three Fir Shelter on Black Mesa had a small living structure with a puddled-adobe floor built within the shelter, and Cave 2 in nearby Kinboko evidenced large, slab-lined features that may have been sleeping areas. Virtually all the shelters contain numerous thermal features as well. Three Fir Shelter had, for example, a large, formal roasting pit filled with fire-cracked rock. In general, features on the sites of the White Dog phase, including storage pits, fire hearths, and roasting pits, virtually cover the rockshelter floors.

A final aspect of the Basketmaker caves of the White Dog phase and in other regions is the ubiquity of painted, incised, and pecked rock images. Plain and embellished hand prints, broad-shouldered figures, and

a variety of designs adorn walls and fallen roof blocks around the sites. Figure 3.4 illustrates some of the embellished hand prints that grace the walls of Three Fir Shelter and numerous other Basketmaker II "cave" sites. All in all, the classic Basketmaker rockshelters of the White Dog phase provide remarkably complete material records of preceramic farming societies from human remains to the art and craft of the former occupants.

Camps of the White Dog Phase

If the hypothesized primary use of rockshelters as habitations in the White Dog phase proves correct, we would still expect to find contemporaneous limited-activity camps and probably open-air habitations as well. In fact, I think we do. The small campsites previously assigned to the Late Archaic Hisatsinom phase (see Smiley and Andrews 1983) appear to fit this category. A small group of sites with calibrated radiocarbon dates falling between about 3700 and 2300 B.P. may be camps occupied by small groups of the White Dog phase in transit or engaged in specific activities such as hunting or pinyon-nut harvesting. The earliest sites appear to be D:7:3003A, D:7:2100, D:7:3144, and D:11:1281. These ephemeral sites evidence no charred remains of corn but yield a few edible wild seeds. The small camps lie in the current zones of pinyon and probably did in earlier times as well. The sites consist entirely of small hearths and lithic scatters.

When the camps came to light in the early 1980s, they provided the primary evidence for the presence of Late Archaic, preagricultural groups on Black Mesa. The period the camps seemed to define was then called the Hisatsinom phase (Smiley and Andrews 1983). The term, Hisatsinom, as an Archaic-period phase name, appears now obsolete in the light of recent chronological discoveries related to the White Dog phase (see also previous chapter). Although the lithic assemblages have been characterized as differing from those of the following Lolomai phase, they do not differ significantly (Parry 1987a) and remain within the range of Lolomai (late Basketmaker II) variability. The lithic assemblages of the small campsites do not appear out of place with the bifaces or biface-manufacturing debris from the later Lolomai phase. The sites cannot be placed with the Lolomai-phase sites, as S. Plog (1986b) suggested, because they date so much earlier and cannot statistically be considered contemporaneous. The side- and corner-notched bifaces from these sites fall within the range of variation of points both for Lolomai-phase sites (Parry and Christenson 1987:plates 5–9) and the Basketmaker II sites in Durango (Morris and Burgh 1954:figures 80–83), as well as for the sites of the White Dog period in the Marsh Pass area and in the Four Corners region (Kidder and Guernsey 1919; Morris and Burgh 1954). Apart from projectile points, comparing the lithic assemblages from the open-air camps on Black Mesa to the lithic assemblages of the classic Basketmaker II caves proves difficult, since, with the exception of the Durango sites, relatively few lithic artifacts have been recovered from sheltered sites.

Although the classic sites were excavated decades earlier by entirely different methods, the scarcity of lithics may not be solely a function of early twentieth-century excavation techniques that failed to employ screening. For example, Three Fir shelter excavations employed nested screens at 1 cm, 0.5 cm, 0.1 cm, and 0.05 cm, a

system that should have recovered samples of all lithic debris present. Even so, Three Fir shelter yielded very few lithic artifacts compared to the far less intensively used open-air habitation sites nearby. If the other regional Basketmaker II rockshelter lithic assemblages are similarly depauperate in lithic debris, the shelters may simply not be the foci of lithic manufacture as were many of the open-air habitations on Black Mesa (Smiley 1985, 1998a).

The campsites exhibit marked similarities in feature types, site size, and artifact assemblages. All sites consist of sparsely distributed lithic scatters, and most exhibit at least one small earthen hearth. Some have as many as twelve. The assemblages from the campsites of the White Dog phase in the Black Mesa study area consist overwhelmingly of chipped stone and a few groundstone items with small but highly variable point assemblages. Projectile points from sites D:7:2100, D:7:3144, and D:11:2191 tend to be large, percussion-flaked, corner-notched specimens with convex bases. Points of this style have been attributed to the En Medio (Basketmaker II) period in some areas (Irwin-Williams 1973). The En Medio phase of the Oshara tradition in the Arroyo Cuervo region of New Mexico (Irwin-Williams 1973) is said to cover the period from approximately 800 B.C. to A.D. 400.

Although stone artifacts prevail in campsite assemblages, some subsistence information derives from intensive flotation of the fills of features. The pattern of plant remains from D:7:3144, similar to that of the Early Archaic recovery from Tsosie Shelter, consisted of abundant carbonized goosefoot seeds as well as trace amounts of purslane and pigweed (Wagner et al. 1984; Parry et al. 1985). The faunal assemblage recovered D:7:3144 contained cottontail, jackrabbit, and a possible mountain sheep specimen (*Ovis canadensis*; Nichols and Smiley 1984b:813–832; Parry et al. 1985). As I have noted elsewhere (Smiley and Andrews 1983), no corn (*Zea mays*) has been recov-

ered from these contexts, although Lolomai-phase campsites routinely produce corn macrofossils. The preponderance of goosefoot seeds in contexts of the White Dog phase parallels the findings of Reinhard et al. (1985) at a sheltered site in southeastern Utah, directly north of Black Mesa. Analysis of coprolites from Dust Devil Cave indicated that goosefoot seeds provided a significant component of the diet during Desha (Early Archaic, 8800 to 6800 B.P.) times.

Discussion

The White Dog peoples who inhabited the limited number of suitable rockshelters in the Marsh Pass/Black Mesa area left an unparalleled material cultural record. They left their dead, their utilitarian tools and materials, their garbage, their works of art and craft, and their cultigens. Careful descriptions by Kidder and Guernsey (1919; Guernsey and Kidder 1921) provide background on what may be the best-known inventory of the material culture of early agricultural societies anywhere in the world. Morris and Burgh (1954) made a significant contribution in reporting the Basketmaker II materials recovered near Durango decades later.

On Black Mesa, the White Dog people left similar archaeological records. The excavations at Three Fir Shelter, though independent of the Black Mesa project, provide numerous links in terms of artifact style, technology, contemporaneity, and subsistence structure. These investigations established without doubt that the rockshelters served not only as graveyards and storage facilities but as habitations as well (Smiley and Parry 1990; Smiley 1998a).

Three Fir Shelter, for example, contains the remains of a small structure with a puddled-adobe floor and central hearth. Midden deposits across the site contain refuse from vigorous cordage and basketry industries. Rock-art images, painted, pecked, and incised, abound on the walls and large boulders. Among the artifacts that link

Three Fir Shelter and Black Mesa with the larger region, are small, distinctive, carefully crafted sticks cached in the shelter that form scissor snares (Spier 1955). Such snares have been found in numerous other Basketmaker II sites in the greater region.

The similarities in assemblage content and style might stem from the desires of the peoples of the White Dog phase to maintain mobility options. Although the Basketmakers clearly held strong views on ownership and place, they did not invest a great deal of labor in elaborate facilities. The sense of propriety in ownership and place manifests itself in the new practice of interring the dead in the immediate site area, for example, in previously used storage facilities. The practice of inhumation in the daily living context stands in sharp contrast to the propensity of hunter-gatherer populations to avoid any sort of contact or association with the dead. The dearth of human remains from the long Archaic, for example, attests the probable disposal of the dead in ways that resulted in destruction of the funerary record. The Basketmakers clearly worked from a very different mind-set that retained or reincorporated the dead in group and family affairs. The inclusion of the dead in the living social structure appears manifest in terms of physical proximity and that may have helped establish stewardship, if not ownership, of sites and facilities.

The apparently low population density during White Dog times may provide another indication of mobility. The advent of agriculture in the Black Mesa region could have occurred as early as about 4000 B.P. and certainly before 3000 B.P. Yet no population expansion appears to occur until about 2000 B.P., a thousand or two thousand years later. We see the same phenomenon with the same timing in the Butler Wash area of southeastern Utah (Smiley and Robins 1997a; Smiley 2000a, b, c). The long period of early agriculture involved the use of caves for effective storage and for shelter rather than the larger

investment and maintenance required for dwellings and facilities built in the open.

The delay between transition and the emergence of surplus-based economies, as Wills notes (1992), occurs in a number of other situations worldwide. For whatever reason, the transition to agriculture does not result in immediate, or continuous, or even punctuated episodes of economic, demographic, or technological expansion. Apparently for early plateau farmers, the difficult part was neither the accomplishment of the transition to what would become a revolutionary new way of life, that is, food production, nor the adaptation of farming to conditions on the plateau. The difficult part may have been changing the patterns of high mobility that had been used successfully for thousands of years.

Mobility and Stability

Primary Food Resources and Early Agriculture on the Colorado Plateau

The longevity of the use of rockshelters on the Colorado Plateau (Smiley 1994), the apparent lack of open-air habitation sites, and the comparatively small number of suitable rockshelters pose explanatory problems unless one posits high mobility and comparatively long-distance travel for early farming groups of the White Dog phase. In fact, other investigators have done this (Wills 1988a). The rockshelters appear to have been in use for centuries, many centuries in some cases (Smiley 1994, 1997a), yet most do not evidence the degree of midden or architectural accumulation one might expect of populations that had, with the advent of farming, begun to settle down.

In contrast, populations in the Tucson Basin of southeastern Arizona may have developed sedentary communities before the agricultural transition, as Fish and Fish (1992) and B. Huckell (1995) argue. A northern Southwest explanation might be that

the groups were indeed farmers but had not yet settled down into particular localities or even into reduced territories. However, in such a scenario, the question arises: Why would groups that *can* farm retain the mobility of hunter-gatherers? Explanation may lie in the other resources on which the populations relied.

One possible way to examine the long, apparently stable period of earliest agriculture in the Black Mesa area involves a companion annual resource to corn, the pinyon. The pinyon pine (*Pinus edulis*) on the Colorado Plateau and over a great portion of the Southwest and the Great Basin produces periodic masts that exceed the consumption capacity of animals and humans alike (Lanner 1981; Little 1940, 1941). Pinyon nuts can be stored for two years or more and provide highly nutritious, well-balanced food (Botkin and Shires 1948). Unfortunately for dependent species, the masts vary tremendously in frequency and quantity for any particular area. The masts occur from four to seven years apart (Gottfried 1992). On a broad regional scale, however, most years bring a usable harvest somewhere.

Pinyon nuts and corn tend to co-occur in early agricultural sites, as inspection of the recovery from Basketmaker II sites in the Marsh Pass area (Kidder and Guernsey 1919) and on Black Mesa attests (Smiley and Parry 1990; Ford et al. 1983). Wills has previously suggested a link between the advent of agriculture on the Colorado Plateau and the significant reliance on pinyon harvest. I see evidence of reliance on corn and pinyon nuts in the White Dog phase as well as in the later, Lolomai-phase sites. In fact, a group might easily have harvested both corn and pinyon nuts in the same year.

Depending on the variety, corn matures early, beginning in late summer. The availability of the pinyon-nut crop runs from mid-September to early November (Gottfried 1992). Robins (1997a) argues that much broader interregional contacts fostered by differential resource distributions, including the distribution of pinyon forest, among the peoples of the White Dog phase may be evident in variability in rock art. The regional similarities and variations in rock art between southeastern Utah groups, Marsh Pass groups, and groups in the Canyon de Chelly area can be linked to subsistence variation that encouraged residents to develop and maintain access to adjoining regions. Groups, thus, worked to maintain ties that insured access to resources such as pinyon that tend to be differentially distributed across the northern Southwest.

Primary dependence on pinyon in any system could, however, be a risky strategy because pinyon masts only occur in any particular locality every four to seven years. Floyd and Kohler (1989) estimate that per land unit, pinyon productivity falls significantly below that of corn. The two are not directly comparable in terms of per unit area production, but even so, pinyon might be a difficult resource on which to depend, even if groups harvested huge amounts in bumper years and successfully stored the nuts over extended periods. On the other hand, corn farming, particularly in the difficult edaphic, topographic, and climatic circumstances of the northern Southwest, remains even today a chancy enterprise. How well might the combination of two chancy resources have worked to reduce risk for these early farmers of the northern Southwest?

Some similarities between corn and pinyon-nut production may help answer the question. Compared to other Colorado Plateau resources, both provide food "bonanzas" that are fairly predictable in the following respects. Humans engineer the predictability of the corn harvest by deciding where and how much to plant. Thus, at least four months ahead of time, humans can determine where, when, and all things being equal, how much corn will be available. Pinyon productivity can also be predicted, given a large enough region.

The pinyon mast can be observed in development long before the mast comes to fruition. The development of cones in quantity signals an impending mast. Groups could theoretically plan and schedule movements and decide on efficient positioning many months, even more than a year, in advance of a particular pinyon mast. Such scheduling would have been important, because, as Floyd and Kohler note, intensive pinyon use requires high mobility. I would add that a large territorial range would be a further requirement of groups with such a subsistence base (see also Robins 1997a).

The corn-pinyon similarities, however, do not stop here. In addition to the positive aspects of predictability and massive productivity, corn and pinyon nuts share some general problems as well. Corn crops, for all the human planting strategies, care, and labor input, remain subject to the vicissitudes of nature. Entire crops can be destroyed right up to harvest by general weather patterns or by specific storms, by erosional events, or even by fires. A particular pinyon mast, too, can appear to be developing properly but can abort in the final months as the individual shells turn out to be "dry" or without nut meats (Gerald Gottfried, personal communication 1994). I have observed this phenomenon in portions of the Colorado Plateau myself.

Thus, both corn and pinyon nuts, as highly nutritious, predictable, bountiful resources, harbor serious drawbacks. In good years, the yields can be overwhelming, but a depressingly significant number of failures may occur as well. A final difficulty in incorporating both corn and pinyon nuts in a subsistence system as primary resources consists of the need for some residential stability in the case of corn and considerable mobility in the case of pinyon harvest.

Even so, human groups working to incorporate a new resource, corn, into the dietary, social-organizational, economic, and technological equation might well opt to stake their year-to-year fortunes on two rather than

only one primary vegetative resource. To use one resource, corn, which requires a certain amount of sedentism, while effectively monitoring the highly variable pinyon mast sounds difficult, at best. However, both resources provide eminently storable commodities. The commodities can be stored upwards of two years and can be harvested in large quantities in successful years. Given the lead time that developing pinyon crops provide to potential users, the scheduling of group movements might have been possible far enough ahead to provide for the transport of seed corn. Successful crops of either resource would set any group up handsomely for the coming year or two. Bumper crops of both would make the subsistence quest a non-problem for a couple of years.

Thus, the earliest farmers in the northern Southwest appear to have had at least three options, two of which were to engage intensively in agriculture and to intensively use the pinyon mast. The archaeological evidence suggests they chose, in good generalist hunter-gatherer fashion, to keep all options open. They chose not to specialize.

The results one might predict from such a strategy include a widely dispersed settlement pattern, low investment in structures and facilities, small populations limited to the regions of pinyon forest, and caches of seed corn and all manner of other items left at many localities for use in the future. Further, we expect the maintenance of stylistic similarities over large areas as groups work to preserve the cultural affiliations needed to insure access to information on the panregional pinyon mast.

In fact, these are the kinds of properties we observe for sites of the White Dog phase and for classic Basketmaker II sites across the Four Corners and in adjacent regions. We see close material cultural similarities in the sites and assemblages ranging from Kane County Utah to the Grand Gulch area, from southwestern Colorado to Canyon de Chelly and the

Marsh Pass region. Even the corn evidences important similarities across some areas, as Wicker's comparative study (1997) of corn from Three Fir Shelter (Smiley 1994) and the Durango sites excavated by Morris and Burgh (1954) attest. Although corn from the Marsh Pass/Black Mesa and Durango regions appears strongly divergent on the basis of some gross metrical characters, Wicker demonstrates that much of the variability can be explained by differences in the growth environments of crops in the respective regions.

The apparent use of particular rockshelters over centuries and even millennia (Smiley 1994), without, in many cases, the accumulation of debris one might expect of a millennium or more of regular seasonal use of a site, suggests to me only sporadic occupation of particular sites. Basketmaker groups probably allowed years, decades, or even longer periods between occupations in particular shelters. Because the number of usable shelters is limited compared to the potential number of habitable open-air locations, we might expect small, highly mobile populations to generate these kinds of sites over many centuries. Such sites might accumulate *net* site occupation time in terms of decades, while the site *use span* ranged over a millennium or more.

The observed pattern fits the stochastic movement and settlement patterns we might infer for groups following the pinyon masts across the Greater Four Corners region and using the available rockshelters in the vicinities of particular mast events. Particularly bountiful mast events combined with the proximity of agricultural land might have combined to provide multiyear stability for fortunate groups. Alternatively, even a series of poor mast years and poor corn harvests might have provided enough to get by year to year. Even so, one can easily imagine the difficulties of groups moving to ultimately failing pinyon masts compounded by problems with the corn harvest and the hard times that such a sequence

might have engendered. The uncertainty of subsistence on the plateau, even using both agricultural and pinyon resources, probably insured the depression of population growth, keeping populations below carrying capacity.

If the model of early Basketmaker II settlement and adaptation I have sketched holds up, the general social evolutionary position of such foraging-dependent, storage-reliant farmers should be an interesting one. The early Basketmakers may have been nearly as wide ranging as typical arid-land hunter-gatherers. Like hunting-gathering bands, they would have maintained panregional social and kinship networks that functioned as safety nets during crashes of local regional resources (e.g., Robins 1997a). Such networks would also have furnished marriage partners and a safety valve for the handling of conflict by group fissioning.

On the other hand, like small-scale tribalists, they were food producers, deciding how much food to raise, when it would be ready, and how much labor to put into the process. They must also have defined their region in terms of labor invested in place and facilities: the storage and habitation shelters. Like tribal agriculturalists, the Basketmaker II symbolic and domestic worlds had room for ancestors to be interred in socially proximate and prominent contexts. The deceased needed material items to help in the afterlife, so the early Basketmaker II peoples furnished the graves in comparatively lavish fashion. The Basketmaker II groups expected to return to particular shelters, so they carefully cached seed corn, hunting and trapping equipment, and numerous kinds of domestic utility items. The remarkably good preservation after two thousand to three thousand years of much of the cached material speaks eloquently of the efficiency of rockshelter storage as a subsistence strategy.

The foregoing suggests that we have learned something about some aspects of Basketmaker II culture

and adaptation. Our advances have chiefly involved inference based on new chronometric data. We did not suspect the antiquity of the Marsh Pass and Black Mesa White Dog–phase Basketmakers, for example. Knowing something of their antiquity and something of the timing of settlement change into the Lolomai phase, we infer differing settlement patterns, differing levels of residential mobility, and different population levels. We can further infer the socioeconomic status of the peoples of the White Dog phase as intermediate between bands and tribes, at least in the classic definitional sense.

In the end, we find that outside the lavish Basketmaker II assemblages and the knowledge that the people who generated those assemblages lived from around 4000 B.P. to about 2000 B.P., we know little about cultural dynamics *within* the White Dog phase. We know that this earliest agricultural period lasts a long time, but we do not know precisely when it begins. We do not, therefore, know how long it lasts. Perhaps most vexing and interesting is that we do not yet know, in an anthropological sense, much about what happened during the period.

The discussion to this point provides only one of several possible explanations for the apparent lack of change, or development, or increase in population, or occupation intensity during the long period of earliest agriculture on the Colorado Plateau. We observe that this sort of developmental hiatus may be characteristic of populations that have just made the transition to agriculture. While the knowledge is exciting that Basketmaker II time depth is far greater than previously thought, important work lies ahead. That work involves finding out what happened during the White Dog phase. We must be cognizant, too, of the evidence for continued use of rockshelters after the advent of open-air habitations (Smiley 1997a). Whether the phenomenon can be tied to specific regions or is a general northern southwestern characteristic remains to be demonstrated.

The First Black Mesa Farming Settlements

The Lolomai Phase

The Lolomai peoples of Black Mesa can hardly be characterized as "early" agriculturalists. People had been farming in the Black Mesa region since as early as 4000 B.P., possibly two thousand years before the Lolomai phase began. In fact, the Lolomai phase has been defined in terms of the significant settlement and demographic-pattern change that occurred among preceramic farming populations just after 2000 B.P. At that time, some of the first open-air settlements, which I term proto-villages, in the northern Southwest arose on Black Mesa, as well as in other areas. Before that time, the region's early farmers seem mostly to have used rockshelters for habitation and storage.

The change at about 2000 B.P. consisted of the appearance of open-air habitation sites of widely varying size and occupation intensity, including small settlements or "proto-villages" of at least six and as many as twelve pit structures. I use the term "proto-village" for a number of reasons. First, the simple term "settlement" is too vague a concept to capture the tight patterning such sites exhibit, particularly on Black Mesa. Second, the small settlements of Basketmaker II peoples really do not qualify as villages in terms of size or in terms of year-round, sedentary occupation. Third, the proto-village settlement form immediately precedes the development of Basketmaker III manifestations in the Southwest that more closely fit the village concept and that likely result from the previous Basketmaker II adaptation to multifamily, open-air, semisedentary settlement.

The recognition and programmatic concentration on sites of the Lolomai phase constitutes a major contribution of the Black Mesa Archaeological Project. The Lolomai-phase groups differ in important respects and appear to represent a cul-

tural evolutionary change from the general adaptation of the previous occupation, the White Dog phase.

I suggested above that the peoples of the White Dog phase occupied an intermediate cultural evolutionary position between bands and tribes. Despite an economy dependent on food production, the White Dog groups appeared to be similar to band societies in a number of respects. The White Dog groups had a high degree of residential mobility. They relied to large extent on wild foods, and they maintained low population levels. The White Dog people put little labor into residence sites and seem to have been careful to maintain panregional social integration.

Given the intermediate status ascribed to the White Dog populations, the peoples of the Lolomai phase appear to have moved further yet toward the sociocultural form normally termed tribal (e.g., Sahlins 1968). The Lolomai people of Black Mesa and probably numerous other groups in numerous other areas built the first small proto-villages in the northern Southwest and appear, on the strength of patterns in the frequencies of some lithic raw materials in site assemblages, to have been more locally oriented. The Lolomai-phase groups built substantial dwellings and storage facilities in the open rather than in rockshelters. No longer constrained by the small number and the locations of the region's rockshelters, the Lolomai people built numerous sites over a period of *only a few hundred years*. In contrast, the White Dog peoples appear to have remained, to a large extent, tied to the region's rockshelters for a period as long as *two thousand years*.

If numbers of sites provide some indication of population levels, the geometric increase in the rate of site construction by Lolomai people compared to the people of the White Dog phase suggests that local or regional population exceeded some critical threshold around 2000 B.P. The simple increase in site counts from the White Dog phase to the Lolomai phase does

not, of course, directly translate into a population increase of like magnitude. The occupants of open-air sites abandon such locations in a few years, while rockshelters last indefinitely and were apparently used, if sporadically, for more than a millennium. Nonetheless, the dramatic increase in the number of habitation sites during the short Lolomai phase can reasonably be taken as evidence of significant population growth. Figure 3.5 shows the locations of the sites of the Lolomai phase surveyed and excavated in the Black Mesa study area.

In all, the study-area survey revealed over one hundred sites that, on surface indications, fit the preceramic, early agricultural category. The sites range from camps consisting of a few hearths to proto-villages. The sites assigned to the Lolomai phase uniformly exhibit a suite of basic characteristics. These include corn macrofossils, lithic assemblages with significant to overwhelming percentages of locally available white-baked siltstone, and no ceramics. The sites yielded projectile points conforming to the several Basketmaker II styles described by Kidder and Guernsey (1919) and Morris and Burgh (1954). Figure 3.6 illustrates selected Lolomai-phase projectile points from sites in the BMAP study area. Many sites with these basic characteristics also provided evidence of earthen pit storage, small pit structures of varying depths, or both. The sites with pit houses often had been located so that the structures would be cut into friable sandstone bedrock.

The Lolomai phase, as the local Basketmaker II manifestation was called (Ware 1984), came to light in 1973 with the excavation of D:7:152, a small pit-structure settlement in Coal Mine Wash. At the time of discovery of the first site of the Lolomai phase, both the presence on Black Mesa and the chronology of the White Dog phase were unknown. The absence of ceramics, the distinctive projectile points, and the comparatively large quantities of charred corn recovered from D:7:152 convinced Euler and Ware of the presence of preceramic

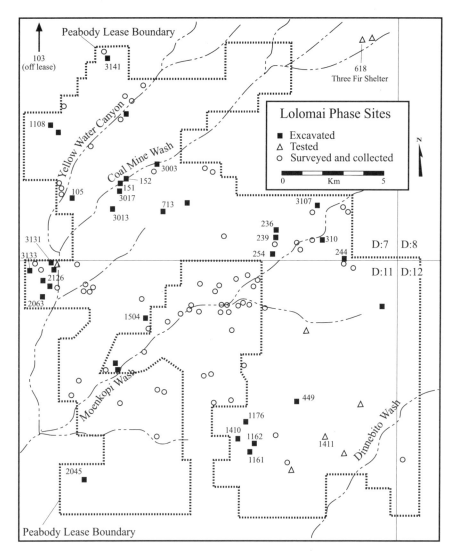

Figure 3.5 Lolomai-phase sites surveyed, tested, and excavated in the Black Mesa study area.

early agricultural groups on Black Mesa. Carefully selected radiocarbon samples from the site dated from 2700 to 2000 B.P. (Robert C. Euler, personal communication 1983), much earlier than the assumed ages of the nearby Marsh Pass rockshelters excavated by Kidder and Guernsey (1919).

Although the initial radiocarbon dates on wood charcoal from D:7:152 eventually proved erroneously early (Smiley 1985), the dates sparked considerable interest in both the early agricultural occupation and the possibility of preagricultural occupation of Black Mesa. Thus the identification of early farming sites in the project area resulted in a programmatic emphasis on the excavation of "early" sites of

all types, including early Puebloan, Basketmaker II, and Archaic manifestations. Between 1974 and the close of field work in 1983, BMAP excavated thirty-five Basketmaker II sites, including D:7:152.

The early agricultural sites of the Lolomai phase provide information on a variety of settlement types, spatial configurations, and the general regional settlement pattern. In contrast to the rockshelter-centered settlement of the preceding millennium, the open-air settlement of the Lolomai phase apparently begins a new social organizational and demographic era in the northern Southwest. The Lolomai phase evidences sites of apparently differing function and

size. In view of the large, aggregate sites of the following Basketmaker III period in the Black Mesa region (see Chapter 4), the Lolomai phase seems to represent another significant step in the process of tribalization.

Still preceramic, the Lolomai phase evidences far less residential mobility than the preceding period. Numerous, large, carefully prepared storage pits and small pit-structure settlements and villages bespeak much greater input into particular locations than we see in the rockshelter facilities of the White Dog–phase peoples. Just as the efforts of the White Dog–phase groups' construction and surplus management represent a quantum change over the Archaic, the dwellings of the Lolomai phase show a significant increase in labor input over the small numbers of dwellings found in a few rockshelters of the White Dog phase (Smiley et al. 1986; Smiley and Robins 1999). In the sections to follow I describe the variability of the Lolomai phase in the study area and compare the sites of the Lolomai phase to those of the greater region.

Environment and Chronometry

The Lolomai phase appears to be the earliest Black Mesa cultural period covered by the definitive dendrochronologically based paleoclimate reconstruction of Dean et al. (1985). Although I touched on this work earlier, extrapolating the climatic and hydrological curves into the period before 2000 B.P. constitutes an exercise in estimation in the absence of hard data. In the present instance, however, Dean et al. provide some solid data for the Black Mesa region during the Lolomai phase.

Over the past decade or so, I have variously placed the Lolomai phase between about 2000 and 1600 B.P. (Smiley 1984, 1985, 1993, 1994). Most recently (Smiley 1997c) and after additional analysis, I have settled on the time span 1900 B.P. to 1600 B.P. This splitting of chronometric hairs results from my desire for chronometric resolution, that is, achieving the high-

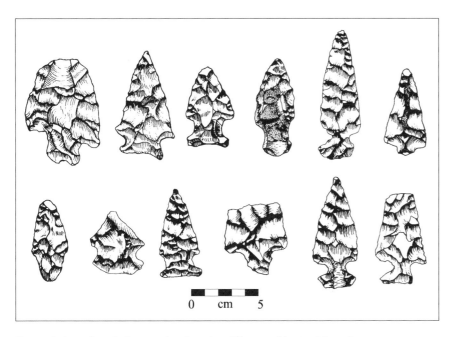

Figure 3.6 Lolomai-phase projectile points (illustrated by Jay Massey).

est possible accuracy and precision through ongoing analysis of the database. The chronological placement results from analysis of the suite of 140 dates on wood charcoal from thirty-one Lolomai-phase sites of all types and AMS dates on corn from six habitation sites (Smiley 1984, 1985, 1997c). The wood dates range from about 2800 B.P. to 1700 B.P. Descriptions of the samples can be found in Smiley 1985 and 1997e. The calibrated (Stuiver and Reimer 1993) dates on cultigens range from 1870 B.P. to 1410 B.P.

The cultigen dates provided a test for a hypothesis derived from tree-ring and simulation studies indicating that most of the radiocarbon dates on wood from the sites of the Lolomai phase overestimated the true site ages by at least two hundred years (Smiley 1984, 1985). The overestimation of site ages, I hypothesized, resulted from the use of old wood by the original site inhabitants for both heating and dwelling construction.

Figure 3.7 shows the relationship between wood dates on Lolomai habitation sites and the more accurate dates on cultigens from the same sites (Smiley 1985, 1994). The dates on corn from the habitation sites form a remarkably tight cluster, with the

exception of the date (1410 B.P.) from site D:11:1162. The D:11:1162 date cannot be dismissed, although it is an outlier. While it may be a statistical anomaly, dates on materials such as annual cultigens can be directly linked to human agency and dictate that the D:11:1162 date be both retained and taken seriously (Smiley 1997f). At two sigmas, the D:11:1162 date overlaps all other corn dates, giving a good deal of assurance that the determination remains useful in the chronometry of the Lolomai phase.

The simulation and tree-ring studies that provided a basis for hypothesizing the magnitude of the old wood error and temporal placement of the Lolomai phase also provided a basis for estimating the duration. I derived the estimate of phase duration from the nature of the distribution of radiocarbon dates on wood from sites of the Lolomai phase. Although the date distribution of the Lolomai-phase wood charcoal dates ranges over about 1,200 years, computer simulation results indicated that the actual human occupation that might produce a 1,200-year distribution might be only about 200 to 300 years long. The five older corn dates cluster between about 1900 and 1700 B.P. The

corn dates clearly support the model just sketched.

The much later date from D:11:1162, however, lies far outside the region expected for the Lolomai phase, given both the wood-date distribution and the cluster of five corn dates. At 95 percent, the D:11:1162 date overlaps the corn-date cluster, which might mean that the date is not a counter example, only a statistical outlier. I am, in fact, inclined to interpret the date in this way. Conversely, I do not discount at all the possibility that the date might be perfectly accurate, and that the Lolomai phase might persist into the sixth century A.D. If that is the case, we have an interesting example of very tight clustering of dates from five sites, using an absolute dating method that is rather famous for failing to produce clear, unequivocally meaningful clusters.

In any case, the duration and position of the Lolomai phase on the Anasazi timeline of Dean et al. (1985:541) appear to be associated with climatic change. Both the onset and end of the phase, if the chronometric reasoning set out above is reasonably accurate, seem to correlate with episodes of significant climatic alteration. The climatic changes on either end of the Lolomai phase have been expressed in various ways by Dean et al. (1985). For example, Dean et al. identify the occurrence of periods of both high-frequency and low-frequency variation in precipitation measured by tree-ring data. Dean et al. also plot the status of the water table in a hydrologic curve that indicates periods of aggradation and degradation of regional flood plains (see also Chapter 6). The resulting combination of plots shows climatic variability from 2000 B.P. to present.

The Lolomai phase, as I currently understand its chronology, falls within a period of climatic amelioration. The period of climatic improvement begins a little before 2000 B.P., running to approximately 1750 or 1700 B.P. The Lolomai phase appears to correlate with a 300-year period of low-frequency dendroclimatic vari-

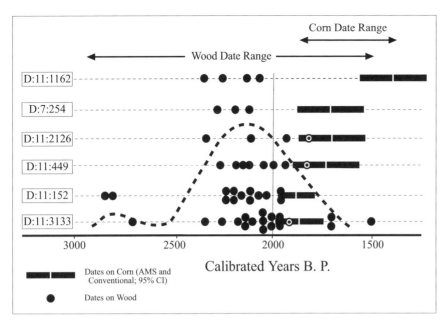

Figure 3.7 Comparison of wood dates and dates on cultigens from the same Lolomai-phase sites (after Smiley and Ahlstrom 1998:figure 7.12).

ability measured by tree-ring precipitation data (Dean et al. 1985:841, Curve C). At approximately 1700 B.P., a precipitous and apparently cyclical "crash" occurs. The crash appears in the record as a rapid lowering of the water table and associated degradation (down cutting) of flood plains. The crash also appears associated with a short period of high-frequency dendroclimatic variability that falls at the end of the Lolomai-phase occupation of northern Black Mesa. Thus, the Lolomai phase appears to begin after the onset of more favorable climatic conditions for agriculture. The phase appears to end with the apparent abandonment of the northern portion, if not all of Black Mesa, at about 1700 or 1600 B.P.

The human occupational and climatic correspondences just outlined appear fortuitous for a simple, environmental explanation of the changes that we see in the Lolomai phase. If a particular climatic amelioration produced the systemic "kick" that sparked the beginnings of Black Mesa village life in terms of increased sedentism and population growth, then we have what can only be called an environmental determinist model of transition toward tribal levels of social organization. If, on the other hand, we have a case of slowly growing population, increasing competition for scarce storage and sheltered dwelling facilities (rockshelters), an increasing emphasis on regionalism over widely distributed styles and technological concepts and ideas, then we have a much more interesting phenomenon in which environment constitutes only one of a number of dimensions of variability.

The implications of the climatic associations of the timing and duration of the Lolomai phase generate a potentially wide-ranging debate that depends on the accuracy and precision of chronometry. These implications will be explored more fully later in this chapter. Such debates are a general feature of archaeological discussions and turn in major respects, on the frequently dubious chronometric and chronological basis for much of the structure and substance of archaeological explanation.

Archaeology of the Lolomai Phase

Black Mesa researchers assigned over one hundred sites within and near the Black Mesa study area to the Lolomai phase. Thirty-five sites have been excavated or tested, and twenty-nine have been dated by radiocarbon. The general site types include habitation rockshelters, small lithic scatters, and pit-structure settlements with as many as twelve structures. In addition to extensive excavation of the sites just mentioned, the crews of the Black Mesa Archaeological Project made surface collections on or tested more than sixty other sites.

Sites of the Lolomai phase typically consist of deposits less than 20 cm deep. Most contain numerous features, and many have structures. Basketmaker II structures on Black Mesa range from ephemeral surface constructions to pit dwellings more than 1.5 m deep. The Lolomai peoples often dug their small pit structures into bedrock, a process that required a considerable investment in labor.

The sites contain a variety of intra- and extramural features, including bell-shaped storage pits, roasting pits, hearths, and slab-lined cists. Chipped-stone tools, debitage, and manos and metates abound at most sites. Site assemblages frequently contain polished stone or shell beads and ornaments similar to those of the classic Basketmaker caves in the Marsh Pass region, as well as abrading stones, a variety of projectile points, many with straight bases and side notches, and bone tools. The sites vary considerably in terms of types and numbers of structures and features present. The variability likely results from differences in site functions, activities, seasons of occupation, and differences in site population size (Smiley 1985; Bearden 1984; Mauldin 1983; Nichols and Smiley 1984b).

Crews sampled all the excavated sites to recover subsistence remains. Excavation units were selected using stratified, unaligned sampling techniques, all excavated matrix was screened, and flotation techniques were used on most sites to recover macrobotanical specimens (Nichols and Karlstrom 1983:16). As a result, excavations recovered minute animal bones and carbonized plant remains from nearly every Basketmaker II site.

In some respects, the sites of the Lolomai phase in the Black Mesa study area appear to be a large-scale palimpsest of occupations. Virtually any mesa-top resource can be reached within a few hours' walk. I am not contending here that the study area constitutes a "center" of Basketmaker II activity in the region. The point is that many sites of a range of types occur within a small area. Such sites probably occur with equal frequency in suitable local areas over the whole northern Southwest. Dohm, for example, has described what appear to be similar settlement circumstances on Cedar Mesa (1994).

The general approach to site classification employed here rests on economic and demographic considerations. The major classificatory criteria involve labor investment in architecture and facilities, population size as indicated by the number of contemporaneous structures, and implications for mobility measured by aspects of both labor investment and population. An additional important criterion is the presence and nature of storage facilities, which have implications for seasonality, mobility, and the intensity of food production (see Gilman 1983).

I divide the Lolomai sites into four classes: (1) proto-villages or settlements with from six to twelve structures; (2) habitation sites with earthen storage pits and a few small subterranean and surface structures as well as external storage pits; (3) non-storage habitation sites with a few surface or shallow pit structures; and (4) campsites consisting of small clusters of hearths surrounded by lithic scatter. I intend the following treatment of site variability and the exercise in classification to provide a functional framework to which the chronometric data may be applied.

The sites of the Lolomai phase yielded a wide range of artifactual and other significant materials. In addition to the projectile-point assemblage already illustrated, the sites produced abundant lithic manufacturing debris and tools, faunal remains, macrobotanicals, and items of per-

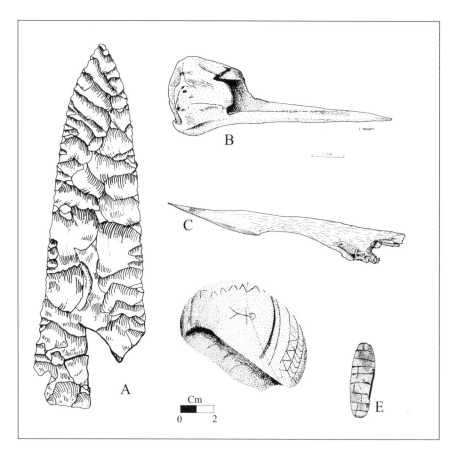

Figure 3.8 Selected artifacts from Black Mesa Lolomai-phase sites (illustrated by Jay Massey).

sonal adornment. Figure 3.8 illustrates selected artifacts from sites of the Lolomai phase on Black Mesa.

Proto-Villages

Proto-villages are the most impressive sites of the Lolomai phase, typically consisting as mentioned of several pit structures, intramural, and extramural features. Although crews found other types of habitation sites, the form of the proto-village site provides an example of one of the most significant changes in settlement in the prehistory of the Southwest. The significance of the rather innocuous proto-villages found on Black Mesa is that such sites were the first indications that populations may have been beginning the process of settling down. Not that the peoples of the White Dog phase had not begun the process a millennium before, but the fact that small groups found it efficient to in-

vest a great deal of labor in particular places, structures, and facilities suggests that the Lolomai proto-villages lie at the base of the Puebloan tradition. Thus, the proto-village site form may provide significant clues to the nature of early Puebloan development.

In previous work (Smiley 1985, 1993), I began calling these kinds of sites "villages," with the proviso that the term did not necessarily imply a high degree of sedentism. The small collections of pit structures on Black Mesa barely qualify as villages in the traditional sense, but they do consist of several single-family dwellings often arranged in orderly fashion, and each site represents a significant labor investment. The problematic aspect of the term "village" lies in the implication of a level of social and political integration indicative of more complex Neolithic societies. I do not see such a level on Black Mesa or in

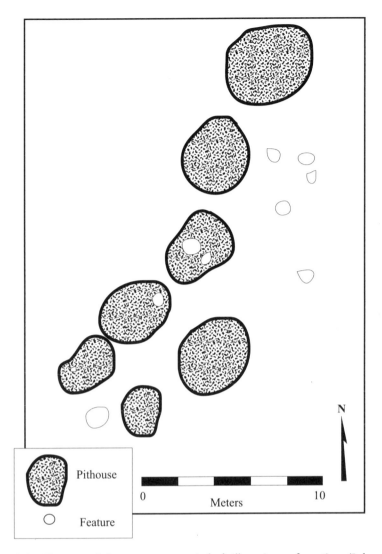

Pithouse

○ Feature

0 Meters 10

N

Figure 3.9 Plan map of site AZ D:7:3107, typical of village site configurations (Lebo et al. 1983:figure 27).

the northern Southwest at the time of the Lolomai phase, and I do not mean to suggest that tribal forms had developed by that time.

Five excavated sites fall within the proto-village settlement category. Figure 3.9 illustrates the site plan of D:7:3107, typical of some of the proto-village site configurations in layout, site size, structure type, and structure count. All such sites exhibit at least four contemporaneously occupied pit structures. Although individual structures cannot yet be dated in absolute terms, structure fill sequences and spatial patterning indicate that the occupants of the Lolomai phase probably did not occupy all structures simultaneously (Smiley 1985, 1997c).

Four attributes in addition to the relatively large number of structures present on proto-village sites help distinguish them as a discrete category. A primary and already noted difference between proto-villages and other habitation sites is the much greater total amount of labor input into proto-villages. For example, for all structures of the Lolomai phase, the mean input per structure is much greater (as measured by estimated structure volume) for proto-villages than for other kinds of habitation sites. When total site input is considered, proto-villages evidence several times the labor input of all other site classes (Smiley 1985).

A second definitional criterion is

the construction by Lolomai builders of excavated pit structures into friable bedrock in four of the five proto-villages. The site builders chose site locations to take advantage of shallow, sandy loam soils underlain by heavily fractured, friable sandstones or shales. In all cases, construction involved the extraction of chunks of rock along jointing fractures, leaving rather irregular floors and walls. The Lolomai builders leveled floors with sand or clay fill, and structures apparently had plastered walls. The number of structures on such sites ranges from six to twelve, although with twelve reported structures, D:7:236 may include one or more intensive outside activity areas consisting of multiple hearths and surface stains that have been assumed to be structures (Cathy J. Lebo, personal communication 1985; Mauldin 1983:appendix 1). However, even this site exhibits three unequivocal subterranean structures.

The third attribute that differentiates proto-villages from other habitation sites is the tendency toward formalized site layout. Three sites (D:7:3107, D:7:236, and D:11:3133) show marked linearity in the arrangement of structures. Structures in the first two sites are laid out along a northeast-southwest axis. The third, D:11:3133, is oriented northwest-southeast, with the structures situated along elevational contours that run northwest-southeast. In each of these sites, a larger or otherwise very different structure lies on the northern end of the site axis. In the case of D:11:3133, a second large structure is slightly, but distinctly, separated to the west-northwest.

A fourth attribute that distinguishes these relatively labor-intensive sites consists of the almost complete lack of visible storage facilities. The only exception, D:7:236, does have extramural bell-shaped storage pits. However, if Gilman's (1983) and Mauldin's (1983) observations and predictions that pit structures of substantial depth are typical of winter occupations are correct, then Lolomai groups should have made some provision for storage of domestic crops and storable wild seeds. Lolomai peoples had a number of options for seed or grain storage (Gilman 1983), one of which might have been basket storage inside dwellings. An alternative storage possibility involves the use of some bedrock pit structures in villages as communal storage facilities.

D:11:3133 again provides an interesting example. Based on two markedly different fill sequences for structures, the site appears to exhibit two construction episodes (Smiley 1985:appendix D). Structures 3 through 6 and Structure 8 contain distinctive levels of yellowish brown to brown clayey matrix mixed with charcoal and lithic debris. Such material likely derives from the excavation of Structures 2, 7, 9, and 10. The clayey material overlies the bedrock into which the structures were excavated. The fills of the latter structures lack the clayey levels and consist entirely of eolian silts and loams. All structures contain burned roof-fall materials. This information, combined with the presence of Structures 1 and 9, large structures with floor areas greater than 28 m², comprises an informative set of dualities. Although Structure 1 is a surface type and cannot be correlated with either of the distinctive fill sequences based on stratigraphy, we can reasonably place it with Structures 3 through 6 and Structure 8. The two apparent temporally discrete occupations, each with two large structures, appear to be more than coincidence.

The dual occupation phenomenon is echoed by D:7:3107 (figure 3.9), which exhibits a similar site layout. In addition, there are two distinct fill sequences more or less evenly divided among the pit structures (Lebo et al. 1983; Smiley 1985, 1997c). In view of the general absence of external storage pits common on many other sites of the Lolomai phase, the possibility that some structures were, themselves, used for storage appears increasingly viable.

In addition, some proto-villages provide at least nominal evidence for a differentiated and/or significantly

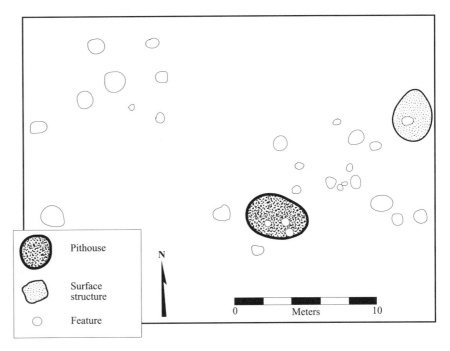

Figure 3.10 Plan map of site AZ D:7:254, typical of earthen pit storage site configurations (after Gilman and Cushman 1983:figure 13).

larger structure. Anyon (1984) suggests ceremonial or communal functions for differentiated structures on early agricultural sites of the Mogollon area dating to the period A.D. 200–600. K. Lightfoot and Feinman investigated the possibility that large, differentiated structures on such sites may be the residences of headmen (1982). However, the pattern is much more robust in the Mogollon area than among the Black Mesa proto-villages.

If some structures functioned as storage or communal facilities rather than habitations, then population size at proto-villages would have been considerably smaller than the numbers of structures suggest. The evidence for multiple construction episodes reduces the likelihood that Lolomai groups occupied all structures in villages simultaneously. By the same token, the stratigraphic evidence for distinct fill sequences on some sites suggests that only about half the structures were simultaneously in use for habitation, storage, or both.

Earthen Pit Storage Habitation Sites

The earthen pit storage (EPS) habitation site class contains sites that had

from one to several formally prepared bell-shaped storage pits. One such site, D:11:449, had at least twenty such pits. The EPS sites further evidenced either surface or subsurface structures. Of the nineteen structures on the ten excavated EPS sites, only three structures appear to be unequivocal surface dwellings. Two of the sites included in this category, D:7:3141 and D:11:1161, had no structures. Figure 3.10 illustrates the plan layout of site D:7:254, which typifies sites in the EPS category.

While the primary criterion for inclusion in the EPS class consists of the presence of earthen storage pits, the ten sites appear similar in a number of other respects. Like villages, all have yielded the charred remains of corn and edible wild seeds. Seven of the ten evidenced no surface structures. The other three sites have one surface structure each. Except for D:11:3131, none of the sites has more than three structures, and five sites have only two structures. Although D:7:3141 and D:11:1161 yielded no evidence of structures, in both cases investigators suspect that structures were destroyed either by erosion (D:7:3141) or by road construction

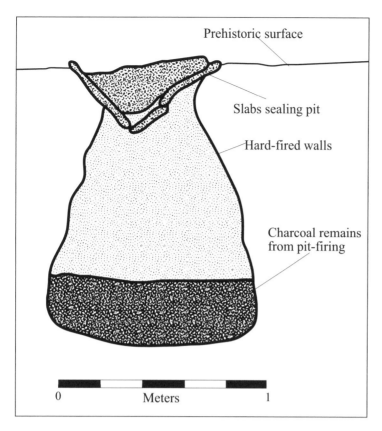

Figure 3.11 Feature 67, a bell-shaped storage pit at site AZ D:7:449 (after Leonard et al. 1985:figure 3.6).

(D:11:1161). In addition, sampling error remains a possibility in both cases, that is, structures may simply not have been located during excavation. The latter possibility seems particularly strong in the case of D:7:3141, since end-of-field-season time constraints limited the area that could be sampled. Site D:7:3141 produced at least three large, formally prepared bell pits, one of which had been used as a mass grave. Seven individuals of both sexes ranging in age from infants to adults over forty years of age came from the storage pit (MacMinn et al. 1984). The presence of structures associated with bell-storage features on the other eight sites, coupled with the conjectural evidence for structures on D:7:3141 and D:11:1161, provide the basis for inclusion of the two latter sites in this class.

A total of forty-nine bell-shaped storage pits have been identified on occupations of the Lolomai phase. Site D:11:449 provides an excellent example, with several well-preserved pits showing the distinctive bell-shaped profile with walls constricted near the top and flaring outward and down to a flat floor. One pit, Feature 67 (figure 3.11), still had cover slabs in place, appeared to have been newly constructed, and never to have been used for storage.

Functionally, the typical pits with hard-fired walls are well suited to storage in the semiarid Black Mesa climate. As Gilman (1983:147) notes, ideal earthen storage pits tend to have narrow openings and well-sealed walls to restrict the supply of oxygen to potentially destructive bacteria, fungi, and insects. In addition, such pits tend to be placed in well-drained areas, for example, in sandy loam. The initial firing of the features hardened and at least partially sealed the walls, probably killing any microorganisms or insect larvae in the process. The mean storage volume for the forty-nine pits

on sites with earthen pit storage falls at .59 m³ and the median at .45 m³, indicating a distribution slightly skewed toward the larger end of the scale. The sample also includes a few small pits that do not appear to be particularly substantial in terms of multiseason storage.

The relationship between settlement patterns and surplus production in the White Dog and Lolomai phases poses an interesting question. Accordingly, I calculated storage capacities for three sites of the White Dog phase, Cave DuPont (near Kanab, Utah) and Caves 1 and 2 in the Marsh Pass area just north of Black Mesa (Smiley 1985). The mean capacity of Basketmaker II storage features in the three dry caves fell at 0.54 m³, close to the 0.57 m³ average value for storage pits in Black Mesa open-air sites. The only available radiocarbon dates on reliable material, that is, corn, for Cave DuPont, interestingly, place occupation coeval with the later portion of the Lolomai phase on Black Mesa at about 1650 B.P. (Smiley 1997d, 1997e, 1998a).

Most of the ten sites in the earthen pit storage category manifest substantial storage capacities, indicating that cultivated and/or gathered seeds were an important source of food and that Lolomai peoples invested a significant amount of labor in storage. Further, if corn were the principal stored commodity, and if earthen storage capacity provides at least an indirect measure of the amount harvested, agricultural production must have made up a significant share of subsistence during the Lolomai phase at these sites. On these sites, moreover, forty-five of the forty-nine bell pits were extramural.

An additional relevant aspect of site morphology is the generally small but variable number of pit structures on such sites. The spatial and contextual data indicate that the sites with more than one structure result from sequential occupations. In this respect, D:11:449 may provide the clearest example. D:11:449 consisted of two nearly identical, medium-depth pit structures, a single surface structure, and two discrete clusters of eight-to-ten bell pits. Each cluster of pits appeared to be associated with a particular pit structure rather than with the lone surface structure. In addition, investigators found some evidence that the storage pits and structures represented sequential construction events. Structure 1, for example, appeared to have been stripped clean of artifacts and slabs before abandonment. Structure 3, on the other hand, still contained grinding implements and had numerous slabs in the fill. If we assume the group of bell pits nearest each pit structure were associated with that particular structure, then the group of pits nearest Structure 3 appears to have been the last used on the site.

The large number (twenty) of substantial storage pits on D:11:449 raises additional questions. No other site in this class has more than four. If the site were occupied by a group or family small enough to be housed in a single pit structure, the storage capacity of D:11:449 appears to be excessive. More likely, a Lolomai group used the site over a long period of time, periodically building new storage facilities. The presence of an intensively used activity area consisting of numerous shallow hearths and amorphous pits supports this interpretation.

Nonstorage Habitation Sites

Nonstorage habitation sites comprise the third class of habitations of the Lolomai phase. These sites have small numbers of structures but provide no evidence of storage features. Figure 3.12 shows the typical configuration of a nonstorage habitation site at site D:11:2126. Five of the excavated sites fall into this class, four of which had two structures each and one of which had four structures. All five sites had at least one surface structure, and two sites consisted of two surface structures each. None of the

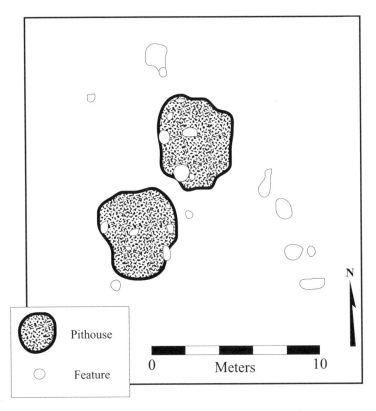

Figure 3.12 Plan map of site AZ D:11:2126, typical of nonstorage habitation site configurations (Wills et al. 1984:figure 3.48).

sites yielded pit structures with depths greater than 1 m.

Two sites, D:11:244 and D:11:2126, provided evidence of reoccupation of two different types. D:11:244 appeared to be a palimpsest of occupations, with at least four activity clusters comprised of pit structures and groups of hearths and amorphous pits. None of the pits fitted the criteria I developed elsewhere (Smiley 1985) to help identify eroded or caved-in bell pits. The pit structures at D:11:244 lay scattered along a low, gently sloping terrace near a wash floodplain. At least one discrete activity area consisted entirely of small hearths and lithic scatter. Structure 1 yielded fragmented human skeletal material from at least three individuals, although investigators could not define the nature of the burial context (D. Martin and Piacentini 1983). The amorphous burial situation in Structure 1, badly disturbed by road grading and rodent activity, appeared different from the mass interment at D:7:3141, described

above. Rynda et al. (1983:169) note the possibility that the burials may be secondary. Rodent disturbance of the shallow deposits, however, remains a likely reason for the fragmentary nature of the skeletal materials.

The spatially discrete activity areas at D:11:244 appeared to represent multiple occupations of the same general locale. Moreover, the absence of the kinds of strong patterns noted for proto-villages and site with earthen pit storage indicated that the various D:11:244 components were small habitation sites related to one another only if, as is likely, the same small group returned seasonally or periodically to this locale.

All but one of the sites had only surface structures, most of which contain internal hearths. D:11:2126 constitutes an exception, with one surface structure and one pit structure. The pit structure had apparently been reused, evidencing a second floor superimposed over the original floor. Hearths occurred in both floor levels (Wills et al. 1984). Reoccupation of such localities appears to be directly confirmed in at least one site (D:11:2126). The lack of evidence of superposition at other nonstorage sites leaves room for speculation only as to whether structures were contemporaneous. The remaining sites in the nonstorage habitation class consist of particularly ephemeral occupations, each with two pit structures located in close proximity.

In summary, if the prevalence of surface structures on nonstorage habitation sites indicates season of use, then sites in this class seem to be non-winter occupations. Some structures on sites such as D:7:236 and D:11:3131 in the village and earthen pit storage classes respectively may represent occupations similar to the nonstorage habitations that were not contemporaneous with other aspects of the site. Thus, a number of sites of the Lolomai phase seem to bridge the seasonal gap left by the proto-villages and sites with earthen pit storage, in that the sites appear to be warm season habitations. Such sites tend to be ephemeral, and there are likely many more among the survey-identified sites that have not yet been classified.

Limited-Activity/Campsites

Six small, ephemeral sites fall within this class, all of which lack evidence of structures and exhibit from one to eleven small hearths amidst scatters of lithic debris. Figure 3.13 shows the plan of site D:11:2045, a typical campsite. All but one of these sites was located on Black Mesa proper. Site D:7:103, comprised of five small hearths (Ware 1984; Parry 1987a), lay near the base of the northwest escarpment in Klethla Valley. In consonance with all other classes of sites, the lithic assemblages for campsites vary a great deal (Parry 1986). At least two sites evidence intensive biface-manufacturing activity (D:11:2063, D:11:1176). Others, such as D:11:2045, produced smaller, though substantial, lithic assemblages. All sites sampled to recover macrobotanical

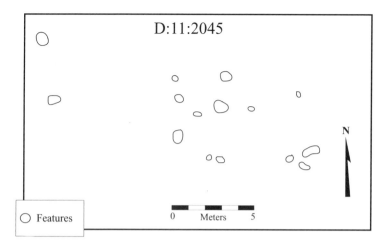

Figure 3.13 Plan map of site AZ D:11:2045, typical of limited activity/campsites (after Smith and Miles 1984:figure 3.34).

remains yielded evidence of corn and various edible wild seeds. The most intensively used of the sites appears to be D:11:2045. The site, with its eleven small hearths and two roasting pits, produced abundant evidence of corn from nearly all features.

The remaining sites (D:7:105, D:7:3017) fall generally within the range of variability already described. The only additional aspect of site variability consists of undated lithic scatters without features of any sort. Sites such as D:11:1014 (S. Smith 1985), D:11:3135 (S. Smith and Wills 1984), D:7:473 (Hays 1983), and probably D:7:3045 (Mauldin et al. 1982) exemplify the subtype. On such sites, the lithic assemblages varied a great deal both in terms of quantity of debris and in the kinds of lithic reduction that took place. The primary attribute used to place the sites in the Lolomai phase was the overwhelming preponderance of white-baked siltstone debris in the artifact assemblages.

In summary, the limited-activity/camp class remains perhaps more variable than the other classes. Such sites are often assumed to be warm season phenomena; however, limited-activity/campsites remain problematical beyond the fact that they could have resulted from occupations in any season.

Surface and Subsurface Remains

In addition to the variability apparent among the excavated and tested sites, the range of site variability has been surprising in terms of the relationship of subsurface to surface remains. For example, lithic debris was the most typical surface manifestation of Lolomai sites. If the density and spatial extent of lithic artifacts on sites provide measures of the intensity and size of occupation, investigators might incorrectly infer the actual nature of a given site in a significant number of cases. The same is true for the visibility of architectural remains and other facilities. Although in no instances have unequivocal sites of the Lolomai phase been located that are deeply buried, structure and feature remains rarely appear on the surface. Lolomai sites uniformly exhibit low surface visibility.

Some examples illustrate the general lack of correlation between surface and subsurface remains on Black Mesa Basketmaker II sites. The first example, D:11:2063, consisted of a dense lithic scatter over a 25 × 30 m area. An apparent rubble concentration raised expectations for the presence of architectural remains. Ultimately, however, excavators found no architectural remains, only thousands of pieces of stone-tool manufacturing debris and a few small features (Leonard et al. 1984b). Much of the debris resulted from biface manufacture (Young 1983). A nearby site, D:11:3133, also exhibited a dense surface scatter of lithic debris and an apparent rubble concentration (Leonard et al. 1984a). Like D:11:2063, the locality eventually produced thousands of pieces of lithic debris, an appreciable amount of which could be attributed to biface manufacture. Unlike D:11:2063, the latter site contained ten structures, nine of which had been cut into bedrock. Although the two sites showed virtually identical surface manifestations and lay close to one another in the study area, the magnitude of subsurface differences cannot be overstated.

As a final example, a survey crew described D:7:3107 (Lebo et al. 1983) on surface indications as a small, sparse lithic scatter with a few upright slabs. The site, thus, showed few lithic artifacts and few solid indications of subsurface architecture. By all indications, D:7:3107 appeared to be a limited activity site. Like D:11:3133, however, the subsurface picture could hardly have been more different. Although excavation produced a total of only fifty-nine pieces of chipped stone, the site contained at least seven pit structures cut into bedrock.

Thus, two artifact scatters, apparently similar on the surface, differed markedly in terms of the nature of subsurface remains. One site was only a surface artifact scatter. In stark contrast, the other turned out to be a substantial proto-village. The sites just described exemplify the differences between the surface and subsurface characters of apparently similar sites.

Site Locational Variability

As intensively investigated localities go, the Black Mesa study area is comparatively large. Relative to the territory used by mobile or even semimobile agricultural/foraging groups, however, the area is comparatively small. Accordingly, I do not view the study area as a regional locus of activity. I view it, instead, as part of the large regional catchment that may have had as much to do with variability in the productivity and cycling of pinyon nuts and other wild resources as with agricultural territoriality. In short, the study area probably comprises only a small portion of the lands used by groups of the Lolomai phase.

The spatial distribution of sites of the Lolomai phase reflects the topographic and vegetative homogeneity of the study area. The Lolomai sites in the study area tend to lie along major drainages such as the Moenkopi and Coal Mine Wash systems. The homogeneity of the distribution of pygmy conifer forest and topographic features such as ridges and valleys makes one location similar to another in important respects. Virtually all sites, for example, lie near major subsistence resources such as arable land, fuel, water, game, and subsistence-related plants. Virtually all such resources can be found within a short distance of all the sites. The site locations, thus, appear not to be particularly sensitive to elevational or resource locational criteria within the pinyon and juniper zones of the study area.

One microenvironmental property common to a majority of the sites is soil type. Lolomai peoples built the vast majority of sites on deep, well-drained eolian sandy loams into which they could relatively easily excavate pit structures and other facilities. The Puebloan groups that occupied the study area after A.D. 800 apparently placed sites on the sandy loams for similar reasons.

Topographically varied situations characterize the sites as well. Nine of the excavated sites were constructed on gently sloping hillsides, and nine on hill tops, while the remainder were scattered among the categories of wash terrace, sage flats, or alluvial floodplain. In addition, the distribution of sites shows no discrete modality in terms of associated vegetation regimes or distance to nearest wash floodplain. Site aspect, the topo-graphic orientation of a site, shows a tendency for Lolomai groups to have selected locations that were level or that had an eastern aspect. Ten sites lie on topographic features that generally face eastward, nine lie on essentially flat terrain, and the remainder vary in aspect from northwest to south. No sites lie on terrain oriented to the west or the southwest, the directions of the prevailing winds.

Settlement and Social Organization in the Lolomai Phase

Seasonality, Mobility, and Population

In the foregoing discussion I evaluated the variability among Lolomai sites on Black Mesa in terms of labor input and placed the sites into four basic classes. Each class contains a certain amount of variability and its own outliers. The site classes suggest settlement types that may, at least nominally, be assigned general parameters of seasonality, population, and length of occupation. Villages, as the largest, most structured, and most labor intensive, were likely cold-season phenomena. If so, some degree of winter aggregation was the pattern for the Lolomai peoples. Population aggregates probably lasted at least several months. However, four to eight families of five to eight persons each may not constitute the maximum size of aggregations for early agriculturalists in the Black Mesa region, and the possibility cannot be ignored that larger, more regional aggregations existed.

If larger groups aggregated periodically for exchange, ritual, or other purposes, the locations have not been identified on either Black Mesa or anywhere else in the Southwest. Sites such as the Hay Hollow site (P. Martin 1967), D:11:3133 (Leonard et al. 1984a), D:7:152 (Ravesloot 1984), and D:7:236 (Whitecotton et al. 1980) are the largest-known regional sites that date to this period. Geib and Spurr (2000) describe at least one other site, Kin

Kahuna on the Rainbow Plateau in northern Arizona, that has at least seven dwellings and may date earlier than the sites of the Lolomai phase on Black Mesa.

The Black Mesa regional sites appear remarkably similar in terms of the numbers of structures (eight to twelve) identified. Moreover, each of these sites produced at least nominal evidence for multiple occupation episodes (M. Berry 1982; Smiley 1985), which potentially reduces the site population estimates. The kinds of sites produced by larger-scale aggregations might, however, have had very low archaeological visibility, particularly if such phenomena were short-term encampments.

Modern-day squaw dance and Yeibichai sites resulting from Navajo regional gatherings in the Black Mesa area that I have observed consist of only surface structures and accompanying hearths. The archaeological condition of such sites in a millennium or two might easily resemble that of a small-scale, short-term encampment, even though hundreds of people occupied the sites for short periods.

The presence of structures in some Black Mesa villages that are both spatially separated from the main cluster of structures and qualitatively and quantitatively different indicates a degree of structure differentiation not previously suspected. If larger or significantly different structures in proto-villages served as ceremonial or other communal facilities and if still other structures were relegated to storage functions, estimates of site populations should be considerably scaled back. In any case, site populations for winter aggregations appear to range from twenty to sixty persons, depending upon whether one assumes simultaneous occupation of all structures.

Earthen pit storage sites, with less substantial, shallower pit structures and formally prepared bell-shaped storage pits, appear to be the next most labor-intensive site class. The large capacity of external storage facilities suggests that stored foods made up an important share of yearly subsistence. While we have little direct evidence of the specific foods stored, the most likely commodities are corn and pinyon nuts, both of which enjoyed seasonal abundance. Of the two, corn would have been most consistently produced year-to-year and, thus, is the probable food for which the Lolomai people constructed most pits. As indicated in the previous chapter, pinyon masts tend to be highly variable over space and time and, accordingly, tend to be less reliable, particularly as a critical resource (see Ford 1984:127; Ford et al. 1985).

Earthen pit storage sites appear to be at least partially cold-season phenomena. The difference in depths between the pit structures in earthen pit storage sites and those in proto-villages indicates that the thermal properties of deeper pit structures were not as critical to subsistence as for proto-villages. This fact further suggests that structures on earthen pit storage sites were not used during the coldest months. In addition, most earthen pit storage sites yielded evidence of surface structures or temporary shelters. The storage pits would have been needed as soon as the harvest came in and had been processed. For corn, the processing essentially involved drying and shelling the ears. Because roasting renders pinyon nuts more perishable, pinyon storage simply amounts to caching the harvest in a storage facility.

The difficulty in articulating earthen pit storage sites with proto-villages within a single settlement system lies in resolving the apparent suitability of the structure/storage facilities on both kinds of sites for cold-weather occupation. Both types of sites have ample storage capacity, and the floor areas of both kinds of habitation structures appear statistically indistinguishable. Only the greater labor investment per structure for proto-villages suggests longer occupation periods and better winter protection.

Annual periods of aggregation for peoples who spend much of the rest of the year as smaller units are well documented in the ethnographic literature (e.g., Steward 1938) and would be expected. On this premise, I suggest that the earthen pit storage sites were late-summer and fall occupations. The ubiquity of surface structures or shelters on such sites further suggests the sites may have been occupied during the growing season as well. Whether nuclear- or extended-family groups occupying a single structure constituted the norm on such sites, or whether two or three structures were in use simultaneously by as many family units, remains open to question. However, the single pit structure sites in this class (D:7:254 and D:11:1410) indicate that groups as small as five to eight persons did spend at least a portion of the year in comparative isolation.

In any case, the ubiquity of corn and the presence of storage features remains the primary link to agricultural activity in connection with the sites. Gilman (1983) found that ethnographic data suggest people tend to use exterior pit storage facilities when a site is to be abandoned for a period. Exterior pits have very low visibility, and in arid and semiarid regions, they have good potential for food preservation. Thus, food for at least a portion of the following year might be left on site as well as seed for the next crop. A portion of the harvest could then be moved to the winter aggregate site.

To judge from the distribution of proto-villages and earthen pit storage sites, transport might have been an easy matter of an hour's walk, but we should consider the possibility of longer transport as part of the process of tracking the pinyon harvest. The advantage in summer dispersal probably lay in the planting of corn plots in varied microenvironmental agricultural situations as insurance against the stochasticity of precipitation and the threat of early and late frosts. In addition, most groups find foraging and hunting in dispersed groups advantageous, since, as Ford (1984:128) notes, the wild resources available in localities such as Black Mesa are sparsely distributed and the environment is generally depauperate in terms of human subsistence.

Nonstorage sites consisting almost entirely of surface structures appear most likely to have been summer habitations or limited-activity sites for pinyon-nut harvesting, an activity still undertaken by local Navajo families (Ford et al. 1985). The near ubiquity of paired structures on such sites suggests some activity for which a single-family group probably would not have sufficed. Nonstorage sites tend to be the least labor intensive of the habitation site types and thus are likely to have been occupied for relatively shorter periods than sites in either of the other two classes.

Last of the site classes is the highly varied, limited-activity/campsite class. Limited-activity sites likely represent a wide range of activities from lithic tool manufacturing to hunting and foraging expeditions requiring stays overnight or of only a few days. Such activities could take place during any season but are more likely to have occurred during the spring, summer, and fall.

Thus the sites assigned to the Lolomai phase appear to fall into functionally and seasonally complementary classes. The curious aspect of the suite of apparent site types remains that so many types appear in the same local area without apparent discrete locational criteria. The settlement pattern might result from use by a population that moved sporadically about the region, using similar areas differently in different years. Such a movement regimen might produce areas with functionally different sites in similar locational situations. Alternatively, the pattern may derive from use by a more localized population that simply constructed different sites according to specific seasonal needs. With the exception of the Cedar Mesa area (Matson and Dohm 1994) and the Rainbow Plateau (Geib and Spurr 2000), we have so few sites across the northern Southwest with which to compare the Black Mesa pattern that

conclusions remain speculative at this point. The lack of sites stems from the paucity of systematic regional survey that specifically and programmatically seeks low-visibility nonceramic sites.

Black Mesa Chronometry

Implications for Early Agricultural Sites in the Northern Southwest

The large body of radiocarbon data from preceramic agricultural sites on and near Black Mesa provides a means for assessing the accuracy and precision for dating regional sites. The long period of use of Three Fir Shelter matches that of other rockshelters, most notably Bat Cave. Even rockshelters dated by only a few samples suggest relatively long periods of use. Thus, rockshelters in the Black Mesa region that have yielded Basketmaker II assemblages may have been used since before 4000 B.P. As I have demonstrated elsewhere, the larger the sample of cultigen or other annual material dates from particular sites, the better the chances for documenting the occupations of sites across centuries (Smiley 1994).

The advent of Lolomai-phase open-air habitation sites on Black Mesa and the relatively short span of time the phenomenon appears to persist may be mirrored in other regional sites as well. I have examined the radiocarbon data from several other open-air habitation sites in the northern Southwest and find a pattern very similar to that of the sites of Black Mesa (Smiley 1985, 1994). The group of sites includes the Hay Hollow site dated by twenty-two determinations on wood charcoal, and the Petri, County Road, and Connie sites located in the Hay Hollow Valley of east-central Arizona, as well as NA 14646 on Hardscrabble Wash approximately 50 km north of St. Johns, Arizona (M. Berry 1982; P. Martin 1967, 1972; F. Plog 1974; Fritz 1974).

The distribution of dates on wood charcoal for these sites considered in the context of wood-age

effects (Smiley 1997f) suggests that the true site ages fall within the Lolomai phase, after 2000 B.P. The possibility that the populations of the earlier White Dog phase also built open-air sites or that the advent of what I term "proto-villages" may, in other regions, predate the Lolomai phase remain tenable and may be indicated by the sites mentioned earlier (Sullivan 1986a; Gilpin 1994; Geib and Spurr 2000). However, the distributions of dates from the several sites considered above, strongly, in my view, suggest occupation after 2000 B.P.

Having argued that a number of open-air habitation sites were occupied later than the wood dates suggest, we must now examine the problem of rockshelter occupation spans. I think more can and should be said of the numerous rockshelters that appear to date somewhat later than the sites of the White Dog phase. The Falls Creek shelters in the Durango area, for example, have been placed near or after 2000 B.P. By 1994, however, dates on corn from Falls Creek North Shelter and the Burial Crevice place that occupation at least three hundred years earlier, calibrated at about 2300 B.P. (Florence C. Lister, personal communication 1994; Stuiver and Reimer 1993).

The newest dates from the Durango shelters suggest occupation from as early as 2800 B.P. The same pattern holds for sites in Butler Wash of southeastern Utah and probably for sites in nearby Grand Gulch as well (Smiley 1997a, d, e). The pattern of long occupational use of rockshelters matches that of the Marsh Pass rockshelters that, before the AMS corn dates I obtained in 1985, had been assumed to date between 2000 and 1500 B.P. The pattern consists of the extension back in time of the occupation span as investigators assay more samples of high-quality materials. High-quality materials consist of annual plants, ideally, cultigens. Accordingly, as archaeologists more intensively investigate northern southwestern rockshelter sites, many, if not virtually all occupations, will eventually date from before 3000 B.P., that is, as early as the Marsh Pass area caves and nearby Three Fir Shelter.

Perspectives on Early Agriculture in the Northern Southwest

Exploring transitions, such as the agricultural transition in the northern Southwest, obviously involves transitional events and processes. Such studies also require that investigators examine events and processes on either side of the transitions, the before and after. I have tried to set out what we know of the preceding, transitional, and following systems and events, moving from Paleoindian and Archaic times to the earliest farmers, and finally the period of the advent of proto-villages during the Lolomai phase. For northeastern Arizona, the archaeological record remains geographically and temporally sparse despite the intensive investigations of the Black Mesa project over a period of nearly twenty years. The scarcity of data results from the small-scale, ephemeral nature of human occupation during most of this time and from the lack of systematic, broad, regional data collection. But that is the current state of the archaeological record with which we must work.

Two primary transitions occurred during this period. Both transitions occurred worldwide at various times, and both command a great deal of archaeological interest on theoretical, methodological, and empirical levels. The process and conditions surrounding both remain highly controversial. The first transition, the change from hunting and gathering to a significant degree of reliance on food production, may have occurred as early as 4000 B.P. and certainly sometime before 3000 B.P. in the northern Southwest. The transition may have occurred rapidly, as I have suggested in other work (Smiley 1993, 1994, 1997a; Smiley and Parry 1990).

The base mechanism of the transition, whether migration, adoption, or, as I suspect, a complex combination of the two, remains poorly documented. We still have too few sites and, more importantly, too few well-dated sites to confirm regional mechanisms. Moreover, the transition itself may have happened so rapidly, that is, in two centuries or fewer (Smiley 1997b), that the progress of agriculture across the Southwest appears archaeologically invisible at the current level of radiocarbon-dating resolution. In any case, the transition appears to have occurred across the Southwest in rapid fashion and may, on the Colorado Plateau, be linked to a dual dependence on two major surplus-producing resources, corn and pinyon nuts.

What we do have from the earliest agricultural period are large, varied, perishable assemblages of much of the Basketmaker II cultural inventory. Few early agricultural manifestations anywhere in the world provide such detailed assemblages. The assemblages give important clues to the nature of the changes that occurred at the transition. One of the most striking and telling changes from Archaic hunter-gatherer times consists of the burial of the dead in the habitation and storage context of the living group. The Basketmaker ancestors, thus, became part of the domestic setting, likely marking proprietary rights to certain rockshelters. The regional rockshelters provided favorable and dry living and storage conditions without the need for construction of elaborate subterranean or surface dwellings and facilities. For groups that apparently required the ability to remain mobile, the use of rockshelters was likely an efficient strategy.

To summarize, the earliest agricultural period, manifested in the White Dog phase of northeastern Arizona, southeastern Utah, southwestern Colorado, and northwestern New Mexico showed marked and fundamental change from the thousands of years of Archaic hunting and gathering. Different ideological structure becomes apparent in the radical new mortuary practices of Basket-

maker II peoples across the northern Southwest. These earliest farmers had a new settlement pattern primarily focused on rockshelters. They also had a vastly different subsistence system that included food production. Basketmaker II groups appear to have been at least somewhat more settled, leaving ample remains of domestic industry in the region's rockshelters.

Curiously, however, once the transition had occurred, the early farming groups appear to have entered a period of adaptive stability. For the next millennium across the northern Southwest, they seem to have maintained populations at low levels. They remained mobile, and they appear, in many areas, to have restricted habitation to caves and rockshelters.

I have frequently used equivocal terms in the foregoing discussion because we have very little information on the events and processes within the long White Dog phase. We have large artifactual and midden assemblages, and we have radiocarbon dates on cultigens. But we have very little temporal resolution.

If populations grew slowly during the White Dog phase, eventually resulting in the necessity to construct the open-air settlements of the Lolomai phase, the archaeological record has not spoken clearly. If reliance on cultigens over pinyon nuts or other resources gradually increased, the record has not been examined in sufficient detail to so reveal. I think, in any case, that the transition to small semisedentary proto-villages does indicate that subsistence, mobility, and population did change, passing some threshold. This transition also looms as highly significant in the process of human adaptation and sociocultural development in the American Southwest.

The second transition, a change from a pattern of mobile farmer/forager groups living primarily in rockshelters to semisedentary groups living in small, open-air proto-villages occurred just after 2000 B.P. in the Black Mesa region. The Black Mesa research revealed previously unsuspected settlement systems for early farmers and provided a large body of temporal data for the northern Southwest. Researchers working on the early agricultural period only two decades ago viewed the agricultural transition as having occurred a little before 2000 B.P. with the appearance of the small Basketmaker II open-air sites on Black Mesa, in Hay Hollow Valley, Cedar Mesa, the Navajo Reservoir District, and the Four Corners area, in general. By the middle and late 1980s, however, much greater antiquity for agriculture in both the northern Southwest (Simmons 1986; Smiley et al. 1986; Wills 1988) and the southern Southwest (Upham et al. 1987) began to be established.

The establishment of considerably greater antiquity for food production placed the Lolomai-phase Basketmaker II peoples in a different interpretive context. No longer were Lolomai groups apparent pioneer immigrants or new recipients of diffused corn farming from the south. Instead, the Lolomai peoples now had to be viewed as heirs to a long tradition, as many as two thousand years of agricultural subsistence.

With so much time depth, could such groups even be considered to still be "early" farmers? In important ways, the answer remains, yes. The groups apparently retained some mobility, and populations remained small. But the threshold to village life appears to have been passed when the Lolomai groups found it necessary to expand from the rockshelter environment to build weatherproof dwellings in the open. The vastly increased labor invested far beyond the labor evident in the rockshelters of the region bespeaks a very different commitment to, and concept of, place: clearly of a changed human/land relationship.

The settlement patterns of the Lolomai phase suggest increased population, decreasing territory sizes, and reduced residential mobility. The patterns appear to be echoed in the variability in structure types among other regional variants of peoples of the Lolomai phase. Pit structures in the Cedar Mesa area differ from those of Black Mesa and Hay Hollow Valley in the configuration of entrances. The Navajo Reservoir District structures evidence large cobble rings. The Durango pit structures show repeated reuse and appear to be of cribbed-log construction. In contrast to the wide regional similarities of rockshelter Basketmaker II assemblages, such variability may indicate the beginnings of regionalization.

The lithic assemblages from virtually all sites of the Lolomai phase consist of high proportions of white-baked siltstone, a locally available raw material frequently used in biface manufacture. The rockshelter sites produce little or no such raw material. The presence and quantities of white-baked siltstone on the Lolomai sites suggests that, in contrast to the lithic procurement habits of the peoples of the White Dog phase, the Lolomai groups more frequently used local materials, which may bolster the case for reduced residential mobility during Lolomai times.

Subsistence may have changed in Lolomai times as well. If the presence of subterranean and surface dwellings indicates greater attachment to locations and territories relative to earlier periods, then such dwellings may also indicate that the opportunity for groups to follow pinyon harvests over a very large region may have been reduced. The reduced access to pinyon nuts, except when the stochastic masts occurred within the territory, would probably encourage increased reliance on agriculture.

While we still lack the data to determine whether Lolomai groups relied more or less on agriculture than peoples of the White Dog phase, one aspect of the Lolomai phenomenon should be carefully considered. The Lolomai phase was quite short, on the order of three hundred years (Smiley 1985, 1998b). The Lolomai phase was, in my view, more of a transition than a phase in and of itself. A few centuries after the long, apparently stable White Dog adaptation, the Anasazi tradition began to emerge, moving toward the status of distinctive, regional, cultural phenomenon. The transition to village life, begun in the small settlements of the Lolomai phase and other regional variants, matured into the large, possibly aggregated Basketmaker III sites of the Western Anasazi region.

Within a relatively short time between the development of small proto-villages of four to twelve structures between 1900 and 1600 B.P., populations may have increased significantly. The more productive, but coincidentally destabilizing, strategy of primary dependence on food production probably had to yield to mobility (abandonment) on the down side of the precipitation cycle I described at the beginning of the chapter. Basketmaker II groups left Black Mesa at that point and seem to disappear from the local region afterwards. A major remaining problem, thus, is tracing and explaining the cultural events and processes between about 1600 B.P., when the Lolomai peoples appear to have abandoned northern Black Mesa, and the fifth and sixth centuries in which we begin to see large nucleated Basketmaker III villages, such as Juniper Cove (Gilpin and Benallie 2000), in the greater region.

Modeling the Agricultural Transition

Southwesternists have developed a variety of models of agricultural beginnings in the Southwest (M. Berry 1982; Berry and Berry 1986; Dean 1985; Smiley 1985, 1994, 1997g; Wills 1988; Matson 1991). Most fall generally into a few basic types. The first type explains the transition as a diffusion phenomenon (Smiley 1994, 1997g; Wills 1988). The second sees migration as a primary mechanism for the movement of agricultural subsistence out of Highland Mexico, into the Basin and Range, and onto the Colorado Plateau (M. Berry 1982). A third approach involves the modeling of agricultural transition as a function of opportunistic adoption (Minnis 1992; Wills 1988). A fourth views the transition as following from conditions that necessitated the transition (Minnis 1992; e.g., Binford 1968; Boserup 1965; Cohen 1977).

The southwestern early agricultural data set, however, remains extremely small in relation to the area over which it is distributed. In this respect, we remain constrained by severe sampling problems that stem not only from low-resolution geographic coverage but also from the typical suite of archaeological context and chronometric problems.

Thus, we work in an environment of endemic sampling problems, and we should exercise care in accepting explanations based on problematic data. Small data sets tend to foster relatively simple explanations, and in my view, the southwestern early agricultural data set has been woefully inadequate to support convincingly any particular model of transition. Things appear to be changing, however, as more complex, multifactor explanations appear in response to increasingly complex and extensive data sets (Matson 1991; Matson and Dohm 1994; Smiley 1994, 1997a, 1997c; Wicker 1997; Robins 1997a, Wills 1992, 1995; B. Huckell 1995).

In fact, we have made significant progress toward what may be termed "chronometric resolution" (Smiley 1997a), which refers to the achievement of appropriate levels of precision and accuracy in the chronology of event and process. Levels of chronometric resolution vary with the kinds of research questions asked, but the numbers of radiocarbon and tree-ring dates amassed and the kinds of materials and contexts dated have vastly raised the level of early agricultural chronometric resolution in the northern Southwest.

In the business of explanation, trends in other world regions may provide useful perspective. Researches on early agriculture in the Middle East and Europe (Gebauer and Price 1992) paint a more complex picture

of regional transition than the basic models thus far developed to account for the agricultural transition in the American Southwest. The most recent examinations tend to characterize the agricultural spread in the Middle East and across Europe as a complex of diffusion and migration events even within regions (Price and Gebauer 1995).

Similar complexity may characterize the agricultural transition in the northern Southwest. While a number of investigators, including myself, lean toward diffusion/adoption within an opportunistic framework as the general transition mechanism, migration may have played a role as well. For example, the accumulating evidence from Cedar Mesa suggests no immediately preagricultural occupation (Matson 1991). Much earlier occupations of nearby portions of southeastern Utah are, however, now well documented (Geib and Davidson 1994; Smiley 1997a, 2000a; Robins 1997a, b; Smiley and Robins 1997a). Accordingly, the early Cedar Mesa farmers must have migrated into the area from nearby locations. B. Huckell makes a migration case for the appearance of agricultural groups contrasting strongly with the previous Middle Archaic patterns as a mechanism in the Tucson Basin (1990). In other situations, investigators argue for diffusion, for example, Wills' case for agricultural transition by diffusion over large portions of the American Southwest (1988a).

Recent computer simulation of the process of agricultural diffusion in hunter-gatherer societies suggests that "the less dense the regional packing of groups, the more rapid the territorial or linear rate of diffusion should be" (Smiley 1997b). Migration as a function of population growth and the budding off of daughter populations as populations grow should require significantly longer. The chronology of the agricultural advance into large portions of Europe from the Middle East tends to corroborate this hypothesis (Cavalli-Sforza 1983).

Alternatively, populations migrating purposefully from one area to a distant destination could also carry an innovation quickly, at least in a linear fashion.

The occupation of large areas, however, requires either population growth with budding off or diffusion. The rate of diffusion, as the simulation suggests, might be surprisingly high, especially in regions of comparatively low population density. My simulation work tentatively indicates that diffusion of corn agriculture could occur within about two hundred years across a region two thousand kilometers square. If even only nominally accurate, this estimate means that given the error term, that is, the fuzziness of radiocarbon chronometry (Smiley 1998a), the *rate* of diffusion could not be measured at the current accuracy and precision of the radiocarbon method. The whole agricultural transition process might take place across a large region *within* the span of the error terms on regional radiocarbon dates. If the advance across the Southwest from the Mexico border to north of the San Juan and Colorado rivers occurred as rapidly as current radiocarbon chronometry indicates (e.g., Lascaux and Hesse 2001, and see Smiley 1994, 1997a, b), then I suggest that the phenomenon can best be explained in terms of an opportunistic, diffusion model that incorporates the concept of preadaptation.

The advent of food production appears to have been rapid across the Southwest, but the entire process of agricultural transition, the change from hunting and gathering to settled farming, required at least fifteen hundred and possibly twenty-five hundred years in the Black Mesa region and apparently across the northern Southwest. The agricultural transition, thus, consists of a long period of human systems in evolutionary flux in one of the most interesting of human rites of passage. The Black Mesa research has provided important data from excavations, surveys, assemblages, and chronometry that have helped advance our knowledge of the agricultural transition in the northern Southwest.

We have raised many new questions ranging from the nature of social dynamics in the poorly understood White Dog phase to the nature of the linkage between the groups of the late Lolomai phase and the succeeding Basketmaker III populations in the Black Mesa/Marsh Pass region. These questions deserve continued attention, which I am confident they will receive.

CHAPTER 4

Basketmaker III

Early Ceramic-Period Villages in the Kayenta Region

Deborah L. Nichols

The Basketmaker III period represents the first highly visible occupation that is known throughout large portions of the northern Southwest, although northern Black Mesa was not permanently occupied during this period (figure 4.1). In the Kayenta area, Basketmaker III is fairly well dated between A.D. 600 and 850. The initial widespread use of pottery is the traditional hallmark of the Basketmaker III period, as originally defined in the Pecos Classification (Kidder 1927), and Basketmaker III is usually thought to be the time when a village lifeway centered on maize agriculture began to develop. The presence of pottery is still the primary criterion for distinguishing between the Basketmaker III and the preceding preceramic Basketmaker II period.

The use of pottery for containers was but one of a series of interrelated technological and economic changes: replacement of spears and darts by bows and arrows, cultivation of beans along with maize, grinding of maize and other seeds on trough metates with oblong manos, and changes in storage facilities and pit-structure architecture that accompanied an apparent increased reliance on agriculture. Population growth is inferred from the larger number of known sites and the large size of some sites. More formal preparation of features and changes in house construction (Le Blanc 1982) along with the preceding

developments suggest less residential mobility.

Formalized site layouts, generally interpreted as reflecting lineage-based organization, begin to appear by the end of the period. The presence of "great kivas" at some sites may reflect new rituals, beliefs (Cordell 1984), and changing social networks (S. Plog 1986a). Thus, during the Basketmaker III period, new organizational forms developed that were elaborated upon in later Puebloan times.

Migrations, diffusion of traits, or both from the Mogollon area were the traditional explanations of these changes, often referred to as the Basketmaker-Pueblo transition (Rouse 1962:38). M. Berry (1982) and more recently Matson (1991) have returned to the idea of migration—with early agricultural groups spreading northward from the southern basin and range into the Colorado Plateau. Other recent explanations see this transition as an in-situ change: a response to stress from population pressure (Glassow 1972; F. Plog 1979a), climatic change (Berry 1982; Euler et al. 1979), increasing risk of subsistence failure because of contracting resource-procurement areas (Braun and Plog 1982; Cordell 1984), an organizational change associated with increasing sedentism and greater reliance of agriculture (S. Plog 1989; Wills 1988a, 1988b, 1991, 1995), or all these changes.

Chronological control for the

Kayenta region within this long timespan, however, is still too imprecise (F. Plog 1979a) for determining the exact timing and rate of the changes noted above (whether they occurred singly or in combination or were rapid or gradual), which is of considerable interest because of new concepts about the general nature of evolutionary change.

Paleoenvironment during Basketmaker III Times

The Basketmaker III period is the first entire archaeological period for which we have detailed paleoenvironmental information (Dean 1988a; Dean et al. 1985; Euler et al. 1979). The end of the Basketmaker II period coincides with 170 years (from A.D. 510–680) of relative dendroclimatic stability with fairly rapid but small oscillations about the mean, but no serious droughts. Just after the Basketmaker III period begins in the late 600s, dendroclimatic variability increased, and subsequently there were long dry intervals (A.D. 700–720, 735–775, 815–845, and 856–880) interspersed with wet periods.

Following a brief drop in water tables at ca. A.D. 600, the first one hundred years of the Basketmaker III period were characterized by stream aggradation, which would have favored alluvial floodplain farming. As long as population densities remained low, people could cultivate land along large drainages that received the most runoff, which might have offset the effects of increasing dendroclimatic variability and periods of drought that began at about the same time.

Beginning ca. A.D. 750, this high temporal dendroclimatic variability was exacerbated by declining water tables and erosion. Moreover, low spatial climatic variability at this time "would have inhibited interactional or exchange responses to the poor low frequency situation" (Dean et al. 1985:543). Hydrologic conditions did not begin improving until A.D. 900, after the end of the Basketmaker III period.

Basketmaker III Subsistence

The adoption of maize farming during the preceding Basketmaker II period ultimately affected most aspects of Anasazi lifeways. Subsequent changes in technology, settlement, and organization were an integral part of the shift from a hunter-gatherer to a horticultural and then an agricultural economy. Beans, *Phaseolus vulgaris*, apparently began to be cultivated during Basketmaker III times (Elizabeth Morris 1980:153), and *Phaseolus limensis* by the ninth century on northern Black Mesa (Ford et al. 1983; Ford et al. 1985; Sink et al. 1983); they represent the last addition to the upper Sonoran agricultural complex. (No remains of domesticated beans have been reported from either open-air or dry-sheltered Basketmaker II sites, despite preservation of many types of perishable food and non-food remains at the latter.) Cultivated legumes would have supplemented animal and wild plant sources of protein and provided a nitrogen-fixing crop that could be grown in semi-arid soils, which are generally low in organic matter. The addition of domesticated plant proteins in Basketmaker III times, which can be stored (as they were at D:11:2068 [Sink et al. 1983]), and the corralling of turkeys (Elizabeth Morris 1980:145) probably reflect increased sedentism stemming

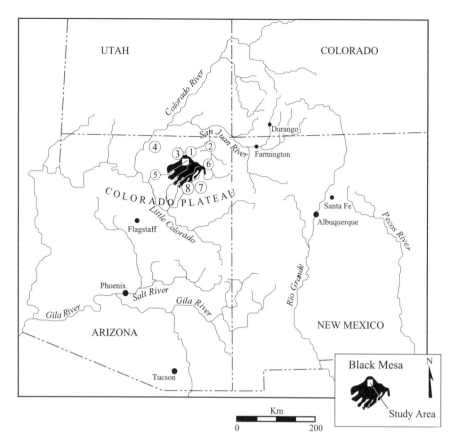

Figure 4.1 The Greater Southwest, showing locations mentioned in Chapter 4: 1–Tsegi Canyon; 2–Laguna Creek; 3–Klethla Valley; 4–Shonto Plateau; 5–Moenkopi Wash; 6–Chinle Valley; 7–Hopi Buttes; 8–Jeddito Valley.

from scheduling changes as more time was spent farming and/or reductions in the size of procurement areas for hunting and wild plant collection.

The conventional view that people became dependent on maize and other cultigens for a significant proportion of their diet during the Basketmaker III period continues to be debated; the different conclusions archaeologists have drawn about the mix of foraging and cultivation (e.g., Kohler 1993; Matson 1991; Paul Reed 2000, Sullivan 1992; Wills 1991) appear to reflect, in part, real regional, and possibly local, differences in subsistence practices and rates of change related to demographic, environmental, and organizational differences. In the Kayenta region some increase in the dietary contribution of domesticates is suggested by the cultivation of beans and technological changes

discussed in the next section; however, the degree of change is problematical. Increased storage during the Basketmaker-Pueblo transition (Gilman 1987) indicates increased agricultural production for storage as well as immediate consumption (Matson et al. 1988:255). A larger sample of Kayenta Basketmaker burials needs to be analyzed in a manner similar to that done by D. Martin et al. (1991) for northern Black Mesa to develop quantitative dietary reconstructions.

There is no direct archaeological evidence of Basketmaker III land-use practices in the area. Matson's (1991) agriculture-development model predicts that most maize cultivation before A.D. 1000 was based on either dry farming or simple run-off farming. The general aridity and short growing season make true rain-fed maize cultivation highly precarious

Figure 4.2 Navajo land-use patterns near Marsh Pass—a model for Basketmaker III land-use patterns (photograph by F. Smiley).

over most of the Kayenta region, if not impossible in some locales. The location of Basketmaker III habitation sites near major drainages indicates that fields were probably situated to take advantage of high water tables and runoff following high-intensity summer storms as well as of stored subsoil moisture from winter snow-melt (Gumerman and Dean 1989:114). This land-use pattern is still practiced today by Navajos in Canyon de Chelly and Tsegi Canyon (figure 4.2). The placement of some Basketmaker III sites in sand dunes suggests to Gumerman and Euler (1976b) that people also cultivated dunes in a manner similar to Hopi agricultural practices (Hack 1942), and swidden cultivation has been proposed for other areas, like Cedar Mesa (Matson et al. 1988).

Evaluating qualitative predictions (Dean et al. 1985) about the impacts of environmental changes on subsistence requires an understanding of the precise effects of hydrologic and climatologic shifts on farming and storage potential and on wild plant and animal populations, as well as quantitative estimates of human population

sizes and densities. Unfortunately, the effects of climatic variability on local wild resource yields, such as pinyon-nut masts, have not been assessed. Longitudinal data necessary to model similar effects on early farming systems are also lacking.

Technology

Pottery

The adoption of pottery throughout the Anasazi region was one of a series of interrelated technological changes during the Basketmaker-Pueblo transition. Their adoption during Basketmaker III times was part of the process of increasing agricultural production (Crown and Wills 1995; Earle 1980; F. Plog 1979a). Le Blanc (1982) proposes that these innovations were adopted relatively rapidly over a large portion of the Southwest as part of a new adaptive complex that reflects the shift to an agriculturally based subsistence economy. At present, dating the appearance of each of these innovations among the Kayenta Anasazi

is too imprecise to determine if they were adopted simultaneously or at different points in time (Dean et al. 1985).

Most early Anasazi pottery is plain and gray; Lino Gray and Lino Fugitive Red are found at the earliest Basketmaker III sites in the Kayenta area, as are small amounts of Lino Black-on-Gray and plain redwares. Bowls and jars are the predominant early grayware vessel forms, the jars having straight vertical necks; pitchers are common, but large jars are also present.

Because pottery is less portable than basketry, its widespread usage implies a decrease in residential mobility. Increased sedentism, however, is not the only factor involved in the adoption of pottery containers, as evidenced by large (and presumably permanent) preceramic settlements in coastal Peru (Quilter 1985). Glassow (1972) argues that the use of pottery containers is due to a restructuring of subsistence activities as more time is spent processing starchy seeds, presumably produced by farming. He points out that pottery not only is more versatile in culinary activities, but it is more efficient: vessels can be set directly on a fire and left unattended while other activities are performed. Stone boiling, however, apparently continued into the Basketmaker III period in the Kayenta region, as indicated by the frequent occurrence in domestic contexts of limestone chunks (Gumerman and Dean 1989:115). Another factor that may underlie the adoption of pottery vessels is a change in techniques of food preparation (Braun 1983; Buikstra et al. 1986). According to Ford (cited in F. Plog 1974:137), cooking maize in water almost doubles the amount of starch available for conversion to glucose, thus increasing the nutritional value of maize, even if the type or amount consumed does not change. As the Basketmaker III people were faced with increasing workloads, scheduling conflicts, and greater reliance on cultigens, Crown and Wills (1995) argue, maize gruel cooked in ceramic pots gave women "a suitable weaning food. The development of pottery and an associated shift in the processing of cultigens [and new maize varieties] would have allowed the early introduction of solid foods and partial weaning" (Crown and Wills 1995:179).

In addition to affording new means of food preparation, pottery also provides a secure storage container that was probably used for short-term storage, while pits and cists (and by A.D. 825/850 above-ground rooms) were employed for long-term storage (Gilman 1987). A well-developed storage system, which buffered temporal variations in resource availability, became a central feature of the Anasazi adaptive system.

Stone Tools

Lithic assemblages also underwent changes during the Basketmaker-Pueblo transition. The atlatl and dart were replaced by the bow and arrow sometime during the Basketmaker III period, resulting in smaller projectile points. The bow and arrow are thought to have been adopted at this time, despite the increased labor involved in bow construction, because of their greater efficiency or greater accuracy (Christenson 1987b). There is also an increase in the proportion of expedient tools relative to formal tools (Leonard et al. 1983, 1984c), and Parry (1987b) argues that the shift to an expedient tool technology corresponds with intensification of agricultural production, declining mobility, or both. Finally, trough metates and two-hand manos replaced basin metates and one-hand manos, suggesting increased grinding efficiency (Christenson 1987a; F. Plog 1974) and flour production but at a cost in terms of increased labor and physical strain on women from grinding for long periods (e.g., J. Adams 1993; Crown and Wills 1995:180).

A further technological innovation during Basketmaker III times

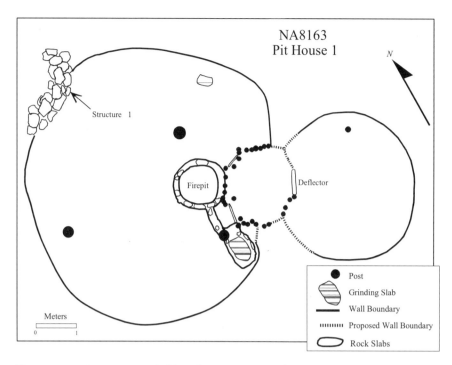

Figure 4.3 Pit House 1 at Klethla Valley site NA 8163 (after Ambler and Olson 1977: figure 5).

was the use of groundstone axes to cut wood. Axes would have facilitated construction of the large Basketmaker III pit structures with their large upright roof supports and heavy roof. Several Basketmaker II sites excavated on northern Black Mesa, however, have pit structures that are over one meter deep. The average depth of Lolomai pit structures is 62 cm (Gilman 1987), while the average depth of the Basketmaker III pit structures from a sample of excavated Kayenta area sites is 96 cm. A variety of roof-construction styles were used on Basketmaker II pit structures; however, the four-post roof-support system becomes increasingly common in Basketmaker III times, and Dean (cited in Le Blanc [1982]) notes that in the northern Anasazi area between Basketmaker II and Basketmaker III, there is a significant increase in the diameter of construction beams that coincides with the use of axes. Presumably groundstone axes facilitated preparation of large beams. The change in house-construction styles and the use of groundstone axes were part of the decrease in residential

mobility and greater investment in structure and feature construction.

Dating Basketmaker III Sites

The earliest recorded Basketmaker III occupation in the Kayenta area is a pit structure in the Klethla Valley (figure 4.3) that yielded one tree-ring cutting date of A.D. 555 (Ambler and Olson 1977). Clusters of dates from the cave sites in the Prayer Rock district to the east provide evidence of a Basketmaker III occupation by the A.D. 620s (Elizabeth Morris 1980:50–51). By A.D. 850, there are several well-dated transitional Basketmaker III–Pueblo I or very early Pueblo I sites in the area— on northern Black Mesa (discussed later) and along Laguna Creek, for example (Bannister et al. 1968:64). The present evidence therefore indicates a Basketmaker III occupation in portions of the Kayenta area by A.D. 550 and lasting until A.D. 825. The total number of independently dated early ceramic sites in the area, however, is small, and so this chronology (especially the initial date) could change as more absolute dates are acquired.

The northern Black Mesa equivalent of the Basketmaker III period, the Dot Klish phase, was defined by Gumerman et al. (1972:30) from sites outside the Peabody leasehold, on the western escarpment of the mesa and Dot Klish Wash, which is another name for the lower reaches of Moenkopi Wash (Ward 1976). No Basketmaker III habitations have been documented in the leasehold, although a concerted effort was made to excavate sites that appeared from surface indications to be early ceramic occupations. Thus there is a lengthy hiatus in the archaeologically visible occupation between A.D. 400 and ca. A.D. 825–850, during which the leasehold was apparently not used for habitation. The area was probably exploited for wild resources (such as pinyon nuts) by people residing in surrounding areas, as suggested by D:11:1296 (Burgett 1985). D:11:1296 originally was designated as Basketmaker II because of two baked siltstone projectile points found on the site's surface. However, a hearth, associated with three undecorated sherds and a siderite flake, was dated using radiocarbon to A.D. 580 ± 70 (Beta-11072). Although a single radiocarbon date is not conclusive, it suggests short-term use of northern Black Mesa during Basketmaker III times.

Several hypotheses have been advanced to account for the absence of Basketmaker III habitation sites in the leasehold. Gumerman and Euler (1976a:165) feel that site locations along major washes and large sand dunes (that are rare on the northern mesa) might have been favored because of an emphasis on floodwater farming and that alluviation on lower terraces subsequently buried the sites. One Basketmaker III–Pueblo I site (D:11:113) that dates to the A.D. 850s was fortuitously found on northern Black Mesa buried beneath alluvial deposits (Gumerman et al. 1972). Other buried cultural strata, which may represent sites, were observed by Eric Karlstrom (personal communication 1983) during his geomorphologic surveys as well as occasionally during

the archaeological inventory surveys. Intensive surveys, however, have never found a buried Basketmaker III site in the leasehold. Ward (1976) was the first to suggest that the Basketmaker III period was a time of depopulation and actual abandonment of the leasehold.

Powell (1983) and S. Plog (1986b) argue that the lack of Basketmaker III sites may result from problems in distinguishing diagnostic Basketmaker III artifacts in surface collections. The relative density of artifacts is low on early ceramic sites compared with later sites (Gumerman et al. 1972), which decreases the likelihood of recovering infrequent diagnostic pottery types.

Stephen Plog (1986b) reexamined the issue of identifying Basketmaker III sites from survey collections and identified other possible temporal characteristics of Kayenta Basketmaker III assemblages. He proposes that Basketmaker III surface samples should be characterized by (1) high relative proportions of plain grayware and very low proportions or absence of banded and corrugated grayware and (2) less than 5 percent whiteware. D:11:1296, the only excavated site in the leasehold possibly dating to the Basketmaker III period, had one plain whiteware and two plain grayware sherds (Burgett 1985:192). However, the other excavated sites exhibiting these characteristics in their surface collections were found to date to the ninth century (e.g., D:7:3194 [Mauldin and Miles 1983] and D:7:135 [Layhe et al. 1976]). Moreover, although some ninth-century sites have essentially the same surface ceramic distribution as Basketmaker III sites, others do have higher relative proportions of painted whiteware (e.g., D:11:2023 [Olszewski 1984] and D:7:135 [Layhe et al. 1976]).

Excavated assemblages from ninth-century sites, however, are distinct from excavated Basketmaker III assemblages. Ninth-century excavated assemblages contain about 10 percent painted whitewares. Thus in the case of sites like D:7:3194, the presence of only graywares or very low proportions of whitewares apparently is a

result of low surface artifact densities and is not uniquely indicative of a Basketmaker III temporal affiliation.

The criteria presently used by archaeologists in the Kayenta area (plain grayware pottery and lack of formalized site plan) for dating surveyed sites thus will incorrectly assign some small early Pueblo I sites to the Basketmaker III period and some Basketmaker III sites to the early Pueblo I period, depending on the analysts' prior assumptions. Assigning temporal affiliations to small sites with plain grayware surface assemblages must be considered tentative. The most promising avenue for improving chronometrics for this time period would be a study of early graywares. This dating problem should be kept in mind during the following review of Basketmaker III settlement in the larger Kayenta area.

Settlement Patterns

Northern Black Mesa was one of several areas abandoned (at least in terms of habitation settlements) after a Basketmaker II occupation (figure 4.1). In southeastern Utah, the Red Rock Plateau was occupied in late Basketmaker II times (Lipe 1970), then abandoned until about A.D. 1100. Cedar Mesa, also in southeastern Utah, was abandoned following a Basketmaker II occupation until the mid-seventh century (Matson and Lipe 1978; Matson et al. 1988). West of Cedar Mesa, in the Glen Canyon project area, Lindsay et al.'s (1968) Rainbow Plateau survey found no Basketmaker III sites north of Navajo Mountain. Surveys by Ambler and his colleagues in the Navajo Mountain area (Cummings Mesa, northeast Navajo Mountain, upper Paiute Canyon, Dzil Nez Mesa, and Paiute Mesa) also indicate "that evidence for Basketmaker III is scanty" (Ambler et al. 1983:7).

However, in lower areas (including those surrounding the Black Mesa leasehold) where surveys have been conducted, there is evidence of Basketmaker III occupations. Between the Kaibito Plateau and Klethla Valley, Anderson (1980) reports a probable Basketmaker III pit structure, and just to the east of White Mesa, in the Laguna Creek and Klethla Valleys, there is substantial evidence of Basketmaker III settlement. These areas also had substantial occupations after A.D. 1150, when people moved away from northern Black Mesa, suggesting that the Basketmaker III period begins the mobility/abandonment pattern characteristic of the Pueblo period. For this reason, it is useful to review just what is known of Basketmaker III settlement in the Kayenta region.

NA 8163, a Basketmaker III site in the Klethla Valley (figure 4.3), produced a single early cutting date at A.D. 555 (Ambler and Olson 1977:5), and Ambler and Olson (1977) excavated a second Basketmaker III site in the area, which has a tree-ring cutting date at A.D. 703 (Bannister et al. 1968). A. V. Kidder reported a large Basketmaker III site near the Old Cow Springs trading post that is described as having over one hundred structures (Jeffrey S. Dean, personal communication 1983), although it has never been systematically recorded. Basketmaker III sites were also found along the Black Mesa–Lake Powell railroad route, where it crosses Klethla Valley and runs onto the Shonto Plateau (Swarthout et al. 1986).

A systematic survey of Long House Valley revealed a Basketmaker III occupation consisting of small habitation sites, with a few pit structures each, located along the edges of the valley floor, and limited-activity sites on the edges of the floodplain and the Shonto Plateau (Lindsay and Dean 1978). Information on the occupation in nearby Tsegi Canyon is principally based on the work of the Rainbow Bridge–Monument Valley Expedition that excavated two sites with Basketmaker III components and conducted some reconnaissance and survey in the area. Swallow's Nest Cave has a pit structure that yielded multiple tree-ring cutting dates at A.D. 667 and 678, and Bannister et al. (1968) conclude from the pattern of

Figure 4.4 Surface indications of large, circular subterranean structure at Juniper Cove site (photograph by F. Smiley).

the noncutting tree-ring dates that the pit structure at RB 1002 (Beals et al. 1945) dates to the late seventh or early eighth century. Based on surface pottery samples, Beals et al. assigned eleven other sites in the canyon to the Basketmaker III period.

Just north of Tsegi Canyon in the Marsh Pass area, the Juniper Cove site (figure 4.4) was excavated by Byron Cummings. Unfortunately, the location of most of the records and artifacts from Cummings's work is unknown. The site consists of over one hundred structures or features, including pit structures, slab-lined cists, and a circular "great kiva." A cutting date of A.D. 666 and the range of noncutting dates place the occupation of the site in the latter half of the seventh century (Bannister et al. 1968), which accords well with dates from other Basketmaker III pit-structure villages.

Basketmaker III sites have also been reported along the western escarpment of Black Mesa and Dot Klish Wash (the lower reaches of Moenkopi Wash) from a survey for a coal-slurry pipeline that runs from the Peabody leasehold on northern Black Mesa to Nevada (Ward 1976). No absolute dates are available for the excavated sites; they were assigned to Basket-

maker III on the basis of architectural patterns and ceramic assemblages, which were dominated by Lino Gray and lacked whitewares.

On Black Mesa, just south of the Peabody leasehold near Forest Lake, two sites (Foose 1982; Legard 1982b), excavated for a road right-of-way, were designated Basketmaker III. Further to the south on Black Mesa, in the vicinity of Pinon, Basketmaker III sites, appearing in the form of small villages, "work areas," and sherd scatters, are reported to occur on or adjacent to ridges that divide major drainages. However, one site is described with at least thirty pit structures (Windham and Dechambre 1978). Because plain grayware sherd scatters continue to occur into the A.D. 900s, some of these sites may date to Pueblo I. The reported absence of painted whitewares at the large pit-structure village, however, is probably not due to sampling and reflects a Basketmaker III affiliation.

A Basketmaker III occupation has also been documented farther to the south on the Hopi Mesas and in the Jeddito Valley. On Second Mesa, Hogan (1984:62) tentatively assigned a site to the Basketmaker III period based on preliminary testing that yielded a radiocarbon date of A.D. 830 ± 70. Subsequent excavation revealed a classic Basketmaker III pit-structure tree ring dated at A.D. 805 that contained no Kana-a Black-on-white pottery (Sebastian 1985).

The Awatovi Expedition excavations of Site 4A (Brew 1941) and Jeddito 264 (Daifuku 1961) in the Jeddito Valley confirmed a Basketmaker III occupation on the Hopi Mesas. A cluster of cutting dates from one of the Site 4A pit structures indicates that it was constructed in A.D. 800–802 (Bannister et al. 1967:82). Jeddito 264 has been dated to the late 600s and early 700s; the pattern of tree-ring dates suggests successive occupations over a period of about fifty years, rather than a single simultaneous occupation of all structures (Bannister et al. 1967).

South of Black Mesa, Gumerman's (1969, 1988b) survey of the Hopi Buttes recorded two possible small Basketmaker III sites, and he excavated the Finger Rock site. East of Black Mesa, a relatively intensive Basketmaker III occupation is known from a series of cave sites excavated between 1930 and 1931 by Earl Morris in Canyon de Chelly and the Red Rock area (Elizabeth Morris 1980). Elizabeth Morris (1980) and Bannister et al. (1966) discuss the dating of the sites, which is quite complicated in some instances. Except for remains dated by tree rings, it is difficult to sort out the components because of the way the sites were excavated. Nonetheless, a Basketmaker III occupation in the area is definitely indicated from the early 600s to 700s. All the cave sites are located along major well-watered drainages.

Near Chilchinbito in the Chinle Valley, Bond et al. (1977) excavated four artifact scatters that they assigned to the Basketmaker III period, along with a two-room slab structure (NA 13806) and a small pit-structure site. The pit-structure site yielded tree-ring dates that range from A.D. 732 to 805. These dates indicate a very late Basketmaker III or early Pueblo I affiliation for the site. Two of the artifact scatters (NA 13805 and NA 13808)

produced large enough excavated assemblages to confirm that the very low relative frequencies of painted whitewares reflect a Basketmaker III affiliation.

Bearing in mind the dangers of generalizing without comparable survey data for all areas, the most intensive Basketmaker III occupations apparently occurred in the Laguna Creek–Klethla valleys, Tsegi Canyon, Canyon de Chelly–Chinle Wash area, and the Hopi Mesas. This pattern supports the standard interpretation that increased agricultural production caused a shift in preferred site locations to better-watered areas where the risk of crop failure was lower and where, presumably, wild plants and animals were more abundant.

It has also been argued that the abandonment of uplands including northern Black Mesa was further stimulated by deteriorating climatological and hydrologic conditions. Yet the reestablishment of habitation sites on northern Black Mesa at the end of the Basketmaker III period took place under similarly adverse conditions, which, as Dean (1986a) correctly observes, implies that changes in the physical environment alone cannot explain the settlement change. He proposes, following well-established ecological principles, that well-watered locales like the Laguna Creek and Klethla valleys were able to support the relatively small Basketmaker III population but that with increasing population density during the late eighth and early ninth centuries, populations expanded into more marginal upland areas. Dean further suggests that high water tables and stream aggradation (which favor alluvial farming) may account for the earlier Basketmaker II occupation in these same upland areas.

The presumed increased reliance on agricultural production during Basketmaker III times, because of environmental perturbations, population increases, or both, would logically be interrelated with a reduction in mobility and increased "logistical" organization (Binford

1980). Accordingly, people might not have abandoned northern Black Mesa but changed their use of the area. They continued to exploit wild resources (especially pinyon nuts), while locating their villages/camps in favorable farming locales elsewhere. A hearth at D:11:1296 — the limited-activity site discussed earlier — provides some evidence, albeit limited, of this kind of use of northern Black Mesa, which has very low archaeological visibility. Increased reliance on cultigens and perhaps environmental changes may account for the concentration of sites in better-watered areas of the Kayenta region. These factors alone, however, do not explain the development of the larger aggregated Basketmaker III villages, and future research needs to focus more on social, political, and economic processes (S. Plog 1990, 1995).

Site Structure

The present sample of excavated sites in the Kayenta region includes artifact scatters (e.g., NA 13805), artifact scatters associated with features like hearths (e.g., NA 13808), small pit-structure sites (e.g., Jeddito 264), and large aggregated pit-structure settlements that were formally laid out (e.g., Juniper Cove and the site at the Old Cow Springs trading post). (Most of the cave sites are probably equivalent to the small, open-air pit-structure sites.) The artifact scatters, which are underrepresented in the sample, probably represent limited-activity loci or temporary camps.

Although there is considerable uniformity in pit-structure architecture, the small pit-structure sites are variable in terms of the number and types of structures present. This variation probably relates to length and seasonality of occupation and household composition. In addition to pit structures, most of these sites have extramural storage cists and hearths; surface dwellings are also present at some sites (e.g., Finger Rock). The evidence from Jeddito 264 indicates that the larger size of some sites is the result of successive occupations of particular locales by one or a few households (Wills 1988b). The absence of burials at the small Basketmaker III pit-structure sites also suggests short occupations. Based on tree-ring dates obtained from three similar but later pit-structure sites in the Peabody leasehold (Nichols and Smiley 1984) and other studies (Ahlstrom 1984; Cameron 1990a; Schlanger 1986), each site or component probably reflects a ten- to fifteen-year occupation.

The issues of site seasonality and sedentism are difficult to address with the extant sample of Kayenta Basketmaker III sites because of differences in excavation methods. Even excluding the large aggregated sites, there is a slight increase in site size during the Basketmaker-Pueblo transition, which could be due to an increase in the average number of occupants per site, a reduction in residential mobility, or both.

Although residential mobility decreased during the Basketmaker-Pueblo transition, Powell's (1983) and Gilman's (1987) studies indicate that sites were probably not occupied on a year-round basis. Gilman, in her model of the transition from pit houses to pueblos, presents convincing ethnographic evidence that pit structures are not associated with fully sedentary site occupations. Groups using pit structures practice some degree of residential mobility, using the pit structures as cold-season dwellings. The presence of surface jacal dwellings as well as pit structures at some Basketmaker III sites, following Gilman's model, would indicate multiseasonal occupations. Gilman's and Powell's models are appealing, given the importance of mobility as a way to deal with spatial differences in agricultural and wild resource productivity that characterize the northern Southwest. Before we can fully accept these analogic models, however, site seasonality must be evaluated using nonarchitectural criteria (see also Kohler 1993:279).

Some Basketmaker III sites, such as Juniper Cove, stand out because of their size. Sites similar to Juniper Cove, as noted earlier, have been reported near Pinon and in the Cow Springs area. Unfortunately, we know virtually nothing about the developmental histories of the sites, nor whether they represent single occupations or successive occupations of favored locations over an extended period of time. I have referred to the sites as aggregated because of their size and the presence of a possible communal structure at Juniper Cove.

Population

Only qualitative and therefore very tenuous generalizations about regional Basketmaker III population trends can be offered at this time. The larger number of reported Basketmaker III and early Pueblo I sites relative to Basketmaker II sites does suggest an increase in the overall size of regional populations during this period. Some areas such as northern Black Mesa, however, experienced population losses; thus the apparent increase in the total number of sites in places like the Laguna Creek must be due to settlement relocation as well as natural rates of increase. Furthermore, the low archaeological visibility of preceramic sites (S. Plog 1978) almost certainly makes the magnitude of population increase between the end of the Basketmaker II period and the beginning of Pueblo I appear greater than it actually was. Nonetheless, the overall increase in the number of known sites from the end of the Archaic period into Pueblo I times suggests increasing population density.

Various propositions have been put forth about the relation between environmental and Basketmaker population dynamics (Berry 1982; Dean et al. 1985; Dean et al. 1994:60; Euler et al. 1979). Euler et al. have indicated that during dry intervals like that beginning at A.D. 750, populations declined and tended to concentrate along drainages. Berry also sees a close relationship between population and climatic change; however, he posits a series of large-scale abandonments of the Colorado Plateau rather than the small-scale settlement shifts proposed by Euler et al. (1979)—a vigorously critiqued proposition (Dean 1985).

Organization

Following Chang's (1958) early work, the appearance of formalized site layouts by the early to mid-ninth century on northern Black Mesa and in much of the Anasazi region is generally thought to reflect the development of lineage-based organization (Dean 1970; S. Plog 1990). Many have argued that lineages were already present by Basketmaker III times (Chang 1958:322; Daifuku 1961:59; P. Martin and Plog 1973:266–267; Steward 1937:95), although extended family households might not have become common until Pueblo I times (Birkedal 1976; Bullard 1962:123; Daifuku 1961). Cordell (1979) and Cordell and Plog (1979) feel that the emphasis on extramural placement of storage facilities and work areas on Basketmaker III sites reflects a strongly egalitarian community organization (see Kohler [1993:280] for an interesting alternative). Nonetheless, as Wills and Windes (1989) note, the presence of "private" storage facilities on some sites suggests that the shift away from the communal storage of mobile foragers had already begun: storage cists have been found inside Basketmaker III pit structures and jacals in the Kayenta region at sites such as Jeddito 264. In the Kayenta area, most small Basketmaker III sites exhibit only slightly more formalization (e.g., east- or southeast-facing pit-structure entryways) than the large Basketmaker II pit-structure settlements.

The presence of a possible "great kiva," or communal structure, at the Juniper Cove site suggests new, more formalized forms of inter- or intracommunity integration and ritual (R. Lightfoot 1988:268–269; S. Plog 1990:190–191) and, perhaps, "interaction with the Mogollon area where such structures have a much longer history" (Gumerman and

Dean 1989:115). If previously dispersed households aggregated at Juniper Cove and a few other locales during part of the Basketmaker III period, then new integrative mechanisms would have been necessary. K. Lightfoot and Feinman (1982) suggest that great kivas in the Mogollon area were residences of village leaders who dominated exchange networks. Schiffer (1983), however, has shown that the failure to consider transformational factors calls into question Lightfoot and Feinman's conclusions. More fundamental is Cordell's (1984) observation that the low population densities did not warrant the kind of organizational structure implied by K. Lightfoot and Feinman. Hegmon's (1995:37) simulation, however, predicts that increasing reliance on agriculture would be accompanied by the development of some form of formal supra-household group.

The sites are large for the time period and by northern southwestern standards. But, in terms of neolithic villages elsewhere in the world, they are not notably large. For example, most Early and Middle Formative Mesoamerican villages range from 3 to 12 ha in size (Marcus 1976:89). Thus almost all Basketmaker III sites are smaller than their Mesoamerican counterparts, even when the large early Mesoamerican villages are excluded from consideration. Although great kivas in the Kayenta region were probably not residences of village leaders, their presence, I think, relates to the development of more formal ritual integration, which we know was a vital part of later Pueblo societies.

Other evidence of Basketmaker III social networks comes from artifactual studies (Gumerman and Dean 1989:115; S. Plog 1986a). By A.D. 825/850 (and probably earlier in areas occupied during Basketmaker III times), lithic assemblages are characterized by expedient tools of local raw materials, while Basketmaker II assemblages have proportionately more formal tools of exotic raw materials. Leonard et al. (1983, 1984c) interpret the change during the Basketmaker-

Pueblo transition as caused by a shift from embedding lithic raw material procurement within subsistence scheduling to embedding it within a formal exchange system.

Compared to later Puebloan times, the distribution of ceramic styles during the early stages of the ceramic sequence is highly homogeneous. This homogeneity is interpreted by Hantman and Plog (1982:250–251; S. Plog 1989:143) as the result of low population density and less formalized open social boundaries. Kohler (1993) sees regional differentiation beginning earlier at ca. A.D. 550, with the start of the Grayware tradition.

The organizational changes evident by the end of the Basketmaker III period—site formalization, physical association of storage buildings with individual dwelling units, increased heterogeneity of ceramic styles, and possibly formalization of exchange networks—are predicted by Braun and Plog (1982) as part of the "tribalization" process. They propose that with increasing population density and reductions in spatial averaging mechanisms such as mobility, there is a corresponding increase in temporal averaging mechanisms that include the intensification of social networks. This intensification entails increased supralocal integration and the development of institutionalized social networks among groups. From an adaptationist perspective, these changes are interpreted as reducing the uncertainties of food production through systems of exchange and sharing (Dean et al. 1994; Ford 1983). Just as important, however, is the instrumental or political nature of exchange in village societies (Brumfiel and Earle 1987:3–4; Ford 1972:43; S. Plog 1989).

Fred Plog (1983) sees alliance systems developing in Basketmaker III times as a response to population-resource imbalance or stress, arguing that alliances developed when spatial variability in rainfall was greater than usual. In his model, times of strong normative patterns in material culture reflect alliances characterized by some

degree of specialized craft production, increased trading, and sometimes, social ranking or stratification.

However, Johnson (1989) has argued that surplus production in the northern Southwest was not sufficient to underwrite proposed hierarchical alliances and that the archaeological data better fit a model of sequential hierarchies—a structure for consensual organization among egalitarian aggregates of increasing inclusiveness. Such a mechanism, he argues, would have facilitated residential mobility and political autonomy. The available data from the Kayenta region, while not adequate to examine details of sociopolitical and economic networks, offer no compelling evidence of a regional political hierarchy in Basketmaker III times. Formalization of site layouts indicative of lineages, storage facilities associated with individual dwellings, and central pit structures at some sites by the end of the Basketmaker III period all point to the development of what Johnson (1989:378) calls "Pueblo social modules," or formal supra-household groups, "that were fundamental units" in Pueblo society. However, the degree of differentiation within and among such units varied between areas and at different times (Hegmon 1995; S. Plog 1995).

Ritual and Ceremonialism

Until the recent work of Robins and Hays-Gilpin (2000), very little could be said about Basketmaker III ritualism or belief systems. The presence of presumed sipapus in pit-structure floors (Wilshusen 1989) suggests continuity with historic Pueblos and their concept of a symbolic entrance to the lower world from which people emerged into this world. Objects, such as pottery, have been found as grave goods accompanying Basketmaker III burials, which implies a concept of an afterlife where goods (or the goods' spirits) would be required (Lister and Lister 1981:191). Although the number of burials reported from Basketmaker III times is small, by the ninth century the regular association of burials with habitation sites reflects the importance of "lineality and locality" (S. Plog 1989:146), as the "burial places of ancestors create a genealogy of place that links descendants to that land" (McAnany 1995:65).

The communal structure, or "great kiva" (if this is indeed what it was), at the Juniper Cove site (and possibly in Broken Flute Cave [Elizabeth Morris 1980]) would have been the focal point of rituals and ceremonies. More regular ritual activity is implied when people build a public structure (Hegmon 1989). Early great kivas mark the start of a change from hunter-gatherer ceremonies conducted in open spaces to the use of enclosed spaces that restrict the number of participants. Some rituals might have become more differentiated according to gender, while other rituals and imagery cross-cut masculine and feminine domains, households, and communities (Robins and Hays-Gilpin 2000:238–244). Ritual burning of ceremonial/sacred structures probably began by the end of the Basketmaker III period (Cameron 1990b; Fowles 1993; Wilshusen 1986), and Ford (1994) thinks that maize ceremonialism also started at this time. The construction of community ritual/public structures reflects the importance of religious rituals among village agriculturalists in societal integration, group decision-making, and status differentiation (Drennan 1983:48).

Conclusions

The Basketmaker III period has long been recognized as a time of important organizational developments. Our knowledge of organizational structures and their relationship to the shift from food collecting to horticultural and agricultural economies is limited in the Kayenta region by the lack of studies of regional settlement patterns, the need for greater chronological refinement within the long Basketmaker III period, and excavations and analyses designed to look at social, economic, and political aspects of Basketmaker III society. Systematic regional surveys would integrate the large areal surveys that have been done to reconstruct population histories and define relations among sites. The scale of our settlement-pattern surveys needs to be commensurate with the scale of the mobility patterns and settlement systems of the ancestral Pueblo people of the region. The composition and development of the aggregated Basketmaker III villages especially warrant problem-oriented excavation so we can go beyond speculating about their significance.

Over the last decade much exciting research has been done on the Basketmaker III period outside the Kayenta region. A comprehensive review of that literature is not possible here, but I have tried to touch, at least briefly, on points and issues that should be explored in future research aimed at documenting the development and history of the foundations of Pueblo society in the Kayenta region.

PART III

The Puebloan Dispersion

Few, if any, archaeological areas have been so intensively researched as the Peabody Coal Company lease area on northern Black Mesa. Here, Shirley Powell synthesizes the mass of information on the most visible and populous periods of occupation on northern Black Mesa—the Pueblo I through the Pueblo II/III transition. Although it was sites from the earlier (Basketmaker II) and later (Tsegi phase) periods that originally attracted pioneer archaeologists to the region in the late 1800s, sites from the intervening periods proved to be more numerous, widespread, and varied.

The lease area florescence, between A.D. 825 and 1125, is but one of several similar phenomena, collectively termed the Puebloan dispersion, occurring throughout the Kayenta region at about the same time. The dispersion ended abruptly in the mid-twelfth century. Archaeologists have long been fascinated by the Puebloan dispersion, offering competing explanations, emphasizing either environmental or social causes, usually one to the exclusion of the other. The BMAP data and interpretations are central to these disputes, and their review offers a history, in microcosm, of Kayenta-area Puebloan archaeological interpretation.

The Black Mesa Archaeological Project research offers many insights on the Puebloan dispersion, but few interpretive resolutions. In many ways, ancestral Puebloan research is the heart of BMAP, continuing and aggravating controversies over interpretation and methods. These controversies spanned the life of the project and continue today.

CHAPTER 5

The Puebloan Florescence and Dispersion

Dinnebito and Beyond, A.D. 800–1150

Shirley Powell

Northern Black Mesa was not occupied between A.D. 400 and the beginning of the ninth century, although people continued to use the area for hunting and gathering, leaving occasional evidence of these activities. For habitation, people chose the lower, better-watered areas surrounding northern Black Mesa, leaving traces of their presence beginning in the mid-sixth century (see Chapter 4). People moved back into the lease area, building and occupying residential sites, during the first half of the ninth century, initiating a period of exuberant growth and expansion. Over fifteen hundred archaeological sites were built, used, and abandoned in less than 350 years.

This chapter describes and interprets those remains, placing them in the larger context of Kayenta-branch archaeology. The reoccupation of northern Black Mesa is but one example of the renown and far-flung expansion of the Kayenta Anasazi, who during this period established notably uniform unit pueblos throughout northern Arizona, southern Utah, and southeastern Nevada (figure 5.1). What archaeologists have come to call the Pueblo II dispersion is all the more intriguing because of its short duration. By A.D. 1150 all but a few of the settlements outside the Kayenta heartland and Tusayan province would be abandoned, including the lease area (see Chapter 6).

In the Kayenta area, the early ninth century marks the transition between the Basketmaker III and Pueblo I periods (Kidder 1927). Pueblo I is distinguished by the replacement of plain gray pottery by neck-banded types, the appearance of above-ground masonry storage rooms and a site configuration termed the "unit pueblo," and the formalization of ceremonial pit structures or kivas. All these trends are continued and elaborated in Pueblo II, when neck-banded pottery was replaced by pottery with all-over corrugations, the unit pueblo became the most apparent residential site type, and Kayenta peoples colonized the peripheries of their territory.

Over time, researchers proposed refinements to the original Pecos Classification tailored to the Kayenta area (Ambler 1985b; Colton 1939), some specific to northern Black Mesa (Gumerman 1984:56; Gumerman et al. 1972:24–27; Klesert 1979). These refinements introduced new phases with new names, including those used in the Peabody leases: Dot Klish (Basketmaker III), Tallahogan (Basketmaker III/Pueblo I), Dinnebito (Pueblo I), Wepo (Pueblo I/II), Lamoki (Pueblo II), and Toreva (Pueblo II/III). These schemes are useful in some contexts, but because they are based on subregional variation in painted pottery assemblages, they cannot be applied consistently throughout the Kayenta area. The lease-area ceramic chronometry is

particularly problematical, since BMAP ceramic analysts ceased using the standard ceramic typology in 1977 (Ahlstrom 1998b), relying instead on an attribute-based dating system (S. Plog and Hantman 1979, 1986). Unfortunately, the full potential of the attribute-based system never was realized. Thus, the lease-area assemblages, analyzed with the attribute-based system, cannot be compared with other Kayenta ceramic assemblages until they are resorted by types or until the other Kayenta assemblages are analyzed by attributes.

Nonetheless, a major transition occurred in the ubiquitous grayware-pottery assemblages: plain and neck-banded graywares were rapidly replaced by corrugated types in the early eleventh century, a pattern observed by Stephen Plog (1978). Thus, all the sites discussed in this chapter can be assigned to one of two periods: the earlier roughly spans the period from the mid-ninth century until the early eleventh century; the later begins in the early to mid-eleventh century and lasts until A.D. 1150, when the lease area and the peripheries of the Kayenta region were abandoned.

Paleoenvironment

The Kayenta Region

The Kayenta region physiography is characterized by uplands (of which

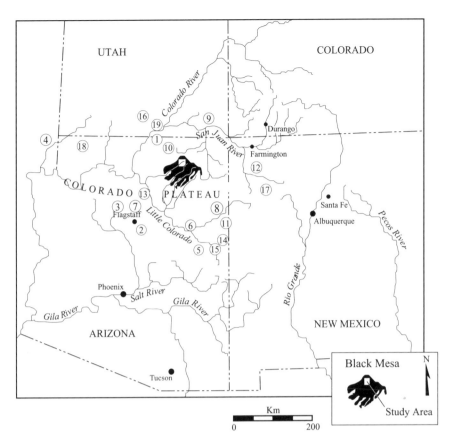

Figure 5.1 The Greater Southwest, showing locations mentioned in Chapter 5: 1–Navajo Mountain; 2–Walnut Canyon; 3–Coconino Plateau; 4–Main Ridge Site; 5–Hay Hollow Valley; 6–Winslow; 7–Sunset Crater; 8–Canyon de Chelly, White House; 9–Cedar Mesa; 10–Rainbow Plateau; 11–Defiance Plateau; 12–Salmon Ruins; 13–Wupatki; 14–Allentown; 15–Navajo Springs; 16–Coombs Site; 17–Chetro Ketl; 18–Arizona Strip; 19–Glen Canyon.

Black Mesa is one), valleys, and canyons, and it provided a varied setting for its human occupants during the ninth through twelfth centuries. Climate, topography, bedrock geology, vegetational zonation, and plant-community composition have changed little over the past two thousand years, and present patterns are a guide to past conditions. Nonetheless, the changes that did occur offered considerable opportunities and challenges to the prehistoric Kayentans (Dean 1988a; Dean et al. 1985; F. Plog et al. 1988).

Beginning about A.D. 750 and continuing until A.D. 900, erosion occurred and water tables declined throughout the Kayenta area. The reoccupation of the lease area in the early ninth century took place during this period. Dendroclimatic values are joint measures of high-frequency

processes (HFP) such as rainfall and temperature, characterized by periodicities shorter than one human generation (twenty-five years) (Dean 1988b:30), and they fluctuated rapidly between A.D. 750 and 1000 (Dean 1988a:138). Regional dendroclimatic variation, however, was comparatively low between A.D. 700 and 975; thus, although oscillating rapidly over time, climatic conditions were similar across large regions at any one point in time.

During periods of alluvial degradation (A.D. 750 until 900), water tables fell, erosion and arroyo-cutting took place, and soil formed on stable alluvial terraces. Under such conditions, pioneer species colonized floodplains, in turn attracting large game such as deer and pronghorn to this habitat. However, the floodplains would have been less than ideal for

agricultural pursuits, as groundwater (the most predictable source of water) would have been in short supply, except in those few places where favorable geologic conditions caused its percolation to the surface as springs or seeps (most commonly in the lowlands and canyons). These conditions worsened with lower-than-average rainfall and possibly ameliorated during periods of higher-than-average rainfall. Wild plants and small-game abundance covary with variation in high-frequency processes; favorable HFP conditions would have increased wild resource availability, offsetting, at least in part, the general pattern of alluvial degradation and poorer agricultural potential.

Environmental conditions were highly variable and localized during the period A.D. 975–1150. A general aggradational trend characterized the Kayenta area from A.D. 925 until 1250, interrupted by a second-order degradation starting around A.D. 1100, peaking about A.D. 1150 (coincident with the abandonment of many parts of the Kayenta region, including the lease area), and ending about A.D. 1175. Substantial fluctuations in the amount of annual precipitation characterized the period between A.D. 1000 and 1150, with periods of above-average rainfall centered at A.D. 1075 and 1110, separated by a drought. A severe and prolonged drought in the middle A.D. 1100s heightened the effects of the second-order degradation cycle. The second-order degradation, accompanied by the drought in the mid-1100s, would have confronted the Kayentans with major obstacles to their farming, hunting, and gathering lifestyle.

Black Mesa

Personnel of the Black Mesa project devoted considerable effort to reconstructing the paleoenvironment and understanding its effects (Gumerman 1988a). As is typical in a complex multiyear research effort, interpretations changed. Early assessments of Black Mesa as "an excellent foraging environment" (Gumerman 1970:118) were later countered by the characterization that major edible plants were "widely distributed, variable in annual yield, and unreliable as dietary staples" (Ford 1984:129). Ford (1984:129) concluded that "calories were a limiting factor for hunters and gatherers in the pre-maize Southwest. Plant foods were not sufficiently abundant in any one location to support large populations or even the annual return of small bands."

Corn agriculture, Ford proposed, changed this situation, even though the corn itself did not produce high yields. Despite its low productivity, corn was "predictable in its location, yield, and caloric contribution" (Ford 1984:130). In addition, the planting of corn created anthropogenic ecosystems. Pioneer annuals invaded the cornfields, and if the farmers permitted them to remain, they formed dense patches of harvestable food (Ford 1984:130). Further, the "abandoned fields were colonized by food-bearing perennials in greater concentration than otherwise occurred in nature" (Ford 1984:130) and by small mammals such as cottontails, jackrabbits, and other rodents that were attracted to the relatively dense stands of edible plants (Semé 1984).

Even though the introduction of cultigens increased the overall productivity and predictability of the landscape, northern Black Mesa remained a precarious environment in which to practice agriculture. Soils formed in the alluvium deposited on wash floodplains were fertile (E. Karlstrom 1983:330), but agricultural potential was still limited by insufficient rainfall and a short frost-free growing season. Navajo farmers residing within the study area today harvest green corn rather than risk the wait until full maturation (Russell 1983:25). Moreover, some Navajo farmers have turned to an alternative, heartier, frost-resistant crop: potatoes (Russell 1981).

Recent studies of animal biomass within the study area indicate that few wild animals and birds live on northern Black Mesa. However, evaluation of the contemporary wild animal biomass must be tempered by the realization that sheep, goats, and cattle are grazed throughout the area today. Data for the Peabody leasehold tallied 1,936 sheep and 703 goats owned by 55 households (Russell 1981, n.d.). Lease-area residents indicated that these figures were comparatively low, that collectively the most sheep ever owned totaled 11,120. However, even though these figures are informative in attempting to evaluate past animal biomass within the area, naturally available graze is supplemented by imported fodder, and water is hauled into the area using pickup trucks.

These data establish a baseline against which the currently available paleoenvironmental data may be compared. Tree rings, pollen, plant macrofossils, and faunal remains all provide information on past environmental conditions, on the productive potential of the landscape, and on how it was exploited.

Pollen

Studies of archaeological and modern pollen from the Colorado Plateaus have helped to identify past patterns of economic plant use, changes in the distribution and composition of major plant communities, and shifts in temperature and moisture conditions. Data from Black Mesa and the Hay Hollow Valley in Arizona, and from the Navajo Reservoir district in northwestern New Mexico, show major and consistent departures from the modern pollen rain (Euler et al. 1979:1095; Hevly 1988). These departures, which exceed the 95 percent confidence limits of the mean of the modern samples, indicate that the "interval A.D. 950 to 1150 is one of the best documented periods of increased effective moisture on the Colorado Plateaus" (Euler et al. 1979:1096).

Analysis of pollen from cultural contexts on northern Black Mesa provide "no significant evidence to suggest major changes in the plant species represented over time" (Murry 1983:107). However, Murry (1983:107) notes that many of the samples from prehistoric contexts contained much less sagebrush pollen and more Cheno-Am pollen than did modern samples and that mesic species are represented in several of the samples from Puebloan sites.

Murry (1983:105) also reported the results of the analysis of seven pollen samples taken from a stratigraphic column in a sagebrush flat "that appeared to be an ideal possible location for an aboriginal corn field." Murry's analyses generally concur with findings (Euler et al. 1979) suggesting that environmental conditions were more mesic during much of the ceramic-period occupation of northern Black Mesa. Murry's "old field" experiment also provided some support for Ford's (1984) contention that human disturbance of the landscape created new edaphic conditions that actually enhanced plant biomass. But Ford (1984) proposed that these anthropogenic ecosystems were the result of agriculture, while Murry (1983:105, 125, 130) offered fire as an alternative cause.

Plant Macrofossils

Soils samples for flotation were recovered from all BMAP sites excavated between 1975 and 1983. Analysis of these materials has been invaluable for providing a qualitative assessment of past economic plant use and paleoenvironmental conditions. The macrobotanical remains from ceramic-period sites support two generalizations about past environmental conditions. First, the presence of the charred remains of plants that grow in the riparian community indicate that climatic conditions were wetter between A.D. 825 and 1150 than they are at present. Charcoal from willow, cottonwood, and reeds is present at sites in the lease area dating from the mid-ninth century (AZ D:11:2027, D:11:2038, and D:11:2068) as well as from sites of the early twelfth century. These plants provide strong support for the past existence of perennial, well-watered zones within the lease area itself. Today, such zones are notably absent.

Second, the plant macrofossils provide "substantial evidence for cornfield agriculture and the anthropogenic ecological changes induced by . . . farmers" (Ford 1984:135). The charred remains of corn and cucurbit are found at sites dating from the Lolomai through Toreva phases, and charred beans were found at sites dating from the mid-A.D. 800s (e.g., AZ D:7:262) through the early A.D. 1100s. In addition, "seeds characteristic of disturbed land, including cultivated fields and older fallow land, were recovered" (Ford 1984:135). These ecological associations were verified by a survey of Navajo fields of various ages within the study area. Certain plants—especially lamb's-quarters, purslane, and pigweed—were found in cornfields and sheep corrals but rarely anywhere else (Ford 1984:135). In addition, buckwheat, milkvetch, prickly pear, four-wing saltbush, and wolfberry were found in greater quantities in disturbed habitats than elsewhere. Remains from all these plants were recovered from archaeological contexts. Lamb's-quarters and pigweed provided the "most outstanding evidence for an abundance of ruderal plants in active fields" (Ford 1984:136). Both these plants were common in archaeological contexts, and Ford (1984:136–137) contends that given the low probability of preservation and recovery, the quantities recovered are highly significant.

Fauna

Analysis of animal species recovered from archaeological sites dating to the period between A.D. 950 and 1150 also suggests environmental changes. At least three species (marmot, bison, and scaled quail) temporarily extended their ranges onto the Colorado Plateaus during this period. Bison and scaled quail normally inhabit grasslands, while the marmot requires green fodder. "The prehistoric existence of animal species dependent on grasslands composed of both

cool and warm season grasses implies moister, warmer conditions during the springs or wetter winters" (Euler et al. 1979:1096).

Within the lease area, several species appearing in the archaeofauna suggest wetter conditions between A.D. 800 and 1150. Two taxa show habitat preference for aquatic environments: spadefoot toad and long-tailed vole (Leonard 1986:table 5-1). The spadefoot toad requires access to standing pools of water for breeding, and so the presence of this animal during the early/middle Puebloan period does suggest more mesic conditions.

Finally, rodent remains provide tentative support for the increasing importance of production of plant food and the establishment of anthropogenic field communities (Semé 1984). Rodents and other small animals that might have been attracted to agricultural fields are especially well represented in the faunal inventories from large, late sites. Semé (1984:172) interprets these findings as indicative of the growing importance of farming in the overall subsistence strategy of the prehistoric Black Mesans.

Geomorphology and Hydrology

Geomorphological and hydrological reconstructions for the Black Mesa region suggest alternating drought and mesic conditions. Droughts peaked at intervals of approximately 550 years, with secondary droughts at 275-year intervals (Dean 1988a; Euler et al. 1979:1097). Most of the ceramic-period occupation of northern Black Mesa coincided with a climatic regime characterized by moister conditions. Drought intervals occurred at A.D. 875, 975, and 1060; however, they appear to be exceptions within a generally moist period.

Evidence suggests that water tables dropped during the dry periods and that the lower water tables initiated arroyo cutting (E. Karlstrom 1983:329, 1988). Moister conditions, characterized by stream aggradation and overbank deposition, occurred between the major drought events

(E. Karlstrom 1983:329, 335). The periodic fluctuations in climate and water table "resulted in alternating depositional and erosional regimes" that greatly changed the character of the landscape (E. Karlstrom 1983:334): "Historic accounts of nearby Tsegi Valley before the 1880 arroyo cutting episode describe a relatively lush, riparian environment with numerous ponds and marshes, tall grasses, and many cottonwood trees. In contrast, alluvial valleys at present are dissected by deep, narrow (post-1880) arroyos, indicating that today's climate is generally drier than previous climates" (E. Karlstrom 1983:334–335).

Karlstrom located a series of lacustrine deposits in the lease area in Yellow Water Canyon that date to the Puebloan period (figure 5.2). Apparently, sediments "transported into the main valley from a large tributary to Yellow Water Canyon built alluvial fans which reduced slope upstream and effectively dammed this portion" of the canyon (E. Karlstrom 1983:335). The remains of aquatic snails in the sediments provide strong support to the interpretation that these deposits are the remains of freestanding bodies of water. The lacustrine deposits indicate that the ponds were probably about 200 m long, 30 m wide, and no deeper than 5 m. Such natural processes may explain place names like Reed Valley in the now-arid lease area, with its prehistoric rock images featuring aquatic birds. Reed Valley was named in the late 1800s when favorable low-frequency processes (LFP) conditions were similar to those that characterized the tenth through thirteenth centuries.

Summary

In general, the data converge nicely and indicate that during the ninth through twelfth centuries, climatic conditions were wetter than at present. Pollen, plant macrofossils, and faunal remains collected from ceramic-period sites all document the presence of plant and animal species that require wetter conditions than now exist

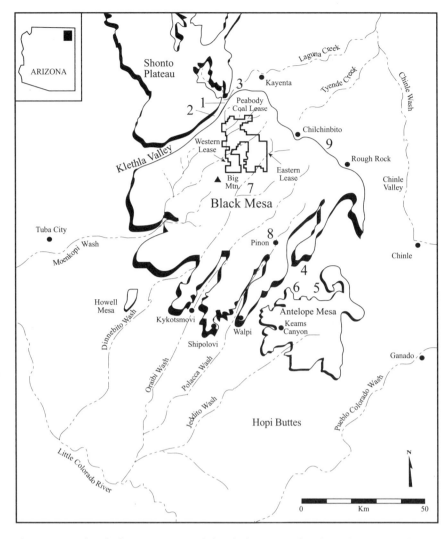

Figure 5.2 The Black Mesa region and the Black Mesa Archaeological Project study area on northern Black Mesa, showing locations mentioned in Chapter 5: 1–Marsh Pass; 2–Long House Valley; 3–Kayenta Valley; 4–Burnt Corn Ruin; 5–Tse Chizzi; 6–Whippoorwill Ruin; 7–J-43-23; 8–D:11:9 (NAU); 9–NA 13805.

The second environmental pattern suggested by the pollen, macrobotanical, and faunal data is human disturbance of the natural environment. Pollen and macrofossils from cultigens and from ruderal plant species, and lagomorph and small rodent remains provide ample evidence for agriculture and for the creation of anthropogenic communities. There are, however, alternative means of creating conditions conducive to the growth of ruderal species; fires and abandoned sites are two such mechanisms. Nonetheless, corn, beans, and squash unambiguously indicate that cultigens were grown.

Wetter climatic conditions between A.D. 825 and 1150, in short, supported plant and animal life not found within the study area today. In addition, direct evidence (the remains of corn, beans, and squash) and indirect evidence (the remains of ruderal plant species and the microfauna often associated with fields) suggest the presence of agricultural fields.

Chronology

There are four options for dating ancestral Puebloan sites in the Kayenta area: radiocarbon, archaeomagnetism, tree rings, and pottery. Each is used with varying frequencies to date samples of all Pueblo I and Pueblo II sites that are more or less representative of the whole. Carbon-14 and archaeomagnetism are rarely used to date suspected Pueblo I and II remains because their precision is less than that of tree rings or cross-dated ceramic assemblages. The use of tree-ring dates is the preferred technique because of its precision, but appropriate wood is not so commonly encountered as archaeologists would hope. Wood samples are recovered most often from excavated sites with burnt structures (Ahlstrom 1985), and wood samples that yield dates come primarily from pit structures and masonry structures, not the jacales that are so prevalent at this time in the lease area. Thus, of the 1,671 lease-area sites occupied between A.D. 800 and 1150, only 72 are tree-ring

within the study area. Elm, cottonwood, willow pollen, and charcoal are found at several sites spanning the period A.D. 825 to 1150. Although less frequent, there also are remains of reeds and cattails at a few sites. The archaeofauna include remains of toads and Mexican voles, both animals that require wetter conditions than now are found within the Peabody leasehold.

Geomorphological data provide unequivocal evidence that environmental conditions could have supported the plant and animal species listed above. Lacustrine deposits exposed in the walls of the arroyo currently eroding Yellow Water Canyon

are the remains of freestanding bodies of water. There are also reasons to believe that similar lakes or ponds might have been characteristic of the landscape during mesic climatic regimes.

Finally, tree-ring studies indicate that there was generally increased available moisture between A.D. 825 and 1150. However, the resolution of tree-ring data, which measure annual variation in available moisture, permits identification of variation in the overall trend of increased available moisture. Although the overall trend was toward increased available moisture, there were dry intervals as well.

dated. These 72 sites are not a representative sample of the 1,671; typically, they are the largest and structurally most complex of the lease-area sites. Tree-ring dates are equally scarce from known sites in the Kayenta area, and the tree-ring dated sites are similarly nonrepresentative of the total.

The vast majority of sites in the Kayenta area are known only through survey and can be assigned dates only on the basis of their ceramic assemblages. This group of sites is probably most representative of the whole. But, unfortunately, many of them are very ephemeral, the results of fleeting activities by few people. Thus, they are assigned to time spans much longer than the span of time during which they were built and used.

At present there is little we can do about this dilemma except to acknowledge that it exists and to attempt to determine how it biases our interpretations of cultural variation. Although the choice between sample representativeness and chronometric precision is problematical, it is somewhat of a nonissue for many of the topics addressed in this chapter, including technology, subsistence, settlement patterns, social organization, and ideology. Most of these topics have been examined primarily with data collected from excavated sites: macrobotanical remains, pollen, fauna, human osteological remains, and architecture are especially pertinent examples. Settlement patterns and social organization are the two topics that have been examined primarily with survey data, and they are the two analytical categories that have suffered most from questions of sample representativeness versus chronological control.

Tree-Ring Dates in the Lease Area

The Black Mesa Archaeological Project produced 642 tree-ring dates from seventy-two sites during its sixteen seasons of excavation (figure 5.3). Ahlstrom (1998a) integrated and interpreted these data; the only previous synthesis of the tree-ring data

is based on materials excavated during the 1968–1972 field seasons (Ward 1972). Ranging from A.D. 656 to 1144, 25 percent are cutting dates, 4 percent "v," and 71 percent noncutting dates (Ahlstrom 1998a). All dates before A.D. 800 are noncutting, and only two cutting dates predate A.D. 840, "both from a structure at D:11:2030 that was probably built in the 870s" (Ahlstrom 1998a:141). These two early cutting dates probably come from reused beams, but despite their incorporation into another structure, someone was present in the lease area to cut the trees. These two dates are the basis for dating the Puebloan reoccupation of the lease area to the early ninth century (Nichols and Smiley 1984b). One other site in the lease area, AZ D:7:136, produced tree-ring dates that may derive from beam cutting at about A.D. 800 (Ahlstrom 1998a:143).

One hundred seventy samples date to the period A.D. 840 to 879, the peak in the tree-ring date distribution in the lease area. One hundred thirty-one of these (77 percent) come from six sites (AZ D:11:113, D:11:2023, D:11:2025, D:11:2027, D:11:2030, and D:11:2068). All six sites are located along the banks of Moenkopi Wash within 5.5 km of one another; three (AZ D:11:2023, D:11:2025, and D:11:2027) were probably occupied sequentially by one community. Ahlstrom (In 1998a:145) notes the concentration of construction activity in one small portion of the lease area, concluding that "whether other sections of northern Black Mesa saw heightened activity during this interval is debatable."

A low median number of dates per decade and a high proportion of noncutting dates characterize the period A.D. 880 to 1069, a period during which the lease area may have been abandoned (S. Plog 1986d). Approximately 50 percent of the dates come from structures with ceramic assemblages that date after A.D. 1070, and Ahlstrom (1998a:145) conjectures that some of the other pre-1070 dates come from reused beams. He concludes that the "small number and poor quality of tree-ring dates falling

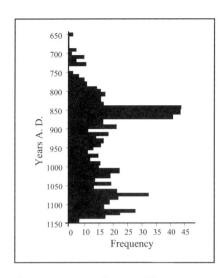

Figure 5.3 Distribution of lease area tree-ring dates (after Ahlstrom 1998a:figure 8-2).

between A.D. 880 and 1069 could have a variety of causes, including poor preservation . . . , biases in the sample of sites and structures chosen for excavation, and even low population in the study area" (Ahlstrom 1998a:145).

The number of tree-ring dates rebounds in subsequent decades, and there is a "small" increase in the number of dates per decade and a "substantial" increase in cutting and "v" dates for the period A.D. 1070 to 1149 (Ahlstrom 1998a:146). The distribution is erratic, matching population reconstructions discussed below. Ahlstrom notes that in contrast to the three decades between A.D. 840 and 870 (when six sites in one small portion of the lease area produced 77 percent of the dates), fourteen sites account for 76 percent of the 136 dates spanning the A.D. 1070s through 1140s, and these are located throughout the lease area. The final tree-ring cutting from a lease-area site dates to A.D. 1144. It follows a steady decrease in the number of dates per decade that commenced in the early twelfth century. Ahlstrom concludes that the decrease in the number of dates mirrors a decline in beam procurement and construction activity that was accompanied by population decrease between A.D. 1130 and 1150 (Ahlstrom 1998a:147).

Ceramic-Based Dating Systems

Within the Kayenta region between the ninth and twelfth centuries, dating most of the sites means using dating systems based on the ceramics. Almost all the sites from this time period have pottery, and those with decorated types can be assigned to typologically based temporal periods, accurate within a range of 40 to 100 years (Ambler 1985b; D. Breternitz 1966; Colton 1939). In addition, whiteware (Kojo 1991; S. Plog and Hantman 1986) and grayware (P. Reed 1981) regression dating formulas have been derived specifically for northern Black Mesa sites. They assign dates to sites within a range of ±19 years and ±40 years respectively; however, numerous problems, especially with sample size and ability to generalize the results, limit the general applicability of both techniques (Ahlstrom 1998b).

Many Pueblo I and II sites, which tend to be small, have few painted whiteware sherds or only graywares in their assemblages and cannot be dated using either typological seriations or regression techniques. Generally, graywares comprise the vast majority of these sites' ceramic inventories, in most cases 80 to 100 percent of the total. Such sites can be assigned to temporal periods delineated by abrupt, but infrequent, grayware ceramic change. On northern Black Mesa, before A.D. 1025, grayware-ceramic assemblages were dominated by plain (Lino Gray) and neck-banded (Kana-a Gray) types; over 90 percent of the grayware assemblages from this period are composed of these two types. After A.D. 1050, Tusayan Corrugated predominates (over 90 percent) (S. Plog 1978:39). These patterns mean that virtually all ceramic-period sites from northern Black Mesa can be assigned to one of three temporal groups: early, A.D. 800 to 900/940; intermediate, A.D. 900/940 to 1030; or late, A.D. 1070 to 1150.

Population Size

If we remember that archaeological population estimates count a surrogate, a material thing, and that one hallmark of the early Puebloan period is the increased number and widespread distribution of archaeological sites (themselves composites of material things), it is not surprising that archaeologists characterize this period as one of population growth. In general, throughout the Kayenta area during the ninth through mid-twelfth centuries, the number of sites increased, and they were more widely distributed (Euler 1988). However, in the mid-twelfth century, this trend abruptly halted; many areas were abandoned for a final time by the Kayenta Anasazi, and populations concentrated in the Kayenta heartland, Navajo and Paiute Canyons, on the Rainbow Plateau and Paiute Mesa, southern Black Mesa, the Hopi Mesas, and Antelope Mesa.

An important question, unsatisfactorily answered at best, is Where did people go after the mid-twelfth century population relocations? Although many regions within the Kayenta area continued to be occupied, most do not show increases in site numbers that would account for the hypothetical number of people that departed the abandoned areas (Dean, Chapter 6, this volume); perhaps there were not so many people as archaeologists suppose, or perhaps the people leaving the peripheral areas emigrated beyond the Kayenta region. Ambler et al. (1983; see also Fairley 1989a) suggest that immigration, possibly from northern Black Mesa, contributed to population growth in the Navajo Mountain area after A.D. 1150. Population growth is also observed in Walnut Canyon (Bremer 1989) and Wupatki National Monument (Downum and Sullivan 1990:5.71, 5.72) starting about A.D. 1130. Downum and Sullivan (1990:5-85) also suggest that some of the people participating in the Wupatki land rush that occurred after the eruption of Sunset Crater in A.D. 1064

may have come from northern Black Mesa, although alternatively they may have come from the Coconino Plateau (Sullivan 1986a; Whittlesey 1992), the Grand Canyon (Euler and Chandler 1978), or the Arizona Strip (Fairley 1989b), all areas that were losing population at this same time.

Population Size in the Kayenta Heartland and Peripheral Areas

In the Kayenta heartland (including Tsegi Canyon, Marsh Pass, and the Klethla, Long House, Kayenta, and Laguna Creek Valleys) there is evidence of occupation beginning in Paleoindian times and continuing until the final abandonment of the Kayenta region in A.D. 1300. Population grew between A.D. 1000 and 1150 (Dean et al. 1978:33), an increase echoed throughout the Kayenta region. However, unlike many of the peripheral areas, the heartland was occupied after A.D. 1150, although population patterns do not suggest that large numbers of emigrants moved there (see Chapter 6).

In many of the peripheral areas, population reconstructions suggest comparable patterns during the Pueblo I and II periods. A period of low population was followed by dramatic increases in approximately A.D. 900–1000. Population climbed precipitously until just before A.D. 1150, when the areas were apparently abandoned. This pattern holds for the Grand Canyon (Euler 1988:198–200; Euler and Chandler 1978), the Virgin Branch (Aikens 1966; Euler 1988:195–198), the western Glen Canyon basin (Euler 1988:204–205; Jennings 1966; Lipe and Lindsay 1983), the Defiance Plateau (Euler 1988:209–210), and, of course, northern Black Mesa (discussed in detail below). Interestingly, all these areas are sparsely watered, and most are uplands.

One peripheral area, Cedar Mesa, was abandoned after the Basketmaker II period and not reoccupied until approximately A.D. 1060. Tree-ring dates suggest construction activity for approximately one

century (A.D. 1060 and 1150), after
which people whose pottery suggests a
Kayenta affiliation may have departed
from Cedar Mesa (Matson et al. 1988).
However, unlike many of the other
Kayenta peripheral areas, this A.D.
1150 abandonment of Cedar Mesa was
not final; after a couple of decades,
people whose pottery suggests a Mesa
Verde affiliation reoccupied the area
and remained until the late thirteenth
century.

Several of the peripheral areas
were not abandoned in A.D. 1150. Well-
watered zones in the Glen Canyon
basin east of the Colorado River were
occupied until the A.D. 1270s (Euler
1988:204–205; Lipe and Lindsay 1983).
The Rainbow Plateau and Navajo
Mountain areas similarly hosted
Kayenta peoples until shortly before
A.D. 1300 (Geib et al. 1993:15; Lindsay
et al. 1968:364–365). In fact, Ambler
et al. (1983) propose that some of the
people departing northern Black Mesa
moved to this area, contributing to an
apparent population influx at about
A.D. 1150.

Between A.D. 1050 and 1150 there
was rapid population growth in
Canyon de Chelly. The canyon system
continued to be occupied after 1150;
however, the demographic patterns do
not suggest major influxes that might
account for the emigrants from the
adjacent Defiance Plateau. Further, as
discussed in Chapter 6, Mesa Verde
peoples showed an increasing presence throughout the Chinle Valley
drainage, including Canyon de Chelly,
during the Transition period and the
Tsegi phase.

Population grew in the Hopi
Buttes starting about A.D. 1000 and
lasting until about 1250; the area was
abandoned by A.D. 1275 (Gumerman
1988b:64–66, figure 2.5; Gumerman
and Dean 1989:108). However, before
A.D. 1075 the area was affiliated stylistically with the Kayenta branch, while
after that date it is part of the Winslow
branch (Gumerman 1988b:65). Thus
the area apparently did not receive
Kayenta peoples in the population
relocations of A.D. 1150; however,
this link may help explain the pos-

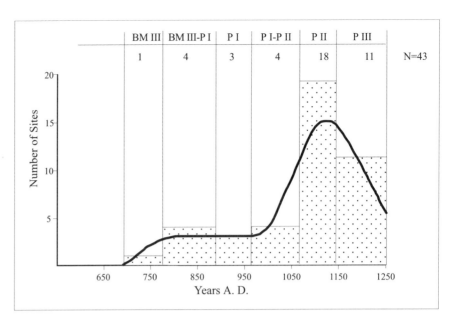

Figure 5.4 Temporal distribution of lease-area sites surveyed prior to 1969.

sible Winslow-branch pit structures
found at sites in the Kayenta heartland
during the Tsegi phase (discussed in
Chapter 6).

Black Mesa

Many archaeological studies focus
on population and the environment
as major causal factors for cultural
variation, and BMAP research is no
exception (Euler et al. 1979; Gumerman 1988a; S. Plog 1986d). Black Mesa
researchers grappled with many of
the theoretical and methodological
issues surrounding the reconstruction
of population size and used numerous
techniques and surrogates. Even now
there is no single, generally accepted
paleodemographic reconstruction for
the Black Mesa study area; researchers
agree on the overall trends of growth
and decline, but they disagree vigorously about the number of people
living within the lease area at any one
time.

The first Black Mesa population
curve was published in 1970 (Gumerman 1970:30), based on forty-one
prehistoric sites located within a small
portion of the lease area (figure 5.4).
The sites were occupied between late
Basketmaker III and early Pueblo III
(Gumerman 1970:13), and all were
habitation sites showing remarkable

similarity in architectural configuration and size (Gumerman 1970:17–18).
These data were combined into a
phase-based population curve that
showed continuous occupation from
the beginning of the Basketmaker III
period (A.D. 650) through Pueblo III
(A.D. 1250). Gumerman employed
many simplifying assumptions to offer
some suggestions about population
dynamics in this little-studied area.
All subsequent population estimates
employed an expanding database
while attempting to refine considerations of site morphology, chronology,
and occupation span (Hantman 1983;
Layhe 1977, 1981; S. Plog 1986d; Swedlund and Sessions 1976).

Despite more data and methodological refinements, there are two recurring points of disagreement about
Black Mesa population estimates: the
choice of a population surrogate and
the chronometric basis for the estimate. Black Mesa researchers have
used rooms as the basis for estimating
population size (except Gumerman
[1970], who used sites); nonetheless,
researchers have differed in which
rooms they counted and how they
counted them. Some (Hantman 1983;
Layhe 1977, 1981) estimated the area
enclosed in the habitation rooms on
each site, while others estimated the
number of rooms on each site (S. Plog

1986d; Swedlund and Sessions 1976). The room-based estimates may be further distinguished by the type of rooms and sites considered sensitive to population size. Layhe (1977, 1981) and Hantman (1983) measured habitation area on all sites, Swedlund and Sessions (1976) measured the number of habitation rooms on habitation sites, while S. Plog (1986d) apparently used all rooms, but only on sites that had either a kiva or a masonry roomblock (which he presumed to be a hallmark of year-round occupation). Simply stated, there is no agreement about the kinds of rooms and sites that should contribute to the population estimate.

The other recurring theme in the development of Black Mesa population estimates is the chronometric basis for the reconstruction. With one exception, each of the population curves makes use of an increasingly small sampling interval and more precise dates. Both Gumerman's and Swedlund and Sessions's curves rely on phases, with their attendant problems of unrealistically long intervals and unequal lengths. The over-long phases are inappropriate as the chronometric basis for Black Mesa population estimates because they are far longer than the likely occupation spans of most sites. This discrepancy has the potential effect of smoothing variation in the curve (F. Plog 1979a) and of masking possible periodic abandonments of the study area (M. Berry 1982). Inappropriately or unequally long phases also have the combined effect of overestimating population size.

Stephen Plog (1986d) dealt with these problems by assigning individual dates to each of the sites used in his population estimate and by constructing two estimates, one using a fifteen-year site occupation span and the other using a twenty-five-year occupation span (figure 5.5). Unlike earlier demographic reconstructions (which showed continuously increasing population), Plog's estimates showed considerable variation in the rate of population growth, including a probable short-term abandonment

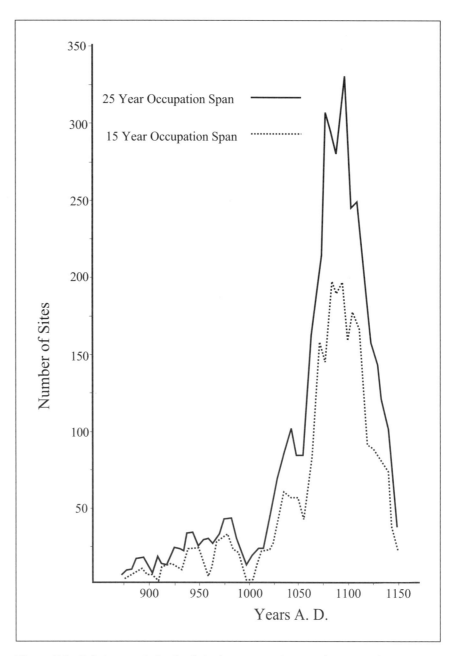

Figure 5.5 Relative population levels in the BMAP study area using occupation span estimates of 15 and 25 years (after Plog 1986f:figure 43).

around A.D. 1000. Plog's chronometric techniques generated much dispute; however, no one disputed the need for accurate and precise dating of the sites and assessments of occupation span.

The many Black Mesa population estimates and the controversies surrounding their construction give rise to a critical question: Of what use are they? Fortunately, each has several common characteristics, suggesting that they are reliable if used with some caution. First, all the more

recent population curves concur that the ceramic-period reoccupation of northern Black Mesa took place in the early to mid-A.D. 800s, and this range of ceramically based dates is well supported by clusters of tree-ring dates from several excavated sites (Ahlstrom 1998a). Population grew relatively slowly for the first one hundred to two hundred years, then the rate of growth accelerated rapidly and erratically, resulting in a population boom lasting one hundred years. The boom was followed by an equally dramatic decline that culminated with the abandonment of the study area by the mid-twelfth century. Finally, virtually all the later population curves agree that northern Black Mesa ceased to be occupied (by Puebloan peoples in an archaeologically visible manner) by approximately A.D. 1150. Once again, this date for the abandonment is well supported by tree-ring dates from excavated sites. The latest tree-ring cutting date is A.D. 1144, and allowing for approximately ten years of use of that structure following its construction or repair, this corresponds remarkably well with the estimated abandonment in A.D. 1150 (Ahlstrom 1998a).

A related issue questions whether there were people living within the study area during the entire period between A.D. 813 and 1150. All the Black Mesa population reconstructions, except one, posit continuous occupation within the study area from the time of initial reoccupation until the final abandonment; the single exception is S. Plog's (1986d) estimate of a fifteen-year occupation span (figure 5.5). This reconstruction shows possible, periodic abandonments of the study area in approximately A.D. 905, 955, and 1000. After A.D. 1000, population increased rapidly until A.D. 1100; however, this growth was punctuated by at least four episodes of decline and recovery. Plog's reconstruction of a twenty-five-year occupation span also shows intervals of population decline between A.D. 850 and 1000; however, population never declined to the zero-point (figure 5.5).

As Plog notes, the differences between his reconstruction and the earlier ones are critical for understanding the processes underlying cultural change on prehistoric Black Mesa (and elsewhere). Most researchers assume cultural stability without stopping to consider the periodicity on which behavioral systems operate. Current archaeological chronometric techniques favor observation of major events, while missing the finer-grained and lower-amplitude variation leading

up to these events. Clearly, these biases in archaeological measurement have major and predictable implications for the kinds of explanations of cultural change favored by most archaeologists: stability punctuated by major change (see also S. Plog 1990).

Almost all the Black Mesa demographic reconstructions have been presented as relative indicators of population size. In the single exception, Hantman (1983) converted Layhe's (1977) floor-area estimates for eastern lease sites into measures of absolute population size. Hantman used the constant, 5 m²/person, as an ethnographically verified estimate of the amount of sheltered space required to house an individual. The calculations indicated that between 22 and 624 people inhabited the eastern portion of the study area between A.D. 850 and 1150.

The resolution of the population question lies in the development of analytical techniques that will permit archaeologists to determine unambiguously the functional interrelationships among rooms and sites, and which of them existed contemporaneously. Until then, given our current state of knowledge and analytical imprecision, the most appropriate use of the various interpretations is as parameters; the two most extreme, empirically based interpretations set the limits within which reality most likely lies (Powell 1988). This approach is more honest than hammering the data to fit a single, monolithic interpretation; plus, it identifies the major points of interpretive contention and their theoretical and methodological underpinnings. If future research deals with these problems, this admission of our interpretive frailties will be far more profitable than continuing with current assumption-based interpretations.

Population Structure, Composition, and Health

Demographic characteristics are poorly understood for the Pueblo I and II periods, a generalization that

applies to the Basketmaker III and Pueblo III periods as well (Nichols, Chapter 4, this volume; Dean, Chapter 6, this volume). The sample of skeletal materials upon which such interpretations are based is small and unevenly distributed over the Kayenta landscape. Compounding the problem for the Pueblo I and II periods is that typical sites are small and were occupied only for short spans of time (perhaps only seasonally). Thus, the likelihood of people dying at any one site, and then being interred in such a way that would promote preservation over the millennia, is much lower than for the subsequent Pueblo III period with its large sites and impressive artifact and trash accumulations.

The single largest mortuary sample from early Puebloan sites in the Kayenta region comes from the Peabody lease area. During sixteen years of BMAP excavations, 194 burial numbers were assigned in the field to remains coming from about 60 sites (Martin et al. 1991:33, 38). Subsequent analyses distinguished 172 individuals and another 100 or so isolated bones (Martin et al. 1991:16). One hundred sixty of these burials date to the period of interest: 49 between A.D. 800–1050, and 111 between A.D. 1050 and 1150.

In 1990, several years after BMAP ended, the Native American Graves Protection and Repatriation Act (P.L. 101-601, NAGPRA) was passed. In response to this law, Peabody Coal Company funded work by the Navajo Nation Archaeological Department (NNAD) to recover any previously undetected human remains at prehistoric archaeological sites in the lease area (Spurr 1993). The NNAD project recovered an additional 32 individuals from thirteen Puebloan sites in the lease area (Spurr 1993:188). These remains were analyzed, using noninvasive techniques, before being reburied in July 1993. The combined lease-area sample of 204 individuals shows no marked biases in age or gender distributions and, with one exception, can be presumed to be fairly representative of the people who lived and died in the area between A.D. 800 and 1150:

there are more young people in the early Puebloan sample, and more old people in the late sample (Martin et al. 1991; Spurr 1993:174).

Two other studies contribute to our knowledge of paleodemography and paleoepidemology in the Kayenta region during the Pueblo II period (Ryan 1977; Sumner 1982). Forty of the 215 individuals analyzed by Dennis Ryan in his dissertation lived and died between A.D. 1000 and 1150; the others date to the Pueblo III and IV periods (Chapter 6, this volume). Most of these 40 were excavated during the Glen Canyon Project excavations from small village sites on the northern periphery of the Kayenta region. Six burials spanning the late Basketmaker III to Pueblo II periods were excavated from five Pinon Project sites on central Black Mesa (Sumner 1982).

Osteological remains from the Pueblo I and II periods have the potential to answer questions about the population growth and spread that are hallmarks of this period. Inferences based on material remains suggest dramatically increasing numbers of people that must be due to immigration or to changes in fertility or mortality. The lease-area osteological remains implicate fertility and immigration, since there are no noticeable changes in mortality rates (Martin et al. 1991:54).

> The analysis of the age structure, in combination with the extrapolated growth and birthrates, suggests an initial early Pueblo population that was growing at least in part because of increased fertility. Immigration to Black Mesa cannot be excluded as a contributing factor, but the regularities in the age structure imply the immigration of entire family units. The late Pueblo population on Black Mesa represents an "older" group (more adults relative to children) that is not producing as many children. [Martin et al. 1991:60]

Gross pathological analyses suggest slightly deteriorating conditions in the lease area between A.D. 800 and 1150. On the average, the late Puebloan people died two years younger (25.7) than did the early Puebloan people (28.0), numbers that are very similar to those for other southwestern skeletal series (e.g., 26.6 for the Kayenta area as a whole, and 26.1 for the Pueblo II component of this sample [Ryan 1977:63]). Early Puebloan children have no hypoplasias on their deciduous dentition, compared with 23.4 percent for late Puebloan children. Hypoplasias suggest that the peak period of stress for these late Puebloan children was between the ages of 3.0 and 4.5, consistent with secondary stresses associated with weaning (Martin et al. 1991:118).

Other indicators suggest comparatively stable, if harsh, conditions. About half the individuals had infectious lesions at the time of death, probably caused by microorganisms, parasites, salmonella, or enteroviruses. These patterns remain fairly constant over time, but are in marked contrast with the individuals from within a hundred-mile radius of the lease area, who show no such lesions (Martin et al. 1991:140). Almost all (87.0 percent) the remains in the lease area also show some form of anemic response; however, most of these cases were mild, "with some healing that only indirectly undermined health" (Martin et al. 1991:162). Compared with the inhabitants of other sites in the Kayenta area, the people of the lease area people had slightly higher frequencies of porotic hyperostosis (Martin et al. 1991:163). See also Spurr (1993) and Sumner (1982, discussed below) for corroboration of these results. Interestingly, the remains in the lease area show no indications of physical trauma or possible cannibalism.[1]

The stable isotope values of the Black Mesa fall well within the range for a "mixed, mainly maize" diet consisting of c4 plants (Martin et al. 1991:73). These interpretations match S. Martin's (1999) assessment based on seventeen individuals from eight Virgin Anasazi sites in southern Utah. He concludes (1999:495, 504) that Virgin Anasazi Basketmakers were "full-time maize agriculturalists and that the diet remained essentially stable throughout the Pueblo (A.D. 700–1250) period," with c4/CAM plants providing 75 percent or more of calories each year. These results are suggestive, however; the "mixed, mainly maize" c4 signature does not tell us conclusively whether the plants were corn or collected plants, such as amaranth. Macrobotanical analyses suggest that corn, which was ubiquitous on the sites of the Puebloan period, must have been a major component of the diet (although collected plants are common as well). Comparison of the Black Mesa Puebloan remains with the seven Basketmaker II individuals suggests that Basketmaker II peoples may have eaten more meat than their descendants.

Only six burials were excavated and analyzed from five sites located between Forest Lake and Pinon on southern Black Mesa (Linford 1982; Sumner 1982). The individuals include two adult males, two adult females, one juvenile, and one infant (Sumner 1982:417), and the remains date from late Basketmaker III to Pueblo II. The individuals had various pathologies, including tooth wear, periodontal disease, enamel hypoplasias, various vertebral problems, and one case of spinal tuberculosis (Sumner 1982:430–431). However, Sumner (1982:431) did not observe the porotic hyperostosis and cribra orbitalia so characteristic of the lease-area burials.

Ryan concurs with Martin et al., Spurr, and Sumner about conditions during the Pueblo II period. His conclusions are intriguing, however, because his mortuary sample includes individuals who lived during Pueblo III and Pueblo IV times, thus providing a perspective on changing conditions. Based on evaluations of enamel hypoplasias, porotic hyperostosis, bone inflammations, and five indicators of oral disease, he concluded that the Pueblo II peoples were "healthier" than their Pueblo III and IV descendants (Ryan 1977:198–200). Conditions deteriorated markedly between A.D. 1150 and 1250 and rebounded somewhat between A.D. 1300 and 1700. Bone inflammations were absent in the Pueblo II sample, occurring only in individuals who lived during the Pueblo III and IV periods. The absence of bone inflammations in the Pueblo II sample suggested to Ryan that the Pueblo II peoples lived in smaller groupings than did their descendants, who might have been subject to infectious diseases (Ryan 1977:200). The occurrence of dental caries increased significantly between the Pueblo II and III periods, indicating that people might have become more reliant on maize in about A.D. 1150 (Ryan 1977:201). Ryan (1977:147) found little evidence of trauma throughout time.

Subsistence

Having addressed the issues of how many people were living in the Kayenta region between A.D. 800 and 1150 and their general health, we now turn our attention to the problem of how those people were making their living. The Pueblo I and II periods mark a transition from the incipient agriculture of the Basketmaker periods (see Smiley, Chapter 3, this volume; Nichols, Chapter 4, this volume), to the intensive cultivation of the Pueblo III period (Dean, Chapter 6, this volume). Archaeologists have assumed incrementally increasing agricultural intensification, meaning reliance on agriculture for the Pueblo I and II periods should be more than during the Basketmaker III period and less than during the Pueblo III period. This assumption is plausible and likely, yet interpretations for different parts of the Kayenta region suggest that hunting and, to an even greater extent, gathering remained important (Sullivan 1986a, 1987). Unfortunately, it is difficult to characterize "important," because subsistence reconstructions are qualitative, and the effects of human activities and natural processes on what archaeologists eventually recover are difficult to assess. Furthermore, characterizations

of "less" agriculture during Basketmaker III and "more" agriculture during Pueblo III can be interpreted as suggesting that the Pueblo I and II intensification took place incrementally and smoothly. Such may not have been the case, and the exceptions to this assumed trend may be contributing to present-day interpretive discrepancies.

BMAP provides a case study in the contributions and pitfalls of subsistence data and their interpretation. The BMAP subsistence analyses, which are still ongoing thirteen years after the final field season, are a microcosm of trends in archaeological subsistence reconstructions throughout the Kayenta region and beyond. Concern for accurate subsistence reconstructions is apparent in questions posed in the first BMAP publication (Gumerman 1970:3):

> Some recent studies have suggested that the Anasazi depended more on hunting and gathering than on agriculture. To what extent did hunting and gathering contribute to the food supply on Black Mesa? Furthermore, what are the natural edible resources on Black Mesa, and what is their distribution and density? Could the people on Black Mesa have utilized the wild plant and animal food to a greater extent than they did? Did the ratio of cultivated to noncultivated food change through time?

At the conclusion of the first year's excavations, tentative answers were offered for these questions. "[I]n spite of what would appear to be an excellent foraging environment, the evidence for hunting and gathering is rare. . . . Yet, the evidence of domesticated plants is great" (Gumerman 1968:118). Data from excavations conducted from 1969 through 1974 reinforced these interpretations (Gumerman et al. 1972; Powell 1984b), although a growing faunal assemblage drew attention to the importance of hunting (Douglas 1972).

By the mid-1970s, generalizations

had been offered about the prehistoric productive potential of northern Black Mesa and about how this potential was exploited by the ancient residents of the region. The region appeared to be "an excellent foraging environment" (Gumerman 1970:118) that was, nonetheless, used primarily for agriculture. Changing patterns of faunal exploitation provided secondary support for these interpretations. The declining dietary importance of artiodactyls over time and their apparent replacement by lagomorphs suggested high human population densities during the Pueblo II period. Presumably, this large population supported themselves by a land-intensive economic pursuit: agriculture (Swedlund and Sessions 1976).

However, there was virtually no direct, unambiguous, and independent evidence to support these interpretations. No empirically based evaluations had been made of either the modern or prehistoric productive potential of the landscape, and although paleoclimatic research was underway, the results had not then been published (Euler et al. 1979; Gumerman 1988a; T. Karlstrom et al. 1974; T. Karlstrom et al. 1976). No work whatsoever had been done on the role of noncultivated plant foods in the subsistence base. The evidence for agriculture was largely circumstantial (e.g., food-processing artifacts and storage rooms). The few findings of corn pollen and macrofossils indicated merely that corn was present, not its relative importance in the diet. Finally, the generalizations were based on a biased sample of sites excavated (for the most part) without screening.

These broad generalizations, based on scanty data, provided a fertile context for a variety of empirical, methodological, and theoretical studies. The early interpretations were challenged on all these grounds by numerous researchers, all with a particular axe to grind. The result was to produce two major interpretive themes: specialization and diversification. Both interpretations agree that subsistence practices intensified over time; more produce was being extracted from the same land base. However, the specialization adherents proposed that this intensification took the form increased agricultural production, while the diversification group argued for intensification through exploitation of a wider variety of plant resources (Gasser 1982). Underlying the two sets of interpretations are additional assumptions about population size, carrying capacity, and the suitability of the landscape for agriculture.

Farming

Reconstructions of the agricultural activities of the Pueblo I and II occupants of the Kayenta region are based on five major classes of data: plant macrofossils, pollen, artifacts, human remains, and to a lesser degree, architecture. All these lines of evidence converge, telling us that corn agriculture played an important role in Pueblo I and II subsistence. As mentioned above, defining "important" is no easy matter. Furthermore, agriculture's contribution may have been different in different parts of the Kayenta region.

Because of the relative scarcity of Pueblo I and II sheltered sites, preservation of organic remains does not begin to match that for the Pueblo III period (for which Dean [Chapter 6, this volume] notes the overwhelming presence of corn). Most Pueblo I and II Kayenta sites are open, and preservation of organic materials is not especially good, perhaps fueling the controversy over subsistence reconstructions. Two Pueblo I and II cliff sites on northern Black Mesa (Standing Fall House [Klesert and Cowan 1978] and Hand House [J. Anderson 1979]) have been systematically mapped and surface finds have been collected. The remains of corn and squash were common at both, and beans were found as well, although in lesser quantities. Interestingly, despite the presence of cultigens at the site, none of the four coprolites analyzed from Standing Fall House contained corn, squash, or beans

(Klesert 1982:figure 6). However, these two sites are unusual for the Pueblo I and II periods, and no researchers have suggested that the patterns at the Standing Fall House and Hand House be generalized to the Kayenta region at large. In fact, as discussed below, Klesert (1982) argues that Standing Fall House was used for storage and redistribution, not habitation.

In the absence of well-preserved macrofloral evidence from sheltered sites, subsistence reconstructions for the Pueblo I and II periods have relied especially on the recovery of materials by flotation. This technique was introduced relatively recently (1975 in the lease area) to archaeological investigations in the Kayenta area, but it has already greatly enriched our understanding of Pueblo I and II subsistence. Investigations by BMAP in the lease area (Ford 1984) and by Pinon Project personnel on central Black Mesa (Gleichman 1982b) found corn (*Zea mays*) to be the plant most commonly recovered in flotation samples from Pueblo I and II sites. In large part, corn's ubiquity was attributable to charred cob fragments, which apparently were used as kindling to start fires. Corn also was identified in flotation samples taken from sites on the Coconino Plateau dating to the Pueblo II period and the Pueblo II/III transition (L. Huckell 1992) but not nearly so frequently as in the central and northern Black Mesa samples. Domesticated plant remains were rare at AZ I:1:17 (ASM), another Coconino Plateau site dating between A.D. 1049 and 1064 (figure 5.1; Sullivan 1986a).

Palynological analyses confirm that the Pueblo I and II Kayenta peoples were eating a mixed diet that included both cultigens and a variety of wild plants (Gasser 1982; Murry 1983; Scott 1982). Pollen washes taken from groundstone found in undisturbed contexts on sites of the lease area recovered maize pollen as well as pollen from a variety of wild plants (Murry 1983). Pollen from sites ranging from the Basketmaker III through Pueblo III on central Black Mesa do not suggest subsistence di-

versification (Scott 1982:415–416); the pollen content of the samples remained remarkably constant over time. Corn was the only cultigen represented in the pollen record, even though macrobotanical evidence of squash was found at two sites. Noncultivated food plants included sagebrush, Compositae (including sunflower), Cheno-ams, beeweed, crucifers or mustards, hackberry, wild tomato/potato, buckwheat, grasses, prickly pear and cholla cactus, *Ephedra*, cattail, purselane, yucca, and members of the parsley or carrot family (Scott 1982:416). No pollen from cultigens was recovered from two Pueblo II sites near Lee Canyon, on the Coconino Plateau (Bozarth 1992). Cheno-ams, agave, *Ephedra*, and possibly sunflower were recovered (Bozarth 1992:144).

Attempts by BMAP researchers to identify actual field locations that might have been used by prehistoric peoples were equivocal; they recovered no maize pollen, but increases in nonarboreal pollen might have been caused in part by human disturbance, including clearing agricultural fields (Hevly 1988:112, 113; Murry 1983). However, on the Coconino Plateau, phytolyth samples from AZ I:1:15 (ASM), a Pueblo II site, demonstrated that maize was cultivated in a probable field area with water-control features (Bozarth 1992:144). Interestingly, there was no evidence of maize in the pollen samples from that same field; the pollen indicates that Cheno-ams and agave were grown, perhaps even cultivated, in the field (Bozarth 1992:144).

The combined data underscore the unpredictability of the environment and the importance of a variety of cultivated and wild resources for subsistence. Cathy Lebo (1991), however, has pointed out that archaeologists have failed to answer two basic questions about agriculture in an unpredictable environment. First, how unpredictable was unpredictable? Second, what impact would this unpredictability have on annual harvests? She developed a computer simulation that combined information on ethnographic Hopi farming practices with dendroclimatological data to retrodict annual corn harvests on northern Black Mesa between A.D. 700 and 1300.

The Hopi data suggest that farmers aim to maintain a one-year reserve of corn in storage. They do so by cultivating twice the amount of land needed to meet their minimum annual dietary requirements (Lebo 1991:45–46). They cultivate about two acres per person per year (M. Bradfield 1971:21), anticipating a "normal" yield of about ten bushels per acre per year (Lebo 1991:table 2.1). Lebo (1991:239) found that simulated prehistoric crop yields averaged 50 percent of "normal" harvests and that the minimum dietary requirement of about 2000 kCal per person per day was met about three years out of four (Lebo 1991:242). Combining harvest and storage information, she found that the maize supply was at a critical level for 60 of the 375 years between A.D. 800 and 1150—18 times during the ninth century, 15 times during the tenth century, 12 times during the eleventh century, and 15 times between A.D. 1100 and 1175. Stored corn had to be used to supplement the current year's harvest 44 percent of the time, and the amount of stored corn ranged from none to three years' supply. Corn stores were depleted only 22 percent of the time. Lebo (1991:242) concluded that "production and storage strategies tempered the hostile environment and sustained the maize-based diet. A single pueblo could withstand significant recurring crop losses." Lebo's point, and an important one, was that despite the much-vaunted unpredictability and hostility of the prehistoric southwestern environment for agriculture, the prehistoric peoples could have anticipated and planned for some of the environment's effects on food availability.

Two lines of architectural evidence suggest change in the importance of agriculture over time to the Pueblo I and II occupants of the Kayenta region; both are discussed in detail later. First, mealing rooms (pit structures or jacales dedicated to plant-food milling) make their appearance in the Kayenta region during the Pueblo II period. The rooms were typically furnished with three to five mealing bins (metates enclosed by upright sandstone slabs), a hearth, and a storage feature. Although they are found most commonly on larger sites, their only consistent structural association is with kivas. Second, in the lease area, storage volume increased by a factor of five between the Pueblo I and II periods (Gilman 1983; Powell 1987). These two patterns suggest an increase in the importance of the storable plant food component of the diet (presumably maize) and changes in how this food was processed and redistributed.

Human osteological data from the lease area (Martin et al. 1991) provide some additional clues to the importance of corn in the diet of the Pueblo I and II peoples. Porotic hyperostosis, infectious lesions, enamel hypoplasias, and dental caries are common during the Pueblo I and II periods, suggesting chronic low-level nutritional stress. Trace element and stable isotope analyses suggest a diet of mixed plant food, with C4 plants (maize and amaranth) contributing up to 80 percent of the caloric intake. CAM plants (prickly pear, agave, and yucca) were also a major component of the diet, with meat making a comparatively small contribution, especially after Basketmaker II times.

Gathering

One finding coincident with the initiation of flotation techniques in the lease area was that nondomesticated plants were common on prehistoric Puebloan sites dating to all periods. No one questions that wild plants contributed substantially to the diet; however (like the quantification of the "importance" of agriculture), there is considerable debate about how "substantial" their contribution actually was and whether their collection was a primary activity or whether it was ancillary to field tending.

In the agriculture camp, Ford (1984:129) points out that the natural biomass of the Upper Sonoran lifezone is low; its gross primary productivity less than one-third that of the eastern woodlands. The introduction of cornfield agriculture improved this situation only slightly (from 2500 kCal/m²/year to 3000 kCal/m²/year), but cornfield agriculture, "even if it was not high-yielding, was predictable in its location, yield and caloric contribution" (Ford 1984:130). Furthermore, the fields themselves became "anthropogenic ecosystems" (Ford 1984:129). The pioneer annuals attracted to the disturbed ground included Portulaca, Cheno-ams, Indian rice grass, sunflower, Eriogonum, legumes, and wolfberry. They formed dense, harvestable patches that were predictable in location and harvest time. Small animals, especially rodents, were a part of these anthropogenic ecosystems as well and could have been harvested in a "garden hunting" strategy (Semé 1984). Thus, although contributing to subsistence, wild plants were secondary to (and dependent on) cornfield agriculture. Ford (1984:131, 135) even questions the contribution of pinyon harvest, noting the paucity of pinyon-nut shells from sites in the lease area and the unpredictability of the harvest.

Alternatively, Robert Gasser (1982) proposed that subsistence intensification may have taken the form of diversification of the resource base rather than increased reliance on a single staple. In support of his argument, he notes that the number of different plant resources exploited by prehistoric Puebloans increased over time and that this apparent diversification occurred in the absence of evidence for intensification of corn agriculture. An important methodological issue, however, clouds Gasser's interpretations. All other things being equal, diversity (or richness, as it is also termed) tends to increase as sample size increases (Leonard 1986). For example, if two samples of macrobotanical remains were drawn from the same site, and if one were larger than the other, the larger sample would likely be more diverse (richer) than the smaller sample, even though they came from the same population of macrobotanical remains. Along this line, Powell (1983:45) noted that the frequency of occurrence of both cultigens and wild plants in flotation samples increased in the lease area between the Pueblo I and II periods (when site size was increasing as well). Thus, the apparent macrofloral diversification that takes place over time may result from the tendency for sites and assemblages from later periods to be larger (and thus more diverse) than those from earlier times. However, unanswered in this methodological debate is the cause of the underlying pattern. Why are later sites and assemblages larger than earlier ones? Undoubtedly, increased site sizes and larger number of artifacts left behind by their prehistoric occupants are important clues to how their lifeways were changing.

Luckily for archaeologists (but unfortunate for the original inhabitants), there is the occasional site that offers a clear glimpse into the past. AZ I:1:17 (ASM), a Pueblo II homestead on the Coconino Plateau, was destroyed by an apparent forest fire in A.D. 1064, before its occupants could remove their belongings. Corn remains were rare, and the catastrophic assemblage was interpreted as a structure devoted to pinyon-nut processing and storage. The evidence prompted Sullivan (1986a:323, 1987) to characterize the Kayenta Anasazi of the region as foragers who were not heavily dependent on horticulture, although his is a minority opinion.

In the Hopi Buttes on the southern periphery of the Kayenta region, recent preliminary analyses suggest little evidence of agriculture before the Pueblo III period (Eck 1994:379). No remains from cultigens were found at Sites 442-36 and 442-130, dating to the Basketmaker III/Pueblo I transition, although beeweed, cholla, *Ephedra*, and Cheno-ams were present. Some corn remains were recovered from Sites 442-25 and 442-136, dating to the Pueblo II period, but they were only one of eight taxa present (Gish et al. 1993).

Hunting

The Pueblo I and II periods mark significant change in game procurement throughout the Kayenta region. The contribution of wild game, especially large-bodied animals, to the diet decreased for a number of reasons: large-game availability may have declined due to human alteration of the landscape; these same alterations may have improved habitat for small animals; and the increasing importance of farming may have caused scheduling conflicts, making logistical hunting forays difficult.

Generalizations about prehistoric hunting on northern Black Mesa echo these themes (Catlin 1986; Douglas 1972; Leonard 1986; Powell 1983; Semé 1984). Douglas' analysis of 2,188 unworked bones from fifteen site components excavated during the 1969 and 1970 field seasons was the methodological and interpretive springboard for all subsequent studies. Douglas (1972) found changes in the relative proportions of artiodactyls and rodents over time (figure 5.6). Before A.D. 1050, artiodactyls were especially characteristic of faunal inventories but declined in importance over time, being replaced by rodents. By A.D. 1100, artiodactyls were comparatively rare in the faunal inventories, which were dominated by lagomorphs and rodents. (Methodological problems with Douglas' sample and subsequent interpretations are discussed below.)

Douglas (1972:237) proposed that the shifting proportional representation of these taxa might have been caused by hunting pressure and increased density in the human population. As a result, it would have become more time-consuming and costly to

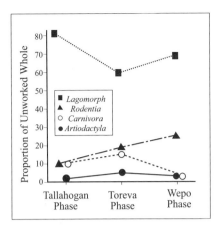

Figure 5.6 Percentage of unworked bones, by taxa, from archaeological sites excavated between 1968 and 1970.

hunt scarce, large-bodied mammals. "Therefore, it would seem to follow that animals, such as rabbits, that could be more readily obtained, would then assume more importance in the diet" (Douglas 1972:237), a conclusion that anticipates garden-hunting models (Semé 1984).

Subsequent BMAP faunal analysts (Eckles 1984; Leonard 1989; Semé 1984) worked with the accumulating faunal assemblages, attempting in various ways to control for the problems of sample representativeness and recovery biases. Despite the number of analysts and analyses, it is very easy to characterize their conclusions: larger sites have larger and more diverse faunal assemblages than do smaller sites.

Leonard (1989) addressed most of the interpretive difficulties inherent in the preceding studies. Leonard demonstrated convincingly that most of the patterns observed by prior researchers are a function of the statistical relationship between assemblage size and assemblage diversity. Leonard argued that before a meaningful diachronic assessment of faunal procurement patterns could be made, the effects of variable sample size on assemblage diversity had to be controlled. He found that surprisingly few assemblages deviated significantly from predicted size/diversity trends. Throughout time, assemblages ranged from very simple to very diverse; the very simple assemblages were also small, while the very complex assemblages were quite large. Thus, faunal assemblages were highly variable at any given time, but there was no observable variation in this overall pattern of variation over time.

Leonard also found that there was no apparent increase in the economic importance of rodents and lagomorphs at the expense of artiodactyls. Apparently, the trend observed by Douglas (1972) was attributable to his sample of sites and the techniques used to excavate them. Douglas analyzed more assemblages (eleven of fifteen) from large late sites, and the deposits were not screened. Thus, the excavated site samples were heavily weighted toward large elements from larger-bodied animals (e.g., artiodactyls). When viewed as a sampling problem, then, there was a greater likelihood for rare taxa (e.g., small elements from small-bodied animals) to occur in the assemblages from the late sites, simply because there were more late sites, and these sites were larger. Thus, earlier assemblages would be weighted toward large elements (artiodactyls), while later assemblages would have both large and small (lagomorphs and rodents) elements.

In conclusion, then, faunal procurement patterns can best be characterized as highly variable at any one point in time and throughout time. There is some suggestion that the fauna predicted by a garden-hunting model occur more frequently on large sites that postdate A.D. 1050 (Semé 1984). However, to focus too strongly on this group of sites ignores the well-demonstrated pattern of noncategorical, continuous variation in faunal assemblages throughout time.

Animal Domestication

There is little evidence of animal domestication in the Kayenta region during the Pueblo I and II periods. The paucity of remains may be due to the unsheltered and ephemeral character of most of the excavated

Kayenta sites dating to this period. The BMAP excavations recovered occasional turkey and dog remains (Leonard 1989:appendix A), typically as isolated bones; however, one small adult female turkey was buried with some eggshells beside her in the fill of a pit structure at AZ D:7:23 (Southern Illinois University [SIU]), a sprawling Pueblo I pit-structure and jacal site located near the confluence of Yazzie Wash and Yellow Water Canyon (J. Anderson 1978:69, 70).

Additional evidence of turkeys is found at Red Turkey Shelter (AZ D:8:1206 [SIU]), a small, unexcavated, stratified shelter located at the headwaters of Moenkopi Wash on northern Black Mesa. The site is named for a pictograph of a turkey shown in rear-end view (Hays 1984). The turkey's shape is masklike and "could . . . represent some sort of head-dress, but the feet are quite prominent and the shape of the tail quite characteristic of a turkey" (Hays 1984:19). In total, the existing evidence for domesticated animals during the Pueblo I and II periods suggests that they contributed little to Puebloan diet during this period.

Exchange[2] and Subsistence

Several studies have postulated the importance of commodities exchange to Pueblo I and II subsistence. A frequently cited theoretical treatise (Braun and Plog 1982), based in part on BMAP data, contends that exchange of both material items and information may have ameliorated the effects of uneven and unpredictable distributions of resources and of population/resource imbalances. Many researchers embraced this model, attempting to quantify the critical variables in the equation: environmental stress, population growth, social integration, and quantities of "exotic" commodities, especially pottery and chipped stone (Fernstrom 1984; Green 1985; Hegmon 1986, 1995; S. Plog 1986a).

In general these studies show that numbers of exotic items increased

on sites in the lease area over time. Basketmaker II sites in the lease area have virtually no nonlocal items in their assemblages. Pueblo I sites have more exotic items, and these objects come from comparatively distant sources (e.g., San Juan Red Wares and certain chipped-stone raw materials). Pueblo II sites have far more exotic items, but these items derive from sources closer to northern Black Mesa (e.g., chipped-stone tools from sources in the Kayenta Valley and Tsegi Orange Ware pottery).

These patterns have been interpreted to suggest that Puebloan peoples from northern Black Mesa maintained close economic and social ties with people living at some distance from them. Over time these relationships became more intense (as measured by the quantities of exchanged goods) but spatially constrained (as measured by the distance over which the exchanged goods were transported). The increased social and economic intensification combined with the decreasing size of the networks is thought to be the product of competition for land and other resources caused by growing population. Presumably, food was exchanged for the pottery and chipped stone, while information and goodwill were "piggy-backed" commodities that were banked until needed.

Summary

The subsistence data indicate that the Pueblo I and II occupants of the Kayenta region relied on numerous resources, all linked with cornfield agriculture and anthropogenic ecosystems. The qualitative floral and faunal records simultaneously point to the ubiquity of corn while underscoring the importance of a variety of resources. However, the occupants of some outlying areas, notably the Coconino Plateau, continued to rely heavily on noncultivated resources. Change over time in Kayenta subsistence practices is suggested by the artifact and architectural patterns. Pottery and chipped stone point to an economic interdependence that spanned great distances. The distribution of these commodities, however, suggests that the exchange networks grew smaller and intensified over time. Increases in storage volume suggest changes in food redistribution and a growing concern with the predictability of harvests and the available food supply, concerns supported by Lebo's (1991) simulation of northern Black Mesa corn harvests between A.D. 700 and 1300. The appearance of mealing rooms during the Pueblo II period suggests changes in milling technology, in the importance of those foods, and in the social units responsible for food processing and redistribution.

Stylistic Distributions

Pottery

Ceramic assemblages at Pueblo I and Pueblo II sites in the Kayenta region are dominated by Tusayan White Ware and Tusayan Gray Ware. The whitewares, for the most part, incorporate much stylistic variation while changing gradually and predictably over time, starting with the fine-line designs of Kana-a Black-on-white and evolving through the subsequent Black Mesa, Sosi, and Flagstaff styles. Over the decades analysts have remarked on these traits, noting the suitability of the Tusayan White Wares for studies focusing on chronometry and social organization (e.g., Beals et al. 1945; Hegmon 1986, 1995; S. Plog 1980a).

One type in the series, Dogoszhi Black-on-white, departs from the gradualism of the other types; it is characterized by wide-line designs that are filled in with hatching. Dogoszhi style is all the more interesting because local variants were produced throughout the northern Southwest and are seen by some as a hallmark of the Chacoan phenomenon and a medium by which stylistic information was disseminated (S. Plog 1990). For the other Pueblo I and II Tusayan White Ware types, however, the sense of gradual transition is very pronounced, and distinguishing between temporally adjacent types is a challenge. The transition from Kana-a to Black Mesa Black-on-white has been so problematical for some ceramic analysts that an attempt was made to resolve the issue by creating a transitional type, Wepo Black-on-white, that shared attributes of both Kana-a and Black Mesa Black-on-white (Gumerman et al. 1972:247–248).

Regional variation within the same type further compounds this issue. Ambler (1992) has studied Black Mesa Black-on-white pottery from throughout the Kayenta region and suggests that there are subregional styles that coincide with variations in paste and temper. Based on this evidence, he argues for two, possibly three, production zones for Black Mesa Black-on-white.

Pueblo I and II pottery assemblages are dominated by the Tusayan Gray Wares. The crudely painted designs on the Basketmaker III type Lino Black-on-gray gave way to unpainted types that were undecorated or decorated by manipulating the clay while it was still plastic. Typical of the early Pueblo I period are Lino Gray and Kana-a Gray, plain and neckbanded types that most often take the form of globular jars. Because neck treatment (plain vs. neck-banded) distinguishes these two types, plain grayware sherds that lack diagnostic attributes are lumped into a catch-all category, Lino Tradition. Until about A.D. 1025, ceramic assemblages were dominated by these two types; typically, 80 percent or more of a given site's ceramic inventory is comprised of Lino Gray, Kana-a Gray, or Lino Tradition, with the other 20 percent made up of Tusayan White Ware, San Juan Red Ware, or Tsegi Orange Ware.

Between A.D. 1025 and 1050 in the lease area there was a dramatic and sudden change in the composition of grayware ceramic inventories. Plain-bodied graywares were replaced almost completely by grayware pottery with overall corrugations, most commonly Tusayan Corrugated. Archaeologists have noted this pattern, making use of the abruptness of the transition and the ease of its identification as a temporal marker (S. Plog and Hantman 1986:92–95; Reed 1981). They have speculated about causes underlying the shift, focusing particularly on technological factors and the thermal and mechanical shock-resistance qualities of plain vs. corrugated surface treatments. Much remains to be done, however, on this intriguing problem.

Rock Images

Rock images are interpretively problematical for archaeologists. They are often located in isolated settings, making them difficult to date, difficult to associate with habitation sites, and difficult to interpret using cultural-historical and processual archaeological theoretical paradigms. For these reasons, many archaeologists have tended to ignore rock images.

The Pueblo I and II periods, characterized as they are by small sites in open settings, are particularly difficult to associate with rock images; thus, there are very few reports of Pueblo I and II rock images in the Kayenta region. Rock images, including both pictographs and petroglyphs, are found on northern Black Mesa, but beyond initial recording and descriptions, they have received little attention. Frequently executed motifs include handprints, anthropomorphs, animals (including snakes, mountain sheep, and lizard men), and geometric and abstract forms (Hays 1984). If, as has been suggested (Hays 1992), making rock images is predominately a male activity, and if they are associated with ritual and ceremonies, they may represent boundary markers, records of clan migrations, or hunting ritual. Recorders presume that the rock images date to the periods of occupation on northern Black Mesa (Basketmaker II, Pueblo I, and Pueblo II), and the observed motifs match those described for other regions of the plateau Southwest for these time periods (Cole 1990; Schaafsma 1980).

Pueblo I and Pueblo II architecture in the Kayenta region is comparatively unremarkable. The great kivas of the preceding Basketmaker III period disappeared (see Nichols, Chapter 4, this volume), and, for the most part, the spectacular cliff dwellings and large plaza-oriented pueblos that characterize the Tsegi phase do not appear in the architectural inventory (see Dean, Chapter 6, this volume).

There are, however, exceptions to this generalization. Standing Fall House, a fifty-five-room cliff site on northern Black Mesa, was used primarily for storage during Pueblo I times, extending into early Pueblo II times, as discussed below (figure 5.7; Klesert 1982; Klesert and Cowan 1978). Hand House (J. Anderson 1979), a seventeen-room cliff dwelling located at the headwaters of Moenkopi Wash on northern Black Mesa, was a habitation site used during Pueblo II times (figure 5.8). Both sites have been mapped and surface finds have been collected; neither has been systematically excavated. Finally, recent interest in the Chacoan phenomenon and in the distribution of pueblos with Chacoan characteristics has resulted in the discovery of likely Chacoan outliers in the southern and eastern portions of the Kayenta range (discussed below) (Gilpin 1987, 1989).

The hallmarks of Kayenta Pueblo I and, particularly, Pueblo II architecture are the unit pueblo and its widespread distribution (which are discussed in detail below). The Pueblo II unit pueblo in the Kayenta region is characterized by a masonry storage roomblock, with habitation rooms (often of jacal construction) abutting either end, a kiva, and a trash midden—all oriented on a northwest to southeast axis. Mealing-pit structures were added to the assemblage sometime during the latter half of the Pueblo II period and were often located northeast of the kiva, between it and the eastern jacal. It is important to note, however, that the

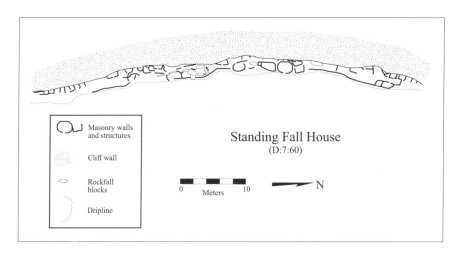

Figure 5.7 Plan map of Standing Fall House, a Pueblo I–II sheltered site on northern Black Mesa (after Klesert and Cowan 1978:figure 14).

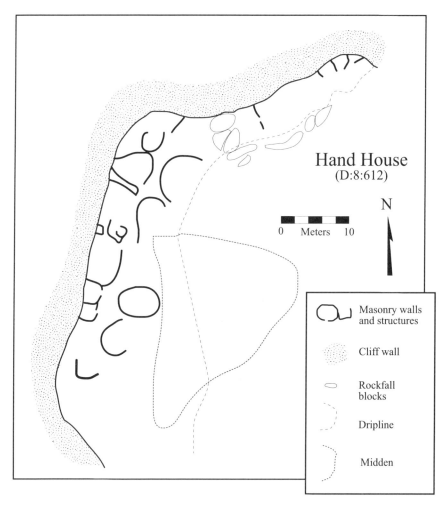

Figure 5.8 Plan map of Hand House, a Pueblo II sheltered site on northern Black Mesa (after J. Anderson 1979:figure 23).

unit pueblo's "cookie cutter" image is overstated; there is notable variation in both Pueblo I and Pueblo II site configuration. Furthermore, the unit pueblo's ubiquity is more apparent in the literature than on the ground. Many areas within the Kayenta region do not have unit pueblos (e.g., the Coconino Plateau [Sullivan 1986a; Whittlesey 1992]) and central Black Mesa [Linford 1982]), and even in those areas with unit pueblos, they are not the only or the major site type (e.g., the lease area and the Navajo Mountain area [Fairley 1989a]).

The shift from Basketmaker III habitation pit structures to below-ground ceremonial chambers (labeled kivas by archaeologists) follows trends outlined elsewhere (Lekson 1988; Wilshusen 1989). Some pit structures lose their habitation qualities, assuming the characteristics that distinguish kivas still in use today by the Hopis and other pueblos. In the Kayenta region this transition is somewhat obscured because habitation pit structures remain an important part of the structural repertoire until the thirteenth century abandonment of much of the Kayenta region (see Dean, Chapter 6, this volume).

Given the longstanding controversy about what attributes distinguish a kiva and when these appear, perhaps the most useful guidelines are those offered by Watson Smith (1952). Smith's definition goes a long way towards explaining why archaeologists cannot agree on criteria that define kivas, yet they share remarkable consensus on what to call a kiva (Lekson 1988):

> [A] kiva was regarded as such because it differed in some way from the other rooms of its unit, or stood apart from them positionally; and not primarily because it possessed or lacked any particular internal feature or complex of features. For example, . . . one room was perhaps circular while all the others were rectangular; it was subterranean while the others

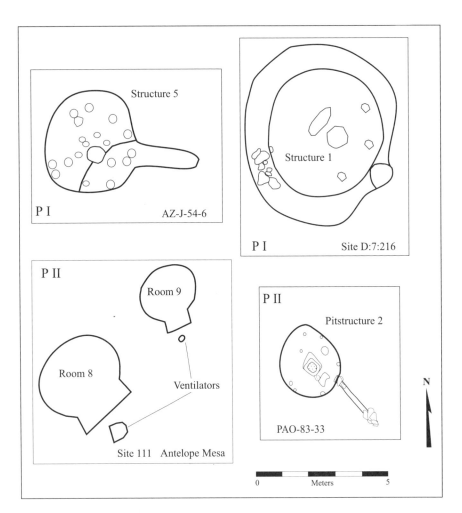

Figure 5.9 Pueblo I and Pueblo II "kivas" from the Kayenta region (after Andrews et al. 1980:figure 9; Fehr 1982:figure 40; Sebastian 1985:figure 4.9; Gilpin 1989:figure 2).

were built upon the surface; it was relatively larger than most of the others; it stood apart from the others, perhaps to the south or southeast; although obviously contemporary, it possessed the only ventilator or the only bench or recess in the unit. Thus it was set apart; to be a kiva it did not have to be square or round, subterranean or surficial, to be equipped with any particular kind of roof, to possess a ventilator or a bench or even a sipapu. It merely had to be different. [Smith 1952:162]

In the Kayenta region some pit structures assume "different" qualities during Basketmaker III times. The so-called Basketmaker III great

kivas (described by Nichols, Chapter 4, this volume) are distinguishable from other pit structures on the sites by virtue of their size: they are large. By the early Pueblo I period such exceptionally large structures cease to be built; however, some pit structures continue to be distinctive by virtue of their larger sizes (Andrews et al. 1980) and by their position (they are placed between the storage features and habitation structures and the trash midden) (figure 5.9; Andrews et al. 1980; Green et al. 1985). Generally these structures have ventilators, a feature often absent on habitation pit structures, and hearths. They may have benches or partial benches, or benches may be absent. Many of these structures have multitudinous small floor features, but it is difficult to assign functions to these features with any certainty (Wilshusen 1989). During Pueblo I times most of these structures have earthen walls and plastered floors.

Large size and location continue to distinguish kivas in the Kayenta area during the Pueblo II period (figure 5.9). Most of the kivas are positioned as described above for the Pueblo I period; however, great kivas were located away from the roomblocks at the Chacoan-style great houses located on southern Black Mesa. Kivas continue to be subterranean, for the most part, although circular structures—presumably kivas—in the Chacoan-style great houses are embedded in the roomblocks (Gilpin 1987, 1989), maintaining a subterranean appearance, although technically not underground.

Kayenta kivas became more predictable in form and content during the Pueblo II period. Many of the structures were masonry lined, and full encircling benches were regular features. Some of the benches have recessed features (Hantman 1980:246, plate 14). The ventilator, slab or masonry deflector, and hearth complex were quite common, often situated in a recess that gave the overall form of the kiva a keyhole shape (Klesert 1977b; Legard 1982a). Kiva floors continue to abound with holes and recessed features, some of which have been labeled vaults, footdrums, loom anchors, or ladder supports. The plastered masonry walls at Kiva A at AZ J-43-23, a site dating to the Pueblo II–III transition on central Black Mesa, were painted with red-on-white geometric designs (Legard 1982a:226, plate 76). Artifacts indicating both male (e.g., lithic debitage [Legard 1982a:234]) and female (e.g., grinding implements and pottery manufacturing tools [Klesert 1977b; Legard 1982a:234]) have been found in Pueblo II kivas in the Kayenta region.

The entrybox complex first appears during Pueblo II times but is more characteristic of the Pueblo III period (see Dean, Chapter 6, this volume). It consists of masonry or

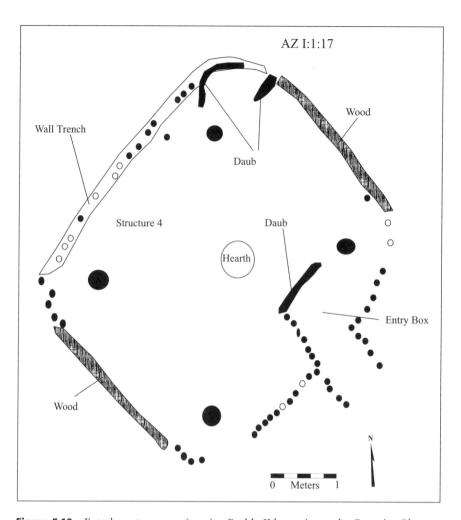

Figure 5.10 Entrybox at AZ I:1:17 (ASM), a Pueblo II homesite on the Coconino Plateau (after Sullivan 1986a:figure 429).

slab wingwalls that connect one or both doorjambs to a deflector situated between the door and hearth and is reminiscent of the Basketmaker III pit-structure wingwalls (Nichols, Chapter 4, this volume). Sullivan (1986a:321) notes an entrybox at Structure 4 (a long-walled jacal) at AZ I:1:17 (ASM), a small Pueblo II Kayenta homesite on the Coconino Plateau (figure 5.10). Entryboxes are not reported from the Pinon Project excavations (Linford 1982) nor from the lease area.

Settlement

The widespread distribution of small sites throughout the Kayenta region distinguishes the period A.D. 800–1150. This pattern marks both a continuity and a departure from previous

and subsequent settlement behavior. The departure: Basketmaker III and Pueblo III settlements are often large and situated unevenly over the landscape (although part of their apparent distribution may be due to uneven survey coverage). In contrast, Pueblo I and II settlements are typically small and so widely distributed that the term for their distribution is the Pueblo II dispersion (figure 5.1). Kayenta settlers reach their furthest extent during the Pueblo II period, when there are comparatively short-lived colonizing efforts as far from the Kayenta heartland as the Grand Canyon (Euler and Chandler 1978), the Coconino Plateau (Sullivan 1986a; Whittlesey 1992), the Arizona Strip (Altschul and Fairley 1989), and the Virgin area (Aikens 1966; Altschul and Fairley 1989; Lyneis 1992) (depending on how one deals with Kayenta-Virgin relationships).

For the most part, the Pueblo I and II occupants of the Kayenta region did not participate in the Chaco phenomenon that dominated the archaeology of the San Juan Basin to the east (Vivian 1990). Except for the southern portion of Black Mesa (Gilpin 1987, 1989), Chacoan outliers are absent from the Kayenta region, an absence that coupled with the simultaneous dispersion of Kayenta settlements to the west, prompts some interesting speculation, as discussed below.

Accompanying the changes in settlement distribution are continuities, especially in community pattern. The front-oriented pueblo—with a trash midden, centrally located kiva, habitation rooms, and specialized storage features, typically oriented on a southwest to northeast axis—begins its evolution during Basketmaker III times. This site configuration continues throughout the Pueblo I period, eventually resulting in the "unit pueblo," or "cookie cutter" site, that is so characteristic of the Pueblo II period (see figure 5.22). Yet despite their apparent popularity, unit pueblos account for only about 25 percent of all sites in the lease area (where they are common) (S. Plog 1986b:table 15), and they are notably absent from parts of the Kayenta region (including central Black Mesa [Legard 1982a] and the Coconino Plateau [Sullivan 1986; Whittlesey 1992]).

The small and widely distributed sites have been characterized as the product of "mobile" peoples, and mobility is a common theme in analyses of Pueblo I and II settlements. The term mobile, however, is used differently by different archaeologists. Some suggest that the Pueblo I and II peoples moved seasonally to take advantage of the highly variable landscape (Euler and Chandler 1978; Gilman 1983, 1987; Jennings 1966; Powell 1983; Schwartz et al. 1981). Others suggest that mobility was "generational," that the small sites were abodes to extended families, and that as the older generation

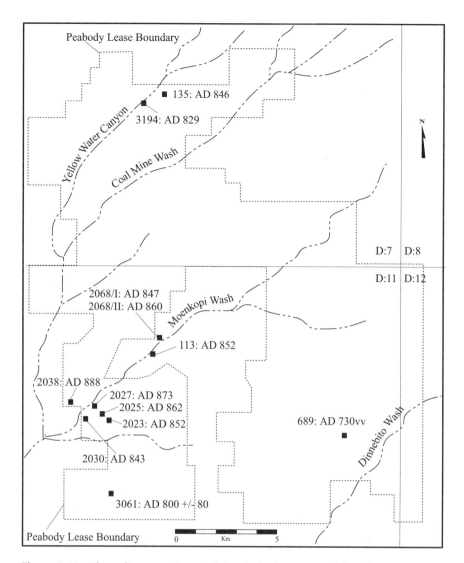

Figure 5.11 The earliest ceramic-period sites in the lease area and their dates.

died, the next moved to establish new homes (Dechambre 1983; Phillips 1972). Generational mobility has been linked functionally with the use-lives of pit structures and jacales, which are thought to be fifteen to twenty years, about the span of one human generation (Hantman 1983).

The Recolonization of Northern Black Mesa

The intensely studied lease area provides a detailed example of the dispersion and colonization that characterize the Pueblo I and II periods in the Kayenta region. The following description of the recolonization of the lease area in the first half of the ninth century is but one example of comparable

population movements throughout the Kayenta area, movements that eventually led to the settlement distributions that archaeologists call the Pueblo II dispersion (figure 5.11).

Three ephemeral sites, all dating to the early ninth century, were built by the first of the colonizers. The earliest securely dated ceramic-period site within the leasehold is located on the floodplain of Yellow Water Canyon. AZ D:7:3194 (Mauldin and Miles 1983:152–160) consists of a pit structure, two posthole concentrations, and fifteen extramural features, of which eight are hearths (figure 5.12). The excavators conjectured that one of the posthole concentrations might have been the remnants of a jacal. Beams from the pit structure produced one cutting

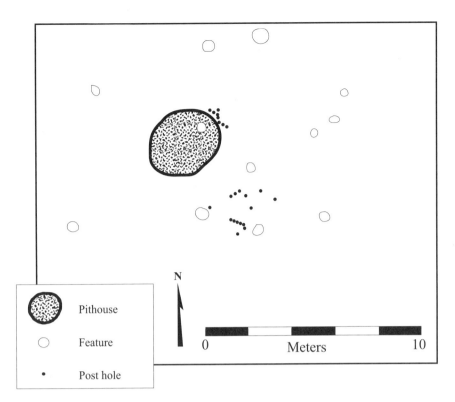

Figure 5.12   Plan map of AZ D:7:3194 (after Mauldin and Miles 1983:figure 31).

date of A.D. 829. This evidence combined with the absence of intramural features, the numerous extramural hearths, and the absence of trash deposits persuaded the excavators that the site had been occupied seasonally, probably during the summer (Mauldin and Miles 1983:157).

Two other sites, each less confidently dated than D:7:3194, may also date to this period. AZ D:11:3061 (Michalik and Bostwick 1983:253–260) overlooks Yucca Flat Wash and consists of a pit structure with slab-lined walls (Structure 1) and a possible shallow pit structure (Structure 2). A hearth was centrally located within Structure 1, and charcoal from the structure was radiocarbon dated to A.D. 800 ± 80 (Beta-5633). Four extramural cists were situated in the vicinity of the structures, as were six possible features with indeterminate functions that were identified by organically stained soil.

AZ D:11:689 consists of one deep pit structure with no internal features and one jacal with a hearth (Leonard et al. 1985a). The site was constructed in the pinyon and juniper woodland

at the headwaters of White House Valley, a tributary to Red Peak Valley, which eventually drains into Moenkopi Wash. Tree-ring samples from the jacal yielded noncutting dates of A.D. 706 and 730; however, the pith dates (A.D. 645 and 663 respectively) compare favorably with those from other sites constructed during the early and mid-800s. (Pith dates from D:11:2023, which dates to A.D. 852, range from A.D. 688 to 804, and the pith date from the A.D. 829 sample from D:7:3194 is A.D. 688.)

Admittedly, the dates from D:11:3061 and D:11:689 lack the precision to assign them confidently to the early A.D. 800s. However, the sites are remarkably similar (to each other and to D:7:3194) in having pit structures and many extramural features and in lacking formalized trash deposits and human osteological remains. Apparently, their prehistoric inhabitants used the sites for too short a period to accumulate large quantities of trash, and none of their inhabitants were buried at the sites. The three sites lacked substantial storage facilities (suggesting short-term occupations),

but each had pit structures (suggesting, in contradiction to the other structural evidence, cold-weather occupation). Additionally, each of the sites had remains that might be interpreted as an ephemeral surface structure: the jacal at D:11:689, one of the posthole clusters at D:7:3194, and the shallow, featureless pit structure at D:11:3061.

If these three sites are contemporaneous, the ceramic-period re-occupation of northern Black Mesa appears to have been a tentative, seasonal exploitation of both floodplain and woodland resources. However, within a few years of the construction of D:7:3194, D:11:3061, and D:11:689, a far more substantial colonizing effort was taking place along Moenkopi Wash and Yellow Water Canyon.

Two Moenkopi Wash site clusters date between A.D. 840 and 888, and two sites on Yellow Water Canyon (AZ D:7:134 and D:7:135, figure 5.13) were constructed in the mid A.D. 840s (Layhe 1984; Layhe et al. 1976). The lower (and probably earlier) Moenkopi Wash cluster consists of four sites on the south bank of the wash and one site on the north side. The four southside sites, all located within 1 km of one another, were constructed between A.D. 840 and 873. AZ D:11:2030 (Green et al. 1985) is a multi-component or sequentially occupied site with three masonry/jacal room-blocks, each facing one or more pit structures (figure 5.14). Seven burials were excavated in the large, deep midden. Radiocarbon assays, which are somewhat contradictory, suggest an occupation as early as A.D. 630 ± 80 (Beta-10082); archaeomagnetic samples indicate a date for cultural activity before A.D. 700 to 725; and two tree-ring samples from one of the pit structures, probably derived from reused beams, dated to A.D. 813(r) and A.D. 814 (+r). However, collectively the tree-ring dates indicate a flurry of construction during the 840s through 870s.

AZ D:11:2023 (figure 5.15; Olszewski 1984) is situated approximately 500 m (1640 ft) upstream from D:11:2030.

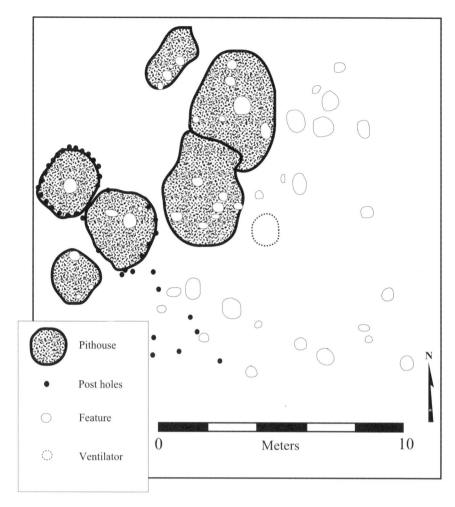

Figure 5.13 Plan map of AZ D:7:135 (after Layhe et al. 1976:figure 3).

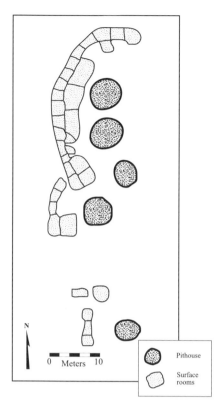

Figure 5.14 Plan map of AZ D:11:2030 (after Green et al. 1985:figure 3.13).

D:11:2023 had three contiguous semi-subterranean storage rooms that faced a large pit structure. A cluster of tree-ring dates firmly placed the pit structure's construction at A.D. 852. Another cluster of cutting dates indicates that the structure was still in use in A.D. 860. An adult male was buried in the pit structure, but no other burials were found at the site. Trash had accumulated to form a shallow midden, suggesting a fairly long occupation or numerous reoccupations of the site.

AZ D:11:2025 (figure 5.16; Stone 1984) was situated down slope from D:11:2023. Three contiguous, semi-subterranean storage rooms and two small masonry rooms (probably also used for storage) partially encircled a large pit structure. Two jacales, located northeast of the pit structure, and a shallow midden attested the like-lihood that two families resided at the site for a number of years. Osteo-logical remains from an adult female and a child and an isolated long bone fragment suggest an occupation of sufficient duration that three individu-als died at the site. Multiple tree-ring samples place the construction of the pit structure at A.D. 861 to 862. Outlier samples that date to A.D. 851 and 853 provide some basis for the supposition that the D:11:2025 inhabitants re-used wood from the then-abandoned D:11:2023.

AZ D:11:2027 (figure 5.17; Olszew-ski et al. 1984) was constructed on the first terrace above Moenkopi Wash in A.D. 873. Although no burials were found there, the structural configu-ration suggests a lengthy occupation by one or more families. A five-unit masonry roomblock was used for stor-ing foods; burned corn was found in two of the rooms. The jacal and the pit structure would have housed people comfortably during all weather condi-tions. The shallow midden (generally less than 10 cm deep) also attests the need for restrictions on trash-disposal patterns. Tree-ring samples from the pit structure indicate that the primary construction took place between A.D. 873 and 877.

The final site in the lower Moen-kopi cluster, AZ D:11:2038 (figure 5.18; Stone and Cunningham 1984:223–231), is situated high above the north bank of the wash. The ceramic-period com-ponent consists of two pit structures, one with slab-lined walls and no intra-mural features and one dug into sand with a centrally located hearth. Two features are situated west of the struc-tures; however, road damage hindered determination of their functions. Tree-ring samples from the second pit structure indicate a construction date of A.D. 888.

The upper Moenkopi cluster consists of two sites, although one of them has two components dated

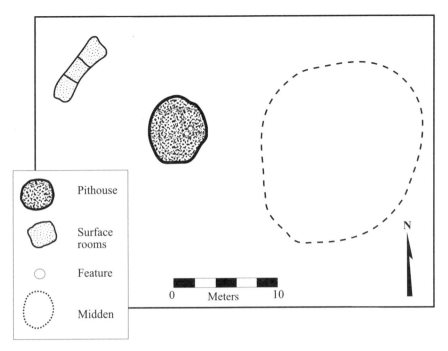

Figure 5.15 Plan map of AZ D:11:2023 (after Olszewski 1984:figure 3.19).

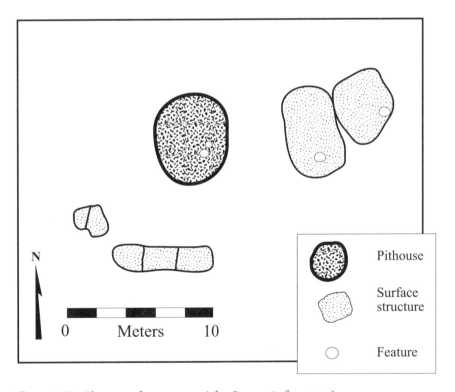

Figure 5.16 Plan map of AZ D:11:2025 (after Stone 1984:figure 3.22).

to the period of interest. D:11:2068 (figure 5.19; Sink et al. 1983) is a multi-component site, and two of the three firmly dated components date to the mid-800s. Component I consists of three deep pit structures, a shallow pit structure, and a masonry storage room. Although the midden was continuously distributed along the eastern edge of the site, it is likely that most of its northern portion was deposited during the occupation of Compo-

nent I. The only tree-ring date from Component I dates Structure 3 (an isolated pit structure at the southern edge of the site) to A.D. 847(+v). Although this is not a cutting date, it is probably close to the actual construction date for the pit structure. Two radiocarbon determinations, also from Structure 3, substantiate this temporal placement for Component I (A.D. 840 ± 60, Beta-5626, and A.D. 820 ± 60, Beta-5628).

Component II at D:11:2068 consists of a masonry-jacal roomblock used for storage, a jacal, two slab-lined storage cists, a deep centrally located pit structure, and a shallow pit structure. The entire component apparently burned in a single conflagration, preserving large quantities of corn that had been stored in the roomblock. A deep midden lay east and down slope of the structural portion of the site. One individual, a woman between 35 and 40 years old, was buried in the Component II midden along with five ceramic vessels (including a unique bird effigy jar, figure 5.20). Tree-ring samples date the construction of Component II to the A.D. 870s. The second upper Moenkopi site, D:11:113 (Gumerman et al. 1972:37–46), was exposed in 1970 during the construction of a water pipeline. Construction activities were halted to allow excavation of a single pit structure, which had been lined with juniper uprights and plastered with clay. Tree-ring samples date the pit structure to A.D. 852. The rest of the site, which had escaped prior notice because it was covered with a thick layer of alluvium, was not excavated.

Two final sites, D:7:134 and D:7:135 (figure 5.13; Layhe 1984:124–134; Layhe et al. 1976), date to this same period. They are located north of the two Moenkopi clusters on Yellow Water Canyon. D:7:134 is a large and complex site whose pottery dates to the Dinnebito phase. Surface evidence included two rubble mounds, a large depression, and an extensive artifact scatter, and excavation disclosed five pit structures (including one possible kiva), ten masonry rooms distributed among

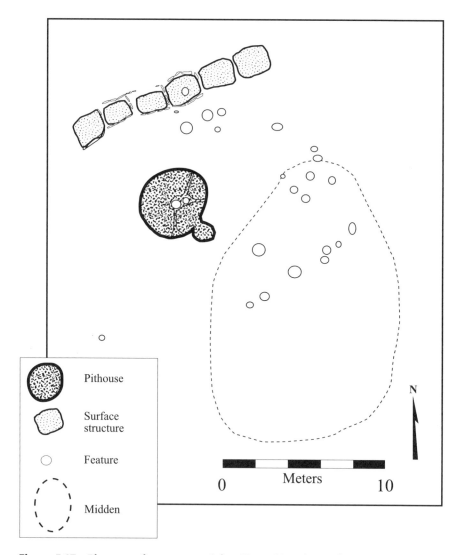

Figure 5.17 Plan map of AZ D:11:2027 (after Olszewski et al. 1984:figure 3.29).

three roomblocks, and three jacales. However, tree-ring dates, analysis of ceramic design, bonding-and-abutting patterns, and stratigraphy suggest multiple building episodes.

The thirty-five tree-ring dates from D:7:134 are all noncutting (Powell et al. 1980:438), and the dated samples range from A.D. 198 (vv) to A.D. 945 (++vv). Twenty-one samples fall between A.D. 804 (+vv) and A.D. 866 (vv). This distribution compares favorably with the noncutting dates from nearby D:7:135, with its one bark date of A.D. 846, suggesting that the sites may be contemporaneous. Analysis of ceramic designs (Klesert 1977a) supports this interpretation, and the combined evidence suggests that the four pit structures, a three-room

masonry roomblock, and one jacal were the earliest structures at the site (Klesert 1977a:20). Wood samples from the masonry rooms and the jacal are among the earliest at D:7:134, but these rooms were comparatively trash-free, suggesting that they were constructed early and were among the last structures abandoned at the site. The builders and occupants of these structures produce a thin scattering of trash that was distributed along the eastern edge of the site; later trash was dumped in abandoned rooms and to the south of the site (Klesert 1977a:24).

Four semisubterranean pit structures were excavated at D:7:135, and all had hearths. The excavators postulated about the existence of an additional two semisubterranean pit

structures, based on the presence of organic soil staining. Structure 1 had tree-ring dates that placed its construction at A.D. 846. One burial was recovered, but there were no trash deposits.

These twelve sites with their thirteen components provide one of the most detailed pictures of a colonizing event in the Kayenta area; one possible reconstruction follows. The earliest sites in the lease area (D:7:3194, D:11:689, and D:11:3061) were temporary camps built by families reconnoitering the area. The well-documented Basketmaker III occupation of Long House Valley (Dean et al. 1978), three Basketmaker III sites found along the western scarp of Black Mesa (Ward 1976), and Basketmaker III sites on Black Mesa south of the lease area (Hogan 1984; Linford 1982; Sebastian 1985) suggest that the occupants of these three northern Black Mesa sites maintained residential bases in the lowlands north, south, or west of the lease area. Macrobotanical remains suggest that the colonists were growing maize and gathering wild plants. The absence of storage facilities indicates that the people moved, with their produce, to another locale after the growing season.

The pit structures on all three sites contradict the growing-season conjecture, suggesting instead cold-weather occupations (their depths range from 0.56 m to 0.78 m, evidence of the builders' concern with thermal efficiency). However, the absence of storage facilities indicates that the colonizers did not winter on the mesa; there is no evidence that they stored enough food to see them through the long winter months. Perhaps the pit structures were used during the pinyon-nut harvest; small amounts of carbonized pinyon-nut shells were found at D:7:3194 (Ford et al. 1983:474). But no pinyon nuts or shell fragments were found at the other two sites (Ford et al. 1983:474; Ford et al. 1985:487). Pinyon nuts certainly would have been attractive to the lowland dwellers, and the fall months can be cold enough to warrant

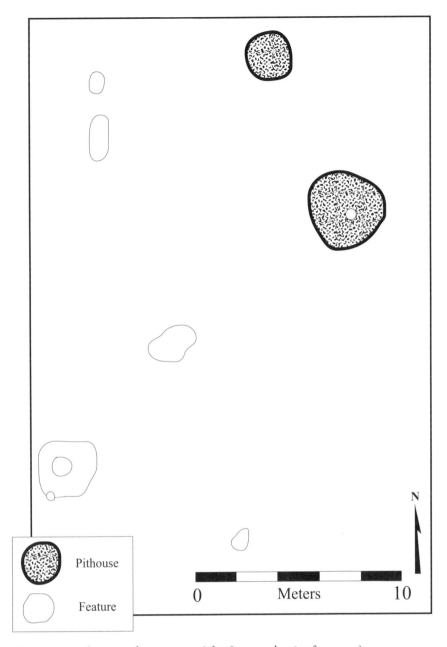

Pithouse

Feature

0   Meters   10

N

Figure 5.18 Plan map of AZ D:11:2038 (after Stone et al. 1984a:figure 3.32).

D:7:134 and D:7:135 and the slightly later sites D:11:2025, D:11:2027, and D:11:2068/Component II) have all the attributes necessary for year-round occupation (Gilman 1983; Powell 1983), and most archaeologists accept that a permanent, year-round occupation of northern Black Mesa was in effect by the mid to late A.D. 800s (S. Plog 1986c).

Based on these patterns and interpretations, the reoccupation of the lease area was a tentative seasonal reconnaissance by potential immigrants to verify the viability of the area for farming and the collection of wild food. Once this viability was established, more people moved into the area, and more labor and capital were expended on the sites. The annual occupation span was extended to include the period of the pinyon harvest, and within thirty years, sites with the full complement of structures and features for year-round habitation were being constructed. Surface and subsurface dwellings would have housed people comfortably during all weather conditions, and storage rooms and cists would have protected perishable foods from spoilage. Thus, we have a picture of growing complexity and refined adaptations to local conditions.

Pueblo I and II Colonization and Dispersion

During the Pueblo I period, Kayenta peoples continued to occupy areas inhabited during the Basketmaker III period (see Nichols, Chapter 4, this volume), but they also moved into previously abandoned or unoccupied areas, constructing a variety of sites. This range expansion creates the impression of a population explosion; estimates of regional site- or room-based population suggest dramatic increases beginning about A.D. 1000 and continuing until the abandonment of many of the peripheral areas about A.D. 1150.

Sites in the peripheral areas are often more ephemeral, lacking the complement of structures present

warm quarters. Yet, the procurement of pinyon nuts would not have demanded year-round occupation of the lease area.

Apparently, the initial scouts found things to their liking, for within a decade, increasingly substantial sites were being built. D:11:2030, the earliest of this second construction phase, is typical in having deep pit structures, masonry storage rooms, consolidated midden deposits, and human osteological remains. The site is imposingly large (by BMAP standards), and

the number of structures (forty-two numbers assigned) and features (sixty-two numbers assigned) (Green et al. 1985:246–268) suggests a substantial investment in labor and building materials. Storage rooms, formal middens, and human osteological remains indicate the elaboration of activities taking place at the site. D:11:2023 and D:11:2068/Component I have similar configurations (figures 5.15 and 5.19), suggesting similar activities were taking place at them. These sites (as well as the contemporaneous

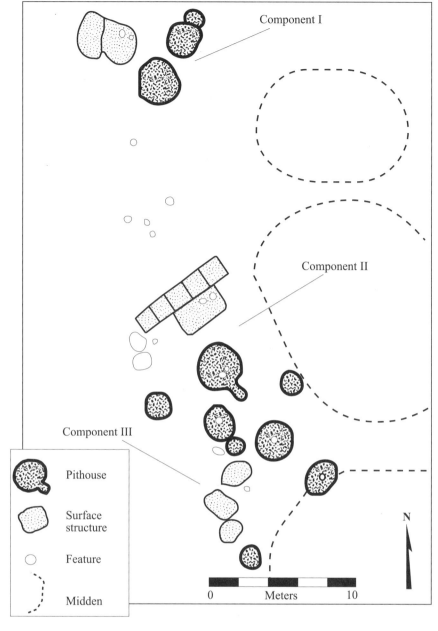

Figure 5.19 Plan map of AZ D:11:2068 (after Sink et al. 1983:figure 52).

Component I

Component II

Component III

Pithouse

Surface structure

Feature

Midden

0 Meters 10

N

Figure 5.20 Bird-effigy jar from Burial 87 at AZ D:11:2068, Component II (BMAP file photograph).

nina peoples, who used the Upper Basin for hunting, making their homes in habitation sites located further west (Cartledge 1979). The Kayenta peoples of the Upper Basin built sites very similar to the earliest BMAP sites of the Puebloan period (AZ D:7:3194, D:11:689, and D:11:3061), with one or two masonry rooms or ephemeral structures and a sparse trash scatter. Notably absent were kivas, trash middens, or burials, suggesting that the Upper Basin peoples had social and ceremonial connections elsewhere. Distributions of site numbers over time suggest that the Anasazi of the Coconino Plateau moved into the area at the beginning of the Pueblo I period, that their numbers increased until about A.D. 1100, and that they abandoned the area beginning in the early twelfth century.

Much of the western part of the Kayenta area is characterized by increasing site numbers during Pueblo I period that peak during Pueblo II, only to be followed by abandonment in about A.D. 1150. Euler and Chandler (1978:73) use the term "halting" to describe efforts dating before A.D. 1000 to colonize the Grand Canyon. Evidence of Kayenta peoples is considerable beginning at A.D. 1000, and "the majority of Anasazi sites [were] occupied between A.D. 1050 and 1150" (Euler and Chandler 1978:73). The distribution of these sites, among many different environmental zones, sug-

on sites in the core area. The sites in the peripheral areas are variable in configuration, fueling debate among archaeologists about the economic activities of the sites' builders and their relationships with neighboring peoples. Archaeologists try, with varying degrees of success, to fit these archaeological remains into the sedentary agricultural model used traditionally to characterize the Kayenta Anasazi. Yet, perhaps these sites are variable because their occupants were engaged in a multiplicity of activities

as they reconnoitered the suitability of these locales for colonization.

For example, during the Pueblo I and II periods, Kayenta peoples lived in the Upper Basin of the Coconino Plateau, just south of the Grand Canyon. Their sites have been interpreted as the year-round abodes of Kayenta peoples, although archaeologists question whether the people were engaged in intensive plant gathering (Sullivan 1986b, 1987) or farming (Whittlesey 1992:186). The Kayenta peoples shared the area with Coho-

gests to Euler and Chandler (1978:83) that they were used seasonally. Similar occupational patterns are inferred for the Arizona Strip (Fairley 1989b), and Lyneis (1992:87) notes that with the exception of the Coombs site (see Chapter 6, this volume) and the Main Ridge site, Kayenta sites in the Virgin area are small.

Unlike much of the western portion of the Kayenta area, Wupatki National Monument and Walnut Canyon, east of Flagstaff, Arizona, witnessed explosive population growth during the twelfth century (figure 5.1; Downum and Sullivan 1990). Both these areas were sparsely occupied before the mid-eleventh century; few sites are recorded in either area before the eruption of Sunset Crater in A.D. 1064. After the eruption, however, the number of sites increased dramatically, coincident with population decline throughout much of the rest of the western Kayenta region. Post-eruptive sites in both areas are varied, including numerous special activity sites, habitations, and ceremonial facilities, suggesting that a full range of activities took place at them.

Convenient though it would be to postulate that the peoples who abandoned portions of the western Kayenta range in the mid-twelfth century relocated to Wupatki and Walnut Canyon, there are some complications. Southwestern archaeologists link ceramic wares with archaeological cultures, and the Kayenta Anasazi are closely associated with Tusayan White Wares and Tusayan Gray Wares. A difficulty arises with the ceramic wares found at Walnut Canyon and Wupatki. Sites at Walnut Canyon are characterized by Alameda Brown Ware pottery, which is associated with the Sinagua and Mogollon archaeological cultures, and Wupatki sites have a mix Alameda and Tusayan types on their surfaces.

If the western Kayenta peoples moved to Walnut Canyon and Wupatki, did they then mix with people from other cultures? What is the association between pottery (and other material culture items) and cultural identity? The mix of Tusayan White and Gray Wares (Kayenta Anasazi), Alameda Brown Wares (Sinagua and/or Mogollon), San Francisco Mountain Gray Wares (Cohonina), and pottery with olivine temper (Virgin) throughout the western Kayenta region has troubled at least four generations of archaeologists. Sullivan's (1986b, 1988) findings of San Francisco Mountain Gray Ware and Tusayan Gray Ware sherds and vessels together in a single feature at AZ I:1:17, a ceramic-manufacturing area on the Coconino Plateau, raises questions about some of the most basic assumptions underlying the definition of archaeological cultures.

Much simplified, Pueblo I and II regional settlement patterns suggest expansion out from low-lying Basketmaker III occupation zones into highlands and to the west. Many of the new sites are small, lacking ceremonial structures, storage facilities, trash accumulations, and burials, suggesting that the people occupying them maintained social and ceremonial ties to more established villages that had these facilities and capabilities. The overall impression is one of population growth and dispersion, yet two patterns lead one to question the population growth. First, because the sites lack some important characteristics of sites occupied year-round—especially storage, ceremonial structures, and trash accumulations—they may have been used seasonally. Second, if population growth characterized the Pueblo II dispersion, and if all the places into which the Kayenta people moved were occupied year-round, where then did the people go at A.D. 1150? Population growth after A.D. 1150 is noted in some areas (as mentioned above and in Chapter 6, this volume), yet the magnitude of growth does not appear sufficient to account for all the abandoned areas.

Perhaps the Pueblo II dispersion did not involve major population growth and instead was, at least in part, a seasonal exploitation of available resources. Or, perhaps the dispersion was a refugee phenomenon similar to Navajo movement into the same western Kayenta areas in response to the U.S. Army's attempts to confine them at Bosque Redondo (see Warburton et al., Chapter 8, this volume). The possibility that refugees might have been the instigations of the Pueblo II dispersion points to the question, To what were the refugees reacting? Perhaps the answer is linked to the presence of Chacoan outliers in the eastern and southern Kayenta area—including three close by on southern Black Mesa, as discussed below.

During the 1970s and 1980s archaeologists turned their attention to the Chacoan phenomenon as a regional expression. Excavations were conducted at outlying great houses (e.g., Bis sa' ani [Breternitz et al. 1982; Doyel et al. 1984], Salmon Ruins [Irwin-Williams and Shelley 1980], and Navajo Springs [Graves 1990]), and surveys were designed to determine the extent of the Chacoan road system and the distribution of outliers (Marshall et al. 1979; Powers et al. 1983). Reasonably enough, these efforts focused initially at the core of Chacoan activity: Chaco Canyon itself and the San Juan Basin. Only gradually did archaeologists take their reconnaissance west into Arizona.

Dennis Gilpin (1987, 1989; see also Benallie 1989:99–100) identified three Chacoan great houses on southern Black Mesa (figures 5.1 and 5.21). Tse Chizzi, the largest of the three, is located at Low Mountain, 14 miles (22 km) northeast of Keams Canyon.

[The site] was occupied between A.D. 1050 and 1125 and consists of a U-shaped great house with an interior kiva and a walled courtyard, surrounded by a swale and berm, the berm being composed of spall middens, earth and trash, interspersed with depression which may represent borrow pits. To the north of the great house is a large, 24-m-diameter, 1-m-deep hole, probably an early great kiva, and north of that is an even deeper hole, 20 m in diameter

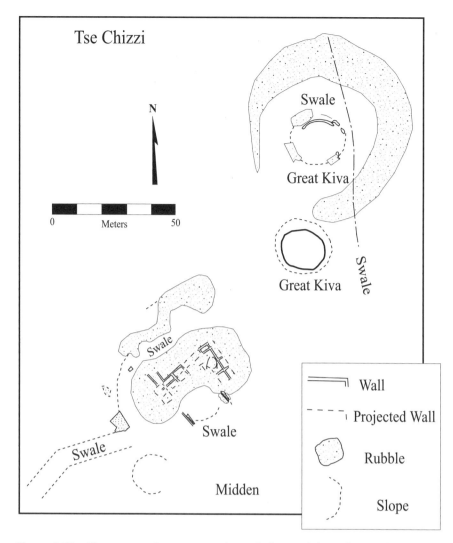

Figure 5.21 Chacoan great houses on southern Black Mesa (after Gilpin 1989).

These ranges are coincident with the burgeoning of site numbers throughout the Kayenta region, especially in the previously unoccupied west. In the Low Mountain area, fifty sites dating to the Pueblo II period, roughly contemporaneous with Tse Chizzi and Whippoorwill Ruins, have been recorded. This represents a fourfold increase from the previous Pueblo I period. In the lease area, population was low between A.D. 800 and 1000, with a possible abandonment in A.D. 1000. Immediately thereafter, population surged, peaking at about A.D. 1100, to be followed by abandonment in A.D. 1150. And throughout the Kayenta region the period A.D. 1000 to 1150 was characterized by expansion of peoples into unoccupied areas, increased numbers of sites, and apparent population increase.

Could the Pueblo II dispersion and the appearance of Chacoan-style great houses in the eastern portion of the Kayenta region be related? The two occurrences certainly are coincident, but the Pueblo II dispersion more typically has been associated with range expansion necessitated by population growth, which, in turn, was facilitated by favorable climatic conditions (Gumerman 1988a). Population growth as a cause of the Pueblo II dispersion is an open question, however. If increasing numbers of people were a primary cause, where did they go after A.D. 1150, when many of the peripheral areas were abandoned? Archaeological evidence does not support a return to the Kayenta heartland after A.D. 1150. (See Dean, Chapter 6, this volume, for a discussion of this issue.)

Alternatively, the Pueblo II dispersion might have been a direct outcome of the appearance of Chacoan great houses along the southern and eastern edges of the Kayenta region. If one views the Chacoan phenomenon as a coercive military and economic presence (Wilcox and Haas 1994; Turner and Turner 1999), then the Pueblo II dispersion might represent an escape from that hegemony. Taking the coercive model several

and 2 m deep with distinct walls, a bench, alcoves, and a surrounding berm. Berms of both the great house and the great kiva are broken by linear swales radiating out away from the site, and are associated with shrines and offering boxes. [Gilpin 1989:2]

The other two outliers are much smaller. Whippoorwill Ruin, also located on Low Mountain, has a great house with sixteen rooms, a courtyard, three kivas situated in the roomblock, two roads, and a berm. The site's surface pottery includes a mix of Tusayan White Ware and Cibola White Ware (60 percent and 40 percent respectively) (Gilpin 1989:table 1). Burnt Corn Ruin, located north of the other two near Pinon, consists of a seven-room great house, one courtyard, three roomblock kivas, and a berm. Three roads radiate from the site. Surface whiteware pottery at Burnt Corn is entirely Tusayan White Ware (Gilpin 1989:table 1). The presence of Chacoan-style core-and-veneer masonry and the design of the roomblocks (with massive construction and kivas incorporated into the roomblock) are primary reasons for these sites' classification as great houses.

These three sites, and White House in Canyon de Chelly, are unusual for the Kayenta region, and Gilpin (1989:3) asks, "What was the context for the great houses?" Tse Chizzi and Whippoorwill Ruins were occupied between A.D. 1050 and 1125, while the pottery at Burnt Corn Ruin spans a longer range, A.D. 940–1250.

steps further, Turner and Turner (1999:482–483) associate the Chacoan phenomenom with violence, cannibalism, and colonizing Toltecs from Mesoamerica:

> We propose that these southerners were practitioners of the Xipe Totec (or Maasaw) and the Tezcatlipoca-Quetzalcoatl (plumed serpent) cults. They entered the San Juan basin around A.D. 900 and found a suspicious but pliant population whom they terrorized into reproducing the theocratic lifestyle they had previously known in Mesoamerica. This involved heavy payments of tribute, constructing the Chaco system of great houses and roads and providing victims for ceremonial sacrifice. The Mexicans achieved their objectives through the use of warfare, violent example, and terrifying cult ceremonies that included human sacrifice and cannibalism. After the abandonment of Chaco, human sacrifice and cannibalism all but disappeared.

Turner and Turner paint a picture of a coercive Chacoan presence that would be well worth avoiding.

If, however, one views the Chacoan presence as more benign, a social and economic community in which people participated willingly, then the Pueblo II dispersion might represent attempts to increase the land base and production levels to support an administrative elite. Various of the Pueblo II inhabitants of the area might have experienced both these perceptions and responses.

Puebloan oral history tells of cases in which people from the same village chose different options when faced with new conditions. One of the better-known examples occurred at Oraibi Pueblo in 1906, where some people stayed and accepted an increasing Euro-American presence while others emigrated, founding two new villages (Titiev 1944). Similarly, Acoma oral history recounts

peoples' responses to a new way of life introduced by the katsinas. Those who accepted the katsinas stayed, saying, "Let us do as we are asked, and learn to carry on as they [the katsinas] want us to" (Stirling 1942:56). Those who rejected the katsinas' teachings "packed up and left in small bands, or perhaps just man and wife would go away. It is not known where they went and they were never heard of any more. (This may account for the other tribes of Indians; but this is not in the tradition.)" [Stirling 1942:56]

If people responded the same way during the twelfth century, some may have chosen to cooperate with the Chacoans, expanding their range to increase production, while others may have chosen to emigrate, rejecting the new social order. Both these models (population growth and Chacoan hegemony), and many others as well could have produced the settlement distribution that archaeologists call the Pueblo II dispersion. The climatic amelioration coincident during this period may have made possible behavioral responses to the Chacoan presence that otherwise might have been unfeasible. Certainly this and other considerations of Chacoan relationships with non-Chacoan populations demonstrate that archaeologists should be looking at large areas with precise chronomteric frameworks (Wilshusen and Ortman 1999).

One final observation about the Pueblo II dispersion: Helen Fairley (1989b:137–138) linked the Pueblo II western and northern expansion with the introduction of cotton into the northern Southwest during the late A.D. 1000s. She suggests that cotton's incorporation into the repertoire of cultigens would have required cultivation of the lowlands to ensure a sufficiently long and warm growing season, possibly necessitating a bi-seasonal settlement pattern. Fairley (1989b:138) links cotton production in the Kayenta region "to the concurrent development of a pan-Southwestern trade network that extended well beyond the boundaries of the Colorado

Plateau." If so, the Pueblo II Kayentans might have been part of two larger socioeconomic networks: the Chacoan to the east, and the Hohokam (perhaps through Wupatki and the ball-court system) to the south.

Social Organization

The span of the Black Mesa Archaeological Project (1967 through 1987) coincided with development of social archaeology in the Southwest (Hill 1970; Longacre 1970). During this period, researchers sought to make anthropological sense of distributions of material items. In the Southwest, they focused especially on architecture and pottery, deriving from the rich southwestern ethnographic literature expectations for forms and distributions that these materials might take and their associations with specific organizational schemes.

The tests for concordances between predicted and actual distributions of archaeological materials require data from excavations or from large-scale surveys. In addition, research requires people with the time and inclination to investigate relationships and patterns in the data. Thus, most archaeological research takes place in the context of large, well-funded projects based at institutions that reward their personnel for research and publication. For the Pueblo I and II periods in the Kayenta region, these constraints point to the Black Mesa Archaeological Project and the Glen Canyon Project, both of which have produced numerous publications, dissertations, and theses on these topics.

Architecture and Site Distributions

Unit Pueblos

Comparatively few studies have been made of the social forces producing Pueblo I and Pueblo II sites nor of those contributing to the sites' abandonment. The assumed ubiquity of the

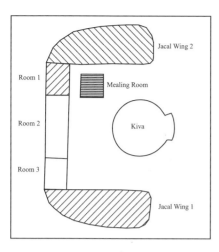

Figure 5.22 Hypothetical social units occupying AZ D:11:93, a Pueblo II/III unit pueblo on northern Black Mesa (after Clemen 1976:figure 43).

unit pueblo form rendered this issue a nonquestion for most researchers. The unit pueblo—with its storage rooms flanked on either side by habitations, centrally situated pit structure/kiva, optional mealing room, and trash midden—seemed so obviously the abode of an extended or multigenerational family that few have questioned this interpretation.

Robert Clemen (1976), following Hill and Longacre, sought to systematize the relationship between this family grouping and the distribution of pottery designs. For his case study he chose AZ D:11:93, a unit pueblo on northern Black Mesa dating between A.D. 1075 and 1150 (figure 5.22). Based on ethnographic analogy and following Hill and Longacre's lead, he postulated that the site was occupied by members of a matrilineage. In a series of statistically questionable analyses, he found that different "design" groups occupied each of the two jacal wings, that the assemblages from the mealing room and one of the storage rooms were mixed, indicating shared use, and that the assemblages from two of the storage rooms and the kiva showed no ceramic-design affinity to either of the jacal groups (Clemen 1976:121). Clemen interpreted his results as support for the conventional wisdom: that D:11:93 and similar sites

as well were occupied by members of a matrilineally related extended family.

Sites with and without Kivas

Although few have questioned the social forms integrating the people occupying unit pueblos, another site type common to the Pueblo I and II periods has been the source of substantial debate. Sites with habitation units, but lacking kivas, are common throughout the Kayenta region during the Pueblo I and II periods. These sites occur on their own, particularly in the western Kayenta region (e.g., in the Arizona Strip [Altschul and Fairley 1989], on central Black Mesa [Linford 1982], and on the Coconino Plateau [Sullivan 1986a; Whittlesey 1992]). In other areas they co-occur with sites that have kivas (e.g., the lease area and Long House Valley [Dean et al. 1978]).

How were sites without kivas used, and what is their relationship to sites with kivas? During the subsequent Pueblo III period there is a substantial size differential between different types of sites. This differential, combined with ethnographic data (use of large pueblos for habitations and small sites as seasonally occupied agricultural field houses) has given credence to the habitation/field house dichotomy (Ward 1978). During the Pueblo I and II periods, however, sites with and without kivas often are similar in size, and archaeologists are more hesitant to assign such functions to the sites.

For the Pueblo I and II periods, habitation sites lacking kivas are commonly interpreted as permanently occupied settlements (Phillips 1972; Sullivan 1986a; Whittlesey 1992). In the lease area, sites with kivas (or primary sites) are viewed as "the basic settlement unit," a continuation of earlier forms (Phillips 1972:207). Sites without kivas (secondary sites, or daughter sites) were a response to growing population and the uneven distribution of resources over the Black Mesa landscape (Phillips 1972:209). Population grew and be-

came too large for the primary site and its resource base. Thus, people left the mother site and established a daughter site near exploitable resources and near the mother site; but the daughter sites lacked kivas, and their occupants looked to the mother site for their integration into the larger social group and participation in socioreligious activities.

The preceding reconstruction emphasizes the social ties between the occupants of the sites, and this social tie is underscored by economic ties. Mother and daughter sites, although in close proximity, often were situated in different ecological zones. For example, Phillips argues that mother sites are found adjacent to major washes—in the "lowlands," while daughter sites are situated in the "uplands" (although, on a larger spatial scale, all are found in the uplands of northern Black Mesa). The upland and lowland sites were situated adjacent to different exploitable resources and subject to different environmental vagaries, creating the potential for economic complementarity. Thus, economic as well as social ties bound the occupants of these two site types (Braun and Plog 1982).

One alternative interpretation questions the need for economic and social ties between the occupants of sites with and without kivas. These interpretations emphasize social and economic autonomy, implicitly painting a picture of rugged individuals colonizing the western Kayenta frontier. This model mirrors the ever-popular autonomous village model that has characterized reconstructions of Kayenta Anasazi social organization for so long (S. Plog 1980b). Typically researchers espousing this alternative work in the western Kayenta region, where many sites lack kivas, and there is no obvious spatial link between sites without kivas (which are the norm) and sites with kivas.

A second alternative derives from research by Gilman (1983, 1987) and Powell (1980, 1983). Both questioned the assumption that the Kayenta Anasazi were sedentary agriculturalists throughout Puebloan prehistory, an interpretation that presumes pressure by human populations on available resources. As an alternative, they propose a spatially extensive model of seasonal exploitation of wild and cultivated resources. In their scenario, population would have been relatively low, subsistence extensive, emphasizing movement to resources, and sites would have been seasonally occupied. Although both Powell and Gilman were working with data from the Peabody lease area, their models might be more applicable to the western Kayenta periphery.

One theme runs through all these interpretations: that economics and population dynamics were major determinants of settlement patterns and social organization. Economics and population dynamics may have driven culture change during prehistory; however, ethnographic literature on the Pueblos offers an interesting alternative. Puebloan accounts of their own past tell of peoples constantly on the move because they were directed to do so by higher powers (see Kuwanwisiwma, Chapter 7, this volume), because of disputes with one another about how to respond to the directives of those same higher powers, or because they could not agree with one another about responses to innovation and change. There are numerous ethnographic accounts of emigration among the Pueblos (M. Bradfield 1971; Levy 1992; Stirling 1942; Titiev 1944; Whiteley 1988), and numerous reasons are offered for these splits. Population/resource imbalances may be one cause underlying such splits; certainly, the ethnographic literature indicates that such was sometimes the case (M. Bradfield 1971; Levy 1992; Whiteley 1988). However, splits sometimes occurred without the apparent provocation of population growth and resource shortages, the two causes on which archaeologists focus their attention. The ethnographic literature points to the supernatural and controversies over acceptance of innovations and change as another major cause of

intravillage strife. These causes do not lend themselves readily to evaluation with archaeological evidence. However, archaeologists, having difficulties explaining ancestral Puebloan remains within the context of environmental and economic models, might find compelling explanations for otherwise inexplicable patterns in the Puebloan oral histories and ethnographies.[3]

Chacoan Outliers in the Kayenta Region

Thus far, this discussion has focused on the two most common types of sites during the Pueblo I and II periods: primary sites (habitation sites with kivas) and secondary sites (habitation sites lacking kivas). However, a third site type, Chacoan outliers, was present. Three Chacoan style sites have been identified on southern Black Mesa (see above), and others exist in the eastern Kayenta region (e.g., White House, in Canyon de Chelly) and just south of the Kayenta region (e.g., Allentown and Navajo Springs). These sites differ from the more typical Kayenta habitation sites in having Chacoan-style masonry, kivas incorporated into the roomblock, great kivas, roads, and berms. In addition, some of the sites have a mixture of Tusayan and Cibola White Ware pottery on their surfaces (Gilpin 1989), contrasting with the more typical Kayenta whiteware ceramic assemblages dominated by Tusayan White Wares (Hantman 1983). Chacoan-style sites are notably absent in the western Kayenta region. It is interesting to note, however, that the construction of Wupatki Pueblo, northeast of present-day Flagstaff, Arizona, coincided with the abandonment of much of the western Kayenta periphery, and some have suggested that Wupatki Pueblo was fortified (Wilcox and Haas 1994:220–221) and that it has characteristics of Chacoan affiliation (Stanislawski 1963:534–543).

The appearance of Chacoan-style great houses in the Kayenta region in about A.D. 1050 coincided with the greatest spread of the Pueblo II dispersion, and the abandonment of

the great houses in about A.D. 1150 coincided with the abandonment of many of the peripheral areas. Could the dispersed settlement distributions so characteristic of the Kayenta Pueblo II period be, at least in part, a reaction to the presence of a "foreign" social and economic presence?

Hantman (1983:293–294) notes that whiteware assemblages from sites in the Pueblo II Kayenta area are dominated by Tusayan White Wares, in contrast to assemblages from sites to the south and east, which have varying mixes of Tusayan, Little Colorado, and Cibola White Wares. At the same time, however, some of the whitewares found on Kayenta sites was decorated with hatched Dogoszhi-style motifs, suggesting links with the Chacoan phenomenon. Hegmon and Plog (1996:28; see also Hantman 1983; S. Plog 1989) raise an important but as-yet unanswered question: "Why do more localized and discrete interaction and exchange networks develop on the peripheries of the [Chacoan] network at the same time that those localities show some evidence of iconographic, if not exchange, ties to Chaco?" Disregarding for the moment the iconographic ties (the Dogoszhi style) with Chaco, Hantman (1983:293–294) interprets the ceramic patterns of the Kayenta area as evidence of closed socioeconomic networks that would have undermined long-term social and economic viability (Kojo [1996] too argues for localized production of Tusayan White Wares especially before A.D. 1150). Hantman proposes that population growth contributed to the formation of a closed social network; however, such patterns of closure might also reflect a refugee phenomenon.

Some of the Kayenta folk may have embraced the Chacoan influence, coalescing around the great houses into communities (Benallie 1989; Gilpin 1989). Others may have rejected the Chacoan presence, choosing instead to emigrate to previously unoccupied areas, both reactions consistent with the variation in response to innovations noted in the Puebloan ethnographic literature and oral histories. Or, people might have established some of the peripheral sites in support of the Chacoan presence, in an attempt to intensify production and diversify the economic base of the Chacoan-style communities.

Other Architectural Evidence for Social Organization

Three additional architectural patterns offer suggestions about Pueblo I and II social organization in the Kayenta region: mealing rooms, storage facilities, and Standing Fall House—the Pueblo I cliff dwelling, located on northern Black Mesa, devoted largely to storage.

Mealing rooms join the architectural repertoire throughout the northern Southwest during the transition from pit structure to pueblo (Mobley-Tanaka 1997:439). They make their first appearance in the Kayenta region during the Pueblo II period. Although precursors to unit pueblos were built during the Pueblo I period, there were no mealing rooms on these sites. For example, AZ D:11:2030 (Green et al. 1985), a large Pueblo I site on northern Black Mesa, had three masonry and jacal roomblocks, associated pit structures, and a large midden and burial area (figure 5.14). But no mealing rooms were found on this site, nor on others like it (e.g., AZ D:7:134 [Layhe et al. 1976:1–14] and AZ D:7:2013 [Sink et al. 1982a]).

Bond et al. (1977:36–38, figure 11) excavated a feature that they designated a disturbed mealing bin at NA 13805, a small Basketmaker III site near Chilchinbito. The feature consisted of a mano, a mano blank, a combination mano and shaft straightener, a metate fragment, several pieces of burnt sandstone, and a slab of worked shale. Irrespective of this feature's function as likely for food processing, it does not resemble the mealing bins that make their appearance during the Pueblo II period, nor was it found with other bins in a structure devoted to milling. Of the nine sites dating to the Pueblo II period

and the Pueblo II/III transition excavated by the Pinon Project, south of the lease area on central Black Mesa (Gleichman 1982a), only AZ J-43-23 had a mealing room. Structure 2, the mealing room, was small (1.7 m by 1.8 m) and constructed of wattle-and-daub. The floor was unplastered, with three mealing bins, one of which had been reused as a hearth. Associated artifacts included a mano and several mano fragments. AZ J-43-23 also had a kiva and several habitation and storage rooms.

Mealing rooms were first constructed on sites in the lease area during the Pueblo II period. They were fairly common but by no means ubiquitous (there are twenty-two mealing rooms on twenty of over seventy excavated sites of the Toreva phase). Sites with mealing rooms are configured quite variably, although most are large by lease-area standards. One unusual site, AZ D:11:2001 (DeMarcay et al. 1982) had only one structure other than the mealing room, a D-shaped kiva. Interestingly, every site on which a mealing room was found also had a kiva.

Mobley-Tanaka (1997) proposes that mealing rooms might have been dedicated to female-dominated rituals surrounding food preparation. Like kivas, a male-dominated ritual place, mealing rooms are largely subterranean and are located in plazas. The two rooms' co-occurrence in plazas might indicate a functional link between ritual activities conducted by men in kivas and by women in mealing rooms. Mobley-Tanaka (1997:445) notes that references to ritual food preparation are common in the ethnographic literature. However, the existence of a "specialized space housing these activities and associated with the public and ritual spheres of kiva and plaza, may indicate both a more prominent role for female ritualism at this period [Pueblo II] and the initial crystallization of gender specific roles in ritual."

Mealing rooms are situated in the plaza area, between the kiva and the habitation and storage rooms, often

northeast of the kiva. Nineteen of the mealing structures are small pit structures (about 3 meters in diameter), dug into sterile soil; three are jacales. They have between one and seven mealing bins, but most have three, four, or five bins; no metates were found in the bins, although whole manos and groundstone fragments were commonly found during excavation in the fill and on the floor. There are few other features in mealing rooms, although a hearth and storage facilities (slab-lined pits or ollas) may be present. Two sites in the lease area have two mealing rooms each. One (AZ D:11:2108 [Sink et al. 1984]) has two components, and one mealing room is associated with each of the components. The other (D:11:2051 [Stone et al. 1984]), however, has only one component, consisting of the two mealing rooms, one kiva, one shallow pit structure, two deep pit structures, one semisubterranean masonry room, and a trash midden (figure 5.23). The latest lease-area tree-ring cutting date, A.D. 1144, comes from AZ D:11:2051, which is located in the southwest corner of the Peabody lease area (adjacent to areas that saw continued occupation after the lease area was abandoned).

The appearance of mealing rooms during the Pueblo II period suggests shifts in the importance of the food item being milled (presumably maize, as discussed above) and in the way people accomplished this task. In some cases, the multiple bins were furnished with graded grinding slabs, from coarse to fine. The millers may have spent a good portion of their day preparing meal from corn, and the mealing room would have allowed the millers to work together at this time-consuming task. Specialized mealing rooms continue into the subsequent Transition and Tsegi phases (Chapter 6, this volume) and are recorded in the ethnographic literature.

Eggan (1950:129, 131) believes that the division of labor among the contemporary Hopi and their ancestors assigned food preparation, including corn milling, to women. He argues that milling could be carried out more

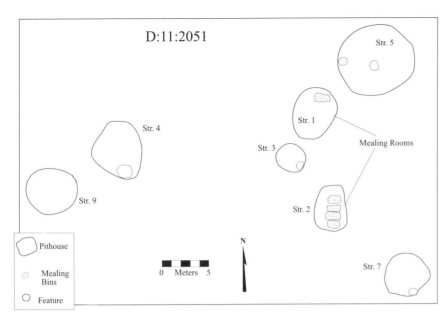

Figure 5.23 Mealing rooms at AZ D:11:2051, a Pueblo II/III habitation site on northern Black Mesa (after Stone et al. 1984b:figure 3.35).

efficiently and pleasantly in groups, and extrapolating from the ethnographic present, Eggan (1950:129) identifies the appearance of facilities for communal grinding with "the development and maintenance of the extended maternal household in the western pueblos."

Generalizations about food storage on ancestral Puebloan sites suggest that storage facilities increased in number and size and were increasingly concentrated on fewer and fewer sites (Martin and Plog 1973:238). One interpretation based on these patterns is that an administrative elite was charged with the collection and redistribution of foodstuffs. On northern Black Mesa, one of the few empirical tests of this generalization shows that storage capacity increases by a factor of five between A.D. 825 and 1150 (Powell 1987:224), and the highest average number of masonry storage rooms per site is found on sites dating to the early Pueblo II period (Gilman 1983). Despite this increase, however, storage facilities were not increasingly concentrated on fewer sites, nor did sites with kivas have more storage volume than sites without (Powell 1987:223–224). Further, although sites with masonry storage roomblocks

continue from Pueblo I into Pueblo II, the form and distribution of storage facilities on sites became far more variable during the Pueblo II period (Nichols and Sink 1984:66, 75).

Habitation sites in the Pinon area were generally smaller than those to the north in the lease area. Storage facilities were more variable in form than in the lease area, and some habitation sites had no storage facilities whatsoever. Legard (1982a:222) notes that during the Pueblo I period, storage roomblocks of "true masonry" were absent from the Pinon Project area and that a reconnaissance survey of the surrounding area "revealed no surface evidence of Pueblo I masonry." Evidence of storage rooms is equally sparse for the Pueblo II period and the Pueblo II/III transition. The combined lease-area and Pinon Project patterns suggest concern with the availability of food but do not suggest an onsite administrative elite. The Chacoan great houses, discussed above, better fit this role.

Standing Fall House (AZ D:7:60), the fifty-five-room cliff ruin dating primarily to the Pueblo I period, is located at some distance from contemporaneous habitation sites and cultivable lands. Although never ex-

cavated, Standing Fall House has been visited numerous times, mapped and surface collected in 1977. The presence of Kana-a, Wepo, Black Mesa, and Dogoszhi Black-on-white sherds coupled with the latest tree-ring date, a bark date of A.D. 1058, suggests that the site was used throughout the Pueblo I period and into early Pueblo II times (Klesert 1982:52–53). Two hundred fifty-four sherds, seven pieces of chipped stone, and "several pieces" of portable groundstone were collected (Klesert 1982:49), surprisingly few artifacts for so large a site. Several hundred dried corn cobs, squash rinds, and some dried beans were collected as well. Using attributes defined by Dean (1969) to assign functions to the site's rooms, Klesert (1982:43) determined that there were thirty-three granaries, fourteen habitations, two kivas, and five courtyards; the function of one room could not be determined. There are proportionally more storage rooms at Standing Fall House than at comparable contemporaneous sites, a characteristic reflected in the small average room size, just 5 m².

Based on this evidence, Klesert (1982:55–59) concluded that Standing Fall House was used primarily for storing and redistributing maize, not as a dwelling place. He proposes that the Pueblo I people of northern Black Mesa were integrated into a social and economic network that extended beyond the boundaries of any single site. Following S. Plog and Powell (1984), Klesert (1982:58) proposed that between A.D. 850 and 1050 these networks were "suggestive of seasonality and widespread exchange networks," and that after A.D. 1050, until regional abandonment in A.D. 1150, the people were less mobile and more closely integrated into smaller socioeconomic networks.

The intra- and intersite distribution of storage facilities is an avenue of research that deserves additional attention. Conventional wisdom argues that over time, storage facilities became increasingly aggregated on fewer sites and that an administrative elite developed to manage the redistribution of the stored goods (Lightfoot and Feinman 1982; Martin and Plog 1973). This pattern, then, would have been part of a larger trend towards increased economic specialization; the appearance of mealing rooms at sites with kivas is supportive of this interpretation. To date, however, the storage-room data from northern Black Mesa do not fit this model (Powell 1987). Overall storage volume does appear to increase over time; however, concentration of storage space on fewer sites may be more characteristic of the Pueblo I period than Pueblo II. By the Pueblo II period, masonry structures were used for habitation as well as storage. Storage facilities take a number of forms and are found throughout the sites, suggesting smaller social units (perhaps families, not an administrative elite) maintained control of the stored resources.

Artifacts and the Evidence against Village Autonomy

Numerous archaeologists have observed the widespread distribution of particular ceramic-design styles in the northern Southwest. Particularly notable are the Kana-a and Dogoszhi styles—the former characterized by thin, uneven lines, triangles, and pendant ticks; the latter characterized by wide linear designs filled in by hatching (figure 5.24). Both design styles occur in the Tusayan White Ware series and on whitewares produced in other areas as well (F. Plog 1979b). Some time between A.D. 1050 and 1150 distinctive regional styles make their appearance (S. Plog 1980a). These observations led archaeologists to question the causes underlying these changes and to investigate the relationships among social organization, the distribution of design styles found on pottery (Hegmon 1986, 1995), and the raw materials used in its manufacture (Ambler 1992; Deutchman 1979, 1980). Fewer studies have attempted to characterize the distributions of the raw materials used in stone-tool

Figure 5.24 Dogoszhi and Kana-a Black-on-white designs (after S. Plog 1980a:figure 4.2).

manufacture (Cameron 1984; Green 1985), although these data, too, are being used to reconstruct prehistoric exchange networks and social organization. In the Kayenta region, most of design studies have used data from the lease area (Hegmon 1986, 1995; S. Plog 1986a), as have some of the studies on the sources of raw materials (Deutchman 1979, 1980; Garrett 1986; Green 1985).

In general, these studies have challenged the very foundations of the village-autonomy models; the exception is Hegmon's (1986, 1995; Hegmon and Plog 1996) analysis of ninth-century pottery in the northern Southwest. Hegmon examined whole vessels and large sherds from lease area and other sites in the northern Kayenta area that had been categorized as Kana-a Black-on-white. She noted that pottery-making equipment was found at most of the sites and that the pottery is technologically homogenous. Furthermore, "the overall compositional heterogeneity of the pottery and the compositional differences between sites and areas suggest that pottery, including decorated white wares, was made at a small scale during the ninth century. It is likely that at least one member of most communities, if not most households, made pottery" [Hegmon 1995:236].

However, Hegmon and her coworkers (1997) also note the concentration of the production of San Juan

Red Wares. During the ninth century, San Juan Red Wares were common across the northern Southwest, including the Kayenta area and Black Mesa. The ware's production, however, was concentrated in southeast Utah, and within southeast Utah, "there is strong evidence that red ware was produced along Montezuma Creek, although it may have been produced in other locations as well" (Hegmon et al. 1997:495). Hegmon et al. (1997:460) conclude that "the concentration of San Juan Red Ware production and its association with ritual contexts suggest that this red ware was special in some way, and it had an important role in social, political, or economic interactions." They further note (1997:460) "that contemporary white ware was not [used or] moved in this way."

Sourcing studies have shown that by the tenth century, many of the raw materials used in pottery and in the manufacture of chipped-stone tools came from nonlocal sources, some from substantial distances from the lease area. For example, Garrett's (1986:140–141) petrographic analysis of pottery from sites in the lease area supports the conclusion that only Black Mesa Black-on-white pottery was made from clay and temper available in the lease area. All other pottery types, including the ubiquitous Kana-a Gray and Tusayan Corrugated, were made on Black Mesa but outside the lease area (Sosi and Dogoszhi Black-on-whites and the graywares), or were made off Black Mesa (San Juan Red Ware and Tsegi Orange Ware) (Garrett 1986). Deutchman's (1979, 1980) neutron-activation analyses of Sosi and Dogoszhi Black-on-white pottery generally support these patterns.

Ambler's (1992) study of Black Mesa Black-on-white sherds from AZ D:11:9 (NAU), a pottery-manufacturing site on central Black Mesa, near Pinon, is also supportive of localized manufacture of Black Mesa Black-on-white pottery. He concludes that tempering materials and design variation suggest at least two local manufacturing traditions for Black Mesa Black-on-white pottery: "one often without dots and with fine sand temper [centered in the northern ranges of the Kayenta region], and the other more frequently with dots and with more temper variation [centered in central Black Mesa]" (Ambler 1992:4).

Analysis of temper found in Tusayan White Wares suggests important changes in production and distribution patterns between Pueblo II and Pueblo III times (Geib and Callahan 1987). Volcanic ash, found in two restricted locales (Blue Canyon and Tonalea), is first used as Tusayan White Ware temper in pottery made in the Klethla Valley, between A.D. 1050 and 1100. At this time, ash-tempered pottery is found only infrequently outside the Klethla Valley, suggesting localized production and use. During middle to late Pueblo III times, however, the frequency of ash-tempered pottery increased dramatically outside the Klethla Valley, suggesting wider-ranging exchange of the tempering material, the pottery, or both (Callahan 1985; Geib and Callahan 1987:106–107).

Green's (1985) research into sources of the chipped-stone raw material indicates that after Basketmaker II times, the vast majority of stone tools found on the sites of the lease area were made from nonlocal raw materials. Green (1985) found that lease-area sites in the Moenkopi Wash area had especially high concentra-

tions of stone tools from imported raw materials, perhaps signifying an exchange route through Black Mesa following Moenkopi Wash. Green concluded that these materials made their way into the lease area by exchange, not direct procurement. Further, Green (1982:208, 216, 1985) proposed that although the size of the lithic exchange networks decreased over time, the intensity of exchange increased, at least until A.D. 1100, when the import of chipped stone raw materials apparently declined. Paradoxically, distribution patterns of material would be similar for the high-mobility models proposed by Gilman (1983, 1987) and Powell (1980, 1983). Regardless of the mechanism moving the materials, however, it is clear that the occupants of the lease area during the Puebloan period were linked economically with outlying areas.

The design-attribute studies (Hantman 1983; Hegmon 1986, 1995) reason that tribal societies are integrated by "lines of . . . transmission of materials and information through reciprocity and reciprocal roles, that is, as lines of cooperation, communication, and control among individuals and groups" (Braun and Plog 1982:507). One mechanism for discerning the presence of these "transmission lines" is stylistic analysis of design variation on pottery. Hegmon (1986:280) concluded: "Increases noted in the quantity of stylistic behavior indicate increases in the contact and communication of socially distant persons and also may indicate elaboration of social group and communication networks." Hegmon (1986, 1995) and S. Plog (1986a) interpret these patterns as indicative of social and economic intensification, which was a response to population growth and perceptions of environmental uncertainty.

Hantman (1983:293) links these processes with the eventual abandonment of the lease area. He observes that northern Black Mesa had the population to support a demographically viable and bounded social network between A.D. 1050 and 1075,

offering the lease area's inhabitants the option to reduce external mate exchange and trade. He argues that the reduction in ceramic-design variation observed by Hegmon (1986, 1995), and the decrease in the distances from which chipped stone raw materials were procured (Green 1985) indicate that the inhabitants of the lease area exercised this option.

Although possibly more efficient on a short-term basis or in a different ecological setting, such a strategy would be a highly precarious one in the marginal Black Mesa upland environment. Without strong linkages to groups in less marginal areas, it is doubtful that Black Mesa populations could have supported a closed social network for an extended period of time. Once isolated, the apparent inability of Black Mesa communities to reestablish any strong systems of nonlocal alliance, as reflected in patterns of ceramic and lithic exchange, may have been a major factor precipitating the abandonment of the area by A.D. 1150. [Hantman 1983:293–294]

All these studies of Pueblo I and Pueblo II social organization rely on architecture, pottery, and distributions of raw material. An assumption underlying all these studies is that similar material items were produced by people who lived and worked in close contact with one another. Conversely, then, distinctive material items would be produced by people who maintained a social distance. In the northern Southwest, the association of ceramic wares with archaeological cultures is perhaps the furthest-reaching interpretation based on this premise. However, Sullivan's (1986a, 1988) discovery of sherds and vessels from two different ceramic wares in a single feature at AZ I:1:17 (ASM) challenges this assumption.

AZ I:1:17, located on the Coconino Plateau, was home to a single household of Kayenta Anasazi people between A.D. 1049 and 1064 (Sullivan 1986a:320). A semisubterranean masonry structure, three log-walled ramadas, and an extramural pottery-making feature were found. The homestead was destroyed, probably by a forest fire, during the summer of A.D. 1064 (Sullivan 1986a:322). No kiva or other ceremonial/integrative architecture was found on the site, and Sullivan (1986a:322) concluded that AZ I:1:17's occupants were relatively autonomous. "If they were linked . . . to some larger social or political entity, the evidence has eluded our investigations." Yet, despite these architecturally based conclusions, Sullivan's crews found sherds and whole vessels of both San Francisco Mountain Gray Ware and Tusayan Gray Ware together in the site's kiln, ceramic wares linked respectively with the prehistoric Cohonina and Kayenta Anasazi archaeological cultures. If, as is frequently argued, women made pottery, the presence of these two wares on a single-household site may be evidence of a Cohonina woman marrying into a Kayenta Anasazi family and maintaining her own ceramic traditions alongside those of Kayenta Anasazi women who lived there as well.

Evidence from Burials

At present, human remains offer little insight into Pueblo I and II social organization. Other than those excavated by the Glen Canyon, Black Mesa, and Pinon projects, few burials dating to this time period have been recovered, and the analyses conducted have targeted issues relating to health and subsistence (Martin et al. 1991; Ryan 1977; Sumner 1982). One preliminary investigation found little variation in Pueblo I and II mortuary behavior within the lease area (Jacobi 1986). Jacobi found no statistically significant patterns over time in burial location (the majority of the burials are found in middens), and there were no patterns by gender, age, or presence/absence of skeletal pathologies. Another pair of analyses suggests that the distribution of ceramic vessels is

associated with the age and gender of the buried person (Hagopian 1995; Hays-Gilpin 1993). "This may indicate high status of women, matrilocal residence leading to more blood relatives present to give offerings, or it may be that older women simply made or used ceramic vessels" (Hays-Gilpin 1993:170).

One final clue about Kayenta Anasazi division of labor comes from osteological analyses conducted on human remains from the lease area. Martin et al. note that both male and female skeletons from the lease area are quite robust. "The fact that robusticity is similar in males and females suggests that the distribution of labor may have been equally divided between the sexes" (Martin et al. 1991:89–90). They conclude that males and females engaged in similar strenuous activities or that different activities resulted in equivalent amounts of stress and strain. One preliminary analysis suggests the possibility of gender-based division of labor in the lease area (Wesson and Martin 1995). Six of eight adult males examined had craggy ischial tuberosities, suggesting prolonged sitting that leads to "weaver's bottom"; only four of eight females had this condition. The females exhibited occupation stress markers indicative of habitual carrying of heavy loads on their backs. Thus, it would appear that men were more commonly engaged in activities requiring prolonged sitting (possibly weaving), while women more commonly carried heavy loads (possibly children).

Ideology and Ritual

Archaeological evidence does not lend itself readily to interpretations of prehistoric ideology and ritual behavior, and when there is evidence, archaeologists often use it to bolster other interpretations. For example, during the Pueblo I and II periods in the Kayenta region, kivas are common. Yet, archaeologists have tended either to assume their likely ceremonial and ideological links or to focus

instead on their possible role in social and economic integration (Braun and Plog 1982; S. Plog 1986f). Some (Lekson 1988) would go so far to say that "kivas" dating to the Pueblo I through III periods were not kivas at all, arguing instead that they served primarily as habitations. Despite these functional interpretive tendencies, some archaeological remains dating to the Pueblo I and II periods are difficult to explain without reference to ritual and ideology.

If one accepts Watson Smith's (1952:162) definition of kivas as distinctive by virtue of their size, configuration, and/or placement on a site, then there are Pueblo I and II kivas throughout the Kayenta region. Some of them have floor features that have been interpreted as sipapus, or the metaphorical opening between the third world and this, the fourth world (Legard 1982a). One distinctive feature of these kivas is that many were burnt upon or soon after abandonment (Gumerman 1970:118), even though other structures on the sites were not burnt. Another unusual characteristic of some kivas is the large number of rabbit bones found in them. For example, at AZ D:11:425 (SIU) (Hantman 1980), a Pueblo II site in the lease area, whole and disarticulated rabbits were found on the kiva floor, and many were found apparently purposefully stuffed in storage features ringing the bench. These rabbits may have entered the kiva after abandonment, and unable to escape, died there (such seems to have been the case at Chetro Ketl, in Chaco Canyon [Voll 1978]). The discovery of some of the animals inside bench features, however, raises some questions about attributing this pattern to natural causes. Finally, a kiva dating to the Pueblo II/III transition at site AZ J-43-23 on central Black Mesa (Legard 1982a:235, figure 76) had "a continuous design of interconnected rectangular and triangular scrolls . . . painted in red on a background on light gray."

In the absence of alternative plausible interpretations, archaeologists often link rock images with ritual and ceremony. The Pueblo I and II rock images recorded in the lease area (Hays 1984) include handprints, anthropomorphs, snakes, mountain sheep, lizard men, and geometric and abstract forms. The images may represent hunting magic, boundary markers, and migration markers; Hopi elders visiting the BMAP excavations during the early 1980s identified some of the motifs and linked them with the migrations of specific Hopi clans (see Chapter 7, this volume).

Burials, both human and nonhuman, offer clues into ritual and ideology. Human remains were interred with preparation and consideration; some of the graves were lined with wood or stone, and although the vast majority burials were in middens, some were in structures, most notably kivas. Many of the bodies were accompanied by grave offerings, most commonly pottery, and preliminary analyses (Hagopian 1995) suggest the possibility of variation based on gender and age.

On occasion, archaeologists discovered and excavated nonhuman burials. The remains of raptors were found in some kivas, and the burial of a young female turkey was excavated at AZ D:7:23, a Pueblo I site in the lease area (J. Anderson 1978).

Conclusions

Archaeologists characterize Kayenta Branch prehistory during the ninth through twelfth centuries as a period of subsistence, settlement, and organizational continuity and elaboration. In this view, the continuity, coupled with population growth, led to the Pueblo II dispersion. The Pueblo II dispersion can be viewed as the maintenance of previous lifeways through emigration that, itself, was possible because of climatic amelioration that allowed transplantation of traditional lifeways in new settings. Archaeologists agree that several trends characterize the period: climatic amelioration, population growth, subsistence intensification, increasing sedentism, architectural innovations, and

increasing formalization of facilities used for social integration and ritual. Thus, a fairly coherent overview can be presented for this period. However, further delving into the archaeological literature discloses substantial disagreement about the particulars of the interpretations of any one of these topics.

Despite the emphasis on continuity, much variation—perhaps the byproduct of intentional experimentation—also occurred. By any archaeological measure, population grew during the period A.D. 800 to 1150. Questions about changing patterns of sedentism do not alter this pattern: a shift from seasonal to year-round occupation of sites means only that the growth was more abrupt and precipitous. Increasing population means that subsistence practices were intensified: the questions of whether this intensification took the form of reliance on a more diversified resource base or whether it meant that reliance was on agriculture are as-yet unanswered. A general shift from below- to above-ground structures continued; however, it can hardly be characterized as a transition from pit structure to pueblo. Prehistoric Kayentans continued to build all the structure and features types present during the Basketmaker III period (see Nichols, Chapter 4, this volume), and pit structures persisted into the subsequent Transition period (see Dean, Chapter 6, this volume). At the same time, they experimented with a variety of new forms, most notably above-ground masonry storage and habitation rooms, mealing rooms, and large, centrally located pit structures (kivas) that appear to have served for ceremonies and social integration.

Unit pueblos made their appearance during the Pueblo I period. The addition of masonry storage/habitation rooms during the Pueblo II period increased the archaeological visibility of the sites; masonry structures are comparatively easy to identify on the ground during archaeological survey. This visibility coupled with the unit pueblo's widespread distribution

created an archaeological phenomenon begging comment: the Pueblo II dispersion. It is important, however, not to be interpretively blinded by the unit pueblo and its widespread distribution. Many other site configurations coexist with unit pueblos, and in some areas, unit pueblos are rare or absent.

Stylistic distributions over time and over space parallel those occurring in other regions in the Southwest. Designs on painted pottery, for the most part, change regularly and predictably. Two of the designs, Kana-a and Dogoszhi styles, are found widely throughout the northern Southwest. The Dogoszhi style has been linked with the Chacoan phenomenon, although most of the Kayenta area was not directly influenced by events taking place in the Chacoan realm. The presence of three Chacoan-style great houses on southern Black Mesa, and another (White House) on the eastern periphery of the Kayenta region, suggests that Kayenta people had some involvement in or reaction to the Chaco hegemony. In fact, it is tempting to link the construction of great houses and the Pueblo II dispersion, which happened about the same time. The great houses are abandoned abruptly at about A.D. 1150, the time at which people left many of the areas colonized during the Pueblo II dispersion. These subregional abandonments also coincided with several decades of environmental deterioration that would have made already precarious adaptations impossible.

Whatever the causes, the twelfth century in the Kayenta region was marked by major population relocations and by the subsistence and settlement experimentation that characterize the Transition period, culminating in the spectacular archaeological remains of the Tsegi phase.

Notes

1. Turner and Turner (1999:395–397) raise the possibility of Pueblo I–II cannibalism in the lease area. They note the isolated human bones, some burned, found in the fill of Structure 33 at site AZ D:7:262, which had burned at or near the

time of its abandonment. They argue that the bones, which represent at least three individuals, "raise questions about violence or an unusual death context" (Turner and Turner 1999:396). The site's excavators assigned the bones both burial and feature numbers (5 and 115 respectively), and postulated that the individuals might have been trapped inside Structure 33 when it burned.

2. This section evaluates the relationship between exchange and subsistence; the archaeological literature for the northern Southwest that evaluates the important connections between social organization and exchange are discussed later in the chapter.

3. Many archaeologists balk at postulating causes for cultural change that leave no material traces, arguing that archaeology's focus of study is material culture and behavior, not culture or the past. Such an attitude is reminiscent of the "drunkard's search": "There is the story of a drunkard searching under a street lamp for his house key, which he had dropped some distance away. Asked why he didn't look where he had dropped it, he replied, 'It's lighter here!'" (Kaplan 1964:11). From certain perspectives, archaeology's emphasis on material culture begins to look suspiciously like a convenient street lamp.

PART IV

Late Pueblo II and Pueblo III in Kayenta-Branch Prehistory

Although Puebloan peoples migrated from northern Black Mesa and other areas throughout the Kayenta periphery between A.D. 1150 and 1175, interesting developments took place in the Kayenta heartland before its final abandonment at the end of the thirteenth century. Jeffrey S. Dean places the twelfth-century abandonment of the Black Mesa study area in the context of later Kayenta Anasazi prehistory. The poorly known A.D. 1150 to 1250 period was an interval of transition, when the pattern of dispersed, comparatively small communities was transformed into the totally dissimilar Tsegi-phase configuration—including the spectacular, in both magnitude and preservation, cliff dwellings that attracted pioneer archaeologists to the region in the late nineteenth century.

Here the author develops the prehistory of aggregation and the construction of the cliff dwellings and large plaza-oriented villages, and he synthesizes research on cultural development around the northern flanks of Black Mesa, linking these developments with the simultaneous withdrawal from the Mesa Verde region to the northeast. The chapter culminates with people migrating from the northern Southwest to the present-day Hopi Mesas to the south.

CHAPTER 6

Late Pueblo II–Pueblo III in Kayenta-Branch Prehistory

Jeffrey S. Dean

One of the major events of Kayenta Anasazi prehistory was the general movement out of upland areas and withdrawal from the far-flung peripheries of the Kayenta distribution in the twelfth century A.D. (figure 6.1). The "abandonment" of the BMAP study area around A.D. 1150 was one local manifestation of the general movement out of upland zones in the Kayenta "core area." A population relocation of the magnitude involved in the abandonment of northern Black Mesa had substantial repercussions for the inhabitants of adjacent areas. These effects ramified across space and time, much like the ripples from a stone dropped into a pond.

The purpose of this chapter is to place the twelfth-century abandonment of the Black Mesa study area in the context of later Kayenta Anasazi prehistory. Typologically, the interval from A.D. 1150 to 1300 is designated Pueblo III (Kidder 1927) or assigned to Colton's (1939:58–59) Klethla and Tsegi phases. The poorly known period from A.D. 1150 to 1250 is recognized as an interval of transition when the Pueblo II pattern of dispersed, comparatively small communities was transformed into the totally dissimilar Tsegi-phase configuration. Although roughly contemporaneous with the Klethla phase, materials of the Transition period are too varied to be confined by the archaeological parameters established for the

phase by Colton (Dean 1970:147–151, 1996a; Dean et al. 1978:29–32; Gumerman and Dean 1989). Later materials, however, still fit comfortably within Colton's system. Therefore, the term "Tsegi phase" is retained for the distinctive settlement pattern of large and small sites, some grouped into spatial clusters that appear to have been hierarchically structured and that emerged after A.D. 1250, prevailing until the abandonment of the Kayenta area by A.D. 1300.

After A.D. 1150, Kayenta prehistory was characterized by a steady decline in spatial extent as peripheral populations collapsed inward on core localities. As contraction continued, gaps opened between centers of population concentration. Thus, while the Kayenta area can be treated as a geographic unit at the beginning of the study period, discrete localities must be isolated for the post-A.D. 1200 portion of the total interval. At least seven loci of high population and slightly divergent development can be provisionally recognized: Tsegi Canyon–Marsh Pass–Kayenta Valley, Navajo Canyon–Rainbow Plateau–Navajo Mountain, Paiute Mesa, Shonto Plateau, Klethla Valley, southern Black Mesa, and Monument Valley (Dean 1996a:figure 3.1). Doubtless, some of these apparent clusters are artifacts of incomplete archaeological knowledge and may have to be collapsed or, perhaps, deleted when complete

coverage of the Kayenta area has been achieved.

Chronology

Ideally, any attempt to establish a chronological framework for the interval from A.D. 1150 to 1300 should involve integrating independent dates from a wide range of pertinent archaeological contexts. Unfortunately, since the vast majority of sites are known only through survey, independent dates are of limited direct application. Furthermore, the sampling biases caused by the selective excavations in the Kayenta area create equally unbalanced chronometric distributions. The principal independent dating technique relevant to the study period is, of course, dendrochronology (Dean 1986b, 1997; Stokes and Smiley 1968). The combination of excellent preservation and disproportionate archaeological attention has made the Tsegi-phase cliff dwellings primary foci of tree-ring dating and the Tsegi phase the best-dated prehistoric archaeological taxonomic unit in the Southwest. Unfortunately, the same cannot be said of the Transition period, whose tree-ring dating corresponds to the lack of attention it has received. Barely half a dozen tree-ring dated sites provide the absolute chronological structure for the interval from A.D. 1150 to 1250. Other independent chronometric techniques

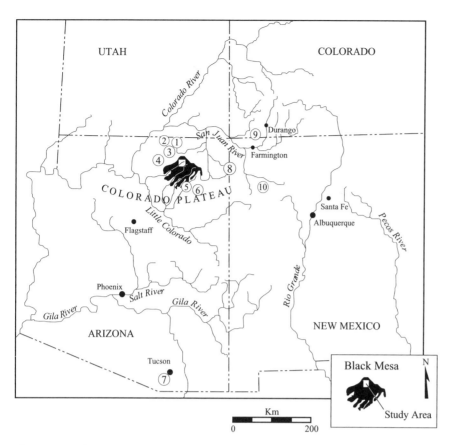

Figure 6.1 The Southwest, showing locations mentioned in Chapter 6: 1–Rainbow Plateau; 2–Navajo Mountain; 3–Shonto Plateau; 4–Klethla Valley; 5–Hopi Mesas; 6–Hopi Buttes; 7–Santa Cruz River; 8–Chuska–Lukachukai Mountains; 9–Mesa Verde; 10–Chaco Canyon.

(1985b:38, figure 2) high-resolution phase system, which discriminates intervals ranging from twenty-five to eighty years in length. Blinman and Schroedl applied multiple regression and mean ceramic-dating techniques respectively to pottery types from several sites along Navajo Route 16 near Inscription House Trading Post (Schroedl and Blinman 1989). Applications of these techniques have been limited, however, and most dating involves the assignment of sites to Pecos Classification periods or phases on the basis of the presence and absence of pottery types.

At present, ceramic-attribute dating systems cannot be applied to the Klethla and Tsegi phases. Only two attribute dating systems have been developed for the Kayenta area (Kojo 1991; S. Plog and Hantman 1986), but both methods apply primarily to the Peabody lease area on Black Mesa. Moreover, they cannot be applied to periods outside the A.D. 800 to 1150 span from which the data come. Consequently, traditional typological techniques will have to suffice for dating the post-A.D. 1150 sites that are the subject of this chapter.

have contributed little to the chronology of the period after A.D. 1150.

Given the preponderance of unexcavated sites and the paucity of independent dates for the Transition period, the basic chronological control for the study period is provided by ceramics. Well over 90 percent of the post-A.D. 1150 Kayenta sites that have been surveyed or excavated are dated solely on the basis of ceramic associations. Ceramic dating works especially well because the pottery of the period is varied, distinctive, and easy to type and because many of the types had discrete, fairly short temporal durations that are well dated. Because the ceramic dating system undergoes repeated revision as new associational data are acquired, the dates assigned to many Kayenta pottery types by Breternitz (1966) are no longer used. Unfortunately, most

of these chronological revisions are known only through the oral tradition of Kayenta archaeology.

The Long House Valley Survey used the combination of pottery types present to identify a span of time within which a site was occupied. Given the resolution of Kayenta ceramic dating, some sites can be placed within intervals as brief as twenty-five years (Dean et al. 1978:29), a considerable improvement on mere phase assignment. Using seriation techniques, Ambler (1985b) intercalated ceramic assemblages from undated contexts with assemblages from dated contexts to delineate and date a succession of ceramic complexes (see also Chapter 5, this volume). These complexes, each defined by a unique configuration of pottery-type percentages, are used to assign sites to time periods that comprise Ambler's

Physical Environment

Stable features of the Kayenta-branch environment—climate type, topography, bedrock geology, vegetational zonation, and species composition of plant communities—have not changed appreciably during the last two millennia, and modern measures of these factors can be projected back into the study period. The three broad habitats of the Kayenta area—uplands, valleys, and canyons—retained their general topographic, geologic, and vegetational characteristics throughout the target interval.

Low-frequency environmental variability (that caused by natural processes with periodicities > twenty-five years) had considerable impact on the three habitats during the A.D. 1150–1300 interval. This period began during a second-order interruption

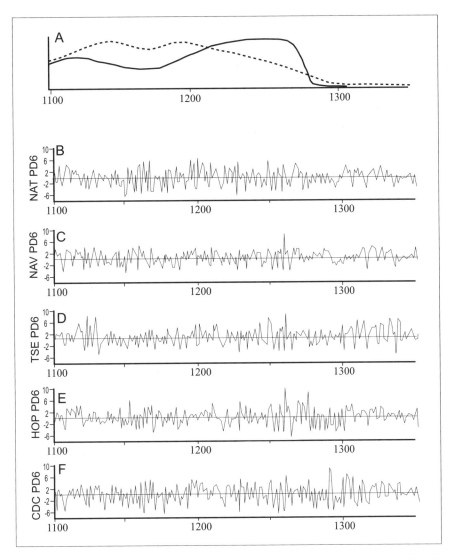

Figure 6.2 Paleoenvironmental variability in the Kayenta area, A.D. 1100–1350: A-alluvial aggradation-degradation (solid line) and ground water fluctuations (dashed line); B to F-reconstructed Palmer Drought Severity Indices for the Natural Bridges, Navajo Mountain, Tsegi Canyon, Hopi Mesas, and Canyon de Chelly areas.

of the general depositional trend that characterized the area from A.D. 925 to 1250 (figure 6.2A). During this hiatus, which was centered on A.D. 1150, alluvial water tables dropped, and floodplains ceased accreting long enough for incipient soils to form on their surfaces. Erosion, in the form of surface stripping (Cooley 1962b) and moderate channel incision (Euler et al. 1979:1096–1097; T. Karlstrom 1988), dissected the floodplain deposits. Around A.D. 1175, the primary fluvial trend was reestablished, causing water tables to rise and terminating

floodplain erosion. During the ensuing seventy-five to one hundred years, water tables rose slightly, stabilized briefly, then began the inexorable plunge associated with the downward limb of the primary hydrologic curve. A moderate amount of alluvial aggradation occurred during this period. Between A.D. 1250 and 1275, transgression of a fluvial system threshold by the falling water tables triggered major floodplain erosion that culminated by A.D. 1300 in a fully integrated system of arroyos similar to that existing today. This arroyo system prevailed

until around A.D. 1450 to 1500, when rising water tables crossed another fluvial threshold and initiated deposition throughout the drainages of the Kayenta country.

Several dendroclimatic measures of high-frequency environmental variability (that due to natural processes with periodicities < twenty-five years) are available. Unlike low-frequency environmental variability, high-frequency variability differed substantially from place to place. As a result, measures of high-frequency conditions and changes in one locale cannot safely be generalized to other localities. Moreover, since spatial variation in climate undoubtedly was a major factor in Kayenta human adaptive behavior, estimates of inter-locality climatic differences are crucial to understanding Kayenta prehistory. Quantitative dendroclimatic reconstructions are available for five localities in and around the Kayenta area: Natural Bridges, Navajo Mountain, Tsegi Canyon, Hopi Mesas, and Canyon de Chelly. Annual Palmer Drought Severity Indices (PDSI) for these areas are plotted for the A.D. 1100 to 1350 interval (figure 6.2B–F) along with a graph of hydrologic and aggradation fluctuations (figure 6.2A).

The PDSI sequences exhibit similar general trends. All are characterized by a prolonged drought in the middle A.D. 1100s, by wetter than average conditions during the first two decades of the thirteenth century, by a severe dry period (the "Great Drought") during the last quarter of the A.D. 1200s, and by pronounced amelioration after A.D. 1300. In addition, all five areas exhibit a marked change from higher- to lower-frequency fluctuations around A.D. 1300. Notable local deviations from these general trends include generally less amplitude variability and a brief wet interval during the Great Drought at Navajo Mountain and a tendency for the Great Drought to be more severe in the Hopi Mesas than in the other localities.

Recent research utilized the chronology of the upper treeline bristlecone pine from the San Francisco Peaks to produce the first dendroclimatic temperature reconstruction for the Southwest (Salzer 2000). Because of the regional scale of temperature variability, relative variations in mean annual maximum temperature revealed by this study apply to the Kayenta area as well as the Flagstaff locality. As would be expected, the droughts of the middle twelfth and late thirteenth centuries were accompanied by high temperatures, and cool conditions prevailed during the wet intervals of 1200–1220 and the 1240s. Especially low temperatures characterized the first decade of the thirteenth century.

Throughout the Colorado Plateau, the period from A.D. 1150 to 1300 was characterized by low temporal variability in climate (Dean et al. 1985:541, figure 1), and the Kayenta area is no exception. Thus, climate during this interval exhibited a high degree of persistence with conditions changing gradually rather than rapidly through time. Spatial variability across the Kayenta area and across the plateau was exceptionally low during the study period (Dean et al. 1985:541, figure 1). Thus, climate conditions were similar throughout the northern Southwest at this time. Principal components analyses reveal that between A.D. 1250 and 1450, the northwestern part of the Southwest experienced a major breakdown in the spatial patterning of the dendroclimate (Dean 1996b; Dean and Funkhouser 1995).

Environmental Change and Productive Potential of the Landscape

Various combinations of stable, low-frequency, and high-frequency environmental conditions and changes significantly affected the productive potential of the Kayenta area for the fairly simple subsistence technology possessed by the Anasazi. Although farming was the principal productive activity during the study period, potential environmental effects on the productivity of other subsistence

resources, primarily wild animals and plants, must also be considered. F. Plog et al. (1988:table 1B) consider this issue in detail, and these conclusions need only be summarized here.

Low-frequency fluvial fluctuations have major impacts on floodplains and on resources found there. The stabilization of floodplains by depressed groundwater levels, as during the period from A.D. 1130 to 1180 and after A.D. 1250, would have favored pioneer plant species adapted to disturbed ground as well as deer and pronghorn. Hunting pressure, however, might have prohibited large-game populations from responding to improved conditions. Small animals, such as rabbits, prairie dogs, pack rats, and field mice, were probably less susceptible to low-frequency environmental variability than were big game because their habitats exist under most fluvial conditions. In fact, some small-animal populations probably grew in response to the increased farming that characterized the period (Ford 1984:137; Semé 1984:143–148). These same fluvial conditions, however, would have been deleterious for floodplain farming, as the most dependable source of agricultural water would have been lost and arable land would have been diminished through erosion and arroyo cutting. During these same intervals, upland areas would have experienced reduced ground cover and, perhaps, minor upward adjustments in the elevational boundaries of non-arboreal plants. Productivity of upland arboreal resources, such as pinyon nuts, would have declined. Upland small-animal populations and mountain sheep were probably less affected by these low-frequency fluctuations.

The period A.D. 1180 through 1250 was characterized by favorable low-frequency conditions for most wild plants and cultigens. Stabilization of alluvial water table levels after A.D. 1200 would have maintained high plant density and productivity in the uplands and stimulated the establishment of riparian vegetation on the lowland floodplains.

High-frequency climatic amplitude variability would have caused corresponding fluctuations in both upland and lowland plant productivity within the fairly relaxed limits established by the favorable low-frequency regime. The sudden onslaught around A.D. 1250 of groundwater decretion and rapid channel incision would have resulted in the colonization of valley and canyon floors by pioneer annuals and in pronounced decreases in upland plant density and productivity. The Great Drought, which began in A.D. 1276, would have magnified all the deleterious effects of the low-frequency deterioration on farming and natural plant distribution, abundance, and productivity. In addition, the transformation of the long-term precipitation regime would have further impacted subsistence systems adopted to more than two hundred years of relative stability.

The Great Drought held the Kayenta area in its grip for a quarter century. Although shorter than the dry interval of the mid-twelfth century, the Great Drought was more severe and would have offered little support to agriculturalists rapidly losing their only dependable water supply, alluvial groundwater, to low-frequency deterioration. Given the desperate water situation, restricted localities where natural factors created conditions suitable for farming under these particular circumstances would have become even more crucial to survival than they had been during the secondary environmental minimum of the twelfth century. Places where alluvial groundwater was forced toward the surface or where alternative agricultural methods, such as irrigation or sand-dune farming, could be applied would have been at a premium. By A.D. 1300, when the fluvial system stabilized at a primary minimum and a climatic maximum succeeded the Great Drought, the Anasazi had vacated the San Juan drainage, and the Kayenta branch had come to an end. Apparently, only a few transient Hopis took sporadic advantage of the return to optimal low-frequency farming conditions near the end of the fifteenth century.

Demographic Factors

Population Size

Powell (1988, Chapter 5, this volume) details the formidable obstacles that plague attempts to estimate prehistoric population sizes from archaeological data. As she points out, no consensus exists concerning the methods to be used in population estimation or regarding the accuracy or reliability of the results of the application of the various methods. The best that can be achieved in the Kayenta area are reconstructions of relative population trends based on numbers of sites or rooms per period of estimation, which commonly is a phase or Pecos Classification period. Often, few points of estimation are available, and in no case can absolute numbers be assigned to points on the curve.

Relative population estimates of the period from A.D. 1150 to 1300 are available for six localities (figure 6.3) within or adjacent to Kayenta territory (Dean 1996a:figure 3.3). All these reconstructions basically are direct representations of numbers of archaeological units (sites or rooms), some of which have been multiplied by estimated average population per unit. In addition, all are based primarily on survey data. A wide variety of population estimators, dating schemes, sampling intervals, and estimation periods is represented. Nonequivalence in these variables renders actual numbers meaningless; only general trends are comparable.

The population rearrangements in the Kayenta area after A.D. 1150 created important changes in local population densities as people forsook less suitable places for more desirable but less widely distributed locations. Before A.D. 1150, Kayenta populations were distributed widely and fairly regularly across broad areas. Population densities were fairly low due to the dispersion characteristic of this inter-

val. Beginning around A.D. 1150, the formerly dispersed population began to aggregate in a few localities. Curiously, although heartland populations continued to grow after A.D. 1150, few localities exhibit the abnormally large increases that should have resulted from the immigration of large numbers of former upland and peripheral people. By the thirteenth century, centers of high population concentration had developed in the Klethla, Long House, and Kayenta Valleys, and Tsegi Canyon of the eastern lowlands, in Navajo and Paiute Canyons and on the Rainbow Plateau and Paiute Mesa in the northwestern area, along the middle reaches of the Tusayan Washes on Black Mesa, and on Antelope Mesa. Between A.D. 1250 and 1300, local population densities peaked in these localities and, except for Antelope Mesa, abruptly fell off as the San Juan drainage was abandoned around A.D. 1300. After A.D. 1300, population density increased on the Hopi Mesas, on Antelope Mesa, and in the Little Colorado River Valley (Adams 1996; Hays et al. 1991:4–5; Lange 1989:211, 1998), where large communities developed in response to population influx from both the north and south.

It has been suggested (F. Plog 1984; Upham 1982) that the apparent disappearance of prehistoric residential populations from areas such as the San Juan drainage does not indicate abandonment but rather reflects behavioral changes that reduce the archaeological visibility of sites. The failure of several large-scale, intensive surveys to locate many Anasazi sites that might postdate A.D. 1300, however, tells against any great number of people remaining behind. The identification in Long House Valley of twenty-six small Hopi farmhouses and campsites (Dean et al. 1978:28) and the presence near Navajo Mountain and along the Colorado River of Hopi petroglyphs and shrines (Turner 1963) identify a transient post-A.D. 1300 Hopi use of the area for hunting and gathering, limited farming, ceremonial activities, and as an access route to other areas (Jenkins, Chapter 7, this

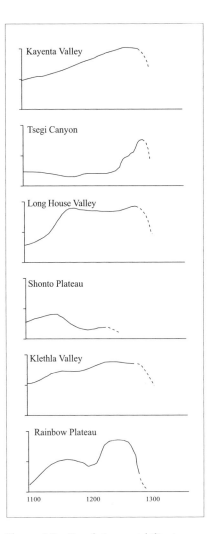

Figure 6.3 Population variability in selected Kayenta-branch areas (after Dean 1996a:figure 3.3).

volume). A historically documented Paiute utilization of the area after A.D. 1800 (Bailey 1964) is carried back in time by Paiute ceramics in post-Anasazi contexts in southern Utah and northern Arizona (Euler 1964); by Paiute pictographs in the Navajo Mountain area (Turner 1963); and by pictographs and simple structures in Long House Valley (Kidder and Guernsey 1919:198–199). By the mid-1700s, Navajos were present on central Black Mesa (Kemrer 1974; Warburton et al., Chapter 8, this volume), and during the next century, they spread northward and westward eventually to occupy the old Kayenta territory south of the San Juan River.

As poorly understood as prehistoric population numbers are, other demographic characteristics are even less well known. Sex composition, age structure, and health of prehistoric populations are comprehended primarily through analysis of human skeletal material. Generalization from such analyses presumes that the skeletal remains constitute a representative sample of the human population from which they were derived. Unfortunately, Kayenta burial data for the interval from A.D. 1150 to 1300 are skimpy, spotty, and skewed. Although 220 individuals have been studied in detail (D. Berry 1983; Ryan 1977), these remains are distributed among 34 sites. Only two adequate site burial populations are available, 32 individuals from Inscription House (Ward 1975:29) in Navajo Canyon and 42 from RB 568 (D. Berry 1983) in the eastern lowlands. The sample from the Inscription House burial represents the Tsegi phase; the RB 568 sample dates at the boundary between the Transition period and the Tsegi phase. Given the low incidence of burials for most Kayenta sites, the available sample is bound to be overwhelmed by the Inscription House and RB 568 collections and undoubtedly is seriously biased in uncontrollable ways.

The assemblages in both the RB 568 and Inscription House burial exhibit age and sex distributions atypical of those found in modern developing countries and in other southwestern burial populations. At RB 568, children under six years of age are "severely underrepresented" (D. Berry 1983:64), and adult females outnumber males twenty-seven to seven (D. Berry 1983:figure 58). Furthermore, with the exception of a single questionably sexed skeleton, all the adult males were between thirty-five and fifty years old at death. In contrast, the adult females displayed a more expectable age distribution, ranging from eighteen to more than fifty years old. A comparable sex ratio exists in the Inscription House adult burial assemblage, which includes ten females and five males (Ward 1975:29). As at RB 568, the Inscription House females apparently were distributed through the expectable age range, that is, ca. twenty years old to "elderly" (Ward 1975:31, figure 5). In contrast to the situation at RB 568, however, the Inscription House males apparently exhibited a more normal age structure, ranging from "adolescent" to "mature adult" (Ward 1975:31, figure 5). With eight infants and five individuals between five and twelve years of age at death (Ward 1975:29), the Inscription House sample is less biased against children than the RB 568 assemblage.

The bias against males evident in both the RB 568 and Inscription House burial assemblages is absent from Ryan's sample of 178 Pueblo II through Pueblo III skeletons (Ryan 1977:57–58). Even his late Pueblo III (Tsegi phase) sample, which includes the Inscription House material but not the RB 568 remains, lacks a bias toward females (Ryan 1977:59, table V). Although Ryan (1977) does not partition the age structure of his sample by sex, apparently he detected no lack of young males similar to that at RB 568. He did, however, discover that infants are underrepresented in his sample (Ryan 1977:58:table VI), a situation similar to that at RB 568. Whether the deviations from "expected" distributions in the total sample and at Inscription House and RB 568 reflect sampling deficiencies, characteristics of the site and areal populations, differential burial practices, or other behavioral factors is unknown. That burial practices varied spatially is shown by the contrast between the "cemeteries" at RB 568 and Inscription House and the virtual absence of interments at places such as Kiet Siel and Betatakin. The degree of behavioral variability implicit in these differences severely constrains demographic inferences from the sample of Kayenta-branch burials.

The general health of Kayenta populations was roughly equivalent to that of other Anasazi groups (D. Berry 1983; El-Najjar 1974; Ryan 1977). In the aggregate, Kayenta adults after A.D. 1150 exhibit the expectable panoply of infirmities, ranging from broken bones to infections to degenerative diseases. As among other Anasazi groups, dental wear, caries, and antemortem tooth loss were common but variable throughout the Kayenta population. Except in Canyon de Chelly on the eastern periphery of the Kayenta area (El-Najjar 1974), nutritional stress was not excessive. Ryan (1977:195–206) noted trends from Pueblo II through Pueblo III toward greater nutritional deficiency, higher infant mortality, and slightly shortened life expectancy, which he attributed to the combined effects of increasingly deficient diets, crowding due to aggregation in large communities, and environmental deterioration. Physical trauma is rare in Ryan's and Berry's skeletal samples and generally occurs in forms most likely attributable to accidents rather than assault by other humans.

Subsistence

The general level of health evident in the admittedly biased post-A.D. 1150 skeletal sample suggests that the subsistence system afforded adequate nutrition for at least some of the Kayenta groups of the period, although the situation was deteriorating to a small degree (Ryan 1977:204–205). If real, the decline in longevity could reflect changes in the nutritional balance of the diet rather than decreasing quantities of food. Thus, increasing reliance on maize at the expense of other foods, and not food shortages per se, may have been responsible for the decline in longevity. Alternatively, the observed change in age structure could be an effect of increasing population densities and only marginally related to the character and magnitude of the food supply.

Whatever the nutritional consequences of Kayenta subsistence practices after A.D. 1150, the available archaeological data do not allow quantitative statements regarding either the contributions of various subsistence practices to nourishment or the composition of the diet. Until more paleodietary analyses have been conducted, compared, and evaluated, less systematic data will have to be used to assess the subsistence behavior of Kayenta populations after A.D. 1150. Most such data come from well-preserved cliff dwellings that were excavated before 1935 and from Glen Canyon Project sites in the San Juan and Colorado River gorges and on the Rainbow Plateau.

Farming

Although wild plant and animal foods contributed significantly to Anasazi subsistence, there can be little doubt that Kayenta populations of the period A.D. 1150 to 1300 relied primarily on agriculture for sustenance. Thousands of corn cobs littering Tsegi-phase cliff dwellings document the importance of farming in the Kayenta economy. Furthermore, the natural resources of the Kayenta area are not capable of supporting large numbers of people. The diversity and quantities of edible wild plants are low, their distributions are spotty, and those that are abundant, such as pinyons, produce irregularly in time and space. Under the best of circumstances, wild animal populations are low. Moreover, human preemption of large areas of land for habitation, farming, and other activities would have diminished the natural plant and animal productivity of the area. Reduced natural productivity may have been offset by the yield of commensal plants associated with the anthropogenic habitats created by agricultural fields (Ford 1984) and of animals drawn to these enriched habitats (Semé 1984).

The available data reveal no differences in the crops grown between the Transition period and the Tsegi phase. Knowledge of changes in the proportions of the various foods produced awaits analyses of pollen, macroscopic plant remains, human coprolites, and, perhaps, the chemical composition of human bones. As in other Anasazi areas, Kayenta farming after A.D. 1150 emphasized the southwestern triumvirate of maize, beans, and squash. Sites of this period throughout the area have yielded corn (*Zea mays*), common bean (*Phaseolus vulgaris*), four species of cucurbits (*C. pepo, C. mixta, C. moschata,* and *C. foetidissima*), and the bottle gourd (*Lagenaria siceraria*) (Harrill 1982:30–33; Lindsay 1969:202–205). Corn is by far the most abundant of these cultigens, reflecting both its primacy in the economy and the greater perishability of squash- and bean-plant parts.

Kayenta agriculture was not restricted to food crops. Cotton-plant parts and a wide variety of cotton textiles testify to the production and processing of *Gossypium* sp. The concentration of stems, bolls, seeds, and unprocessed fibers in lowland sites indicates that cotton was cultivated primarily in the valleys and canyons where conditions were optimal for the survival of this relatively sensitive plant (Lindsay 1969:204). The occurrence of cotton fabric in upland sites indicates that either the textiles or the raw materials for their production were transferred from the lowlands to the uplands. Although obviously cultivated as a raw material for textiles, cotton probably filled two other major economic roles. First, raw cotton or cotton textiles could have been exchanged locally and regionally for food or other items. Such behavior has been identified at Antelope House in Canyon de Chelly, whose residents may have specialized in cotton production (Magers 1986:269–272). The existence of a cotton blanket painted with a Kayenta Black-on-white pottery design at Hidden House in the Verde Valley (Dixon 1956) hints at the scope of this trade. Second, as at Antelope House, cotton seeds could have been consumed as an alternative to beans as a source of protein and fat (D. Morris 1986:221). The presence of cotton seeds in human feces from Inscription House (Harrill 1982:40) suggests this practice, although beans also were present in these coprolites.

The economic importance of farming is indicated by the amount of energy devoted to the control of soil and water in the cause of agricultural production. Agricultural intensification of this sort first appeared in the Kayenta area early in the Transition period and continued through the Tsegi phase. During the interval from A.D. 1150 to 1300, formal agricultural soil- and water-control facilities occurred in all three habitats—upland, valley, and canyon—throughout the area. Such facilities are less abundant in the eastern core locality than they are around Navajo Mountain, probably because the natural topographic and geologic concentration of water in the eastern lowlands reduced the need for human efforts (Dean et al. 1978:27–28). Lindsay (1969:209–210) describes the range of these features:

> Such devices . . . include terraces and linear series of cobble alignments . . . ; windscreens and gridded field plots for soil and moisture control; rock, stone, and earthen-lined ditches and an aqueduct for water transport . . . ; water diversion devices; masonry platforms for soil beds at seeps; dams for soil impoundment; tank-like reservoirs with water metering devices; water flow and gradient maintenance devices; and open reservoirs at bedrock exposures.

Kayenta water- and soil-control facilities are rather simple compared to other southwestern agricultural systems (Haury 1976:120–151; Masse 1981). Anasazi irrigators did not tap large rivers, probably because most of the flowing streams had gradients too steep for the technology of Anasazi water management. Instead, Anasazi water-control systems were designed to collect, move, and distribute slope runoff or to capture the intermittent flow of minor drainage channels (Vivian 1974). The Kayenta Anasazi focused their water- and soil-control efforts on check dams, linear borders and terraces in small drainage basins, and localized ditch and terrace systems that diverted runoff from small, intermittent drainages and slopes and directed the water onto the fields. As limited as these efforts seem compared to Hohokam, Chacoan, and Mesa Verde accomplishments, they do establish that the Kayenta Anasazi were conversant with and capable of implementing a broad range of agricultural intensification techniques.

Gathering

Even though Kayenta subsistence after A.D. 1150 relied predominantly on farming, wild plant resources undoubtedly contributed substantially to the diet. The relative impoverishment of natural plant resources in the area is due more to the limited quantities and patchy distribution of these resources than to a deficiency of kinds of edible wild plants. Clark (1966) documents nearly one thousand plant species that occur naturally in the Kayenta country, and a great many of these are edible. Unfortunately, except for pinyon trees and some annuals, few of these species are abundant or densely distributed over wide areas. Although a large number of edible and inedible wild plant species has turned up in Kayenta sites (Harrill 1982:table 1), it is difficult to estimate the relative contribution of the edible varieties to the total diet. Thus, although the gathering of wild plants was an archaeologically discernible activity during the period from A.D. 1150 to 1300, the precise role this activity played in the economy remains conjectural.

It often is assumed that the gathering of wild plant food was a crisis behavior mobilized to offset diminished agricultural production. While this assumption probably is valid to a degree, gathering may have been a less effective buffer against crop failure than is commonly supposed. The same environmental factors that reduce crop yields adversely affect the production of wild plants. Storage is a much more dependable buffer against episodic agricultural failures than is reliance on wild plant resources. It seems more likely that gathering was a

fairly regular but opportunistic subsistence activity that supplemented and added variety to the products of the fields. In addition to the purposeful exploitation of fairly dependable or predictable resources, such as periodic crops of pinyon nuts, wild plant foods undoubtedly were collected as the opportunity arose on trips away from the residences for other purposes.

A strong basis exists for inferring the utilization of commensal wild plant species that would have flourished in the artificially enriched habitats created by the preparation and planting of fields. Ford (1984) develops the case for the abundance of edible wild plants—such as lamb's-quarters, purslane, and pigweed—in the anthropogenic habitats of agricultural fields. Most of these species are not abundant in the natural environment of the pinyon-juniper forest. That Anasazi farmers did not ignore this convenient, easily exploited, artificially concentrated resource is attested by the frequent recovery of these ruderal species in post-A.D. 1150 sites (Harrill 1982:table 1). As Ford (1984:136–137) contends, the very presence of such fragile, perishable remains indicates a reliance out of proportion to the numbers of fragments assignable to these species.

Hunting and Animal Domestication

Faunal remains are poorly represented in Kayenta sites of the Transition period and Tsegi phase; far fewer animal bones are present than would be expected given even a minimal amount of hunting (Harrill 1982:33; Lindsay 1969:206). This apparently anomalous lack of bone could be due to a variety of factors, including poor preservation, lack of screening during excavation, differential discard practices, butchering animals at kill loci away from the villages, and the scavenging of dogs. Whatever the causes, the paucity of animal bone in Kayenta sites hampers evaluation of the economic role of hunting. Clark (1966:101–110) identifies nearly three hundred animal and bird species in

the Kayenta area, and around sixty of these species have been recovered from archaeological sites (Harrill 1982:table 2). Changes in the proportions of various species among different sites allow some inferences about game procurement.

Big-game hunting during the period from A.D. 1150 to 1300 probably would have involved forays at fairly long distances from areas of dense human occupation. Within the large-game category, remains of mountain sheep outnumber those of deer and pronghorn, a distribution that may reflect the degree of human impact on these species' habitats rather than selective procurement. In the Kayenta area, human activity would have affected pronghorn habitats most and mountain sheep habitats least. On the other hand, the preponderance of mountain sheep may reflect ritual, gustatory, or raw material (horn, bone, hides) preferences. Deer and mountain sheep probably were hunted individually, although a petroglyph in West Creek Canyon near Navajo Mountain (Turner 1963:55, figure 34) suggests that dogs were used to drive mountain sheep toward waiting hunters. Pronghorns probably were driven into enclosures. Other fairly large wild animals whose remains occur in small numbers in Kayenta sites—such as bears, wolves, coyotes, raccoons, and beavers—probably were taken expediently rather than in any organized fashion.

Changing reliance on small game cannot be documented due to procedural differences in the collection of faunal samples and to a paucity of comparative analyses. It is likely that procurement of small animals attracted to the lush resources of Anasazi fields, as outlined by Semé (1984) for Black Mesa, also was important after A.D. 1150. Since such crop predators would have to be eliminated as pests anyway, it would have been only practical to consume them as well. The common occurrence of such field pests in Kayenta sites (Harrill 1982:table 2) indicates that this strategy of small-game procurement was in fact employed. Some small game, particularly rabbits and prairie dogs, probably was taken away from the fields as well. Prairie dogs could have been hunted individually or trapped, while rabbits probably were taken individually or driven into nets or groups of waiting hunters.

A wide variety of wild birds is present in Kayenta sites after A.D. 1150 (Harrill 1982:table 2). Apart from ducks and quail, most of these are unpalatable raptors (golden eagles, hawks, owls), vultures, or small birds such as jays, flickers, swifts, ravens, crows, and blackbirds. Remains of two scarlet macaws, an exogenous species imported from Mexico (Hargrave 1970), were recovered from Kiet Siel. Most or all of these birds probably were exploited for their feathers, which were prominent items in the material culture of the Kayenta branch. Given the low frequencies of remains of edible species, it seems unlikely that wild birds were important components of the Kayenta diet.

Turkey remains occur in low frequencies in most Kayenta residential sites of the period from A.D. 1150 to 1300. These remains include disarticulated bones and bone artifacts in trash deposits (Stein 1984:935); articulated elements in human burials (Beals et al. 1945:209, plate 18a); and complete or nearly complete skeletons in architectural contexts (K. Anderson 1969:31, figure 18), as burials or as furnishings of human interments (K. Anderson 1980:54). In addition, sheltered sites have produced turkey feathers and feather artifacts, eggshell fragments, and extensive deposits of turkey droppings.

In view of the widespread occurrence of turkeys in sites dating after A.D. 1150, surprisingly little attention has been given to the place of this domesticated animal in Kayenta social and economic life. A number of possible functions of the bird can be inferred. First, turkeys would have provided a ready and easily exploited source of protein, in which the Anasazi diet was deficient. Butchering marks on some bones show that turkeys were eaten. Second, the abundance of cordage incorporating turkey feathers in Tsegi-phase cliff dwellings indicates that these birds were used as sources of feathers. Third, some may have achieved the status of "pets," as suggested by the interment of entire turkeys with humans. Fourth, turkeys may have served important ceremonial functions involving sacrifice or ritual consumption. Only the interment of individual turkeys and, perhaps, the manufacture of whistles from turkey bones support this inference. Fifth, as suggested by the turkey "headdress" pictographs at Kiet Siel (Schaafsma 1966, 1980), these birds may have had important symbolic connotations. Finally, they may have served as items of exchange between villages that produced turkeys and those that did not or between Kayenta and non-Kayenta groups. It seems probable that turkeys fulfilled most or all of these functions, but only problem-oriented investigation of this badly neglected animal will permit the true situation to be sorted out (Breitburg 1988).

The relative contribution of big game, small game, and domestic turkeys to the meat diet of Kayenta groups after A.D. 1150 is difficult to determine due to the vagaries of preservation and archaeological excavation, to the biased nature of the faunal sample, and to the paucity of analyses designed to elucidate this problem. There can be no doubt that the proportions of these sources varied over time and space in response to habitat differences, changing local conditions, and fortuitous encounters with game. The "harvesting" of small-animal "pests" in the fields may have provided the most stable source of wild meat, at least during the farming season. Turkey management, however, may have provided the most dependable, even though fairly small, year-round supply of meat. Big-game hunting probably was a seasonal activity that contributed large but relatively infrequent increments to the meat diet.

Trade

The role of trade in Kayenta subsistence is difficult to assess because of the consumable, perishable nature of the evidence for the direct exchange of food. Furthermore, most prehistoric southwestern foodstuffs are so uniform that source areas could not be identified even if the materials were available. The widespread distribution of Kayenta pottery and design styles coupled with the presence in the Kayenta area of "foreign" ceramic-design elements and architectural forms and of trade pottery establish that Kayenta populations interacted with the Mesa Verde Anasazi to the northeast and with the Tusayan-branch Anasazi, Sinagua, and Mogollon groups to the south. Whether any or all of this interaction involved the direct exchange of food or involved other economic or sociocultural materials is unknown. That Kayenta people apparently did not receive "foreign" pottery in return for their ceramic exports (Lindsay 1969:329–330) may indicate that they were importing more perishable items such as food. Cotton and/or cotton products probably were exported from the Kayenta area, but it is not known what might have been acquired in exchange for such commodities.

Stylistic Distributions

The Kayenta branch is defined archaeologically on the basis of stylistic similarities among materials assigned to this taxon and of consistent stylistic differences between these materials and those of other stylistically homogeneous manifestations such as the Mesa Verde and Chaco branches of the Anasazi and the Sinagua and Mogollon "cultures" of Arizona's central mountains to the south. Diagnostic stylistic attributes are manifested chiefly in ceramics and architecture and to a lesser extent in other categories of archaeological materials. For purposes of comparison within the Kayenta branch and with other archaeological manifestations, only ceramics and architecture are considered here.

Ceramics

Even after fifty-five years, Beals et al. (1945) remains the most comprehensive and sophisticated analysis of Kayenta ceramic stylistic variability and continuity, complemented by Crotty's (1983:24–63) analysis of the RB 568 mortuary pottery, Kojo's (1991) study of Kayenta ceramic chronology, and W. Smith's (1971) analysis of Tusayan-branch ceramics from the Antelope Mesa area. Given the quality of these efforts, only a brief summary of late Kayenta ceramic-design relationships is necessary here.

Kayenta potters maintained three separate traditions of ceramic production and design: (1) plain and textured grayware, (2) black-on-white painted ware, and (3) bichrome and polychrome red-slipped and unslipped orangeware. Despite evidence that individual potters produced at least two and perhaps all three of these types of pottery (Beals et al. 1945:138), there is little overlap in design layouts, motifs, and elements between the two painted ceramic traditions. Ambler (1983) and Crotty (1983:57–59) use the Kayenta ceramic trichotomy to argue for individual specialization in the production of gray, white, and orange pottery. Obviously, the mechanisms by which these three disparate traditions were maintained require further research.

Unpainted ceramic styles of the period after 1150 did not differ substantially from those associated with the terminal occupation of the Peabody lease area. Tusayan Corrugated, which possesses indented corrugations over the entire exterior of the vessel, is the preponderant textured form in late sites of the lease area (P. Reed 1981), and the style persisted virtually unchanged until abandonment of the Kayenta area around A.D. 1300. Toward the end of the lease-area occupation, a second textured style developed. Moenkopi Corrugated is identified by the downward flattening of the coils,

which imparts a clapboard effect. This type burgeoned after A.D. 1150 and predominated over Tusayan Corrugated by the Tsegi phase. During the Tsegi phase, coarse, thick walled, plain gray vessels (Kiet Siel and Rainbow Grays) were produced in large numbers. The vast majority of plain and textured vessels of the period after A.D. 1150 are jars. Grayware styles analogous to Tusayan and Moenkopi Corrugateds and Kiet Siel Gray persisted for some time after A.D. 1300 in the area of the Hopi Mesas (Gifford and Smith 1978; Lindsay 1969:323).

An unpainted ceramic form that appears to have originated in the Kayenta area during Pueblo II times is the perforated-rim plate (Crotty 1983:55–56; Lindsay 1969:291–292; Lyons 2001:392–403). This form is a shallow, concave, plain or exterior-corrugated vessel usually fitted with a broad, flat rim ringed with evenly spaced perforations produced before it was fired. Such plates occur on Tusayan White Ware, Gray Ware, or Orange Ware paste. The appellation Tsegi Corrugated is the only type name that commemorates a pottery form that crosscuts three different wares and two different styles of surface treatment, plain and corrugated. Tsegi Corrugated plates may have served several functions, of which one could have been as a base for forming pots (Crotty 1983:56; Haury and Hargrave 1931:68; Hough 1903:337; Lyons 2001).

Whatever its function, this distinctive form has a wide and interesting geographical distribution. Its abundance on Pueblo IV sites in the Tusayan area (Gifford and Smith 1978:97; Lindsay 1969:292) is not surprising in view of its occurrence in the Tsegi phase. Nor is its presence in late Mogollon pueblos, such as the Pinedale Ruin (Haury and Hargrave 1931:68), unexpected. Its occurrence along with several other Kayenta traits at the Reeve and Davis Ruins on the San Pedro River in southern Arizona (Di Peso 1958), however, is intriguing. In addition, perforated plates have been recovered from Los Muer-

tos (Haury 1945a:111) and Las Colinas (Hammack and Sullivan 1981:165), Classic-period Hohokam sites in the Salt River drainage. The form also occurs at Casas Grandes in northern Chihuahua, Mexico (Lindsay 1969:292). The spread of perforated plates from a modest beginning in hamlets scattered across the Colorado Plateau to the Classic-period Hohokam riverine communities of the Sonoran Desert and ultimately to a fourteenth-century urban center in northern Chihuahua provides a fascinating, albeit hazy, glimpse of the dynamics of prehistoric southwestern sociocultural interaction.

Black-on-white ceramic-design styles of the period from A.D. 1150 to 1300 are, by and large, direct outgrowths of the designs of the preceding period. The broad line style, represented just before A.D. 1150 by Sosi Black-on-white, evolved by around A.D. 1175 into the somewhat more complex but often less well executed designs of Flagstaff Black-on-white. In the eastern Kayenta area, Flagstaff Black-on-white appears in lower frequencies than one would expect for a major indigenous type, rarely occurs by itself or even as a predominant type, and is found on far fewer sites than would be expected. Although some of these problems may reflect the difficulty of sorting a type that grades into preceding and following styles, they also seem to accurately reflect the "behavior" of this type. Paradoxically, the type "Flagstaff Black-on-white" exists in two different wares, Tusayan White Ware and Little Colorado White Ware, the only difference being the nature of the paste. The apparent higher frequency of the Little Colorado White Ware variant in the Flagstaff area has led to the hypothesis that the Flagstaff style represents an infusion of "foreign" design elements into the Kayenta tradition of design (Beals et al. 1945:109, 133).

Around A.D. 1200, the Flagstaff style evolved into the more complex Tusayan Black-on-white style, which is characterized by heavier line work, a higher proportion of black painted area to white background, a different symmetrical structure, more complex layouts, and improved execution. Around A.D. 1270, the distinctive Kayenta variety of Tusayan Black-on-white appeared alongside the established variety. The Kayenta variant is characterized by the predominance of black painted area over white background and the development of the narrow-line, rectilinear underframing known as "mosquito bar." In contrast to the grayware types, Kayenta-branch whiteware types after A.D. 1150 occur in all forms: jars, bowls, seed jars, colanders, "canteens," and other, more specialized shapes.

The Tusayan-Kayenta style represents the culmination of the Tusayan White Ware tradition. Potters of the Tsegi phase fashioned vessels that are technical and artistic equals of any pottery produced in the Southwest. This style marks the end of the tradition in the Kayenta heartland. The style itself, however, survived the demise of the Kayenta branch around A.D. 1300 and persisted in the Hopi Mesas–Hopi Buttes area (W. Smith 1971) and on the western flanks of the Defiance Plateau (Colton 1956).

During the Tsegi phase, Tsegi Orange Ware design ramified into a number of different types and styles in addition to the continuing Tusayan Black-on-red and Tusayan Polychrome styles (Beals et al. 1945:125–133). Several simple, linear styles were created by applying designs in red or black paint or both to the unslipped orange paste to produce Tsegi Red-on-orange, Black-on-orange, and Polychrome. Kiet Siel Black-on-red features broadline black designs on a red slip over the orange vessel, while Kiet Siel Polychrome has white-outlined bold black designs painted on a red slip. Kiet Siel Black-on-red vessels that exhibit black-on-white pottery designs are rare examples of the cross-ware occurrence of ceramic-design patterns. A four-color scheme, designated Kayenta Polychrome, was created by appending white outlines to the red or black elements of Tusayan Polychrome. Orange pottery exhibits a

narrower range of forms than is found in the whitewares. Jars are far less numerous than bowls and tend to cluster toward the small end of the range of jar sizes. Except for a few high-shouldered forms with constricted necks (Lindsay et al. 1968:350, figure 248), large orangeware jars equal in size to the wide-mouthed grayware jars and the elegant whiteware ollas are not found. Small, handled pitchers are common.

The design exuberance evident in the orangeware pottery of the Tsegi phase contrasts markedly with the rigid adherence to a narrower range of design conventions apparent in the whiteware vessels. Although the whiteware is unequaled in technical quality, excellence of execution, and beauty of outcome within prescribed design limits, it represents the apex of the Tusayan-Kayenta style. Apparently, the orangeware was not so rigidly bound by convention as the whiteware and was the subject of considerable experimentation in paint colors and design configurations. Late in the Tsegi phase, experimentation with firing procedures produced a wide variety of paste and paint colors, including tans and purples. The exhilarating variation in late Tsegi Orange Ware pottery reflects the creative efforts of a group of craftsmen to explore the possibilities of a vital, still-evolving, artistic tradition.

The white outlining that occurs on Kiet Siel and Kayenta polychromes is shared with the late black- and white-on-red polychromes of the White Mountain Red Ware (Carlson 1970), which was produced south of the Puerco and Little Colorado Rivers. Since white outlining appears to have originated in the White Mountain Red Ware, it is likely that the practice was adopted by Kayenta potters as a result of interaction with late Mogollon groups. Such long-distance interaction could have been mediated by the Tusayan-branch peoples of southern Black Mesa. The possibility of ceramic-design interchange between Kayenta and late Mogollon potters is supported by occasional occurrences

of White Mountain Red Ware pottery in sites of the Tsegi phase and by the shared design attributes diagnostic of the Pinedale style (Carlson 1982:217–218). The late thirteenth-century Kayenta or Tusayan immigration into Point of Pines (Haury 1958; Lindsay 1986; Reed 1958) and a western Anasazi presence at Grasshopper Pueblo (Reid 1989; Reid and Whittlesey 1999) provide further evidence of interaction between these groups. Local copies at Point of Pines of Tsegi Orange Ware polychromes document the spread of Kayenta ceramic-design styles far beyond the boundaries of the Kayenta-Tusayan areas. Even wider dissemination of these design conventions is evident in Tucson Polychrome, a post-A.D. 1300 derivative of Kiet Siel Polychrome that occurs in the San Pedro (Di Peso 1958; Lindsay 1992) and Santa Cruz (Hayden 1957) Valleys of southern Arizona. Thus, elements of the Tsegi Orange Ware design tradition were widely distributed throughout the western Southwest and persisted for some time after the demise of the Kayenta branch itself around A.D. 1300.

During the period from A.D. 1150 to 1300, ceramic design was virtually identical across the entire Kayenta area. Nonetheless, minor design differences in Tsegi-phase painted pottery from the Navajo Mountain and Marsh Pass core localities exist. Detailed design analyses, particularly of the possible "potter's marks" that occur on many Tsegi Orange Ware vessels, would go a long way toward elucidating these areal differences. An overt acknowledgment of spatial variation lies in the identification of local varieties of coarse, plain gray pottery; Rainbow Gray (Ambler 1985b) in the Navajo Mountain area and Kiet Siel Gray elsewhere. Local differences in frequencies of particular design elements, wares, and types also have been recognized (K. Anderson 1971; Crotty 1983:59–60), but much more work along these lines remains to be done.

Potters of the Kayenta branch participated in a number of design styles that crosscut local ceramic traditions. The spread of ceramic-design conventions across large areas of the Southwest is one of the markers of episodes of increased interareal interaction that F. Plog (1983, 1984) terms "alliances." Before A.D. 1150, Kayenta potters participated in the widespread Lino, Kana-a, and Dogoszhi horizon styles. This type of artistic sharing continued after A.D. 1150, although the horizon styles of this period seem to be less geographically extensive than the earlier ones. The previously noted occurrence of the Flagstaff style in both the Little Colorado and Tusayan White Wares is an example of this phenomenon. The Tusayan-Kayenta Black-on-white style also seems to have been produced outside the core localities of the Kayenta and Tusayan branches.

Architecture

Several attributes differentiate Kayenta-branch architecture from that of neighboring groups. Masonry style has long been thought to distinguish the Kayenta branch from the Mesa Verde and Chaco branches. However, masonry is quite variable across the Kayenta area. So-called typical Kayenta masonry (Kidder 1924:plate 20; McGregor 1965:337) is found primarily in cliff dwellings, where the structures are protected by the overhanging rockshelters. Generally, higher-quality masonry is found in open sites that are exposed to the elements. Double-thick masonry walls (Lindsay 1969:140–141) are found primarily in open sites, often in central roomblocks or as dividers between major sections of a pueblo. This kind of wall is rare in cliff dwellings. Large-scale adobe construction is mostly limited to Navajo Canyon cliff dwellings (Ward 1975:43). Jacal walls seem to be more common in cliff dwellings, but this apparent association could be due to poor preservation of this perishable form in open sites. BMAP recovered abundant evidence of jacal construction at open sites. Intersite differences in the occurrence of jacal walls are evident at Betatakin and Kiet

Siel. The distribution of such walls is highly regular at Betatakin, where in all instances but one they occur as front walls of living rooms. At Kiet Siel, on the other hand, jacal walls appear in a variety of contexts, ranging from storerooms to dwellings and forming up to three of a room's four walls (Dean 1969:132, figure 32).

Perhaps the most diagnostic feature of Kayenta domestic architecture is the entrybox complex (Dean 1969:27–28, figure 7; Jennings 1966:figure 40; Lindsay 1969:143–145, figure 10). An entrybox (figure 5.10, Chapter 5, this volume) consists of one or two masonry or slab wingwalls that connect one or both doorjambs to a masonry or slab deflector set between the doorway and fire pit. This feature originated in the Pueblo II period and is virtually unique to the Kayenta branch. Entryboxes are found nowhere else in the Southwest, except at the Goat Hill site in the Safford Valley of Arizona (Woodson 1995), at the Reeve Ruin on the San Pedro River in southern Arizona (Di Peso 1958; Lindsay 1987), and at Mariana Mesa Site 616 in west-central New Mexico (McGimsey 1980:37–170, figures 22, 26).

Kayenta-branch architecture varies considerably in form both within and between communities. Although present in other Navajo Canyon sites (Morss 1931:12), entryboxes are absent from Inscription House (Ward 1975:43), which also lacks grooved jambs on granary doorways, a feature present at most other sites. In contrast, Inscription House has a higher than average incidence of T-shaped doorways, which are relatively scarce in other cliff dwellings. Slab paving of granary floors is more frequent in open sites than in cliff dwellings, where the bedrock floors of the rockshelters prevented vermin from burrowing into the food supply.

Religious architecture exhibits some consistent differences between sites and between localities. As Lindsay (1969:174) points out, rectangular kivas have not yet been found in plaza-oriented sites, while

both rectangular and circular kivas exist in open and sheltered courtyard sites. Kivas in the Navajo Mountain locality seem to be somewhat more standardized in shape and features than do kivas in other localities. Slab floor paving is more common around Navajo Mountain. Many Navajo Mountain area Tsegi-phase kivas, paved or unpaved, have large circular slabs set into the floors (Cummings 1945; Lindsay 1969:177), a trait absent from the eastern localities. D-shaped or rectangular ceremonial annexes are abutted to some kivas, and there seems to be no geographic patterning to the distribution of these structures. At present, however, they are not known to occur in open sites. The number of habitation units per kiva varies widely from site to site; however, there is a tendency for larger sites and plaza-oriented sites to have higher ratios of secular rooms to kivas. Important differences exist between kivas in the Kayenta heartland and those of the Tusayan branch on the southern extremity of Black Mesa. Although D-shaped kivas are unknown in the former area, they are abundant in Pueblo III sites on Antelope Mesa (W. Smith 1972). It is tempting to posit a link between these kivas and the D-shaped ceremonial annexes of the Tsegi phase; however, confirmation of such connection will involve considerable problem-oriented research.

Settlement

Kayenta settlement during the period from A.D. 1150 to 1300 can be comprehended in terms of two primary aspects of settlement behavior. The term *settlement pattern* (Sears 1961:226) refers to the manner in which different types and sizes of sites are distributed across the landscape and the ways in which they are related to one another and to aspects of the physical environment. The term *community pattern* (Sears 1961:226) refers to the basic units of site architecture and the ways in which they are articulated to form different kinds of sites. In combination, these two concepts provide useful, consistent, and comparable descriptions of archaeologically visible aspects of this important behavioral phenomenon. Because of major differences in settlement, the Transition period and the Tsegi phase are considered separately.

The Transition Period (A.D. 1150 to 1250)

The entire Transition period is represented by fewer than twenty excavated sites, most of which are located in the vicinity of Navajo Mountain, on the Shonto Plateau, and in the Klethla Valley; thus, the data are heavily biased geographically. Moreover, in the Klethla Valley and on the Shonto Plateau, only portions of sites lying within narrow highway and railroad rights of way have been excavated. As a result of these shortcomings, this period is known primarily through survey and only secondarily through excavation. Because of these sampling biases, Transition-period settlement pattern, although imperfectly understood, is much better known than community patterning.

The Transition period was an era of substantial change in Kayenta society. During the century between A.D. 1150 and 1250, the small, dispersed, relatively autonomous communities that dotted the countryside around A.D. 1150 evolved into the large, aggregated, interdependent communities of the Tsegi phase. These changes are manifested in and in some measure caused by major shifts in settlement pattern that in turn were responses to increasing imbalances within the Kayenta adaptive system (Gumerman and Dean 1989). Thus, the Kayenta settlement pattern underwent a drastic and relatively sudden transformation at the beginning of the Transition period. The range expansion that had characterized the preceding three hundred years ceased, and the Kayenta system collapsed back toward its center. Huge areas north and west of the San Juan and Colorado Rivers were vacated by Kayenta peoples, the Virgin branch declined, and the Kayenta presence

in the Chinle Valley and Canyon del Muerto waned. Although the greater part of this settlement shift occurred early in the Transition period, the process of abandoning areas peripheral to the core localities continued throughout the period. Toward the end of the period, Monument Valley was abandoned (Neely and Olson 1977:72–73), and habitation of the San Juan and Colorado River canyons fell precipitously (Adams and Lindsay 1961; Long 1966).

Circumstances surrounding twelfth-century population movements on the southern Kayenta periphery are poorly understood. The nature of interactions between Kayenta-Tusayan groups of southern Black Mesa and Winslow branch groups east and south of the Hopi Mesas during the Transition period is unknown. If, as seems likely, the people of the Wupatki area were Kayentans, their behavior during the contraction after A.D. 1150 would be most enlightening. It is clear that this area was not vacated soon after A.D. 1150 and that, unlike other peripheral Kayenta groups, the Wupatki population did not participate in the initial withdrawal toward the Kayenta heartland (Sullivan and Downum 1991). In fact, Ambler (1985a:48) feels that the Wupatki area was a major locus of Kayenta-branch activity in the late twelfth century. Population declined rapidly thereafter, probably as a result of emigration, and the Wupatki locality was abandoned by A.D. 1225 (Hartman and Wolf 1977:17; Sullivan and Downum 1991).

Archaeologically, the Kayenta spatial contraction that began around A.D. 1150 seems to be a straightforward withdrawal of a population from the perimeter to the center of its distribution. As noted previously, however, core-locality population curves fail to exhibit the increments that should reflect the absorption of immigrants from the peripheries. The possibility that the apparent abandonments really reflect reversion to or adoption of different lifeways or absorption by local populations merits investigation.

Such processes would account for the apparent disappearance of Kayenta groups from peripheral areas without concomitant population increases in the supposed heartland destinations of these people.

Two interesting anomalies mar the generally consistent archaeological picture of the Kayenta disappearance from the peripheries after A.D. 1150. Eighty km (50 mi) northwest of the Colorado River near the head of the Escalante drainage at the foot of the Aquarius Plateau lies the Coombs Site (R. Lister 1959; Lister et al. 1960; Lister and Lister 1961). Consisting of several masonry and jacal roomblocks and a number of pit houses, the Coombs site is identified by its excavators as a Kayenta manifestation showing minor infusions of Virgin branch and Fremont traits. Tree-ring dates (Bannister et al. 1969:12–13) place the occupation of this site in the A.D. 1170s, twenty years after the Kayenta Anasazi are supposed to have withdrawn from these far northern fringes of their Pueblo II range. Roughly 320 km (200 mi) southwest of the Coombs Site, on the Coconino Plateau near the south rim of the Grand Canyon, is a small, seemingly isolated group of Kayenta sites, only one of which has been excavated. The Tusayan Ruin (Haury 1931) is a U-shaped masonry pueblo of eight living rooms, eight storage chambers, and two kivas. Tree-ring dates in the 1180s and 1190s (Bannister et al. 1968:11) reveal that the Tusayan Ruin, like the Coombs site, postdates the presumed Kayenta abandonment of its locality.

The apparent existence in the late twelfth century of at least two Kayenta "outposts" in areas supposedly forsaken by Kayenta populations several decades earlier raises a number of intriguing questions. Are these apparent anomalies real? Could contemporaneous Kayenta sites in these areas have escaped the notice of archaeologists? Could there be, as Jennings (1966:55–56) suggests, problems in the dating of pottery types that produce anomalously early date estimates for frontier sites lacking dendrochronological placement? Given the amount of survey and excavation in these areas, both these possibilities seem unlikely. Could both sites have been misidentified as Kayenta phenomena? Perhaps, but there seem to be no compelling reasons to question the assessments of the excavators. If we provisionally accept the reality of both situations, are the Coombs Site and the Grand Canyon ruins the only instances of this phenomenon, or are there other examples as yet unrecognized? What do such frontier outposts signify within the context of the archaeology of the Transition-period Kayenta branch? Could they be the outliers of a Kayenta regional interaction system? Could they be Kayenta enclaves maintained to ensure continued access to natural resources present in these recently abandoned localities? Could they be Kayenta trading centers located to facilitate exchange with non-Kayenta populations in the two localities? Could they represent small groups of obstinate Kayentans who refused to join the exodus to the heartland or to be absorbed by local populations? Could they be centers where local non-Kayentans, who had maintained trade or other ties with the Kayenta heartland, funneled imported Kayenta goods into the local economies? None of these questions can be answered at present, but they offer fascinating opportunities for further research.

Coincident with the twelfth-century settlement changes on the peripheries were major settlement rearrangements within the Kayenta nuclear area. Except in the Navajo Mountain locality, upland areas were virtually abandoned as loci of permanent habitation. In both east and west, populations began to aggregate in localities where alluvial or eolian arable land and water were available. Around Navajo Mountain, sites were concentrated along alluviated drainages and dune areas of the broad upland surfaces. With the exception of middle Paiute Canyon (Ambler et al. 1983:21) and Navajo Canyon, the western canyons are not notably suitable for farming. Many,

including the gorges of the San Juan and Colorado Rivers, are cut into bare rock and possess only isolated patches of arable land. Others, such as lower Paiute Canyon and Nakai Canyon, are incised into the Chinle formation, which is notoriously inimical to plant life. After A.D. 1150, these canyons were used sparingly for permanent habitation as the Kayenta Anasazi focused on the more favorable uplands. The opposite elevational trend prevailed in the east, where the most favorable conjunctions of soil and water occur in the lowlands. Here, the large, open valleys were the principal loci of settlement concentration as the less-favorable uplands were vacated. During the Transition period, the alluviated Kayenta, Long House, and Klethla Valleys became major foci of settlement (Dean et al. 1978; Haas and Creamer 1993) as did the lower, heavily duned, southwestern flanks of the Shonto Plateau. Settlement behavior in the Tusayan area during this period is unknown, due to the lack of large-scale survey. A shift from upland to lowland habitation similar to that in the eastern core locality is noted farther east, where the Defiance Plateau was abandoned and settlement concentrated in Canyons de Chelly and del Muerto (Fall 1981:31; McDonald 1976:60; D. Morris 1983:3).

A major outcome of the internal settlement shifts that began around A.D. 1150 was the development of "empty" areas between local population centers. The abandonment of northern Black Mesa created a large uninhabited zone between the eastern core locality centered on Marsh Pass and the Tusayan populations of southern Black Mesa. A similar gap that eventually encompassed the entire Shonto Plateau widened during the Transition period, as did a breach between the Klethla Valley and Long House Valley settlements. Despite the increasing geographical isolation of Kayenta settlement groups, interaction among these centers was high, as indicated by strong similarities in ceramic design and an apparently lively trade in ceramic raw materials or finished

products (Ambler 1983; Geib and Callahan 1987).

Settlement shifts also occurred within inhabited areas in the eastern lowlands. A generalized upstream movement toward the upper reaches of the drainages began in the Transition period. Even within fairly small headwater localities, major settlement changes occurred during the Transition period. These shifts are most thoroughly documented for the Kayenta and Long House Valleys (Dean et al. 1978; Lindsay and Dean 1978; Effland 1979; Haas and Creamer 1993).

The coincidence of major settlement shifts in the Kayenta heartland and peripheries with significant environmental fluctuations suggests that the former might have been caused at least in part by the latter (Dean 1988b; Dean et al. 1985:538–540; Gumerman and Dean 1989; F. Plog et al. 1988). Between about A.D. 1130 and 1170, low- and high-frequency environmental degradation (figure 6.2) substantially lowered the environmental limits that regulated Kayenta adaptive systems. These drastically altered adaptive circumstances would have required equally drastic responses if the Kayenta population was to continue to thrive.

The far-flung Kayenta populations that had expanded across a vast territory during two and a half centuries of favorable environmental and demographic conditions were ill-equipped to cope with simultaneous deteriorations in both low- and high-frequency environmental conditions. Given that farming was no longer equally possible everywhere, settlement was reoriented around the more restricted localities favorable for farming under the altered conditions. Not surprisingly, the areas most affected by these settlement adjustments were upland localities, where precipitation was crucial to agriculture, and fringe areas, where the Kayenta adaptive system was stretched to its limits. In the west, the greater precipitation associated with the orographic effects of Navajo Mountain coupled with greater areas of arable land favored the uplands over the barren canyons. In the east, abundant arable land combined with localized sources of groundwater favored the lowlands over the uplands, where diminished groundwater supplies would have been insufficient to offset the lower precipitation of the period.

During the Transition period, Kayenta-branch community patterning underwent changes comparable in magnitude to that seen in settlement pattern. Two new community configurations arose to coexist with the "unit pueblo" pattern, which persisted into the Transition period, though in reduced numbers. The plaza community type may represent an expansion of the Pueblo II unit pueblo (see figure 5.17, Chapter 5, this volume). The simplest variant consists of a single or double row of masonry rooms fronted by an open plaza or a plaza bounded by walls extending from the ends of the roomblock. More complex variants feature rows of masonry rooms projecting at right angles from the ends and middle of the primary roomblock to form L-, U-, or E-shaped groundplans (Beals et al. 1945:15, figure 2; Ambler et al. 1964:11, figure 3) with open or closed plazas.

The abundance of jacal rooms in Pueblo II sites of the lease area suggests that such chambers might also exist in the later plaza sites; however, none have been recognized in the handful of Transition-period pueblos that have been excavated. Occasionally, pit houses are arrayed along one or more sides of the plaza in addition to the masonry roomblock at the back. Usually, the row of masonry rooms at the rear of the plaza contains facilities for community food storage and preparation, while living rooms are situated in the masonry, jacal, or pit-house wings that flank the plaza. Toward the end of the Transition period, sites of this type became quite large, in terms of both area and height of rubble mounds, some of which suggest two-story construction. Surprise Pueblo (figure 6.4) on Cummings Mesa (Ambler et al. 1964:figure

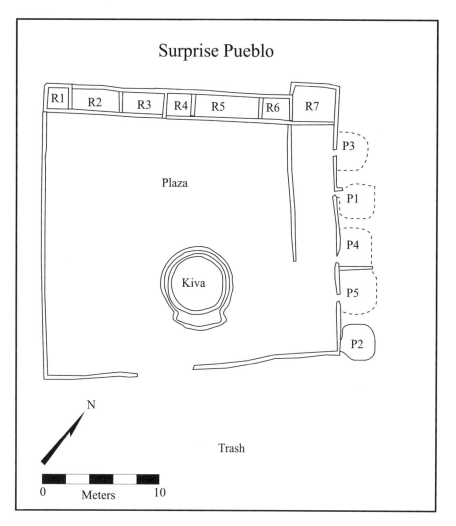

Figure 6.4 Transition-period plaza-oriented site, Surprise Pueblo (NA 7498) on Cummings Mesa (after Ambler et al. 1964:figure 41).

41) and NA 12062 (Dean 1996a:figure 3-4a) in Long House Valley exemplify the late configuration of this community type as it takes on attributes of the Tsegi-phase plaza-oriented community plan.

The second major community pattern of the Transition period consists of scattered pit houses associated with surface and subterranean storage facilities and a detached kiva (K. Anderson 1980:7, figure 4; Dean 1996a:figure 3-4b). Semisubterranean grinding rooms are present at many of these pit-house hamlets, as are surface work areas and ramadas. Since a Transition-period pit-house village has never been completely excavated, the extent and composition of this type of community remain problematical. In the preceding Pueblo II period, this

community pattern occurred in the Klethla Valley (Adams 1973), in the Peabody Coal Company lease area, and on central Black Mesa (Gleichman 1982b). Like the unit pueblo and plaza pueblo community types, the pit-house village persisted through the Transition period and into the Tsegi phase.

The pit houses found in the Transition-period pit-house villages are extraordinarily varied, ranging from circular to square to utterly amorphous (figure 6.5; Adams 1973:figures 18, 24; Ambler et al. 1964:25, figures 9, 12, 13; Ambler and Olson 1977; K. Anderson 1980; Beals et al. 1945:82–83, figure 17, plate 20; Foose 1982:184, figure 63). A distinctive constellation of architectural features that contrasts sharply with the

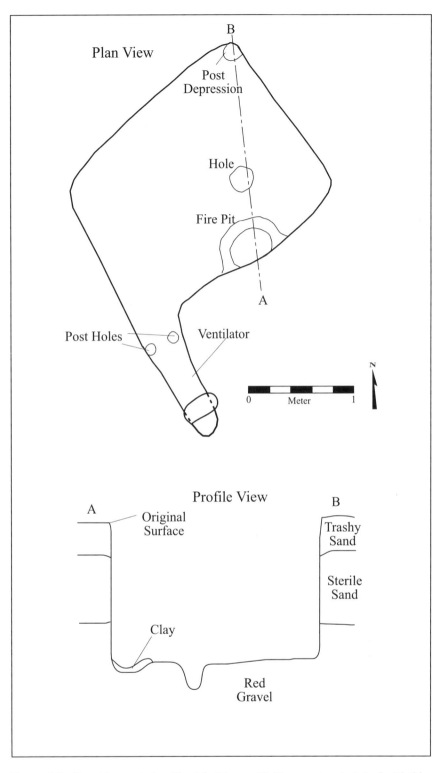

Plan View

B

Post
Depression

Hole

Fire Pit

A

Post Holes

Ventilator

N

0   Meter   1

Profile View

A

Original
Surface

B

Trashy
Sand

Sterile
Sand

Clay

Red
Gravel

Figure 6.5 Transition-period residential pit house, Pit House 7 at NA 8163 in the Klethla Valley (after Anderson 1980:7, figure 4).

except the masonry-lined Room P at RB 568 (Beals et al. 1945:82–83, figure 17, plate 20) are unlined. The front walls of these structures, as identified by ventilators in the middle or at one end of the wall, range from south-southeast to east-southeast in orientation. Fire pits commonly are adjacent to or actually abut the front wall, although occasionally they are situated about one-third the distance from the front to the back wall (Ambler and Olson 1977:16–17, figures 17–18). A unique feature of these structures is twin roof-support posts set opposite one another within the side walls slightly to the rear of the fire pit.

Pit structures of this type are widely distributed in late Transition-period pit-house villages throughout the Kayenta country. The five examples cited by Ambler and Andrews come from Paiute Mesa (the early component of Neskahi Village), the Klethla Valley (NA 8163, NA 11055, and the Shonto Junction Doghouse), and the Parrish Creek drainage (RB 568). An unequivocal sixth example is present in Structure 4 at AZ J-58-4 in the upper Wepo drainage near Pinon on central Black Mesa, some 40 km south of the Peabody Coal Company lease area (Gleichman 1982b:172, figures 57–58; Legard 1982a:228, figure 77). At present, this kind of pit structure occurs in the Kayenta area primarily in Transition-period pit-house villages. It has not been recognized in the Pueblo II sites excavated by BMAP in the lease area; it does not appear in the few Transition-period unit pueblos and plaza pueblos that have been sampled; and it is absent from Tsegi-phase courtyard and plaza sites.

The antecedents of the Transition-period specialized pit structure are as yet unknown. Ambler and Andrews (1981:75–76) see a possible origin for some features of these chambers in a couple of earlier kivas, one at RB 1008 (Beals et al. 1945:69–70, figure 13) and the other at NA 8171 (Ambler 1994; Ambler and Olson 1977:47–48, figures 43–44). Compared to the major differences in form between these kivas and the pit structures, however, these

general heterogeneity of Transition-period pit houses led Ambler and Andrews (1981:72–77, figure 16; Ambler 1994) to identify a specialized type of pit structure. These structures

(figure 6.6) are rectangular to square in plan, averaging from two to three meters on a side, and are noticeably deeper than the "ordinary" pit houses with which they are associated. All

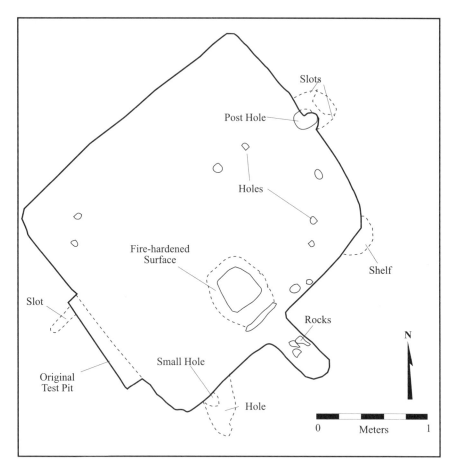

Figure 6.6 Transition-period specialized pit structure, Feature 16 at the Shonto Junction Dog House (AZ-D-10-16 [NAU]) in the Klethla Valley (after Ambler and Andrews 1981:figure 16).

minor concordances seem rather inconclusive. Similarly, it is impossible to recognize any morphological descendants of these pit structures in the Tsegi Phase. However, the failure to find Tsegi-phase equivalents of these pit structures may be nothing more than a consequence of the lack of excavation in Tsegi-phase pit house villages, where such structures would be expected to occur.

The functions of these distinctive pit structures remain unknown. Because of their intersite uniformity, their morphological differences from associated pit structures, and the existence of only one per site, it is tempting to assign them ceremonial status. In fact, Legard (1982a:228) identifies Structure 4 at AZ J-58-4 as a kiva. Although Ambler and Andrews (1981:76; Ambler 1994) consider including this form in the kiva category,

they ultimately reject this assignment because these structures would have been too small for public observances and because they lack many of the attributes of unequivocal contemporaneous kivas. To these reasons should be added that in at least two instances (NA 8163 and Neskahi Village), specialized pit structures and unambiguous kivas are found together. These associations coupled with the pronounced size and morphological differences suggest that these two kinds of structures performed different functions. For the present at least, the term kiva should be restricted to structures that conform to the recognizable kiva form.

Based on the occurrence of loom anchors in the Shonto Junction Doghouse and the possible presence of such features in Pit house 6 at NA 8163, Ambler and Andrews (1981:76–77;

Ambler 1994) hypothesize that these pit structures were used for weaving activities not performed in the kivas, specifically, for producing narrow fabrics such as sashes and belts. This inference gains some support from the recovery of a possible weaving implement of wood from the floor of Structure 4 at AZ J-58-4 on central Black Mesa (Legard 1982a:228).

The specialized-function hypotheses of Ambler and Andrews (weaving facility) and Legard (kiva) are, to a great extent, confounded by the fact that this type of pit structure is the principle domiciliary structure of sites of the McDonald phase (A.D. 1150 to 1250) in the Winslow branch of the central Little Colorado River Valley far to the south of the Kayenta heartland (Gumerman 1988b; Gumerman and Skinner 1968). In the Hopi Buttes, for example, five of the eight pit houses that comprise the McDonald phase component of the Ramp Site (Gumerman 1988b:108–142) are indistinguishable from the specialized pit structure of the pit-house villages of the Kayenta branch. The occurrence in at least five Kayenta-branch Transition-period pit-house villages of single examples of a common Winslow-branch domiciliary form has important implications for the function of these structures and their place within Transition-period pit-house communities. That they represent local ceremonial or craft specialization alone seems unlikely.

That these structures denote interaction between people of the Kayenta and Winslow branches seems inescapable. The nature of such interaction, however, is less obvious. The presence of a foreign architectural form implies the presence of a foreigner, or foreigners, to construct and use it. Could the specialized pit structures in Kayenta sites represent southern men, perhaps craftsmen (weavers?), who married into the Kayenta villages, or whole families who immigrated to provide the village with a particular craft or service? Could they represent more formal economic or political relationships involving the presence of southern "agents" in the Kayenta villages? If these structures do represent a southern presence in the Kayenta area, why only one structure per pit-house village, and why are they seemingly absent from contemporaneous unit pueblo and plaza-oriented sites? These and a host of other important questions regarding this pattern can be answered only through problem-oriented excavation. Understanding the place of the specialized pit structure in Transition-period pit-house villages is crucial to understanding the interrelationships between these communities and similar communities in the Winslow-branch area, which in turn clearly is vital to an adequate understanding of the prehistory of the Kayenta and Winslow branches.

In addition to the three major community patterns of the Transition period—unit pueblo, plaza pueblo, and pit-structure village—are ad hoc site configurations dictated by location. Principal among these are cliff sites, most of which consist of linear arrangements of rooms in low recesses in cliffs and along ledges. NA 7485 and NA 7486 on Cummings Mesa (Ambler et al. 1964:43–53, figures 31–38) exemplify this type of site. Cliff dwellings of the sort common in the Tsegi phase are rare in the Transition period, primarily because of low population densities in localities with suitable rockshelters. Two Transition-period rockshelter occupations are known for Tsegi Canyon, one at Kiet Siel (Anderson 1971), and one at a small, possibly defensive site in the notch between Kiet Siel Canyon and the main Tsegi. Other ad hoc site "types" of this period include walled-up crevices in cliffs (Neely and Olson 1977:36, figure 7) and slump-boulder sites (Neely and Olson 1977:34, figure 5).

The three main Transition-period site types appear to occur in different proportions in different areas. Unit pueblos and plaza pueblos are more abundant in the Marsh Pass and Navajo Mountain localities. Pit-house villages, on the other hand, seem to be concentrated in the Klethla Valley (Haas and Creamer 1993; Swarthout

et al. 1986:349–425), on the southern Shonto Plateau, and on central Black Mesa (Linford 1982). Pit houses are found with masonry pueblos in the Navajo Mountain area, but only one Transition-period pit-house community of the type found in the Klethla Valley—the early component of Neskahi Village on Paiute Mesa (Hobler 1964, 1974)—has been noted in this locality. As Ambler and Andrews (1981:72–75) point out, masonry-lined pit structures are known in the eastern Kayenta core locality; however, pit-house villages are as yet unknown there. It must be stressed that these apparent differential distributions could be artifacts of the poor and geographically skewed sample of excavated sites dating to this interval.

As poorly understood as Transition-period community pattern is in the Kayenta heartland, it is even less well known in other localities, owing to lack of intensive surveys and excavations. In the Wupatki area, local groups seem to have aggregated into fairly large masonry pueblos, if the tree-ring dates from Wupatki Ruin can be accepted at face value. The internal structure of these sites, however, is virtually unknown, and it is impossible to compare Wupatki area structural units with those of the Kayenta heartland. Superficially, the large pueblos of the Wupatki area seem not to conform to the community patterns of the nuclear area, but the apparent differences could be due in part to these sites having been accommodated to the conformations of the rock outcrops on which they were built. Transition-period community patterns in the Tusayan branch are virtually unknown, and it would be fruitless to speculate on that subject here. In the Hopi Buttes area (Gumerman 1969; 1975:111–112, figure 3; 1983; 1988b; Gumerman and Skinner 1968), small pit-house hamlets were accompanied by a single plaza pueblo that—as indicated by its unique size and layout, two kivas, and a great kiva—probably served community integrative and religious functions.

Tsegi Phase (A.D. 1250 to 1300)

The Tsegi phase is one of the most thoroughly investigated and best-understood archaeological taxons in southwestern archaeology. Numerous sites in the Navajo Mountain and Tsegi Canyon–Marsh Pass core localities have been intensively studied. In addition, much systematic archaeological survey has been accomplished in both these areas. In contrast, sites of the Tsegi phase in the Laguna Creek and Klethla Valleys and in the canyons of the Shonto Plateau are known mainly through survey. The Tsegi-phase archaeology of central Black Mesa, south of Peabody Coal Company's lease area, is known primarily through unsystematic visitation and the personal impressions of scholars who have traversed this vast area. Thanks to the work of the Awatovi Expedition, the Tusayan-branch equivalent of the Tsegi phase is much better known than its Transition-period counterpart.

The settlement pattern of the Tsegi phase represents the culmination of trends set in motion at the beginning of the Transition period a century earlier. Peripheral areas continued to be vacated as settlement density continued to grow in the core localities. Around the end of the Transition period, Monument Valley on the northeastern margin of the Kayenta range was virtually abandoned as a place of permanent residence (Neely and Olson 1977:72). In the northwest, the canyons draining northward into the San Juan and Colorado Rivers were used almost exclusively in a logistic manner, as habitation was concentrated in the uplands surrounding Navajo Mountain. To the southwest, the Wupatki area seems to have been largely abandoned, at least by Kayenta peoples, by A.D. 1225 (B. Anderson 1990; Hartman and Wolf 1977:17; Sullivan and Downum 1991). In the south, many settlements in the Hopi Buttes and Little Colorado desert were abandoned, as the population aggregated into medium to large sites on the Hopi Mesas (Gumerman 1983:23–24; Gumerman and Skinner

1968) or adjacent to the Little Colorado itself (Hays et al. 1991; Lange 1989). In the Chinle Valley and its tributaries, Kayenta "influence" continued to diminish, although the picture is complicated by a growing Mesa Verde presence. Thus, instead of a Kayenta contraction, there may have been an intermingling of two populations, two cultural traditions, or both. Either the putative Kayenta outposts at the Coombs Site and the south rim of the Grand Canyon were abandoned or their connections with the Kayenta heartland were severed before the beginning of the Tsegi phase.

The continued contraction of Kayenta settlement into the nuclear area widened the gaps between these people and their neighbors. Paradoxically, interaction with some of these neighboring populations seems to have increased despite the growing spatial disjunctions separating them. Paiutes (Euler 1964) and Fremont peoples presumably were present to the north and west of the Kayenta area, but no material evidence links these groups to the Tsegi phase. Similarly, there is little evidence for interchange with the Cerbat peoples of the Grand Canyon area. Virtual identity in ceramic-design styles and a few imported vessels indicate that the people of the Kayenta heartland remained in close contact with the peoples of the Tusayan branch to the south, despite the widening separation across northern Black Mesa. Even more distant southern connections, probably mediated by peoples of the Tusayan branch, are signified by the occasional occurrence of Kayenta and White Mountain Red Ware pottery in areas of opposite affiliation, the occurrence of Kayenta-like ceramic-design styles in large pueblos beyond the Little Colorado, and the addition of white outlining to some Tsegi Orange Ware polychromes. Kayenta or Tusayan migrations to Homol'ovi, Point of Pines, and the San Pedro Valley provide further evidence of interaction across long distances (Woodson 1999).

Considerable evidence supports the position that in the eastern Kayenta area at least, particularly strong ties were maintained with peoples of Mesa Verde affiliation. Mesa Verde ceramics are far and away the most abundant trade pottery in sites of the Tsegi phase. Interestingly, Kayenta ceramics are not equally abundant in Mesa Verde sites. If one-to-one exchange was involved, the Mesa Verdeans received something other than ceramic vessels for their pottery; however, there is no evidence as to what this other commodity might have been. The infrequent occurrence in sites of the Tsegi phase of novel architectural forms that are far more abundant and have long developmental histories in the Mesa Verde area attest to contact between these groups. Kiva pilasters are an example of this phenomenon, although the Kayentans ignored the roof-support function of these features and raised flat instead of corbeled roofs over them (Morss 1927:32). Another example is provided by the circular or rectangular towers found at a few Kayenta cliff dwellings, notably Poncho House on the Chinle (Guernsey 1931:plates 38–39), Ruin 8 in Long House Valley (Kidder and Guernsey 1919:57–58, plate 18), and Kiet Siel (Dean 1969). Particularly telling in this regard are a granary (Room 68) and an attached wingwall in Room Cluster 10 at Kiet Siel (Dean 1969:125–126). The masonry of these features contrasts sharply with that of the rest of the pueblo and, in fact, is a reasonable facsimile of the Mesa Verde style characterized by large, blocky, carefully dressed stones set in regular courses. Moreover, the granary possesses a Mesa Verde–style entry with a lowered lintel (Lekson 1984:25–28) and slanted, recessed jambs rather than the grooved doorway with flanking loops that occurs in every other granary in Tsegi Canyon. The unique occurrence of an identifiably "foreign" architectural form in a context for which there is a perfectly good "native" equivalent is unambiguous evidence for direct contact between the two groups.

While Mesa Verde ceramics penetrated all the way to Navajo Mountain and both ceramics and architectural forms appeared in the eastern Kayenta territory, the center of Mesa Verde–Kayenta interaction clearly was the Chinle Valley. Joining the San Juan River near a fordable crossing, the Chinle drainage provides a natural access route into the country west of the Lukachukais for Mesa Verde populations of southwestern Colorado or southeastern Utah. Before around A.D. 1150, the Chinle Valley marked the eastern edge of the contiguous territory of people who produced material items of the Kayenta branch. Kayenta materials are abundant as far south as Canyon del Muerto but are in a distinct minority in Canyon de Chelly, which is dominated by Cibola White Ware pottery. After A.D. 1150, the Kayenta presence waned in the Chinle drainage and the Canyon de Chelly area, which was dominated thereafter by a mixture of Kayenta, Mesa Verde, Chuska, and Western Pueblo elements (McDonald 1976:59; D. Morris 1983:6; Thornton 1981).

Not long before A.D. 1250, a distinctive pattern developed in the Chinle drainage that bespeaks a high degree of interaction between Mesa Verde and Kayenta peoples and may signify the actual coresidence of members of both groups in individual villages. Several late thirteenth-century cliff dwellings exhibit styles of architectural execution similar to those of the Kayenta nuclear area. Produced in these styles, however, are characteristically Mesa Verdean forms such as pilastered kivas (Morss 1927:32), towers (Guernsey 1931:plates 38–39), and "masklike" arrangements of apertures (Gaede and Gaede 1977:figure 6). Except for Poncho House (Neely and Olson 1977:69–70), these sites appear to be dominated by Mesa Verde black-on-white pottery. In contrast, cotton textiles from Painted Cave bear polychrome designs painted in the style of Kayenta Black-on-white pottery (Haury 1945b:plates 10–12). Based on the division of craft production and postmarital residence practices that are usually assumed for the Anasazi, it is possible to infer that Kayenta males, who wove and painted blankets and used Kayenta construction techniques to produce Mesa Verde architectural forms, married into Mesa Verde–affiliated villages, where their wives produced and painted pottery in the Mesa Verde tradition. This hypothesis undoubtedly fails to capture the complexity of the true situation but does indicate possibilities for future research.

The position of Poncho House in the late Pueblo III organization of the Chinle Valley is a critical issue requiring additional research that should be undertaken while there still is enough left of the site to reward investigation (Gaede and Gaede 1977). W. Adams (1951:43) and Hargrave (1935:39) consider the site to be a Mesa Verde pueblo with some Kayenta affiliations, while Neely and Olson (1977:70) believe the site to have been "a Kayenta outpost with many Mesa Verde connections." Whichever assignment is correct, the size, configuration, and strategic location of this once magnificent cliff dwelling (Jackson 1878:422–423, plate L) attest to its importance as the probable pivot of thirteenth-century interactions in the Chinle Valley and of Kayenta–Mesa Verde social relations.

Within the Kayenta heartland, settlement trends that began during the Transition period persisted into the Tsegi phase. Upland areas continued to be forsaken as major loci of permanent habitation. Even the Navajo Mountain locality was no longer immune to this trend. Cummings Mesa had been vacated by around A.D. 1225 (Ambler et al. 1983:figure 4b), and the Dził Nez area of the Shonto Plateau was abandoned only slightly later (Ambler et al. 1983:figure 5c). In the western uplands, settlement persisted into the Tsegi phase only on the Rainbow Plateau and Paiute Mesa, and both these localities were abandoned before the Tsegi phase ended in the eastern Kayenta area (Ambler et al. 1983:figure 6). Of the two major inhabited western canyons, Paiute and Navajo, the former was abandoned shortly after A.D. 1250, while the latter appears to have supported settlement throughout the Tsegi phase. Occupation of two other upland areas, White and Tyende mesas, might have persisted into the early Tsegi phase.

In the eastern Kayenta area, the relocation of settlements toward the upper reaches of drainages and the agglomeration of populations in large sites located in a few restricted localities continued. These processes account for the concentration of settlements in headwater localities, such as the upper Klethla Valley, the Kayenta Valley, and Long House Valley, and the influx of population into Tsegi Canyon (figure 6.3). Casual survey on central Black Mesa reveals a trend toward aggregated settlements along the middle reaches of the Tusayan washes. Farther south, in the Tusayan area proper, the trend in the late Transition period toward aggregation in large sites on the edges of Antelope Mesa (W. Smith 1971:1–12), on the Hopi Mesas, and in the Homol'ovi area (Hays et al. 1991; Lange 1989, 1998) intensified. These settlement rearrangements continue the trend to concentrate around increasingly restricted localities favorable for farming.

The internal settlement shifts of the early Tsegi phase widened the gaps between the centers of population. A major break comprising most of the Shonto Plateau separated the Tsegi–Marsh Pass locus from the Navajo Mountain center. Contraction of settlement opened a gap 15 km wide between the Long House Valley and Klethla Valley loci (Haas and Creamer 1993:85). Additional southward withdrawal increased the space between nuclear area groups and their cohorts on central Black Mesa. The magnitude of the separation, if any, between the central Black Mesa groups and the large Tusayan branch centers on the southern edge of the mesa is at present unknown.

As during the Transition period, the spatial gaps between Kayenta settlement concentrations did not appreciably hinder interaction. Close similarities among the centers in terms of ceramic technology and design conventions, architectural forms and styles, and community pattern bespeak a correspondingly intense interchange among these loci. Differences in ceramic designs and type frequencies, architectural features, and community pattern do not negate the overall evidence for the sharing of items and ideas among these groups. Formal means of interlocality communication probably developed during this period. Contact between the Klethla Valley and central Black Mesa settlements could have been maintained through the Valley View site on the rim of the mesa overlooking the valley to the north and the mesa interior to the south (Haas and Creamer 1993:76–77). Although there is no apparent connection between the Klethla Valley and Long House Valley, the latter area appears to have been joined with the Kayenta Valley (Haas and Creamer 1993:69–70). A line of intervisible sites along Laguna Creek might have linked the Kayenta Valley locus with the "mixed" Kayenta–Mesa Verde communities of the Chinle Valley. Long-distance line-of-sight relationships also may have linked the Navajo Mountain and Klethla Valley centers (Dean 1998).

Settlement shifts also occurred within inhabited areas. Ambler et al.'s (1983:figure 3.5) population curves reflect changes in settlement distributions throughout the uplands and lowlands of the Navajo Mountain locality. In the east, major settlement rearrangements were focused on Tsegi Canyon, which had been only sparsely occupied immediately before the Tsegi phase. Transition-period occupations are known for some open sites (Beals et al. 1945:tables 1 and 2), the Kiet Siel rockshelter (K. Anderson 1971), and Hostile House, a small cliff site in the gap between Kiet Siel Canyon and the main Tsegi. The nature of the Kiet Siel rockshelter occupation is unknown, since the pueblo was razed during the construction of Kiet Siel. The strategic location and minimal defensive arrangements of Hostile House may identify it as the locus of a small vanguard sent out to explore the potential of the canyon for "colonization." The size of Hostile House (it probably housed no more than two families) removes it from the category of a "fort" established by invaders. Whatever the preparation, during the A.D. 1250s, Betatakin, Kiet Siel, and perhaps Swallow's Nest Cliff Dwelling were founded by small groups consisting of two to five households (Dean 1969:193–196). Betatakin and Kiet Siel grew slowly for twenty years or so until large population increments took place in the middle A.D. 1270s. This major population influx was also responsible for the founding of other villages in suitable locations throughout the canyon system. Among the sites probably begun in this decade are Scaffold House, Batwoman House, Twin Caves Pueblo, Nagashi Bikin, and a number of smaller hamlets. Betatakin, Kiet Siel, and Scaffold House were augmented in the A.D. 1280s, and most of the other sites were probably occupied into that decade as well. The evidence indicates that between A.D. 1250 and 1286, nearly seven hundred people moved into the Tsegi Canyon system and established at least twenty villages that ranged in size from one or two households to more than one hundred individuals (Dean 1969:194).

Long House Valley (Dean et al. 1978) provides a good example of local settlement distributions during the Tsegi phase (figure 6.7). Habitation sites were restricted to the northern half of the valley. In a major departure from previous periods, limited-activity sites tended to be closely associated with residences, a change that reflects the increased number of water-control facilities near habitations. Only a few "gathering" camps were located on the valleyside slopes and in Kin Biko, a small canyon at the northwest corner of the valley. A few farming camps were situated on

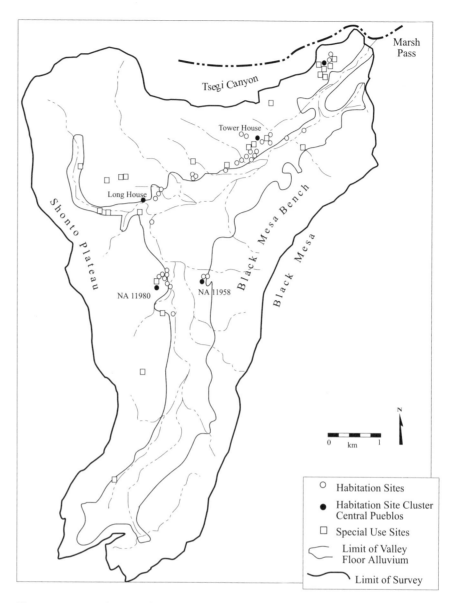

Figure 6.7 Distribution of habitation and special-use sites in Long House Valley, A.D. 1250–1300 (after Dean et al. 1978:figure 3).

the valley floor at varying distances from the residential loci. Habitation and nonhabitation sites are grouped into five clusters, four on the margins of the floodplain and one on a mesa overlooking the mouth of the valley at Marsh Pass. These clusters are associated with areas of arable land and sources of domestic water. Site clusters of this type are common throughout the eastern Kayenta valleys (but not the canyons) and in the Navajo Mountain uplands.

The settlement shifts of the Tsegi phase can be seen as responses to the

adaptive crisis triggered by the combination of high population densities and deteriorating low- and high-frequency environmental conditions. As shown most clearly in Long House Valley but evident elsewhere as well, site clusters are located near restricted patches of land farmable under the prevailing conditions of depressed alluvial water tables and active stream entrenchment (figure 6.8). Furthermore, the sizes of the site clusters, in terms of numbers of rooms, are highly correlated with the areas of arable land. The prevalence at these sites of facilities for the capture and storage of domestic water reflects a major concern for another precious resource that would have been adversely affected by the falling alluvial groundwater levels. An intensive analysis of the Long House Valley data allowed Dean et al. (1978:43) to rank the resource correlates of the site locations of the Tsegi phase. Residential loci were situated with reference first to arable land, second to domestic water supply, third to wild plant resources, and fourth (i.e., not at all) to game. Systematic surveys (Haas and Creamer 1993) indicate that similar relationships prevail in the Klethla and Kayenta Valleys.

Tsegi-phase community patterning is characterized by considerable morphological and functional differentiation of sites and units within sites. Functionally distinct types of rooms are recognized on the basis of the presence or absence of features indicative of the use of the chambers. Living rooms (Dean 1969:27–28; Lindsay 1969:142–146) are identified by low-silled doorways, entrybox complexes, fire pits, prepared floors, interior plastering, interior smoke blackening, and a host of minor features. These attributes are not limited to masonry surface structures but occur also in residential pit houses, as at Neskahi Village on Paiute Mesa (Hobler 1964, 1974). These features established that living rooms were used for domestic activities, including sheltering from the elements, the preparation and consumption of food, and sleeping. Courtyards (Dean 1969:33–34; Lindsay 1969:157–164) are unroofed areas that have many of the attributes of living rooms as well as other features, such as mealing bins, storage pits, and abrading grooves. Courtyards were outdoor work areas as well as loci of some activities that also took place in living rooms. Granaries (Dean 1969:28–29; Lindsay 1969:146–149) are denoted by features designed to keep the weather and vermin out (high-silled entries, grooved doorways for seating slab doors secured by sticks

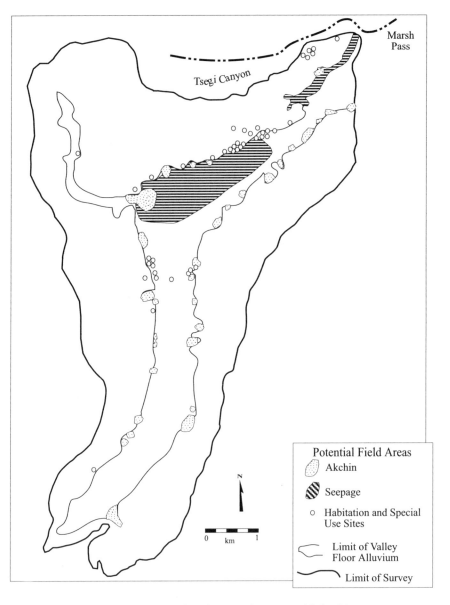

Figure 6.8 Tsegi-phase settlement distribution relative to arable land in Long House Valley (after Harrill 1982:figure 12).

shot through withe loops, clay copings around the edges of entries, superior masonry, exterior plastering, bedrock or stone-slab paved floors) and by the lack of floor features and interior smoke blackening. Granaries were clearly used for the storage and protection of perishable food. Storerooms (Dean 1969:29; Lindsay 1969:149–152) are recognized by the absence of the attributes of living rooms and granaries. Basically, they are small chambers used for storing nonperishable items. Grinding rooms (Dean

1969:33; Lindsay 1969:152–156) are small rooms, often unroofed and sometimes open on one side, that contain batteries of mealing bins used for the grinding of corn with manos and metates. Galleries consist of low walls along the lips of ledges behind the main roomblocks in cliff dwellings. Although galleries occasionally have some defensive characteristics (Kidder and Guernsey 1919:53), evidence from Swallow's Nest Cliff Dwelling (Dean 1969:158) and Olla House (Kidder and Guernsey 1919:53) clearly indicates a storage function as well. Plazas bounded on one to four sides by roomblocks or wingwalls occur in some open sites. The presence of kivas and work areas indicate that these large, open features served both secular and ceremonial functions.

The basic structural component of most excavated Tsegi-phase sites is the room cluster (Dean 1969:34–35; Lindsay 1969:157–158). Usually, this unit (figure 6.9) consists of one or two living rooms, one to a dozen storage chambers (granaries and storerooms), and occasionally a grinding room, all grouped around a courtyard through which access to the rooms is gained. In crowded circumstances, courtyards may be situated on the roofs of the rooms, as in Room Cluster 10 at Kiet Siel (Dean 1967:136, figure 11b; Dean 1969:125), or in rare instances, absent. Occasionally, two or more room clusters are grouped around a courtyard to form a courtyard complex (Dean 1969:35; Lindsay 1969:157), such as the two complexes oriented around Courtyards 1 and 3 (figure 6.10) at Pottery Pueblo (Stein 1984:188, figure 24).

The grouping of domestic rooms, open areas, and kivas into discrete habitation units characteristic of Mesa Verde cliff dwellings (Fewkes 1909:8; Rohn 1965:67) was once thought not to exist in the Kayenta heartland (Dean 1970:157). This still seems to be the case as far as cliff dwellings are concerned. Large, open sites where construction space is less restricted are another matter, however. In some sites, groups of room clusters and courtyard complexes with associated kivas define discrete units within larger villages, as at Segazlin Mesa (figure 6.11) and Pottery Pueblo (figures 6.10 and 6.12). Long House (figure 6.13) exhibits a variant of this pattern in which discrete, plaza-oriented units comprise the entire site. In many ways these subvillage units are equivalent to small- or medium-sized villages that have been integrated into larger communities while still retaining at least a modicum of separation from like units.

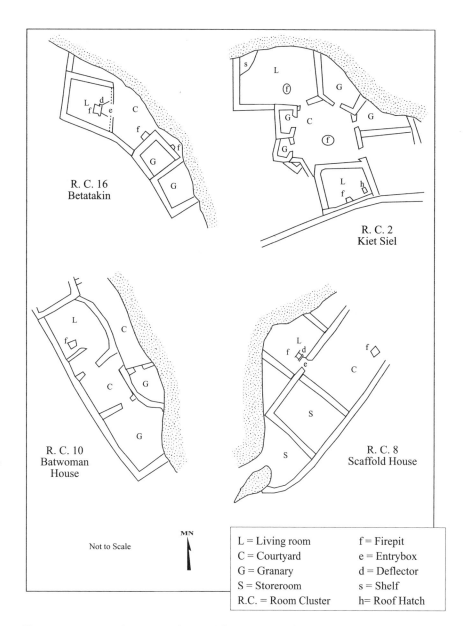

Figure 6.9 Tsegi-phase room clusters (after Dean 1969:figure 9).

The architectural and structural units described above combine to form four archaeologically recognizable types of residential sites. To Lindsay's (1969:243–246) plaza and courtyard types must be added pithouse villages (Ambler 1985a:51) and ad hoc forms dictated by the peculiarities of the construction sites. While four distinct types can be conceptualized, at some level and under some circumstances they intergrade into one another and become indistinguishable.

Plaza pueblos consist of masonry roomblocks or pit houses situated on one to four sides of a partially or wholly enclosed plaza that contains one or more kivas. As noted previously, this site configuration may have evolved from the unit-pueblo layout during the Transition period (figure 6.4). Although strongly patterned, the general plaza-pueblo category subsumes wide variation in size, complexity, and configuration. The simplest form, which occurs in large and small sites, involves a single large plaza surrounded by masonry and jacal rooms and sometimes, as at Neskahi Village (figure 6.14), pit

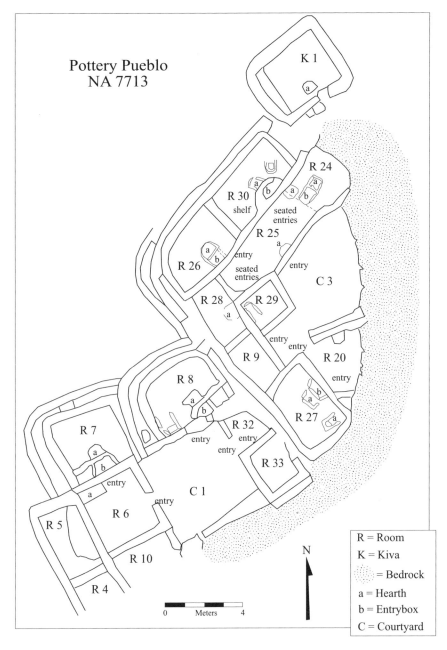

Pottery Pueblo
NA 7713

K 1

R 24

R 30
shelf

seated
entries

R 25

R 26
seated
entries

entry

entry

C 3

R 28   R 29

entry
entry

R 9   R 20

entry

R 8

R 32
entry   entry

R 27

R 7
entry

entry

R 33

C 1
entry

R 6

R 5

R 10

R 4

N

R = Room
K = Kiva
⋯ = Bedrock
a = Hearth
b = Entrybox
C = Courtyard

0   Meters   4

Figure 6.10 A representative Tsegi-phase courtyard complex, Courtyard 1 and 3 Complex, Pottery Pueblo (NA 7713) on Paiute Mesa (after Stein 1984:figure 24).

houses. Red House (figure 6.15) exhibits a more complex form involving two main plazas. The largest-known Kayenta site, Long House (figure 6.13), also is one of the most complex of the plaza pueblos, with at least six individual plazas bounded by walls and roomblocks. Plaza pueblos range in size from Long House, which probably has more than three hundred rooms, to sites comprising but one or

two room clusters, as exemplified by NA 10830 (figure 6.16) in Long House Valley (Haas and Creamer 1993:figure 3.5). Figures 6.4, 6.13, 6.14, 6.15, and 6.16 provide only an indication of the variety of ground plans that characterize plaza pueblos. This variability is due in part to the necessity to adjust the pueblos to the conformations of the building sites and in part to other factors that exist when site loca-

tion does not constrain construction. Plazas are oriented in the arc from east to south, with the main roomblock at the back, that is, to the north or west. Despite the degree of "community planning" that can be inferred from the regular patterning of plaza pueblos, all such sites that have been investigated are composed of individual room clusters whose courtyards ring the perimeter of the plaza, a pattern particularly evident at Neskahi Village (figure 6.14; Hobler 1964, 1974).

Courtyard sites lack formal plazas. Instead, room clusters and courtyard complexes are grouped around courtyards, as at Pottery Pueblo (figure 6.12); are oriented along "streets," as at Kiet Siel (figure 6.17), or linear open areas, as at Segazlin Mesa (figure 6.11); or are arranged to conform to the available space, as at Betatakin (figure 6.18). Lacking the unifying influence of formal plazas, courtyard sites exhibit an even wider range of variability in size, complexity, and configuration than do plaza sites. The two largest courtyard sites, Pottery Pueblo and Kiet Siel (figures 6.12 and 6.17) have between one hundred and fifty and two hundred rooms each, while the smallest examples of this type consist of only one or two room clusters, as at Lolomaki (figure 6.19). Complexity varies from the simplicity of Lolomaki to the street arrangement of Kiet Siel and the discontinuous scatter at Pottery Pueblo. Courtyard sites most commonly occur in situations where external factors—such as the size, composition, and conformation of the building site—constrain construction.

Courtyard-site layouts range from the linear arrangements found in most cliff dwellings (figures 6.17 and 6.18) and on Segazlin Mesa (figure 6.11) to the relatively amorphous configuration of Pottery Pueblo (figure 6.12). In the absence of plazas, kivas are associated with subvillage habitation units, as at Segazlin Mesa and Pottery Pueblo (figures 6.11 and 6.12), or with the village as a whole, as in the Tsegi Canyon

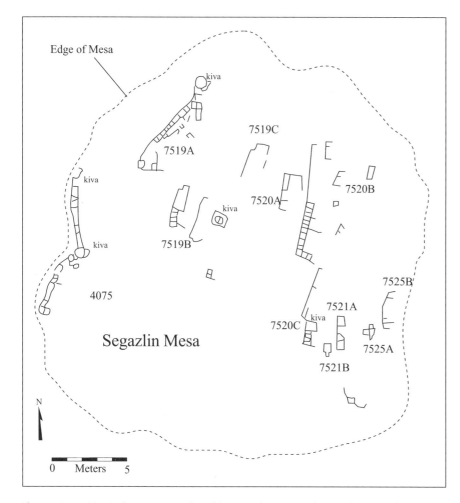

Figure 6.11 Tsegi-phase courtyard pueblo, Segazlin Mesa (after Lindsay 1969:figure 25).

cliff dwellings (figures 6.17 and 6.18). The secular activities performed in plazas probably were concentrated in the courtyards of courtyard sites, while the "streets" and open areas of courtyard sites may have taken on some of the plaza's ceremonial functions. There are few pre-Tsegi-phase precedents for the courtyard type of site, although the room cluster itself existed in the Transition period.

No Tsegi-phase pit-house village has been fully excavated. In fact, only one excavated Tsegi-phase pit house (Ambler and Olson 1977:23–24, figures 24–25) has been described: a small, squarish structure with a ramp entry and an entrybox (figure 6.20). Nonetheless, fairly large sites apparently consisting of scattered pit structures and a few masonry structures have been surveyed in the Klethla Valley

(Haas and Creamer 1993:73–78). The two such sites that have been adequately recorded, Thief Site and Kin Klethla (Haas and Creamer 1993:78–85), have forty-three and seventy-five pit houses respectively, and the latter has a substantial masonry component as well (figure 6.21). The complete size range of these sites is unknown. Clear antecedents in the Pueblo II and Transition periods exist for this type of site (Ambler 1994; Ambler and Andrews 1981; Ambler and Olson 1977), especially in the Klethla Valley. As yet unpublished Navajo Nation Archaeology Department excavations at a Tsegi-phase pit-house village on the Rainbow Plateau will help alleviate our ignorance of the extent, structure, and configuration of Tsegi-phase pit-house villages and to illuminate the nature and interrelationships

of the structures of which they are composed.

As was the case throughout Kayenta history, a number of sites that conform to no particular pattern exist. As usual, these generally represent adjustments to space constraints established by the locations in which the sites were built. Ledges, low overhangs, slump boulders, crevices, and bedrock features are common determinants of the layouts of these sites. Many such sites are limited-activity loci, but many others are habitations. Most of the latter comprise one or more recognizable room clusters.

As Ambler (1985a:51) points out, the different kinds of sites are not uniformly distributed across the countryside. Plaza pueblos and courtyard sites are found throughout the Kayenta heartland; however, they are somewhat differentially distributed relative to local terrain features. Plaza pueblos tend to occur on eminences that slope fairly gently toward the southeast. These eminences range from abrupt, steep-sided rock buttes to long, gentle bajadas with little vertical relief. The main roomblock usually is situated on the highest point, with the plaza sloping away in front. Courtyard sites also are situated on eminences, commonly steeper and less accessible than those where plaza sites are found. Defensive arrangements may be more abundant at open courtyard sites. Open sites of this type appear to be more numerous in the Navajo Mountain locality and less common in the east. This apparent distinction, however, may be an artifact of the poor sample of excavated sites in the eastern locality. All cliff dwellings appear to be courtyard sites, if only because rockshelters cannot accommodate plazas. Although pit-house sites seem to be concentrated in the western areas, Bliss (1960) suggests that they also may occur in Long House Valley. Ad hoc site configurations are abundant wherever local circumstances constrain construction.

Community patterning outside the Kayenta nuclear area is poorly

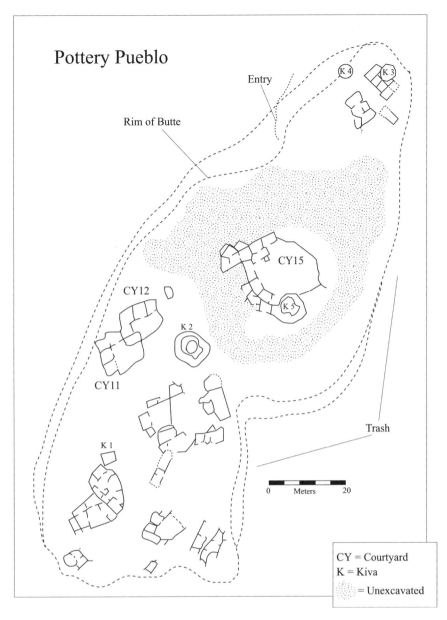

Figure 6.12 Tsegi-phase courtyard pueblo, Pottery Pueblo (NA 7713) on Paiute Mesa (after Lindsay 1969:figure 30).

understood. Both large, open sites and cliff dwellings occur along the middle reaches of the Tusayan Washes on Black Mesa south of the lease area. Few have been systematically investigated, and none have been intensively studied. Linford (1982:39–40, figure 8) describes a late Pueblo III site in the Wepo drainage that includes as many as ten noncontiguous roomblocks, each appearing to consist of sets of rooms fronted by a plaza. This site could represent the amalgamation of several small- to medium-sized plaza pueblos into a single community. A late Pueblo III site on Oraibi Wash (Linford 1982:49, figure 16) possesses a large rubble mound, but too little testing was done to delineate its configuration. Other large, multiple plaza sites are known in this locale. Farther south in the areas of the Tusayan branch and middle Little Colorado River, large pueblos, such as Homol'ovi IV (E. Adams 1991:171–172, figure 6.3; Lyons 2001:136–138, figure 4.1), appear late in the Pueblo III period.

New theoretical perspectives combined with recent research has compelled the recognition that levels of integration beyond the individual site existed during the Tsegi phase. Intensive archaeological survey in Long House Valley led to the realization that Tsegi-phase habitation and limited-activity sites were interrelated in a "hierarchical" settlement system (Dean et al. 1978:33; Effland 1979) that seems to be characteristic of the eastern Kayenta valleys in general (Haas and Creamer 1993). In this system, individual residential sites representing two or possibly three levels of complexity are spatially and structurally related to form multisite communities. Spatial relationships and communication linkages integrate these communities into larger interactional systems.

The lowest community level in this system comprises habitation sites located adjacent to plots of arable land. Such sites range from one room cluster (figure 6.16) to more than fifty rooms and include both plaza and courtyard configurations. No matter how small, these sites have attributes indicative of a full range of secular and ceremonial activities (Haas and Creamer 1993:37–47). All possess the features that denote room clusters and the domestic functions associated with this architectural unit. Artifacts and trash associated with these sites specify a full range of maintenance and discard behaviors. Even the smallest usually has a kiva, and the number of kivas per site increases with site size. Though commonly, but not exclusively, situated above the valley floor and footed on bedrock, there is nothing defensive about either the locations or features of these sites. All in all, these sites seem to represent functionally self-contained, relatively autonomous social units ranging from one to several households.

The highest single-village organizational level consists of a few sites that appear to have had special, extra-residential functions related to the maintenance of communities made up of several residential pueblos. In

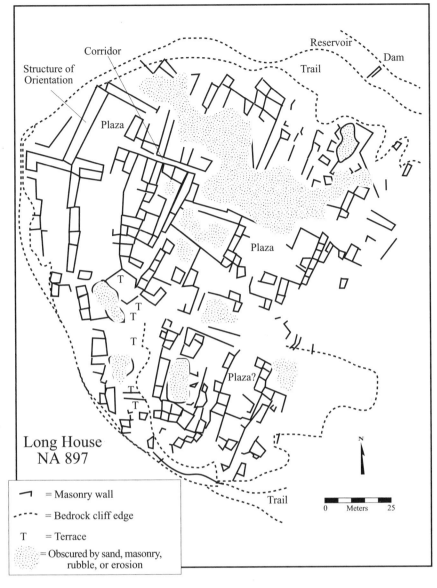

Figure 6.13   Tsegi-phase plaza-type central pueblo, Long House (NA 897) in Long House Valley (after plane table map by Dean and Lindsay 1978).

pueblos, the latter have several attributes that clearly distinguish them from the former. Most central pueblos are plaza-type sites, the most notable possible exception to this generalization being the Moki Rock site at the confluence of Parrish and Laguna Creeks (Dean 1967:98, figure 56; Haas and Creamer 1993:55–57). Nearly all central pueblos have "spinal" roomblocks constructed of double-faced, sometimes rubble-cored masonry. These spinal roomblocks have been named the "structure of orientation" (Lindsay 1969:245) because they usually are located on the apices of the eminences and establish the orientations of the main plazas directly in front of them (figure 6.13). The function of these roomblocks is poorly known; defense and communal storage have been suggested. Although the two excavated spinal roomblocks, at Red House (Cummings 1953:39) and Upper Desha Pueblo (Lindsay et al. 1968), have both living and storage chambers, only additional excavation will reveal the range of functions served by these features. Most central pueblos have facilities for the capture and storage of domestic water (figure 6.13; Kidder and Guernsey 1919:plate 23a). In most cases, the current absence of a reservoir at a central pueblo probably means that this feature has been destroyed or obscured by natural processes in the years since the site was occupied.

Some central pueblos have features designed to restrict access to their interiors, particularly the main plazas (figure 6.13). In combination with the elevation of the sites above the surrounding countryside, such features (ramps, corridors, crosswalls, and limited entries) have been interpreted as defensive arrangements. It is equally possible that they regulated access to sacred precincts within the pueblos and channeled actions connected with ceremonial observances or other community activities. The long entrance ramps and corridor at Long House (figure 6.13) would have served admirably as staging areas for processions whose simultaneous or

any given locality, there are far fewer of these central pueblos than there are ordinary habitation sites. In Long House Valley, there are only five central pueblos as compared to thirty-five residential pueblos. Central pueblos have all the features diagnostic of a full range of secular and ceremonial activities: room clusters, courtyard complexes, plazas and plaza-oriented room groups, kivas, and the artifacts and debris indicative of the same maintenance activities that were performed in the residential pueblos. No artifact types are present at central pueblos that are not also present at

residential pueblos. Lack of information, however, precludes determining whether these kinds of sites differ in frequencies of particular artifacts or design characteristics. Central pueblos seem not to have frequencies of "foreign" items disproportionate to their relative sizes nor burials with richer offerings than those at residential pueblos. Central pueblos and residential sites exhibit no consistent size relationship; some residential sites are larger than the central pueblos with which they are associated.

Despite the numerous similarities between residential and central

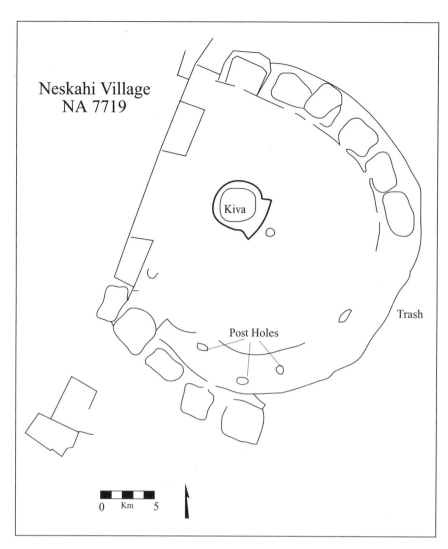

Neskahi Village
NA 7719

Kiva

Post Holes

Trash

0   Km   5

Figure 6.14   Tsegi-phase plaza pueblo with pit house dwellings, Neskahi Village (NA 7719) on Paiute Mesa (after Lindsay 1969:figure 34).

staggered entry into the main plaza from three different directions would have been most impressive. Speculation aside, the combination of situation and features that distinguishes central pueblos clearly specifies extra-village functions related to the maintenance of multivillage communities. Among such possible functions are the storage and redistribution of community water and food supplies, community integration, communication, and possibly refuge in times of strife. Explication of these functions through careful, problem-oriented excavations is one of the major unfinished tasks of Kayenta-branch archaeology.

Large pueblos, ranging from fifty to one hundred rooms, that lack the specialized features and locational attributes of central pueblos may constitute an intermediate level in the village hierarchy between "ordinary" residential sites and central pueblos. On the other hand, they may be nothing more than large members of a single but quite varied class of residential pueblos. Superficially, nothing but size (some are larger than some central pueblos) distinguishes them from the smaller residential pueblos. The possibility of an intermediate village level is another problem whose solution will come only through excavation.

Open habitation sites are grouped into localized communities that are

exemplified by the four valley-floor site clusters in Long House Valley (figure 6.7). Each community consists of a number of residential sites clustered around a central pueblo situated on an eminence overlooking the cluster. These clusters are spatially discrete and include from three to fifteen habitation sites apiece. Ranked in descending order by number of rooms—Long House, Tower House, NA 11980, and NA 11958—size of cluster covaries strongly with area of arable land (figure 6.8). The structural, size, and spatial relationships within each cluster suggest that the residential pueblos, despite a recognizable degree of integrity, were organized into an interdependent community by activities and, probably, deliberations that took place in the central pueblos. Between-cluster spatial distributions suggest that these multivillage communities probably were comparatively autonomous and perhaps competed with one another for access to or control over subsistence or other resources.

Despite the centrifugal effects of competition, evidence exists for yet a higher level of social interaction. In Long House Valley, the four valley-floor central pueblos are situated so that each site can be seen from the other three. In fact, there can be little doubt that clear lines of sight were important factors in locating these central pueblos. Were the spinal unit of NA 11958 situated 25 m farther east on a level ridge top instead of on the sloping toe of the ridge, its view of Tower House would be obscured by a landslide deposit on the flank of Black Mesa (Haas and Creamer 1993:30, figures 2.6, 2.7). Similarly, Tower House is situated somewhat precariously on the only eminence in its vicinity high enough to be seen from Long House. The visual relationships among these central pueblos seem best explained as means of facilitating communication among the four main valley communities. Communication may have been necessitated by the potential of conflict with groups

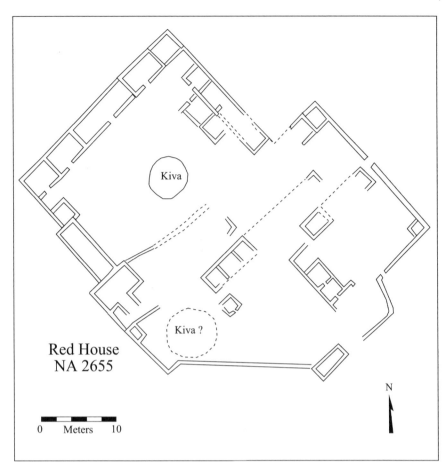

Figure 6.15 Tsegi-phase plaza pueblo with multiple plazas, Red House (NA 2655) on the Rainbow Plateau (modified by Lindsay and Dean from Lindsay 1969:figure 32).

somewhat less structured than that of the valleys and uplands. Although sites of all sizes exist in both areas, they are rarely clustered into groups. Rather, individual, functionally complete sites are situated near drainage junctures, where the combination of land and water is most favorable for agriculture. A few cliff dwellings, notably Kiet Siel, might have served as loci of some activities, principally ceremonial, shared with residents of nearby small, "satellite" sites. As a rule, however, cliff dwellings have few of the attributes of central pueblos and seem to have functioned as residential loci where the full range of secular and ceremonial activities was performed. The severely limited view from most rockshelters precluded line-of-sight communication systems. While the residents of canyons undoubtedly interacted with one another, it more likely was by foot than by eye, as attested by the many hand and toehold trails traversing the canyon walls. Hierarchical settlement systems like those of the valleys probably existed only in attenuated form if at all in the confined environments of the canyons.

Social Organization

Architecture has been heavily relied on for reconstructing Anasazi social behavior and organization for four principal reasons. First, Anasazi architectural units are morphologically varied but possess a high degree of within-category uniformity that can be used for functional assignments. Second, Anasazi architecture is extremely durable and exceptionally well preserved, even in sites excavated long ago. Third, few detailed studies of artifact distributions, task residues, and work and discard deposits have been published. Fourth, site-abandonment practices of the Kayenta Anasazi militate against using artifact distributions to measure social behavior. Unlike other populations who commonly left quantities of material items when they deserted a site, the Kayentans usually took everything portable and

from outside the valley or by a need to coordinate activities, perhaps ritual observances, at all four sites. In any case, the intervisibility implies valleywide communication and cooperation, and the considerable effort expended to ensure line-of-sight relationships among the central pueblos testifies to fairly intense advanced planning and coordination on the scale of the whole valley. Similar intervisibility relationships among central pueblos in the Klethla and Kayenta Valleys (Haas and Creamer 1993) and in the Navajo Mountain and Paiute Mesa areas (Dean 1998) reveal the existence of comparable intercommunity interactional system elsewhere in the Kayenta area.

Haas and Creamer (1993:69–70) found central sites located so as to suggest a connection between Long House Valley and the Kayenta Val-

ley to the east. Interestingly, there appears to be no corresponding westward connection with the Klethla Valley (Haas and Creamer 1993:85). As mentioned previously, there is a strong possibility that the Klethla Valley was connected with the interior of Black Mesa through the Valley View Ruin (Haas and Creamer 1993:76), a central pueblo situated on the rim of the mesa overlooking the valley. Recently, long-range between-mesa relationships have been recognized in the Navajo Mountain area (Dean 1998). A similar visual network along the course of Laguna Creek could link the Kayenta heartland with the Chinle Valley. Thus, a strong case can be made for the existence of a fifth interaction level, one that links valley and mesa-top systems.

Settlement in the eastern and western canyon systems appears to be

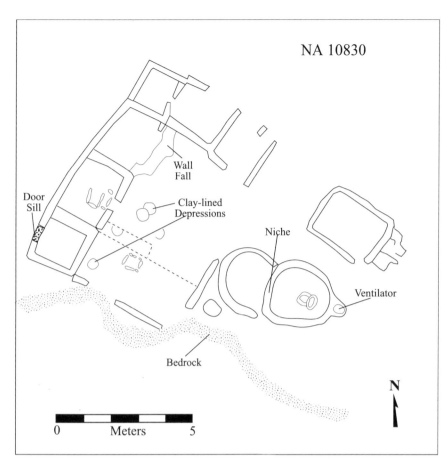

NA 10830

Wall Fall

Door Sill

Clay-lined Depressions

Niche

Ventilator

Bedrock

0   Meters   5

N

Figure 6.16 Small Tsegi-phase habitation site NA 10830 in Long House Valley (after Haas and Creamer 1993:figure 3-5).

destroyed the rest, leaving only the structures they had built and the materials they had discarded while living there. Given these circumstances, the following discussion of the social organization of the Kayenta branch after A.D. 1150 is based primarily on architectural and site distributional data, supplemented whenever possible by information on artifacts and their distributions.

Transition Period (A.D. 1150 to 1300)

Too few Transition-period sites have been excavated to provide an accurate picture of social organization during this extremely varied and perhaps somewhat chaotic period of major settlement adjustment. The degree of variability in social arrangements is suggested by the variety of residential structures and the variation in site configurations that characterize

this interval. This variability contrasts sharply with the relative homogeneity of the Pueblo II period and undoubtedly reflects social adjustments to the altered environmental and settlement conditions of the period after A.D. 1150. The differences within and between individual locations may reflect attempts to integrate different groups thrown together by settlement responses to the worsening environmental conditions of the period, or they could represent local adjustments to the changed adaptive situation.

The nature of the social units that made up a Transition-period community is poorly known. Individual living rooms and pit houses generally possess features (entryboxes, fire pits, storage bins and pits, mealing bins) and artifacts (cooking and serving vessels, manos and metates, stone, wood, and bone implements) that specify a range of domestic activi-

ties associated with the shelter and maintenance of a small residential unit that can be termed a household (Dean 1970:163; Dozier 1965:38–40). The size of these structures indicates that most households consisted of a nuclear family composed of a married couple, their unmarried children, and perhaps occasionally an older relative. Although living rooms and residential pit structures are too small to have accommodated a larger group, individual families forming an extended family could have occupied contiguous living rooms or pit houses.

The occurrence of apparently isolated pit houses and individual masonry dwellings testifies to the fundamental independence of Transition-period households. Nevertheless, most households were organized into larger social units, as indicated by agglomerations of pit houses into small villages and the existence of multi-dwelling unit and plaza pueblos. In the absence of extensive excavation, almost nothing is known about the organization of the pit-house villages. These communities could have been loose aggregations of independent households, or the households could have been organized into larger sub-village social units, such as localized lineage and clan segments. Some evidence for cooperation among households may be found in the detached surface (Ambler and Olson 1977:45–46, figure 41) and semisubterranean (Ambler and Olson 1977:18, figures 21–22) grinding complexes. If Ambler and Andrews' (1981; Ambler 1994) hypothesis that the specialized pit structures represent specialization in the weaving of narrow fabrics is confirmed, a further degree of social differentiation will have been established for these seemingly amorphous villages. On the other hand, if future work affirms a relationship between these structures and their counterparts in the Winslow branch, the Transition-period pit-house villages will be tied into a widespread interaction network that spanned the settlement gap produced by the abandonment of the Peabody lease area. Whatever the in-

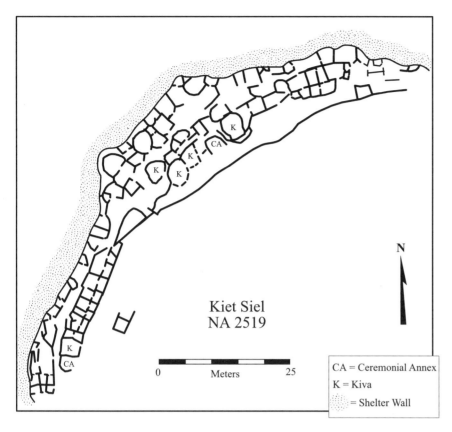

Figure 6.17 Tsegi-phase courtyard cliff dwelling site, Kiet Siel (NA 2519) in Tsegi Canyon (after Dean 1969:figure 20).

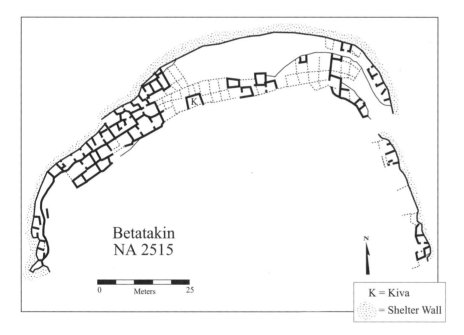

Figure 6.18 Tsegi-phase courtyard cliff dwelling site, Betatakin (NA 2515) in Tsegi Canyon (after Dean 1969:figure 13).

ternal social relationships and external linkages of the pit-house villages, the presence of kivas suggests that these multihousehold communities were integrated by ceremonial activities focused on these structures.

Sounder empirical and inferential bases exist for assessing the social organization of the unit pueblos. There is little reason to suppose that these pueblos were organized differently from the earlier pueblos described in Chapter 5. Individual households are specified by well-defined living rooms and pit houses, and some small hamlets apparently consisted of single households. In larger sites, multihousehold organization is represented by the jacal or masonry living rooms appended to the main masonry roomblock. The presence of two wings may indicate two different, though obviously related, multihousehold residential units. Community integration is indicated by the use of the back row of masonry rooms for communal food storage. Semisubterranean corn-grinding rooms are not noted for Transition-period pueblos; however, the occasional presence of grinding rooms in the masonry roomblocks suggests that communal mealing also was a unifying activity. As in the pit-house villages, the primary mechanism of community integration probably was ceremonies performed in the kivas.

Since only one Transition-period plaza site, Surprise Pueblo on Cummings Mesa (figure 6.4; Ambler et al. 1964:53–83), has been excavated, it is difficult to generalize about the organization of this type of community. Single-family households inhabited the pit structures flanking the northeast side of the plaza. All seven chambers in the masonry roomblock on the northwestern side of the pueblo were apparently devoted to activities involving multiple households. Six of the rooms appear to be divided into three identical two-room units, each unit consisting of a storeroom and a mealing room. It is tempting to infer from this pattern the existence of three extended family households,

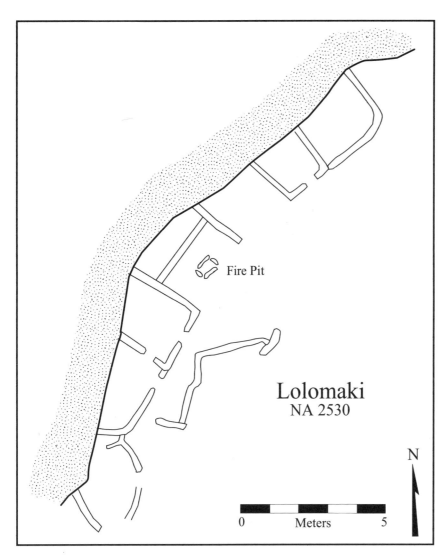

Figure 6.19 Small Tsegi-phase site, Lolomaki (NA 2530) in Tsegi Canyon (after Dean 1969:figure 42).

Fire Pit

Lolomaki
NA 2530

N

0   Meters   5

though individually not uncommon in Kayenta kivas, rarely occur in such complete array as here. This unusual constellation of features suggests that Surprise Pueblo might have been the locus of integrative activities involving participants from several nearby villages on Cummings Mesa. If so, it would bear a striking resemblance in layout and inferred function to the Plaza Site in the Hopi Buttes far to the south (Gumerman 1969, 1988b). As tantalizing as this possible example of intervillage integration is, much more research is necessary to confirm the existence of social organization above the hamlet and village level during the Transition period.

The lack of architectural and artifactual evidence for high social complexity during the Transition period is paralleled by the absence of what, by even the lowest of standards, could be recognized as "high status" burials. Although only one site has produced an adequate sample of interments, the utter lack of rich burials undoubtedly accurately reflects the general situation. RB 568 yielded forty-two burials that date to the end of the Transition period and the beginning of the Tsegi phase. The distribution of mortuary furnishings favors older women and, to a lesser extent, older men over younger individuals (Crotty 1983). This pattern reflects social differentiation based primarily on sex, age, and perhaps kin affiliations. The RB 568 data show that status differences based primarily on achievement and secondarily on ascription characterized Kayenta society by the end of the Transition period. The implications of the RB 568 situation for Kayenta social organization in general can be fully developed only when much more data on burial associations from throughout the area have been analyzed.

To summarize, archaeological data provide only a hazy glimpse of the social organization of the Kayenta branch during the Transition period. Moderately independent nuclear-family and extended-family house-

each with its own suite of food-storage and preparation rooms in the communal roomblock. The seventh room also contains mealing bins and might have been used by all the households. The pueblo seems to have been integrated by activities centered on the kiva in the plaza. The formal, clearly demarked plaza suggests a more encompassing integrating principle than those of the unit pueblos. Activities associated with this feature may have been important in integrating the five households into a functioning community. It also is possible that the plaza served as an integrating mechanism for several hamlets.

Lack of excavation precludes firm assessment of the possibility of intervillage organization during the Transition period. The use of four of the seven rooms at Surprise Pueblo for grinding indicates an amount of food processing somewhat excessive for five nuclear families, and some of this food preparation might have been for visitors to the site. In addition, the plaza itself seems too grandiose to have served only the twenty or so people estimated by Ambler et al. (1964:82) to have inhabited the village. The kiva has an unusually varied complement of features (Ambler et al. 1964:59–60, figures 50–51) that al-

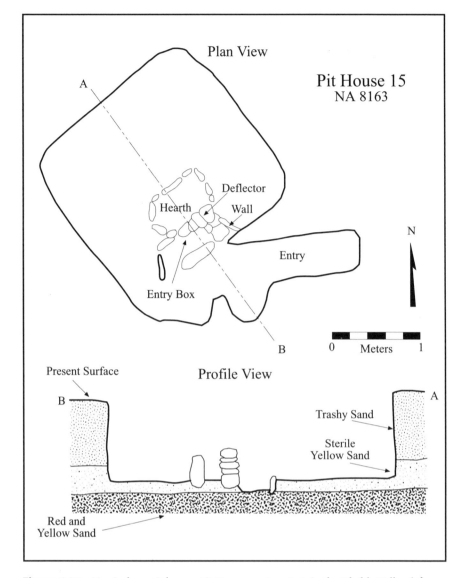

Figure 6.20 Tsegi-phase pit house, Pit House 15 at NA 8163 in the Klethla Valley (after Ambler and Olson 1977:figure 24).

conducted during the last thirty years. More important, no evidence to refute these postulations has come to light. Recent research has, moreover, produced new information on aspects of social organization in the Tsegi phase not apparent in the cliff dwellings; the overall situation has proved to be far more complex than the situation in Tsegi Canyon.

The highly regular composition and the ubiquity of the room clusters in sites of the Tsegi phase suggest that its associated social unit occupied a comparably uniform and widespread position in the social structure of the Tsegi phase. Room clusters occur in basically the same form in all types of sites except, perhaps, the pit-house villages, about which little is known. Given the unambiguous evidence that room clusters provided shelter from the elements, delimited territory, and served as the primary locus of domestic activities (including the storage, preparation, and consumption of food; the manufacture, use, and repair of implements; and the discard of unwanted items), this architectural unit can be defined as the residential locus of a household. In most cases, room clusters are too small to have accommodated more than a nuclear family; however, a few room clusters with more than one living room probably housed extended families. Courtyard complexes may indicate the existence of extended families as well; however, when the complexes also have kivas, as at Pottery Pueblo (figure 6.10; Stein 1984), they probably housed a larger multihousehold unit such as a lineage segment or clan segment. In some instances, all these social units might have been collapsed into a single courtyard complex.

The Tsegi phase saw the concentration within the household of functions, such as food storage and corn grinding, that had been performed communally in the unit pueblos, plaza pueblos, and pit-house villages of the Transition period. This change undoubtedly reflects the increasing differentiation of Kayenta society. The

holds were integrated by kinship, residence, and ceremonialism into small, relatively autonomous communities ranging in size from two to perhaps a dozen households. These communities took several forms, including amorphous agglomerations of pit structures, unit pueblos, and formalized plaza pueblos. The multi-community organization evident in the Tsegi phase may have begun in the Transition period, but the only concrete evidence of this comes from one site, Surprise Pueblo. Obviously, much additional problem-oriented archaeological research on a num-

ber of fronts is necessary to elucidate Transition-period social organization.

Tsegi Phase (A.D. 1250–1300)

Dean (1969:36–39, 191–192, 1970) presents a series of hypotheses about social organization in the Tsegi phase, developed from archaeological-dendrochronological analyses of cliff dwellings in Tsegi Canyon. Although the opportunity has not yet arisen to formally test these hypotheses with data gathered specifically for that purpose, considerable support has resulted from archaeological research

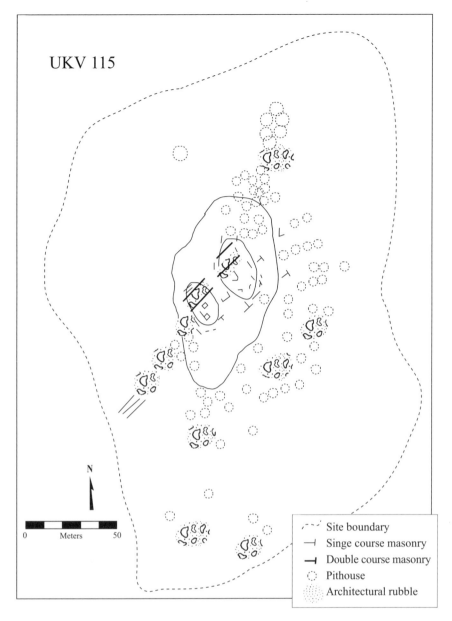

UKV 115

- - -	Site boundary	
⊣	Singe course masonry	
⊣	Double course masonry	
◌	Pithouse	
⣿	Architectural rubble	

N

0   Meters   50

Figure 6.21 Tsegi-phase pit house village UKV 115 in the Klethla Valley (after Haas and Creamer 1987:figure 12).

"new," functionally differentiated, and economically self-contained household was the basic social building block of villages in the Tsegi phase. The stability and independence of the household is shown by the fact that at Kiet Siel and elsewhere households moved in and out of villages more or less at will (Dean 1969:149). Interestingly, the greater intracommunity social differentiation, as manifested in the expanding self-sufficiency of the household, was accompanied by increased scope of social integration as communities grew larger and more internally diverse.

The Tsegi Canyon cliff dwellings possess no architectural or chronological components intermediate between the courtyard complex and the village itself, and the kivas are associated with the sites only, not with room clusters or other architectural units (Dean 1969:38, 1970:165). The next level of organizational complexity beyond the extended family household was the village. These villages were aggregations of quasi-independent, fairly

mobile nuclear- and extended-family households integrated into the village as a whole by ritual observances and obligations focused on the kivas and ceremonial annexes. This form of organization was flexible enough to accommodate the comings and goings of households at Kiet Siel and stable enough to maintain a much tighter social order at Betatakin. Apart from a couple of small sites that might have been ceremonially integrated into larger villages, there is no evidence that the Tsegi Canyon cliff dwellings were organizationally linked into larger communities.

More complex organization is indicated for the two major types of open sites. Both large courtyard sites that have been excavated have residential units larger than the household but smaller than the village. Pottery Pueblo (figure 6.12; Stein 1984) consists of several single- and multiple-household units scattered across the surface of a low butte on the eastern edge of Paiute Mesa. The largest of these units are identifiable as courtyard complexes. They differ from those of the cliff dwellings in that some, such as the Courtyard 1 and 3 Complex (figure 6.10), have kivas. The association of kivas with courtyard complexes suggests a level of interhousehold integration based on mechanisms different from the principles of kinship and residence that are thought to have integrated the Tsegi Canyon nuclear- and extended-family households. A large detached kiva near the middle of the site (figure 6.12; Stein 1984:115–118, figure 19), and the unusually large Courtyard 15 (figure 6.12; Stein 1984:201–204), might have been loci of activities important to the integration of the village as a whole. Alternatively, these features could have functioned solely to integrate the inhabitants of nearby room clusters and courtyard complexes. A large rock-outlined enclosure on the bald-rock below the eminence may have served communal functions like those performed by plazas at other sites.

While the grouped courtyard complex layout of Pottery Pueblo could be attributed to the conformation of the baldrock knob on which it is situated, the same cannot be said for the community of Segazlin Mesa (Lindsay et al. 1968:231–363), where topography did not seriously constrain construction. Here (figure 6.11), a half-dozen linear pueblos, each composed of room clusters and courtyard complexes backed up against a long north-south trending wall, are scattered across the surface of the mesa. The pueblos consisted of one to a dozen nuclear- and extended-family households integrated by ceremonies conducted in the kivas. Some of the smaller pueblos lack kivas and might have been components of nearby units with kivas. Each pueblo is a highly structured unit of residence intermediate in size and level of complexity between the household and the village as a whole. Community-level cooperation is indicated by the location of Guardian Pueblo (NA 4075) astride the main access route onto the mesa, which it controlled for the benefit of the other pueblos. If the detached kiva at NA 7519B (Lindsay et al. 1968:328–331, figures 239–240) did not have a communal function, the community was probably integrated through activities associated with the extremely large courtyards at some of the pueblos or with the open spaces between pueblos.

Lack of excavation precludes considering the organization of eastern Kayenta open courtyard sites. The most prominent of these, Moki Rock, seems quite similar to Pottery Pueblo, but the apparent congruence could be due to their being located on baldrock eminences. RB 568 may also fall into the courtyard-site category, but too little excavation was done in the pueblo (Beals et al. 1945:80–86) to elucidate this possibility.

Plaza sites clearly represent a social order quite different from that of the courtyard sites. Only two of these sites, Upper Desha Pueblo near Navajo Mountain (Lindsay et al. 1968:155–184) and Neskahi Village on Paiute Mesa (Hobler 1964, 1974), have been thoroughly excavated.

Like Red House (figure 6.15), Upper Desha Pueblo has two plazas fronting a continuous block of masonry rooms along the back (west) side of the pueblo. Neskahi Village (figure 6.14) exhibits the customary masonry roomblock on the west side of the plaza, but the north and south sides are formed by rows of contiguous pit houses. Room clusters attest the presence of households in both sides. Both plaza pueblos have communal storage and grinding facilities in the main roomblock. At Neskahi Village, in fact, individual households had no storage chambers and apparently drew their food from the community stock. As Lindsay (1969:367) points out, this pattern represents a continuation of communal food-storage and preparation practices evident in the unit pueblos of the Pueblo II period and the unit and plaza pueblos of the Transition period.

Communal structures, facilities, and activities of this sort clearly indicate tighter interhousehold organization than that evident in the courtyard sites. Probably, closer kinship and residence ties bound the households of the plaza pueblos into larger units such as lineage and clan segments. The tighter, more unitary social structure of plaza pueblos is probably reflected in the lower incidence of kivas apparent at these sites. Even large plaza pueblos, such as Red House (figure 6.15), seem to have only one or two kivas, and the largest of all, Long House (figure 6.13), has yet to produce evidence of even one kiva. Contrast this situation with that at Kiet Siel, which had at least eight kivas during its occupation. Fewer kivas probably were necessary at plaza pueblos because fewer but larger social units had to be integrated into the village social structure. It also seems likely that the plazas themselves had assumed some of the community integrative functions of kivas, thus necessitating fewer of the latter. The epitome of this development is probably represented by Long House (figure 6.13) where individual plaza-oriented units seem to have been integrated into a large

plaza pueblo without benefit of kivas. Plaza pueblos, then, probably consisted of nuclear- and extended-family households and lineage or clan segments bound together by kinship and residence ties, cooperative economic behavior, and village-level ceremonial activities centered on the kivas and plazas.

Recent research in the Kayenta area also has disclosed at least two levels of supravillage organization. The first involves the bounded clusters of residential pueblos grouped around central pueblos. Position and special features show that the central pueblos integrated the other villages into the communities represented by the clusters. In addition to functioning as loci for the storage and redistribution of communal food and water supplies, central pueblos undoubtedly also served as symbols of identity and solidarity for the members of the cluster and legitimized the community's claim to critical resources, particularly arable land. They might also have served as defendable refuges in times of real or imagined threats. The central pueblos probably were quasi-administrative centers that arose in response to the social pressures that accompanied the major increases in population density as groups congregated in the few localities still suitable for farming. Increased population densities would require the development of mechanisms to mediate disputes over land and other resources, to schedule and organize activities for the benefit of the community as a whole, to organize task groups, to coordinate economic activities, to regulate potentially troublesome interaction with other groups, and generally to handle the host of problems that arises when large numbers of people assemble in a small area. Given the paucity of kivas in central pueblos and the effort expended to restrict access to the plazas, it is likely that activities associated with these open areas within the central pueblos had become critical to the management of unprecedented organizational problems that could not be resolved through the extant integrative system built around kinship, residence, and kiva ceremonialism.

The second supravillage organizational level is manifested by the line-of-sight relationships that linked central pueblos, and through them their village clusters, into multicommunity communication networks and interaction systems. The purpose and organizational bases of such systems are unknown at present. They undoubtedly involved the interchange of information and very likely the management of activities. It has been suggested that they acted as early warning systems and to direct defensive activities in case of attack (Haas and Creamer 1993). Distance relationships, however, militate against a primary defensive rationale for these intervisibility networks (Dean 1998). The central pueblos in Long House Valley are so close together that no formal communication system would be necessary to announce an attack, which would be obvious to everyone in the valley. Conversely, sight-linked central pueblos on Paiute Mesa and the Rainbow Plateau are so far apart that any attack would long be over before aid could arrive in response to a signal for help. It seems equally plausible, therefore, that these communications networks served to coordinate economic and ceremonial activities that required the cooperation of all communities within a particular system. Whatever their precise functions, these networks clearly integrated the residents of localized multivillage communities into even larger social units that encompassed broad areas. Even wider spheres of interaction are indicated by possible line-of-sight relationships between valley systems (Haas and Creamer 1993:69–70).

Despite abundant evidence for a settlement hierarchy in the Tsegi phase, there are few indications of social stratification involving "elite" individuals or social units. Although communal features—food-storage facilities, reservoirs, plazas, central pueblos—are common and access to some of these features is sometimes restricted, exclusive residential

or ceremonial precincts that might have been loci of elite activities are not distinguishable. Similarly, neither exotic nor local artifacts appear to be differentially distributed within or between sites. The meager sample of burials also lacks any indication of major social differentiation among individuals. In the one large burial assemblage, thirty-two interments at Inscription House (Ward 1975:29–34), the most abundant and varied furnishings accompanied adult women and consisted for the most part of utilitarian items such as manos, metates, ceramic vessels, and bone tools. This depauperate (and, therefore, not representative?) mortuary pattern suggests that as at the beginning of the Tsegi phase at RB 568, social asymmetry among individuals was based primarily on achievement rather than ascription.

In summary, social organization in the Tsegi phase is fairly well understood. The nuclear- or extended-family household appears to have been the irreducible building block of society. Households existed alone, as at NA 10829 (Haas and Creamer 1993:39–41), or, when incorporated into larger residential units, behaved fairly independently, as at Kiet Siel (Dean 1969:82–84), or they acted in concert with other households, as at Betatakin (Dean 1969:148–150). Households commonly were organized into multihousehold units that were integrated by ceremonial activities in associated kivas. Multihousehold units existed separately, as at NA 10830 (Haas and Creamer 1993:41–43), or as components of larger settlements, a pattern manifested in open sites such as the courtyard sites of Pottery Pueblo (Stein 1984) and Segazlin Mesa (Lindsay et al. 1968:231–363) and the plaza sites of Long House and Upper Desha Pueblo (Lindsay et al. 1968:155–184). Multihousehold units are not evident in cliff dwellings, where the only suprahousehold unit is the village itself. Large and small settlements were organized into multisite communities by secular and religious activities in the central

pueblos, and these communities were linked into mesa- or valley-wide systems by activity coordination through visual communication among central pueblos. Finally, even larger cooperative arrangements were effected by visual connections between some mesa and valley systems.

Haas and Creamer (1993) argue that warfare caused by competition for dwindling resources was a major force in generating the hierarchical organization of Tsegi-phase settlements. While there is little doubt that resources declined markedly during this period and that increased competition was an important cause of Tsegi-phase settlement patterns, the degree and influence of overt conflict remain problematical. This uncertainty arises in part from problems with the definition of warfare and in part from differences of opinion over what constitutes acceptable archaeological evidence for warfare and defense against attack. With regard to the latter, the virtual absence of skeletal trauma ascribable to physical combat places the onus primarily on putatively defensive site locations and architectural features. Most of these attributes, however, could equally well be due to other factors such as the desire to control crucial natural resources and to regulate access to communal or ceremonial activities. Additional problem-oriented research is necessary to elucidate the ramifications of Haas' and Creamer's warfare hypothesis.

Ideology

The material remains and relationships available to archaeological investigation leave few clues to such intangible aspects of past cultures as belief systems and ideology. Often, archaeological attempts to deal with these nonmaterial topics involve projecting of the scholar's own preconceptions or presumed ethnographic analogues onto the prehistoric past. To avoid the pitfalls of subjectivity, circularity, and the inability to verify hypotheses that afflict such exercises, attention must be limited to matters that leave archaeological traces and that can be tested against archaeological data.

Given these limitations, only a few rather general inferences can be drawn about Kayenta ideology during the interval from A.D. 1150 to 1300. It is reasonable to suppose that these people held fairly egalitarian values that inhibited individual accumulation of wealth and power and, perhaps, even helped them remain relatively independent of the Chacoan regional interaction system and its northern and southern successors (Dean 1996a:40–41). Despite the emphasis on independence, Kayenta people were not reluctant to join with relatives and others in mutually beneficial activities and to form large communities. Religious beliefs and observances appear to have been focused on the kivas and, later, on the plazas where ceremonies for the benefit of all took place. The presence of sipapus and sipapu-like features in kivas suggests that Kayentans shared the generalized Puebloan origin tradition that exhibits considerable time depth in the Anasazi area. Differences in kiva morphology from those of other Anasazi branches and the wide variety of kiva forms and accoutrements attest to, respectively, beliefs somewhat different from those of the eastern Anasazi and a high degree of ideological variability among the various Kayenta groups. The total absence of items that resemble Katsina paraphernalia supports E. Adams' (1991) contention that the Katsina Cult postdates the abandonment of the Kayenta area and was not a part of the Kayenta Anasazi belief system.

Conclusions

Kayenta Anasazi prehistory between the abandonment of northern Black Mesa around A.D. 1150 and the abandonment of the San Juan drainage around A.D. 1300 marks the transition from a fairly simple society of dispersed, relatively autonomous hamlets to a much more complex, hierarchical settlement system characterized by large communities and groups of communities. By and large, these changes represent behavioral adjustments to increasing subsistence and social stresses resulting from the combination of greater population densities, caused by settlement relocations, and severe environmental degradation. The concentration of population in limited localities favorable for farming under conditions characterized by severe floodplain erosion created numerous density-dependent social problems having to do with the allocation of subsistence resources (particularly arable land), the management of communal facilities, the accumulation and distribution of domestic water supplies and stored food reserves, the organization and supervision of communal activities, the resolution of disputes, and the conduct of interactions with other groups. These problems generally were resolved through increasing social complexity that resulted in the Tsegi-phase pattern of a four- or five-tiered settlement hierarchy within the framework of a generally egalitarian society.

These adjustments were unsuccessful in the sense that the entire adaptive system disappeared from the area around A.D. 1300. In reality, however, the system was simply moved to a different area, where the level of social organization that had evolved by the Tsegi phase could be maintained. Although this movement probably was triggered by the continuing deterioration of the environment, strong attractive forces undoubtedly determined the movement's target area and sustained the migration after population had dropped to levels that could have been sustained locally. Among these forces were more favorable environmental conditions, a tradition of interaction with a culturally affiliated population, social obligations between emigrant groups, and enticing new socioreligious developments that eventually produced the Katsina Cult. The bulk of the Kayenta population joined closely related groups of the Tusayan branch in the Hopi Mesas and Homol'ovi areas of the middle Little Colorado drainage, where productive farming was possible under the prevailing conditions of regional channel entrenchment. Some Kayentans continued past the Hopi area, paused at Point of Pines, reappeared in the Safford and San Pedro Valleys of southern Arizona, and then disappeared from the stage of Southwestern prehistory. Those that remained behind constituted an important increment to the growing societies of the middle Little Colorado area that evolved into the modern Hopi cultural pattern.

PART V

A View from the Present

Most of this volume was written between 1985 and 1987, and it recounts an archaeological story. Chapter 7 ("*Hopit Navotiat*, Hopi Knowledge of History") and Chapter 8 ("The Navajos and Black Mesa") continue the story from a different perspective. Leigh Kuwanwisiwma, Miranda Warburton, and Richard Begay were recruited as authors after Peabody Coal Company submitted the original manuscript to the Office of Surface Mining in 1986. By the early 1990s, when work resumed on the manuscript, archaeology's social and legal contexts had changed dramatically. New laws, amended laws, and new regulations legislated a voice in archaeological decision-making and interpretation to people claiming cultural affinity with the makers of the archaeological remains. BMAP was not affected directly by this changing context; however, the invitations to Begay, Kuwanwisiwma, and Warburton are explicit acknowledgment that there are interpretations other than those offered in Chapters 2 through 6, and we welcome their telling.

Chapter 7 tells of the Hopi emergence from *Sipapuni* and of each clan's covenant with Maasaw to wander the landscape until receiving a sign to return to Hopi, the spiritual center. The clans were to leave a record (or footprints) of their passage in the form of archaeological sites. Kuwanwisiwma tells us that the Hopis know that the environmental perturbations that many archaeologists believe contributed to cultural change were, in fact, reminders from *Masaaw* to the Hopi that they had stayed long enough in one place and that it was time to continue their migrations to the spiritual center.

After Puebloan peoples departed much of the Kayenta region at about A.D. 1300, archaeologists pick up their story again with the arrival of the Navajos by the late eighteenth century. Chapter 8 presents the ethnographic, ethnohistoric, and archaeological data on this period, integrating it with data from Navajo ethnoarchaeological research conducted by BMAP. It offers a materialistic interpretation while simultaneously reminding us that Navajos view this landscape from a sacred stance as well. Much of the Kayenta region, including Black Mesa, is part of a metaphorical female figure, who along with her male counterpart to the east, reminds us of the beauty and balance in the world.

Chapters 7 and 8 acknowledge interpretations based on archaeological remains, yet the authors examine northern Black Mesa, the Peabody lease area, and BMAP from Hopi and Navajo perspectives. They represent a very preliminary effort at collaboration—an effort to communicate the existence of other voices, other interpretations. The authors show that the combination of perspectives enhances our understanding of Black Mesa and of the past.

CHAPTER 7

Hopit Navotiat, Hopi Knowledge of History

Hopi Presence on Black Mesa

Leigh Kuwanwisiwma

ALIKSAII! Listen!

Much has been said about the evolution of cultures in the Southwest. Cultural anthropologists and archaeologists have attempted to piece together the puzzle of human habitation on Black Mesa and the Colorado Plateau, a puzzle that goes back ten thousand years.

Anthropologists and archaeologists characterize themselves as scientists who study human cultures, past and present. But, science, while credible within its own standards, will never answer all the questions that seemingly pop up whenever new evidence is found. Moreover, because new evidence is always being discovered, scientific "answers" will always be professionally argued and debated.

Recently, anthropologists, especially archaeologists, have begun to pay more attention to a new source of evidence—what historically has been relegated to the categories of "myth," "legend," and "folktale." Myths, legends, and folktales are a tribe's knowledge of its own past, and this knowledge plays a continuing and important part in maintaining a people's cultural identity. This chapter explores the understanding of Hopi history based on contemporary ethnohistorical research efforts by the Hopi Tribe and knowledge gained from Hopi experiences within a complex cultural and religious setting.

Context is important. Hence, the viewpoint presented in this chapter is based in the complexity of the Hopi mind as it conceptualizes time and sequences. An awareness and understanding of these conceptualizations are necessary to explain adequately the past to a predominantly western-oriented audience.

Let us begin.

The beginning of time in the current Fourth World of the Hopis was at the place of emergence, a shrine known as Sipapuni. Here the Hopi clans began to emerge one by one to seek a newer, humble way of life.

As clan after clan emerged to this world, each was challenged to commit itself to a life plan that was dictated by the guardian deity, who Hopis know as Maasaw. As it is told, this life plan of the fourth world necessitated each clan to enter into a spiritual covenant with Maasaw.

The Hopi way is a way of humility, cooperation, and respect for the lifeblood of humanity: Earth. Maasaw spoke: "If you are able to accept and live my way of life, then be my people and live here with me. I will ask that you mark the lands with your footprints. Go as far as you can, and there will be a sign from above to let you know when you are to return back to the spiritual center of this earth, back to my place called Hopi. Upon your return, you will be judged one more time to see if you have earned final spiritual stewardship over the earth. If you have fulfilled these migrations to the four corners of this world, then you will have truly become my people—people who will henceforth be Hopi."

These "footprints" that are the hallmark of Hopi stewardship over these lands are described as ruins, burials, artifacts, shrines, springs, trails, rock writings (petroglyphs, pictographs, or other forms), and other physical evidence of occupation and use. Thus, archaeological sites (which can be seen as silent reminders of the past) are not mere vestiges; Hopi rites and liturgies recognize them as living entities.

The clans' spiritual covenant with Maasaw dictated migrations—deliberate movements over the landscape. Decisions to move on by these clans were purposeful with one thing in mind: to fulfill the spiritual covenant by returning to the spiritual center of the earth, thus earning final stewardship of the earth.

In Orayvi (Oraibi, Third Mesa) traditions, it is told that a clan was to stay at one site for a minimum of sixteen years but no longer. Sixteen years was long enough for the people to gather their physical strength, rejuvenate their spirit, and stock up on food supplies for yet another journey.

In many cases, signs required clans to locate their villages in places that seemingly had inadequate water supply and poor farming areas. Clans then called upon their respective spiritual deities to come to their aid. Through the use of ritual and prayer, clans brought forth blessings from these guardian spirits, sometimes resulting in the development of ritual springs. As Maasaw dictated, through the exercise of humility, industry, cooperation, and respect, Hopis were ensured of survival.

With this background, let us examine Hopi clan traditions in the Black Mesa area.

First, it is important to acknowledge clan traditions about Black Mesa and their association with other major Hopi ancestral sites such as Salapa (Mesa Verde); Kawestima, Talastima, and Tokonavi (Betatakin, Kiet Siel, and Inscription House); Hoo'ovi (Aztec National Monument), and even Palangwu (Chaco Culture National Historical Park) and Wupatki (Wupatki National Monument).

Traditional western anthropological viewpoints all too often confine themselves to a narrow scientific theory. As a result, archaeologists have chosen to pursue their inquiries and offer conclusions within neatly bounded material cultural packages (e.g., Mogollon, Sinagua, and Anasazi—the last a term offensive to Hopi people, who prefer the term, Hitsotsinom). Convenient? Yes. But nevertheless narrow and restricted.

The area known as Black Mesa is called Nayavuwaltsa (na-ya-vu-wal-tsa) in Hopi. It is interpreted as the "place of the gap where there is clay." Among the contemporary clans that have a direct interest in this area are the Deer and Flute clans of First Mesa; the Sand Clans of both Mishongnovi and Orayvi; the Rattlesnake and Lizard Clans of Orayvi; the Fire Clans of First, Second, and Third Mesa; and the Coyote Clans of all three mesas.

Other clans that migrated through the area are the Badger, Grey Badger, Butterfly, and Tobacco clans, represented at all three Hopi Mesas. As a matter of fact, the Badger phratry's origin story talks about this place, Black Mesa, as their place of emergence. Significant Badger Clan shrines are still visited with the area.

Later, the Third Mesa Eagle Clan gained rights to conduct eagle-gathering pilgrimages into the Black Mesa area. Several Eagle Clan shrines exist within the Peabody Coal Company's lease area.

How much can be said of specific clan traditions remains a sensitive issue. The heart and soul of clan traditions rest on the maintenance of privacy by clans within Hopi society. Clan traditions are highly respected and privileged information. This system of control begets integrity, and it is not for others outside the clan to know or publicly discuss esoteric knowledge. Thus, this chapter is inherently limited by how much the author can feel comfortable in disclosing for public consumption.

Nevertheless, a dynamic evolutionary process was happening. Guiding this process was the covenant to mark the lands with our "footprints." One can imagine the diversity of clans interacting with one another. Clans migrating from the Mimbres culture in southern New Mexico came into contact with clans who, in the opinion of Hopis, descended from the Mogollon, Salado, Sinagua, and Cohonina cultural groups.

The Hopi clans talk of facing harsh environmental conditions during the migration period. Many archaeological scholars surmise that changes in the environment caused people to move to areas more favorable for survival. Although this theory is a worthy and valid conclusion within a scientific context, it explains only half the story. Hopi traditions tell the other half.

Earlier, it was mentioned that the spiritual covenant dictated habitation at one particular site for a period of sixteen years. When the sixteen years were up, the clans had to continue their migrations. Well, basic human nature says that if you have a "good thing" going, you stick with it.

A case in point: some of the migrating clans found themselves with an abundance of natural resources to support their livelihood. Abundant water and arable lands influenced many clans to forego their covenant with Maasaw in favor of ensured survival. Subsequently, such clans had to be reminded by nature that they were in violation of their pact with Maasaw. If they stubbornly persisted and refused to move on, the forces of nature brought forth calamities such as drought and pestilence as a direct reminder that a mission was still at hand. Hence, clans were forced to move on.

Black Mesa was visited several times by clans during this period. Clans such as the Flute and Deer clans visited the area during their initial migrations from down south. But, they later traveled back through the same area towards their final destination and destiny—the Hopi Mesas, which are referred to as Tuuwanasavi, or the spiritual center of the earth.

Physical evidence of human habitation indicates that Black Mesa and the surrounding area were occupied and used for as long as ten thousand years. Archaeologists further record Puebloan-type habitations back at least one thousand years, the same time that villages were established on the Hopi Mesas and in surrounding areas. In addition, there is evidence of even earlier Paleoindian, Archaic, and Basketmaker occupations throughout the Black Mesa region. Is it mere coincidence that Hopi traditions speak of some clan originating in this area? Or are these traditions merely to be relegated to the category of self-serving legends, as they have in the past?

How does Hopi knowledge, which says that some clans "greeted" emerging clans, corroborate archaeological evidence of human habitation patterns? Important to remember here is that there are still living clans within Hopi society that claim direct ancestral ties into different southwestern cultures at varying times.

Today the Hopis still see the Black Mesa area as culturally and religiously significant. Key, for example, to this contemporary connection are the more than fifteen hundred ancestral Puebloan archaeological sites that have been documented within Peabody Coal Company's mining leasehold. These sites have cultural meaning to the Hopis; the Hopis consider prehistoric human remains to be the remains of their ancestors and the footprints of their migrations.

Important Hopi clan sites exist today on Black Mesa and are still visited annually by Hopis for various reasons. Clans still conduct ritual pilgrimages, homage is paid to important shrines, and Hopis still collect important ceremonial minerals from throughout Black Mesa. As well, today the Hopis regularly benefit from the availability of coal for heating. In this context, many Hopi families are still

directly associated with a geographic area that once sustained their ancestral people long ago.

Black Mesa and its history are not frozen in time. Rather, Nayavuwaltsa is a very real part of a living culture called Hopi, and the Hopis see Black Mesa as part their spiritual stewardship over the earth.

CHAPTER 8

The Navajos and Black Mesa

Miranda Warburton and Richard M. Begay

Prologue

'Ałk'idą́ą́' dahojilne', A long time ago, people told these stories. The history of our people began below us, in another world altogether. Here First Man and First Woman were created and the all the animals and birds spoke and lived together in harmony and in conflict. The people traveled through several worlds to get where we are today. The people emerged into this world at a place we call Hajíínáí, the Place of Emergence. After the emergence, the world was put into order, and the people began to disperse and find their niches upon this land. Over time, Monsters emerged and began to feed on the people. Changing Woman, the great goddess, came into being, and she gave birth to the Twin Warriors to rid the earth of the monsters.

The Twins cleansed the earth of monsters, and balance and harmony were restored. Changing Woman then left the People and went to the western sea where her husband, the Sun, built a home for her. After many years, the People missed their goddess, their mother, and journeyed to visit her. After they found her, they spent many years with her until she sent them home. She told them, "The land was created for you; it is decorated with all the things that you need to live your lives. Beauty is reflected in our land, the rain is your hair, the rivers

are your blood, and so on—you must return to your home." Before they left for their home, she created four clans of people and sent them along with the original travelers. When they returned home, the people, and the new clans and others who they befriended along the way spread again over Navajo lands, including Black Mesa.

When the people returned to their former lands, they found physical evidence of their ancestors who had lived there generations earlier. Those places are what we now call archaeological sites. They also found the other places mentioned in their oral history, such as sacred places. To this day, for the Navajo people, the natural land features and archaeological sites testify to the validity of our version of our own history. Our history is preserved in ceremonial life, in family and clan histories, and in community history and is intricately tied to the landscape. Therefore it's important that we tell the Navajo history from a Navajo point of view, to keep our land, and to live the life that was given to us by Holy People.

The traditional life we live today and the ceremonies we perform honor our creation, our history and our gods. For the Navajo people our life and history began before archeologists and others estimate the settlement of Navajos on Black Mesa. We were on Black Mesa and other places countless

generations before the arrival of the Spanish and Mexicans, the Nakaii, and the Americans, the Bilagáana.

[Richard M. Begay, 2001]

The Landform of Black Mesa

The archaeological field work conducted at historic sites was complemented by ethnographic interviews with the former residents of these sites or their descendents, relatives, or friends. In this manner, the fieldwork and subsequent research have allowed us to construct a fairly complete picture of Navajo economy and subsistence on Black Mesa during the nineteenth and twentieth centuries. The rather one-dimensional picture of Navajo life derived from the archaeological emphasis can be augmented with the rich body of traditional history that exists about Black Mesa.

Black Mesa as a landform is mentioned by VanValkenburgh (1941:105):

> This isolated dome [Navajo Mountain] dominating the horizon of the western Navajo country is regarded as sacred by the Navajos. They tell in their Blessingside stories that Navajo Mountain represents the head of the female and pollen figure of Navaholand, of which Black Mountain [Black Mesa] is the body and Balukai Mesa the lower extremities. In ceremonial parlance, the whole

system is called tádídíín dził, Pollen Mountain.

He also describes the male counterpart of the female aspect (Van Valkenburgh 1941:41–42):

> Chuska Peak figures prominently in Navajo mythology, particularly in the Tledji Hathal, Night Chant. The Blessing Chant stories tell that it is a part of the Goods of Value Range which embraces the Chuska, Tunichia, Lukachukai, and Carrizo Mountains. Chuska Peak is the head of this mythic grouping, Washington Pass, the neck, the Tunichias and Lukachukais, the body, Carrizos, the lower extremities. This is the Male Figure and is called in all its part, Yo'didził, Goods of Value Range.

The female Pollen Mountain, of which Black Mesa is a part, is integrated with the male counterpart of Yo'didził. In the Navajo worldview, there is always a pairing of male and female entities, and the male and female pollen figures are an integral part of Navajo sacred landscape.

BMAP Research on Navajo Sites

Archaeologists say that Puebloan peoples left the Kayenta uplands, including the Peabody lease area, in A.D. 1150, coalescing in the more clement Kayenta heartland. These people then left the heartland by the beginning of the fourteenth century, founding new villages and joining already established settlements on the Hopi Mesas (see Chapters 5 and 6, this volume). Sometime between the thirteenth and sixteenth centuries (the date is disputed, in part, because of the limitations of archaeological data) some of the ancestors of the Navajos, Athabaskan speakers, arrived in the Southwest from the north (Brugge 1983; A. Reed and Horn 1990; Towner 1996, 1997).

The Dine'tah (Navajo homeland) in northwestern New Mexico is considered by many archaeologists to be one of the earlier centers of Navajo

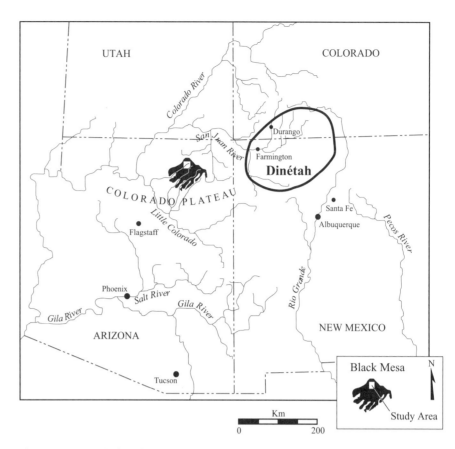

Figure 8.1 Dine'tah and the distribution of Athabaskan-speaking peoples in the southwestern United States (after Sundberg 1995:map 4).

occupation. Over time, Navajos intermingled with other people living in the area and moved east and south and west, spreading into the area now known as Navajo land (figure 8.1). Two tree-ring dates place the Navajo on Black Mesa in the seventeenth century (Kemrer 1974:129–131), and Spanish accounts relate that Navajos were trading with and raiding the Hopis on southern Black Mesa by the late seventeenth or early eighteenth century (Hester 1962:21). Archaeological evidence records their presence in the Peabody lease area during the 1830s and 1840s (Blomberg and Smiley 1982; Rocek 1984b:413).

This chapter presents a chronology of Navajo economy and subsistence on northern Black Mesa and endeavors to portray this picture as a part of a comprehensive Navajo worldview. Several kinds of information are brought together, and two interpretive perspectives are offered—historic

and anthropological, encompassing both archaeology and ethnography. Historic documents provide the primary framework used here for viewing Navajo culture. Because these documents were written by Europeans and Euroamericans, their perspective is, of course, Euro-western; however, archaeology and ethnography offer some insights into the Navajo perspective.

Archaeological surveys identified 1,039 Navajo sites; all were recorded in varying detail, and 9 were excavated. Over the years, BMAP researchers accumulated a massive archaeological database and wrote several articles, theses, and dissertations (Blomberg 1983; Blomberg and Powell 1983; Nichols and Powell 1987; Oswald 1993; Powell 1980, 1983; Rocek 1985, 1995; Russell and Dean 1985; Warburton 1985).

Throughout the late 1960s and into the mid-1970s BMAP emphasized prehistoric sites; beginning in 1975, however, field crews began to be more systematic about recording these types of sites. This trend echoed archaeological research activity throughout the Southwest; early twentieth-century archaeologists gravitated to the most grandiose and scenic of the ruins, which predated Coronado's arrival in the Southwest. When archaeological attention finally turned to Navajo remains, it focused on the highly visible and spectacular Navajo pueblitos of the Dine'tah area of northern New Mexico (Carlson 1965; Farmer 1942; Keur 1944; Kidder 1920; Mera 1937). Before the late 1970s, most archaeological projects (research and contract alike) did not routinely record small Navajo habitation sites.

The establishment of the Navajo Nation Cultural Resource Management Program (now known as the Navajo Nation Archaeology Department, or NNAD) in the mid-1970s, and the operation of a number of contract projects on the Navajo Reservation with Navajo oversight (Vogler et al. 1982, 1983), corrected this omission. The projects called attention to the importance of these sites for understanding the ancient and modern history of our nation's largest Indian tribe. Consistent with this trend, BMAP did not collect substantial data on Navajo sites during the late 1960s and 1970s. From its inception, however, BMAP archaeologists did assign numbers to Navajo sites and gathered information such as site location, numbers and kinds of structures, type of building material, size of sites and structures, probable function, and date of sites (Warburton 1985:69).

In 1975, historic-site research became an integral part of the project and remained so until the end (Blomberg and Smiley 1982; S. Plog and Powell 1984; Powell et al. 1983). This shift in research orientation came about for a number of reasons. First, for all archaeologists working on the Navajo Reservation, the mid-1970s signaled increasing awareness of the number and variety of Navajo sites; there was a growing sense of their potential contribution to understanding Navajo culture. On Black Mesa this concern for documentation was heightened by the archaeologists' first-hand exposure to the rapid cultural change brought about by the presence of Peabody Coal Company (Powell and Gumerman 1987:125).

Second, most of the BMAP archaeologists had been trained to study prehistoric sites. Yet, their exposure to the lease area's historic archaeology had led some to question aspects of their interpretations of the prehistoric remains. They saw in the Navajo sites an opportunity for ethnoarchaeological research that would enhance their interpretations of the puebloan remains (Blomberg and Powell 1983; Nichols and Powell 1987; Powell 1983, 1984b; Russell and Dean 1985; Russell and McAllister 1978). Eventually, the archaeologists recognized that the Navajo sites were inherently interesting and could help answer questions of general anthropological import (Blomberg 1983; Oswald 1993; Rocek 1985, 1995; Warburton 1985).

Despite the growing awareness of their importance, lease-area Navajo sites remained in legal limbo for a number of years. Between 1967 and 1977, oversight authority and legal procedures for complying with federal legislation were hazy at best. BMAP archaeologists recorded all Navajo sites encountered on survey. Many were fewer than fifty years old, however, which at that time made them ineligible for nomination to the National Register (by general consensus, they were not of outstanding national heritage value). If they were ineligible for National Register nomination, the Peabody Coal Company had no obligation to fund data recovery. Nonetheless, because of these sites' research potential, BMAP continued to record them and to excavate some, and Peabody Coal Company supported the work financially, seeing their continued support as cautious and farsighted management.

Some federal archaeologists questioned this decision and, by implication, the importance of the Navajo sites, stating that the coal company had no compelling reason to fund data recovery at Navajo sites; the BMAP archaeologists disagreed. Finally, Frances Levine, at that time with the National Park Service, ended this uneasy situation. Levine argued emphatically for the value of the Navajo sites and for the importance of the precedent that was being set by Peabody's compliance with federal laws and regulations. She worked with the BMAP directors, who shared her view of the sites' importance, establishing the case for the sites' determination of eligibility for nomination to the National Register and developing a long-term data-recovery plan for the Navajo sites.

In 1978, the American Indian Religious Freedom Act (AIRFA, P.L. 95-341) was passed to "protect the rights of Native Americans to practice their traditional lifeways and religions." BMAP directors expected that they would have to comply with AIRFA, but they took no initiative to do so (Powell et al. 1983:244), nor did any of the lead agencies ever suggest conducting an inventory and evaluation of sacred and ceremonial places and traditional-use areas. Such places thus were never systematically recorded during the course of BMAP.

Field and Analytical Procedures

The Black Mesa project investigated Navajo sites throughout its history, and procedures changed greatly over the seventeen years in the field. A systematic recording method was in place by 1980, and all sites that were as yet undisturbed by mining were recorded using these procedures, even if they had been recorded previously. Sites were mapped, all artifacts were point-provenienced and identified, any unidentifiable or unusual artifacts were collected for laboratory analysis, many nonartifactual samples were collected and studied, and consultants were taken to all sites. In addition, an ethnographer collected ethnohistoric, economic, and demographic data. Together, these data provide an unparalleled basis for reconstructing Black Mesa's cultural history and examining the hows and whys of cultural change. Because of the time of the project (1968–1983) and circumstances surrounding it, Navajos were not consulted at the Research Design stage nor did they have any input in the analysis of ethnographic data. It is likely that if they had been, the emphasis on clans, clan origins, and clan migrations would be greatly increased, and the emphasis on sites and specific structures would be greatly reduced.

Until around 1975, historic sites were recorded on forms designed for prehistoric sherd and lithic scatters, and the quality of the data varied with the recorder. Some recorders were interested in the architectural details of hogans, others were interested in the features or artifacts, and some had no interest in Navajo sites at all. Because there was no standardized format for recording characteristics specific to Navajo sites, field archaeologists were free to indulge their personal and professional preferences. Consequently, Navajo site data from this period of BMAP range from excellent to useless.

After 1975, historic sites in the lease area were recorded in a three-stage procedure (Rocek 1985:89–90). During survey, crews identified sites, plotted them on USGS topographic maps, and briefly described and sketched them. Next came field mapping, when crew members drew detailed site and structure maps (to scale), identified and point-provenienced artifacts, collected tree-ring and flotation samples, and interviewed residents. Finally, a small sample of Navajo sites, representative of different site types, was excavated (Haley et al. 1983). These procedures evolved over the years, with the detail and amount of effort continually increasing.

In 1980 and 1981, six Navajo sites were excavated to determine the extent of their subsurface remains (Andrews et al. 1982; Smiley et al. 1983). Project directors' suspicions that such remains might be scant proved correct. Surface information, includ-

ing the position and relation of the structures in conjunction with the artifactual remains, therefore, provided as much information as time-consuming and costly excavation. (Navajo sites had been excavated in 1976 [Sessions and Spalding 1977] and 1977 [Russell and McAllister 1978]; however, the focus had been large ceremonial and habitation sites.) The 1980 through 1983 field seasons concentrated on accurate and thorough recording of Navajo sites. All sites that had been surveyed before 1980 were re-recorded by historic-site crews (unless they had been destroyed in the interval between their original and second, more thorough, recordings).

Numerous samples were collected from each site, including wood samples from hogans, corrals, and features for tree-ring dating, flotation samples from hearths or ash piles, and pollen samples from any feature that the crew chief determined might be important in site interpretation. Faunal remains, shell, or other unidentified organic material were recovered on occasion; however, collection of such samples from Navajo sites was rare.

Although all historic artifacts were recorded on a site map, most of these were identified in the field and left in place. If the material was unusual or unfamiliar, however, it was collected and returned to the field laboratory for analysis. The analytical system emphasized function and was modeled after that developed by the Coal Gasification Project survey of the lower Chaco River (L. Jacobi 1984; Ward et al. 1977).

Ethnography

Many of the sites under investigation had been occupied by a project employee or relative, who was often willing to discuss his or her personal history or events related to the site occupation. This ethnographic information provided a vibrant counterpart to the often economically deterministic and lackluster archaeological information (Warburton 1985:71).

Crew chiefs took consultants, usually former residents, to each historic site and conducted interviews based on a standardized set of questions. If a former resident was not available, the crew chief generally interviewed relatives or people who lived nearby. Consultants were asked to identify all the structures on the site and briefly discuss their function. More information was usually collected when it was clear that the field crew had misidentified a structure during recording. In these cases, the field personnel tried to determine why the misidentification occurred and how this type of feature might be correctly identified in the future. Consultants were asked about the former site occupants and their relatives, the number of occupations of the site, and the date of the site or component, whether it was occupied seasonally or year-round, and what kind of transportation (wagon or motor vehicle) its occupants used. The open-ended nature of the interview process often elicited more information than strictly required by the form. If appropriate, this information was included in the site report.

Between 1975 and 1980 the Black Mesa project hired an ethnographer, Scott C. Russell, to collect ethnohistoric and ethnographic information about the Peabody lease area. Russell's work focused on economic issues, and he collected much data on livestock, agriculture, hunting, wild plant collection, trade with Hopis, wage labor both on and off Black Mesa, arts and crafts production, wood use, and the effects of motorized transportation on local economic and settlement patterns. He also gathered data on genealogy and demographic trends (Russell 1981, n.d.).

Unfortunately, at that time (and even today) most archaeological investigators questioned the legitimacy of ethnographic data and traditional history for learning about the past; thus, no ethnographic information from Navajo consultants was collected about prehistoric sites. The complexity of prehistoric and protohistoric interethnic relationships, including relationships among Navajo and their non-Navajo neighbors, was not investigated.

Cultural History

> The key to comprehending the Navajo history of Black Mesa . . . is understanding the ruralness of the area. Black Mesa was historically, and continues to be today, one of the most rural and isolated areas of the Navajo occupied lands. Black Mesa, which is an imposing geological feature, has kept this area isolated by limiting until (and even after) the introduction of automobiles within the last 30 years. The location of Black Mesa in the middle of the reservation far from the towns that border the reservation has also contributed to its isolation. [Russell 1983:21]

The following chronology describes Black Mesa's integration into Euroamerican culture with information summarized from numerous sources (Downs 1972; Kelley 1982; Kemrer 1974; Kozlowski 1972; Oswald 1993; Rocek 1984b, 1985, 1995; Russell 1981, 1983; Warburton 1985:123–146). In addition, some Navajo autobiographies (Dyk 1938; Dyk and Dyk 1980; Frisbie and McAllester 1978) mention Black Mesa and provide insights into Navajo social and economic patterns during the late nineteenth and early twentieth centuries.

Settlement and Warfare before 1864

For Black Mesa, written documents from the period before 1864 are minimal and fragmentary (Russell 1983:11). Undoubtedly, a thorough documentation of Navajo traditional history from this area would provide a more complete history than the one presented here. Ethnohistorical evidence documents Navajo and Hopi contact, such as intermarriage, ceremonial exchange, and trade during the late seventeenth or early eighteenth centuries (Rocek 1984b:413). Only two

tree-ring dates point to Navajo use of the area in the seventeenth century (Kemrer 1974). A series of seven tree-ring dates from the early eighteenth century signal construction activity on Black Mesa, but this is followed by a gap from 1730 to 1750 (Kemrer 1974:127). Between 1750 and 1799 the southeastern portion of the Black Mesa, west to Oraibi, was occupied by Navajos (Kemrer 1974:129). Between 1800 and 1868, all of Black Mesa was occupied by Navajos, except the extreme western edge and those areas right around the Hopi Mesas (Kemrer 1974:130).

During this period the Navajos were reputed raiders; representatives of Spain, Mexico, and the United States retaliated against the Navajo for raids on livestock, food, or stores. Governor Vizcarra's Mexican journal provides a glimpse of a march by Mexican troops across Black Mesa in search of Navajos in 1823. Vizcarra's descriptions of the Navajos with whom he came into contact suggest that they lived in settled home sites on Black Mesa (Russell 1983:16–17).

As Rocek (1984b:414) notes:

> During the early 1860s, hostilities intensified between Navajos and the United States. At that time the U.S. embarked upon a systematic campaign to pacify the entire tribe by capturing and imprisoning all Navajos. A plan was developed to transport the entire Navajo Tribe to Fort Sumner in eastern New Mexico, where a permanent Navajo agricultural community was to be established. United States forces moved throughout much of the Navajo territory, killing Navajos who resisted and destroying their fields and herds, in a largely successful effort to force them to surrender.

Many Navajos, including some inhabitants of Black Mesa, went to Fort Sumner (Attakai in Roessel 1973:124–125). Stories illustrate the role of Black Mesa, Wupatki, Gray Mountain, Grand Canyon, and other areas as successful hideouts for people

who refused to go to Fort Sumner. Individuals recall that the military came into the Black Mesa area, tracking evaders and their families, forcing them to go to Fort Defiance and on to Fort Sumner (Draper in Roessel 1973:44; Tso in Roessel 1973:103; Beck in Roessel 1973:176–177; Denejolie in Roessel 1973:241).

The Limbo after Conquest, 1868–1881

A final treaty was negotiated between the Navajos and the United States government in 1868. Its terms freed the incarcerated Navajos and required them to relocate on a reservation located in northwestern New Mexico—a mere fragment of their former territory (Rocek 1984b:414). Upon release from Fort Sumner, many Navajos returned to their former traditional use areas, including Black Mesa, irrespective of whether they were on the newly defined reservation. Those people returning to Black Mesa and other places found some of the evaders living there.

> My great-grandfather and great-grandmother were among the first people to arrive back from Fort Sumner. Surprisingly, they discovered some people living on Dziłíʼjiin [Black Mesa]. They were living peacefully. It seems that while most Navajos were herded to Fort Sumner, some had managed to hide and survive. [Burbank in Roessel 1973:134]

Two sites in the lease area, AZ D:7:4089 (Smiley et al. 1983) and AZ D:7:4044 (Haley 1984), date to the period of the Fort Sumner incarceration and may have sheltered their inhabitants from the U.S. military.

It is unclear whether Black Mesa was occupied only seasonally or year-round at this time. The autobiographies of three Navajo former residents of the area, Left Handed, Frank Mitchell, and Old Mexican (Dyk 1938; Dyk and Dyk 1980; Frisbie and McAllester 1978), all describe winter use of Black Mesa. The mesa held four attractions for the Navajo during the winter months: (1) the dense cover of trees over much of the mesa prevented the snow from blanketing the understory, thus providing grazing opportunities for sheep; (2) varieties of small plants were available on the mesa that were unobtainable elsewhere; (3) the abundance of trees provided plenty of fuel to get through the cold winter months; and (4) snow could easily be melted, thus ensuring adequate water for the winter months. In summer, people moved off Black Mesa to the valleys where conditions for agriculture were better.

For the general Navajo population during this period, the primary means of subsistence were livestock and agriculture, supplemented by hunting, gathering, and raiding. Because Black Mesa, apart from the perennial springs in the Hopi areas, was not optimal for agricultural pursuits, livestock traditionally was the most important economic pursuit (Russell 1983:19). Hopi presence and the opportunities for trade, however, were among the factors that attracted Navajos to the Black Mesa area both prior and subsequent to their release from Fort Sumner. Hopi agriculture complemented the Navajo pastoralism, and the opportunities for trade were obvious and probably began early (Russell 1983:19). Virtually no documents, however, exist concerning Navajo lifestyle on Black Mesa before the late nineteenth century.

The Railroad, Trading Posts, and Filling of the Land, 1881–1910

In 1875, surveyors entered the reservation to map out the continuation of the railroad; it had already reached Albuquerque and was scheduled to pass through Fort Wingate and west to Flagstaff. Although the Navajos who had signed the peace treaty had agreed not to impede the railroad's progress in any way, they were horrified to learn it would pass through some of their best grazing land and destroy some of their finest water holes. An agreement, thus, was reached with the government whereby the tribe would

be given a strip of land north of the San Juan River in exchange for lands taken over by the railroad (Mitchell 1972:113).

With the advance of the railroad and railroad workers, new items infiltrated Navajo material culture and began to influence their lives. Pieces of scrap iron were picked up and carried home to the hogan or taken to a blacksmith to be made into tools. Railroad ties were used to make many-sided hogans: "Soon hogans made of railroad ties could be seen, not only along the tracks in every direction but also in many isolated places" (Mitchell 1972:114).

The first train reached Fort Wingate in 1881 and brought with it bandits armed with Winchester rifles and six-shooters, increased land values, and traders attracted by high wool prices. In addition, thousands of white Americans swarmed into New Mexico and Arizona to homestead. According to Kelley (1982), the railroad and ensuing negotiations for this major transportation and communication corridor across the reservation were the main forces that transformed the Navajo political economy and land-use patterns. Due to Black Mesa's topography and isolation, the railroad did not go anywhere near it nor affect its inhabitants in any appreciable way at this time, although some years later it drew some local inhabitants away from the mesa for wage labor.

Trading posts, however, affected the Navajos of Black Mesa, as they did virtually all Navajos on the reservation. One of the first trading posts to open on the reservation was at Keams Canyon, some sixty miles (96 km) south of the project area. Left Handed remembers going there to trade during the mid-1870s, when his family was able to obtain "different kinds of grub, flour, coffee, sugar, all different kinds of calico and colored blankets and dishes, and . . . matches" (Dyk and Dyk 1980:37) in exchange for wool, skins, and blankets. In the late 1800s, due to the difficulty of transportation, trips were infrequent, and purchases consisted only of the essentials.

After Keams, other trading posts opened in the vicinity of Black Mesa, including Tonalea between 1881 and 1885, Red Lake in 1881, Blue Canyon in the mid-1880s, Chinle and Tuba City between 1886 and 1890, Cow Springs and Lukachukai between 1891 and 1895, and Kayenta between 1906 and 1910 (Russell 1981:35). Apparently, the lack of transportation and discretionary income were limiting factors for Black Mesa Navajo; Navajo sites on Black Mesa from this time period contain few or no items of Anglo material culture (Russell 1981:36). Some women report selling as many as three rugs a year to traders, but it is not clear how far back this pattern goes. Art and craft production was not a large source of income for people in the project area.

Beyond the trading posts, trading relationships were an important economic resource for the Black Mesa residents in the late 1800s. The usual trading pattern with Hopi consisted of male Navajos traveling to the Hopi villages with "mutton, goat meat, sheep and goat skins, and pinyon nuts [and sometimes firewood] to trade" (Russell 1981:28). For these items they would receive "corn, cornmeal, peaches, dry peaches, apples, piki bread, watermelons, muskmelons, beans, and Hopi pottery" (Russell 1981:28). Trips to the Hopi villages were usually made in the fall, after crop and pinyon-nut harvests. The round trip, by wagon, took approximately three days. Russell's consultants state that their grandparents or someone in the family established a trading relationship with a Hopi man, and this trading relationship between families was then passed down the generations.

Black Mesa Navajos regularly interacted and traded with Navajos and other tribes as well, including trading with Paiutes for baskets. Even today, Navajo chanters prize Paiute baskets for their technical quality, beauty, and spiritual value. Most of these relationships ended in the 1950s and 1960s, replaced by easy transportation to stores and participation in the cash economy, although informal trading relationships between Hopi, Navajo, and Paiute continue to this day. Others mentioned that occasionally Hopis would travel to northern Black Mesa for mutton from their Navajo trading partners. During the late nineteenth century, trading relationships with the Hopi were probably of the utmost importance due to limited access to trading posts.

Between 1880 and 1910, hunting small animals such as rabbits and prairie dogs, and gathering a variety of wild plants including chokecherry, ribes, prickly pear, and broad leaf yucca, also contributed to the subsistence base (Russell 1981:15). One of the most important wild plant foods, today and throughout the span of human occupation, is pinyon nuts. "Areas of higher elevation on Black Mesa are one of the more important areas for gathering pinyon nuts on the western portion of the Navajo reservation. Navajos from as far away as 250 kilometers come to gather pinyons on Black Mesa" (Russell 1981:16). There are large stands of pinyon trees within the project area today that residents identified as pinyon-collecting sites. At the turn of the century, most pinyon nuts were probably gathered for home consumption or trade with the Hopi; today, they are sold to tourists and trading posts.

The land-use pattern on Black Mesa at this time was primarily seasonal: grazing herds of sheep, goats, and horses in the winter. Some people occupied Black Mesa year-round, but agricultural fields were generally planted off the mesa in the summer, near Kayenta or in the Long House and Klethla Valleys. Others report a reverse pattern for the late nineteenth century, of wintering off Black Mesa and summering on it (Russell 1981:51). This pattern of seasonal round also allowed for greater social interaction with non–Black Mesa Navajos. Russell (1981:18) notes that agriculture continues to have been secondary to animal husbandry as a subsistence activity.

In the early 1900s, with no designated family grazing areas, people grazed their herds where feed and water were available. Animal husbandry was critical for home consumption, for exchange, and for generating income. Perhaps more important to the Navajo people, however, they felt (and many still feel) a spiritual connection to the livestock. Livestock were and are a means to be a part of the landscape created by the Holy People. People, then, can recognize and be recognized by the landscape through herding and caring for sheep and other livestock. As one woman from the Big Mountain community observed: "I am well-known among the hills; among the ditches; rivers; streams; plants. I have touched them in various ways and they have touched me the same" (Bedoni in Wood and Stemmler 1981:ii).

Population growth in the area was similar to patterns elsewhere on the reservation. Russell (1981:54–55) reports that the current residents of the eastern portion of Peabody Coal Company's lease, except for some spouses, all trace their descent from four couples who occupied the land by 1880 or 1890. "Because of intermarriage between the children of the founding families all camps within and around the Eastern Lease Area . . . can be placed on a common genealogy."

Between 1880 and 1910, matrilocal residence was the norm, and kinship ties were strong. Religion was part of all aspects of life, with no distinction between the sacred and secular, and most people followed traditional lifeways. The traditional, large forked-stick hogan, with a diameter of 6–8 meters, was the most common house type. These hogans also had large and elaborate vestibules or entrances (Russell 1983:40).

The End of Semicommercial Herding, 1910–1930

This period on Black Mesa is characterized by increased involvement in the Anglo economy, increased herd size, increased sedentism, and increased pressure by Anglo development to assert rights to grazing areas. Because this time is within the memory of some of the current inhabitants of the mesa, more detailed information is available.

In addition to the trading posts mentioned previously, new trading posts were established at Dinnebito and Pinon between 1911 and 1915 and at Shonto between 1915 and 1920. Both Pinon and Dinnebito are on Black Mesa, however, the location of the Dinnebito trading post is unknown. It may have been located to the south of the lease where some stone foundations have been found but appears to have closed in the 1930s (Russell 1981:35). The trading post at Pinon is important because once founded, it became the nucleus for the settlement of Pinon, the only major settlement on Black Mesa, some 19 miles (30 km) south of the lease area.

A Navajo-owned trading post (AZ D:11:36, Rocek 1984a) operated for a few years in the lease area during the mid-1910s and into the 1920s (figure 8.2). The site was originally misidentified as the Big Mountain trading post (Gumerman et al. 1972:28), but excavation disclosed it to be an earlier and smaller operation. The post was run by local Navajos, Dághaa Yázhí (Small Mustache) and his older brother Bikooh (Arroyo), with the help of their parents, who herded their stock (Rocek 1984a:429). Bikooh later opened another post in the lease area to the north of AZ D:11:36, which may be AZ D:11:4283 (located about two miles north and west of AZ D:11:36). Archaeological surveyors originally identified D:11:4283 as an agricultural field house; however, several consultants said that it was a trading post located on a former wagon trail (Michalik 1984:509).

Dághaa Yázhí and Bikooh stocked their posts from Winslow, Keams Canyon, Holbrook, and Oraibi, trading clothing, blankets, canned food, and soda for locally produced items, including sheep, goats, corn, animal skins, wool, mohair, rugs, and pinyon nuts (Rocek 1984a:430). The traders lived at two nearby settlements, AZ

Figure 8.2 AZ D:11:36, Dághá Yazhi's and Bikooh's trading post on northern Black Mesa (photograph by F. Smiley).

D:11:4144 and D:11:4145 (Semé and Joha 1984). Large corrals and many lamb pens were found at these sites, along with a large number of beads "not found in any significant numbers on other historic sites in the area" (Rocek 1984a:430). Consultants related that Dághaa Yázhí was a silversmith, which perhaps explains the many beads.

The two Navajo-owned and operated posts in the lease area were never the primary trading outlets for occupants of the lease area, which perhaps explains why they closed during the mid-1920s. Rocek (1984a:431) notes that an unusual range of artifacts was recovered from AZ D:11:36 and that the site would have been identified as a trading post even without confirmation by consultants. (The smaller trading post, AZ D:11:4283, was misidentified by archaeological surveyors; its actual function was later revealed by consultants.) Also unlikely would be the identification of AZ D:11:36 and AZ D:11:4283 as local Navajo endeavors (for example, Gumerman et al. [1972:28–29] identified AZ D:11:36 as the Big Mountain Trading Post, a part of Lorenzo Hubbell's Ganado trading operation).

Residents of the lease area mention Pinon, Shonto, Kayenta, and Rough Rock most commonly as places at which they or their parents traded between 1910 and 1930. The once-a-month trip to the trading post in those days was made by wagon and might take as much as a day, depending on the post. Russell (1981:35) points out that Kayenta may have been the most important post because of seasonal movement to agricultural fields located nearby. The Black Mesa Navajos used trading posts primarily to obtain the essentials of life in return for lambs, wool, and mohair. Art and craft production for sale to the trader continued to play a small role in the family economy. Agriculture, trade, and hunting and gathering were important but secondary economic activities during this period.

This period marks the introduction of substantial U.S. government interference, in the form of "assistance programs" in Navajo lifeways. As Rocek (1984b:417) notes:

Considerable government-sponsored well and reservoir construction occurred on the reservation in the 1920s, along with efforts at stock improvement, control of excess horse populations, and further efforts at promoting sheep dipping. . . . A growing overgrazing problem resulted in government efforts to improve range conditions for livestock. References to overgrazing date as early as 1883, and an 1894 report by a Navajo Indian agent suggested that the Navajo land base was insufficient.

For the inhabitants of Black Mesa there was a new source of income: wage labor. Before 1920, there was virtually no wage labor on the mesa, but between 1920 and 1930, job opportunities picked up sporadically, consisting of "small and temporary governmental projects constructing stock tanks, roads, and dams" (Russell 1981:30).

This period marks a shift in land-use patterns from seasonal to year-round occupation. One family curtailed seasonal movements between 1910 and 1915 (Russell 1981:43), and most families stopped by about 1920, except occasionally, when people lived on the mesa's scarp or had access to irrigated fields near Kayenta (Russell 1981:43). Local residents say that they discontinued seasonal movements because other inhabitants would no longer allow them to move through their land, thus cutting off access to summer grazing areas, perhaps indicating deteriorating environmental conditions on the mesa. Increasing population and amassing of large herds on Black Mesa as elsewhere on the reservation corresponded with overgrazing and erosion. Lack of water and available feed may have been one of the reasons that some inhabitants would not allow other people to cross their land with their herds.

Population grew continuously, sometimes rapidly, until the influenza epidemic hit in 1918. This epidemic is a key time marker for the Black Mesa Navajo, one whose "importance cannot be over-emphasized" (Russell 1981:52), ranking with incarceration at Fort Sumner and the stock-reduction program of the 1930s (see below). Many of the burials in the project area date to this epidemic, and sadly almost no families in the area escaped the epidemic without loss of life

Figure 8.3 The chapter house at Forest Lake on northern Black Mesa (photograph by M. Warburton).

(Russell 1981:52); one family died out completely from the epidemic. When people died, their livestock and lands were distributed among the survivors.

Navajo residence patterns change slightly between 1910 and 1930. Formerly, the most common postmarital residence was matrilocal. After about 1920, there seems to have been a slight shift toward patrilocal or neolocal residence. Neolocal residence, however, retains somewhat of a matrilineal aspect, because the new residence is often located on the traditional use area of the wife's family (Russell 1981:55).

On a broader political scale, the establishment of the Navajo Nation Tribal Council on January 27, 1923 (Iverson 1981:20), probably had little effect on the residents of northern Black Mesa. Chapters and Chapter Houses were also established in the early 1920s. Chapter Houses were started at Pinon and Hard Rock, north of Hopi, and at Forest Lake, just south of the project area (figure 8.3). Chapter Houses form the basis of local government on the Navajo Reservation. They were initiated as a means of trying to improve agricultural conditions at the local level and later served as the basic political subdivision of the tribal government. Each chapter elects a representative to the government: a Tribal Council delegate.

By 1930, two trading posts, three Chapter Houses, and very sporadic wage labor are the only avenues of contact for the inhabitants of Black Mesa with the greater reservation-wide social trends. Religion on the mesa was still predominantly traditional.

The Transformation of the Black Mesa Economy, 1930–1950

The traditional Navajo economy on northern Black Mesa was transformed between 1930 and 1950 by increased involvement in the Anglo economy. Wage labor, stock reduction, and attendant economic pressures all became increasingly a part of Navajo economic life. In 1931, a subcommittee of the U.S. Senate Committee on Indian Affairs held hearings in Navajo Country to determine the social and environmental conditions on the reservation at the start of the depression. Subsequently, in 1933, President Franklin D. Roosevelt appointed John Collier as Commissioner of Indian Affairs. Collier, a member of the Indian Rights Association and strong supporter of Native American rights and self-government, is nonetheless considered "Number One Enemy" by the Navajo because of his decision to enforce a stock-reduction program through the Department of the Interior. The stock-reduction policy was based on studies conducted on

the reservation that showed most of the land was disastrously overstocked (Human Dependency Survey 1939). For example, in 1930 the Black Creek Valley area (near Window Rock) was determined to be 276 percent overstocked (Kelley 1982:114).

Collier's stock-reduction program altered the economy throughout the reservation, including Black Mesa. Downs (1972) notes that stock reduction was more difficult for inhabitants . of Black Mesa than other parts of the reservation. Because of its remote and rural nature, stock-reduction enforcement came late to Black Mesa. Stock reduction was enforced on the mesa in 1938–1940, after years of rumors about the insensitivity of program management and the disdainful attitude of program personnel toward Navajo people. Stock reduction also hit Black Mesa residents toward the end of the Great Depression, a time of extreme financial hardship for Navajos (Downs 1972:19).

Firsthand accounts of stock reduction (Roessel 1973) relate some of the impacts on people who worked or lived in Pinon during the program. For example, Gorman (Roessel 1973:66–69) recollects:

> The people became hopeless and helpless. Some were saying, "Suppose you were the one to be penalized; suppose your wages were cut in half or a third cut off, what would you do? You wouldn't like it, would you?"
>
> That's what the Navajos said, and it was very true. I think that drastic stock reduction in the 1930's and 1940's was one of the worst things that ever happened to the Navajos because it ruined them economically. It cut off their livelihood. It ruined many Navajos to the point where they had to go on relief. To this day, I think many of them have never recovered from it.

In the lease area, stock reduction brought about the necessity for off-mesa wage work. Although this exposed Black Mesa inhabitants to the broader economic milieu, they were still generally unable to participate in it.

In 1936 the residents of Land Management District (LMD) 4, on Black Mesa, participated very little in the Anglo economy in comparison with the rest of the reservation; the residents relied on animal husbandry and agriculture (Human Dependency Survey 1939). Ironically, while the percentage of income from both livestock and agriculture was very high, the amount of cash generated in this part of the reservation was very low compared with other areas. The final figure for per capita income per land management unit shows LMD 4 residents at $70.28, substantially lower than the mean for all Navajo districts, $132.30, and the lowest for the entire reservation. Herding and agriculture remained the major sources of subsistence, and grazing areas on Black Mesa were quite large. Grazing areas began to be subdivided among siblings, as population grew and camps divided (Russell 1981:24).

Hunting and gathering in the lease area continued to be important economic pursuits. Gathering of wild pinyon nuts took on increased importance because there was a wider market for the nuts. Traders began buying pinyon nuts from the pickers, and pinyon-nut collection shifted from a subsistence activity to a commercial pursuit. According to Russell (1981:17), "one informant indicated that her family had gathered 2000 pounds of nuts during a single fall and winter."

Wage labor became increasingly important, and with stock reduction, an economic necessity. The temporary Civilian Conservation Corps provided some jobs in the late 1930s. Not until the 1940s, however, did wage labor become a common economic pursuit for men in the lease area; many mention their participation in summer railroad work at this time. Two coal mines operated in the western lease area during the 1930s and 1940s. One, the Maloney Mine, a joint Anglo/Navajo endeavor, was recorded by BMAP as AZ

D:7:38 (Prescott College) (Gumerman et al. 1972:28). Coal from the mine was shipped to Tuba City, where it was used to heat the boarding school. The mine eventually shut down because two of the three main shafts flooded and because of difficulties transporting the coal from Black Mesa to customers. These mines did not provide men from the lease area much opportunity for wage labor because their owners were from off the mesa and did not hire local Navajo laborers (Russell 1981:30–31).

World War II did not directly affect many of the inhabitants of the lease area. There is virtually no record of people within the project area having joined the Armed Forces. Nonetheless, the wartime economy provided jobs that were otherwise unavailable for residents of Black Mesa and elsewhere on the reservation.

Between 1930 and 1950, even with increased participation in the Anglo economy, the trading posts still provided only the essentials for the residents of Black Mesa. Luxuries remained out of the reach of most inhabitants of the project area, as reflected in the virtual absence of Anglo material items on Navajo sites dating before 1950 (Russell 1981:36).

Until 1950, Navajos in the lease area were still living predominantly in hogans. Forked-stick hogans were rarely built, cribbed log and corbeled log hogans remained the most popular forms, and square houses/cabins were built in small numbers. Christianity made few, if any inroads in the project area; residents still practiced traditional Navajo religion. There appeared to be no Navajo-owned automobiles on northern Black Mesa; trips to the trading post were still made in wagons. Herds were no longer moved seasonally between grazing areas; instead, they grazed year-round within grazing areas atop Black Mesa. Population continued to grow, and grazing area size decreased somewhat.

Black Mesa's population grew; the community of Pinon, formed around the trading post, expanded with the Chapter House, and in the 1940s a

school was built, the first on the mesa north of the Hopi area. Before its construction, some local Navajos went off the mesa to boarding schools, however, most people born in the lease area before 1940 received no formal education.

Industrialization and Government Expansion, 1950–Present

Economic information about Black Mesa during the 1940s, 1950s, and 1960s is virtually nonexistent. A report on Shonto (Ruffing 1973) details economic information for that area in 1955, and Russell (1983:34) argues that Shonto is comparable to Black Mesa because both are rural, traditional, and isolated. The combined effects of the depression, stock reduction, and post-war economy on the reservation led most adult males from Shonto in search of off-reservation wage work, primarily with the railroad. In 1955, approximately 51 percent of all Shonto income came from this source; local labor work accounted for only 13.2 percent of all Shonto income during this same year (Russell 1983:34). Russell (1983:34) asserts that for Black Mesa, especially from Forest Lake northward, the amount of local wage labor was probably lower during the same time period, adding:

> Livestock and agriculture accounted for 18.3 and 5.0 percent of Shonto income respectively in 1955. For Black Mesa, this figure was probably slightly higher. Also in 1955, residents of Shonto received 7.9 percent of their income from welfare. This figure was probably similar to that for Black Mesa. Per capita income in Shonto in 1955 was only $291. Black Mesa per capita income may well have been even lower.

Trade with the Hopi began to decline in the 1950s, and decreased further in the 1960s. Hunting continued to provide a small percentage of food, although it, too, declined in importance. Gathering was still undertaken and contributed a small

Figure 8.4 The main access to the Peabody Coal Company leases and northern Black Mesa (photograph by D. Barr).

amount to the household, although its importance decreased due to increased reliance on wage labor and competitive grocery stores. For the decade 1950–1960 on Black Mesa, agriculture was probably important in filling the subsistence gap caused by stock reduction and local dearth of wage-labor opportunities. Russell (1981:18) reports that the primary nine eastern lease camps "currently have or have had agricultural fields within their grazing areas." Sheep and goat herds, although smaller than their former size, were still spiritually and economically important. While the percentage of income from domestic animals tangibly decreased over the previous forty years, animal husbandry still ranked as the primary means of subsistence in the eyes of the Navajo residents (Russell 1981:31). Furthermore, care of the herds was (and still is) critical for maintaining relationships—with the landscape and within and between families—and for perpetuating ceremonial practices.

During the 1950s and 1960s, men were seeking off-reservation wage labor, and children were sent to boarding schools. This out-migration left the women and elderly men to care for the flocks and fields. Short tribal work projects and seasonal railroad labor offered additional wage-labor opportunities for Black Mesa

Navajos during the 1960s (Russell 1981:31).

By the late 1960s, the Peabody Coal Company arrived on the mesa and opened mines for work, dramatically increasing wage-labor opportunities. Peabody mining operations required transporting supplies and workers, thereby increasing the mesa's accessibility. The main mesa access road was paved in 1979 (figure 8.4).

In 1972, just before Peabody expanded operations, Kozlowski (1972) undertook a study in the northwestern portion of Black Mesa, including the project area. His goal was to determine the demographic, economic, and social characteristics of western Black Mesa before the impact of the mines. Although his research was thwarted by a very high refusal rate among the local people, he, nonetheless, calculated a mean household income of $2,400 and a per capita income of $400 for twenty-three of the twenty-five households in his sample (Kozlowski 1972:16). Kozlowski concluded that the inhabitants of his study area were poverty stricken and elderly and that younger people migrated to other areas for possible wage work.

A subsequent study by Callaway et al. (1976) surveyed thirty-six households from northeastern Black Mesa and the Klethla and Long House Valleys. A substantial change had

taken place in the five years that had elapsed since Kozlowski's (1972) study: for the 202 members of the thirty-six households sampled, a per capita income of $1,108 was reported (Callaway et al. 1976:67). "Of this amount 77% was from wage labor, 5% from livestock, 16% was unearned (welfare, social security, scholarships, pensions, etc.), and 1% was from craft activities. Eighty percent of the household heads in this sample, who resided on Black Mesa, were employed at the time of the study in mine-related jobs."

During the 1970s, expanded mining operations created even more wage-labor opportunities. In fact, many of the able-bodied men who had left the mesa for off-reservation employment returned in the hopes of being hired by Peabody. Russell (1981:31) reports that by the late 1970s, some camps in the eastern lease had two or three members working for the coal company. He adds that most camps, however, had no one employed by Peabody because of the advanced age of camp adults, mostly over or near retirement age (Russell 1981:32).

At this same time, operations secondary to the mine such as the Black Mesa Archaeological Project employed quite a few of the local elderly, female, and younger members of the camps. By 1980, BMAP was hiring up to 225 Navajos for summer employment and had a seasonal payroll of several hundred thousand dollars. Most of the wage-labor opportunities until the mid- to late 1970s had been exclusively for males. The pattern has been changing off the mesa because clinics, offices, hotels, restaurants, and retail stores were hiring female staff and secretarial help in greater numbers than males. On the mesa, with the exception of BMAP, most wage-labor opportunities were, and continue to be, for men.

Wood et al. (1982) undertook an assessment of a second stock-reduction program imposed by the U.S. government on the Navajos of Black Mesa. The reduction was, in part, a response to the Navajo-Hopi Joint Use Area dispute. The study was undertaken in the Former Joint Use Area (FJUA) while the reduction program was in effect. The FJUA encompasses virtually all of Black Mesa, including approximately the southern 60 percent of the lease area. Interviews conducted in 146 households indicated that the per capita income was $1,267, comprising 52.8 percent wages, 18.2 percent livestock sales, 6.9 percent livestock consumed, 0.7 percent livestock received, 0.7 percent wool sales, 14.5 percent unearned, 2.6 percent weaving, 3.5 percent silversmithing, and 0.1 percent other crafts (Wood et al. 1982:111). The authors point out that income from livestock is higher than expected because of incentive payments offered by the Bureau of Indian Affairs for stock sold to them by residents of the FJUA. Russell (1981:41) adds that upon completion of this new stock-reduction program, herds were reduced by 90 percent, portending severe reduction in income from livestock and far greater economic and social change.

From 1950 to the present, a new source of income—government assistance programs and Social Security—became available to Black Mesa Navajos. Older people started receiving Social Security payments in the 1960s and 1970s as they became eligible (Russell 1981:32). Before mining operations on Black Mesa, the Bureau of Indian Affairs General Assistance Program was an important source of income for many families in the project area (Russell 1981:32). Government surplus-food commodities also became available to low-income families. Government assistance, however, has not played as major a role on Black Mesa as it has in other areas of the reservation, because just as the assistance was beginning, the mines started operating, thus reducing the need for these programs. Nonetheless, camps with older members still rely heavily on Social Security as their major source of cash (Russell 1981:33).

The economic changes mentioned above are reflected in the material culture from sites of this time period (Russell 1981:36):

A Navajo habitation site occupied in the 1950s in the Eastern Lease Area can contain ten times or more the number of Anglo items of material culture than a similar site, in terms of length of occupation and site function, that was occupied in the 1930s. As we approach even closer to the present, Navajo involvement in the Anglo economy and in its material culture goods continue to increase.

One of the material-culture items that contributes heavily to site debris from this period is the automobile. Cash from wage labor enabled many of the inhabitants of the lease area to buy pickup trucks, and the newly built roads contributed to the trucks' usefulness. Informants indicated that some inhabitants of the project area had trucks as early as 1950, but they were not common until after 1960.

Habitation structures also changed after 1950. Although hogans continued to be built in the 1990s, wood frame and cinder-block houses and some trailers replaced them as the predominant type of housing on the mesa. Plank and frame hogans often appear on sites as an intermediate type of housing between traditional structures and Anglo-style houses (Russell 1983:411). Habitations from this period were occupied year-round and are no longer considered temporary or seasonal structures.

The community of Pinon continued to grow. By the 1960s, churches, a school, a second trading post, a Chapter House, a post office, a sheep dipping vat, a police station, a small clinic, and a rodeo ground had sprung up around the trading post (Russell 1981:301). The road to Chinle was paved in the 1980s, linking Pinon to the population centers to the east, and a Basha's supermarket was constructed.

There were also significant changes in religion at this time; for the first time, Christianity became important. Formerly, informants note that virtually all the occupants of

the project area practiced traditional Navajo ceremonialism. A few mention that missionaries came into the area on donkeys in the 1920s but were unsuccessful in their conversion attempts. The longest any informant would admit to being a Christian was twenty-six years. Apparently, in the 1950s, dedicated Protestant missionaries from Hard Rock Mission (just north of the Hopi Villages) converted a number of people in the project area. There is evidence that the Native American Church is popular on the mesa; two informants mentioned that they had been practicing this religion for over forty years in conjunction with a traditional lifestyle. By 1980, many people had converted to Christianity and endeavored to raise their children in a very strict and conservative Christian manner. At this same time, however, almost one-third of the families said that they still practiced traditional Navajo ceremonialism.

Since the mid-1960s, the promise of work at the Peabody Coal Company mines has been inextricably linked with population growth in the lease area. Mining operations, however, are disturbing large tracts of land (figure 8.5) making them virtually useless to the local inhabitants for traditional activities for the period of mining and reclamation (until the mid-twenty-first century, in some cases). The Navajo families who have traditional use of the disturbed lands are compensated monetarily by Peabody, but such compensation cannot address the peoples' spiritual relationship with the landscape and ignores the interconnectedness of all beings within and beyond the lease area (Kelley and Francis 1994:101). Further, disputes over who can lay claim to the land have and will continue to cause conflicts. In many cases, people using certain grazing areas had no formal claim or title to the land and thus were not compensated by Peabody. Additionally, Navajos have not traditionally demarcated the boundaries of their grazing areas by any official means such as fences, often leaving boundaries disputed. Finally, determination

Figure 8.5 Peabody Coal Company lease-area view of natural habitat in the foreground, mining activity in the center background, and reclaimed terrain to the right and left of the longwall mining activity (photograph by M. Warburton).

of land ownership and the recipient of compensation are often matters of dispute. Sometimes the dispute is between families, but increasingly, it is within families. This unfortunate process weakens the strong kin ties that have been so important in the project area.

Comparison with Other Areas

The following brief comparison of Black Mesa with other areas of the reservation uses as a foundation Kelley's study (1986) of the area around Black Creek Valley near Window Rock, Arizona, and the work of Vogler et al. (1982) on Gallegos Mesa, New Mexico. These studies were selected from among many because their depth of analysis and recording procedures are comparable to those used on Black Mesa. Both the Black Creek Valley and the Gallegos Mesa, however, were more immediately affected by both reservation-wide and national politics and economy than Black Mesa. This comparison, then, highlights the remote and rural nature of the Black Mesa.

Looking first at the Black Creek Valley area, Kelley's study (1986) is an economic analysis of Navajos within this region. She examines the shift from "family production for direct consumption to production for the market" (Kelley 1986:203), arguing that this transition serves as the foundation for a basic class transformation in Navajo social organization. Kelley (1986:204) notes that

intensified and diversified production is what distinguishes Navajo family production in the railroad era and in the transitional era of grazing regulation from production in the industrial era. The reason for this trend, again, is that families suffer at once from shrinking land bases and a growing burden of indebtedness that forces them to produce goods in greater volume, variety, or both. Through the judicious use of both technology and space, therefore, families must enlarge output in proportion to the land and labor input. If these means do not suffice, families have no choice but to overexploit and degrade their resource base. Industrial-era families feel less pressured to enlarge

land-based production because it is not their main source of livelihood.

To support her interpretation, Kelley looked for archaeological evidence of intensified and diversified use of space. The number of what many archaeologists call "special-activity" sites—sheep camps, campsites, and isolated corrals—diminished with land subdivision. Family members used such sites while exploiting lands far from their homestead; customary use areas diminished in size, because families traveled less in their seasonal rounds. Special sites for exploiting the farthest lands therefore ceased being used. (Sites for exploiting lands nearer the homesite—isolated corrals—continued to be used, however, for the family was pushed to use its land base as evenly as possible.)

Another source of archaeological evidence for intensification and diversification of the use of the land base is the increase in the overall size and complexity of homesites. This increase coincided with and was caused by longer annual stays due to range subdivision; people simply had nowhere else to go and engaged in more activities at their primary homesite. Technological correlates of this change (larger dwellings, more facilities on homesites, and wider spacing of features in front of dwellings) signaled intensification and diversification of production. Finally, homesites did not begin to cluster noticeably near major transportation links to the outside world until this transformation was well underway.

The general trends that Kelley (1986) outlined for the Black Creek Valley are also present on northern Black Mesa (cf. Oswald 1993; Rocek 1985, 1995). The difference, however, is that these trends are present in the Black Creek Valley area as early as the late 1800s to early 1900s but do not occur on Black Mesa until the 1960s, with the arrival of large-scale mining operations. The Black Mesa residents were certainly affected by these pressures, but they did not have to succumb as rapidly as did residents of the Black Creek Valley. On Black Mesa we have seen the gradual trend toward sedentism and the decreasing per capita land base as a result of increasing population. The stock reduction of the 1930s forced some of Black Mesa's inhabitants to search for wage labor, but subsistence-based, family-oriented production remained on the mesa until the wage economy provided by Peabody Coal supplanted it. This sudden transformation may have effects that we cannot yet anticipate. In the Black Creek Valley region, the residents have had almost one hundred years to adjust to the pressures of a market-based economy, whereas on Black Mesa this transformation has taken place in less than twenty years. It is likely that this sudden transformation of a rural traditional area to a wage labor, Anglo-influenced society has had bewildering effects on many of its inhabitants, including feelings of disenfranchisement. Local health care workers note the increase of stress-related disorders, including hypertension and heart disease.

Gallegos Mesa is located in the San Juan River Basin, south of Farmington, New Mexico. The settlement history of the Gallegos Mesa area is analogous with the Gallup/Window Rock area, although because of the richness of its natural resources, it was subjected to Anglo pressures even more rapidly and dramatically than Window Rock/Gallup. Anglo settlement of the San Juan River Basin began in 1876, coincident with the founding of Farmington (Gilpin 1982:534); shortly thereafter, trading posts were established along the San Juan River and, later, on Gallegos Mesa itself. At about this time (1880–1907, the Incipient Trading Post Period [Gilpin 1982:534]), Euroamerican ranchers began using the area in and around Gallegos Mesa for grazing.

Permanent camps were built on the flat grasslands of the mesa top after about 1900; they were occupied by both Navajos and Euroamericans.

This permanent occupation . . . was made possible by improvements in transportation, in the form of both roads and wagons, and by the introduction of new technology for establishing permanent water sources, such as wells, reservoirs, on the formerly waterless grasslands. These innovations opened up the mesa top for the first time to permanent occupation and ushered in the Developed Trading Post Period, . . . between 1907 and 1933. [Gilpin 1982:534–535]

Navajo families began to move away from washes and onto the grasslands during the Developed Trading Post Period. They "experienced their greatest expansion, both economically and demographically" during this period (Gilpin 1982:535). Euroamerican ranchers increased their use of the Gallegos Mesa area as well.

The economic boom of the Developed Trading Post Period ended in the late 1920s and early 1930s with the Great Depression, which was accompanied on the Navajo Reservation by several years of severe weather. . . . With the products of herding selling for much less than had been customary during the 1910s and 1920s and the weather ravaging the pastures, the Navajo herds increased beyond the carrying capacity of the range. The government response was to reduce the size of reservation herds by half. . . . This program ended the commercial-herding economy, and forced the Gallegos Mesa Navajo to diversify their economy.

This economic downswing ended in 1950, when oil and natural-gas development contributed to an economic boom in the San Juan Basin.

Wage work became the most important aspect of the Gallegos Mesa Navajo subsistence strategy. The Gallegos Mesa Navajo began to participate extensively in the

local cash economy. Most of the younger people took jobs which required that they move off the mesa, and hence, most mesa-top camps came to be occupied primarily by older people. [Gilpin 1982:536]

This brief economic history illustrates conditions similar to those on Black Mesa for the Window Rock area, except that the Anglo influence and the effects of the national economy have been even stronger and more pronounced in the latter locale. The contrast between Gallegos Mesa and Black Mesa is striking. By virtue of its geographical character, distance from population centers, absence of Euroamerican desired resources (until the exploitation of coal in the 1960s), and distance from major transportation routes, Black Mesa remained a bastion of traditional Navajo lifeways until the 1960s. Because this change on Black Mesa was so sudden and recent, it remains to be seen whether the inhabitants will be able to retain some of the traditional Navajo ways or will be forced to accommodate the Anglo economy to such a degree that Black Mesa loses its unique character.

The Navajo-Hopi Land Dispute and Relocation

On June 1, 1868, a treaty was signed that created a reservation for the Navajo in northwestern New Mexico (figure 8.6). The Executive Order of December 16, 1882, signed by President Chester A. Arthur, set aside 2.5 million acres around the Hopi Mesas for the Hopis and "such other Indians as the Secretary of the Interior may see fit to settle thereon." In 1891, Navajo-Hopi boundary conflicts appeared to have been resolved with the establishment of a 519,000-acre area for the Hopis (Kammer 1980:xiii). Disagreements persisted, however, and in 1931 the Commissioner of Indian Affairs and the Secretary of the Interior agreed that "a reasonable area of land" should be reserved for ex-

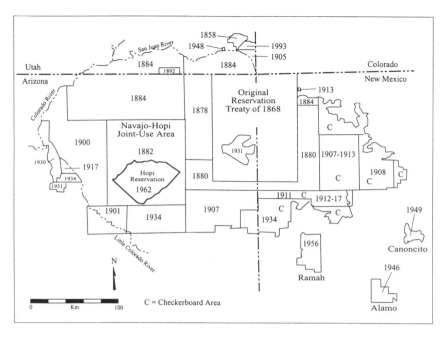

Figure 8.6 Boundaries of the Navajo Reservation over time (after Goodman 1982: map 28).

clusive Hopi use (Kammer 1980:xii). Accordingly, discussions held between 1936 and 1943 led to the designation of Grazing District 6 for Hopi use; an expansion of that area to 650,013 acres thus initiated the first relocation of Navajo families (Hasgood 1994; Kammer 1980:xiii).

Subsequently, in 1958, Congress passed legislation that authorized a lawsuit to determine ownership of the 1882 Reservation. Four years later, in 1962, a "special three-judge federal court rule[d] that 1.8 million acres of the 1882 Reservation are owned jointly by the two tribes. This area bec[ame] known as the Joint Use Area [JUA]. A year later the [U.S.] Supreme Court summarily affirm[ed] the district court decision" (Kammer 1980:xiii). The northern portion of the JUA (figure 8.6) overlaps the Peabody Coal Company lease area. In 1972, the district court in Arizona ordered Navajo livestock reduction to allow Hopi use of half the JUA range; the order also barred Navajo construction in the JUA. In 1974, Congress passed the Navajo-Hopi Land Settlement Act, which provided for equal partition of the JUA and the relocation of members

of one tribe living on land partitioned to the other (Kammer 1980:xiv). The actual partitioning of the land was undertaken by a district court in 1977, but Navajo appeals delayed the effective date of the partition until April 18, 1979 (Kammer 1980:xiv).

The Navajo and Hopi Indian Relocation Commission was established to plan and oversee the relocation of people affected by the court's decision. By now, virtually all Navajo families living in what is now referred to as the FJUA have been relocated.

This brief and dry chronology does not begin to convey the human suffering caused by legal machinations to resolve the ongoing disputes between the Navajo and Hopi tribal governments over this land. For peoples whose entire being is intertwined with their land, relocation is not a simple matter of substituting one parcel of land with an economically equivalent parcel. Equivalence is an Anglo-American concept linked to their cash economy. For those relocated, "There is no place but here" (Bedoni in Wood and Stemmler 1981:ii).

Navajo Sacred and Ceremonial Use of Black Mesa

Traditional Navajo life and ceremonialism centers around the maintenance and restoration of Hózhǫ́ǫ́, beauty and balance with one's self, community, and the natural and spiritual worlds. The Blessing Way ceremony, Hózhǫ́ǫ́jí epitomizes this concept. Other branches of Navajo ceremonialism, the Life Way, Evil Way and Holy Way branches work to restore balance and harmony, Hózhǫ́ǫ́, by getting rid of (eliminating) barriers to Hózhǫ́ǫ́. The execution of any Navajo ceremony or ritual involves the natural world. Each Navajo ceremony (there are many within the three major branches) has its own history of development that identifies peoples, places, and resources that make up the ceremonial repertoire. Some ceremonial traditions specifically identify Black Mesa as a location, thereby weaving the significance of this landform into the broad practice of Navajo ceremonialism; thus Black Mesa cannot be separated from the larger Navajo landscape.

The maintenance of traditional life and land centers around boundaries defined by four sacred mountains. Within these boundaries, all Navajo life, history, ceremony and language are centered. When ceremonies are performed at a specific locale it recalls, and re-enacts, events and places that happened generations ago, and/or in far-away places. A ceremonial event on Black Mesa, as in other places, would require the use of local resources, plants, minerals, soils, local knowledge, and so on and in that respect merges the local landscape to the larger Navajo landscape. Just as important is that ceremony brings together people from across vast distances, allowing them to socialize, renew family relationships, share knowledge, and bind them together as a people.

Furthermore, the Earth is the Mother of Navajo People, Nihosdzáán, Earth Mother. In the Navajo creation history, the mountains were created so that all mountains are the repository of knowledge and contain the basic elements of life: water, wildlife, and plants. As a people we must protect all mountains, and consider the danger to all life if the mountains are destroyed by humans. The mountains, indeed Black Mesa, are a part of the Earth Mother and cannot be separated. In local traditions, Black Mesa is a generous female mountain, and she readily gives gifts of herself to her children. Many Black Mesa residents have told me that you never go on Black Mesa and leave without a gift from her; it may be knowledge, medicine, or materials for domestic use. Black Mesa, Dziłíjiin, keeps the Navajo people strong.

[Richard M. Begay, 2001]

In addition to the overarching sacred significance of Black Mesa, there are many natural resources such as plants, water, and minerals that contribute to continuing presence of people on the Mesa. Residents of the Mesa attest to the sacredness of the landscape, noting their lifelong interrelationship with the land.

All of this made me think of the land, water, and grazing for livestock. I needed all that to survive. Then besides that there are offerings needed along the way. There are songs and prayers needed to help me along, so they taught me some songs and I learned prayers. I learned of sacred places where I go to make my offerings and give my thanks . . . . And we know the land, we know the sacred places, and we know where all the waters are, and the land knows us. And so will my children. We will know it and the land knows us. [Dine' Yázhí in Wood and Stemmler 1981:9]

These resources help Navajos to modify their environment through building various structures such as hogans, sweat houses, and corrals; resources also provide land for farming and grazing, and forage for livestock.

Remnants of material culture are generally what are recorded by archaeologists, and the most prominent of these remains on Black Mesa—structures such as hogans and sweat houses.

Human habitation structures (and some corrals) have significance that goes beyond the mere function of providing shelter. For Navajo people, the larger cultural landscape is a home. Each of the four sacred mountains makes up a side of the fork-stick hogan, the earliest known hogan type recorded on Black Mesa. Thus the hogan is a microcosm of the larger landscape. This significance is imposed onto other hogan types found on Black Mesa such as the cribbed-log and corbeled hogans, or even sweatlodges. The architecture and construction of habitation structures (and other types of structures) were prescribed by Holy People to reflect the Navajo landscape. The final act of this prescription is to bless the home as the land itself is blessed so the structure becomes sacred, allowing both mundane and sacred activity to take place within the structures. Everything within the four cardinal mountains such as archaeological sites, structures, and natural features, decorate the home and give it greater value. Within this space, life goes on, both secular and ceremonial, and for the Navajos on Black Mesa, in the lease area and elsewhere, sacred and secular are indistinguishable because they are one and the same.

Yet, even though Peabody's mining activities completely reconfigure the landscape, they may not have destroyed some of these places' sacredness. People still consider the whole mesa sacred; even though the landscape is different, it is still referred to in ceremonies and sacred mountain songs. Indeed, other sacred areas that have been mined, disturbed, or both are still considered sacred, even after fairly intense damage (Klara Kelley, personal communication 1989).

Locations in the lease area that were recorded as ceremonial sites are places where major ceremonies were

held, such as an Enemy Way (Ndáá), Mountaintop Way (Dziłk'ijí), and Night Way (Tł'éé'jí). BMAP differentiated between ceremonial sites and habitation sites; however, even though some sites were constructed specifically for ceremonies, most are held at habitation sites. Thirteen ceremonial sites have been identified within Peabody's lease (Warburton 1985:appendix II), including Enemy Way sites, Mountain Way sites (Sessions and Spalding 1977), one Night Way site, and unspecified healing/ceremonial sites. In addition, Kinaaldá (puberty ceremony) sites were identified (Estes et al. 1984; Rocek 1984c).

The ceremonial significance of most of these sites was identified by former residents or neighbors or by Navajo archaeologists. In most cases, even though they could recognize distinctive patterns on the sites, the BMAP Anglo archaeologists could not attribute meaningful significance to these patterns. For example, several sites (e.g., AZ D:11:301 [Warburton 1985:327], AZ D:11:4316 [Michalik 1984:503]) had hogans built specifically for ceremonies and outbuildings placed in special relationship to these hogans. Although the Anglo archaeologists did observe these distinctive patterns, they were unable to determine what had caused the patterns. People familiar with Navajo culture, almost always Navajo people themselves, were needed to make these determinations.

Site AZ D:7:718 had material clues to the past that were correctly identified; archaeologists found "material used in sandpainting, located under a sagebrush northeast of the hogan ring" (Russell 1979:161). They included four different-colored rocks and a small log with cut marks that might have been used as a base when chipping sections from the rocks "so they could then be ground into sand for use in sandpainting associated with . . . curing ceremonies" (Russell 1979:161).

The Navajo hogan is both a sacred and secular structure and likely has been blessed before its occupation.

Thus, any site at which there is a hogan may be considered sacred or ceremonial. If a ceremony has been held at a habitation site that has no observable hogan remains, there may be other features and structures that indicate the religious observance. It depends, however, on the type of ceremony, the events related to the ceremony, and the family who hosted the ceremony whether or not a ceremonial location has any special sacred significance. Because of these complex issues regarding the identification of Traditional Cultural Places (TCPs), and because during the life of BMAP these kinds of data were not mandated, TCP identification on Black Mesa remains incomplete to this day. It is especially in regard to TCP identification and related interviews where indigenous anthropologists can provide so much information and insight. The fact that a ceremony was held in a place, however, does not necessarily imbue that place with any special sacred quality. Nonetheless, the hogan generally does have special significance because of its place in Navajo religion.

Other structures on the landscape include what are referred to by most Southwestern archaeologists as Anasazi sites; these structures are also important to Navajo people. Navajos came from many different places and people, and today over sixty clans exist. Each of these clans has their history of how they became Navajo people. Among the sixty or so existing clans, a few trace their ancestry to the Ánaasází ("ancient peoples"). Navajos do not distinguish between prehistoric and historic as do archaeologists. The Anasazi cultural tradition, as well as other cultural periods distinguished by archaeologists, are not separate developments, according to Navajo people. To them, the Anasazi are a part of Navajo history, some of whom became Navajos, and others become other modern peoples. Anasazi sites and people figure prominently in Navajo history, and tradition and may be considered sacred (Downer 1991:33). The Night Way ceremony is one example of this interaction. Many of the major,

named archaeological sites were still occupied when the Night Way ceremony was given to the people. In the ceremonial history recounted in the Night Way, the Navajo people went to such places as Mesa Verde and Canyon de Chelly to visit, sing, and dance with the Anasazi people and with the gods residing there.

Black Mesa is important as a natural sacred landscape, but within that landscape there are specific smaller places that are important in and of themselves. These include archaeological and historic sites as well as many natural features such as sacred plants and springs. Outside forces brought on by development needs are threatening the integrity of these sacred places.

One of the inhabitants of the lease area, when questioned in 1980 about mining on Black Mesa, remarked that all Black Mesa is sacred; it symbolizes the body of the female aspect, and the coal is her liver. Thus, disturbing or destroying the Black Mesa landscape will cause disease and other problems (Russell 1981:51). When questioned further about specific sacred places, the same person said: "Areas where steam comes out of ground, Holy People in legend keep warm by burning coal. Shouldn't disturb them. Even told in story not to burn coal." Another person noted that surface coal mining "destroyed places where we make prayers, prayer hills." He then added that "coal is the liver of the world" (Russell 1981:99). These responses reflect the sacredness of all Black Mesa (Kelley and Francis 1994:150–152).

Black Mesa is significant for all Navajo people, whether they live on Black Mesa or in Los Angeles. It holds a place in their ceremonial lives.

Concluding Remarks

Until the mid-1950s, Black Mesa was one of the most rural, isolated, and traditional areas of the reservation. Some changes among the inhabitants of the lease area took place during this time, especially in land-use patterns,

but generally these changes were gradual and not incompatible with the traditional Navajo culture prevailing on Black Mesa. Stock reduction was, of course, a glaring exception. Looking at the record, many, if not all, of the changes after 1950 arose as a result of interactions with Anglos; nonetheless, Navajo culture remains distinctively Navajo, incorporating "foreign" elements. This pattern is increasingly clear since the arrival of Peabody Coal Company; the inhabitants of the lease area have been confronted with an entirely new lifestyle. This lifestyle requires far greater participation in the Anglo wage economy, less reliance on livestock and animal husbandry, children attending schools, roads and automobiles providing access off-mesa and off-reservation, new religion, new types of housing, and, in some cases, forced relocation from their homes of many generations. All the above-mentioned items from the dominant culture virtually supplant the traditional way of life, yet Navajo culture retains its distinctiveness.

Epilogue

It has been many years since we have written this chapter, but we continue to work occasionally on Black Mesa. There are many changes there, the mine has expanded and is moving into new areas, most of the children no longer speak primarily Navajo, some people have access to the internet, and there are more roads and modern homes (thanks to Peabody Western and the Relocation Commission). The people of Black Mesa have greater access to goods and services that many people both off and on the reservation take for granted. The only constant is that the people of Black Mesa still pride themselves as residents of Black Mesa and continue to value all that is Black Mesa. Many of them continue to defend Black Mesa as they know it. However, a whole new generation of people has now grown up with the mine and the recent developments and will not know Black Mesa before all the changes. It is important that we continue to encourage the retention of traditional culture and language, so that the younger people, the people who don't know Black Mesa as the parents and generations before knew it, will learn of this magnificent place when our ancestors first set their footprints many countless generations ago.

Off Black Mesa, Navajo people respect this place too. As a child, my family spoke of the people of Black Mesa and of our relatives who moved there three generations before my time. They spoke of Navajo traditions that remained strong there, of people still living the old way of life, of the differences in language, and of their ability to sit on the ground without shame or uneasiness. It was only later in life that I got to know Black Mesa; granted I don't know all there is to know of Black Mesa, but I have learned about some of the historic and traditional history, its place in Navajo ceremonialism, and have come to know some of the people. I have realized that the people of Black Mesa are strong people and will survive the development, the mine, and the relocation. They have my admiration.

[Richard M. Begay, 2001]

Note

Most of the chapters in this volume were written between 1985 and 1987, and these chapters recount an archaeological story. This chapter was written later, several years after BMAP ended and after important changes in the laws governing the conduct of archaeology. During the late 1980s, legislative and regulatory changes required consultation and collaboration with native peoples. Although BMAP was exempt from most of these regulatory shifts, this chapter and Chapter 7 (by Leigh Kuwanwisiwma of the Hopi Cultural Preservation Office) were written in hindsight. They represent a very preliminary effort at collaboration, an effort to communicate the existence of other voices, other interpretations of the Black Mesa landscape. Here we tried to show, by example, that a combination of perspectives enhances our understanding of Black Mesa and that multiple perspectives in no way detract from the archaeological story.

CHAPTER 9

Black Mesa Present and Past

Shirley Powell and Francis E. Smiley

What was the Black Mesa Archaeological Project? BMAP was people doing archaeology in northeastern Arizona, and as time fades, the written record becomes the source to which we look for an answer to this question. BMAP was one of the most expensive, longest-running, and best-published archaeological endeavors in the history of American archaeology. The project was large by many standards, and its magnitude and productivity offer many perspectives from which to view Kayenta prehistory, archaeological theory, and the history of American archaeology. Because BMAP involved such a large research area, because BMAP involved so many people, and because BMAP enjoyed unusual longevity, this volume takes the form of both a research synthesis and a chronicle of research effort.

In this final chapter, we intend not only to present summaries of aspects of Black Mesa prehistory but also to pull together the threads of the study, the research process, and to examine some of the links we think the project forged with American archaeology past and present. We also discuss problems and responsibilities that archaeological research encounters in today's archaeological arena.

The year 1983 marked BMAP's final field season, although Peabody Coal Company funded analyses and writing up until 1987. When the Office of Surface Mining accepted the final

report, Peabody had completed all compliance responsibilities. Before 1987, especially between 1968 and 1983 while field work continued, BMAP consisted of people, their activities, and the places in which they worked. The people filled numerous roles—excavation, survey, laboratory analyses, interpretation, writing, planning, and management. These people worked in the Black Mesa field site and/or the academic settings, from which BMAP was administered (Prescott College, in Prescott, Arizona; Fort Lewis College, in Durango, Colorado; and Southern Illinois University at Carbondale). When funding ended in 1987, the people left, most of the activities ceased, university administrators committed the project offices to other uses, and Peabody had crossed one more regulatory hurdle.

At this point, what remains of BMAP? The curated records and materials, the memories of the participants, and the written words. Eventually the records and materials accumulate dust, and participants forget them; a new generation of archaeologists chooses to work with new materials, collected using up-to-date techniques. Then the participants' memories fade, and only the written words remain, accumulating their own share of dust. The printed words then shape perceptions and eventually *become* the project for those people who did not experience it firsthand.

But how well do the written and printed words communicate the cumulative experiences that made BMAP? Who wrote those words, how did the writers choose the topics, and were there topics that never received attention? A review of the "References Cited" in this volume provides clues to the identities of the BMAP chroniclers, as does the volume's "List of Contributors." For the most part, the people who published books, chapters, and articles on BMAP are BMAP archaeologists. During the project, they were graduate students or young (at least at that time) professionals or seasoned veteran professionals. They were either practicing archaeologists or archaeologists-in-training, and they wrote from the theoretical archaeological perspectives of the time. Their words constructed a past populated with artifacts, bones, and plant remains, and these objects inhabited a harsh and unpredictable environment reconstructed using these same objects.

What of the stories and reconstructions that never were written? What about the BMAP personnel who wrote but tailored their stories to mesh with prevailing positivist theory, or those who had stories but did not write or publish them? Do these stories matter? Does their existence denigrate the stories that were published? We could be systematic and compare the people who wrote and published (archaeological professionals and graduate students) with those who did not (summer workers and students who decided not to continue their training in archaeology). The comparison probably would suggest that the untold stories are markedly different from those that were told. A modicum of imagination offers images of these non-authors: a worker impatiently awaiting Friday's paycheck, a grandmother washing and labeling potsherds while she watched a baby, a screener—teeth covered with dust, or a disheartened student covered with scabs and fresh bites from June's gnats. One student's field notebook, written in the late 1960s and still curated in the files at Southern Illinois University, reflects one individual's reactions to the rigors of field research and the remoteness of the field camp. The notebook contains page after page of the words, "I want to go home."

Clearly there are many different interpretations that can be offered on the archaeology of northern Black Mesa and the Kayenta region. Similarly, there are many different stories that can be recounted about doing BMAP archaeology in Peabody's lease area. There are also many different people who could offer their accounts of both these topics. However, the choice of interpretation and the teller depends, in part, on the audience. We professional archaeologists and cultural preservationists have written this volume for professional archaeologists. The volume emphasizes material remains, especially how changes in those remains articulated with changes in the physical and social environments.

At the same time, we do not deny that other stories can and should be told. We welcome their telling. We believe, however, that archaeology makes a contribution to our understanding of the human condition; its interpretations reflect the concerns of contemporary Euroamerican culture. In attempting to balance these considerations, we have come to understand that BMAP was a significant force in

American archaeology for more than twenty years and that it both shaped and was shaped by concurrent events in American archaeology and the larger context of American culture.

BMAP's history is the recent history of American archaeology in microcosm. BMAP anticipates and reflects many of the changes in American archaeology during the past three decades. BMAP people witnessed the shifts from archaeology as an academic pursuit to archaeology as business (now often conducted in the private sector); the change from a small project guided by a few major players to large and multidisciplinary endeavors requiring the orchestrated cooperation of many people; and the shift from no oversight or legal accountability to oversight by and accountability to peoples with cultural affinity to the creators of the archaeological remains, to multiple governmental agencies, and to the tax-paying public. Not surprisingly, this growth and elaboration introduced new players to archaeology and its management, people with very different perspectives on archaeological remains and the past. The inevitable broadening of the cast of players and introduction of new perspectives accompanied and enabled the introduction of a new paradigm, post-processualism, in American archaeology.

Beyond BMAP's role in the recent history of American archaeology, however, the project made major contributions to our understanding of Kayenta prehistory and the dynamics of cultural change in the northern Southwest. BMAP research substantially enhanced our understanding of the transition from hunting and gathering to an agricultural lifeway. BMAP research has produced a richer understanding of the origins of settled life, including the roles of mobility on many temporal and spatial scales and of episodic abandonments in the lifeways of the prehistoric Puebloan peoples.

To reiterate, professional archaeologists wrote this volume primarily

for other professionals. Accordingly, the volume is "archaeological." Most of the chapters are archaeological, interpreting the material remains from the perspective of cultural ecology. The authors, for the most part, focus on the changing physical environment and how humans responded to those changes under varying demographic and social conditions. Chapters 2 through 6 recount what we know of the physical environment for the different time periods, describe the known archaeological remains, and integrate these pieces of information into a cultural ecological tale.

Because we wrote and edited this text over the fifteen-year period 1985 to 2000, the volume preparation itself spanned important changes in the social context and theoretical orientation of American archaeology. To acknowledge and address the changes in social context and in theoretical orientation that occurred after initial preparation of the manuscript, we solicited two additional chapters. Chapters 7 and 8 present Hopi and Navajo perspectives on Black Mesa respectively. Thus, changes in the original design of this text from the materials we submitted to Peabody Coal Company in 1986 to the text that appears in this publication hint at some of the changes challenging the foundations of American archaeology. What follows is a more comprehensive discussion of BMAP's contributions to the profession and of the reflexivity linking BMAP and American archaeology writ large.

Approaches and Contributions

The Black Mesa research story consists of a complex braid of sometimes disparate topical threads. Some threads appear at the project's beginnings, demonstrating continuity over three decades; some begin later. Together, the research threads provide a reasonably coherent general approach to learning about the past. All aim to contribute to understanding the people of Black Mesa and the greater region and to understanding the ways in which the structure of human societies changed over a period of nine thousand years. In the interest of brevity in the summary below, we cite only a few of the numerous works and apologize in advance to any researchers we have omitted from citation.

The primary threads of continuity in Black Mesa research can probably be said to have begun with the necessity to develop a useful cultural chronology for a new piece of archaeological real estate (Gumerman and Skinner 1968; Gumerman et al. 1972). Efforts to establish a sequence of the breaks and patterns in human behavior that make up the Black Mesa culture history continued to the end of the project (e.g., Layhe 1977; Hantman 1983; S. Plog 1986b; Christenson and Bender 1994).

A second early topical focus of the research involved the study of the human population, the paleoenvironment, and the geologic context. The research on the environment/culture linkage achieved high visibility in the efforts of a number of investigators to link the frequency and types of environmental change to changes in the behaviors of area peoples (Euler et al. 1979; Gumerman 1988a; Gumerman and Dean 1989). Research along this front continues as well.

A third primary research thread consists of chronometry, the measuring of the archaeological ages of events and processes. The business of chronometry took a number of forms based on exhaustive dendrochronological studies directed by Jeffrey Dean (1982) over many field seasons. Ahlstrom (1998a), Smiley (1985, 1998c), and Rocek (1985) carried out some of the primary analyses of the mass of tree-ring data gathered by Dean. Ceramic assemblage studies by Plog (1980a) and Christenson and Bender (1994) sought to help date sites and site components. Radiocarbon chronometry studies (Smiley 1985, 1998b) grounded in the tree-ring database developed means for assessing the relation between the age of wood in archaeological contexts and the true age of the contexts for Black Mesa preceramic sites.

A fourth thread includes research on the demographics of Black Mesa prehistoric populations. A number of investigators worked to develop population estimates for the various periods (S. Plog 1986d; Hantman 1983; Layhe 1981). Because demographic trends have such profound implications for cultural development, investigators examined and reexamined the premises on which they based the analyses and reconstructions (Powell 1988). The demographic work provided a corpus of data against and upon which numerous other studies could be established.

Some researchers worked to link population trends with changes in technology and exchange. Parry and Christenson (1987) found that lithic technological change corresponds with changing mobility patterns, while Green (1982, 1985), Hegmon (1986), Hantman (1983), and S. Plog (1986e; Hantman and Plog 1982) investigated the interrelationships among population, exchange, and social organization.

A fifth research thread consists of work on settlement and mobility for groups in the study area. Powell focused on settlement and site structure to examine the nature of mobility strategies for the ancestral Puebloan occupations (1980, 1983, 1984). S. Plog (1986f) examined mobility and settlement strategies. Bearden tested hypotheses about Basketmaker II settlement (1984). Klesert examined the settlement patterns of areas adjacent to the leasehold (1980, 1983), and Blomberg (1983), Rocek (1985), and Warburton (1985) examined a range of questions on historic period Navajo settlement. In addition, Leonard et al. (1983) and Parry and Christenson (1987) examined lithic assemblages, in part to link stone-tool technology and frequencies of raw material with mobility strategies.

A sixth research thread, studies in subsistence, includes works by Martin et al. (1991) that identify patterns in diet, disease, life, and death on prehistoric Black Mesa. Leonard (1989) conducted an exhaustive examination of faunal assemblages from prehistoric sites. Ford (1984; Ford et al. 1985) engaged in research on the consequences of early agriculture and directed the large-scale paleoethnobotanical flotation recovery and analysis effort in BMAP field work.

A final research thread consists of a general methodological effort by numerous investigators to uncover the range of variability in Black Mesa archaeological manifestations, including, among others, assemblages of ceramic and lithic artifacts, faunal remains, settlement patterns, site configurations, and the relation between surface and subsurface assemblages. Leonard's faunal analytical work explicitly seeks to reveal the full range of inter- and intrasite variability (1989). Powell (1983) examines variation in site structure to reveal seasonal mobility patterns. Parry (1987b) reviews the range of variation in lithic debitage to identify patterns of technological change in tool production. Christenson (1987b) examines the Black Mesa projectile-point assemblage for new ways to characterize temporal and functional variability. Plog (1980a) examines design variation in ceramic assemblages, while Marion Smith (1991) delineates the variability in ceramic assemblages from the perspective of function.

Other significant research initiatives could doubtless be included here. Black Mesa researchers have closely examined a wide range of ideas, models, topics, and materials from the various occupations on Black Mesa during the prehistoric and historic periods. Nonetheless, the diverse research group of variable composition over the years tended to approach the work from the same general perspective, that of developing a picture of Black Mesa peoples and the structures of their societies, in terms of demographics, economy, technology, environmental and geological context, and subsistence.

Black Mesa and American Archaeology

As most archaeologists would agree, a project's contributions can be broken down into theoretical, methodological, and empirical areas. In such a schema, BMAP contributions fall into all three. One, perhaps more general, contribution lies in the early, intensive, and consistent application of processualist methods to the massive and rapidly growing database and to the research problems of a large-scale project.

The identity and definition of major theoretical problems in archaeology vary by paradigm and from one generation of researchers to the next. BMAP researchers have largely approached the study from the perspective of processual archaeology. Nonetheless, from the processual perspective, we must acknowledge that we have relied heavily on previous approaches and on other bodies of research in the Greater Southwest as well.

Most archaeologists active over the past three or four decades would probably have no problem characterizing the two approaches used by southwesterners for doing archaeology over the past four or five decades as paradigms in the sense in which Thomas Kuhn (1970) defined them. Paraphrasing Kuhn, paradigms consist of approaches to particular scientific fields of inquiry that (1) originally attracted a group of adherents because of the utility of some body of new ideas and that (2) present sufficient opportunity for intraparadigm problem solving to occupy those adherents for the foreseeable future (1970:10).

The two archaeological paradigms, variously termed the Classificatory-Historical and Explanatory (Willey and Sabloff 1973), or as most archaeologists know them, the Culture Historical and Processual paradigms, have successively dominated American archaeology over the past seventy years. Kuhn viewed paradigms as essentially "incommensurable" (1970:103), that is, each paradigm at-tracts its own adherents, who turn out to be incapable of interparadigm communication.

In contrast with Kuhn's view, we see the operation of the two paradigms as largely commensurable, at times fraught with conflict, but essentially commensurable in the sense that adherents of each find a great deal of common ground and a great many common interests. Investigators who have applied the processual approach have regularly used, and even relied on, the data and conclusions of the culture-history approach. In fact, the chronometry, the identified temporal and spatial patterning, and other data classes developed by "culture historians" provided a number of starting points for hypothesis development and testing.

Although BMAP has enjoyed great longevity, the project started after the beginning of the interparadigm shift to processual archaeology. Accordingly, BMAP did not actually span the paradigmatic gulf between culture-history and "new" archaeology. Nonetheless, the BMAP approach, with nearly all other southwestern projects during the period, employed many of the classificatory systems developed during the culture historical phase. For evidence of continuity, one only need examine the continuity of use of classificatory systems to see both the continued employment of the culture historical approach and the utility of the patterns recognized, classified, and codified during the previous paradigm.

Primary among such systems, the type-variety ceramic classification and the various projectile-point classifications played important roles in the processual analytical frameworks and in the process of hypothesis testing. S. Plog (1978:32) worked, for example,

to formalize our classification, reduce subjectivity, and increase consistency between individuals in the way they sorted ceramics. . . . "Diagnostic" attributes for each type were defined first on the basis of previous type descriptions. To classify a given sherd, the number of diagnostic attributes of each type were counted. If the majority of attributes on a sherd were of one type . . . then the sherd was classified as that type. If a sherd had an equal number of diagnostic attributes of two types, then the sherd was classified as an intermediate type.

As Ahlstrom (1998b) also points out, true to the nature of paradigm shifts, processualist researchers harbored a great deal of skepticism about the system of type-variety ceramic classification and even the phase system introduced for Black Mesa chronology in 1972 (Gumerman et al. 1972). Nonetheless, they continued to use the type-variety system in tandem with the attribute system, because types tended to be helpful and easy to understand. Moreover, familiarity with the old classificatory systems enabled communication with a far greater audience of scholars. A typical example is the study to improve ceramic-type chronology by Christenson and Bender (1994), who refined the dating of ceramic types defined during the culture historical period (Colton 1937, 1956).

Both ceramic and projectile-point classificatory systems remain in use today in continuing research on BMAP materials. In fact, processually motivated attempts to test, refine, and improve the accuracy and precision of the chronologies associated with the classificatory systems have comprised a significant share of BMAP research over the years (S. Plog 1980a; Christenson and Bender 1994; Smiley 1985, 1998b; Ahlstrom 1998a).

We think the enduring utility of previous classificatory systems demonstrates a different sort of paradigmatic relationship than that described by Kuhn. Kuhn viewed paradigms as essentially unrelated, except that one follows another in time. We, on the other hand, see an example in which a new paradigm structure *builds* on the previous one. We do not imply that the archaeological paradigm shift occurred without spirited argument or a great deal of skepticism on the parts of the various paradigm adherents. We do mean that, in our experience, one paradigm provided the foundation upon which researchers in the next would build. We only hope that the work of processual archaeology can provide such a basis for the benefit of new paradigms that will inevitably arise in the future.

BMAP's Contributions to an Archaeological Understanding of Kayenta and Southwestern Prehistory

In archaeology, scarcity of data on a given phenomenon often enables the development of simple, elegant explanations. The environmental explanations of culture change on Black Mesa and in the Kayenta region, for example, developed from the early stages of the analysis of the excavations of relatively few sites and a careful gathering of geological and dendrochronological data.

The explanations appeared powerful, explaining the cycles of occupation, demographic flux, and regional abandonment. Such cycles usually leave remains, often architectural, that exhibit the highest archaeological visibility in a given region. Accordingly, such remains tend to claim the earliest investigators' attention. Later, however, with the recovery of more data, variability tends to increase. Larger samples tend to have more outliers, and often the shapes of distributions change as the sizes of the data sets increase. Such changes occur particularly frequently if the original data sets derive from nonrandom sampling of site populations or of the contents of individual sites. As the data proliferate, variability increases, and as variability increases, simple, elegant explanations may require a great deal of adjustment to fit new, more variable data. Sometimes the range of variability exceeds the power of previously useful explanations.

In the case of Black Mesa archae-ology, initial explanations tend to hold up relatively well but have required some adjustments. In addition, a second trend issuing from changing theoretical interests in American archaeology impels archaeologists frequently to want to move beyond environmentally based explanations to understand the role of the components of culture in the processes of culture change. While new questions and explanatory systems beckon, any scientific research in archaeology must have firm grounding in precisely the domains that early BMAP archaeologists labored to develop: geological and archaeological context, chronometry, and the identification of patterns in remains that indicate culture change over time.

Perhaps the most important ingredient in the process, chronometry, requires that researchers place the remains along a time scale. For useful work in the rarified regions of sociopolitical-ideological research that many have come to think of as post-processual archaeology, investigators require an absolute scale. Research in the cognitive and symbolic areas consists to a significant degree of questions about meaning, that is, communication. Making inference about communication among prehistoric individuals or groups requires that the individuals or groups be basically contemporaneous. Establishing contemporaneity in archaeological remains is notoriously difficult.

In addition, archaeologists really have to know something of the rates and placement of temporally recognized change. In other words, the social dimensions of human societies tend to be strongly conditioned by demographics and by the natural environment, so that if archaeologists wish to learn about the social dimensions of change, they must know something about the size, location, and cultural similarities of the groups that might have interacted. While many modern-day investigators want to move from studies of environment in which researchers often view humans as just another species on the game board

and into the uniquely *human* and interesting research areas of symbolism, ideology, and individual intention, such research remains contingent on foundational data that come from careful work in the ground.

Because information on environment, population size, site location, and cultural similarities comprised the first priorities of the early BMAP investigations, the BMAP material is useful for a wide range of inquiry. On one hand, such a research foundation can underwrite even the most ephemeral of postmodern research approaches. On the other, for scientifically motivated research, the database just described remains elemental.

The data gathering and analysis from twenty years of intensive archaeological work on Black Mesa changes our perceptions of regional prehistory along a number of dimensions. We have achieved better understandings of regional chronology and of changes in regional demographics, economic and sociopolitical interaction, ideological variation, social organization, and technology.

Important advances in the understanding of the preceramic peoples who moved through and lived in the Kayenta region have revealed the base of Puebloan development. BMAP demonstrated the existence and examined the nature of the Archaic occupation. The ephemeral presence of Archaic groups in the region across at least five millennia suggests extremely high mobility in a depauperate, stochastic environment that required *extensive*, that is, large-scale, territorial adaptations. While the existence of Archaic hunter-gatherer groups in the Kayenta region that BMAP documented came as no archaeological surprise, the BMAP-derived discoveries in chronology and culture change in the immediately post-Archaic cultural phenomenon, the Basketmaker II period, significantly altered perceptions of early farming peoples across the northern Southwest.

BMAP research demonstrates that when domestication and food production passed a productivity and reliability threshold in Highland Mexico, groups from central Mexico to southern Utah appear to have adopted farming in relatively rapid succession (Smiley 1994, 1997a, b). The dates for early agriculture from the Mexico border to the northern Southwest currently appear radiometrically contemporaneous (Smiley 1997a).

In the Kayenta environs, the earliest farmers, early Basketmaker II groups, lived in rockshelters and caves in deeply incised canyons that abound in the region. The groups appear to have been poised between band and tribal levels of social organization. Populations remained small, and groups appear to have retained the relatively high levels of mobility typical of band societies.

At the same time, they grew corn and squash, built significant storage facilities, and stored large amounts of food. Moreover, they began to inter their deceased in domestic contexts, that is, in storage facilities or in graves in the caves and rockshelters in which they lived. The latter behaviors, food production and a view of the dead that enabled domestic-context burial, typify tribal societies. Because they appear to occupy the conceptually transitional territory between bands and tribes, the Basketmaker II groups of the Kayenta region afford an important social evolutionary case (Smiley 1997a).

BMAP research revealed unsuspected temporal placement and relationships for late Kayenta–region Basketmaker II peoples as well. In 1972, BMAP crews recognized and began to excavate small, open-air settlements in the Peabody leasehold. By the close of field operations in 1983, more than thirty such sites revealed a wide range of variability within a limited temporal frame. The sites appear to have been occupied from about 1900 to 1600 B.P., a relatively short period. The sites vary from camps to sites with one to twelve small surface or subterranean structures. As evolving, foundational Puebloan societies, the Basketmaker II development of small, open-air settlements appears to

comprise the archetype of Puebloan villages, so highly visible and well known across the Southwest.

Accordingly, BMAP provided a sample, large by archaeological standards, of the foundations of Puebloan society. In the process of delineating the nature of preceramic, early agricultural adaptation, BMAP enabled advances in the accuracy and precision of the interpretation of radiometric data (Smiley 1985, 1998b).

While much is known about the ancestral Puebloans of the Kayenta region, much remains to be discovered, and much already-completed field work awaits interpretation and integration into the larger picture. Early regional syntheses emphasized growth, intensification, and elaboration: population grew, the number of sites increased, sites became larger and more complex, people relied increasingly on the products of agriculture for subsistence, and social organization became more complex and hierarchical. These trends were symptomatic of a stability that could be disrupted only by dramatic and catastrophic events: the Great Drought of A.D. 1276 or invasion by enemies from the north.

Alternatively, the interpretations offered from the perspective of the Black Mesa Archaeological Project are far less dramatic and undermine the interpretation of cultural stability. Interpretations emphasize variation, both over time and at any one point in time. Population growth was a deviation amplifying process, and regional abandonments were the rule rather than the exception. Sites were variable in configuration and, in hindsight, do not appear to have been evolving toward a single norm. Although agricultural products were important, they were not equally important throughout the Kayenta region. People relied on numerous resources and were opportunistic in resource exploitation. Throughout the ancestral Puebloan period, some sites were large, suggesting comparatively complex social organization. At the same time, other sites were small, perhaps isolated by

choice from population centers like the Chacoan-style great houses on southern Black Mesa.

Contemporary researchers differ on the relative importance of physical or social environments in causing change; however, they agree that the magnitude of any individual causal factor has been overestimated in the past. Archaeologists favoring the physical environment as triggering cultural change have refined their measurements and found that smaller and smaller perturbations correlate with cultural change. Further, they agree that the social environment is important in determining how people might respond to changes in the physical environment. Archaeologists favoring social causes also emphasize the importance of perceptions of risk and the relationship of these perceptions to changes in the physical environment. Interestingly, Kuwanwisiwma (Chapter 7, this volume) suggests that environmental perturbations were reminders to the ancestral Hopi of their covenant with Maasaw, that they had settled in one place long enough, and setting complacency and comfort aside, it was time to move on.

So, how has this diminution of the causes of changes altered our interpretations of the Puebloan prehistory of the Kayenta region? Clearly, we view the situation as more complex, partly because we tend now to consider more variables and partly because we have a great deal more information than those who developed the initial interpretive structures.

Research Controversy

Are there still areas of disagreement? Certainly, and some disagreements raise questions about the very foundations on which subsequent interpretations rest. This research has opened a world of options suggesting, if not establishing, that prehistoric people did not walk in lockstep through the past. Instead, the wide ranges of variation in material culture suggest that people solved problems both creatively and idiosyncratically.

Here, as in so many other areas, the problem of establishing contemporaneity rears its ugly head. For the most part, BMAP researchers attacked the problem head on through tree-ring and radiocarbon studies. Nonetheless, the contemporaneity problem remains in a number of time periods at a number of sites, vigorously resisting solution. Some general examples follow.

Certainly Archaic-period populations barely registered on the archaeological preservation scale. We have few sites, but the site occupations appear to have occurred across a five- or six-millennium period. While researchers debate the reality of occupational hiatuses on the Colorado Plateau (M. Berry 1982; Wills 1988a), the Black Mesa evidence remains equivocal. The sparse distribution of chronometric data during the long Black Mesa Archaic could accommodate long occupational hiatuses, or they could indicate relatively continuous use of the region. The paucity of data in the latter case could result from preservation problems, sampling error, the impermanent nature of Archaic occupations, or all these factors.

Similar levels of disagreement persist for the Basketmaker II occupation. The indications from the Black Mesa/Marsh Pass area suggest that Basketmaker II groups occupied sheltered locations and maintained low population levels for at least a millennium (Smiley 1994, 1997e, 1998b). Some preliminary indications of open-air settlements of Basketmaker II groups dated by radiocarbon to about 3000 B.P., however, come from the Lukachukai area east of Black Mesa. Whether the Lukachukai sites (Gilpin 1994) comprise an outlier or indicate the contemporary existence of open-air settlements with the rockshelter occupations now so well documented and dated to the same period across the northern Southwest (Smiley 1997a) remains to be determined.

Another area over which southwesterners tend to disagree is the extent to which early farming groups relied on cultigens. Chisholm and Matson (1994) find evidence for major dependence on consumption of C-4 plants for Basketmaker II groups in southeastern Utah. Archaeologists usually interpret dependence on C-4 plants as dependence on corn agriculture. While wild C-4, pathway plants, and animals that eat wild C-4 plants, can influence the levels of C-4 dependence interpreted by researchers, Black Mesa evidence suggests a similar conclusion.

As for the demographics of Basketmaker II populations, no estimates have yet been possible because so few sites in the greater region have been scientifically excavated. We can be sure, however, that during the initial millennium of occupation, populations remained extremely low, on the scale of extensively adapted band societies, probably with large territories, significant reliance on wild foods, especially pinyon nuts, and retaining a measure of seasonal or year-to-year mobility.

The groups of the Black Mesa Lolomai phase who built small settlements of earthen pit structures and storage pits represent a significant population increase. The density of the low-visibility sites across the Peabody leasehold is geometrically higher than the density of Archaic sites or of Basketmaker II rockshelters in the region. Nonetheless, populations must have continued to number within the range of band societies. A settlement of five or six contemporaneously occupied pit structures cannot represent a group of more than twenty or thirty people. Most settlements of the Lolomai phase evidence only a few pit structures, representing very small groups. The use-span of pit structures could have ranged from a few years to a decade or more. Still, the one hundred or so sites of the Lolomai phase discovered in the leasehold could easily have been generated by an occupation in the Lolomai phase lasting only two or three centuries (Smiley 1985, 1998) and a population of twenty to thirty people who separated into smaller units and moved seasonally about the area, abandoned sites or dwellings every few years, and built new sites or new dwellings on the same sites.

The level of social complexity of Basketmaker II groups seldom comes into question. In this volume, Smiley emphasizes the importance to human social evolutionary studies of the Basketmaker II adaptation as transitional between band and tribal levels of social organization. In the western portion of the northern Southwest where social complexity rarely, if ever, passed beyond tribal level, the Basketmaker transition looms as particularly significant, providing the behavioral model of *settling and moving, moving and settling* (Smiley 1995b) that seems to characterized Puebloan adaptation for the next two millennia.

While the Basketmaker II occupations appear remote from modern Native American occupation of the Black Mesa area, Hopi elders have identified Basketmaker rock images as symbolic of Hopi migrations. The Hopi continue to use some of the same technologies as the Basketmaker II groups. The regional occupational history clearly links the Basketmaker II groups with later Basketmaker III peoples and thence to Puebloans. In any case, Hopi culture probably has significant connections to the Basketmaker II peoples. Hopi oral tradition and history may provide important insights into and perspectives on Basketmaker development.

Puebloan Period Archaeology

Most basically, we still lack a consensus on the number of people living in the Kayenta region during the prehistoric Puebloan period. Unfortunately, most archaeologists fail to address this question explicitly. Rather, they implicitly assume the presence of the number of people required to support their particular interpretations on such questions as settlement patterns, subsistence base, and organizational complexity (Powell 1988). However,

BMAP and other research have raised questions about interpretations of archaeological remains that investigators usually use to infer population levels. The BMAP researchers delved frequently in the problems associated with determining the use-life of dwellings and sites in small-scale societies (Hantman 1983), about mobility and the temporal scales on which mobility might have operated (Gilman 1983; Powell 1980, 1983), about the role of abandonments and their frequency (S. Plog 1986c), and about the relationship between material items and the number of people who used those items.

In a sense, these ancillary studies raised continuing questions about the number of people living in the Kayenta region during Puebloan prehistory. If people built, used, and abandoned sites at a rapid rate, then larger numbers of sites during a given period might not mean larger numbers of peoples. These unresolved issues converge on the question of the Pueblo II dispersion: Do the large numbers of far-flung sites represent the colonizing efforts of a growing population? Or were they the result of a refugee population fleeing the hegemony of Chacoan overlords? Both reconstructions are plausible, but the former begs the question of where the people went after the dispersion ended.

Most basically, many of the unanswered questions about the ancestral Puebloan occupation of the Kayenta region remain unanswerable—for the time being. They are unanswerable because the temporal and spatial resolution of the archaeological materials does not begin to match the temporal and spatial requirements of the questions we would like to answer. Archaeological materials typically have broad temporal context (i.e., they can be dated to a block of time) and narrow spatial context (i.e., they come from a specific location). Alternatively, the questions archaeologists would like to answer require tight temporal control and broad spatial focus (i.e., we need to know specifi-

cally when something occurred and the spatial extent of its repercussions).

For example, to return to the population question, we are unable to answer reliably such basic questions as, How long was a site occupied?, With whom did its occupants interact?, Was it occupied seasonally or year-round?, If occupied seasonally, how far did the site's occupants travel to their off-season site?, and Did they use the same set of sites each year? Clearly, similar questions of scale impact our approaches to problems such as settlement patterns, subsistence, exchange, and social complexity as well. BMAP and other archaeologists continue to acknowledge problems of scale, and they continue their attempts to articulate the spatial and temporal scales of the archaeological record with the questions we are asking of it.

BMAP and the History of American Archaeology

BMAP's history is the history of American archaeology from the 1960s through the 1980s. The project was shaped by larger trends and, in turn, played a part in forming those trends. During BMAP's twenty-year span, archaeology changed from a primarily academic endeavor to a business based on contracts and bureaucratic oversight. Accountability broadened beyond the discipline to include responsibility to the larger public and oversight by multiple governmental agencies. Throughout the history of American archaeology, big projects have been the exception, but they are exceptions that served as harbingers of what was to come. Complementing these changes, processualism's explicitly positivist interpretive stance has been challenged by the multiple, ephemeral perspectives of post-processualism. In short, the mix of perspectives in American archaeology in the 1990s differs greatly from that of the 1960s.

Much of that difference stems from the legal climate and larger acknowledged social milieu in which archaeology gets done. Archaeological

excavations for the purposes of mitigating the adverse effects of Peabody Coal Company mining operations started in 1968. The National Historic Preservation Act (NHPA) had been made law just two years earlier; however, regulations for implementing the legislation had not yet been drafted. In the absence of implementing regulations, BMAP archaeologists Robert C. Euler and George J. Gumerman set the compliance agenda by doing *archaeological research*. Euler and Gumerman thus established a standard of state-of-the-art archaeological research as an appropriate response to the spirit of NHPA.

By the late 1970s, the legal climate for archaeology had begun to be "regulation-ized." Archaeologists from the National Park Service's Southwest Regional Office in Santa Fe worked with new BMAP director Shirley Powell to create a plan for complying with NHPA, a process made difficult by the lack of a complete inventory of sites in the Peabody lease.

Archaeological data recovery had been ongoing for more than ten years at that point, yet much of the area had not been surveyed. BMAP personnel quickly planned for completion of the archaeological survey, evaluation of sites for legal significance under the guidelines established by Section 106 of 36 CFR 800 of the NHPA. They then developed a data-recovery plan that would ensure collection of representative data from a representative suite of "significant" (in the legal sense) sites.

Peabody Coal Company, paying for the archaeology as a necessary prerequisite to mining, expressed increasing and valid concern that the rules had changed, requiring the company to redo archaeology by a new set of standards. Peabody responded to the regulatory situation by expediting the archaeology, planning closure mutually agreed in a memorandum of agreement signed by Peabody, the Navajo Nation, the Hopi Tribe, the Arizona State Historic Preservation Office, and various federal agencies. These changes signaled the shift from a BMAP driven by strong research agendas set by the director to a BMAP driven by federal and industry management priorities.

At this point BMAP changed. Gone were the comparatively leisurely days of archaeological excavations paced to stay just ahead of the active mining, as had been done for thirteen years. Gone, too, were the days of the director setting the research agenda. Instead, BMAP began a massive effort to complete archaeological field work in a three-season blitz. The new data-recovery program, detailed in the memorandum of agreement, was co-drafted by the researchers, federal and state regulators, and Peabody Coal Company environmental specialists. The adequacy of the archaeology now could be assessed legally with reference to the memorandum of agreement, and changes to the data-recovery program had to be negotiated with the signers of the MOA.

The impact of these changes on BMAP were surprisingly few. Thirteen years of cumulative research had constructed a framework for understanding the lease area's archaeological remains. By 1980 many questions had been answered: we thought we understood the Puebloan-period archaeology fairly well, patterns had emerged, and continuing excavations were not producing surprises. But two other issues required further investigation. First, the preceramic occupation of the lease area was discovered belatedly in 1973, and by 1980, few patterns had emerged. Second was Navajo archaeology. Who were these people? Where did they come from and when? How dependent were they on agriculture? How did they articulate with the preceramic peoples of Long House Valley?

BMAP 2000 and Beyond

We are frequently asked, What would the Black Mesa Archaeological Project be like if it were being done today? The answer is simple because it can be answered in one word: different. But the answer is complex because it

would be *so* very different. The differences and complexities can best be understood by considering changes in archaeology's social context over the past three decades.

When BMAP started in 1967, Robert C. Euler and George J. Gumerman set the archaeological agenda in consultation with representatives from Peabody Coal Company. Peabody concern focused not on the archaeology per se but on getting what the company paid for: legal compliance for the mining operation. Beyond that "bottom line," company concerns were minimal. The company paid Euler and Gumerman to do state-of-the-art archaeology that would be beyond reproach from the discipline and the federal government. Moreover, they trusted Euler and Gumerman to define and implement "state of the art." Gumerman and Euler did so by reconstructing the paleoenvironment and the cultural responses to changes in the paleoenvironment (e.g., Euler et al. 1979; Gumerman 1988a).

The ensuing years brought more federal legislation, more regulations, and additional voices to archaeological decision-making. The regulations for implementing the NHPA established procedures for determining which archaeological sites met eligibility standards for protection, preservation, or data recovery. The regulations also created a federal archaeological bureaucracy with the authority to determine how protection, preservation, or data recovery should take place, effectively adding an entire suite of overseers to the process. In our view, adding superstructure and complexity, in this case, resulted in archaeology by committee. In addition, although the term "cultural resource management" had been coined to describe the activities conducted under these laws and regulations, the activities consisted primarily of archaeology monitored by archaeologists.

Then, in 1990, the Advisory Council on Historic Preservation issued Bulletin 38 (Parker and King 1990). Bulletin 38 broadened the definition of cultural resources to include

places important in contemporary cultures, places that need not be archaeological sites nor identifiable by archaeologists. Instead, such places might simply have significant symbolic or social-functional meaning to the members of a particular contemporaneous culture.

About the same time, the Native American Graves Protection and Repatriation Act (NAGPRA) redefined human remains and grave-associated objects. In the legal arena, such materials acquired a new status not solely based on scientific or art-historical archaeological significance. The new status for human remains and associated grave objects, as defined by NAGPRA, became significant under the law as contextualized parts of living cultures. Accordingly, primary responsibility for determining what happened to these kinds of remains shifted from archaeologists to descendants or to other people with cultural affinity.

Almost simultaneously, the 1992 amendments to the NHPRA required consultation with people of established cultural affinity before an archaeological project could take place on federal lands or with federal funding. Suddenly, archaeologists were required to talk to people outside archaeology, and to do so, they needed skills beyond the typical range of archaeological training. At the same time, the "archaeology-by-committee" effect proliferated. The congregation of overseers of archaeological activities had grown to include descendants and other people with cultural affinity to the past that archaeologists were trying to reconstruct.

Coincident with the changing legal context, the base from which archaeologists worked changed. During the mid-1970s, and continuing to the present, the academic market for archaeologists dried up. At the same time, federal laws and regulations required that archaeology be done before many kinds of development projects could proceed. Thus, the laws and regulations created a "civilian" market for archaeologists at the same time that academic market, the traditional consumer of archaeologists, declined. For a while, academic departments added cultural-resource management wings staffed by personnel paid from project funds, that is, soft money. Such units and positions, however, were typically viewed as "second-best" to academic situations. Over time, some archaeological entrepreneurs moved from academic settings to the private sector, where they could operate in a more profitable manner, unencumbered by academic bureaucracy. The numbers of such firms have multiplied, now providing employment to a significant percentage of archaeologists.

So, given this dramatically altered social environment, how might the remains of the past be dealt with in this present? How might a large archaeological project like BMAP be run? We intend the following short prognostication to characterize a probable, not necessarily an ideal, BMAP.

In our view, "BMAP 2001" would retain much of the operational structure but would advance a number of new goals and operate on a far different time scale. The operational structure worth retaining consists of the large-scale, multidisciplinary, and complementary field personnel that included archaeologists from many institutions and archaeologists, workers, and consultants from groups with cultural affinity. A large-scale field-lab effort would insure that all recovered materials received preliminary analysis and inventory in the field. In addition, we envision different institutions working together in the analytical effort, with one or more representatives from each participating in the field effort.

With all the structural-operational similarities, a primary difference, however, would be the relatively short span of project operation. The project might likely be required to complete compliance action within five years, not twenty. The field effort would, under such constraints, consist of a year for consultation, investigations of

Traditional Cultural Properties, and survey inventory; two or three years for excavations; and another two or, possibly, only a single year for writing and curation. Under such a schedule, the number of sites excavated might fall from 188 to as few as 40.

Given the likelihood of the use of some variant in stratified random sampling in site selection for excavation, most occupational components would be likely to be included in the sample. But a sample of 40, even 60, sites would be unlikely to capture the range of variation within occupation periods. Moreover, the detailed mapping and surface collection of sites could not have been accomplished in a single-year survey operation.

Accordingly, the investigators involved in BMAP 2001 project would likely proceed with analysis of a very small sample of a highly variable universe of sites from each occupation period. What can one do if one has, as our imagined investigators might, a sample of five Basketmaker II sites of five unequivocally different types or a sample of five sites of only a couple of the several defined site types. In such cases, one concludes either that the suite of Basketmaker II sites on the landscape exhibits little patterning or that the sites tend to be extremely tightly patterned. Both conclusions would be dead wrong. But that, as we all know, is archaeology. And as we all often say, "Sampling error is a !%#@!!!." Time constraints on the order of those sketched above and on the scale of modern-day government-mandated projects would very likely result in seriously deficient archaeology.

A particularly valuable and useful aspect of a BMAP 2001 might be the articulation of salvage research with Native American cultural preferences and practices. Doubtless, BMAP 2001 would operate under very different rules and develop very different procedures for excavation, avoidance, preservation, and curation of sites that might be likely to contain human burials, the burials themselves, and

the associated funerary objects. Some aspects of the rapidly evolving cultural sensitivity by archaeologists to the Native American record would have deleterious scientific research results, however. The limits implied and explicit in NAGPRA on invasive analysis and the requirement for reburial of human remains and associated materials would place significant constraints of the kinds of information that archaeologists could recover on prehistoric behavior.

Most of these problems remain poorly defined, and solutions remain only developmental. How such problems can be overcome remains to be seen. The prognosis for future large-scale projects remains obscure, at least to us. Government-spending priorities appear to have changed dramatically, making funding on the scale at which BMAP received monies (adjusted for inflation) appear equally unlikely. Projects that might "enjoy" time for analytical, methodological, and theoretical introspection appear unlikely to occur in the current CRM/bureaucratic/regulation-ized environment. The number of players, having increased almost geometrically, poses problems that accrue from committee governance.

In any case, we hope we have made clear our view of the successes and problems of the Black Mesa Archaeological Project, one of the largest, longest-running in the history of American archaeology. In this volume, we have tried not to oversimplify the problems, the difficulties, the analytical conclusions or the complexity of articulating researches by many, many major investigators on surely one of the largest archaeological databases in history. Any attempt to articulate so many and such disparate elements in a single, coherent volume, however, presents a daunting task. We hope that future investigators will take up the challenge to wring additional knowledge from the massive collections, records, and writings that flowed over a thirty-year period from Black Mesa.

References Cited

Adams, E. Charles
  1973 Dead Horse Site. Unpublished Master's thesis, Department of Anthropology, University of Colorado, Boulder.
  1991 *The Origin and Development of the Pueblo Katsina Cult.* University of Arizona Press, Tucson.

Adams, E. Charles (editor)
  1996 *River of Change: Prehistory of the Middle Little Colorado River Valley, Arizona.* Arizona State Museum Archaeological Series 185. Arizona State Museum, University of Arizona, Tucson.

Adams, Jenny L.
  1993 Toward Understanding the Technological Development of Manos and Metates. *Kiva* 58:331–344.

Adams, William Y.
  1951 Archaeological and Culture History of Navajo Country: Report on Reconnaissance for the Pueblo Ecology Study, 1951. Manuscript on file, Museum of Northern Arizona, Flagstaff.

Adams, William Y., and Alexander J. Lindsay Jr.
  1961 *Survey and Excavations in Lower Glen Canyon, 1952–1958.* Bulletin No. 36. Museum of Northern Arizona, Flagstaff.

Agenbroad, Larry D.
  1967 The Distribution of Fluted Points in Arizona. *Kiva* 32:113–120.
  1990 Before the Anasazi: Early Man on the Colorado Plateau. *Plateau* 61(2):2–32.

Ahlstrom, Richard Van Ness
  1984 *A Comparative Approach to the Interpretation of Tree-Ring Data.* Paper presented at the 49th Annual Meeting of the Society for American Archaeology, Portland, Oregon.
  1985 The Interpretation of Archaeological Tree-Ring Dates. Ph.D. dissertation, Department of Anthropology, University of Arizona, Tucson. University Microfilms, Ann Arbor, Michigan.
  1998a The Black Mesa Tree-Ring Distribution. In *Working at Archaeological Chronometry*, edited by F. E. Smiley and Richard V. N. Ahlstrom, pp. 137–148. Center for Archaeological Investigations Occasional Paper No. 16. Southern Illinois University, Carbondale.
  1998b Evaluating Ceramic Dating on Black Mesa. In *Working at Archaeological Chronometry*, edited by F. E. Smiley and Richard V. N. Ahlstrom. Center for Archaeological Investigations Occasional Paper No. 16. Southern Illinios University, Carbondale.

Aikens, C. Melvin
  1966 *Virgin-Kayenta Cultural Relationships.* University of Utah Anthropological Papers No. 79. University of Utah Press, Salt Lake City.

Altschul, Jeffrey H., and Helen C. Fairley
  1989 *Man, Models and Management: An Overview of the Archaeology of the Arizona Strip and the Management of Its Cultural Resources.* U.S.D.A., Forest Service and U.S.D.I. Bureau of Land Management, Albuquerque, New Mexico.

Ambler, J. Richard
  1983 Kayenta Craft Specialization and Utilization. In *Proceedings of the Anasazi Symposium 1981*, edited by Jack E. Smith, pp. 75–82. Mesa Verde Museum Association, Mesa Verde National Park, Colorado.
  1985a *Navajo National Monument: An Archaeological Assessment.* Archaeological Series No. 1. Northern Arizona University, Flagstaff.
  1985b Northern Kayenta Ceramic Chronology. In *Archaeological Investigations near Rainbow City, Navajo Mountain, Utah*, edited by Phil R. Geib, J. Richard Ambler, and Martha M. Callahan, pp. 28–68. Archaeological Report No. 576. Northern Arizona University, Flagstaff.
  1992 Design Variation in Black Mesa Black-on-white From a Site on Black Mesa. *Pottery Southwest* 19(3):1–5.
  1994 The Shonto Junction Doghouse: A Weaver's Field House in the Klethla Valley. *Kiva* 59:455–473.

Ambler, J. Richard, and Michael J. Andrews
  1981 The Shonto Junction Doghouse: A Pueblo III Pithouse in the Klethla Valley. Manuscript on file, Department of Anthropology, Northern Arizona University, Flagstaff.

Ambler, J. Richard, Helen C. Fairley, and Phil R. Geib
  1983 *Kayenta Anasazi Utilization of Canyons and Plateaus in the Navajo Mountain District.* Paper presented at the Second Anasazi Symposium, Bloomfield, New Mexico.

Ambler, J. Richard, Alexander J. Lindsay Jr., and Mary Anne Stein
  1964 *Survey and Excavations on Cummings Mesa, Arizona and Utah, 1960–1961.* Bulletin No. 39. Museum of Northern Arizona, Flagstaff.

Ambler, J. Richard, and Alan P. Olson
  1977 *Salvage Archaeology in the Cow Springs Area.* Technical Series No. 15. Museum of Northern Arizona, Flagstaff.

Anderson, Bruce A. (compiler)
  1990 *The Wupatki Archeological Inventory Survey Project: Final Report.* Southwest Cultural Resources Center Professional Paper No. 35. U.S. National Park Service, Southwest Regional Office, Division of Anthropology, Santa Fe, New Mexico.

Anderson, Joseph K.
  1978 Arizona D:7:23. In *Excavation*

*on Black Mesa, 1977: A Prelimi-
nary Report*, edited by Anthony L.
Klesert, pp. 65–71. Southern Illinois
University, Carbondale.

1979   Arizona D:8:612. In *Excavation
on Black Mesa, 1978: A Descriptive Report*, edited by Anthony L.
Klesert and Shirley Powell, pp.
143–154. Center for Archaeological Investigations Research Paper
No. 8. Southern Illinois University,
Carbondale.

Anderson, Keith M.
1969   *Archaeology on the Shonto Plateau,
Northeast Arizona.* Southwestern
Monuments Association, Globe,
Technical Series, Vol. 9. Globe,
Arizona.

1971   Excavations at Betatakin and Keet
Seel. *Kiva* 37:1–29.

1980   *Highway Salvage on Arizona State
Highway 98: Kayenta Sites between
Kaibito and the Klethla Valley.*
Archaeological Series No. 140. Ari-
zona State Museum, University of
Arizona, Tucson.

Andrews, Peter P., Jean French, and Julie Mur-
phy
1980   Arizona D:7:216. In *Excavation on
Black Mesa, 1979: A Descriptive
Report*, edited by Shirley Powell,
Robert Layhe, and Anthony L.
Klesert, pp. 73–90. Center for
Archaeological Investigations Re-
search Paper No. 18, Southern
Illinois University, Carbondale.

Andrews, Peter P., Robert Layhe, Deborah L.
Nichols, and Shirley Powell (editors)
1982   *Excavations on Black Mesa, 1980:
A Descriptive Report.* Center for
Archaeological Investigations Re-
search Paper No. 24. Southern
Illinois University, Carbondale.

Antevs, Ernst
1955   Geologic-Climatic Dating in the
West. *American Antiquity* 20:317–
335.

Anyon, Roger
1984   Mogollon Settlement Patterns and
Communal Architecture. Unpublished Master's thesis, Department
of Anthropology, University of New
Mexico, Albuquerque.

Ayers, James E.
1966   A Clovis Fluted Point from the
Kayenta, Arizona, Area. *Plateau*
38(4):76–78.

Bailey, L. R. (editor)
1964   *The Navajo Reconnaissance: A
Military Exploration in the Navajo
Country in 1859.* Westernlore Press,
Los Angeles.

Bannister, Bryant, Jeffrey S. Dean, and Elizabeth
A. M. Gell
1966   *Tree-Ring Dates from Arizona E:
Chinle–Canyon de Chelly–Red Rock
Area.* Laboratory of Tree-Ring

Research, University of Arizona,
Tucson.

Bannister, Bryant, Jeffrey S. Dean, and William J.
Robinson
1968   *Tree-Ring Dates from Arizona
C–D: Eastern Grand Canyon–Tsegi
Canyon–Kayenta Area.* Laboratory
of Tree-Ring Research, University
of Arizona, Tucson.

1969   *Tree-Ring Dates from Utah S–W:
Southern Utah Area.* Laboratory of
Tree-Ring Research, University of
Arizona, Tucson.

Bannister, Bryant, William J. Robinson, and
Richard L. Warren
1967   *Tree-Ring Dates from Arizona J:
Hopi Mesas.* Laboratory of Tree-
Ring Research, University of
Arizona, Tucson.

Beals, Ralph L., George W. Brainerd, and
Watson Smith
1945   *Archaeological Studies in Northeast
Arizona.* Publications in Ameri-
can Archaeology and Ethnology
Vol. 44(1). University of California,
Berkeley.

Bearden, Susan E.
1984   *A Study of Basketmaker II Settlement on Black Mesa, Arizona:
Excavations, 1973–1979.* Center
for Archaeological Investigations
Research Paper No. 44. Southern
Illinois University, Carbondale.

Benallie, Larry, Jr.
1989   Anasazi Settlement Patterns at Low
Mountain, Navajo Nation, Arizona.
Unpublished Master's thesis, De-
partment of Anthropology, Arizona
State University, Tempe.

Bender, Marilyn J.
1979   A Discussion of the Collected
Chipped Stone Artifacts from
the Former Navajo-Hopi Joint
Use Area, Arizona. Manuscript
on file, Navajo-Hopi Relocation
Commission, Flagstaff.

Berry, Claudia F., and Michael S. Berry
1986   Chronological and Conceptual
Models of the Southwestern Archaic. In *Anthropology of the Desert
West*, edited by Carol Condie and
Don Fowler, pp. 253–327. University
of Utah Press, Salt Lake City.

Berry, David R.
1983   Skeletal Remains from RB 568.
In *Honoring the Dead: Anasazi
Ceramics from the Rainbow Bridge–
Monument Valley Expedition*,
edited by Helen K. Crotty, pp.
64–69. Monograph Series No. 22.
UCLA Museum of Cultural His-
tory, University of California, Los
Angeles.

Berry, Michael S.
1982   *Time, Space, and Transition in Anasazi Prehistory.* University of Utah
Press, Salt Lake City.

Betancourt, Julio L.
1984   Late Quaternary Plant Zonation
and Climate in Southeastern Utah.
Great Basin Naturalist 44:1–35.

Betancourt, Julio L., and Owen K. Davis
1984   Packrat Middens from Canyon
de Chelly, Northeastern Arizona:
Paleoecological and Archaeological
Implications. *Quaternary Research*
21:56–64.

Betancourt, Julio L., Thomas R. Van Devender,
and T. W. Gardner
1983   Fossil Packrat Middens from Chaco
Canyon, New Mexico: Cultural and
Ecological Significance. In *Chaco
Canyon Country: A Field Guide to
the Geomorphology, Quaternary
Geology, Paleoecology, and Envi-
ronmental Geology of Northwestern
New Mexico*, edited by S. G. Wells
and D. Love, pp. 207–217. 1983
Field Trip Guidebook, American
Geomorphological Field Group.
N.p.

Binford, Lewis R.
1968   Post-Pleistocene Adaptations. In
Prehistoric Agriculture, edited by
Stewart Struever, pp. 22–49. Natu-
ral History Press, Garden City, New
York.

1979   Organization and Formation Processes: Looking at Curated Technologies. *Journal of Anthropological
Research* 35:255–273.

1980   Willow Smoke and Dogs' Tails:
Hunter-Gatherer Settlement Systems and Archaeological Site
Formation. *American Antiquity*
45:4–20.

Birkedal, Terje G.
1976   Basketmaker III Residence Units:
A Study of Prehistoric Social
Organization in the Mesa Verde
Archaeological District. Ph.D.
dissertation, Department of An-
thropology, University of Colorado,
Boulder. University Microfilms,
Ann Arbor, Michigan.

Bliss, Wesley L.
1960   Impact of Pipeline Archaeology
on Indian Prehistory. *Plateau*
33(1):10–13.

Blomberg, Belinda
1983   *Mobility and Sedentism: The Navajo
of Black Mesa, Arizona.* Center
for Archaeological Investigations
Research Paper No. 32. Southern
Illinois University, Carbondale.

Blomberg, Belinda, and Shirley Powell
1983   An Ethnoarchaeological Approach
to the Detection of Navajo and
Anasazi Remains on Black Mesa,
Arizona. *Kiva* 49:3–18.

Blomberg, Belinda, and F. E. Smiley
1982   Ethoarchaeological Research: The
Black Mesa Navajo. In *Excavations
on Black Mesa, 1980: A Descriptive*

Report, edited by Peter P. Andrews, Robert Layhe, Deborah Nichols, and Shirley Powell, pp. 197–200. Center for Archaeological Investigations Research Paper No. 24. Southern Illinois University, Carbondale.

Bond, Mark, Toni Sudar-Murphy, and Fred P. Frampton
1977   *Highway Salvage Archaeology in the Vicinity of Chilchinbito, Arizona.* Occasional Paper No. 4. New Mexico State University Museum, Las Cruces.

Boserup, Esther
1965   *The Conditions of Agricultural Growth: The Economics of Agrarian Change under Population Pressure.* Aldine, Chicago.

Botkin, C. W., and L. B. Shires
1948   *The Composition and Value of Pinon Nuts.* Bulletin of the Agricultural Experiment Station, New Mexico College of Agriculture and Mechanic Arts, State College, New Mexico, No. 344. State College, New Mexico.

Bozarth, Steven
1992   Fossil Pollen and Phytolith Analysis. In *Archaeological Investigations at Lee Canyon: Kayenta Anasazi Farmsteads in the Upper Basin, Coconino County, Arizona,* edited by Stephanie M. Whittlesey, pp. 135–144. Statistical Research Technical Series No. 38, Tucson, Arizona.

Bradfield, George
1976   *Paleo Points: An Illustrated Chronology of Projectile Points.* George R. Bradfield, Preston, Ontario, Canada.

Bradfield, Maitland M.
1971   *The Changing Pattern of Hopi Agriculture.* Occasional Paper No. 30. Royal Anthropological Institute of Great Britain and Ireland, London.

Braun, David P.
1983   Pots as Tools. In *Archaeological Manners and Theories,* edited by James A. Moore and Arthur S. Keene, pp. 107–134. Academic Press, New York.

Braun, David P., and Stephen Plog
1982   Evolution of "Tribal" Social Networks: Theory and Prehistoric North American Evidence. *American Antiquity* 47:504–525.

Breitburg, Emanuel
1988   Prehistoric New World Turkey Domestication: Origins, Developments, and Consequences. Ph.D dissertation, Southern Illinois University, Carbondale. University Microfilms, Ann Arbor, Michigan.

Bremer, J. Michael
1989   *Walnut Canyon: Settlement and Land Use.* The Arizona Archaeolo-

gist No. 23. Arizona Archaeological Society, Flagstaff.

Breternitz, Cory D., David E. Doyel, and Michael P. Marshall (editors)
1982   *Bis sa'ani: A Late Bonito Phase Community on Escavada Wash, Northwest New Mexico.* Navajo Nation Papers in Anthropology No. 24. Window Rock, Arizona.

Breternitz, David A.
1966   *An Appraisal of Tree-Ring Dated Pottery in the Southwest.* Anthropological Papers of the University of Arizona No. 10. University of Arizona Press, Tucson.

1993   The Dolores Archaeological Program. In Memoriam. *American Antiquity* 58:118–125.

Brew, John O.
1941   Preliminary Report of the Peabody Museum Awatovi Expedition of 1939. *Plateau* 13(3):37–48.

Brown, B.
1928   Recent Finds Relating to Prehistoric Man in America. *Bulletin of the New York Academy of Medicine* 4:824–828.

Brugge, David M.
1983   Navajo Prehistory and History to 1850. In *Handbook of North American Indians,* vol. 10: *Southwest,* edited by Alfonso Ortiz, pp. 489–501. Smithsonian Institution Press, Washington, D.C.

Brumfiel, Elizabeth M., and Timothy K. Earle
1987   Specialization, Exchange, and Complex Societies: An Introduction. In *Specialization, Exchange, and Complex Societies,* edited by Elizabeth M. Brumfiel and Timothy K. Earle, pp. 1–9. Cambridge University Press, Cambridge.

Buikstra, Jane E., Lyle W. Konigsberg, and Jill Bullington
1986   Fertility and the Development of Agriculture in the Prehistoric Midwest. *American Antiquity* 51:528–546.

Bullard, William, Jr.
1962   *The Cerro Colorado Site and Pithouse Architecture in the Southwestern United States Prior to A.D. 900.* Papers of the Peabody Museum of American Archaeology and Ethnology Vol. 44(2). Harvard University, Cambridge, Massachusetts.

Burgett, Galen R.
1985   Arizona D:11:1200, D:11:1281, D:11:1294, and D:11:1296. In *Excavations on Black Mesa, 1983: A Descriptive Report,* edited by Andrew L. Christenson and William J. Parry, pp. 185–202. Center for Archaeological Investigations Research Paper No. 46. Southern Illinois University, Carbondale.

Burgett, Galen R., Alison Rautman, James K. Feathers, and Monica M. Bargielski
1985   Arizona D:7:2085. In *Excavations on Black Mesa, 1983: A Descriptive Report,* edited by Andrew L. Christenson and William J. Parry, pp. 87–123. Center for Archaeological Investigations Research Paper No. 46. Southern Illinois University, Carbondale.

Callahan, Martha M.
1985   Excavations at Dogtown: A Pueblo III Pithouse Village in the Klethla Valley. Unpublished Master's thesis, Department of Anthropology, Northern Arizona University, Flagstaff.

Callaway, D. G., J. E. Levy, and E. B. Henderson
1976   *The Effects of Power Production and Strip Mining on Local Navajo Populations.* Lake Powell Research Bulletin No. 22. University of California Institute of Geophysics and Planetary Physics, Los Angeles.

Cameron, Catherine M.
1984   A Regional View of Chipped Stone Raw Material Use in Chaco Canyon. In *Recent Research on Chaco Prehistory,* edited by W. James Judge and John D. Schelberg, pp. 137–152. Reports of the Chaco Center No. 8. Division of Cultural Research, National Park Service, Albuquerque, New Mexico.

1990a   The Effect of Varying Estimates of Pit Structure Use-Life on Prehistoric Population Estimates in the American Southwest. *Kiva* 55:155–166.

1990b   Pit Structure Abandonment in the Four Corners Region of the American Southwest: Late Basketmaker III and Pueblo I Periods. *Journal of Field Archaeology* 17:27–38.

Carlson, Roy L.
1965   *Eighteenth Century Navajo Fortresses in the Gobernador District.* Earl Morris Papers No. 2. Series in Anthropology No. 10. University of Colorado, Boulder.

1970   *White Mountain Red Ware: A Pottery Tradition of East-Central Arizona and Western New Mexico.* Anthropological Papers of the University of Arizona No. 19. University of Arizona Press, Tucson.

1982   The Polychrome Complexes. In *Southwestern Ceramics: A Comparative View* No. 15, edited by Albert H. Schroeder, pp. 201–234. Arizona Archaeologist. Arizona Archaeological Society, Phoenix.

Cartledge, Thomas R.
1979   Cohonina Adaptation to the Coconino Plateau: A Re-Evaluation. *Kiva* 44:297–317.

Catlin, Mark C.

1986   Intersite Diversity and the Role of Limited-Activity Sites in Subsistence-Settlement Systems on Black Mesa. In *Spatial Organization and Exchange: Archaeological Survey on Northern Black Mesa*, edited by Stephen Plog, pp. 169–186. Southern Illinois University Press, Carbondale.

Cavalli-Sforza, L. L.

1983   The Transition to Agriculture and Some of Its Consequences. In *How Humans Adapt*, edited by Donald S. Ortner, pp. 103–127. Smithsonian Institution Press, Washington, D.C.

Chang, Kwang-Chih

1958   Study of the Neolithic Social Groupings: Examples from the New World. *American Anthropologist* 60:298–334.

Christenson, Andrew L.

1987a   The Prehistoric Tool Kit. In *Prehistoric Stone Technology on Northern Black Mesa, Arizona*, edited by William J. Parry and Andrew L. Christenson, pp. 43–94. Center for Archaeological Investigations Occasional Paper No. 12. Southern Illinois University, Carbondale.

1987b   Projectile Points: Eight Millennia of Projectile Point Change on the Colorado Plateau. In *Prehistoric Stone Technology on Northern Black Mesa, Arizona*, edited by William J. Parry and Andrew L. Christenson, pp. 143–198. Center for Archaeological Investigations Occasional Paper No. 12. Southern Illinois University, Carbondale.

Christenson, Andrew L., and Marilyn J. Bender

1994   Appendix G: A Method for the Chronological Classification of Black Mesa Sherd Assemblages. In *Function and Technology of Anazazi Ceramics from Black Mesa, Arizona*, edited by Marion F. Smith Jr., pp. 223–236. Center for Archaeological Investigations Occasional Paper No. 15. Southern Illinois University, Carbondale.

Christenson, Andrew L., and William J. Parry (editors)

1985   *Excavations on Black Mesa, 1983: A Descriptive Report*. Center for Archaeological Investigations Research Paper No. 46. Southern Illinois University, Carbondale.

Clark, Susan R.

1966   A Tabular Summary of Plant and Animal Resources of the Glen Canyon Area. In *Corn, Cucurbits, and Cotton from Glen Canyon*, edited by Hugh C. Cutler, pp. 63–116. University of Utah Anthropological Papers 80. University of Utah Press, Salt Lake City.

Clemen, Robert T.

1976   Aspects of Prehistoric Social Organization on Black Mesa. In *Papers on the Archaeology of Black Mesa, Arizona*, edited by George J. Gumerman and Robert C. Euler, pp. 113–135. Southern Illinois University Press, Carbondale.

Cohen, Mark N.

1977   *The Food Crisis in Prehistory*. Yale University Press, New Haven, Connecticut.

Cole, Sally J.

1990   *Legacy on Stone: Rock Art of the Colorado Plateau and Four Corners Region*. Johnson Books, Boulder, Colorado.

Colton, Harold S.

1939   *Prehistoric Culture Units and Their Relationships in Northern Arizona*. Bulletin No. 17. Museum of Northern Arizona, Flagstaff.

1956   *Pottery Types of the Southwest: Wares 5A, 5B, 6A, 6B, 7A, 7B, 7C, San Juan Red Ware, Tsegi Orange Ware, Homolovi Orange Ware, Winslow Orange Ware, Awatovi Yellow Ware, Jeddito Yellow Ware, Sichomovi Red Ware*. Ceramic Series 3c. Museum of Northern Arizona, Flagstaff.

Colton, Harold S., and Lyndon L. Hargrave

1937   *Handbook of Northern Arizona Pottery Wares*. Bulletin No. 11. Museum of Northern Arizona, Flagstaff.

Cook, H. J.

1928   Glacial Age Man in New Mexico. *Scientific American* 139:38–40.

Cooley, Maurice E.

1962a   Geomorphology and the Age of Volcanic Rocks in Northeastern Arizona. *Arizona Geological Society Digest* 5:97–115.

1962b   *Late Pleistocene and Recent Erosion and Alluviation in Parts of the Colorado River System, Arizona and Utah*. Professional Paper 450-B, pp. 48–50. U.S. Geological Survey, Washington, D.C.

Cooley, Maurice E., J. W. Harshbarger, and W. F. Hardt

1969   *Regional Hydrogeology of the Navaho and Hopi Indian Reservations, Arizona, New Mexico, and Utah*. Professional Paper No. 512A. U.S. Geological Survey, Washington, D.C.

Cordell, Linda S.

1979   Prehistory: Eastern Anasazi. In *Handbook of North American Indians*, Vol. 9: *Southwest*, edited by Alfonso Ortiz, pp. 131–151. Smithsonian Institution Press, Washington, D.C.

1984   *Prehistory of the Southwest*. Academic Press, New York.

Cordell, Linda S., and Fred T. Plog

1979   Escaping the Confines of Normative Thought: A Reevaluation of Puebloan Prehistory. *American Antiquity* 44:405–429.

Crotty, Helen K.

1983   *Honoring the Dead: Anasazi Ceramics from the Rainbow Bridge–Monument Valley Expedition*. Monograph Series No. 22. UCLA Museum of Cultural History, University of California, Los Angeles.

Crown, Patricia L., and W. H. Wills

1995   The Origins of Southwestern Ceramic Containers: Women's Time Allocation and Economic Intensification. *Journal of Anthropological Research* 51:173–186.

Cummings, Byron

1945   Some Unusual Kivas near Navajo Mountain. *Kiva* 10:30–35.

1953   *First Inhabitants of Arizona and the Southwest*. Cummings Publication Council, Tucson, Arizona.

Daifuku, Hiroshi

1961   *Jeddito 264: A Report on the Excavation of a Basket Maker III–Pueblo I Site in Northeastern Arizona with a Review of Some Current Theories in Southwestern Archaeology*. Papers of the Peabody Museum of American Archaeology and Ethnology 33(1). Harvard University, Cambridge, Massachusetts.

Danson, Edward B.

1961   Early Man Points from the Vicinity of Sanders, Arizona. *Plateau* 34(2):67–68.

Davis, William E.

1985   The Montgomery Folsom Site. *Current Research in the Pleistocene* 2:11–12.

Dawson, Jerry, and Dennis Stanford

1975   The Linger Site: A Reinvestigation. *Southwestern Lore* 41(4):11–16.

Dean, Jeffrey S.

1967   Chronological Analysis of Tsegi Phase Sites in Northeastern Arizona. Ph.D. dissertation, Department of Anthropology, University of Arizona, Tucson. University Microfilms, Ann Arbor, Michigan.

1969   *Chronological Analysis of Tsegi Phase Sites in Northeastern Arizona*. Laboratory of Tree-Ring Research Papers No. 3. University of Arizona Press, Tucson.

1970   Aspects of Tsegi Phase Social Organization: A Trial Reconstruction. In *Reconstructing Prehistoric Pueblo Societies*, edited by William A. Longacre, pp. 140–174. University of New Mexico Press, Albuquerque.

1982   *Dencroclimatic Variability and Demography, Black Mesa*. Paper presented at the 47th Annual Meeting of the Society for American Archaeology, Minneapolis, Minnesota.

1985 Review of *Time, Space, and Transition in Anasazi Prehistory*, by Michael S. Berry. *American Antiquity* 50:704–705.

1986a Delineating the Anasazi. In *Emil W. Haury's Prehistory of the American Southwest*, edited by J. Jefferson Reid and David E. Doyel, pp. 407–413. University of Arizona Press, Tucson.

1986b Dendrochronology. In *Dating and Age Determination of Biological Materials*, edited by Michael R. Zimmerman and J. Lawrence Angel, pp. 126–165. Croom Helm, London.

1988a Dendrochronology and Paleoenvironmental Reconstruction on the Colorado Plateaus. In *The Anasazi in a Changing Environment*, edited by George J. Gumerman, pp. 119–167. Cambridge University Press, Cambridge.

1988b A Model of Anasazi Behavioral Adaptation. In *The Anasazi in a Changing Environment*, edited by George J. Gumerman, pp. 25–44. Cambridge University Press, Cambridge.

1996a Kayenta Anasazi Settlement Transformations in Northeastern Arizona, A.D. 1150 to 1350. In *The Prehistoric Pueblo World, A.D. 1150–1350*, edited by Michael A. Adler, pp. 29–47. University of Arizona Press, Tucson.

1996b Demography, Environment, and Subsistence Stress. In *Evolving Complexity and Environmental Risk in the Prehistoric Southwest*, edited by Joseph A. Tainter and Bonnie Bagley Tainter, pp. 25–56. Santa Fe Institute Studies in the Sciences of Complexity, Proceedings Volume 24. Addison-Wesley Publishing Company, Reading, Pennsylvania.

1997 Dendrochronology. In *Chronometric Dating in Archaeology*, edited by R. E. Taylor and Martin J. Aitken, pp. 31–64. Advances in Archaeological and Museum Science, Vol. 2. Plenum Press, New York and London.

1998 Intervisibility of Tsegi Phase Sites. Paper presented at the Fall 1998 Meeting of the Arizona Archaeological Council, Flagstaff.

Dean, Jeffrey S., William H. Doelle, and Janet D. Orcutt

1994 Adaptive Stress, Environment and Demography. In *Themes in Southwest Prehistory*, edited by George J. Gumerman, pp. 53–86. School of American Research Press, Santa Fe, New Mexico.

Dean, Jeffrey S., Robert C. Euler, George J. Gumerman, Fred Plog, Richard H. Hevly, and Thor N. V. Karlstrom

1985 Human Behavior, Demography, and Paleoenvironment on the Colorado Plateaus. *American Antiquity* 50:537–554.

Dean, Jeffrey S., and Gary S. Funkhouser

1995 Dendroclimatic Reconstructions for the Southern Colorado Plateau. In *Climate Change in the Four Corners and Adjacent Regions: Implications for Environmental Restoration and Land-Use Planning*, edited by W. G. Waugh, pp. 85–104. U.S. Department of Energy, Grand Junction Projects Office, Grand Junction, Colorado.

Dean, Jeffrey S., Alexander J. Lindsay Jr., and William J. Robinson

1978 Prehistoric Settlement in Long House Valley, Northeastern Arizona. In *Investigations of the Southwestern Anthropological Research Group: An Experiment in Archaeological Cooperation—The Proceedings of the 1976 Conference*, edited by Robert C. Euler and George J. Gumerman, pp. 25–44. Museum of Northern Arizona, Flagstaff.

Dean, Jeffrey S., and William J. Robinson

1978 *Expanded Tree-Ring Chronologies for the Southwestern United States*. Laboratory of Tree-Ring Research, Chronology Series III. University of Arizona, Tucson.

Dechambre, David J.

1983 The Settlement of East-Central Black Mesa, A.D. 600–1250. Unpublished Master's thesis, Department of Anthropology, Northern Arizona University, Flagstaff.

DeMarcay, Gary B., Jeff Setzer, and Laura Michalik

1982 Arizona D:11:2001. In *Excavations on Black Mesa, 1980: A Descriptive Report*, edited by Peter P. Andrews, Robert Layhe, and Shirley Powell, pp. 185–191. Center for Archaeological Investigations Research Paper No. 24, Southern Illinois University, Carbondale.

Deutchman, Haree L.

1979 Intraregional Interaction on Black Mesa and Among the Kayenta Anasazi: The Chemical Evidence for Ceramic Exchange. Ph.D. dissertation, Department of Anthropology, Southern Illinois University, Carbondale. University Microfilms, Ann Arbor, Michigan.

1980 Chemical Evidence of Ceramic Exchange on Black Mesa. In *Models and Methods in Regional Exchange*, edited by Robert E. Fry, pp. 119–133.

Society for American Archaeology Papers No. 1, Washington, D.C.

Di Peso, Charles C.

1958 *The Reeve Ruin of Southeastern Arizona*. Publication No. 8. Amerind Foundation, Dragoon, Arizona.

Dick, Herbert W.

1965 *Bat Cave*. School of American Research Monograph No. 27. Santa Fe, New Mexico.

Dixon, Keith A.

1956 *Hidden House: A Cliff Ruin in Sycamore Canyon, Central Arizona*. Bulletin No. 29. Museum of Northern Arizona, Flagstaff.

Dohm, Karen

1994 The Search for Anasazi Village Origins: Basketmaker II Dwelling Aggregation on Cedar Mesa, Southeast Utah. *Kiva* 60:257–276.

Donaldson, Marcia L.

1982 Environmental Setting of the Gallo Wash Mine Lease. In *Prehistoric Adaptive Strategies in the Chaco Canyon Region, Northwestern New Mexico*, Vol. 1, edited by Alan H. Simmons, pp. 81–128. Navajo Nation Papers in Anthropology No. 9. Navajo Nation Cultural Resource Management Program, Window Rock, Arizona.

Douglas, Charles L.

1972 Analysis of Faunal Remains from Black Mesa: 1968–1970 Excavations. In *Archaeological Investigations on Black Mesa: The 1969–1970 Seasons*, edited by George J. Gumerman, Deborah Westfall, and Carol S. Weed, pp. 225–238. Prescott College Studies in Anthropology No. 4. Prescott College Press, Prescott, Arizona.

Downer, Alan S.

1991 Navajo Nation Historic Preservation Plan Pilot Study: Identification of Cultural and Historic Properties in Seven Arizona Chapters the Navajo Nation. Manuscript on file, Navajo Nation Historic Preservation Department, Window Rock, Arizona.

Downs, James F.

1972 *The Navajo*. Holt, Rinehart and Winston, New York.

Downum, Christian E., and Alan P. Sullivan, III

1990 Settlement Patterns. In *The Wupatki Archeological Inventory Survey Project: Final Report*, edited by Bruce A. Anderson, pp. 5.1–5.90. Southwest Regional Office, Division of Anthropology, Professional Paper No. 35. Southwest Cultural Resources Center, National Park Service, Santa Fe, New Mexico.

Doyel, David E., Cory D. Breternitz, and Michael P. Marshall

1984 Chacoan Community Structure:

Bis sa'ani Pueblo and the Chaco Halo. In *Recent Research on Chaco Prehistory*, edited by W. James Judge and John D. Schelberg, pp. 37–54. Report of the Chaco Center No. 8, Division of Cultural Research, National Park Service, Albuquerque, New Mexico.

Dozier, Edward P.
1965   Southwestern Social Units and Archaeology. *American Antiquity* 31:38–47.

Drennan, Robert D.
1983   Ritual and Ceremonial Development at the Early Village Level. In *The Cloud People*, edited by Kent V. Flannery and Joyce Marcus, pp. 46–50. Academic Press, New York.

Dyk, Walter
1938   *Son of Old Man Hat: A Navajo Autobiography*. University of Nebraska Press, Lincoln.

Dyk, Walter, and Ruth Dyk
1980   *Left Handed: A Navajo Autobiography*. Columbia University Press, New York.

Earle, Timothy K.
1980   A Model of Subsistence Change. In *Modeling Change in Prehistoric Subsistence Economics*, edited by Timothy K. Earle and Andrew L. Christenson, pp. 1–29. Academic Press, New York.

Eck, David C.
1994   *The Anasazi of Wide Ruin Wash and the Hopi Buttes*. Across the Colorado Plateau: Anthropological Studies for the Transwestern Pipeline Expansion Project, Vol. 11. Office of Contract Archaeology and the Maxwell Museum of Anthropology, University of New Mexico, Albuquerque.

Eckles, David
1984   Intersite Variation in Faunal Remains on Black Mesa. In *Papers on the Archaeology of Black Mesa, Arizona*, Vol. 2, edited by Stephen Plog and Shirley Powell, pp. 158–172. Southern Illinois University Press, Carbondale.

Eddy, Frank W.
1958   A Sequence of Cultural and Alluvial Deposits in the Cienega Creek Basin, Southeastern Arizona. Unpublished Master's thesis, Department of Anthropology, University of Arizona, Tucson.
1966   *Prehistory in the Navajo Reservoir District, Northwestern New Mexico*. Papers in Anthropology No. 15. Museum of New Mexico, Santa Fe.

Eddy, Frank W., and Beth Dickey
1961   *Excavations at Los Pinos Phase Sites in the Navajo Reservoir District*. Papers in Anthropology No. 4. Museum of New Mexico, Santa Fe.

Effland, Richard Wayne, Jr.
1979   A Study of Prehistoric Spatial Behavior: Long House Valley, Northeastern Arizona. Ph.D. dissertation, Department of Anthropology, Arizona State University, Tempe. University Microfilms, Ann Arbor, Michigan.

Eggan, Fred
1950   *Social Organization of the Western Pueblos*. University of Chicago Press, Chicago, Illinois.

El-Najjar, Mahmoud Yousef
1974   People of Canyon de Chelly: A Study of Their Biology and Culture. Ph.D. dissertation, Department of Anthropology, Arizona State University, Tempe. University Microfilms, Ann Arbor, Michigan.

Emery, Sloan, and Dennis Stanford
1982   Preliminary Report on Archaeological Investigations at the Cattle Guard Site, Alamosa County, Colorado. *Southwestern Lore* 48(1):10–20.

Estes, Byron, Kelley Hays, and Elizabeth Nelson
1984   Navajo Sites Investigated in the J-10 Mining Area. In *Excavations on Black Mesa, 1982: A Descriptive Report*, edited by Deborah L. Nichols and F. E. Smiley, pp. 483–488. Center for Archaeological Investigations Research Paper No. 39. Southern Illinois University, Carbondale.

Euler, Robert C.
1964   Southern Paiute Archaeology. *American Antiquity* 29:379–381.
1984   Descriptive Reports for the 1973 Field Season. In *Excavations on Black Mesa, 1971–1976: A Descriptive Report*, edited by Shirley Powell, pp. 199–217. Center for Archaeological Investigations Research Paper No. 48. Southern Illinois University, Carbondale.
1988   Demography and Cultural Dynamics on the Colorado Plateau. In *The Anasazi in a Changing Environment*, edited by George J. Gumerman, pp. 192–229. Cambridge University Press, Cambridge.

Euler, Robert C., and Susan M. Chandler
1978   Aspects of Prehistoric Settlement Patterns in Grand Canyon. In *Investigations of the Southwestern Anthropological Research Group: An Experiment in Archaeological Cooperation: The Proceedings of the 1976 Conference*, edited by Robert C. Euler and George J. Gumerman, pp. 73–85. Museum of Northern Arizona, Flagstaff.

Euler, Robert C., George J. Gumerman, Thor N. V. Karlstrom, Jeffrey S. Dean, and Richard H. Hevly
1979   The Colorado Plateaus: Cultural Dynamics and Paleoenvironment. *Science* 205:1089–1101.

Fairley, Helen C.
1989a   Anasazi Settlement Dynamics in Upper Paiute Canyon, Northeastern Arizona. Unpublished Master's thesis, Department of Anthropology, Northern Arizona University, Flagstaff.
1989b   Culture History. In *Man, Models and Management: An Overview of the Archaeology of the Arizona Strip and the Management of Its Cultural Resources*, edited by Jeffrey H. Altschul and Helen C. Fairley, pp. 85–152. U.S.D.A. Forest Service and U.S.D.I. Bureau of Land Management, Albuquerque, New Mexico.

Fall, Patricia L.
1981   Culture History of Canyon del Muerto. In *The Canyon del Muerto Survey Project: Anasazi and Navajo Archeology in Northeastern Arizona*, edited by Patricia L. Fall, James A. McDonald, and Pamela C. Magers, pp. 25–40. Publications in Anthropology No. 15. U.S. National Park Service, Western Archeological Center, Tucson, Arizona.

Farmer, Malcolm
1942   Navaho Archaeology of Upper Blanco and Largo Canyons, New Mexico. *American Antiquity* 8:65–79.

Feathers, James K., and Julie K. Stein
1985   Site Formation at D:7:2085, Black Mesa: A View from the Sediments. In *Excavations on Black Mesa, 1983: A Descriptive Report*, edited by Andrew L. Christenson and William J. Parry, pp. 411–442. Center for Archaeological Investigations Research Paper No. 46. Southern Illinois University, Carbondale.

Fehr, Russell T.
1982   AZ-J-54-6. In *Kayenta Anasazi Archaeology on Central Black Mesa, Northeastern Arizona: The Pinon Project*, edited by Laurance D. Linford, pp. 111–120. Navajo Nation Papers in Anthropology No. 10, Navajo National Cultural Resource Management Program, Window Rock, Arizona.

Fernstrom, Katharine W.
1984   The Effect of Ecological Fluctuations on Exchange Networks, Black Mesa, Arizona. In *Papers on the Archaeology of Black Mesa, Arizona*, Vol. 2, edited by Stephen Plog and Shirley Powell, pp. 189–208. Southern Illinois University Press, Carbondale.

Fewkes, Jesse Walter
1909   *Antiquities of the Mesa Verde*

National Park: Spruce-Tree House. Bulletin No. 41. Bureau of American Ethnology, Smithsonian Institution, Washington, D.C.

Fish, Suzanne K., and Paul R. Fish

1992   Comparative Aspects of Paradigms for the Neolithic Transition in the Levant and the American Southwest. In *Perspectives on the Past: Theoretical Biases in Mediterranean Hunter-Gatherer Research*, edited by Geoffrey A. Clark, pp. 396–410. University of Pennsylvania Press, Philadelphia.

Flannery, Kent V.

1968   Archaeological Systems Theory and Early Mesoamerica. In *Anthropological Archeology in the Americas*, edited by Betty J. Meggers, pp. 67–87. Anthropological Society of Washington, Washington, D.C.

Floyd, M. L., and T. A. Kohler

1989   Current Productivity and Prehistoric Use of Pinon (Pinus edulis, Pinaceae) in the Dolores Archaeological Project Area, Southwestern Colorado. *Economic Botany* 44(2):141–156.

Foose, Benjamin M., III

1982   AZ-J-55-2. In *Kayenta Anasazi Archaeology on Central Black Mesa, Northeastern Arizona: The Pinon Project*, edited by Laurance D. Linford, pp. 182–186. Navajo Nation Papers in Anthropology No. 10. Navajo Nation Cultural Resource Management Program, Window Rock, Arizona.

Ford, Richard I.

1972   Barter, Gift, or Violence: An Analysis of Tewa Intertribal Exchange. In *Social Exchange and Interaction*, edited by Edwin N. Wilmsen, pp. 21–46. Museum of Anthropology Paper No. 46. University of Michigan, Ann Arbor, Michigan.

1983   Inter-Indian Exchange in the Southwest. In *Handbook of North American Indians, Southwest*, Vol. 10, edited by Alfonso Ortiz, pp. 711–722. Smithsonian Institution Press, Washington, D.C.

1984   Ecological Consequences of Early Agriculture in the Southwest. In *Papers on the Archaeology of Black Mesa, Arizona*, Vol. 2, edited by Stephen Plog and Shirley Powell, pp. 127–138. Southern Illinois University Press, Carbondale.

1994   Corn is Our Mother. In *Corn and Culture in the Prehistoric New World*, edited by Sissel Johannessen and Christine A. Hastorf. Westview Press, Boulder, Colorado.

Ford, Richard I., Jean French, Janet Stock, Tristine Smart, Gretchen Hazen, and David Jessup

1983   1981 Ethnobotanical Recovery: Summary of Analysis and Frequency Tables. In *Excavations on Black Mesa, 1981: A Descriptive Report*, edited by F. E. Smiley, Deborah L. Nichols, and Peter P. Andrews, pp. 459–480. Center for Archaeological Investigations Research Paper No. 36. Southern Illinois University, Carbondale.

Ford, Richard I., Pamela Vander Werf, Carol Goland, and Heather B. Trigg

1985   Paleoethnobotany of Anasazi Sites. In *Excavations on Black Mesa, 1983: A Descriptive Report*, edited by Andrew L. Christenson and William J. Parry, pp. 473–487. Center for Archaeological Investigations Research Paper No. 46. Southern Illinois University, Carbondale.

Fowles, Severin

1993   *Moving On: Pit Structure Abandonment on Northern Black Mesa.* Department of Anthropology, Dartmouth College, Hanover, New Hampshire.

Freeman, C. E.

1972   Pollen Study of Some Alluvial Deposits in Dona Ana County, Southern New Mexico. *Texas Journal of Science* 24:203–220.

Frisbie, Charlotte J., and David P. McAllester (editors)

1978   *Navajo Blessingway Singer: The Autobiography of Frank Mitchell, 1881–1967.* University of Arizona Press, Tucson.

Frison, George C.

1974   *The Casper Site.* Academic Press, New York.

1978   *Prehistoric Hunters of the High Plains.* Academic Press, New York.

Fritz, John M.

1974   The Hay Hollow Site Subsistence System, East Central Arizona. Ph.D. dissertation, Department of Anthropology, University of Chicago, Chicago. University Microfilms, Ann Arbor, Michigan.

Gaede, Marc, and Marnie Gaede

1977   100 Years of Erosion at Poncho House. *Kiva* 43:37–48.

Garrett, Elizabeth M.

1986   A Petrographic Analysis of Black Mesa Ceramics. In *Spatial Organization and Exchange: Archaeological Survey on Northern Black Mesa*, edited by Stephen Plog, pp. 114–142. Southern Illinois University Press, Carbondale.

Gasser, Robert E.

1982   Anasazi Diet. In *The Coronado Project Archaeological Investi-* *gations: The Specialists' Volume: Biocultural Analyses*, edited by Robert E. Gasser, pp. 8–95. Coronado Series No. 4, Research Paper No. 23. Museum of Northern Arizona, Flagstaff.

Geib, Phil R.

1994   Archaic Occupation of the Glen Canyon Region. In *Glen Canyon Revisited: Summary and Conclusions of Recent Archaeological Investigations in the Glen Canyon National Recreation Area*, edited by Carl J. Phagan, pp. Chapter 5. Archaeological Report No. 1047. Northern Arizona University, Flagstaff.

Geib, Phil R., and Martha M. Callahan

1987   Ceramic Exchange within the Kayenta Anasazi Region: Volcanic Ash-Tempered Tusayan White Ware. *Kiva* 52:95–112.

Geib, Phil R., and Dale Davidson

1994   Anasazi Origins: A Perspective from Preliminary Work at Old Man Cave. *Kiva* 60:191–202.

Geib, Phil R., and Kimberly Spurr

2000   The Basketmaker II–III Transition on the Rainbow Plateau. In *Foundations of Anasazi Culture: The Basketmaker-Pueblo Transition*, edited by Paul F. Reed. University of Utah Press, Salt Lake City.

Geib, Phil R., Miranda Warburton, and Kelley Ann Hays-Gilpin

1993   *Economic Specialization and Social Differentiation in the Northern Kayenta Region: A Data Recovery Plan for Prehistoric Sites along the Navajo Mountain Road.* Navajo Nation Archaeology Department, Window Rock, Arizona.

Gifford, James C., and Watson Smith

1978   *Gray Corrugated Pottery from Awatovi and Other Jeddito Sites in Northeastern Arizona.* Papers of the Peabody Museum of American Archaeology and Ethnology No. 69. Harvard University, Cambridge, Massachusetts.

Gilman, Patricia A.

1983   Changing Architectural Forms in the Prehistoric Southwest. Ph.D. dissertation, Department of Anthropology, University of New Mexico, Albuquerque. University Microfilms, Ann Arbor, Michigan.

1987   Architecture as Artifact: Pit Structures and Pueblos in the American Southwest. *American Antiquity* 52:538–564.

Gilman, Patricia A., and David W. Cushman

1983   Arizona D:7:254. In *Excavations on Black Mesa, 1981: A Descriptive Report*, edited by F. E. Smiley, Deborah L. Nichols, and Peter P. Andrews, pp. 84–93. Center for Archaeological Investigations Research Paper No. 36. Southern Illinois University, Carbondale.

Gilpin, Dennis

1982 Introduction to the Historic Sites Research. In *Gallegos Mesa Settlement and Subsistence: A Set of Explanatory Models for Cultural Resources on Blocks VII, XI, X, and XI, Navajo Indian Irrigation Project*, Vol. 2, edited by L. E. Vogler, Dennis Gilpin, and J. K. Anderson, pp. 527–547. Navajo Nation Papers in Anthropology No. 12. Navajo Nation Cultural Resource Management Program, Window Rock, Arizona.

1987 *Current Research on Large, Thirteenth- and Fourteenth-Century Sites in the Black Mesa, Pueblo Colorado Valley, Chinle Valley, and Defiance Plateau Region of the Navajo Indian Reservation, Apache and Navajo Counties, Arizona.* Paper presented at the 1987 Pecos Conference, Pecos National Monument, New Mexico.

1989 *Great Houses and Pueblos in Northeastern Arizona.* Paper presented at the 1989 Pecos Conference, Bandelier National Monument, New Mexico.

1994 Lukachukai and Salina Springs: Late Archaic/Early Basketmaker Habitation Sites in the Chinle Valley, Northeastern Arizona. *Kiva* 60:203–218.

Gilpin, Dennis, and Larry Benallie Jr.

2000 Juniper Cove and Early Anasazi Community Structure West of the Chuska Mountains. In *Foundations of Anasazi Culture: Basketmaker-Pueblo Transition*, edited by Paul F. Reed, Shirley Gorenstein, and Elizabeth Ann Morris, pp. 175–202. University of Utah Press, Salt Lake City.

Gish, J. W., J. E. Hammett, M. E. Brown, P. McBride, J. C. Winter, K. L. Brown, J. J. Ponczynski, and J. L. DeLanois.

1993 *Subsistence and Environment.* Across the Colorado Plateau: Anthropological Studies along the San Juan Basin and Transwestern Mainline Extension Pipeline Routes, Vol. 15. Office of Contract Archeology and the Maxwell Museum of Anthropology, University of New Mexico, Albuquerque.

Glassow, Michael A.

1972 Changes in the Adaptations of Southwestern Basketmakers: A Systems Perspective. In *Contemporary Archaeology*, edited by Mark P. Leone, pp. 289–302. Southern Illinois University Press, Carbondale.

Gleichman, Peter J.

1982a AZ-J-43-23. In *Kayenta Anasazi Archaeology on Central Black Mesa, Northeastern Arizona: The Pinon Project*, edited by Laurance D. Linford, pp. 161–167. Navajo Nation Papers in Anthropology No. 10, Navajo National Cultural Resource Management Program, Window Rock, Arizona.

1982b AZ-J-58-4. In *Kayenta Anasazi Archaeology on Central Black Mesa, Northeastern Arizona: The Pinon Project*, edited by Laurance D. Linford, pp. 169–173. Navajo Nation Papers in Anthropology No. 10. Navajo Nation Cultural Resource Management Program, Window Rock, Arizona.

1982c Ethnobotanical Remains. In *Kayenta Anasazi Archaeology on Central Black Mesa, Northeastern Arizona: The Pinon Project*, edited by Laurance D. Linford, pp. 376–401. Navajo Nation Papers in Anthropology No. 10, Navajo Nation Cultural Resource Management Program, Window Rock, Arizona.

Gold, Peter

1994 *Navajo and Tibetan Sacred Wisdom: The Circle of the Spirit.* Inner Traditions International Press, Rochester, Vermont.

Goodman, James M.

1982 *The Navajo Atlas.* University of Oklahoma Press, Norman.

Graves, Donna

1990 Navajo Springs: An Examination of the Great House and Surrounding Community. Unpublished Master's thesis, Department of Anthropology, Northern Arizona University, Flagstaff.

Green, Margerie

1982 Chipped Stone Raw Materials and the Study of Interaction. Ph.D. dissertation, Department of Anthropology, Arizona State University, Tempe. University Microfilms, Ann Arbor, Michigan.

1985 *Chipped Stone Raw Materials and the Study of Interaction on Black Mesa, Arizona.* Center for Archaeological Investigations Occasional Paper No. 11. Southern Illinois University, Carbondale.

Green, Margerie, Keith Jacobi, Bruce D. Boeke, Helen O'Brien, Elizabeth S. Word, Richard L. Boston, Heather Trigg, Gilbert D. Glennie, and Melissa Gould

1985 Arizona D:11:2030. In *Excavations on Black Mesa, 1983: A Descriptive Report*, edited by Andrew L. Christenson and William J. Parry, pp. 223–260. Center for Archaeological Investigations Research Paper No. 46. Southern Illinois University, Carbondale.

Gottfried, Gerald J.

1992 Ecology and Management of Pinyon-Juniper Southwestern Woodlands. In *Ecology and Management of Oak and Associated Woodlands: Perspectives in the Southwestern United States and Northern Mexico*, edited by Peter F. Folliott, pp. 78–86. United States Department of Agriculture; U.S. Forest Service; Rocky Mountain Forest and Range Experiment Station, Fort Collins, Colorado, Sierra Vista, Arizona.

Guernsey, Samuel J.

1931 *Explorations in Northeastern Arizona: Report on the Archaeological Field Work of 1920–1923.* Papers of the Peabody Museum of American Archaeology and Ethnology Vol. 12, No. 1. Harvard University, Cambridge, Massachusetts.

Guernsey, Samuel J., and Alfred V. Kidder

1921 *Basket Maker Caves of Northeastern Arizona: Report on the Explorations, 1916–1917.* Papers of the Peabody Museum of American Archaeology and Ethnology Vol. 8, No. 2. Harvard University, Cambridge, Massachusetts.

Gumerman, George J.

1966 A Folsom Point from the Area of Mishongnovi, Arizona. *Plateau* 38(4):79–80.

1969 The Archaeology of the Hopi Buttes District, Arizona. Ph.D. dissertation, University of Arizona, Tucson. University Microfilms, Ann Arbor, Michigan.

1970 *Black Mesa: Survey and Excavation in Northeastern Arizona, 1968.* Prescott College Studies in Anthropology No. 2. Prescott College Press, Prescott, Arizona.

1975 Alternative Cultural Models for Demographic Change: Southwestern Examples. In *Population Studies in Archaeology and Biological Anthropology: A Symposium*, edited by Alan C. Swedlund, pp. 104–115. Memoirs of the Society for American Archaeology No. 30.

1983 *Prehistoric Social and Economic Survival on the Little Colorado Desert.* Paper presented at the 2nd Anasazi Symposium, Bloomfield, New Mexico.

1984 *A View from Black Mesa: The Changing Face of Archaeology.* University of Arizona Press, Tucson.

1988b *The Archaeology of the Hopi Buttes District, Arizona.* Center for Archaeological Investigations Research Paper No. 49. Southern Illinois University, Carbondale.

Gumerman, George J. (editor)

1988a *The Anasazi in a Changing Environ-*

ment. Cambridge University Press, Cambridge.

Gumerman, George J., and Jeffrey S. Dean
1989   Prehistoric Cooperation and Competition in the Western Anasazi Area. In *Dynamics of Southwest Prehistory*, edited by Linda S. Cordell and George J. Gumerman, pp. 99–148. Smithsonian Institution Press, Washington, D.C.

Gumerman, George J., and Robert C. Euler
1976a   Black Mesa, Retrospect and Prospect. In *Papers on the Archaeology of Black Mesa, Arizona*, edited by George J. Gumerman and Robert C. Euler, pp. 162–170. Southern Illinois University Press, Carbondale.

Gumerman, George J., and Robert C. Euler (editors)
1976b   *Papers on the Archaeology of Black Mesa, Arizona.* Southern Illinois University Press, Carbondale.

Gumerman, George J., and J. Alan Skinner
1968   A Synthesis of the Prehistory of the Central Little Colorado Valley, Arizona. *American Antiquity* 33:185–199.

Gumerman, George J., Deborah Westfall, and Carol S. Weed
1972   *Archaeological Investigations on Black Mesa: The 1969–1970 Seasons.* Prescott College Studies in Anthropology No. 4. Prescott College Press, Prescott, Arizona.

Haas, Jonathan, and Winifred Creamer
1987   *Warfare and Tribalization in the Prehistoric Southwest.* Final report submitted to the Harry Frank Guggenheim Foundation. School of American Research, Santa Fe.
1993   *Stress and Warfare among the Kayenta Anasazi of the Thirteenth Century.* Fieldiana: Anthropology, New Series Vol. 21. Field Museum of Natural History, Chicago, Illinois.

Hack, John T.
1942   *The Changing Physical Environment of the Hopi Indians of Arizona.* Papers of the Peabody Museum of American Archaeology and Ethnology Vol. 35, No. 1. Harvard University, Cambridge, Massachusetts.

Hagopian, Janet
1995   Status Differentiation and Ceramic Vessels: A Case Study from Black Mesa, Arizona. Unpublished Master's thesis, Department of Anthropology, Northern Arizona University, Flagstaff.

Haley, Brian D.
1984   Navajo Sites Investigated in the N-11 Mining Area. In *Excavations on Black Mesa, 1982: A Descriptive Report*, edited by Deborah L. Nichols and F. E. Smiley, pp. 443–446. Center for Archaeological Investigations Research Paper No. 39. Southern Illinois University, Carbondale.

Haley, Brian D., Thomas R. Rocek, Belinda Blomberg, and Dana Anderson
1983   Ethnoarchaeological and Historical Excavations on Black Mesa, 1981. In *Excavations on Black Mesa, 1981: A Descriptive Report*, edited by F. E. Smiley, Deborah L. Nichols, and Peter P. Andrews, pp. 281–299. Center for Archaeological Investigations Research Paper No. 36. Southern Illinois University, Carbondale.

Hammack, Laurens C., and Alan P. Sullivan, III (editors)
1981   *The 1968 Excavations at Mound 8, Las Colinas Ruins Group, Phoenix, Arizona.* Arizona State Museum, Archaeological Series No. 154. University of Arizona, Tucson.

Hantman, Jeffrey L.
1980   Arizona D:11:425. In *Excavation on Black Mesa, 1979: A Descriptive Report*, edited by Shirley Powell, Robert Layhe, and Anthony L. Klesert, pp. 237–252. Center for Archaeological Investigations Research Paper No. 18, Southern Illinois University, Carbondale.
1983   Social Networks and Stylistic Distributions in the Prehistoric Plateau Southwest. Ph.D. dissertation, Department of Anthropology, Arizona State University, Tempe. University Microfilms, Ann Arbor, Michigan.

Hantman, Jeffrey L., and Stephen Plog
1982   The Relationship of Stylistic Similarity to Patterns of Material Exchange. In *Contexts for Prehistoric Exchange*, edited by Jonathan E. Ericson and Timothy K. Earle, pp. 237–263. Academic Press, New York.

Hargrave, Lyndon L.
1935   Archaeological Investigations in the Tsegi Canyons of Northeastern Arizona in 1934. *Museum Notes* 7(7):25–28. Museum of Northern Arizona, Flagstaff.
1970   *Mexican Macaws: Comparative Osteology and Survey of Remains from the Southwest.* Anthropological Papers of the University of Arizona 20. University of Arizona Press, Tucson.

Harrill, Bruce G.
1982   Prehistoric Agricultural Adaptation and Settlement in Long House Valley, Northeastern Arizona. Ph.D. dissertation, Department of Anthropology, University of Arizona, Tucson. University Microfilms, Ann Arbor.
n.d.   The Discovery of a Paleo-Indian Site in Northeastern Arizona. Manuscript on file, Museum of Northern Arizona, Flagstaff.

Hartman, Dana, and Arthur H. Wolf
1977   *Wupatki: An Archaeological Assessment.* Anthropology Research Report No. 6. Museum of Northern Arizona, Flagstaff.

Hasgood, Eugene
1994   Dine' Evictees of District 6. Manuscript on file, Navajo Nation Archaeology Department, Window Rock, Arizona.

Haury, Emil W.
1931   *Kivas of the Tusayan Ruin, Grand Canyon, Arizona.* Medallion Papers 9. Gila Pueblo, Globe, Arizona.
1945a   *The Excavations of Los Muertos and Neighboring Ruins in the Salt River Valley, Southern Arizona.* Papers of the Peabody Museum of Archaeology and Ethnology No. 24, Vol. 1. Harvard University, Cambridge, Massachusetts.
1945b   *Painted Cave, Northeastern Arizona.* Publication No. 3. Amerind Foundation, Dragoon, Arizona.
1953   Artifacts with Mammoth Remains, Naco, Arizona. *American Antiquity* 19:1–14.
1958   Evidence at Point of Pines for a Prehistoric Migration from Northern Arizona. In *Migrations in New World Culture History*, edited by Raymond H. Thompson, pp. 1–6. Social Science Bulletin No. 27. University of Arizona, Tucson.
1976   *The Hohokam: Desert Farmers and Craftsmen.* University of Arizona Press, Tucson.

Haury, Emil W., and Lyndon L. Hargrave
1931   *Recently Dated Pueblo Ruins in Arizona.* Smithsonian Miscellaneous Collections Vol. 82(11). Smithsonian Institution, Washington D.C.

Haury, Emil W., E. B. Sayles, and William W. Wasley
1959   The Lehner Mammoth Site, Southeastern Arizona. *American Antiquity* 25:2–30.

Hayden, Julian D.
1957   *Excavations, 1940, at University Indian Ruin, Tucson, Arizona.* Technical Series No. 5. Southwestern Monuments Association, Globe, Arizona.

Haynes, C. Vance, Jr.
1968   Geochronology of Late Quaternary Alluvium. In *Means of Correlating Quaternary Successions*, edited by Roger B. Morrison and Herbert E. Wright, pp. 591–618. Proceedings of the VIII INQUA International Congress. University of Utah Press, Salt Lake City.
1973   Geochronology and Paleohydrology of the Murray Springs

Site, Arizona. Manuscript on file, Arizona State Museum Library, University of Arizona, Tucson.

Hays, Kelley A.

1983 Arizona D:7:473. In *Excavations on Black Mesa, 1981: A Descriptive Report*, edited by F. E. Smiley, Deborah L. Nichols, and Peter P. Andrews, pp. 95–98. Center for Archaeological Investigations Research Paper No. 36. Southern Illinois University, Carbondale.

1984 Rock Art of Northern Black Mesa. In *Excavations on Black Mesa, 1982: A Descriptive Report*, edited by Deborah L. Nichols and F. E. Smiley, pp. 517–540. Center for Archaeological Investigations Research Paper No. 39. Southern Illinois University, Carbondale.

1992 Anasazi Ceramics as Text and Tool: Toward a Theory of Ceramic Design "Messaging." Ph.D. dissertation, Department of Anthropology, University of Arizona. University Microfilms, Ann Arbor, Michigan.

Hays, Kelley A., E. Charles Adams, and Richard C. Lange

1991 Regional Prehistory and Research. In *Homol'ovi II: Archaeology of an Ancestral Hopi Village, Arizona*, edited by E. Charles Adams and Kelley Ann Hays, pp. 1–9. Anthropological Papers of the University of Arizona No. 55. University of Arizona Press, Tucson.

Hays-Gilpin, Kelley

1993 Mortuary Ceramics. In *NAGPRA and Archaeology on Black Mesa, Arizona*, edited by Kimberly Spurr, pp. 161–170. Navajo Nation Papers in Anthropology No. 30. Navajo Nation Archaeology Department, Window Rock, Arizona.

Hegmon, Michelle

1986 Information Exchange and Integration on Black Mesa, Arizona, A.D. 931–1150. In *Spatial Organization and Exchange: Archaeological Survey on Northern Black Mesa*, edited by Stephen Plog, pp. 256–281. Southern Illinois University Press, Carbondale.

1989 Social Integration and Architecture. In *The Architecture of Social Integration in Prehistoric Pueblos*, edited by W. D. Lipe and Michelle Hegmon, pp. 5–14. Occasional Papers of the Crow Canyon Archaeological Center No. 1, Cortez, Colorado.

1995 *The Dynamics of Pottery Style in the Early Pueblo Southwest*. Occasional Papers of the Crow Canyon Archaeological Center No. 5, Cortez, Colorado.

Hegmon, Michelle, James R. Allison, Hector Neff, and Michael D. Glascock

1997 Production of San Juan Red Ware in the Northern Southwest: Insights in to Regional Interaction in Early Puebloan Prehistory. *American Antiquity* 62:449–463.

Hegmon, Michelle, and Stephen Plog

1996 Regional Social Interaction in the Northern Southwest: Evidence and Issues. In *Interpreting Southwestern Diversity: Underlying Principles and Overarching Patterns*, edited by Paul R. Fish and J. Jefferson Reid, pp. 23–34. Anthropological Research Papers No. 48, Arizona State University, Tempe.

Hemmings, E. Thomas, and C. Vance Haynes Jr.

1969 The Escapule Mammoth and Associated Projectile Points, San Pedro Valley, Arizona. *Journal of the Arizona Academy of Science* 5(3):184–188.

Hesse, India Sun, William J. Parry, and Francis E. Smiley

1996 *A Unique Late Paleoindian Site near Inscription House, Northeastern Arizona.* Paper presented at the 61st Annual Meeting of the Society for American Archaeology, New Orleans, Louisiana.

2000 New Investigations at Southwestern Paleoindian Sites: Badger Springs. *Archaeology Southwest* 14:2.

Hester, James J.

1962 *Early Navajo Migrations and Acculturation in the Southwest.* Museum of New Mexico Papers in Anthropology No. 6, Santa Fe.

1975 Paleoarchaeology of the Llano Estacado. In *Late Pleistocene Environments of the Southern High Plains*, edited by Fred Wendorf and James J. Hester, pp. 247–256. Fort Burgwin Research Center Publications No. 9. Southern Methodist University, Dallas, Texas.

Hevly, Richard

1988 Prehistoric Vegetation and Paleoclimates on the Colorado Plateaus. In *The Anasazi in a Changing Environment*, edited by George J. Gumerman, pp. 92–118. Cambridge University Press, Cambridge.

Hevly, Richard H, and Thor N. V. Karlstrom

1974 Southwest Paleoclimatic and Continental Correlations. In *Geology of Northern Arizona with Notes on Archaeology and Paleoclimate, Part II—Area Studies and Field Guides*, edited by Thor N. V. Karlstrom, Gordon A. Swann, and Raymond L. Eastwood, pp. 257–296. Geological Society of America, Flagstaff, Arizona.

Hill, James N.

1970 *Broken K Pueblo: Prehistoric Social Organization in the American Southwest.* Anthropological Papers of the University of Arizona No. 18. University of Arizona Press, Tucson.

Hobler, Philip M.

1964 The Late Survival of Pithouse Architecture in the Kayenta Anasazi Area. Unpublished Master's thesis, Department of Anthropology, University of Arizona, Tucson.

1974 The Late Survival of Pithouse Architecture in the Kayenta Anasazi Area. *Southwestern Lore* 40(2):1–44.

Hogan, Patrick

1984 *Archaeological Test Excavations along the Turquoise Trail.* Office of Contract Archaeology, University of New Mexico, Albuquerque.

Hough, Walter

1903 *Archaeological Field Work in Northeastern Arizona: The Museum-Gates Expedition of 1901.* Report of the U.S. National Museum, 1900–1901, pp. 279–358. Smithsonian Institution, Washington, D.C.

Hrdlicka, A.

1928 The Origin and Antiquity of Man in America. *Bulletin of the New York Academy of Medicine* 4:802–820.

Huckell, Bruce B.

1977 *The Hastqin Site: A Multicomponent Site near Ganado, Arizona.* Arizona State Museum Contribution to Highway Salvage Archaeology in Arizona No. 61. University of Arizona, Tucson.

1982 *The Distribution of Fluted Points in Arizona: A Review and an Update.* University of Arizona Archaeological Series No. 145. Cultural Resource Management Division, Arizona State Museum, Tucson.

1987 *Agriculture and the Late Archaic Settlements in the River Valleys of Southeastern Arizona.* Paper presented at the Hohokam Symposium, Tempe, Arizona.

1990 Late Preceramic Farmer-Foragers in Southeastern Arizona: A Cultural and Ecological Consideration of the Spread of Agriculture into the Arid Southwestern United States. Ph.D. dissertation, Arid Lands Resource Sciences, University of Arizona, Tucson. University Microfilms, Ann Arbor, Michigan.

1995 *Of Marshes and Maize: Preceramic Agricultural Settlements in the Cienega Valley, Southeastern Arizona.* Anthropological Papers of the University of Arizona No. 59. University of Arizona Press, Tucson.

Huckell, Bruce B., and Lisa W. Huckell

1988 *Crops Come to the Desert: Late Preceramic Agriculture in Southeastern Arizona.* Paper presented at the 53rd Annual Meeting of the

Society for American Archaeology, Phoenix, Arizona.

Huckell, Lisa W.
1992 Plant Remains. In *Archaeological Investigations at Lee Canyon: Kayenta Anasazi Farmsteads in the Upper Basin, Coconino County, Arizona*, edited by Stephanie M. Whittlesey, pp. 119–133. Statistical Research Technical Series No. 38, Tucson, Arizona.

Human Dependency Survey
1939 *Statistical Summary: Human Dependency, Navajo and Hopi Reservation*. U.S. Department of Agriculture, Soil Conservation Service, Window Rock, Arizona.

Hurst, C. T.
1941 A Folsom Location in the San Luis Valley, Colorado. *Southwestern Lore* 7(2):31–34.

Irwin-Williams, Cynthia
1973 *The Oshara Tradition: Origins of Anasazi Culture*. Contributions in Anthropology Vol. 5, No. 1. University of New Mexico, Albuquerque.
1979 Post-Pleistocene Archaeology, 7000–2000 B.C. In *Handbook of North American Indians*, Vol. 9: *Southwest*, edited by Alfonso Ortiz, pp. 31–42. Smithsonian Institution Press, Washington, D.C.

Irwin-Williams, Cynthia, Henry Irwin, George Agogino, and C. Vance Haynes Jr.
1973 Hell Gap Paleo-Indian Occupation of the High Plains. *Plains Anthropologist* 18:40–53.

Irwin-Williams, Cynthia, and Phillip H. Shelley (editors)
1980 *Investigations at the Salmon Site: The Structure of Chacoan Society in the Northern Southwest*. Final report to funding agencies. Eastern New Mexico University, Portales, New Mexico.

Iverson, Peter
1981 *The Navajo Nation*. University of New Mexico Press, Albuquerque.

Jackson, William H.
1878 *Report on the Ancient Ruins Examined in 1875 and 1877*. Tenth Annual Report of the U.S. Geological and Geographical Survey of the Territories, 1876, pp. 411–450. Washington, D.C.

Jacobi, Keith
1986 An Examination of Population Mobility through the Mortuary Record at Black Mesa, Northeastern Arizona. Unpublished Master's thesis, Department of Anthropology, Southern Illinois University, Carbondale.

Jacobi, Lori M.
1984 Historic Period Artifacts. In *Excavations on Black Mesa, 1983: A Descriptive Report*, edited by Andrew L. Christenson and William J. Parry. Center for Archaeological Investigations Research Paper No. 46. Southern Illinois University, Carbondale.

Jennings, Jesse D.
1966 *Glen Canyon: A Summary*. University of Utah Anthropological Papers No. 81. University of Utah Press, Salt Lake City.
1978 *The Prehistory of Utah and the Eastern Great Basin*. University of Utah Anthropological Papers No. 98. University of Utah Press, Salt Lake City.

Johnson, Gregory A.
1989 Dynamics of Southwestern Prehistory: Far outside—Looking in. In *Dynamics of Southwest Prehistory*, edited by Linda S. Cordell and George J. Gumerman, pp. 371–389. Smithsonian Institution Press, Washington, D.C.

Judge, W. James
1973 *PaleoIndian Occupation of the Rio Grande Valley in New Mexico*. University of New Mexico Press, Albuquerque.
1982 The Paleo-Indian and Basketmaker Periods: An Overview and Some Research Problems. In *The San Juan Tomorrow: Planning for the Conservation of Cultural Resources in the San Juan Basin*, edited by Fred Plog and Walter Wait, pp. 5–58. National Park Service, Southwest Region, and the School of American Research, Santa Fe, New Mexico.

Judge, W. James, David Breternitz, Linda Cordell, George Gumerman, Leigh Jenkins, Edmund Ladd, and William Lipe
1981 *The Anasazi: Why Did They Leave? Where Did They Go?* Southwest Natural and Cultural Heritage Association, Albuquerque, New Mexico.

Kammer, Jerry
1980 *The Second Long Walk: The Navajo-Hopi Land Dispute*. University of New Mexico Press, Albuquerque.

Kaplan, Abraham
1964 *The Conduct of Inquiry: Methodology for Behavioral Science*. Chandler Publishing Company, San Francisco, California.

Karlstrom, Eric T.
1983 Soils and Geomorphology of Northern Black Mesa. In *Excavations on Black Mesa, 1981: A Descriptive Report*, edited by F. E. Smiley, Deborah L. Nichols, and Peter P. Andrews, pp. 317–342. Center for Archaeological Investigations Research Paper No. 36. Southern Illinois University, Carbondale.
1985 Soils and Geomorphology of Excavated Sites. In *Excavations on Black Mesa, 1983: A Descriptive Report*, edited by Andrew L. Christenson and William J. Parry, pp. 387–409. Center for Archaeological Investigations Research paper No. 46. Southern Illinois University, Carbondale.
1986 Stratigraphic and Pedologic Evidence for a Relatively Moist Early Holocene on Black Mesa, Northeastern Arizona. Manuscript in possession of the author, Flagstaff, Arizona.

Karlstrom, Thor N. V.
1975 Cenozoic Time—Stratigraphy of the Colorado Plateau: Continental Correlations and Some Paleoclimatic Implications. Manuscript in possession of author, Flagstaff, Arizona.
1988 Alluvial Chronology and Hydrologic Change of Black Mesa and Nearby Regions. In *The Anasazi in a Changing Environment*, edited by George J. Gumerman, pp. 45–91. Cambridge University Press, Cambridge.

Karlstrom, Thor N. V., George J. Gumerman, and Robert C. Euler
1974 Paleoenvironmental and Cultural Changes in the Black Mesa Region, Northeastern Arizona. In *The Geology of Northern Arizona with Notes on Archaeology and Paleoclimate*, edited by Thor N. V. Karlstrom, pp. 768–792. Twenty-seventh Annual Meeting, Rocky Mountain Section, Geological Society of America. Flagstaff, Arizona.
1976 Paleoenvironmental and Cultural Correlates in the Black Mesa Region. In *Papers on the Archaeology of Black Mesa, Arizona*, edited by George J. Gumerman and Robert C. Euler, pp. 149–161. Southern Illinois University Press, Carbondale.

Kelley, Klara Bonsack
1982 The Black Creek Valley: Ethnohistoric and Archaeological Evidence of Navajo Political Economy and Land Use. In *Prehistoric and Historic Occupation of the Black Creek Valley, Navajo Nation*, edited by Russell T. Fehr, Klara B. Kelley, Linda Popelish, and Laurie E. Warner, pp. 55–138. Navajo Nation Papers in Anthropology No. 7. Navajo Nation Cultural Resource Management Program, Window Rock, Arizona.
1986 *Navajo Land Use*. Academic Press, New York.

Kelley, Klara Bonsack, and Harris Francis

1994   *Navajo Sacred Places.* Indiana University Press, Bloomington.

Kelly, Robert L.

1995   *The Foraging Spectrum: Diversity in Hunter-Gatherer Lifeways.* Smithsonian Institution Press, Washington, D.C.

Kelly, Robert L., and Lawrence C. Todd

1988   Coming into the Country: Early Paleoindian Hunting and Mobility. *American Antiquity* 53:231–244.

Kemrer, Meade F.

1974   The Dynamics of Western Navajo Settlement: An Archaeological and Dendrochronological Analysis. Ph.D. dissertation, Department of Anthropology, University of Arizona, Tucson. University Microfilms, Ann Arbor, Michigan.

Keur, Dorothy

1944   A Chapter in Navaho-Pueblo Relations. *American Antiquity* 10:75–86.

Kidder, Alfred V.

1920   Ruins of the Historic Period in the Upper San Juan Valley, New Mexico. *American Anthropologist* 22:322–329.

1924   *An Introduction to the Study of Southwestern Archaeology with a Preliminary Account of the Excavations at Pecos.* Phillips Academy Southwestern Expedition No. 1. Yale University Press, New Haven, Connecticut.

1927   Southwestern Archaeological Conference. *Science* 66:489–491.

Kidder, Alfred V., and Samuel J. Guernsey

1919   *Archaeological Explorations in Northeastern Arizona.* Bureau of American Ethnology Bulletin No. 65. Smithsonian Institution, Washington, D.C.

Klesert, Anthony L.

1977a   An Analysis of Intra-site Ceramic Design Variability. Unpublished Master's thesis, Department of Anthropology, Southern Illinois University, Carbondale.

1977b   Arizona D:11:352. In *Excavation on Black Mesa, 1976: A Preliminary Report*, edited by Stephen Plog, pp. 89–95. University Museum Archaeological Service Report No. 50. Southern Illinois University, Carbondale.

1979   Black Mesa Culture History and Research Design. In *Excavation on Black Mesa, 1978: A Descriptive Report*, edited by Anthony L. Klesert and Shirley Powell, pp. 27–54. Center for Archaeological Investigations Research Paper No. 8. Southern Illinois University, Carbondale.

1982   Standing Fall House: An Early Puebloan Redistribution Center in Northeastern Arizona. *Kiva* 48:39–61.

Klesert, Anthony L., and C. W. Cowan

1978   Arizona D:7:60. In *Excavation on Black Mesa, 1977: A Preliminary Report*, edited by Anthony L. Klesert, pp. 73–84. Center for Archaeological Investigations Research Paper No. 1. Southern Illinois University, Carbondale.

Kluckhohn, Clyde, W. W. Hill, and Lucy Wales Kluckhohn

1971   *Navajo Material Culture.* Belknap Press of Harvard University, Cambridge, Massachusetts.

Kohler, Timothy A.

1993   News from the North American Southwest: Prehistory on the Edge of Chaos. *Journal of Archaeological Research* 1:267–321.

Kojo, Yasushi

1991   Rethinking Methods and Paradigms of Ceramic Chronology. Ph.D. dissertation, Department of Anthropology, University of Arizona, Tucson. University Microfilms, Ann Arbor, Michigan.

1996   Production of Prehistoric Southwestern Ceramics: A Low-Technology Approach. *American Antiquity* 61:325–339.

Kozlowski, Edwin

1972   The Economic Condition of Navajos on Black Mesa. Manuscript on file, Museum of Northern Arizona, Flagstaff.

Kuhn, Thomas S.

1962   *The Structure of Scientific Revolutions.* University of Chicago Press, Chicago.

Lange, Richard C.

1989   Survey of the Homolovi Ruins State Park. *Kiva* 54:195–216.

1998   Prehistoric Land-Use and Settlement of the Middle Little Colorado River Valley: The Survey of Homol'ovi Ruins State Park, Winslow, Arizona. *Arizona Museum Archaeological Series 189.* University of Arizona, Tucson.

Lanner, Ronald M.

1981   *The Pinon Pine: A Natural and Cultural History.* University of Nevada Press, Reno.

Lascaux, Annick, and India S. Hesse

2001   *The Early San Pedro Phase Village: Las Capas, AZ AA:12:11 (ASM).* SWCA Cultural Resource Report No. 01-100. SWCA Inc., Environmental, Tucson, AZ.

Layhe, Robert W.

1977   A Multivariate Approach for Estimating Prehistoric Population Change: Black Mesa, Northeastern Arizona. Unpublished Master's thesis, Department of Anthropology, Southern Illinois University, Carbondale.

1981   A Locational Model for Demographic and Settlement System Change: An Example for the American Southwest. Ph.D. dissertation, Department of Anthropology, Southern Illinois University, Carbondale. University Microfilms, Ann Arbor, Michigan.

1984   The Black Mesa Archaeological Project: Descriptive Reports for the 1975 Excavations. In *Excavations on Black Mesa, 1971–1976: A Descriptive Report*, edited by Shirley Powell, pp. 119–138. Center for Archaeological Investigations Research Paper No. 48. Southern Illinois University, Carbondale.

Layhe, Robert W., Steven Sessions, Charles Miksicek, and Stephen Plog

1976   *The Black Mesa Archaeological Project: A Preliminary Report for the 1975 Season.* Archaeological Service Report No. 48. University Museum, Southern Illinois University, Carbondale.

Le Blanc, Steven A.

1982   The Advent of Pottery in the Southwest. In *Southwestern Ceramics: A Comparative Review*, edited by Albert A. Schroeder, pp. 27–57. Arizona Archaeologist No. 15. Arizona Archaeological Society, Phoenix.

Lebo, Cathy J.

1991   *Anasazi Harvests: Agroclimate, Harvest Variability, and Agricultural Strategies on Prehistoric Black Mesa, Northeastern Arizona.* Department of Anthropology, Indiana University, Bloomington. University Microfilms, Ann Arbor, Michigan.

Lebo, Cathy J., Byron M. Estes, and Janet E. Belser

1983   Arizona D:7:3107. In *Excavations on Black Mesa, 1981: A Descriptive Report*, edited by F. E. Smiley, Deborah L. Nichols, and Peter P. Andrews, pp. 138–151. Center for Archaeological Investigations Research Paper No. 36. Southern Illinois University, Carbondale.

Legard, Carol L.

1982a   Architecture Analysis. In *Kayenta Anasazi Archaeology on Central Black Mesa, Northeastern Arizona: The Pinon Project*, edited by Laurance D. Linford, pp. 207–248. Navajo Nation Papers in Anthropology No. 10. Navajo Nation Cultural Resource Management Program, Window Rock, Arizona.

1982b   AZ-J-54-7. In *Kayenta Anasazi Archaeology on Central Black Mesa, Northeastern Arizona: The Pinon Project*, edited by Laurance D. Linford, pp. 71–83. Navajo Nation

Papers in Anthropology No. 10. Navajo Nation Cultural Resource Management Program, Window Rock, Arizona.

Lekson, Stephen H.

1984   Great Pueblo Architecture of Chaco Canyon, New Mexico. *National Park Service Publications in Archaeology 18B: Chaco Canyon Studies*, National Park Service, Albuquerque, New Mexico.

1988   The Idea of the Kiva in Anasazi Archaeology. *Kiva* 53:213–234.

Leonard, Robert D.

1986   Patterns of Anasazi Subsistence: Faunal Exploitation, Subsistence Diversification and Site Function in Northeastern Arizona. Ph.D. dissertation, Department of Anthropology, University of Washington, Seattle. University Microfilms, Ann Arbor, Michigan.

1989   *Anasazi Faunal Exploitation: Prehistoric Subsistence on Northern Black Mesa, Arizona.* Center for Archaeological Investigations Occasional Paper No. 13. Southern Illinois University, Carbondale.

Leonard, Robert D., Janet E. Belser, David A. Jessup, and James Carucci

1984a   Arizona D:11:3133. In *Excavations on Black Mesa, 1982: A Descriptive Report*, edited by Deborah L. Nichols and F. E. Smiley, pp. 371–394. Center for Archaeological Investigations Research Paper No. 39. Southern Illinois University, Carbondale.

Leonard, Robert D., Catherine M. Cameron, and F. E. Smiley

1983   *Diversification in Anasazi Lithic Assemblages: Implications for the Study of Social and Technological Change on Black Mesa.* Paper presented at the 48th Annual Meeting of the Society for American Archaeology, Pittsburgh.

Leonard, Robert D., Melissa Gould, James Carucci, and Peter H. McCartney

1985a   Arizona D:11:689. In *Excavations on Black Mesa, 1983: A Descriptive Report*, edited by Andrew L. Christenson and William J. Parry, pp. 155–170. Center for Archaeological Investigations Research Paper No. 46. Southern Illinois University, Carbondale.

Leonard, Robert D., David A. Jessup, and Janet E. Belser

1984b   Arizona D:11:2063. In *Excavations on Black Mesa, 1982: A Descriptive Report*, edited by Deborah L. Nichols and F. E. Smiley, pp. 281–286. Center for Archaeological Investigations Research Paper No. 39. Southern Illinois University, Carbondale.

Leonard, Robert D., Peter H. McCartney, Melissa Gould, James Carucci, and Gilbert D. Glennie

1985b   Arizona D:11:449. In *Excavations on Black Mesa, 1983: A Descriptive Report*, edited by Andrew L. Christenson and William J. Parry, pp. 125–154. Center for Archaeological Investigations Research Paper No. 46. Southern Illinois University, Carbondale.

Leonard, Robert D., F. E. Smiley, and Catherine M. Cameron

1984c   *Changing Strategies of Anasazi Lithic Procurement on Black Mesa, Arizona.* Paper presented at the 49th Annual Meeting of the Society for American Archaeology, Portland, Oregon.

Levy, Jerrold E.

1992   *Orayvi Revisited: Social Stratification in an "Egalitarian" Society.* School of American Research Press, Santa Fe, New Mexico.

Libby, Willard F.

1955   *Radiocarbon Dating*, Second Edition. University of Chicago Press, Chicago, Illinois.

Lightfoot, Kent G., and Gary M. Feinmen

1982   Social Differentiation and Leadership Development in an Early Pithouse Village in the Mogollon Region of the American Southwest. *American Antiquity* 47:64–86.

Lightfoot, Ricky R.

1988   Roofing an Early Anasazi Great Kiva: Analysis of an Architectural Model. *Kiva* 53:253–272.

Lindsay, Alexander J., Jr.

1969   The Tsegi Phase of the Kayenta Cultural Transition in Northeastern Arizona. Ph.D. dissertation, Department of Anthropology, University of Arizona, Tucson. University Microfilms, Ann Arbor, Michigan.

1986   *Late 13th-Century Pit House and Pueblo Occupations at the Point of Pines Ruin, Arizona.* Paper presented at the 51st Annual Meeting of the Society for American Archaeology, New Orleans, Louisiana.

1987   Anasazi Population Movements to Southeastern Arizona. *American Archaeology* 6:190–198.

1992   Tucson Polychrome: History, Dating, Distribution, and Design. In *Proceedings of the Second Salado Conference*, edited by Richard C. Lange and Stephen Germick, pp. 230–237. Arizona Archaeological Society, Tucson, AZ.

Lindsay, Alexander J., Jr., J. Richard Ambler, Mary Anne Stein, and Philip M. Hobler

1968   *Survey and Excavations North and East of Navajo Mountain, Utah, 1959-1962.* Bulletin No. 45, Glen

Canyon Series No. 8. Museum of Northern Arizona, Flagstaff.

Lindsay, Alexander J., Jr., and Jeffrey S. Dean

1978   Special Use Sites in Long House Valley, Northeastern Arizona: An Analysis of the Southwestern Anthropological Research Group Data File. In *Limited Activity and Occupation Sites: A Collection of Conference Papers*, edited by Albert E. Ward, pp. 109–117. Contributions to Anthropological Studies No. 1. Center for Anthropological Studies, Albuquerque, New Mexico.

Linford, Laurance D. (editor)

1982   *Kayenta Anasazi Archaeology on Central Black Mesa, Northeastern Arizona: The Pinon Project.* Navajo Nation Papers in Anthropology No. 10. Navajo Nation Cultural Resource Management Program, Window Rock, Arizona.

Lipe, William D.

1966   Anasazi Culture and its Relationship to the Environment in the Red Rock Plateau Region, Southeastern Utah. Unpublished Ph.D. dissertation, Department of Anthropology, Yale University, New Haven, Connecticut.

1970   Anasazi Communities on the Red Rock Plateau. In *Reconstructing Prehistoric Pueblo Societies*, edited by William A. Longacre, pp. 84–139. University of New Mexico Press, Albuquerque.

Lipe, William D., and Alexander J. Lindsay Jr.

1983   *Pueblo Adaptations in the Glen Canyon Area.* Paper presented at the 2nd Anasazi Symposium, Bloomfield, New Mexico.

Lipe, William D. and R. G. Matson

1971   Human Settlement and Resources in the Cedar Mesa Area S. E. Utah. In *The Distribution of Prehistoric Population Aggregates*, edited by George J. Gumerman, pp. 126–151. Prescott College Anthropological Reports No. 1, Prescott, Arizona.

Lister, Florence C., and Robert H. Lister

1968   *Earl Morris and Southwestern Archaeology.* University of New Mexico Press, Albuquerque.

Lister, Robert H.

1959   *The Coombs Site.* University of Utah Anthropological Papers No. 41. University of Utah Press, Salt Lake City.

Lister, Robert H., J. Richard Ambler, and Florence C. Lister

1960   *The Coombs Site: Part 2.* University of Utah Anthropological Papers No. 41. University of Utah Press, Salt Lake City.

Lister, Robert H., and Florence C. Lister

1961   *The Coombs Site, Part 3: Summary and Conclusions.* University of Utah

Anthropological Papers No. 41. University of Utah Press, Salt Lake City.

1981   *Chaco Canyon: Archaeology and Archaeologists.* University of New Mexico Press, Albuquerque.

Little, Elbert L., Jr.

1940   Suggestions for Selection Cutting of Pinon Trees. In *Southwestern Forest and Range Experiment Station Research Notes* No. 90, pp. 1–3. Forest Service, U.S. Department of Agriculture, Tucson, Arizona.

1941   Managing Woodlands for Pinon Nuts. *Chronica Botanica* VI(15):348–349.

Lockett, H. Claiborne, and Lyndon L. Hargrave

1953   *Woodchuck Cave: A Basketmaker II Site in Tsegi Canyon, Arizona.* Bulletin No. 26. Museum of Northern Arizona, Flagstaff.

Long, Paul V., Jr.

1966   *Archaeological Excavations in Lower Glen Canyon, Utah, 1959–1960.* Bulletin No. 42. Museum of Northern Arizona, Flagstaff.

Longacre, William A.

1970   *Archaeology as Anthropology: A Case Study.* Anthropological Papers of the University of Arizona No. 17. University of Arizona Press, Tucson.

Longacre, William A., and Michael W. Graves

1976   Probability Sampling Applied to an Early Multi-Component Surface Site in East-Central Arizona. *Kiva* 41:227–287.

Lyneis, Margaret M.

1992   *The Main Ridge Community at Lost City: Virgin Anasazi Architecture, Ceramics, and Burials.* University of Utah Anthropological Papers No. 117. University of Utah Press, Salt Lake City.

Lyons, Patric Daniel

2001   Winslow Orange Ware and the Ancestral Hopi Migration Horizon, Ph.D. dissertation, Department of Anthropology, University of Arizona, Tucson. University Microfilms, Ann Arbor, Michigan.

MacMinn, Margaret, Helen O'Brien, and Elizabeth S. Word

1984   Arizona D:7:3141. In *Excavations on Black Mesa, 1982: A Descriptive Report*, edited by Deborah L. Nichols and F. E. Smiley, pp. 167–178. Center for Archaeological Investigations Research Paper No. 39. Southern Illinois University, Carbondale.

Magers, Pamela C.

1986   Weaving at Antelope House. In *Archeological Investigations at Antelope House*, edited by Don P. Morris, pp. 224–276. National Park Service, Washington, D.C.

Mangelsdorf, Paul C., and Robert H. Lister

1956   *Archaeological Evidence of the Diffusion of Maize in Northern Mexico.* Botanical Museum Leaflets No. 17:151–178, Harvard University, Cambridge, Massachusetts.

Marcus, Joyce

1976   The Size of the Mesoamerican Village. In *The Early Mesoamerican Village*, edited by Kent V. Flannery, pp. 79–90. Academic Press, New York.

Marshall, Michael P., John R. Stein, Richard W. Loose, and Judith E. Novotny (editors)

1979   *Anasazi Communities of the San Juan Basin.* Public Service Company of New Mexico and the New Mexico Historic Preservation Bureau, Albuquerque and Santa Fe.

Martin, Debra L., Alan H. Goodman, George J. Armelagos, and Ann L. Magennis

1991   *Black Mesa Anasazi Health: Reconstructing Life from Patterns of Death and Disease.* Center for Archaeological Investigations Occasional Paper No. 14. Southern Illinois University, Carbondale.

Martin, Debra L., and Carol Piacentini

1983   1981 Osteological Recovery: Summary of Analysis and Frequency Tables. In *Excavations on Black Mesa, 1981: A Descriptive Report*, edited by F. E. Smiley, Deborah L. Nichols, and Peter P. Andrews, pp. 499–506. Center for Archaeological Investigations Research Paper No. 36. Southern Illinois University, Carbondale.

Martin, Paul Sidney

1963   *The Last 10,000 Years: A Fossil Pollen Record of the American Southwest.* University of Arizona Press, Tucson.

1967   Hay Hollow Site (200 B.C.–A.D. 200). *Chicago Field Museum of Natural History Bulletin* 38(5):6–10.

1972   Foreword and Introduction to Paleoecology of the Hay Hollow Site, Arizona. *Fieldiana* 63(1):1–5.

Martin, Paul Sidney, and Fred T. Plog

1973   *The Archaeology of Arizona: A Study of the Southwest Region.* American Museum of Natural History, Garden City, New York.

Martin, Steve L.

1999   Virgin Anasazi Diet as Demonstrated through the Analysis of Stable Carbon and Nitrogen Isotopes. *Kiva* 64:495–514.

Masse, W. Bruce

1981   Prehistoric Irrigation Systems in the Salt River Valley, Arizona. *Science* 214:408–415.

Matson, R. G.

1991   *The Origins of Southwestern Agriculture.* University of Arizona Press, Tucson.

Matson, R. G., and Brian Chisholm

1986   *Basketmaker II Subsistence: Carbon Isotopes and Other Dietary Indicators from Cedar Mesa, Utah.* Paper presented at the Third Anasazi Symposium, Monument Valley, Utah.

Matson, R. G., and Karen M. Dohm

1994   Introduction to Anasazi Origins: Recent Research on the Basketmaker II. *Kiva* 60:159–163.

Matson, R. G., and William D. Lipe

1978   Settlement Patterns on Cedar Mesa: Boom and Bust on the Northern Periphery. In *Investigations of the Southwestern Anthropological Research Group*, edited by Robert C. Euler and George J. Gumerman, pp. 1–12. Museum of Northern Arizona, Flagstaff.

Matson, R. G., William D. Lipe, and William R. Haase, IV

1988   Adaptational Continuities and Occupation Discontinuities: The Cedar Mesa Anasazi. *Journal of Field Archaeology* 15:245–264.

Mauldin, Raymond

1983   An Inquiry into the Past: Basketmaker II Settlement on Northeastern Black Mesa, Arizona. Unpublished Master's thesis, Department of Anthropology, University of Texas, Austin.

1993   The Relationship between Ground Stone and Agricultural Intensification in Western New Mexico. *Kiva* 61:317–330.

Mauldin, Raymond, Denise Hutto, and Jackson Underwood

1982   Arizona D:7:3045. In *Excavations on Black Mesa, 1980: A Descriptive Report*, edited by Peter P. Andrews, Robert Layhe, Deborah Nichols, and Shirley Powell, pp. 174–177. Center for Archaeological Investigations Research Paper No. 24. Southern Illinois University, Carbondale.

Mauldin, Raymond, and Jo Ellen Miles

1983   Arizona D:7:3194. In *Excavations on Black Mesa, 1981: A Descriptive Report*, edited by F. E. Smiley, Deborah L. Nichols, and Peter P. Andrews, pp. 152–160. Center for Archaeological Investigations Research Paper No. 36. Southern Illinois University, Carbondale.

McAnany, Patricia A.

1995   *Living with the Ancestors: Kinship and Kingship in Ancient Maya Society.* University of Texas Press, Austin.

McDonald, James A.

1976   *An Archaeological Assessment of Canyon de Chelly National Monument.* Publications in Anthropology No. 5. Western Archaeological

Center, U.S. National Park Service, Tucson, Arizona.

McGimsey, Charles R., III
1980   *Mariana Mesa: Seven Prehistoric Settlements in West-Central New Mexico.* Papers of the Peabody Museum of Archaeology and Ethnology No. 72. Harvard University, Cambridge, Massachusetts.

McGregor, John C.
1965   *Southwestern Archaeology.* University of Illinois Press, Urbana.

Mehringer, Peter J.
1967   Pollen Analysis and the Alluvial Chronology. *Kiva* 32:96–101.

Meltzer, David J.
1989   Why Don't We Know when the First People Came to North America? *American Antiquity* 54:471–490.

Mera, H. P.
1937   Some Aspects of the Largo Cultural Phase, Northern New Mexico. *American Antiquity* 3:236–243.

Michalik, Laura K.
1984   Navajo Sites Investigated in the J-15 Mining Area. In *Excavations on Black Mesa, 1982: A Descriptive Report*, edited by Deborah L. Nichols and F. E. Smiley, pp. 503–510. Center for Archaeological Investigations Research Paper No. 39. Southern Illinois University, Carbondale.

Michalik, Laura K., and Todd Bostwick
1983   Arizona D:11:3061. In *Excavations on Black Mesa, 1981: A Descriptive Report*, edited by F. E. Smiley, Deborah L. Nichols, and Peter P. Andrews, pp. 253–260. Center for Archaeological Investigations Research Paper No. 36. Southern Illinois University, Carbondale.

Minnis, Paul E.
1985a   Domesticating Plants and People in the Greater Southwest. In *Prehistoric Food Production in North America*, edited by Richard I. Ford, pp. 309–340. Anthropological Papers No. 75. Museum of Anthropology, University of Michigan, Ann Arbor.
1985b   *Social Adaptation to Food Stress: A Prehistoric Southwestern Example.* University of Chicago Press, Chicago.
1992   Earliest Plant Cultivation in the Desert Borderlands of North America. In *The Origins of Agriculture: An International Perspective*, edited by C. Wesley Cowan and Patty Jo Watson, pp. 121–140. Smithsonian Institution Press, Washington, D.C.

Mitchell, Marie
1972   *The Navajo Peace Treaty 1868.* Mason and Lipscomb, New York.

Mobley-Tanaka, Jeanette L.
1997   Gender and Ritual Space during the Pithouse to Pueblo Transition: Subterranean Mealing Rooms in the North American Southwest. *American Antiquity* 62:437–448.

Morris, Don P.
1983   *Settlement Pattern Adjustments and Node Relationships, Canyon de Chelly, Arizona.* Paper presented at the 2nd Anasazi Symposium, Bloomfield, New Mexico.

Morris, Don P. (editor)
1986   *Archeological Investigations at Antelope House.* National Park Service, Washington, D.C.

Morris, Earl H.
1925   Exploring the Canyon of Death. *National Geographic* 48(3):262–300.

Morris, Earl H., and Robert F. Burgh
1954   *Basketmaker II Sites near Durango, Colorado.* Publication No. 604. Carnegie Institution of Washington, Washington, D.C.

Morris, Elizabeth Ann
1958   A Possible Early Projectile Point from the Prayer Rock District, Arizona. *Southwestern Lore* 24(1):1–5.
1980   *Basketmaker Caves in the Prayer Rock District, Northeastern Arizona.* Anthropological Papers of the University of Arizona No. 35. University of Arizona, Tucson.

Morss, Noel
1927   *Archaeological Explorations on the Middle Chinlee, 1925.* Memoirs 34. American Anthropological Association, Menasha, Wisconsin.
1931   *Notes on the Archaeology of the Kaibito and Rainbow Plateaus in Arizona.* Papers of the Peabody Museum of American Archaeology and Ethnology Vol. 12(2). Harvard University, Cambridge, Massachusetts.

Murry, Robert E., Jr.
1983   *Pollen Analysis of Anasazi Sites at Black Mesa, Arizona.* Unpublished Master's thesis, Department of Anthropology, Texas A & M University, College Station.

Neely, James A., and Alan P. Olson
1977   *Archaeological Reconnaissance of Monument Valley in Northeastern Arizona.* Research Paper No. 3. Museum of Northern Arizona, Flagstaff.

Nichols, Deborah L., and Erik T. Karlstrom
1983   The Cultural resources of the 1981 Mitigation Areas. In *Excavations on Black Mesa, 1981: A Descriptive Report*, edited by F. E. Smiley, Deborah L. Nichols, and Peter P. Andrews, pp. 1–42. Center for Archaeological Investigations Research Paper No. 36. Southern Illinois University, Carbondale.

Nichols, Deborah L., and Shirley Powell
1987   Demographic Reconstructions in the American Southwest: Alternative Behavioral Means to the Same Archaeological Ends. *Kiva* 52:193–207.

Nichols, Deborah L., and Clifton W. Sink
1984   The 1982 Field Season. In *Excavations on Black Mesa, 1982: A Descriptive Report*, edited by Deborah L. Nichols and F. E. Smiley, pp. 1–86. Center for Archaeological Investigations Research Paper No. 39. Southern Illinois University, Carbondale.

Nichols, Deborah L., and F. E. Smiley
1984b   A Summary of Prehistoric Research on Northern Black Mesa. In *Excavations on Black Mesa, 1982: A Descriptive Report*, edited by Deborah L. Nichols and F. E. Smiley, pp. 89–107. Center for Archaeological Investigations Research Paper No. 39. Southern Illinois University, Carbondale.

Nichols, Deborah L., and F. E. Smiley (editors)
1984a   *Excavations on Black Mesa, 1982: A Descriptive Report.* Center for Archaeological Investigations Research Paper No. 39. Southern Illinois University, Carbondale.

Nusbaum, Jesse L.
1922   *A Basketmaker Cave in Kane County*, Utah. Indian Notes and Monographs, Museum of the American Indian, New York.

Olszewski, Deborah I.
1984   Arizona D:11:2023. In *Excavations on Black Mesa, 1982: A Descriptive Report*, edited by Deborah L. Nichols and F. E. Smiley, pp. 183–192. Center for Archaeological Investigations Research Paper No. 39. Southern Illinois University, Carbondale.

Olszewski, Deborah I., Margaret C. Trachte, and Rhonda M. Kohl
1984   Arizona D:11:2027. In *Excavations on Black Mesa, 1982: A Descriptive Report*, edited by Deborah L. Nichols and F. E. Smiley, pp. 209–222. Center for Archaeological Investigations Research Paper No. 39. Southern Illinois University, Carbondale.

Oswald, Dana
1993   *Navajo Space Use under Conditions of Increasing Sedentism.* Ph.D. dissertation, Department of Anthropology, University of New Mexico, Albuquerque. University Microfilms, Ann Arbor, Michigan.

Parker, Patricia L., and Thomas F. King
1990   *Guidelines for Evaluating and Documenting Traditional Cultural Properties.* National Register Bulletin No. 38. U.S. Department of

the Interior, National Park Service, Interagency Resources Division, Washington, D.C.

Parry, William J.

1984   Lithic Artifacts from Arizona D:7:103. In *Excavations on Black Mesa, 1971–1976: A Descriptive Report*, edited by Shirley Powell, pp. 238–239. Center for Archaeological Investigations Research Paper No. 48. Southern Illinois University, Carbondale.

1987a   Sources of Chipped Stone Materials. In *Prehistoric Stone Technology on Northern Black Mesa, Arizona*, edited by William J. Parry and Andrew L. Christenson, pp. 21–42. Center for Archaeological Investigations Occasional Paper No. 12. Southern Illinois University, Carbondale.

1987b   Technological Change: Temporal and Functional Variability in Chipped Stone Debitage. In *Prehistoric Stone Technology on Northern Black Mesa, Arizona*, edited by William J. Parry and Andrew L. Christenson, pp. 199–256. Center for Archaeological Investigations Occasional Paper No. 12. Southern Illinois University, Carbondale.

Parry, William J., Galen R. Burgett, and F. E. Smiley

1985   *The Archaic Occupation of Black Mesa, Arizona*. Paper presented at the Symposium on Archaic Hunter-Gatherer Archaeology in the Northern Southwest, 50th Annual Meeting of the Society for American Archaeology, Denver, Colorado.

Parry, William J., and Andrew L. Christenson

1987   *Prehistoric Stone Technology on Northern Black Mesa, Arizona*. Center for Archaeological Investigations Occasional Paper No. 12. Southern Illinois University, Carbondale.

Parry, William J., and F. E. Smiley

1990   Hunter-Gatherer Archaeology in Northeastern Arizona and Southeastern Utah. In *Perspectives on Southwestern Prehistory*, edited by Paul E. Minnis and Charles L. Redman, pp. 47–56. Westview Press, Boulder, Colorado.

Patterson, David, and George A. Agogino

1976   The Linger Skull: A Find of Possible Folsom Age. *The Greater Llano Estacado Southwest Heritage* 6(2).

Pepper, George H.

1902   *The Ancient Basketmakers of Southeastern Utah*. American Museum Journal Vol. 2, No. 4; Guide Leaflet No. 6, New York.

Petersen, Kenneth Lee

1981   10,000 Years of Climatic Change Reconstructed from Fossil Pollen, La Plata Mountains, Southwestern Colorado. Ph.D. dissertation, Department of Anthropology, Washington State University, Pullman. University Microfilms, Ann Arbor, Michigan.

Phillips, David A., Jr.

1972   Social Implications of Settlement Distributions on Black Mesa. In *Archaeological Investigations on Black Mesa: The 1969–1970 Seasons*, edited by George J. Gumerman, Deborah Westfall, and Carol S. Weed, pp. 199–210. Prescott College Studies in Anthropology No. 4. Prescott College Press, Prescott, Arizona.

Plog, Fred T.

1974   *The Study of Prehistoric Change*. Academic Press, New York.

1979a   Alternative Models of Prehistoric Change. In *Transformation: Mathematical Approaches to Culture Change*, edited by C. Renfrew and K. I. Cooke, pp. 221–236. Academic Press, New York.

1979b   Prehistory: Western Anasazi. In *Handbook of North American Indians*, Vol. 9: *Southwest*, edited by Alfonso Ortiz, pp. 108–130. Smithsonian Institution, Washington, D.C.

1983   Political and Economic Alliances on the Colorado Plateaus, A.D. 600–1450. In *Advances in World Archaeology*, Vol. 2, edited by Fred Wendorf and Angela E. Close, pp. 289–302. Academic Press, New York.

1984   Exchange, Tribes, and Alliances: The Northern Southwest. *American Archeology* 4:217–223.

Plog, Fred T. (editor)

1981   *Cultural Resources Overview: Little Colorado Area, Arizona*. U.S.D.A. Forest Service, Southwest Region, Albuquerque, New Mexico.

Plog, Fred T., George J. Gumerman, Robert C. Euler, Jeffrey S. Dean, Richard H. Hevly, and Thor N. V. Karlstrom

1988   Anasazi Adaptive Strategies: The Model, Predictions, and Results. In *The Anasazi in a Changing Environment*, edited by George J. Gumerman, pp. 230–276. Cambridge University Press, Cambridge.

Plog, Stephen

1978   Black Mesa Research Design. In *Excavation on Black Mesa, 1977: A Preliminary Report*, edited by Anthony L. Klesert, pp. 21–42. Center for Archaeological Investigations Research Paper No. 1. Southern Illinois University, Carbondale.

1980a   *Stylistic Variation in Prehistoric Ceramics: Design Analysis in the American Southwest*. Cambridge University Press, Cambridge.

1980b   Village Autonomy in the American Southwest: An Evaluation of the Evidence. In *Models and Methods in Regional Exchange*, edited by Robert E. Fry, pp. 135–146. Society for American Archaeology Papers No. 1, Washington, D.C.

1986a   Change in Regional Trade Networks. In *Spatial Organization and Exchange: Archaeological Survey on Northern Black Mesa*, edited by Stephen Plog, pp. 282–309. Southern Illinois University Press, Carbondale.

1986b   Chronology and Cultural History. In *Spatial Organization and Exchange: Archaeological Survey on Northern Black Mesa*, edited by Stephen Plog, pp. 50–86. Southern Illinois University Press, Carbondale.

1986c   Group Mobility and Locational Strategies: Tests of Some Settlement Hypotheses. In *Spatial Organization and Exchange: Archaeological Survey on Northern Black Mesa*, edited by Stephen Plog, pp. 187–223. Southern Illinois University Press, Carbondale.

1986d   Patterns of Demographic Growth and Decline. In *Spatial Organization and Exchange: Archaeological Survey on Northern Black Mesa*, edited by Stephen Plog, pp. 224–255. Southern Illinois University Press, Carbondale.

1986f   Understanding Cultural Change in the Northern Southwest. In *Spatial Organization and Exchange: Archaeological Survey on Northern Black Mesa*, edited by Stephen Plog, pp. 310–338. Southern Illinois University Press, Carbondale.

1989   Ritual, Exchange, and the Development of Regional Systems. In *The Architecture of Social Integration in Prehistoric Pueblos*, edited by William D. Lipe and Michelle Hegmon, pp. 132–154. Occasional Paper No. 1. Crow Canyon Archaeological Center, Cortez, Colorado.

1990   Agriculture, Sedentism, and Environment in the Evolution of Political Systems. In *The Evolution of Political Systems: Sociopolitics in Small-Scale Sedentary Societies*, edited by Steadman Upham, pp. 177–202. Cambridge University Press, Cambridge.

1995   Equality and Hierarchy: Holistic Approaches to Understanding Social Dynamics in the Pueblo Southwest. In *Foundations of Social Inequality*, edited by T. Douglas

Price and Gary M. Feinman, pp. 189–206. Plenum Press, New York.

Plog, Stephen (editor)
1986e   *Spatial Organization and Exchange: Archaeological Survey on Northern Black Mesa*. Southern Illinois University Press, Carbondale.

Plog, Stephen, and Jeffrey Hantman
1979   Measuring Ceramic Variation: The Black Mesa Classification System. In *Excavation on Black Mesa, 1978: A Descriptive Report*, edited by A. L. Klesert and Shirley Powell, pp. 217–220. Center for Archaeological Investigations Research Paper No. 8. Southern Illinois University, Carbondale.
1986   Multiple Regression Analysis as a Dating Method in the American Southwest. In *Spatial Organization and Exchange: Archaeological Survey on Northern Black Mesa*, edited by Stephen Plog, pp. 87–113. Southern Illinois University Press, Carbondale.

Plog, Stephen, Fred T. Plog, and Walter Wait
1978   Decision Making in Modern Survey Research. In *Advances in Archaeological Method and Theory*, Vol. 1, edited by Michael B. Schiffer, pp. 383–421. Academic Press, New York.

Plog, Stephen, and Shirley Powell
1984   Patterns of Cultural Change: Alternative Interpretations. In *Papers on the Archaeology of Black Mesa, Arizona*, Vol. 2, edited by Stephen Plog and Shirley Powell, pp. 209–216. Southern Illinois University Press, Carbondale.

Powell, Shirley
1980   Material Culture and Behavior: A Prehistoric Example from the American Southwest. Ph.D. dissertation, Department of Anthropology, Arizona State University, Tempe. University Microfilms, Ann Arbor, Michigan.
1983   *Mobility and Adaptation: The Anasazi of Black Mesa, Arizona*. Southern Illinois University Press, Carbondale.
1984a   The Effects of Seasonality on Site Space Utilization: A Lesson from Navajo Sites. In *Papers on the Archaeology of Black Mesa, Arizona*, Vol. 2, edited by Stephen Plog and Shirley Powell, pp. 117–126. Southern Illinois University Press, Carbondale.
1987   Food Storage and Environmental Uncertainty: An Example from Black Mesa, Arizona. In *Coasts, Plains and Deserts: Essays in Honor of Reynold J. Ruppé*, edited by Sylvia W. Gaines, pp. 213–225. Anthropological Research Papers

No. 38. Arizona State University, Tempe.
1988   Anasazi Demographic Patterns and Organizational Responses: Assumptions and Interpretive Difficulties. In *The Anasazi in a Changing Environment*, edited by George J. Gumerman, pp. 168–191. Cambridge University Press, Cambridge.

Powell, Shirley (editor)
1984b   *Excavations on Black Mesa, 1971–1976: A Descriptive Report*. Center for Archaeological Investigations Research Paper No. 48. Southern Illinois University, Carbondale.

Powell, Shirley, Peter P. Andrews, Deborah L. Nichols, and F. E. Smiley
1983   Fifteen Years on the Rock: Archaeological Research, Administration, and Compliance on Black Mesa, Arizona. *American Antiquity* 48:228–252.

Powell, Shirley, and George J. Gumerman
1987   *People of the Mesa*. Southern Illinois University Press, Carbondale.

Powell, Shirley, Robert Layhe, and Anthony L. Klesert, editors
1980   Excavation on Black Mesa, 1979: A Descriptive Report. Center for Archaeological Investigations Research Paper No. 18. Southern Illinois University, Carbondale.

Powers, Robert P., William B. Gillespie, and Stephen H. Lekson
1983   *The Outlier Survey: A Regional View of Settlement in the San Juan Basin*. Reports of the Chaco Center No. 3. Division of Cultural Research, National Park Service, Albuquerque, New Mexico.

Price, T. Douglas, and Anne Birgitte Gebauer (editors)
1995   Last Hunters-First Farmers: New Perspectives on the Prehistoric Transition to Agriculture. *School of American Research Advanced Seminar Series*, Santa Fe, New Mexico.

Prudden, T. Mitchell
1897   An Elder Brother to the Cliff-Dwellers. *Harper's New Monthly Magazine* 95(565):56–62.

Quilter, Jeffrey
1985   Architecture and Chronology at El Pariso, Peru. *Journal of Field Archaeology* 12:279–297.

Ravesloot, John
1984   Arizona D:7:152. In *Excavations on Black Mesa, 1971–1976: A Descriptive Report*. Center for Archaeological Investigations Research Paper No. 48, pp. 176–198. Southern Illinois University, Carbondale.

Reed, Alan D., and Jonathon C. Horn
1990   Early Navajo Occupation of the American Southwest: Reexami-

nation of the Dinetah Phase. *Kiva* 55:283–300.

Reed, Erik K.
1958   Comment on Evidence at Point of Pines for a Prehistoric Migration from Northern Arizona by Emil H. Haury. In *Migrations in New World Culture History*, edited by Raymond H. Thompson, pp. 7–8. Social Science Bulletin 27. University of Arizona, Tucson.

Reed, Pamela K.
1981   Variability in Gray Ware Ceramics, Black Mesa, Arizona. Unpublished Master's thesis, Department of Anthropology, Southern Illinois University, Carbondale.

Reed, Paul F., ed.
2000   *Foundations of Anasazi Culture: The Basketmaker-Pueblo Transition*. University of Utah Press, Salt Lake City.

Reher, Charles A. (editor)
1977   *Settlement and Subsistence along the Lower Chaco River: The CGP Survey*. University of New Mexico Press, Albuquerque.

Reher, Charles A., and George C. Frison
1980   The Vore Site, 48CK302, A Stratified Buffalo Jump in the Wyoming Black Hills. *Plains Anthropologist Memoir* 16.

Reher, Charles A., and D. C. Witter
1977   *Archaic Settlement and Vegetative Diversity*. University of New Mexico Press, Albuquerque.

Reichard, Gladys A.
1950   *Navaho Religion: A Study of Symbolism*. Pantheon Books, New York.

Reid, J. Jefferson
1989   Grasshopper Perspective on the Mogollon of the Arizona Mountains. In *Dynamics of Southwest Prehistory*, edited by Linda S. Cordell and George J. Gumerman, pp. 65–97. Smithsonian Institution Press, Washington, D.C.

Reid, J. Jefferson, and Stephanie Whittlesey
1999   *Grasshopper Pueblo: A Story of Archaeology and Ancient Life*. University of Arizona Press, Tucson.

Reinhard, Karl J., J. Richard Ambler, and Magdalene McGuffie
1985   Diet and Parasitism at Dust Devil Cave. *American Antiquity* 50:819–824.

Roberts, Frank H. H., Jr.
1929   *Shabik'eshchee Village: A Late Basket Maker Site in the Chaco Canyon, New Mexico*. Bulletin No. 92. Bureau of American Ethnology, Smithsonian Institution, Washington, D.C.

Robins, Michael R.
1997a   Modeling the San Juan Basketmaker Socio-economic Organiza-

tion: A Preliminary Study in Rock Art and Social Dynamics. In *Early Farmers in the Northern Southwest: Papers on Chronometry, Social Dynamics, and Ecology*, edited by Francis E. Smiley and Michael R. Robins, pp. 73–120. Animas—La Plata Archaeological Project Research Paper No. 7. Northern Arizona University, Flagstaff.

1997b   A Brief Description of a Selection of Basketmaker II Rockshelter Sites in the Northern Southwest. In *Early Farmers in the Northern Southwest: Papers on Chronometry, Social Dynamics, and Ecology*, edited by Francis E. Smiley and Michael R. Robins, pp. 43–58. Animas—La Plata Archaeological Project Research Paper No. 7. Northern Arizona University, Flagstaff.

Robins, Michael R., and Kelley A. Hays-Gilpin
2000   The Bird in the Basket: Gender and Social Change in Basketmaker Iconography. In *Foundations of Anasazi Culture: The Basketmaker-Pueblo Transition*, edited by Paul F. Reed, pp. 231–250. University of Utah Press, Salt Lake City.

Rocek, Thomas R.
1984a   Arizona D:11:36. In *Excavations on Black Mesa, 1982: A Descriptive Report*, edited by Deborah L. Nichols and F. E. Smiley, pp. 422–435. Center for Archaeological Investigations Research Paper No. 39. Southern Illinois University, Carbondale.

1984b   Navajo Cultural History. In *Excavations on Black Mesa, 1982: A Descriptive Report* No. 39, edited by Deborah L. Nichols and F. E. Smiley, pp. 413–421. Southern Illinois University, Carbondale.

1984c   Navajo Sites Investigated in the J-2 Mining Area. In *Excavations on Black Mesa, 1982: A Descriptive Report*, edited by Deborah L. Nichols and F. E. Smiley, pp. 451–461. Center for Archaeological Investigations Research Paper No. 39. Southern Illinois University, Carbondale.

1985   Correlates of Economic and Demographic Change: Navajo Adaptations on Northern Black Mesa, Arizona. Ph.D. dissertation, Department of Anthropology, University of Michigan, Ann Arbor. University Microfilms, Ann Arbor, Michigan.

1995   *Navajo Multi-Household Social Units: Archaeology on Black Mesa, Arizona*. University of Arizona Press, Tucson.

Roessel, Ruth (editor)
1973   *Navajo Stories of the Long Walk Period*. Navajo Community College Press, Tsaile, Arizona.

Rogge, Allen Eugene
1983   Little Archaeology, Big Archaeology: The Changing Context of Archaeological Research. Ph.D. dissertation, Department of Anthropology, University of Arizona, Tucson. University Microfilms, Ann Arbor, Michigan.

Rohn, Arthur H.
1965   Postulation of Socio-Economic Groups from Archaeological Evidence. In *Contributions of the Wetherill Mesa Archeological Project*, edited by Douglas Osborne, pp. 65–69. Society for American Archaeology Memoirs 19. Society for American Archaeology, Washington, D.C.

Roth, Barbara J.
1992   Sedentary Agriculturalists or Mobile Hunter-Gatherers? Evidence on the Late Archaic Occupation of the Northern Tucson Basin. *Kiva* 57(4):291–314.

Rouse, Irving
1962   Southwestern Archaeology Today. In *An Introduction to the Study of Southwestern Archaeology*, edited by Alfred Vincent Kidder, pp. 1–55. Yale University Press, New Haven, Connecticut.

Ruffing, Lorraine Turner
1973   An Alternative Approach to Economic Development in a Traditional Navajo Community. Ph.D. dissertation, Department of Anthropology, Columbia University, New York. University Microfilms, Ann Arbor, Michigan.

Russell, Scott C.
1979   Navajo Sites Investigated During 1978. In *Excavations on Black Mesa, 1978: A Descriptive Report*, edited by Anthony L. Klesert and Shirley Powell, pp. 155–165. Center for Archaeological Investigations Research Paper No. 8. Southern Illinois University, Carbondale.

1981   The Navajo Oral History and Ethnohistory of Northeastern Black Mesa, Arizona. Manuscript on file, Center for Archaeological Investigations, Southern Illinois University, Carbondale.

1983   *The Navajo History and Archaeology of East-Central Black Mesa, Arizona* (CRMP-83-046). Navajo Nation Papers in Anthropology No. 21. Navajo Nation Cultural Resource Management Program, Window Rock, Arizona.

n.d.   Unpublished field notes. Manuscript on file, Center for Archaeological Investigations, Southern Illinois University, Carbondale.

Russell, Scott C., and Jeffrey S. Dean
1985   The Sheep and Goat Corral: A Key Structure in Navajo Site Analysis. *Kiva* 51:3–18.

Russell, Scott C., and Shirley Powell McAllister
1978   Arizona D:7:21. In *Excavation on Black Mesa, 1977: A Preliminary Report*, edited by Anthony L. Klesert, pp. 59–64. Center for Archaeological Investigations Research Paper No. 1. Southern Illinois University, Carbondale.

Ryan, Dennis John
1977   The Paleopathology and Paleoepidemiology of the Kayenta Anasazi Indians in Northeastern Arizona. Ph.D. dissertation, Department of Anthropology, Arizona State University, Tempe. University Microfilms, Ann Arbor, Michigan.

Rynda, Ann E., Joyce Gerber, Raymond Mauldin, and Diane Hirsch
1983   Arizona D:11:244. In *Excavations on Black Mesa, 1981: A Descriptive Report*, edited by F. E. Smiley, Deborah L. Nichols, and Peter P. Andrews, pp. 161–177. Center for Archaeological Investigations Research Paper No. 16. Southern Illinois University, Carbondale.

Sahlins, Marshall D.
1968   *Tribesmen*. Prentice-Hall, Englewood Cliffs, New Jersey.

Salzer, Matthew W.
2000   Dendroclimatology in the San Francisco Peaks Region of Northern Arizona, USA. Ph.D dissertation, Department of Geosciences, University of Arizona. University Microfilms, Ann Arbor, Michigan.

Sayles, Edwin B.
1965   Late Quaternary Climate Recorded by Cochise Culture. *American Antiquity* 30:476–480.

1984   *The Cochise Cultural Sequence in Southeastern Arizona*. Anthropological Papers of the University of Arizona No. 42. University of Arizona Press, Tucson.

Sayles, Edwin B., and Ernst Antevs
1941   *The Cochise Culture*. Medallion Papers No. 29. Gila Pueblo, Globe, Arizona.

Schaafsma, Polly
1966   A Survey of Tsegi Canyon Rock Art. Manuscript on file, Navajo National Monument, Tonalea, Arizona.

1980   *Indian Rock Art of the Southwest*. University of New Mexico, Albuquerque.

Schiffer, Michael B.
1983   Toward the Identification of Formation Processes. *American Antiquity* 48:675–706.

Schlanger, Sarah
1986   Population Studies. In *Dolores*

Archaeological Program: Final Synthetic Report, edited by David A. Breternitz, Christine K. Robinson, and G. Timothy Gross, pp. 492–524. Bureau of Reclamation, U.S. Department of the Interior, Bureau of Reclamation, Denver.

Schroedl, Alan R.
1977   The Paleo-Indian Period on the Colorado Plateau. *Southwestern Lore* 43(3):1–9.

Schroedl, Alan R., and Eric Blunman
1989   Dating and Site Chronologies. In *Kayenta Anasazi Archaeology and Navajo Ethnohistory on the Northwestern Shonto Plateau: The N-16 Project*, edited by Alan R. Schroedl, pp. 53–87. P-III Associates, Inc., Salt Lake City, Utah.

Schroedl, Alan R., and Eric Blinman
1989   Dating and Site Chronologies. In *Kayenta Anasazi Archaeology and Navajo Ethnohistory on the Northwestern Shonto Platueau: The N-16 Project*, edited by Alan R. Schroedl, pp. 53–87. P-III Associates, Inc., Salt Lake City, Utah.

Schumm, S. A.
1977   *The Fluvial Systems*. J. Wiley and Sons, New York.

Schwartz, Douglas W., Jane Kepp, and Richard C. Chapman
1981   *The Walhalla Plateau*. School of American Research Press, Santa Fe, New Mexico.

Scott, Linda
1982   Pollen Analysis in the Pinon-Forest Lake Region. In *Kayenta Anasazi Archaeology on Central Black Mesa, Northeastern Arizona: The Pinon Project*, edited by Laurance D. Linford, pp. 403–416. Navajo Nation Papers in Anthropology No. 10, Navajo Nation Cultural Resource Management Program, Window Rock, Arizona.

Sears, William H.
1961   The Study of Social and Religious Systems in North American Archaeology. *Current Anthropology* 2:223–231.

Sebastian, Lynne
1985   *Archaeological Excavation along the Turquoise Trail: The Migration Program*. Office of Contract Archaeology, University of New Mexico, Albuquerque.

Semé, Michele
1984   The Effects of Agricultural Fields on Faunal Assemblage Variation. In *Papers on the Archaeology of Black Mesa, Arizona*, Vol. 2, edited by Stephen Plog and Shirley Powell, pp. 139–157. Southern Illinois University Press, Carbondale.

Semé, Michele, and John E. Joha
1984   Navajo Sites Investigated in the J-13/14 Mining Area. In *Excavations on Black Mesa, 1982: A Descriptive Report*, edited by Deborah L. Nichols and F. E. Smiley, pp. 489–502. Center for Archaeological Investigations Research Paper No. 39. Southern Illinois University, Carbondale.

Sessions, Steven, and Joan A. Spalding
1977   Arizona D:11:351. In *Excavation on Black Mesa, 1976: A Preliminary Report*, edited by Stephen Plog, pp. 83–88. University Museum Archaeological Service Report No. 59. Southern Illinois University, Carbondale.

Simmons, Alan H.
1982a   Modeling Archaic Adaptive Behavior in the Chaco Canyon Region. In *Prehistoric Adaptive Strategies in the Chaco Canyon Region, Northwestern New Mexico*, Vol. 3, edited by Alan H. Simmons, pp. 881–932. Navajo Nation Papers in Anthropology No. 9. Navajo Nation Cultural Resource Management Program, Window Rock, Arizona.
1986   New Evidence for the Early Use of Cultigens in the American Southwest. *American Antiquity* 5:73–89.

Simmons, Alan H. (editor)
1982b   *Prehistoric Adaptive Strategies in the Chaco Canyon Region, Northwestern New Mexico*. Vol. 3. Navajo Nation Papers in Anthropology No. 9. Navajo Nation Cultural Resource Management Program, Window Rock, Arizona.

Sink, Clifton W., Brenda J. Baker, James K. Feathers, Greg Reed, and James Carucci
1984   Arizona D:11:2108. In *Excavations on Black Mesa, 1982: A Descriptive Report*, edited by Deborah L. Nichols and F. E. Smiley, pp. 287–308. Center for Archaeological Investigations Research Paper No. 39. Southern Illinois University, Carbondale.

Sink, Clifton W., Douglas M. Davy, and Anne T. Jones
1982a   Arizona D:7:2013. In *Excavations on Black Mesa, 1980: A Descriptive Report*, edited by Peter P. Andrews, Robert Layhe, and Shirley Powell, pp. 121–132. Center for Archaeological Investigations Research Paper No. 24. Southern Illinois University, Carbondale.

Sink, Clifton W., Douglas M. Davy, A. Trinkle Jones, Laura Michalik, and Diane Pitz
1982b   Arizona D:7:262. In *Excavations on Black Mesa, 1980: A Descriptive Report*, edited by Peter P. Andrews, Robert Layhe, and Shirley Powell, pp. 87–108. Center for Archaeological Investigations Research Paper No. 24. Southern Illinois University, Carbondale.

Sink, Clifton W., Margaret C. Trachte, Laura K. Michalik, Byron M. Estes, Todd Bostwick, Lisa Anderson, and David Jessup
1983   Arizona D:11:2068. In *Excavations on Black Mesa, 1981: A Descriptive Report*, edited by F. E. Smiley, Deborah L. Nichols, and Peter P. Andrews, pp. 218–252. Center for Archaeological Investigations Research Paper No. 36. Southern Illinois University, Carbondale.

Smiley, Francis E.
1979   Changes in the Cursorial Ability of Wyoming Holocene Bison. Unpublished Master's thesis, Department of Anthropology, University of Wyoming, Laramie.
1984   *The Black Mesa Basketmakers: A Reevaluation of the Chronometry of the Lolomai Phase*. Paper presented at the 49th Annual Meeting of the Society for American Archaeology, Portland, Oregon.
1985   The Chronometrics of Early Agricultural Sites in Northeastern Arizona: Approaches to the Interpretation of Radiocarbon Dates. Ph.D. dissertation, Department of Anthropology, University of Michigan, Ann Arbor. University Microfilms, Ann Arbor, Michigan.
1993   Early Farmers in the Northern Southwest: A View from Marsh Pass. In *Anasazi Basketmaker: Papers from the 1990 Wetherill-Grand Gulch Symposium*, edited by Victoria M. Atkins, pp. 243–254. Cultural Resource Series No. 24. U.S.D.I., Bureau of Land Management, Salt Lake City, Utah.
1994   The Agricultural Transition in the Northern Southwest: Patterns in the Current Chronometric Data. *Kiva* 60:165–189.
1995a   Typology and Temporal Variation: A Consideration of Projectile Points from Ridges Basin and the Northern Southwest. In *Lithic Assemblage Structure and Variation: Animas–La Plata Archaeological Project 1992–1993 Investigations in Ridges Basin, Southwestern Colorado*, edited by Francis E. Smiley, pp. 33–81. Animas–La Plata Archaeological Project Research Paper No. 2. Northern Arizona University, Flagstaff.
1995b   Regional Packing, Group Size, and the Diffusion of Innovation. Paper presented at the 53rd Annual Plains Anthropology Conference, Laramie, Wyoming, October 19–21, 1995.
1997a   The American Neolithic and the Animas–La Plata Archaeological

Project. In *Early Farmers in the Northern Southwest: Papers on Chronometry, Social Dynamics, and Ecology*, edited by Francis. E. Smiley and Michael R. Robins, pp. 1–12. Animas–La Plata Archaeological Project Research Paper No. 7. Northern Arizona University, Flagstaff.

1997b   Appendix A: List of New Radiocarbon Dates from A-LP Chronometric Research in the Northern Southwest. In *Early Farmers in the Northern Southwest: Papers on Chronometry, Social Dynamics, and Ecology*, edited by Francis. E. Smiley and Michael R. Robins, pp. 165–170. Animas–La Plata Archaeological Project Research Paper No. 7. Northern Arizona University, Flagstaff.

1997c   Appendix B: Selected Photographs of A-LP Radiocarbon Samples. In *Early Farmers in the Northern Southwest: Papers on Chronometry, Social Dynamics, and Ecology*, edited by Francis. E. Smiley and Michael R. Robins, pp. 171–186. Animas–La Plata Archaeological Project Research Paper No. 7. Northern Arizona University, Flagstaff.

1997d   Regional Packing, Group Dynamics and the Diffusion of Innovation. In *Early Farmers in the Northern Southwest: Papers on Chronometry, Social Dynamics, and Ecology*, edited by Francis. E. Smiley and Michael R. Robins, pp. 59–72. Animas–La Plata Archaeological Project Research Paper No. 7. Northern Arizona University, Flagstaff.

1997e   Toward Chronometric Resolution for Early Agriculture in the Northern Southwest. In *Early Farmers in the Northern Southwest: Papers on Chronometry, Social Dynamics, and Ecology*, edited by Francis. E. Smiley and Michael R. Robins, pp. 13–42. Animas–La Plata Archaeological Project Research Paper No. 7. Northern Arizona University, Flagstaff.

1998a   Appendix A: Radiocarbon Dates from Early Agricultural Sites on Black Mesa. In *Archaeological Chronometry: Radiocarbon and Tree-Ring Models and Applications on Black Mesa, Arizona*, edited by Francis E. Smiley and Richard V. N. Ahlstrom, pp. 225–235. Center for Archaeological Investigations Occasional Paper No. 16. Southern Illinois University, Carbondale.

1998b   Applying Radiocarbon Models: Lolomai Phase Chronometry on Black Mesa. In *Archaeological Chronometry: Radiocarbon and Tree-Ring Models and Applications on Black Mesa, Arizona*, edited by Francis E. Smiley and Richard V. N. Ahlstrom, pp. 99–134. Center for Archaeological Investigations Occasional Paper No. 16. Southern Illinois University, Carbondale.

1998c   Old Wood and Natural Processes: A Simulation Approach to Site Age Determination. In *Archaeological Chronometry: Radiocarbon and Tree-Ring Models and Applications on Black Mesa, Arizona*, edited by Francis E. Smiley and Richard V. N. Ahlstrom, pp. 83–97. Center for Archaeological Investigations Occasional Paper No. 16. Southern Illinois University, Carbondale.

1998d   Wood and Radiocarbon Dating: Interpretive Frameworks and Techniques. In *Archaeological Chronometry: Radiocarbon and Tree-Ring Models and Applications on Black Mesa, Arizona*, edited by Francis E. Smiley and Richard V. N. Ahlstrom, pp. 25–48. Center for Archaeological Investigations Occasional Paper No. 16. Southern Illinois University, Carbondale.

2000a   *First Farmers: Models and Methods for Examining Early Agriculture on the Colorado Plateau.* Paper Presented at the Southwest Symposium, Santa Fe, New Mexico.

2000b   *First Farmers: New Basketmaker II Research in the Northern Southwest.* Paper presented at the 65th Annual Meeting of the Society for American Archaeology, Philadelphia, Pennsylvania.

2000c   *Infra-Tribal Systems and Cultural Evolutionary Studies of Early Agriculture on the Colorado Plateau.* Paper presented at the 65th Annual Meeting of the Society for American Archaeology, Philadelphia, Pennsylvania.

Smiley, F. E., and Peter P. Andrews

1983   An Overview of Black Mesa Archaeological Research. In *Excavations on Black Mesa, 1981: A Descriptive Report*, edited by F. E. Smiley, Deborah L. Nichols, and Peter P. Andrews, pp. 43–60. Center for Archaeological Investigations Research Paper No. 36. Southern Illinois University, Carbondale.

Smiley, F. E., Deborah L. Nichols, and Peter P. Andrews (editors)

1983   *Excavations on Black Mesa, 1981: A Descriptive Report.* Center for Archaeological Investigations Research Paper No. 36. Southern Illinois University, Carbondale.

Smiley, Francis E., and William J. Parry

1990   *Early, Rapid, Intensive: Rethinking the Agricultural Transition in the Northern Southwest.* Paper presented at the 55th Annual Meeting of the Society for American Archaeology, Las Vegas, Nevada.

Smiley, Francis E., William J. Parry, and George J. Gumerman

1986   *Early Agriculture in the Black Mesa/Marsh Pass Region of Arizona: New Chronometric Data and Recent Excavations at Three Fir Shelter.* Paper presented at the 51st Annual Meeting of the Society for American Archaeology, New Orleans, Louisiana.

Smiley, F. E., and Michael R. Robins

1997a   *Chronometric Sampling and Disturbed Contexts.* Paper presented at the 62nd Annual Meeting of the Society for American Archaeology, Nashville, Tennessee.

1998   *The Butler Wash Rockshelters Project: Preliminary Data Recovery from Extensively Looted Archaeological Contexts.* Paper presented at the 63rd Annual Meeting of the Society for American Archaeology, Seattle, Washington.

1999   *Early Agriculture and Intersite Variation: The Basketmaker II Peoples of Southeastern Utah.* Paper presented at the 64th Annual Meeting of the Society for American Archaeology, Chicago, Illinois.

Smiley, F. E., and Michael R. Robins (editors)

1997b   *Early Farmers in the Northern Southwest: Papers on Chronometry, Social Dynamics, and Ecology.* Animas–La Plata Archaeological Project Research Paper No. 7. Northern Arizona University, Flagstaff.

Smith, Marion F., Jr.

1991   *Function and Technology of Anasazi: Ceramics from Black Mesa, Arizona.* Center for Archaeological Investigations Occasional Paper No. 16. Southern Illinois University, Carbondale.

Smith, Shelley J.

1985   Arizona D:11:1014. In *Excavations on Black Mesa, 1983: A Descriptive Report*, edited by Andrew L. Christenson and William J. Parry, pp. 171–184. Center for Archaeological Investigations Research Paper No. 46. Southern Illinois University, Carbondale.

Smith, Shelley J., Richard L. Boston, Gilbert D. Glennie, and Helen L. O'Brien

1985   Arizona D:11:1410. In *Excavations on Black Mesa, 1983: A Descriptive Report*, edited by Andrew L. Christenson and William J. Parry, pp. 203–222. Center for Archaeological Investigations Research Paper No. 46. Southern Illinois University, Carbondale.

Smith, Shelley J., and Jo Ellen Miles

1984 Arizona D:11:2045. In *Excavations on Black Mesa, 1982: A Descriptive Report*, edited by Deborah L. Nichols and F. E. Smiley, pp. 232–238. Center for Archaeological Investigations Research Paper No. 39. Southern Illinois University, Carbondale.

Smith, Shelley J., and Elizabeth O. Wills

1984 Arizona D:11:3135. In *Excavations on Black Mesa, 1982: A Descriptive Report*, edited by Deborah L. Nichols and F. E. Smiley, pp. 395–401. Center for Archaeological Investigations Research Paper No. 39. Southern Illinois University, Carbondale.

Smith, Watson

1952 *Excavations in Big Hawk Valley, Wupatki National Monument, Arizona*. Bulletin No. 24. Museum of Northern Arizona, Flagstaff.

1971 *Painted Ceramics of the Western Mound at Awatovi*. Papers of the Peabody Museum of American Archaeology and Ethnology Vol. 38. Harvard University, Cambridge, Massachusetts.

1972 *Prehistoric Kivas of Antelope Mesa, Northeastern Arizona*. Papers of the Peabody Museum of American Archaeology and Ethnology Vol. 39(1). Harvard University, Cambridge, Massachusetts.

Spier, Leslie

1955 *Mojave Culture Items*. Museum of Northern Arizona Bulletin 28.

Spurr, Kimberly

1993 *NAGPRA and Archaeology on Black Mesa, Arizona*. Navajo Nation Papers in Anthropology No. 30. Navajo Nation Archaeology Department, Window Rock, Arizona.

Stanislawski, Michael B.

1963 Wupatki Pueblo: A Study in Cultural Fusion and Change in Sinagua and Hopi Prehistory. Ph.D. dissertation, Department of Anthropology, University of Arizona, Tucson. University Microfilms, Ann Arbor, Michigan.

Stein, Mary Anne

1984 Pottery Pueblo: A Tsegi Phase Village on Paiute Mesa, Utah. Ph.D. dissertation, Department of Anthropology, Southern Methodist University, Dallas, Texas. University Microfilms, Ann Arbor, Michigan.

Steward, Julian H.

1937 Ecological Aspects of Southwestern Society. *Anthropos* 32:87–104.

1938 *Great Basin Aboriginal Sociopolitical Groups*. Bureau of American Eth-

nology Bulletin 120, Smithsonian Institution, Washington, D.C.

Stirling, Matthew W.

1942 *Origin Myth of Acoma and Other Records*. Bureau of American Ethnology Bulletin 135, Smithsonian Institution, Washington, D.C.

Stokes, Marvin A., and Terah L. Smiley

1968 *An Introduction to Tree-Ring Dating*. University of Chicago Press, Chicago, Illinois.

Stone, Glenn Davis

1984 Arizona D:11:2025. In *Excavations on Black Mesa, 1982: A Descriptive Report*, edited by Deborah L. Nichols and F. E. Smiley, pp. 193–208. Center for Archaeological Investigations Research Paper 39. Southern Illinois University, Carbondale.

Stone, Glenn Davis, C. Michael Barton, and Anne F. Cunningham

1984a Arizona D:11:2051. In *Excavations on Black Mesa, 1982: A Descriptive Report*, edited by Deborah L. Nichols and F. E. Smiley, pp. 239–254. Center for Archaeological Investigations Research Paper No. 39, Southern Illinois University, Carbondale.

1984b Arizona D:11:2038. In *Excavations on Black Mesa, 1982: A Descriptive Report*, edited by C. Michael Barton, Deborah L. Nichols, and F. E. Smiley, pp. 223–231. Center for Archaeological Investigations Research Paper 39. Southern Illinois University, Carbondale.

Stuiver, M., and P. J. Reimer

1993 Extended 14C Data Base and Revised CALIB 3.0 14C Age Calibration Program. *RadioCarbon* 35(1):215–230.

Sullivan, Alan P., III

1986a *Prehistory of the Upper Basin, Coconino County, Arizona*. Arizona State Museum Archaeological Series No. 167. University of Arizona, Tucson.

1986b Sherd and Lithic Scatter Archaeology and the Reconstruction of Prehistoric Land-Use Patterns. In *Prehistory of the Upper Basin, Coconino County, Arizona*, edited by Alan P. Sullivan III, pp. 213–275. Arizona State Museum Archaeological Series No. 167. University of Arizona, Tucson.

1987 Seeds of Discontent: Implications of a "Pompeii" Archaeobotanical Assemblage for Grand Canyon Anasazi Subsistence Models. *Journal of Ethnobiology* 7:137–153.

1988 Prehistoric Southwestern Ceramic Manufacture: The Limitations of Current Evidence. *American Antiquity* 53:23–35.

1992 Pinyon Nuts and Other Wild Resources in Western Anasazi Subsistence Economies. In *Long-term Subsistence Change in Prehistoric North America*, edited by Dale Croes, Rebecca A. Hawkins, and Barry L. Isaac, pp. 195–239. Research in Economic Anthropology Supplement No. 6. JAI Press, Greenwich, Connecticut.

Sullivan, Alan P., III, and Christian E. Downum

1991 Aridity, Activity, and Volcanic Ash Agriculture: A Study of Short-Term Prehistoric Cultural-Ecological Dynamics. *World Archaeology* 22:271–287.

Sumner, Dale R.

1982 An Analysis of Six Anasazi Burials from the Kayenta Region: Biological and Cultural Variables. In *Kayenta Anasazi Archaeology on Central Black Mesa, Northeastern Arizona: The Pinon Project*, edited by Laurance D. Linford, pp. 417–432. Navajo Nation Papers in Anthropology No. 10, Navajo Nation Cultural Resource Management Program, Window Rock, Arizona.

Sundberg, Lawrence D.

1995 *Dinétah: An Early History of the Navajo People*. Sunstone Press, Santa Fe, New Mexico.

Swarthout, Jeanne, Sara Stebbins, Pat Stein, Bruce Harrill, and Peter J. Pilles Jr.

1986 *The Kayenta Anasazi: Archaeological Investigations Along the Black Mesa Railroad Corridor*. MNA Research Paper Vol. 2, No. 30. Museum of Northern Arizona, Flagstaff.

Swedlund, Alan C., and Steven E. Sessions

1976 A Developmental Model of Prehistoric Population Growth on Black Mesa, Northeastern Arizona. In *Papers on the Archaeology of Black Mesa, Arizona*, edited by George J. Gumerman and Robert C. Euler, pp. 136–148. Southern Illinois University Press, Carbondale.

Thomas, Alston V.

1994 Knocking Sense from Old Rock: Typologies and the Narrow Perspective of the Angostura Point Type. *Lithic Technology* 18 (1 and 2):16–27.

Thornton, Barrie

1981 Anasazi Ceramics: Chronology and Prehistoric Trade. In *The Canyon del Muerto Survey Project: Anasazi and Navajo Archeology in Northeastern Arizona*, edited by Patricia L. Fall, James A. McDonald, and Pamela C. Magers, pp. 269–280. Publications in Anthropology No. 15. National Park Service, Western Archeological Center, Tucson, Arizona.

Titiev, Mischa
1944   *Old Oraibi: A Study of the Hopi Indians of Third Mesa.* Papers of the Peabody Museum of American and Ethnology 22(1). Harvard University, Cambridge, Massachusetts.

Towner, Ronald H.
1996   *The Archaeology of Navajo Origins.* University of Utah Press, Salt Lake City.
1997   The Dendrochronology of Navajo Pueblitos of Dinétah. Ph.D. dissertation, Department of Anthropology, University of Arizona, Tucson. University Microfilms, Ann Arbor, Michigan.

Trigg, Heather B.
1985   Ethnobotanical Analysis of Arizona D:7:2085. In *Excavations on Black Mesa, 1983: A Descriptive Report*, edited by Andrew L. Christenson and William J. Parry, pp. 489–511. Center for Archaeological Investigations Research Paper No. 46. Southern Illinois University, Carbondale.

Turner, Christy G., II
1963   *Petroglyphs of the Glen Canyon Region: Styles, Chronology, Distribution, and Relationships from Basketmaker to Navajo.* Bulletin No. 38. Museum of Northern Arizona, Flagstaff.

Turner, Christy G., II, and Jacqueline A. Turner
1999   *Man Corn: Cannibalism and Violence in the Prehistoric American Southwest.* University of Utah Press, Salt Lake City.

Two Bears, Davina
1995   A Navajo Student's Perception: Anthropology and the Navajo Nation Archaeology Department Student Training Program. Society for American Archaeology *Bulletin* 13(1):4–6.

Upham, Steadman
1982   *Polities and Power.* Academic Press, New York.

Upham, Steadman, Richard S. MacNeish, Walton Galinat, and Christopher M. Stevenson
1987   Evidence Concerning the Origin of Maiz de Ocho. *American Anthropologist* 89:410–419.

Van Valkenburgh, Richard F
1941   *Diné Bikeyah.* Office of Indian Affairs, Navajo Service, Window Rock, Arizona.

Vierra, Bradley J.
1985   Hunter-Gatherer Settlement Systems: To Reoccupy or Not to Reoccupy, That Is the Question. Unpublished Master's thesis, Department of Anthropology, University of New Mexico, Albuquerque.

Vivian, R. Gwinn
1974   Conservation and Diversion: Water-Control Systems in the Anasazi Southwest. In *Irrigation's Impact on Society*, edited by Theodore E. Downing and McGuire Gibson, pp. 95–112. Anthropological Papers of the University of Arizona No. 25. University of Arizona, Tucson.
1990   *The Chacoan Prehistory of the San Juan Basin.* Academic Press, San Diego, California.

Vogler, Lawrence E., Dennis A. Gilpin, and Joseph K. Anderson
1982   *Gallegos Mesa Settlement and Subsistence: A Set of Explanatory Models for Cultural Resources on Blocks VII, IX, X, and XI, Navajo Indian Irrigation Project.* Volumes 1, 2, and 3. Navajo Nation Papers in Anthropology No. 12. Navajo Nation Cultural Resource Management Program, Window Rock, Arizona.
1983   *Cultural Resource Investigations on Gallegos Mesa: Excavations in Block VII and IX, and Testing Operations in Blocks X and XI, Navajo Indian Irrigation Project, San Juan County, New Mexico.* Vol. 1. Navajo Nation Papers in Anthropology No. 24. Navajo Nation Cultural Resource Management Program, Window Rock, Arizona.

Voll, Charles B.
1978   Appendix E: The Excavation of Room 92, Chetro Ketl. In *Wooden Ritual Artifacts from Chaco Canyon: The Chetro Ketl Collection*, edited by R. Gwinn Vivian, Dulce N. Didgen, and Gayle H. Hartmann. Anthropological Papers of the University of Arizona No. 32. University of Arizona Press, Tucson.

Wagner, Gail, Tristine Smart, Richard I. Ford, and Heather Trigg
1984   Ethnobotanical Recovery, 1982: Summary of Analysis and Frequency Tables. In *Excavations on Black Mesa, 1982: A Descriptive Report*, edited by Deborah L. Nichols and F. E. Smiley, pp. 613–632. Center for Archaeological Investigations Research Paper No. 39. Southern Illinois University, Carbondale.

Warburton, Miranda
1985   Culture Change and the Navajo Hogan. Ph.D. dissertation, Department of Anthropology, Washington State University, Pullman. University Microfilms, Ann Arbor, Michigan.

Ward, Albert E.
1972   Appendix II. The Tree-Ring Dating of the Black Mesa Project: 1968–

1971. In *Archaeological Investigations on Black Mesa: The 1969–1970 Seasons*, edited by George J. Gumerman, Deborah Westfall, and Carol S. Weed, pp. 211–223. Prescott College Press, Prescott, Arizona.
1975   *Inscription House: Two Research Reports.* Technical Series No. 16. Museum of Northern Arizona, Flagstaff.
1976   Black Mesa to the Colorado River: An Archaeological Traverse. In *Papers on the Archaeology of Black Mesa, Arizona*, edited by George J. Gumerman and Robert C. Euler, pp. 3–105. Southern Illinois University Press, Carbondale.

Ward, Albert. E. (editor)
1978   *Limited Activity and Occupation Sites.* Contributions to Anthropological Studies No. 1, Albuquerque, New Mexico.

Ward, Albert E., Emily K. Abbink, and John R. Stein
1977   Ethnohistorical and Chronological Basis of the Navajo Material Culture. In *Settlement and Subsistence Along the Lower Chaco River: The C.G.P. Survey*, edited by Charles Reher, pp. 217–278. University of New Mexico Press, Albuquerque.

Ware, John A., III
1984   Descriptive Reports for the 1972 Field Season. In *Excavations on Black Mesa, 1971–1976: A Descriptive Report*, edited by Shirley Powell, pp. 219–237. Center for Archaeological Investigations Research Paper No. 48. Southern Illinois University, Carbondale.

Wesson, A. L., and Debra L. Martin
1995   *Women Carried Heavy Loads while Men Were Weaving: Precontact Sexual Division of Labor at Black Mesa, Arizona.* Paper presented at the Twentieth Annual Meeting of the American Association of Physical Anthropologists, Oakland, California.

Whitecotton, Steven, Cathy J. Lebo, and Anthony L. Klesert
1980   Arizona D:7:236. In *Excavation on Black Mesa, 1979: A Descriptive Report*, edited by Shirley Powell and Robert Layhe, pp. 129–170. Center for Archaeological Investigations Research Paper No. 18. Southern Illinois University, Carbondale.

Whiteley, Peter
1988   *Deliberate Acts: Changing Hopi Culture through the Oraibi Split.* University of Arizona Press, Tucson.

Whittlesey, Stephanie M. (editor)
1992   *Investigations at Lee Canyon: Kayenta Anasazi Farmsteads in the Upper Basin, Coconino County, Arizona.* Technical Series No. 38,

Statistical Research, Tucson, Arizona.

Wicker, G. Christy

1997 Morphological Variability of Maize from Selected Basketmaker II Rockshelters. In *Early Farmers in the Northern Southwest: Papers on Chronometry, Social Dynamics, and Ecology*, edited by Francis E. Smiley and Michael R. Robins, pp. 121–164. Animas–La Plata Archaeological Project Research Paper No. 7. Northern Arizona University, Flagstaff.

Wilcox, David R., and Jonathan Haas

1994 The Scream of the Butterfly: Competition and Conflict in the Prehistoric Southwest. In *Themes in Southwest Prehistory*, edited by George J. Gumerman, pp. 211–238. School of American Research Press, Santa Fe, New Mexico.

Wills, Wirt H., III

1985 Early Agriculture in the Mogollon Highlands of New Mexico. Ph.D. dissertation, Department of Anthropology, University of Michigan. University Microfilms, Ann Arbor, Michigan.

1988a *Early Prehistoric Agriculture in the American Southwest*. School of American Research Press, Santa Fe, New Mexico.

1988b Early Agriculture and Sedentism in the American Southwest: Evidence and Interpretations. *Journal of World Prehistory* 2:445–488.

1991 Organizational Strategies and the Emergence of Prehistoric Villages in the American Southwest. In *Between Bands and States*, edited by Susan A. Gregg, pp. 161–180. Center for Archaeological Investigations Occasional Paper No. 9, Southern Illinois University, Carbondale.

1992 Plant Cultivation and the Evolution of Risk-Free Economies in the Prehistoric American Southwest. In *Transitions to Agriculture in Prehistory*, edited by Anne Birgitte Gebauer and T. Douglas Price. *Monographs in World Archaeology* 4:153–176. Prehistory Press, Madison, Wisconsin.

1995 Archaic Foraging and the Beginning of Food Production in the American Southwest. In *Last Hunters First Farmers*, edited by T. Douglas Price and Birgitte Gebauer, pp. 215–242. School of American Research Press, Santa Fe, New Mexico.

Wills, Wirt H., and Thomas C. Windes

1989 Evidence for Population Aggregation and Dispersal during the Basketmaker III Period in Chaco Canyon, New Mexico. *American Antiquity* 54:347–369.

Wills, Wirt H., III, Elizabeth S. Word, Joni Manson, and Heather Trigg

1984 Arizona D:11:2126. In *Excavations on Black Mesa, 1982: A Descriptive Report*, edited by Deborah L. Nichols and F. E. Smiley, pp. 309–322. Center for Archaeological Investigations Research Paper No. 39. Southern Illinois University, Carbondale.

Wilmsen, Edwin N.

1970 *Lithic Analysis and Cultural Inference: A PaleoIndian Case*. Anthropological Papers of the University of Arizona No. 16. University of Arizona, Tucson.

1974 *Lindenmeier: A Pleistocene Hunting Society*. Harper and Row, New York.

Wilshusen, Richard H.

1986 The Relationship Between Abandonment Mode and Ritual Use in Pueblo I Anasazi Protokivas. *Journal of Field Archaeology* 13:245–254.

1989 Unstuffing the Estufa: Ritual Floor Features in Anasazi Pit Structures. In *The Architecture of Social Integration in Prehistoric Pueblos*, edited by W. D. Lipe and Michelle Hegmon, pp. 89–112. Occasional Papers of the Crow Canyon Archaeological Center No. 1, Cortez, Colorado.

Wilshusen, Richard H. and Scott G. Ortman

1999 Rethinking the Pueblo I Period in the San Juan Drainage: Aggregation, Migration, and Cultural Diversity. *Kiva* 64:396–399.

Windham, Michael, and David Dechambre

1978 Report on the Cultural Resources in the Former Joint Use Area. Manuscript on file, Department of Anthropology, Northern Arizona University, Flagstaff.

Witherspoon, Gary

1974 The Central Concepts of Navajo World View (I). *Linguistics* 119:41–59.

Witter, D. C.

1977 Vegetative Ecology. In *Settlement and Subsistence Along the Lower Chaco River: The CGP Survey*, edited by Charles A. Reher, pp. 165–188. University of New Mexico Press, Albuquerque.

Wobst, Martin

1974 Boundary Conditions for Paleolithic Social Systems: A Simulation Approach. *American Antiquity* 39:147–178.

Wood, John J., and Kathy Mullin Stemmler

1981 Land and Religion at Big Mountain: The Effects of the Navajo-Hopi Land Dispute on Navajo Well-being. A report to the Congress of the United States of America, on file, Museum of Northern Arizona, Flagstaff.

Wood, John J., Walter M. Vannette, and Michael J. Andrews

1982 *"Sheep Is Life," An Assessment of Livestock Reduction in the Former Navajo-Hopi Joint Use Area*. Anthropological Paper No. 1. Northern Arizona University, Flagstaff.

Woodson, Michael Kyle

1995 The Goat Hill Site: A Western Anasazi Pueblo in the Safford Valley of Southern Arizona. Master's thesis, Department of Anthropology, University of Texas, Austin.

1999 Migrations in Late Anasazi Prehistory: The Evidence from the Goat Hill Site. *Kiva* 65:63–84.

Wormington, H. M.

1957 *Ancient Man in North America*. Popular Series No. 6. Denver Museum of Natural History, Denver, Colorado.

Wyman, Leland C.

1970 *Blessingway*. University of Arizona Press, Tucson.

Young, Lisa C.

1983 Basketmaker Bifaces: A Case Study from Black Mesa, Arizona. Unpublished B.A. honor's thesis, Museum of Anthropology, University of Michigan, Ann Arbor.

List of Contributors

Richard M. Begay is Deputy Executive Division Director for the Division of Natural Resources for the Navajo Nation. Previously, he served as head of the traditional cultural program of the Navajo Nation Historic Preservation Department.

Jeffrey S. Dean is professor of dendrochronology in the Laboratory of Tree-Ring Research at the University of Arizona, Tucson. Dr. Dean has participated in BMAP cooperative research since the early 1970s. His particular interests are the tree-ring dating of Navajo and puebloan archaeological sites and dendroclimatic reconstruction. The dendroclimatic reconstructions formed the foundation of the environmental and cultural reconstructions published in the *Anasazi in a Changing Environment* (Gumerman 1988a). Currently, he is working on tree-ring dating of Mesa Verde cliff dwelling and Dinetah Navajo sites and on dendroclimatic reconstructions on scales ranging from one year to centuries.

Robert C. Euler, who holds a Ph.D. in anthropology from the University of New Mexico, was founding director of the Black Mesa Archaeological Project, which began in 1967. He headed the Center for Anthropological Studies at Prescott College and has taught at Northern Arizona University, the University of Utah, and Fort Lewis College. He has published papers and books on southwestern archaeology, ethnology, applied anthropology, and ethnohistory.

George J. Gumerman is Director of the Arizona State Museum at the University of Arizona, Tucson. He was hired as the Black Mesa Archaeologist Project's first field director in 1968, and in 1975 he (and BMAP) moved to Southern Illinois University, where he founded the Center for Archaeological Investigations, serving as its director through 1991. Dr. Gumerman has written many books and articles on the archaeology

of the Southwest, including *A View from Black Mesa* (Gumerman 1984). He also serves on the steering committee of the Science Board for the Santa Fe Institute.

Leigh Kuwanwisiwma heads the Hopi Tribe's Cultural Preservation Office. He has authored several articles that examine management of cultural resources from a Hopi perspective and contributed to the volume *The Anasazi: Why Did They Leave? Where Did They Go?* (Judge et al. 1981). He is a graduate of Northern Arizona University in business administration and has served as assistant director of the Hopi Tribal Health Department.

Deborah L. Nichols was an assistant director for the Black Mesa Archaeological Project between 1981 and 1985. Among her BMAP responsibilities, she coordinated data recovery at historic sites. Currently, Dr. Nichols is professor of anthropology at Dartmouth College, where she served as chair from 1991 through 1994. She has published several articles and edited several volumes on southwestern archaeology. Since 1985 she has researched the evolution of Aztec city-states, with support from the National Science Foundation. Dr. Nichols is presently collaborating on a book about the archaeology of city-states that will be published by the Smithsonian Institution Press.

Shirley Powell directed the Black Mesa Archaeological Project between 1978 and 1987, also serving as co-principal investigator with George J. Gumerman. She is the author of numerous books and articles on the archaeology of Black Mesa and the northern Southwest, including *Mobility and Adaptation* (Powell 1983) and *People of the Mesa* (Powell and Gumerman 1987). She was a professor in the Department of Anthropology and former director of the Anthropology Laboratories at Northern Arizona University, where she helped to implement

cooperative agreements for student training and research with the Navajo Nation Archaeology Department and the Hopi Tribe's Cultural Preservation Office. Between 1992 and 1995 she served as principal investigator, with Francis E. Smiley, of the Animas–La Plata Archaeological Project, a large contract operation in southwestern Colorado. Until 2000, she worked and lived in Dolores, Colorado, where was mayor of the town. Currently, she is a principal investigator with Archaeological Consulting Services in Tempe, Arizona.

Francis E. Smiley is a professor of anthropology and chair of the Department of Anthropology at Northern Arizona University. He filled many roles with the Black Mesa Archaeological Project. Dr. Smiley's research interests range from method and theory in archaeological chronometry, faunal and lithic analyses, and computer simulation. His primary research focus continues to be small-scale societies and the transition to agriculture. Dr. Smiley has worked in several locations in the northern Southwest, the American High Plains, northern Europe, and the southwestern United States.

Miranda Warburton is Director of the Navajo Nation Archaeology Department (NNAD), Northern Arizona University branch office. She was a site supervisor for the Black Mesa Archaeological Project during the 1980 and 1983 field seasons and received funding from BMAP during the 1983 and 1984 academic year for research on hogans (Warburton 1985). Dr. Warburton currently coordinates a Native American archaeological training program for NNAD, whose primary goal is reintroducing native voices to archaeological site management and interpretation. At present, she is researching symbolic approaches to lithic analysis and Navajo history and ethnohistory.

Index

AA:12:111, 40

Abandonment, 10–11, 27, 107–8, 112, 125, 183, 186–87, 189; of Black Mesa/Kayenta region, 97, 104–5, 110, 114–17, 119, 121, 130, 133–34, 157; environmental change and, 7–8, 52, 63, 70–73, 85–88; of sites, 57, 70, 149

Acoma, 108

Adaptation: agricultural, 37, 49, 187; Archaic, 11, 13, 26–37, 50; collecting, 26, 75, 170; foraging, 16, 26, 28, 35, 37–38, 41, 48, 59–61, 67, 80, 90; Paleoindian, 21–28

Agave, 91–92

Agriculture: computer simulation of dispersal of, 40, 51, 64, 74, 92, 95; origins of, 9, 39, 183; soil control and, 127; Upper Sonoran agricultural complex, 67, 92; water control and, 127, 141

American Indian Religious Freedom Act (AIRFA), 166

Antelope Mesa, 85, 125, 130, 132, 140

Antevs, Ernst, 16–18, 20

Aquarius Plateau, 133

Archaic, 15, 20, 26–34

Architecture: courtyard, 106–7, 126, 132, 136, 142–47, 153–56; entrybox, 98, 132, 142, 145, 150; granary, 132, 139; jacal, 73, 83, 92, 99, 109, 111, 132–33, 135, 151; Kayenta-style masonry, 79, 96, 98; kiva, 73–75, 79, 87, 92, 96–99, 102, 105–7, 109, 110–13, 115–16, 132–33, 135–39, 143–44, 147, 150–52, 155, 157; mealing pit structure, 92, 95, 96, 109, 111, 113, 116, 142, 150; pit structure, 49, 52–63, 69, 71–74, 83, 86, 92, 94, 96–104, 109, 111, 116, 136, 143, 188; roomblock, 96, 98, 100–103, 107, 110, 112, 132–33, 135, 142–47, 151, 155; sipapu, 74, 97, 115, 157, 159, 161; storage room, 79, 96, 101–2, 104, 109, 111–12; unit pueblo, 79, 96–97, 99, 108–9, 111, 116, 135–36, 138, 151–53, 155

Arizona State Historic Preservation Office, 5, 189

Arizona Strip, 85, 98, 106, 109

Athabaskan, 165

Awatovi Expedition, 17, 72, 138

Aztec National Monument, 162

Badger Springs site (D:5:13, NA 10924), 15, 22, 24

Basketmaker-Pueblo transition, 66–69, 72–74

Basketmaker II, 7–9, 28, 32, 37–65; rockshelters, 30, 38, 42–43, 188. *See also* Open-air Basketmaker II sites

Basketmaker III, 7, 10–11, 35, 49–50, 63, 66–75

Bat Cave, 39–41, 61

Beans, 9, 66–67, 82–83, 91, 112, 127, 169

Betatakin, 126, 132, 141, 144, 155–56

Big Mountain, 170–71

Black Mesa Archaeological Project (BMAP): history of, 1–6; research design, 4, 6

Broken Flute Cave, 75

Bureau of Indian Affairs (BIA), 5

Burials, 1; Basketmaker II and, 28, 39, 43, 57, 61–62, 67, 187; Basketmaker III and, 72, 74–75; Hopis and, 161; NAGPRA and, 191; Navajos and, 171; Paleoindian, 24; Puebloan, 88–89, 100–101, 103, 105, 106, 111, 115–17, 126, 129, 147, 152, 156

Burnt Corn Ruin, 107

Butler Wash, 39, 46, 61

Canyon de Chelly: Basketmaker II, 43, 47; Basketmaker III, 72; Chacoan outliers, 107, 110; climate, 19–21, 123; cotton, 127; health of Pueblo populations, 86, 126; Kayenta ceramics, 139; Navajo land use, 180; Puebloans, 68

Canyon del Muerto, 39, 130, 133–34, 139

Casas Grandes, 130

Cave DuPont, 56

Cave two, 44

Cedar Mesa, 39, 53, 61, 63–64, 68, 70, 85–86

Ceramics, general: as burial accompaniments, 74, 115–16, 156; dating, 122; distribution, 70; exchange, 94, 110, 114, 129; production, 95, 130; sourcing, 113

Ceramics, types and wares: Alameda Brown Ware, 106; Black Mesa Black-on-white, 95, 113–14; Cibola White Ware, 107, 110, 139; Dogoszhi Black-on-white, 70, 72, 85, 95, 100, 102–3; Flagstaff Black-on-white, 130; Kana-a Black-on-white, 72, 95, 112–13, 116, 132; Kana-a Gray, 85, 95, 113; Kayenta Polychrome, 131; Kiet Siel Black-on-red, 131; Kiet Siel Gray, 130, 131; Kiet Siel Polychrome, 131; Moencopi Corrugated, 130; Lino Black-on-gray, 68, 95; Lino Fugitive Red, 68; Lino Gray, 68, 71, 85, 95; Lino Tradition, 95; Little Colorado White Ware, 130; Rainbow Gray, 130–31; San Francisco Mountain Gray Ware, 106, 115; San Juan Red Ware, 94–95, 113–14; Tsegi Black-on-orange, 131; Tsegi Corrugated, 130; Tsegi Orange Ware, 94–95, 114, 131, 139; Tsegi Polychrome, 131; Tsegi Red-on-orange, 131; Tusayan Black-on-red, 131; Tusayan Black-on-white, 130–31; Tusayan Corrugated, 85, 95, 113, 130; Tusayan Gray Ware, 95, 106, 115; Tusayan Polychrome, 131; Tusayan White Ware, 9, 95, 106–7, 110, 113–14, 130–32; Wepo Black-on-white, 95, 112, 136, 146; White Mountain Red Ware, 131, 139

Chaco Canyon, 19–21, 106, 115; Chacoan, 95–96, 99, 106, 110–11; great house, 98, 106–8, 116, 187; outlier, 96, 99, 106, 110; phenomenon, 95–96, 106–8, 110, 116; road system, 106

Chilchinbito, 72, 111

Chinle Wash, 72

Chipped stone: exchange, 113–14; expedient technology, 74; formal tools, 31, 74; sourcing, 31, 34

Cienega Creek, 39

Clans, Hopi, 116, 161–62

Coal Mine Wash, 18, 49, 59

Cochise Tradition, 27

Coconino Plateau, 85, 91, 93–94, 97–99, 105–6, 109, 114, 133

Cohonina, 105–6, 115, 162

Colorado Plateau, 2, 11, 188; Basketmaker II, 9, 37–38, 40, 46–48, 62–63; Basketmaker III, 66, 73, 81–82; Hopis and, 161; Paleoindian, 15, 16, 21–27, 30; Puebloan, 108, 124, 130

Colton, Harold S., 30, 121

Comb Ridge, 42

Computer simulation, 40, 51, 64, 74, 92, 95

Coombs site, 106, 133–34, 139

Corn, 9, 41–42, 82; Basketmaker II, 37, 41, 44–66, 187; Basketmaker III, 66–69, 75, 81; chronometry of, in Southwest, 40, 42, 51, 61; diet and, 89, 92, 188; Hopis and, 92, 111, 169; Navajos and, 170; pinyon nuts and, 46–47, 62; Pueblo, 90–95, 101–12, 126–27, 141–42, 152

Cow Springs, 71–73, 169
Cummings, Byron, 24, 71, 132

D:7:23, 94, 116, 145
D:7:38, 173
D:7:60, 91, 96, 111–12
D:7:102, 8
D:7:103, 9, 58
D:7:105, 58
D:7:134, 100, 102–4, 111
D:7:135, 70, 100, 102–4
D:7:136, 84, 143
D:7:152, 49–50, 59
D:7:236, 54, 58–59
D:7:254, 55, 60
D:7:262, 82, 116
D:7:473, 58
D:7:618, 34
D:7:619, 34
D:7:718, 179
D:7:2085, 18, 29, 30–31
D:7:2100, 30, 44–45
D:7:3003A, 30, 44
D:7:3045, 58
D:7:3107, 54–55, 59
D:7:3141, 55–57
D:7:3144, 30, 44–45
D:7:3194, 70, 99–100, 103, 105
D:8:612, 91
D:10:16, 137
D:11:9, 114
D:11:36, 170–71
D:11:93, 109
D:11:113, 70, 84, 102
D:11:244, 57
D:11:425, 115
D:11:449, 55–57
D:11:689, 100, 103, 105
D:11:1014, 58
D:11:1161, 55–56
D:11:1162, 51
D:11:1176, 58
D:11:1281, 30, 34, 44
D:11:1296, 70, 72
D:11:2001, 111
D:11:2023, 70, 84, 100–101, 104
D:11:2025, 84, 101, 104
D:11:2027, 81, 84, 101, 104
D:11:2030, 84, 100, 104, 111
D:11:2038, 81, 101
D:11:2045, 58
D:11:2051, 111
D:11:2063, 58–59
D:11:2068, 67, 81, 84, 102, 104
D:11:2108, 111
D:11:2126, 57–58
D:11:2191, 30–45
D:11:3061, 100, 103, 105
D:11:3063, 25, 30–34
D:11:3131, 55, 58
D:11:3133, 54–55, 59
D:11:3135, 58
D:11:4144, 171
D:11:4145, 171
D:11:4283, 170
Dating: ceramic, 122; radiocarbon, 7, 9; tree ring, 7, 9

Davis Ruin, 130
Dead Juniper Wash, 7
Defiance Plateau, 85–86, 131, 134
Depression, Great, 172, 177
Desert Culture Tradition, 27
Desha Complex, 32, 45, 147, 155–56
Dine'tah, 165–66
Dinnebito phase, 102
Dot Klish phase, 70–71, 79
Dot Klish Wash, 70
Dzil Nez Mesa, 70

En Medio period, 28, 45
Environment: change, 16, 68, 72, 82, 124, 184; Great Drought, 123–24, 187; high-frequency processes, 8, 51–52, 80, 123–24, 134, 141; low-frequency processes, 51, 82, 122–24; Palmer drought severity indices, 123
Euler, Robert C., 1, 3–4, 7, 9, 49
Exchange: ceramics, 74, 94, 110, 113–14, 139; chipped stone, 34, 74; macaws, 129

Falls Creek Shelters, 61
Finger Rock site, 72
First Mesa, 162
Forest Lake, 71, 89, 172, 173
Fort Defiance, 168
Fort Lewis College, 4, 10, 182
Fort Sumner, 168–69, 171
Fort Wingate, 169
Four Corners region, 37, 43–48, 61, 63

Gallup, 177
Ganado, 25, 28–29, 171
Glen Canyon, 70, 85–86, 89, 108, 115, 127
Government Mountain, 31
Grand Canyon, 4, 85, 98, 105, 133–34, 139, 168
Grand Gulch, 38–39, 42, 47, 61
Grasshopper Pueblo, 31
Gray Mountain, 168
Great kiva, 66, 71, 73–75, 96–98, 106–7, 110, 138
Groundstone artifacts: axes, 69; manos, 32, 52, 66, 69, 111, 142, 150, 156; metates, 32, 52, 66, 69, 92, 111, 142, 150, 156
Guardian Pueblo, 155
Guernsey, Samuel, 37, 42, 43, 45
Gumerman, George J., 4, 7–8, 10, 189–90

Habitat: canyon, 33, 37, 80, 149; upland, 35, 72, 85, 109, 114, 122, 124, 127, 134; valley, 80, 124, 134
Hack, John T., 17–18
Hand House. See D:8:612
Hastqin site (K:6:19), 25, 28–29
Hay Hollow Valley, 39, 59, 61, 63, 81
Hisatsinom phase, 27, 30–31, 34, 44–45
Historic archaeology, 1, 10, 74, 164, 166–67, 171, 180–81, 184
Hitsotsinom, 162
Hogans, 169–70, 179–80
Holocene, 13, 16–21, 25–27, 29–30, 33–34
Homol'ovi, 139–40, 146, 157
Hopi Buttes, 7, 72, 86, 93, 131, 137–38, 152
Hopi Mesas, 1, 7, 23, 177; Basketmaker III occupation of, 72; ceramics and, 130–31; environment and, 123, 157; Hopi clans and, 162;

Navajos and, 168, 177; prehistoric populations and, 125, 133, 138, 140
Hopis, 10, 157, 161, 163, 177; agriculture and, 92; Basketmaker II and, 188; emergence of, 159, 161; kiva style, 97; Navajo trading with, 165, 169–70, 173; Tribe, 3, 10, 161, 181, 189
Hostile House, 140–41

I:1:17, 96; Katsina Cult, 157; ritual burning, 75; rock images, 82, 95, 115–16, 188
Inscription House, 122, 126–27, 132, 156, 162

Jeddito, 264, 72
Jeddito Valley, 17, 71–72
Joint Use Area (JUA), 29, 174–75, 178
Juniper Cove site, 63, 71–75

Kaibito Plateau, 24, 71
Katsina Cult. See Ideology
Kayenta: core area, 105, 121; periphery, 105
Kayenta–Mesa Verde communities, 86, 129, 139–40
Kayenta Valley, 94, 140, 149
Keams Canyon, 106, 169–70
Kidder, A. V., 38, 42–43
Kiet Siel, 126, 129–32, 138–41, 144, 149, 153, 155–56, 162
Kinboko Canyon, 44
Kin Kahuna, 59
Kin Klethla, 145
Klethla phase, 121
Klethla Valley: Basketmaker II occupation of, 9, 58; Basketmakr III occupation of, 69, 71–72; ceramics and, 114; Navajos and, 170; Puebloan occupation of, 121, 133–36, 138, 140, 145

Laguna Creek, 23, 69, 71–73, 85, 138, 140, 149
Lamoki phase, 79
Land-use patterns, 47, 66, 92
La Plata Mountains, 16, 18, 20–21, 41–42
Las Colinas, 130
Left Handed, 168–69
Limited activity sites, 59
Lolomai phase, 9, 30, 35, 39, 45, 48–64, 188
Long House (NA 897), 28, 143–44, 147–48, 155–56
Long House Valley, 7, 190; abandonment of, 134; Archaic occupation of, 28; Basketmaker III occupation of, 71, 103; Puebloan occupation of, 109, 135, 139–41, 144, 147–49; survey of, 122, 125
Los Muertos, 130

Maasaw, 108, 161–62
Maize. See Corn
Marsh Pass: Basketmaker II occupation of, 8, 28, 37–61, 188; Basketmaker III occupation of, 71. See also Klethla Valley; Long House Valley
Matty Canyon, 39
Mesa Verde, 86, 119, 127, 129, 132, 139–43, 180
Migration, 41, 62–64, 116, 157, 162
Moapa phase, 39
Moenkopi Wash, 59, 70–71, 84, 94, 96, 100–102, 114, 130
Mogollon, 55, 66, 73–74, 106, 129, 131, 162
Moki Rock site, 147, 155

Monument Valley, 121, 133, 138
Museum of Northern Arizona, 23–24, 28

NA 7159B, 155
NA 7485, 138
NA 7486, 138
NA 8163, 71, 136–37
NA 8171, 136
NA 8278, 23
NA 10824, 28
NA 10829, 156
NA 10830, 144, 156
NA 10924, 24
NA 11958, 148
NA 11980, 148
NA 12062, 135
NA 13805, 72
NA 13806, 73
NA 13808, 72
NA 14646, 61
Nagashi Bikin, 141
Nakai Canyon, 134
National Park Service, 5–6, 189
Native American Graves Protection and Re-
    patriation Act (NAGPRA), 8, 88, 190–91
Navajo-Hopi Joint Use Area. See Joint Use Area
Navajo Mountain: environment and, 123; Hopis
    and, 125; kiva architecture, 132; Mesa Verde
    peoples and, 139; Navajos and, 164; Paiutes
    and, 125; Pueblo ceramics and, 131; Puebloan
    occupation of, 97, 121, 138, 145, 149, 155; re-
    gional abandonments and, 85–86, 134, 140;
    soil control and, 127
Navajo Nation: Archaeology Department, 10,
    145, 166; Historic Preservation Office, 10
Nayavuwaltsa, 162–63
Neskahi Village, 136–38, 142–44, 155
Northern Arizona University, 10, 23–24, 28, 60,
    79, 125

Office of Surface Mining, 5–6, 159, 182
Olla House, 142
Open-air Basketmaker II sites, 7, 9, 25, 30, 37–50,
    61–63, 72, 187–88
Oraibi, 108, 161, 168, 170
Oshara Tradition, 27–28, 32, 34, 45
Osteology: cannibalism, 89, 108, 116; dietary
    reconstruction, 67, 81, 92, 126; human, 57, 61,
    88–89, 92, 115, 184; paleodemography, 86, 89;
    paleoepidemiology, 89

Painted Cave, 139
Paiute Canyon, 70, 85, 125, 134
Paiute Mesa: Basketmaker III, 70; intervisibility
    sites, 156; Plaza sites, 155; Puebloan sites, 85,
    121, 125, 136, 138, 149
Paleoenvironment, 7–8, 16, 25, 41, 66, 79, 80–81,
    184, 190
Paleoindian, 7, 10–11, 13, 15–16, 21–29, 34, 38, 62,
    85, 162
Peabody Coal Company, 174–75; BMAP and, 1, 3,
    159, 166, 182–83, 189; federal agencies and, 5,
    190; Joint Use Area and, 178; leasehold of, 1,
    77, 135–36, 138, 162, 170; NAGPRA and, 88

Pecos classification, 38, 66, 79, 122, 125
Pinedale Ruin, 130–31
Pinon (Ariz.), 70, 136, 174–75
Pinyon (P. Edulis): archaeological recovery of,
    20, 103; climatic reconstruction and, 41–42,
    forestation, 2, 19–21, 25, 46–47, 59, 128
Pinyon nuts: Basketmaker II use of, 44, 46–47,
    59, 60, 62, 70, 72, 188; mast events, 48, 63, 68;
    Navajo use of, 61, 169–70, 173; Pueblo use of,
    92–93, 103–4, 124, 127
Plaza site, 136, 144–46, 151–52, 155–56
Pleistocene, 13, 15–16, 19, 21, 26, 33
Plog, Stephen, 4, 8–9
Point of Pines, 131, 139, 157
Poncho House, 139–40
Population: size, 85–94, 125; surrogates, 86
Pottery Pueblo, 143–44, 153, 155–56
Prescott College, 3–4, 8, 173, 182
Proto-villages, 49, 53–55, 57–63
Pueblo I, 69–79, 83–116
Pueblo II, 79–117
Pueblo III, 7, 86–93, 98, 114, 119–46
Pueblo IV, 89, 130

Rainbow Plateau, 39, 60–61, 70, 85–86, 121, 125,
    127, 140, 145, 156
RB 568, 126, 130, 136, 152, 155–56
RB 1002, 71
Red House, 144, 147, 155
Red Peak Valley, 18, 100
Red Rock Plateau, 70
Reed Valley, 82
Reeve Ruin, 130, 132
Ritual burning, 75
Rock images, 44, 82, 95, 115–16, 188

Salado, 162
San Juan Basin, 22, 24, 28, 33, 39, 99, 106, 108,
    177
San Pedro Valley, 139, 157
Scaffold House, 141
Second Mesa, 71
Segazlin Mesa, 143–44, 155–56
Settlement pattern: hierarchy, 156–57; inter-
    visible sites, 140, 148–49, 156; logistical
    mobility, 26–27, 31, 33, 72, 93; residential
    mobility, 25–26, 33–34, 41, 48–50, 63, 66, 68–
    69, 73–74; sedentism, 9, 47, 52–53, 66–68, 72,
    116, 170, 177
Shonto Plateau, 71, 121, 133–34, 138, 140
Sinagua, 106, 129, 162
Sipapuni, 159, 161
Social organization: alliance systems, 74; divi-
    sion of labor, 111, 115; lineage-based, 66, 73;
    relationship to population size, 50, 59, 110
Sociopolitics, 10
Sourcing studies: ceramics, 113, chipped stone,
    31, 34
Southern Illinois University at Carbondale
    (SIUC), 4–5, 94, 182–83
Squash, 83, 91, 112, 127, 187
Standing Fall House. See D:7:60
Starling site, 15, 23–25, 28–29, 32
Stock reduction, 172–74, 177–78, 180

Subsistence: animal domestication, 94; cotton
    growing, 108, 127, 129, 139; dietary recon-
    struction, 67, 81, 92, 126; farming, 9, 27, 35,
    37–65, 67, 91, 124, 127; foraging, 16, 26, 48,
    59–61, 67, 80, 90; hunting, 15, 22, 25, 44, 61,
    67, 90, 92–94, 105, 124, 128, 167, 170; plant
    remains, 45, 52, 91, 127, 182
Sunset Crater, 85, 106
Surprise Pueblo, 135, 151–53
Swallow's Nest Cave, 71
Swallow's Nest Cliff Dwelling, 141–42

Tachini Point, 24
Tallahogan phase, 79
Talus Village, 39
Thief site, 145
Third Mesa, 161–62
Three Fir Shelter, 40–48, 61–62, 102
Toreva phase, 79, 82, 111
Tower House, 148
Traditional Cultural Properties (TCP), 180, 191
Transition period, 86, 116, 121–22, 126–28, 133–55
Tse Chizzi Ruin, 106–7
Tsegi Canyon, 68, 71–72, 85, 121, 123, 125, 130,
    138–41, 144, 153–55
Tsegi phase, 77, 86, 96, 111, 116, 121, 126–41,
    152–53, 156–57
Tsosie Shelter (D:7:2085), 15, 18–21, 25, 30–32,
    34, 45
Tucson Basin, 41, 43, 46, 64
Tusayan Ruin, 133
Twin Caves Pueblo, 141

U.S. Geological Survey, 5
Upper Desha Pueblo, 147, 155–56

Verde Valley, 127
Virgin Branch, 85, 133
Virgin River, 39

Walnut Canyon, 85, 106
Warfare, 108, 156, 168
Wepo phase, 79, 95, 112
Wepo Wash, 136, 146
Whippoorwill Ruin, 107
White-baked siltstone, 49, 58, 63
White Dog Cave, 42
White Dog phase, 30–31, 34–35, 39–50, 53, 56,
    61–65
White House, 107, 110, 116
White Mesa, 71
Window Rock, 172, 176–77
Winslow Branch, 86, 133, 137–38, 150
Wupatki, 85, 106, 108, 110, 133, 138, 162, 168

X-ray fluorescence, 31

Yazzie Wash, 19, 94
Yellow Water Canyon, 18, 82–83, 94, 99, 100,
    102

Zea mays. See Corn